Introduction to Pascal and Structured Design

SECOND EDITION

Introduction to Pascal and Structured Design

NELL DALE
University of Texas at Austin

CHIP WEEMS
University of Massachusetts at Amherst

D. C. HEATH AND COMPANY

Lexington, Massachusetts   Toronto

This book is dedicated to you,
and to all of our other students for whom it was begun and
without whom it would never have been completed.

Acquisitions Editor: Pam Kirshen
Developmental Editor: Lee Ripley
Production Editor: Marret McCorkle
Designer: Mark Fowler

Production Coordinator: Michael O'Dea
Photo Researcher: Martha Shethar
Text Permissions Editor: Margaret Roll

Trademark Acknowledgements: Turbo Pascal is a trademark of Borland International, Inc. Macintosh is a trademark of Apple Computer, Inc. VAX Pascal is a trademark of Digital Equipment Corporation. CDC is a trademark of Control Data Corporation. UCSD is a trademark of the Regents of the University of California. Pascal/M is a trademark of Sorcim. Pascal/MT+ and CP/M are trademarks of Digital Research. Pascal/Z is a trademark of Ithaca Intersystems.

Cover: 1984 Los Angeles Olympics Site Structure. Bill Gallery/Stock Boston

Published simultaneously in Canada.

Printed in the United States of America.

International Standard Book Number: 0-669-09570-2 (paperback)

International Standard Book Number: 0-669-10399-3 (hardcover)

Library of Congress Catalog Card Number: 86-80506

In the past there have been two distinct approaches used in introductory computer science texts. One approach focused on problem solving and algorithm design in the abstract, leaving the learning of a particular language to a supplemental manual or to a subsequent course. The second approach focused on the syntax of a particular programming language, and assumed that the problem-solving skills would be learned later through practice.

We believe that neither approach is adequate. Problem solving is a skill that can and should be taught—but not in the abstract. Students must be exposed to the precision and detail required in actually implementing their algorithms in a real programming language.

The introduction to the Preface of the first edition of *Introduction to Pascal and Structured Design* (quoted above) proved to be prophetic as to the direction that computer science education would take. That edition came out in early 1983.

In 1983 the College Board published the description of an advanced placement course in computer science. In 1984 the ACM published the revised recommended curriculum for CS1, the first course in computer science. Both guidelines emphasize problem solving and algorithm design within the context of a block-structured language such as Pascal.

Since the first edition of this book has been widely accepted as a model for textbooks for CS1 and the first section of the AP exam in computer science, the temptation is to make only minimal changes for this second edition. We have resisted that temptation: to succumb would be to betray those students for whom the book was written.

The first edition of *Introduction to Pascal and Structured Design* was the first of a new wave of introductory textbooks. We trust this second edition will also make waves, for it is based on our vision of where computer science education is going: toward more testing, more abstraction, and more attention to the development of control structures and data structures.

Many topics considered advanced are introduced right from the beginning. Loop invariants are introduced as a way to design loops, not verify them. Designing test data is included as an integral part of the programming process. Data types are defined as a set of values and the operations defined on those values. Parallel decomposition of problem and data structure is introduced with the first structured data types. Control and data abstraction are introduced early and encouraged throughout.

In response to your feedback, we have also included many more exercises and examples, earlier coverage of procedures, and more emphasis on interactive programming.

With all the changes, however, we have kept in mind the pedagogical philosophy that the best examples are those drawn from everyday experience. All problems and examples have been carefully chosen to require only high school algebra.

Organization

The order of presentation has been altered slightly to reflect our own changing view and the view of our colleagues who used the first edition.

Chapter 1 is still designed to create a comfortable rapport between the student and the subject. Most students now take their first course in an interactive programming environment. The discussion of the program entry, compilation, and execution process reflects this change with a shift in orientation toward timesharing systems and personal computers. Because it is still widely used in production environments, batch processing is also discussed.

By the end of Chapter 1 students should have a basic knowledge of what computers are, what programming is, and the mechanics of getting a program to run. The goal of Chapter 2 is to bring students to the point where they can design a simple program of their own. Because this involves so many fundamental concepts, we have chosen to divide the chapter into two parts. The first part introduces the bare minimum necessary to design and write a very simple program. The second part fleshes out the details of Pascal syntax for more complex expressions and output.

The top-down design methodology is a major focus of Chapter 3. Our discussion of the methodology builds on the problem-solving techniques that are introduced in Chapter 2 by providing a concrete framework in which to apply them. Chapter 3 also covers input from fundamental concepts to the finer points of style in writing prompting messages. Files other than Input and Output are introduced at this stage in order to allow instructors to assign programming problems that require the use of sample data files.

Both Chapters 2 and 3 contain discussions of procedures and functions, with an introduction to the basic concepts of subprogram calls, parameter passing, and subprogram libraries. Chapter 3 also relates subprograms to the principles of modular design that are used throughout the text.

Chapters 4 and 5 are devoted to the concepts of flow of control and the logical versus physical ordering of statements. In Chapter 4 we introduce selection with the IF-THEN-ELSE and IF-THEN statements. The concept of nested control structures is also developed in this chapter.

Chapter 5 is devoted to looping structures. As in the first edition, all of the structures are introduced using the syntax of the WHILE statement. Rather than confuse the student with multiple syntactical structures, our approach is to teach the concepts of looping using only the WHILE. Students are first introduced to the basic loop control strategies and common looping operations. We then present a step-by-step process for designing loops using loop invariants.

Because there are so many new concepts associated with designing and writing user-defined procedures and functions, we have devoted three chapters to this topic. Chapter 6 covers flow of control in procedures, formal and actual parameters, interface design, local variables, and multiple calls to a procedure. Chapter 7 expands the discussion to include value parameters, nested scope, stubs and drivers, and more on interface design. Chapter 8 covers user-defined functions and briefly introduces recursion. Because of the numerical orientation of Chapter 8, we also take the opportunity to discuss the problems of representation and precision associated with Real numbers.

Chapter 9 represents a transition between the control structure orientation of the first half of the book and the abstract data type orientation of the second half. The chapter begins by introducing the first new data type since Chapter 3 (Sets) and ends by covering the remaining "ice cream and cake" control structures in Pascal (CASE, REPEAT, and FOR). Chapter 9 forms a natural ending point for the first quarter of a two-quarter introductory programming course.

In keeping with the increased emphasis on abstraction, simple data types are given a chapter all of their own, Chapter 10. The built-in simple data types are examined in terms of the set of values that variables or constants of that type can contain and the allowable operations on values of that type. Enumerated and subrange types are covered in detail. The functions Pred, Succ, and Ord are defined as Pascal implementations of the corresponding operation on scalar data types. Type compatibility is defined, and anonymous typing is strongly discouraged.

The array data type is introduced in Chapter 11. Arrays are the last big conceptual hurdle for the students to cross: A variable to access another variable? Three case studies and numerous small examples successfully make the jump. Three typical types of array processing are covered in the case studies: using only a portion of the array (subarray processing), using two or more arrays in parallel (parallel arrays), and using indices that have more meaning other than just representing a position (indexes with semantic content).

Chapter 12 represents a radical departure from the first edition. Algorithms that are commonly applied to lists of data are developed and coded as general-purpose Pascal procedures. Strings are described. A concluding Problem Solving in Action applies several of the procedures written in the first part of the chapter to strings to demonstrate the general applicability of the procedures.

Multidimensional arrays are discussed in Chapter 13; records are presented in Chapter 14 along with a lengthy discussion on how to choose an appropriate data structure. Data abstraction is demonstrated by creating an abstract data type Date and several useful operations on dates.

The remaining data types, files and pointers, are discussed in Chapter 15. Pointers are presented as a way to make programs more efficient. The use of pointers to create dynamic data structures is handled in a chapter by itself, Chapter 16. Linked lists in general and linked-list representations of stacks, queues, and binary trees are described briefly.

Chapter 17 deals with recursion. There is no consensus as to the best place to cover recursion. We personally feel that it is a topic that requires more maturity than many first semester students possess. We have included it, however, for two reasons: many instructors have requested it and there are those students for whom recursion seems natural. Although it is the last chapter, the examples are divided into two parts: those that require only simple data types and those that require structured data types. The first part is appropriate after Chapter 8. The second part contains examples from simple arrays to binary trees. These examples could be used singly after the appropriate chapter or as a unit after Chapter 16.

Additional Features

Problem Solving in Action Problem solving is demonstrated using case studies. A problem is presented followed by a discussion of how the problem might be solved by hand. An algorithm is developed using top-down design, and the algorithm is coded in Pascal. Sample test data and output are shown, followed by a discussion of what is involved in thoroughly testing the program.

Goals Goals for each chapter are listed at the beginning of the chapter. These goals are then tested in the end-of-chapter exercises.

Quick Checks At the end of each chapter there are questions to test the student's recall of major points keyed to the appropriate pages. The answers immediately follow in the body of the text.

Exam Preparation Exercises Thought questions to help students prepare for tests are presented. Answers to selected questions from each chapter are in the back of the book. Answers to the remaining questions are in the Instructor's Guide.

Preprogramming Exercises Questions that provide students with experience in writing Pascal code fragments or procedures are given in this section. This allows students to practice the syntactic constructs in each chapter without the overhead of writing a complete program. Solutions to selected questions from each chapter appear in the back of the book; the balance are given in the Instructor's Guide.

Programming Problems Specifications for problems from a wide range of disciplines are included. Students are required to write complete programs.

Supplements

Instructor's Guide Prepared by the authors, the Instructor's Guide includes teaching notes, answers to the balance of the exercises, a carefully worked out solution and discussion to one programming problem per chapter, and an example advanced placement exam question with a sample solution and the actual grading rubrics used by the AP exam graders.

Test Item File   Prepared by Tom Parks, the Test Item File includes over 1200 possible test questions. It is available in Archive, a computerized test generator, for the IBM PC.

Compiler Supplements   Supplementary booklets are available with compiler-specific information keyed to pages in the text. Three versions are available: MacIntosh™ Pascal, VAX Pascal™, and Turbo Pascal™.

In addition to the elements listed above, the programs in the text are available on disk in either Turbo format or ANSI format. A separate set of transparency masters is available to adopters of the text.

Acknowledgments

We would like to thank the many individuals who have helped us. We are indebted to the members of the faculties of the Computer Sciences Department at the University of Texas at Austin and of the Computer and Information Science Department at the University of Massachusetts at Amherst.

Among those in Austin, we would like to thank the following people: colleagues Jean Rogers and Joyce Brennan, who many times acted as a sounding board for new ideas; Carolyn Goldston, who never forgets birthdays; the Advance Placement CS readers who shared their ideas so willingly during those weeks at Rider College; and most especially Al Dale.

From among our colleagues in Amherst, we especially thank Caxton Foster, Alan Hanson, Steven Levitan, Edward Riseman, William Verts, and Beverly Woolf. Thanks also to Jeffrey Bonar of the Learning Research and Development Center at the University of Pittsburgh.

For their many helpful suggestions, we thank the lecturers, teaching assistants, consultants, and student proctors who run the courses for which this book was written, and the students themselves.

We would like to thank the following people who reviewed the manuscript: Randy Bartell, Syracuse University; James Case, Hiram College; Thomas Copeland, Middlebury College; John A. Koch, Wilkes College; Russell B. Lee, Allan Hancock College; Teck-Kah Lim, Drexel University; Ken Loach, State University of New York at Plattsburgh; Joseph Mayne, Loyola University; Randall Jay Molmen, University of North Dakota; Jean Rogers, University of Texas at Austin; Harbans Sathi, University of Southern Colorado; Mary Lou Soffa, University of Pittsburgh; Richard St. Andre, Central Michigan University; Bernard Taheny, Chicago Public Schools; Tim Thurman, University of Kansas; Darrell R. Turnidge, Kent State University; Frank T. Vanecek, Norwich University; Greg Wetzel, University of Kansas; D. Franklin Wright, Cerritos College.

For this impressive list of reviewers, as well as her tremendous support, we must thank our editor, Pam Kirshen. To all the others at D. C. Heath who contributed so much, especially Lee Ripley, Susan Gleason, Ruth Thompson, and Marret McCorkle, we are indeed grateful.

Special thanks go to David Orshalick for his input at the early stages of the development of this edition.

Anyone who has ever written a book—or is related to anyone who has—knows the amount of time involved in such a project. To our families who learned this first hand, all we can say is: "To Sarah, Susy, June, Judy, Bobby, Phil, Carol, and Lisa, thanks for your tremendous support and indulgence."

N.D.
C.W.

Contents

1 OVERVIEW OF PROGRAMMING _____ 1

Why Programming?   1
What Is Programming?   3
Data Representation   7
What Is a Computer?   8
Personal Computers and Mainframes   13
What Is a Programming Language?   16
What Is Pascal?   21
Program Entry, Correction, and Execution   24
    Interactive Program Entry   25
    Batch Program Entry   31
SUMMARY 32 • QUICK CHECK 33 • EXAM PREPARATION EXERCISES 34

2 PROBLEM SOLVING, SYNTAX/SEMANTICS,
AND PASCAL PROGRAMS _____ 36

Part 1   ALGORITHMS, DATA, AND PROGRAM
CONSTRUCTION   36
Problem-Solving Process   37
    Ask Questions   38
    Look for Things That Are Familiar   38
    Divide and Conquer   38
    Solve by Analogy   39

xi

The Building Block Approach   40
Means-Ends Analysis   40
Mental Blocks: The Fear of Starting   42
Syntax/Semantics   44
Syntax Diagrams   44
Identifiers   45
Data Types   47
Data Storage   49
Assignment   53
Output   57
Program Construction   59
Compound Statements   61
Blocks   61
Program Formatting   62
SUMMARY 65 • QUICK CHECK 66

Part 2   MORE OUTPUT MORE EXPRESSIONS   69
The Writeln Statement   70
The Appearance of Output   72
Formatting Output   73
Formatting Integer and Character Output   74
Program ForMom, Written with a Procedure   78
Formatting Real Output   79
More Expressions   80
Precedence Rules   80
Functions   81
Programs in Memory   86
SUMMARY 86 • QUICK CHECK 88 • EXAM PREPARATION EXERCISES 89 •
PREPROGRAMMING EXERCISES 92 • PROGRAMMING PROBLEMS 93

3   *INPUT AND DESIGN METHODOLOGY* _____ 94
Getting Data into Programs   95
Read   96
Readln   98
The Reading Marker and <eoln>   99
Reading Character Data   100
More About Procedures and Parameters   103

Interactive Input/Output 103

Batch Input/Output 105

Files Other Than Input and Output 106

Using Files 107

Listing File Names in the Program Heading 107

Declaring Files in the VAR Section 108

Preparing Files with Reset or Rewrite 108

Specifying Files in Read, Readln, Write, and Writeln 110

The Impact of Data Formats on Program Design 112

Top-Down Design 112

Modules 113

Methodology 117

Documentation 119

Testing and Debugging 126

SUMMARY 128 • QUICK CHECK 129 • EXAM PREPARATION EXERCISES 129 • PREPROGRAMMING EXERCISES 131 • PROGRAMMING PROBLEMS 132

4 *SELECTION* _____ 134

Conditions and Boolean Expressions 136

Boolean Expressions 136

Precedence of Operators 140

Writing Boolean Expressions 141

Relational Operators with Real and Boolean Data Types 142

The Boolean Function Odd 142

Selection Control Structures 143

Flow of Control 143

Selection 143

The IF Statement 143

The IF-THEN-ELSE Form of IF Statement 144

Compound Statements 145

The IF-THEN Form of IF Statement 147

Nested IF Statements 151

Testing and Debugging 161

Testing and Debugging Hints 163

SUMMARY 165 • QUICK CHECK 165 • EXAM PREPARATION
EXERCISES 166 • PREPROGRAMMING EXERCISES 168 • PROGRAMMING
PROBLEMS 170

5 LOOPING _____ 172

WHILE Statement   173
Loops Using the WHILE Statement   175
    Count-Controlled Loops   176
    Event-Controlled Loops   177
    Looping Subtasks   183
How to Design Loops   186
    Determining the Loop Invariant   188
    Designing the Flow of Control for a Loop   188
    Designing the Process Within the Loop   190
Nested Logic   206
    Designing Nested Loops   209
    Printing Headings and Columns   210
Testing and Debugging   217
    Testing and Debugging Hints   218
SUMMARY 219 • QUICK CHECK 220 • EXAM PREPARATION
EXERCISES 221 • PREPROGRAMMING EXERCISES 223 • PROGRAMMING
PROBLEMS 224

6 PROCEDURES _____ 226

Top-Down Structured Design with Procedures   227
An Overview of User-Defined Procedures   234
    Flow of Control in Procedure Calls   234
    When to Use Procedures   234
    Procedures and Blocks   235
    Parameters   236
    An Analogy   236
Procedure Declarations   238
Procedure Call (Invocation)   238
    Naming Procedures   239
Parameters   239
Local Variables   242

Multiple Calls to the Same Procedure   243
Testing and Debugging   249
    Testing and Debugging Hints   250
SUMMARY 250 • QUICK CHECK 251 • EXAM PREPARATION
EXERCISES 252 • PREPROGRAMMING EXERCISES 254 • PROGRAMMING
PROBLEMS 256

7   *VALUE PARAMETERS AND NESTED SCOPE* _____ 258

VAR/Value Parameters   259
    Value Parameter Semantics   260
    Interface Design   260
    Value Parameter Syntax   262
Local versus Global Declarations   270
Scope Rules   272
Side Effects   277
    Global Constants   280
Designing Programs with Nesting   280
Testing and Debugging   282
    Stubs and Drivers   287
    Testing and Debugging Hints   291
SUMMARY 292 • QUICK CHECK 293 • EXAM PREPARATION
EXERCISES 293 • PREPROGRAMMING EXERCISES 297 • PROGRAMMING
PROBLEMS 299

8   *FUNCTIONS, PRECISION, AND RECURSION* _____ 302

Functions   303
    Boolean Functions   306
    Function Interface Design and Side Effects   307
    When to Use Functions   308
More on Real Numbers   316
    Representation of Real Numbers   316
    Arithmetic with Real Numbers   319
    How Pascal Implements Real Numbers   320
    Practical Implications of Limited Precision   322
Recursion   323
Testing and Debugging   326
    Testing and Debugging Hints   326

SUMMARY 327 • QUICK CHECK 328 • EXAM PREPARATION
EXERCISES 328 • PREPROGRAMMING EXERCISES 330 • PROGRAMMING
PROBLEMS 330

9 SETS AND ADDITIONAL CONTROL STRUCTURES _____ 332

Sets   333
Additional Control Structures   343
   REPEAT Statement   343
   FOR Statement   346
   Guidelines for Choosing a Looping Statement   348
   CASE Statement   349
Testing and Debugging   356
   Testing and Debugging Hints   356

SUMMARY 357 • QUICK CHECK 358 • EXAM PREPARATION
EXERCISES 359 • PREPROGRAMMING EXERCISES 360 • PROGRAMMING
PROBLEMS 362

10 SIMPLE DATA TYPES _____ 364

Data Types   365
   Ord, Pred, and Succ Functions   367
   Chr Function   369
User-Defined Scalar Data Types   370
   Enumerated Data Types   371
   Subrange Types   383
   Anonymous and Named Data Types   385
Type Compatibility   386
Sets and Additional Control Structures Revisited   389
Testing and Debugging   397
   Testing and Debugging Hints   401

SUMMARY 402 • QUICK CHECK 402 • EXAM PREPARATION
EXERCISES 403 • PREPROGRAMMING EXERCISES 404 • PROGRAMMING
PROBLEMS 404

11 ONE-DIMENSIONAL ARRAYS _____ 406

Structured Data Types   407
One-Dimensional Arrays   414
   Defining Arrays   414
   Accessing Individual Components   416

      Examples of Defining and Accessing Arrays   416
   Processing an Array   421
   Using Arrays in Programs   423
      Subarray Processing   423
      Parallel Arrays   423
      Indices with Semantic Content   424
   Special Note on Passing Arrays as Parameters   438
   Testing and Debugging   438
      Testing and Debugging Hints   439

SUMMARY 440 • QUICK CHECK 440 • EXAM PREPARATION
EXERCISES 442 • PREPROGRAMMING EXERCISES 443 • PROGRAMMING
PROBLEMS 444

12   APPLIED ARRAYS _____ 448

   Algorithms on Lists   449
      Sequential Search in an Unordered List   450
      Sorting   453
      Sequential Search in a Sorted List   456
      Inserting into an Ordered List   458
      Binary Search in an Ordered List   461
   Working with Words   466
   Testing and Debugging   485
      Testing and Debugging Hints   487

SUMMARY 487 • QUICK CHECK 488 • EXAM PREPARATION
EXERCISES 489 • PREPROGRAMMING EXERCISES 491 • PROGRAMMING
PROBLEMS 492

13   MULTIDIMENSIONAL ARRAYS _____ 494

   Two-Dimensional Arrays   496
   More on Array Processing   508
      Initialize the Table   510
      Sum the Rows   511
      Sum the Columns   512
      Print the Table   513
   Another Way of Defining Two-Dimensional Arrays   525
   Multidimensional Arrays   527

Choosing a Data Structure   529
Testing and Debugging   531
   Testing and Debugging Hints   532

SUMMARY 532 • QUICK CHECK 533 • EXAM PREPARATION
EXERCISES 534 • PREPROGRAMMING EXERCISES 537 • PROGRAMMING
PROBLEMS 538

14 RECORDS AND DATA ABSTRACTION _____ 542

Records   543
Arrays of Records   549
Hierarchical Records   564
WITH Statement   565
More on Choosing Data Structures   569
   *Representing Logical Entities with Hierarchical
      Records*   569
   Style Considerations in Choice of Data Structure   577
Testing and Debugging   588
   Testing and Debugging Hints   591

SUMMARY 591 • QUICK CHECK 592 • EXAM PREPARATION
EXERCISES 593 • PREPROGRAMMING EXERCISES 595 • PROGRAMMING
PROBLEMS 598

15 FILES AND POINTERS _____ 602

Files   603
   Text Files Reviewed   604
   Other Files   608
File Buffer Variable   618
Pointers   622
Testing and Debugging   637
   Testing and Debugging Hints   637

SUMMARY 638 • QUICK CHECKS 638 • EXAM PREPARATION
EXERCISES 639 • PREPROGRAMMING EXERCISES 640 • PROGRAMMING
PROBLEMS 641

16 DYNAMIC DATA STRUCTURES _____ 642

Static Versus Dynamic Structures   643
Linked Lists   646
   Algorithms on Linked Lists   654

Pointer Expressions   666
Choice of Data Structure   685
Other Data Structures   686
    Stacks   687
    Queues   690
    Binary Trees   694
Testing and Debugging   714
    Testing and Debugging Hints   715
SUMMARY 716 • QUICK CHECK 716 • EXAM PREPARATION
EXERCISES 717 • PREPROGRAMMING EXERCISES 719 • PROGRAMMING
PROBLEMS 720

17 RECURSION _____ 722

What Is Recursion?   723
Recursive Algorithms with Simple Variables   727
Towers of Hanoi   733
Recursive Algorithms with Structured Variables   737
Recursion Using Pointer Variables   741
    Printing a Linked List in Reverse Order   742
    Recursion with Trees   744
Recursion or Iteration?   749
Testing and Debugging   750
    Testing and Debugging Hints   750
SUMMARY 750 • QUICK CHECK 751 • EXAM PREPARATION
EXERCISES 751 • PREPROGRAMMING EXERCISES 751 • PROGRAMMING
PROBLEMS 753

APPENDIXES _____ A1

A Reserved Words   A1
B Standard Identifiers   A1
C Pascal Operators and Symbols   A3
D Precedence of Operators   A4
E Syntax Diagrams   A4
F Compiler Error Messages   A8
G Program Style, Formatting, and Documentation   A10
H Additional Features of Pascal   A18

I   Implementations   A24
J   Character Sets   A32

GLOSSARY _____ A34

ANSWERS TO SELECTED EXERCISES _____ A42

INDEX _____ A66

Problem Solving in Action

Happy Birthday #1   63

Happy Birthday #2   76

Miles Per Gallon   81

Weighted Average   120

Length of the Hypotenuse   123

Product or Sum of Three Integers   148

Sports at Different Temperatures   152

Failing Notices   157

Average Income   191

Half-life of Plutonium   196

High and Low Temperatures   201

Shipping Invoices   212

Sum Data Sets   227

Comparison of Department Store
    Sales   243

Reformat Names   263

Words of a Given Length   308

Integrating a Function   311

Read and Print Alphanumeric
    Characters   338

Final Grades   352

Rock, Paper, Scissors   375

Birthday Reminder   390

Comparison of Two Lists   409

Frequency of Certain Characters   424

Frequency of All Characters   432

Birthday Reminder Revisited   469

Exam Attendance   473

City Council Election   500

Absenteeism Pattern   513

Automated Address Book   551

Keeping Track of Dates   570

Birthday Calls   581

Campaigning for a Candidate   612

Sports Banquet   620

Personnel Records   630

Solitaire Simulation #1   652

Solitaire Simulation #2   667

SAT Scores   700

Converting Decimal Integers to Binary
    Integers   729

Minimum Value in an Integer
    Array   740

- *To gain an understanding of what a computer program is.*
- *To be able to list the basic steps involved in writing a program.*
- *To be able to define what an algorithm is.*
- *To learn what the major parts of a computer are and how they work together.*
- *To learn the difference between interactive and batch processing.*
- *To learn the difference between hardware and software.*
- *To know what a programming language is.*
- *To understand the compilation and execution processes.*
- *To learn some of the history and features associated with the Pascal programming language.*
- *To learn the steps involved in entering a program into the computer and getting it to run correctly.*

1

Overview of Programming

com·put·er \kəm-ˈpyüt-ər\ *n. often attrib* (1646): one that computes; *specif*: a programmable electronic device that can store,
retrieve, and process data*

What a brief definition for something that has in 35 short years changed the way of life in industrialized societies! We come in contact with computers in all areas of our daily lives: when we pay our bills, when we drive our cars, when we use the telephone, when we go shopping. In fact, it would be easier to list those areas of our lives *not* affected by computers.

It is sad that a device that does so much good is so often feared and maligned. How many times have you heard someone say, "I'm sorry, our computer fouled things up," or "I just don't understand computers; they're too complicated for me"? The very fact that you are reading this book, however, means that you are ready to set aside prejudices and learn about computers. Be forewarned: This book is not just about computers in the abstract. This is a text to teach you how to use them.

WHY PROGRAMMING?

Human behavior and human thought are characterized by logical sequences. Since infancy, you have been learning how to act, how to do things. You learn to expect certain behavior from other people as well as what is expected of you. Your life has a certain order to it; this is what you feel most comfortable with.

*By permission. From Webster's Ninth New Collegiate Dictionary © 1985 by Merriam-Webster, Inc.,
publishers of the Merriam-Webster® Dictionaries.

A lot of what you do every day is done automatically, on an unconscious level. Fortunately, it is not necessary for you to consciously think of every step involved in a process as simple as turning this page by hand. If it were necessary to consciously think

Lift hand.

Move hand to right side of book.

Grasp corner of top page.

Move hand from right to left until page is positioned so that what is on the other side can be read.

Let go of page.

we would all be illiterate. Think how many neurons must fire and how many muscles must respond, all in a certain order or sequence, to achieve a smooth motion of arm and hand. Yet you do it unconsciously.

Much of what you do unconsciously you once had to learn. Watch the intense concentration of a baby putting one foot before the other while learning to walk. Then watch a group of three-year-olds playing tag. Another example of a learned logical sequence of steps is the process of brushing your teeth. You were taught to put the toothpaste carefully on the brush, put it in your mouth, and clean your teeth in a certain way. Now the action is completely automatic.

On a broader scale, mathematics could never have been developed without logical sequences of steps for solving problems or proving theorems. Music requires a definite sequence of notes in order to be recognizable. A logical sequence of steps is also needed for mass production of many of the products we use; certain operations must take place in a prescribed order. Our whole civilization is based on the order of things and actions.

Ordering, both conscious and unconscious, is an important part of our lives. This ordering is achieved through a process we call *programming.*

Programming The planning, scheduling, or performing of a task or an event.

This book is concerned with the programming of one of our tools, the computer.

Computer Programming The process of planning a sequence of instructions for a computer to follow.

Just as a program for a concert or play is an outline of the actions to be performed by the players, a *computer program* is an outline of the steps to be performed by the computer.

Computer Program A sequence of instructions outlining steps to be performed by a computer.

From now on, when we use the words *program* and *programming,* we will mean *computer program* and *computer programming.*

The computer allows us to do tasks more efficiently, quickly, and accurately than we could do them by hand—if we could do them by hand at all. In order to use this powerful tool, we must specify exactly what we want done and the order in which it should be done. This is accomplished through programming.

WHAT IS PROGRAMMING?

Our definition of programming leaves a lot unsaid. In order to write a sequence of instructions for a computer to follow, we must go through a certain process. This process is composed of a *problem-solving phase* and an *implementation phase.* (See Figure 1-1.)

Problem-Solving Phase

Analysis—Understand (define) the problem.

General Solution (Algorithm)—Develop a logical sequence of steps to be used to solve the problem.

Test—Follow the exact steps as outlined to see if the solution truly solves the problem.

Implementation Phase

Specific Solution (Program)—Translate the algorithm into a programming language (code).

Test—Have the computer follow the instructions. Check the results and make corrections until the answers are correct.

Use—Use the program.

Figure 1-1
Programming
Process

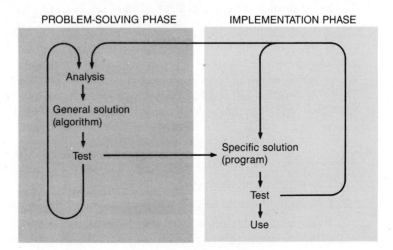

PROBLEM-SOLVING PHASE   IMPLEMENTATION PHASE

Analysis

General solution
(algorithm)

Test

Specific solution
(program)

Test

Use

The computer, alas, is not intelligent. It cannot analyze a problem and come up with a solution. The programmer must arrive at the solution and communicate it to the computer. The problem solving is done by the programmer—not the computer. So, you may ask, what's the advantage of using a computer if it can't solve any problems? The advantage is that once we have a solution for a problem and have prepared a version of it for the computer, the computer can rapidly repeat the solution again and again and again. Thus the computer may be used to free people from tasks that are repetitive and boring or that require great speed or consistency.

The programmer begins the programming process by analyzing the problem and developing a general solution called an *algorithm*. Understanding and analysis of a problem take up much more time than Figure 1-1 implies. They are the heart of the programming process; more will be said about them in Chapter 2.

Algorithm A step-by-step procedure for solving a problem in a finite amount of time.

We use algorithms every day. An algorithm is simply a verbal or written description of a logical sequence of actions. Cooking recipes, laundry detergent instructions, and refrigerator-defrosting instructions are examples of written algorithms.

When you start your car, you go through a step-by-step procedure. The algorithm might look something like this:

1. Insert the key.
2. Make sure the transmission is in Park (or Neutral).
3. Depress the gas pedal.
4. Turn the key to the start position.
5. If the engine starts within six seconds, release the key to the ignition position.
6. If the engine doesn't start in six seconds, wait ten seconds and repeat steps 3 through 6 (but not more than five times).
7. If the car doesn't start, call the garage.

Without the phrase "but not more than five times" in step 6, it would be possible to get stuck trying to start the car forever. Why? Because if something is wrong with the car, repeating steps 3 through 6 over and over again will not start it. That never-ending situation is known as an infinite loop. So if the phrase "but not more than five times" is left out of step 6, the procedure does not fit the definition of an algorithm. An algorithm must terminate in a finite amount of time for all possible conditions.

Suppose a programmer needed an algorithm to determine an employee's wages for the week. The algorithm would reflect what would be done by hand:

1. Look up the employee's pay rate.
2. Determine the number of hours worked during the week.
3. If the number of hours worked is less than or equal to 40.0, multiply the number of hours by the pay rate to get the regular wages.

4. If the number of hours worked is greater than 40.0, multiply the pay rate by 40.0 to get the regular wages and multiply $1\frac{1}{2}$ times the pay rate by the difference between the number of hours worked and 40.0 to get the overtime wages.

5. Add the regular wages to the overtime wages (if any) to get the total wages for the week.

The steps followed by the computer are very often the same as those you would use to do the calculations by hand.

After developing a general solution, the programmer "walks through" the algorithm by performing each step mentally or manually. If this testing of the algorithm doesn't produce satisfactory answers, the programmer repeats the problem-solving process, analyzing the problem again and coming up with another algorithm. Often the second algorithm is just a variation of the original one. When the programmer is satisfied with the algorithm, it is translated into a *programming language*. We use the Pascal programming language in this book.

Programming Language A set of rules, symbols, and special words used to construct a program.

We use a programming language, rather than English, because a programming language restricts us to writing only instructions that the computer can carry out. English is far too complicated a language for today's computers to be able to follow instructions written in it. A programming language is essentially a simplified form of English (with math symbols) that adheres to a strict set of grammar rules. If we write instructions using only this language, they will be simple enough for the computer to follow. Using this language is not as easy as it sounds, though. Try giving someone directions to the nearest airport using a vocabulary of no more than 36 words and you'll begin to see the problem. Programming will require you to develop a skill for writing very simple and exact instructions.

Translating an algorithm into a programming language is called *coding* the algorithm. The resulting program is tested by running (*executing*) it on the computer. If the program fails to produce the desired results, the programmer must determine what is wrong and modify the algorithm and program as needed. The combination of coding and testing an algorithm is often referred to as *implementing* an algorithm.

There is no unique way of implementing an algorithm. For example, an algorithm can be translated into more than one programming language. Each different translation of the algorithm produces a different implementation. Even two different people translating an algorithm into the same programming language are likely to come up with different implementations. (See Figure 1-2.) Variations occur because a programming language allows some flexibility in how the algorithm is translated. Given this flexibility, two people will usually adopt different *styles* in writing programs, just as people have different styles in writing English. Once you have gained some experience in writing programs, you will develop a style of your own. Throughout this book, we will offer tips on good programming style.

If the definitions of a computer program and an algorithm look suspiciously alike, it is because all programs are algorithms. An algorithm can be expressed in a

Figure 1-2
Differences in
Implementation

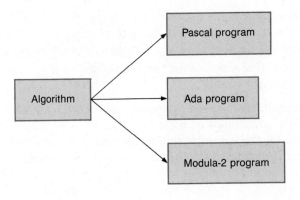

IN DIFFERENT LANGUAGES

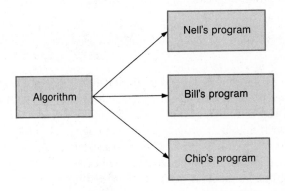

RESULTING FROM PERSONAL PROGRAMMING STYLES

programming language or in English; when it is expressed in a programming language, it is also called a program.

Some students try to take a shortcut in the programming process by going directly from the problem definition to the coding of the program. (See Figure 1-3.) This shortcut is very tempting, and it might seem at first to save a lot of time. However, for many reasons that will become obvious to you as you read this book, this approach actually takes *more* time and effort. If you don't take the time initially to think out and polish your algorithm, you will spend a lot of extra time correcting errors (debugging) and revising an ill-conceived program. So think first and code later! The sooner you start coding, the longer it will take to get a correct program.

Programming involves more than simply writing a program. First, a programmer must analyze the problem in order to develop a strategy that can be used in the program to solve the specific problem correctly. Developing a general solution before actually writing the program helps the programmer manage the problem, keep thoughts straight, and avoid unnecessary errors. In addition, since most programs will be used over and over again, program *documentation* and *maintenance* are important parts of programming.

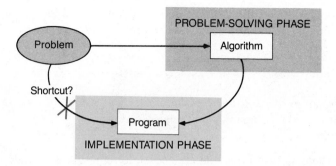

Figure 1-3
Programming
Shortcut?

Documentation	Written text and comments that make a program easier for others to under-stand, use, and modify.
Maintenance	The modification of a program, after it has been completed, in order to meet changing requirements or take care of any errors that show up.

DATA REPRESENTATION

In a computer information is represented electronically by pulses of electricity. Electric circuits, in their simplest form, may be either on or off. Usually a circuit that is on will represent the number 1 and a circuit that is off will represent the number 0. Any kind of information can be represented by combinations of enough 1's and 0's. We simply have to choose which pattern of 1's or 0's will represent each piece of information we will be using. For example, we could arbitrarily choose the pattern 1101000110 to represent the name "Pascal."

When information is represented by 1's and 0's, it is said to be in *binary* form, since the binary (base 2) number system uses only 1's and 0's to represent numbers. The word *bit* (short for *binary digit*) is often used to refer to a single 1 or 0. Thus the pattern 1101000110 is said to have ten bits. The process of assigning bit patterns to pieces of information is called *coding*—the same name as is given to the process of translating an algorithm into a programming language. Both processes have the same name because the only language that the first computers could work with was binary in form. In the early days of computing, programming meant translating an algorithm into patterns of 1's and 0's.

Fortunately we no longer have to know how to use binary coding schemes. With modern computers, the process of coding—putting something into a form that is usable by the computer—is usually just a matter of writing down the information in letters and numbers. The computer automatically converts the numbers and letters we use to represent information into binary form.

From now on, we will use the term *data* rather than the word *information*. *Information* is a general term that encompasses abstract ideas and concepts. *Data* is information in symbolic form, such as numbers and letters. We have to represent information as data before it can be used by the computer.

Information	Any knowledge that can be communicated.
Data	Information that has been put into a form usable by a computer, that is, a form suitable for analysis or decision making.

The patterns of bits that are chosen to represent data and instructions will vary from one computer to another. Even on the same computer, different programming languages may use different binary representations for the same data. A single programming language may even use the same pattern of bits to represent different things in different contexts. (Humans do this too. The four letters that represent the word *tack* have different meanings depending on whether you are talking about upholstery, sailing, sewing, paint, or horseback riding.) The point is that the patterns of bits are, by themselves, meaningless. It is the way the patterns are used that gives them their meanings.

WHAT IS A COMPUTER?

You don't need to know much about a computer in order to use it as an effective tool. You can learn a programming language such as Pascal, write programs, and learn the procedure for running (executing) these programs. However, if you know something about the parts of a computer, you can better understand the effect of each instruction in the programming language.

Computer	A programmable electronic device that can store, retrieve, and process data.

The verbs *store, retrieve,* and *process* imply the five basic components of most computers: memory, arithmetic/logic, control, input, and output.

The *memory unit* is an ordered sequence of storage cells, each capable of containing a piece of data. It is similar to an old-fashioned post office with pigeonholes for mail. These memory storage cells are known variously as memory cells, memory locations, or places in memory. Each memory cell has a distinct address to which one refers in order to store or retrieve information.

Memory Unit	The internal data storage of a computer.

The memory holds data (input data or results of computation) and instructions (programs). (See Figure 1-4.) The part of the computer that follows these instructions is called the *central processing unit.*

Figure 1-4
Memory

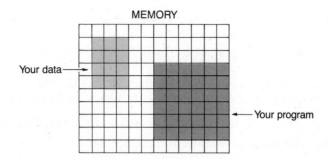

Central Processing Unit (CPU) The part of the computer that executes the instructions of a program stored in memory; computer component composed of the *arithmetic/logic unit* and the *control unit.*

Arithmetic/Logic Unit (ALU) The computer component that performs arithmetic operations (addition, subtraction, multiplication, division) and logical operations (comparison of two values).

Control Unit The computer component that controls the actions of the other components in order to execute instructions (the program) in sequence.

In order for us to use computers, we must have some way of getting data into and out of them. *Input and output devices* perform this function.

Input/Output (I/O) Devices The parts of the computer that accept data to be processed (input) and/or present the results of the processing (output).

A video display terminal is typical of devices that are used for both input and output. The keyboard of the terminal is the input component, and the video display is the output component. Terminals that use liquid crystal displays (LCDs) are also becoming available. Another form of terminal uses a printer mechanism to provide output. A printer is an example of a device that is used only for output from the computer. An example of a device that is used only for input is a punch-card reader. Figure 1-5 is a stylized diagram of the basic components of a computer.

Figure 1-5
Basic Components
of a Computer

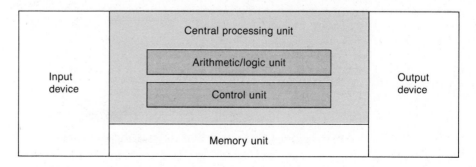

For the most part, computers simply move and combine data in memory. The differences among various computers basically involve the size of the memory and the speed with which data can be recalled from it, the efficiency with which data can be moved or combined, and limitations on I/O devices.

When a program is executing (when the instructions are being followed), the computer proceeds step by step through the instruction execution cycle:

1. The control unit fetches the next coded instruction from memory.
2. The instruction is decoded into control signals.
3. The control signals tell the appropriate unit (arithmetic/logic unit, memory, or I/O device) to perform the instruction.
4. The sequence is repeated from step 1.

Computers can have a wide variety of *peripheral devices* attached to them. (See Figure 1-6.)

(a) CPU behind two terminals   Digital Equipment Corporation

(b) Desktop printer   Dataproducts

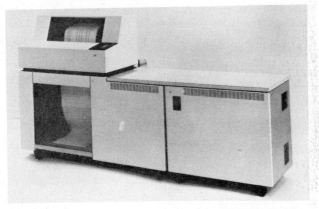

(c) Line printer   International Business Machines

Figure 1-6
CPU and
Peripheral Devices

(d) Disk drive   Digital Equipment Corporation

(e) Tape drive   Control Data

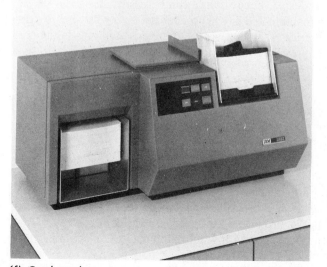

(f) Card reader   International Business Machines

(g) CRT   Digital Equipment Corporation

Peripheral Device An input, output, or auxiliary storage device of a computer.

An *auxiliary storage device* (sometimes called a *secondary storage device*) is used to hold coded data, ready for use by the computer, in between the times when we actually want to use the data. Instead of inputting the data to the computer every time we want to use it, we can input the data once and have the computer store it on the auxiliary storage device. From then on, whenever we need to use the data, we tell the computer to transfer the data from the auxiliary storage device to its memory. Typical auxiliary storage devices are magnetic tape drives and disk drives. A magnetic tape drive is similar to a tape recorder. A disk drive may be thought of as a cross between a record player and a tape recorder because it uses a thin platter made out of a magnetic material. A read/write head (similar to the record/playback head in a tape recorder) travels across the spinning disk and retrieves or records data.

Auxiliary Storage Device A device that stores data in encoded form, external to the computer's memory.

The operation of all these physical components, known as *hardware*, depends on the presence of *software*.

Hardware The physical components of a computer.

Software The computer programs; the set of all programs available to a computer.

Hardware is usually fixed in design, but software can be easily changed. The ease with which software can be manipulated is what makes the computer such a versatile and powerful tool. In addition to our programs, there are programs in the computer that are designed to simplify the user/computer *interface*, thus making it easier for us to use the machine.

Interface A connecting link at a shared boundary, permitting independent systems to meet and act on or communicate with each other.

The user and the computer can be considered to be the "independent systems" in the definition of interface. The interface between us and the computer is provided by some device, such as a terminal, which allows us to communicate with the computer. The terminal, for example, provides a keyboard and screen that we work with on our side of the interface boundary and a wire that carries the electronic pulses that the computer works with on its side of the interface boundary. At the boundary itself, the terminal provides a mechanism for translating between the two sides.

When we communicate directly with the computer through a terminal, we are using an *interactive system.*

> **Interactive System** A system for direct communication between the user and the computer; a terminal/computer connection allowing direct entry of programs and data and providing immediate feedback to the user.

When, on the other hand, we submit a program and data on cards through a device such as a card reader, we are using a form of *batch processing.*

> **Batch Processing** A technique for entering data and executing programs without intermediate user interaction with the computer.

Typically, batch processing involves input of programs and data on cards and output in printed form from the line printer.

As we have seen, a computer is composed of different functional parts. It can store data in memory and on tape or disk, manipulate this data (through the arithmetic/logic and control units), and communicate with the user (through input and output devices).

PERSONAL COMPUTERS AND MAINFRAMES

So far we have discussed computers in general terms. There are, however, many different sizes and kinds of computers. Not all of the features we mentioned may be easily recognizable in every computer you encounter. The different parts of a computer are easiest to distinguish in the larger models, called *mainframes.*

> **Mainframe** A large computing system designed for high-volume data processing or for use by many people at once.

Mainframes are large, very fast computers that may fill an entire room. A typical mainframe computer consists of several cabinets full of electronic components. You may very well see mainframe cabinets labeled "Central Processing Unit," "Memory Unit," and "Input/Output Unit." It is easy to spot the various peripheral devices: separate cabinets labeled "Disk Drive" and "Tape Drive," plus some other units that are obviously terminals, card readers, line printers, and other such devices. Figure 1-7 shows an example of what you might see in a typical mainframe computer installation.

At the other end of the spectrum are the microcomputers called *personal computers (PCs).* These are so small that they fit comfortably on a desktop.

Figure 1-7
Mainframe
and two
terminals

Digital Equipment Corporation

Figure 1-8
Personal Computer

International Business Machines

Personal Computer (PC) A small computer system (usually intended to fit on a desk top) that is designed to be used primarily by a single person.

It isn't always quite as easy to spot the individual parts within a personal computer. Many PCs are made up of only a single box, such as the one shown in Figure 1-8, and a keyboard. You must open up the case in order to see the central processing unit, which is usually just a single, large integrated circuit. Figure 1-9 is a view of the inside of a PC. The small black, rectangular components are the integrated circuits.

In personal computers the human-computer interface, rather than being a separate terminal, is just a keyboard and a display screen. Personal computers rarely have tape drives or card readers, but they often have disk drives and printers. The disk drives of a personal computer typically hold much less data than the disk drives used with mainframes. Similarly, the printers that are typically attached to personal com-

Figure 1-9
The Inside of a PC.
(The CPU is not
visible.)

Input/Output

Power Supply

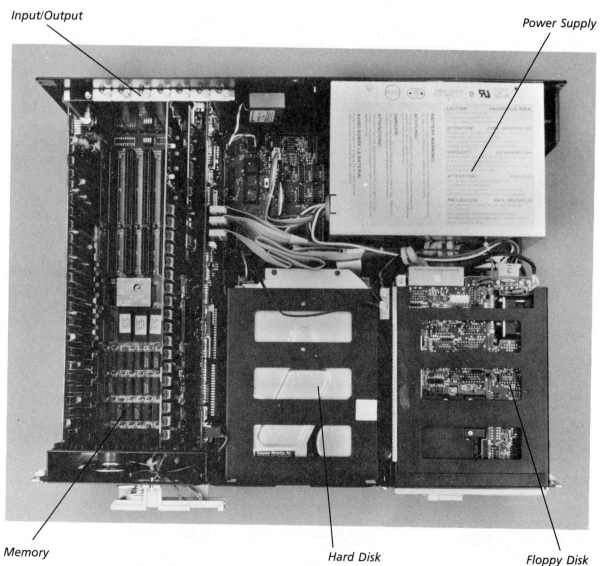

Memory

Hard Disk

Floppy Disk

puters are much slower than the line printers commonly used with mainframes. Figure 1-9 points out some of the different parts of a personal computer.

Between personal computers and mainframes are *minicomputers*. These intermediate-size computer systems are designed to be more powerful than a personal computer and less expensive than a mainframe.

Minicomputer A computer system larger than a personal computer but smaller than a mainframe; sometimes called an entry-level mainframe.

WHAT IS A PROGRAMMING LANGUAGE?

Remember that in the digital computer all data, whether it is alphabetic or numeric data or instructions, is stored and used in binary codes of 1's and 0's. When computers were first developed, the only programming language available was the primitive instruction set of each machine, known as *machine language* (or machine code).

Machine Language The language used directly by the computer and composed of binary-coded instructions.

Even though most computers perform the same kinds of operations, different designers have chosen different sets of binary codes of 1's and 0's to stand for each instruction. So the machine code for one computer is not the same as for another.

When programmers used machine language for programming, they had to enter the binary codes for the various operations of the computer, a tedious and error-prone process. The resulting programs were difficult to read and modify, so *assembly languages* were developed to make the programmer's job easier.

Assembly Language A low-level programming language in which a mnemonic is used to represent each of the machine language instructions for a particular computer.

An instruction in assembly language is in an easy-to-remember form called a mnemonic (pronounced "ni-mon'ik"). Typical instructions for addition and subtraction might look like this:

Assembly Language	Machine Language
ADD	100101
SUB	010011

The only problem with assembly language was that instructions written in it could not be directly executed by a computer. So a program called the *assembler* was written to translate the assembly language instructions into machine language instructions (machine code).

Assembler A program that translates an assembly language program into machine code.

Development of the assembler was a step in the right direction, but a programmer was still forced to think in terms of individual machine instructions. Eventually high-level programming languages were developed that were closer to natural languages such as English and thus less limiting than machine code. (See Figure 1-10.) Programs in these high-level languages (such as Pascal, COBOL, and FORTRAN) must be translated into machine language instructions by a translator program called the *compiler*.

Compiler A program that translates a high-level language into machine code.

*Figure 1-10
Levels of
Abstraction*

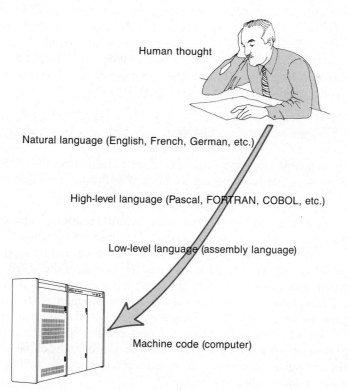

Human thought

Natural language (English, French, German, etc.)

High-level language (Pascal, FORTRAN, COBOL, etc.)

Low-level language (assembly language)

Machine code (computer)

Figure 1-11
Use of High-Level
Programming
Language

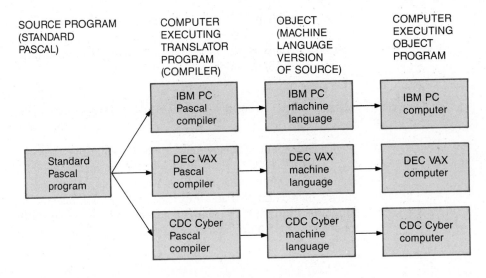

If we write a program in a high-level language, we can run it on any computer that has the appropriate compiler. This is because most high-level languages are *standardized,* meaning that an official description of the language exists.

A program in a high-level language is called a *source program.* When the source program is compiled by running the compiler with the program as data, a machine language program called an *object program* results. The object program can be run directly on the computer. (See Figure 1-11.)

Source Program A program written in a high-level programming language.

Object Program The machine language version of a program that results when a compiler translates a source program into binary codes for a particular computer.

Notice in Figure 1-12 that compilation/execution is a two-step process. During the compilation phase of the process, the computer is running the compiler program.

To the compiler program, a source program is just input data. The compiler program outputs a machine language translation of the source program. In the execution phase of the process, the machine language version of the program (object code) replaces the compiler program in the computer's memory. The computer then runs the object program, doing whatever the program instructs it to do.

We saw that a computer system is composed of both hardware and software. *System software* is a set of programs that improves the efficiency and convenience of the computer's processing. It includes the compiler as well as the *operating system* and the *editor.* (See Figure 1-13.)

Figure 1-12
Compilation/
Execution

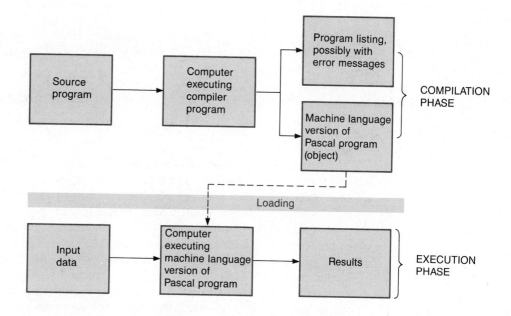

Figure 1-13
Human/Machine
Interface

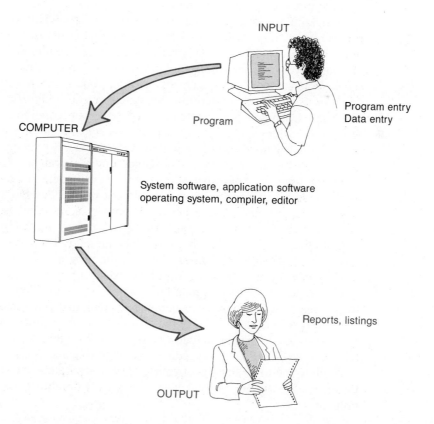

Operating System A set of programs that manages all computer resources (it can input a program, call the compiler, execute the resulting object program, and carry out any other system commands).

Editor An interactive program that is used to create and modify source programs or data.

The instructions available in a programming language reflect the functions a computer can actually perform. The computer can transfer data from one place to another. It can input data from an input device such as a terminal and output data to an output device such as a printer. Most programming languages have Read and Write statements for these purposes. The computer can store data in and retrieve data from its memory and its secondary storage (such as tape or disk). The computer can also compare two data values for equality or inequality, and it can perform arithmetic operations such as addition and subtraction very quickly.

When designing an algorithm, a programmer should keep in mind the things a computer can do. A programmer who is aware of the computer's limitations won't make the mistake of including an impossible step such as "perform a somersault" in an algorithm meant for the computer.

Programming languages require that we use certain structures to express algorithms as programs. There are four basic ways of structuring statements (instructions) in Pascal and in other languages: sequentially, conditionally, repetitively, and procedurally. These structures are known by the names shown in Figure 1-14. The *sequence* is composed of statements executed one after another. The conditional structure (*selection*) executes different statements depending on certain conditions. The *loop* structure repeats statements while certain conditions are met. And the *procedure* enables us to replace a group of statements with a single statement.

To visualize how each of these structures works, let's compare executing a program to driving a car down a road. Going down a straight stretch of road is like following a *sequence* of instructions. But when you come to a fork in the road, you must decide which way to go and then take one or the other branch of the fork. This is what the computer does when it encounters a *selection* (sometimes called a branch or decision) in the program. And sometimes you have to go around the block several times to find a place that you are looking for. The computer does the same sort of thing when it encounters a *loop* in the program.

A *procedure* is a combination of the basic structures that is considered as a single instruction in the program. For example, you know how to get from home to work, even though that may be a complicated path to drive. Someone might tell you, "The party is four blocks west of the office." Your algorithm for getting to the party from home would then be to follow your "going from home to work" procedure and then go four blocks west. Procedures are often called subprograms or subroutines. They allow you to write parts of your programs separately, then assemble them into final form. We will see that procedures can greatly simplify the task of writing a large program.

Figure 1-14
Basic Structures
of Programming
Languages

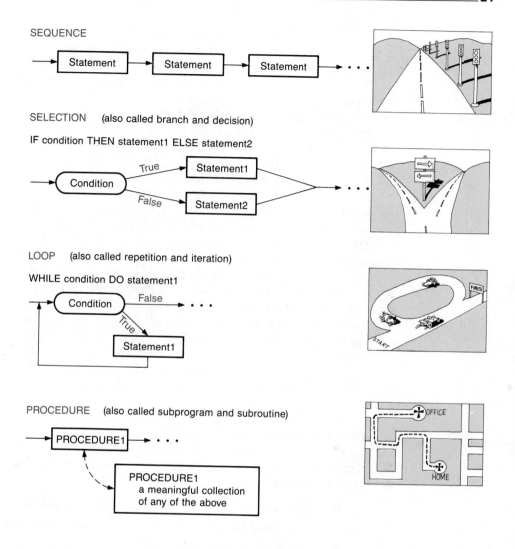

SEQUENCE

SELECTION   (also called branch and decision)

IF condition THEN statement1 ELSE statement2

LOOP   (also called repetition and iteration)

WHILE condition DO statement1

PROCEDURE   (also called subprogram and subroutine)

PROCEDURE1
a meaningful collection
of any of the above

WHAT IS PASCAL?

The programming language Pascal was designed by the Swiss computer scientist Niklaus Wirth in 1968 and revised in 1972. In 1984, Wirth received the prestigious Turing Award, the highest honor in computer science, in part for his work on Pascal. Wirth created Pascal to avoid many of the problems and pitfalls of the programming languages in widespread use at the time. It includes their better features and more, in a streamlined format that is easy to use. The language is named after the famous French mathematician Blaise Pascal (1623–1662), who is credited with designing a very early mechanical calculating machine, a forerunner of the modern digital computer.

Originally intended to be a teaching tool for programming concepts, Pascal has become very popular for use in business, industry, and personal computing. The language is simple to learn, yet embodies a wide range of programming concepts. Pascal encourages programmers to write programs that are clear and can be easily understood by other programmers.

After learning Pascal, you will find it easy to learn other programming languages such as FORTRAN, COBOL, BASIC and Modula-2. The bonus is that you can apply concepts, methods, techniques, and habits that you learn with Pascal to other languages as well, thus increasing your skill and value as a programmer.

The International Standards Organization (ISO) established an official description of the Pascal programming language in 1981. Whenever a program is written according to the ISO standard for Pascal, it can be translated into the machine language of any computer for which there exists a compiler that also adheres to the ISO Pascal standard. Unfortunately, not all compiler writers (people who write compiler programs) adhere strictly to the standard. For one reason or another, various compilers recognize slightly different versions of the Pascal language.

Throughout this book, we will adhere to the ISO Pascal standard unless we specifically say otherwise. If something we tell you doesn't seem to work on your computer, you should check the manuals for your specific computer and compiler to see if the compiler differs from the standard. To help you out, we will note some things that are done differently on some of the more widely used computers and compilers. For your convenience, Appendix I describes the difference between ISO standard Pascal and two more widely used compilers (CDC Pascal and UCSD Pascal).*

Let's look at a sample algorithm and then at the coded Pascal program. The following algorithm parallels what is done by hand to compute the wages for each employee in a company and the total wages for the company. The program was designed to be interactive—the person using the program interacts with the program via a terminal.

1. Prepare to write a list of the employees' wages (open file Payfile).
2. Prompt the user for the employee number (put message on the screen).
3. Read the employee number.
4. If the employee number is zero then continue with step 13.
5. Prompt the user for the employee's pay rate.
6. Read the pay rate.

*We have provided special supplementary materials for Turbo Pascal, Macintosh Pascal, and VAX Pascal. These materials are coordinated with the order of presentation of topics in the text. Whenever a special feature of one of these Pascal systems pertains to the topic at hand, the ⇦ symbol will appear in the margin along with one or more letters (T for Turbo, M for Macintosh, V for VAX). If you are using one of these systems, you should then turn to the appropriate supplement, where the pertinent information will be marked with a corresponding ⇨ symbol and the number of the page that referred to the supplement.

T,M,V ⇦ For example, the symbol T, M, V ⇦ to the left of this sentence indicates that if you are using Turbo, Macintosh, or VAX Pascal, you should now turn to the corresponding supplement and read the part marked 22 ⇨.

7. Prompt the user for the hours worked.

8. Read the hours worked.

9. Perform the procedure for calculating pay (shown below).

10. Add the employee's wages to the total payroll.

11. Write the employee number, pay rate, hours worked, and wages on the list (file Payfile).

12. Continue with step 2.

13. Write the total company payroll on the screen.

14. Stop.

Procedure for Calculating Pay

1. If the hours worked is greater than 40.0, then

1A. wages = (40.0 × pay rate) + (hours worked − 40.0) × 1.5 × pay rate otherwise

1B. wages = hours worked × pay rate

Following is the Pascal program for this algorithm. This sample program is shown just to give you an idea of what you'll be learning. If you have had no previous exposure to programming, you probably won't understand most of the program. Don't worry about it; you will soon. In fact, as each new construct is introduced, we will refer you back to its occurrence in Program Payroll.

NOTE: The comments enclosed by the symbols "(*" and "*)" are only for the benefit of readers of the program and are ignored by the compiler.

```
PROGRAM Payroll (Input, Output, Payfile);

(* This program computes the wages for each employee and the total
   payroll for the company *)

CONST
  MaxHours = 40.0;        (* Maximum normal work hours *)
  Overtime = 1.5;         (* Overtime pay rate factor  *)

VAR
  PayRate,                (* Employee's pay rate     *)
  Hours,                  (* Hours worked            *)
  Wages,                  (* Wages earned            *)
  Total:                  (* Total company payroll *)
    Real;
  EmpNum:                 (* Employee ID number      *)
    Integer;
  Payfile:                (* Company payroll file  *)
    Text;
```

```
PROCEDURE CalcPay (    Payrate,        (* Employee payrate *)
                       Hours:          (* Hours worked     *)
                       Real;
                VAR Wages:             (* Wages earned      *)
                       Real);

(* CalcPay computes wages from hours worked and the employee pay rate,
   taking overtime into account *)

BEGIN (* CalcPay *)
   IF Hours > MaxHours                          (* Check for overtime *)
      THEN
         Wages : = (MaxHours * Payrate) +
                   (Hours - MaxHours) * Payrate * Overtime
      ELSE
         Wages : = Hours * Payrate
   END;   (* CalcPay *)


BEGIN (* Payroll *)
   Rewrite(Payfile);                            (* Open file Payfile *)
   Total : = 0.0;
   Write('Enter employee number:  ');           (* Prompting message *)
   Readln(EmpNum);                         (* Read employee ID number *)
   WHILE EmpNum <> 0 DO
      BEGIN
         Write('Enter payrate:  ');             (* Prompting message *)
         Readln(Payrate);                   (* Read hourly payrate *)
         Write('Enter hours worked:  ');            (* Prompt *)
         Readln(Hours);                       (* Read hours worked *)
         CalcPay(Payrate, Hours, Wages);        (* Compute wages *)
         Total : = Total + Wages;            (* Add wages to total *)
         Writeln(Payfile, EmpNum, Payrate, Hours, Wages);
                         (* Put employee wage data in file Payfile *)
         Write('Enter employee number:  ');          (* Prompt *)
         Readln(EmpNum)
      END;
   Writeln('Total payroll is ', Total:10:2)
                              (* Print total payroll on screen *)
   END.   (* Payroll *)
```

PROGRAM ENTRY, CORRECTION, AND EXECUTION

Up to this point we have talked about programming in the abstract. We have described the programming process as having two phases: problem solving and implementation. It isn't until the implementation phase that the computer actually figures in computer programming. Remember, the computer is only a tool. First we analyze and solve our problem intellectually for the general case. Then we code our solution in a programming language, often on paper, before we test our solution by using it on a computer.

Once we have the program written on paper, how do we get it into the machine? The most common way is to type it on the keyboard of a computer terminal or personal computer. An alternative method is to copy the program onto punch cards using a machine called a keypunch.

Interactive Program Entry

Recall that an interactive system is one in which the user communicates directly with the computer. Generally the user does this through the keyboard and display screen of a terminal or personal computer.

Unfortunately, the process is not quite as simple as it sounds. First of all, you have to learn some commands that you must give to the computer to tell it that you want to type in a program. You also have to learn how to correct typing mistakes—unless, of course, you are a perfect typist! In this section we will go over the interactive program entry process in general. You will need to consult the manuals for your specific computer in order to get the details. On most computers, however, the process is basically the same as what we will describe here.

Getting Started on a Personal Computer The first step in entering a program is to get the computer's attention. With a personal computer, this usually means turning it on and inserting a system disk. The system disk contains a collection of programs, called the operating system, which comes with the computer and allows you *T,M* ⬅ to use it. The process of using the system disk is called *booting the system.* The term comes from the phrase "pulling yourself up by your own bootstraps"—when the computer is first turned on, this is basically what it must do in order to get the essential programs into its memory. (Most computers forget everything in their memory when they are turned off.) Once the system is "booted," you have its attention. It is ready to accept commands from you.

Getting Started on a Mainframe Larger computers (mainframes) are left running all of the time, except when some component fails. Such a failure is called a *crash.* When a large computer is not running, it is said to be *down.* Assuming the computer is up, you get its attention by sitting down in front of a terminal, turning the terminal on if it isn't already (usually the switch is located somewhere on the back of the terminal), and pressing a key. Usually the key you will press is labeled "Return." Since use of a particular large computer is often restricted to a small number of people, you must identify yourself to the computer before it will let you give it any commands. Most computers will first ask you for a *user name*, which is the name by which the computer knows you. Your user name may be your real name, a student number, or some other sequence of letters and numbers uniquely assigned to you for that particular computer.

Figure 1-15
Logging on to the
Computer

```
<return>
Username: SMITH
Password: ZYMURGY


        Welcome to VAX1:: running VMS 4.4
        *********************************

Last Login was Friday, Feb. 14, 1986 at 10:27:35
```

After you type in your user name, you press the return key. The computer will then ask you for a *password*. This is a series of letters that has been assigned to you and that only you know. Other people may be able to guess your user name, but your password should be something that nobody else can guess. The password system protects information that you store in the computer from being tampered with or destroyed by someone else using the computer. After you type your password, you press the return key.

If you typed your user name and password correctly, the computer will greet you with a welcoming message. If you mistyped either of them, the computer will type a message telling you that you are not a valid user. Then you must start over. This entire process is called *logging on* to the computer. Once you have successfully logged on, the computer is ready to accept commands from you. Figure 1-15 shows how to log on to a typical computer.

Entering Your Program Once the computer is ready to accept your commands, you can tell it that you want to type in a program. You do this by typing a command that tells the operating system to make the computer run a program to let you type information into its memory. This program is the editor we mentioned earlier. The editor program does more than simply let you type in lines of characters—it also lets you go back and make corrections or changes to anything you have typed.

There are many different types of editor programs. On many computers there are several editors that you can use, each with different features. We won't attempt to describe them all here—you will have to consult the manual for your computer to find out about its editors. We will, however, describe two basic types of editors: line-oriented editors and screen editors.

Entering Your Program with a Line-Oriented Editor Line-oriented editors, or line editors, are the simpler of the two types of editors. When you use a line editor, your basic unit of information is a line of characters that have been typed in. You may look at any line that has been typed in, add new lines, delete lines, change words within lines, and so on.

Usually a line editor has two modes of operation: command mode and input mode. In command mode, you type commands to the editor which cause it to perform actions such as deleting lines, printing out lines, and so on. In input mode, you simply type lines and the editor stores them in the computer's memory. You use input mode to type your program into the computer.

While you are in input mode, most line editors will let you back up and make changes to the line you are typing. Usually a key marked "Backspace," "BKSP," "Delete," or "Del" is provided to let you back up on a line. Each time you press this key, one character is deleted from the right end of the line.

When you have finished typing a line and are satisfied that it is correct, you press the return key to tell the editor to save the line in the computer's memory. You also must press the return key when you have finished typing a command in command mode—the editor will not perform a command until you press the return key. Until that point, you can use the backspace or delete keys to correct any typing mistakes in the command.

Once you have typed all of the lines in your program into the computer's memory, you must tell the editor that you have finished entering lines. You do this by switching to command mode and giving a command to the editor that tells it to quit and let you communicate directly with the operating system. After you exit from the editor, your program will be stored in an area of the computer's memory called a *file*.

File An area in secondary storage that has a name and is used to hold a collection of data; the collection of data itself is also often referred to as a file.

A file in the computer's memory is just like a file folder in a filing cabinet. It is a collection of information that has a name tag attached to it. You get to choose the name you want the file to be tagged with, usually when you first type it in with the editor. From that point on, you can refer to the file by the name you gave it.

Figure 1-16 shows a sample editing session with a line-oriented editor.

Entering Your Program with a Screen Editor The screen editor is more complex but easier to use than the line-oriented editor. Until recently screen editors were found only on special computers designed for word processing. Now screen editors have become available on almost every kind of computer.

The basic unit of information in a screen editor is a display screen full of lines. Unlike a line editor, which restricts you to directly correcting only the line you are typing, a screen editor will let you directly change anything that you see on the screen of your terminal. Most modern computer terminals have a special group of keys called *cursor control keys*. (The cursor is a little mark on the screen that indicates the point where you are typing.) The cursor control keys are most often a set of arrows that point up, down, right, and left. (See Figure 1-17.) Each time you press one of these keys, the cursor moves one character position in the direction shown.

Figure 1-16
Editing Session
for Line-
Oriented Editor

```
$ edit myprog.pas

EDIT Version 2.0     Creating file MYPROG.PAS

Command Mode

?input

Input Mode

00010: PROGRAM MyProg <Input, Output>;
00020: BEGIN
00030:    Writeln('This is my first program.')
00040: END
00050: <ESC>

Command Mode

?exit

File MYPROG.PAS contains 4 lines.
End Editing
```

Using these keys, you can move the cursor to any point on the screen to make a correction.

The terminal may also contain other special keys that let you view other parts of the file on the screen, delete lines on the screen, insert new lines, and so on. These keys take the place of many of the commands a line editor would require you to type in command mode. Generally a screen editor is always in input mode.

Figure 1-17
Cursor Control
Keys

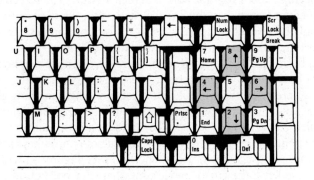

When you first create a file with a screen editor, the editor will clear the screen to show you that there is nothing in the file. You can then begin typing in the lines of your program, using the cursor control keys to go back and make corrections as necessary. When you have filled the screen with lines of program, the screen editor will automatically roll some of the lines off at the top of the screen and give you more space to type in at the bottom of the screen. If you want to go back to lines that have gone off the top of the screen, you press a key that tells the editor to roll the material back down onto the screen.

Most screen editors have far more commands than there are special keys on terminals. There will be keys for all of the frequently used commands, but the less frequently used commands won't have keys associated with them. To issue one of these commands to the editor, you have to switch to a mode analogous to command mode in a line editor. This is usually called *extended command mode.* One of the special keys will be reserved for switching to this mode. Usually, when you press this key the cursor will move to a blank line at the top or bottom of the screen. You can then type the extended command in the space provided. When you press return, the editor does whatever the command told it to do; then the editor puts the cursor back to where it belongs on the screen and automatically switches back to input mode. Usually the command to quit the editor is one of the extended commands. Figure 1-18 shows what the display screen looks like for a typical screen editor.

T,M ⟵

Compiling and Running a Program   Once your program has been typed into a file, you tell the operating system to compile the Pascal program stored on that file. For example, if you named your program file "myprog.pas," you might issue the following command to the operating system:

            pascal myprog.pas /list=myprog.lis

Figure 1-18
Display Screen
for Screen Editor

```
PROGRAM MyProg (Input, Output);
BEGIN
   Writeln('This is my first program.')
END.




================================================================
SCREEN EDIT version 3.0    File MYPROG.PAS   4 Lines   100%
Command: exit
```

This command tells the operating system to run the Pascal compiler, translating the program on file myprog.pas into machine language. A *compiler listing* will also be stored in a file called myprog.lis. A listing is a copy of the program with messages from the compiler inserted into it. Usually the messages indicate errors in the program that prevent the compiler from translating the program into machine language.

If there are errors in your program, you will have to go back to the editor and fix them. Then you must run the compiler again. When there are no more errors in the program, the compiler will create a file containing the machine language version of the program. You can then tell the operating system to run your program. If the file with the machine language version of your program is called myprog.exe, then the command might be

```
run myprog.exe
```

Even though your program compiles without any errors, it may still have errors in its design. The computer will try to do exactly what you tell it, even if that's not what you wanted it to do. If your program doesn't do what it should, you have to go back to the algorithm and fix it. Then you have to log on to the computer again, get into the editor, and fix the program. Finally, you have to compile and run the program again. This process (known as *debugging*) is repeated until the program does

T,M,V ⟵ what it is supposed to do. (See Figure 1-19.)

Finishing Up On a large computer, after you have finished working on your program (or if you just need to take a break), you have to *log off*. You do this by typing a command to the operating system that looks something like

V ⟵   ```logoff```

*Figure 1-19
Debugging
Procedure*

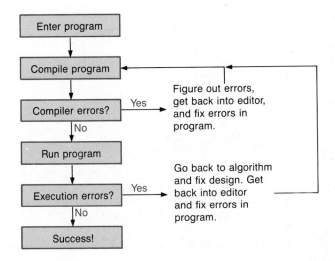

This frees up the terminal so that someone else can use it. It also prevents someone from walking up to the terminal after you leave and tampering with your files. The next time you log on, you will find that all of your files are still stored in the computer's memory.

T,M ⬅   On a personal computer, when you are done working, you simply remove any disks on which you've stored material and then turn off the power. Turning off the power wipes out the computer's memory, but your files are safely stored on the disks. The next time you use the computer, you simply reinsert the disks and the computer will be able to recall the files from them.

Be sure to read the manual for your particular operating system and editor before you type your first program into the computer. The commands you use will almost surely be different from those we've shown you, although the overall process will be the same as what we have described here. Don't panic if you have trouble with these steps at first—almost everyone does. It becomes much easier with practice.

Batch Program Entry

As we mentioned, an alternative to interactive program entry is batch program entry. In this method the program is prepared without using the computer, often through the use of punched cards. After the program is prepared, a series of operating system commands is prepared. The commands specify how the program is to be compiled and executed. If the program will input data, the data must also be prepared.

Once the program, system commands, and data (if any) have been prepared, they are submitted together for processing. If cards are being used, this involves running the cards through a card reader. The computer then compiles the program and (if there are no compiler errors) executes the object code using the prepared data. During this process the user has no interaction with the computer. Eventually a compiler listing and the output from the program are printed along with an *execution summary,* which lists all of the commands that were processed and any system messages that were generated. The user must examine the printout to see if everything worked correctly.

In another variation of batch processing, the user logs on to the computer from a terminal and uses an editor to enter the program, commands, and data. This is almost like interactive processing except that the user does not directly issue the commands to compile and execute the program. Instead, the commands are entered and stored in a file. A command is then issued to submit the file of commands for batch processing. The user may log off and go away, returning some time later to log on again and examine the results of processing.

As we have seen, in interactive processing the computer responds directly to each command. In batch processing the commands are submitted all at once, in a single batch, and the responses to those commands are returned to the user all at once. (See Figure 1-20.)

Figure 1-20
Processing Methods
Compared

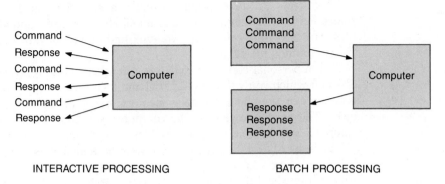

SUMMARY

We think nothing of turning on a TV and sitting down to watch it. It's a communication tool we use to enhance our lives. Someday computers will be as widespread as television sets and just as normal a part of our lives. Like television sets, computers are based on complex principles but are designed to be easy to use.

Computers are dumb—they must be told what to do. A true computer error is extremely rare (usually due to a component malfunction or an electrical fault). Since we tell the computer what to do, most errors in computer-generated output are really human errors.

As problem solvers, we use the computer to implement our solutions. Computer programming involves a problem-solving phase and an implementation phase. After analyzing a problem, we develop and test a general solution called an algorithm. This general solution becomes a specific solution, our program, when we write it in some convenient high-level programming language. The sequence of instructions that makes up our program is then compiled into the language that the computer uses. After correcting any errors or "bugs" that show up during testing, we can use our program.

Data and instructions are represented as binary numbers (numbers consisting of only 1's and 0's) in electronic digital computers.

Computers are composed of five basic parts: memory, arithmetic/logic, control, input, and output (I/O). The arithmetic/logic and control units together are called the central processing unit (CPU). Some I/O peripheral devices are the card reader, the line printer, and the CRT terminal. Disk drives provide backup storage for the memory unit. These physical parts are called hardware. Whether interactive or batch oriented, mainframe or PC, a computer system is composed of both hardware and software.

System software improves the user/computer interface. The operating system obeys the system commands entered. It can do things such as translate a program into machine language by calling the compiler and then run a translated program with specified data. Other programs, such as the editor, provide further services.

A programming language reflects the range of operations a computer can perform. The basic control structures (sequence, selection, loop, and procedure) of a programming language are based on these fundamental operations. In this text you will learn to write programs in the high-level programming language called Pascal.

Users of an interactive system can communicate and interact with the computer. A batch-processing system allows no interaction during program execution.

Interactive programming usually involves preparing a program at a terminal using an editor program. The commands to the operating system to compile and then run a program are entered directly at the terminal when the user has finished editing the program.

Modern computer systems find wide usage in science, engineering, business, and government. Learning to program in Pascal, using its highly structured design, will allow you to use this powerful tool effectively.

QUICK CHECK _____

1. What is a computer program? (p. 2)

2. What are the two phases in writing a program? (p. 3)

3. Is an algorithm the same as a program? (pp. 4–6)

4. What is the difference between interactive and batch processing? (p. 13)

5. What is the difference between hardware and software? (p. 12)

6. What are the advantages of using a standardized high-level programming language? (pp. 18, 22)

7. How does the object program fit into the compilation/execution process? (pp. 18–19)

8. What are some of the features of the Pascal programming language? (pp. 21–22)

9. How does the editor program fit into the process of getting a program to run on the computer? (pp. 26–29)

Answers

1. A computer program is a sequence of instructions outlining steps to be performed by a computer.
2. The two phases are problem solving and implementation.
3. No. All programs are algorithms, but not all algorithms are programs.
4. Interactive processing involves direct communication between the user and the computer. In batch processing the user and computer communicate indirectly through terminals, cards, and printouts.
5. Hardware is the physical components of the computer, whereas software is the collection of programs that run on the computer.
6. Programs written in a standardized programming language can be run on many different computers. High-level languages are easier to use than assembly language or machine language.
7. The object program is the binary, machine-language version of the program, which is created by the compiler or assembler. The object program can be loaded into the computer's memory and executed.
8. Pascal is simple to learn but embodies a wide range of programming concepts. Pascal also encourages programmers to write programs that can be easily understood by others.
9. The editor is used to enter a source program into the computer's memory interactively and store it on a file. The editor is used in the debugging process to make changes and corrections to the source program.

EXAM PREPARATION EXERCISES

1. Use the manuals for the computer you will be using or information your instructor has given you to answer the following questions:
   (a) Is the computer a mainframe, a PC, or something in between?
   (b) Will you be using interactive or batch processing (or a combination) when you implement your programs?
   (c) Will you be using a screen editor or a line-oriented editor?
   (d) Does the Pascal compiler that you will be using conform to the ISO standard?

2. The compiler program takes one file as input and outputs two other files. What are these three files, and which one is the input file?

3. Which of the following are peripheral devices?
   (a) Disk drive
   (b) Arithmetic/logic unit
   (c) Tape drive
   (d) Printer
   (e) Card reader
   (f) Memory
   (g) Auxiliary storage
   (h) Control unit
   (i) Terminal

4. Which of the following are hardware and which are software?
   (a) Disk drive
   (b) Memory
   (c) Compiler
   (d) Arithmetic/logic unit
   (e) Editor
   (f) Operating system
   (g) Object program
   (h) Terminal
   (i) CPU

5. In the following recipe for chocolate pound cake (an example of an algorithm), identify steps that are branches, steps that are references to procedures outside of the algorithm, and places where there are loops (that is, where steps are repeated).

   Preheat oven to 350 degrees.

   Line the bottom of a 9-inch tube pan with wax paper.

   Sift $2\frac{3}{4}$ c flour, $\frac{3}{4}$ t cream of tartar, $\frac{1}{2}$ t soda, $1\frac{1}{2}$ t salt, and $1\frac{3}{4}$ c sugar into a large bowl.

   Add 1 c shortening to bowl.
       If using butter, margarine, or lard,
           then add $\frac{2}{3}$ c milk to bowl,
           else (for other shortenings) add 1 c minus 2 T of milk to bowl.

   Add 1 t vanilla to mixture in bowl.

   If mixing with a spoon,
       then see the instructions in the introduction to the chapter on cakes,
       else (for electric mixers) beat contents of bowl for 2 minutes at medium speed, scraping bowl and beaters as needed.

Add 3 eggs plus 1 extra egg yolk to bowl.

Melt 3 squares of unsweetened chocolate and add to mixture in bowl.

Beat mixture in bowl for 1 minute at medium speed.

Pour batter into tube pan.

Put pan into oven and bake it for 1 hour and 10 minutes.

Perform the test for doneness, described in the introduction to the chapter on cakes. Repeat the test once each minute until it shows that the cake is done.

Remove pan from oven and allow cake to cool for 2 hours.

Follow the instructions for removing the cake from the pan, given in the introduction to the chapter on cakes.

Sprinkle powdered sugar over cracks in top of cake just prior to serving.

PART 1 ALGORITHMS, DATA, AND PROGRAM CONSTRUCTION

■ *To be able to choose an appropriate problem-solving method for developing an algorithmic solution to a problem.*

■ *To be able to read syntax diagrams in order to construct and identify legal Pascal statements and declarations.*

■ *To be able to create and/or recognize Pascal identifiers.*

■ *To be able to declare variables of type Integer, Real, Char, and Boolean.*

■ *To be able to distinguish Pascal reserved words from user-defined identifiers, given a list of words.*

■ *To be able to declare named constants.*

■ *To be able to construct simple arithmetic expressions made up of variables, constants, and arithmetic operators (+, −, *, /, DIV, MOD).*

■ *To be able to evaluate simple Pascal arithmetic expressions.*

■ *To be able to construct a specified Write statement.*

■ *To be able to determine what would be printed, given a Write statement.*

■ *To be able to recognize examples of procedure usage.*

■ *To be able to recognize the parameters in a procedure call.*

■ *To be able to construct simple Pascal programs.*

2

Problem Solving, Syntax/Semantics, and Pascal Programs

As a programmer, you will develop solutions to problems, solutions that transform given data into required results. You will implement these solutions on a computer using a programming language. In this chapter we will look at some of the strategies you can use to solve problems. Then we will start looking at the rules and symbols that make up the Pasal programming language.

PROBLEM-SOLVING PROCESS

We solve problems every day, but we are often unaware of the process we are going through. In a learning environment we are usually given most of the information we need: a clear statement of the problem, the given input, and the required output. In real life this is not always the case; we often must come up with the problem definition ourselves, decide what we have to work with and what the results should be.

After we have understood and analyzed the problem, we must come up with a solution—an algorithm. In Chapter 1 we defined an algorithm as a step-by-step procedure for solving a problem in a finite amount of time. Although we work with algorithms all the time, most of our experience with them is in the context of following them. We follow a recipe, play a game, assemble a toy, take medicine. We are all taught how to follow directions, that is, execute an algorithm.

In Chapter 1 we described the programming process as being composed of a problem-solving phase (analysis, general solution, test) and an implementation phase (specific solution, test, use). In the problem-solving phase of computer programming you will be designing algorithms, not following them. You will be given a problem and asked to devise the algorithm—to design the set of steps to be carried out in order to solve the problem. Actually, we do this kind of problem solving all the time at an unconscious level. We don't write down our solutions, however; we just execute them.

In learning to program you will have to make conscious some of your underlying problem-solving strategies in order to apply them to programming problems. Let's look at some of these strategies we all use every day.

Ask Questions

If you are given a task orally, you ask questions until what you are to do is clear. You ask when, why, where until your task is completely specified. If your instructions are written, you might put question marks in the margin; underline a word, group of words, or sentence; or in some other way indicate that the task is not clear. Perhaps your questions will be answered by a later paragraph, or you might have to discuss them with the person giving you the task.

Some typical questions you will be asking in the programming context are as follows:

■   What am I given to work with; that is, what are my data?

■   What does the data look like?

■   How much data is there?

■   How will I know when I have processed all the data?

■   What must my output look like?

■   How many times is the process I am doing to be repeated?

■   What special error conditions might come up?

Look for Things That Are Familiar

Never reinvent the wheel. If a solution exists, use it. If we have solved the same or a similar problem before, we just repeat the successful solution. We don't consciously think, "I have seen this before, and I know what to do"; we just do it. Humans are good at recognizing similar situations. We don't have to learn how to go to the store to buy milk, then to buy eggs, then to buy candy. We know that going to the store will be the same, and only what is bought is different.

In computing you will see certain problems again and again in different guises. A good programmer will immediately see a subtask that has been solved before and plug in the solution. For example, finding the daily high and low temperature is exactly the same problem as finding the highest and lowest grade on a test. You want the largest and smallest numbers among a set of numbers. (See Figure 2-1.)

Divide and Conquer

We often break up large problems into smaller units that we can handle. The task of cleaning the house or apartment may seem overwhelming. The tasks of cleaning the

Figure 2-1
Look for Things
That Are Familiar

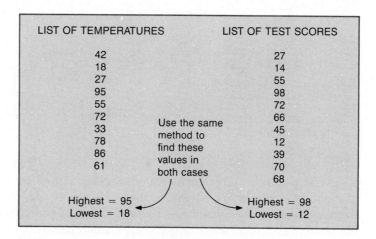

living room, the dining room, the kitchen, the bedrooms, and the bathrooms seem more manageable. The same principle applies to programming. We break up a large problem into smaller pieces that we can solve individually. In fact, the methodology we will outline in Chapter 3 for top-down design is based on this principle. (See Figure 2-2.)

Figure 2-2
Divide and
Conquer

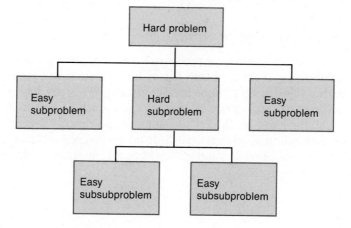

Solve by Analogy

Often, when you are presented with a problem, it will remind you of a similar problem that you have seen before. The two problems may be in completely different areas of expertise. For example, something you once had to solve in a chemistry class might pop into your head when you are presented with a problem in business statistics. You may gain useful insight into solving the problem at hand if you just recall how you solved the other problem. In other words, you are making an analogy between the two problems. (See Figure 2-3.)

Figure 2-3
Analogy

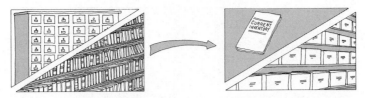

A library catalog system may give some insight into how to organize
a parts inventory.

Analogy can be a powerful means of attacking a problem. It can open up a plan
of action when you have otherwise run out of ideas. As you work your way through
the new problem, you will encounter things that are different than they were in the
old problem, but these are usually just details that you can easily deal with one at a
time. By the time you have dealt with all of the "minor" differences, you may discover that the solution you've reached bears little resemblance to the solution you
started working from. Don't worry if your analogy doesn't match perfectly—the
only reason for starting with an analogy is that it gives you that necessary place to
begin.

The best programmers are those people who have broad experience in solving
problems of different types.

The Building-Block Approach

One way of attacking large problems is to see if there are any existing solutions for
smaller pieces of the problem. It may be possible to put some of these together to
solve most of the big problem. This strategy is really just a combination of the
familiar-things and divide-and-conquer approaches. You look at the big problem
and see that it can be divided into subproblems that correspond to smaller problems
for which solutions already exist. Solving the bigger problem is then simply a matter
of putting the existing solutions together, like mortaring together blocks to form a
wall. (See Figure 2-4.)

Means-Ends Analysis

Many problems can be characterized as having a beginning state and a desired
ending state, with a set of actions that can be used to get from one state to the other.
For example, if you want to go from Boston, Massachusetts, to Austin, Texas, you
know that the beginning state is that you are in Boston and the desired ending state
is to be in Austin. The set of actions that you could perform to accomplish this is
quite large. You could drive there, you could hitchhike, you could bicycle, you could
take a boat most of the way, or you could fly there on an airplane. The method you
choose will depend on the circumstances associated with the problem. If you are in
a hurry, you will probably want to fly. If you are broke, you may want to hitchhike.

Once you have narrowed down the set of actions, say to flying, you still may
have to work out the details. There may be several routes that you can choose (go

Figure 2-4
Building-Block
Approach

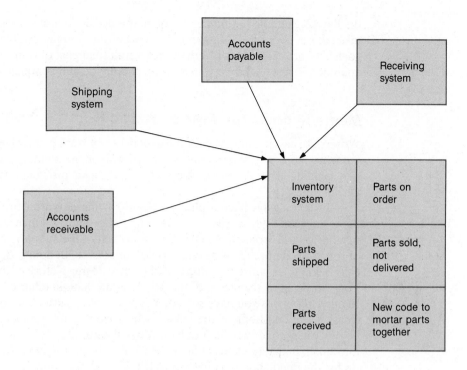

through Atlanta or Chicago?). You may set up intermediate goal states between the two ends. Perhaps there is a really cheap, direct flight out of Newark. Your intermediate goal would then be to get to Newark from Boston. Now you must examine what means are available to reach your intermediate goal. (See Figure 2-5.)

The overall strategy of means-ends analysis is to pin down what the ends are and then to analyze what means you have of getting between them. In developing a solution that will become a computer program, you first write down what the input will look like and what the desired output will be. You then consider the actions that the computer can perform and begin to work out a series of these actions that will transform the data into the results. It may help to establish intermediate goals. For

Figure 2-5
Means-Ends
Analysis

Start: Boston Goal: Austin	Means: *Fly*, walk, hitchhike, bicycle, drive, sail, bus

Start: Boston
Goal: Austin
	Revised Means: Fly to Chicago, then Austin;
	        fly to Newark, then Austin; fly to Atlanta,
	        then Austin

Start: Boston Goal: Austin Intermediate goal: Newark	Means: *Commuter flight*, walk, hitchhike, bicycle, drive, sail, bus
Solution: Take commuter flight to Newark and then catch cheap flight to Austin	

the Payroll example in Chapter 1, you might decide to first compute wages and then take care of overtime. In making these decisions, you are establishing intermediate goals that are easier to get to than the overall final goal of printing the payroll. This approach is just slightly different from the divide-and-conquer method.

Mental Blocks: The Fear of Starting

Writers are all too familiar with the experience of staring at a blank page, not knowing where to begin. Programmers also encounter the mental block associated with first tackling a big problem. You look at a difficult problem and it seems to overwhelm you.

But you always have a place to begin solving any problem: Write it down on paper in your own words, so that you understand it. Once you begin to try to paraphrase the problem, you can focus on each of the subparts individually instead of trying to comprehend the entire problem at once. In doing so, you will automatically begin to organize the subparts to form a clearer picture of the overall problem. You will begin to see pieces of the problem that look familiar or that are analogous to other problems you have solved. You may notice parts that are unclear and have to ask more questions of the person who gave you the problem.

As you write down the problem, you will naturally tend to group things together into small, understandable chunks, which may be natural places to split the problem up for the divide-and-conquer approach. Your description of the problem may collect all of the information about data and results into one place for easy reference. Then you will be able to see the beginning and ending states and perhaps apply means-ends analysis.

Most mental blocks are caused by not really understanding the problem. Rewriting the problem in your own words is a good way to get yourself to focus on the subparts of the problem, one at a time, and to gain insight into what is required for a solution.

Now let's apply these strategies (called *heuristics*) to a specific problem.

Problem

How can I get to the party?

Questions

Where is the party?
Where am I coming from?
What is the weather like (or likely to be like)?
Will I be walking? Driving a car? Taking a bus?

Once these questions have been answered, you can begin to design your algorithm.

If it is raining, your car is in the shop, and the buses have stopped, your best solution (algorithm) might be to call a taxi and give the driver the address.

If you look at a map and see that where you are going is six blocks west of the building where you work, the first part of your algorithm might be to repeat what you do each morning to get to work (providing you are leaving from home). The next part would be to turn west and go six blocks. If you have trouble remembering how many blocks you have gone, you might take a pencil and make a hash mark on a piece of paper each time you cross a street.

Though hash marking might be stretching the human algorithm a little too much, this is a technique you will use frequently in your programs. If you wish to repeat a process ten times, you will have to write instructions to count each time the process is done and check to see when the count reaches ten. This is the repetition (loop) construct mentioned in Chapter 1.

If you wanted to write a set of directions for other people, some of whom would be leaving from one place and some from another, you would have to have two sets of instructions prefaced by a statement: If you are coming from place A, follow the first set of directions; otherwise follow the second set of directions. This would be an example of the selection construct referred to in Chapter 1.

Coming up with a step-by-step procedure for solving a particular problem is not always cut and dried. In fact, it is usually a trial-and-error process requiring several attempts and refinements. Each attempt is tested to see if it truly solves the problem. If it does, fine. If it doesn't, we try again.

When designing algorithms for computer programs it is important to keep in mind that the computer manipulates data—that information which we have reduced to symbolic form. We have looked at some algorithms which require physical actions by a human being. These algorithms are not suitable for use on a computer. Our primary concern, then, is how the computer can transform, manipulate, calculate, or process the input data to produce the desired output or results. We can analyze the content (what it is composed of) and the form (what the order or pattern is) of the input data as well as the required content and form of the output to help us develop an algorithm to process the data.

Program Payroll in Chapter 1 was coded from an algorithm that paralleled how the payroll was figured by hand. The algorithm for doing something by hand can very often be used with little or no modification as the general solution. Just keep in mind the things a computer can do. If, when writing an algorithm for a program, you keep in the back of your mind the allowable instructions in a programming language, you won't design an algorithm that would be difficult or impossible to code.

When you have hand-tested your algorithm and feel that you have a working solution, you can proceed to translate your algorithm into a programming language. This implementation phase is similar to the problem-solving phase in that the program (algorithm) must be tested with input data to see that it produces the desired output. If it doesn't, you must locate the errors in the program. If your algorithm is faulty, you must go back to the problem-solving phase to see where you went wrong. Sometimes you have a correct algorithm but have failed to translate it correctly into the programming language.

We will now leave the general topic of programming and begin to look at the specifics of the Pascal language.

SYNTAX/SEMANTICS

A programming language is a set of rules, symbols, and special words used to construct a program. There are rules for both *syntax* (grammar) and *semantics* (meaning).

Syntax The formal rules governing how one writes valid instructions in a language.

Semantics The set of rules that gives the meaning of instructions written in a programming language.

We will discuss the syntax and semantics of Pascal throughout this text.

Syntax Diagrams

A useful tool for accurately describing syntax rules is the syntax diagram. The following is an example to explain how syntax diagrams work.

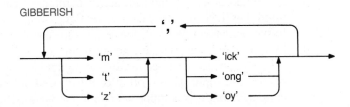

This syntax diagram shows how to form a piece of gibberish. By following the arrows from entry to exit, we can construct a syntactically correct piece of gibberish such as

moy, toy, zick, zong, mick

There is no pattern for using the diagram other than beginning at the left and obeying the direction of the arrows. At a branching point you may go either way. At the first branch you could take an 'm', 't', or 'z'. Then add 'ick', 'ong', or 'oy'. You could stop there, or you could add a ',' and then go back to the beginning and start again.

Another way of writing this diagram is as follows:

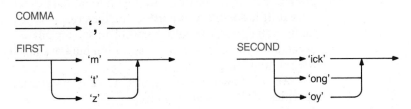

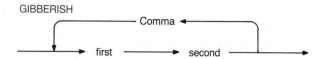

Syntax diagrams are one way of writing algorithms. If you look closely at the gibberish diagrams, you will see all four of the basic structures of algorithms represented. There are sequences of instructions (first write an 'm', 't', or 'z', then write 'ick', 'ong', or 'oy'); there are selections (places where you can branch to different choices); and there are loops (writing a comma and going back to the start). The second way of writing the gibberish diagrams involves subprograms (called Comma, First, and Second) and references to them. The two ways of writing the syntax diagrams demonstrate, once again, that there is more than one way to write any algorithm.

Appendix E is a collection of syntax diagrams used to describe the syntax rules of Pascal. You are urged to refer to these diagrams whenever you are in doubt concerning the syntax of a Pascal construct.

Identifiers

Identifiers are used in Pascal to name things. Some are defined in the language and are reserved for specific uses. Any other names can be defined for your own use. These identifiers are formed using letters and digits.

Identifiers Names associated with processes and objects and used to refer to those processes and objects. Identifiers are made up of letters (A–Z, a–z) and numbers (0–9), but must begin with a letter.

It is important to remember that an identifier *must* start with a letter.

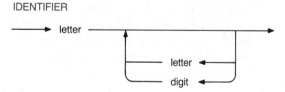

Examples of valid identifiers:

 Hello J9 Box22 GetData Bin3 Count

Identifiers are not limited in length, but some compilers do not look beyond the first few characters to distinguish different names. If, for example, a compiler does not look beyond the first six characters in an identifier, the valid identifiers

 DataItem1
 DataItem2

will be treated as if they were the same. You might solve this problem by using the identifiers

Data1   or   Data1Item

Data2   Data2Item

T,M,V ⇦

and so on. You should check the manual for your compiler to see if it places this sort of restriction on identifier names.

In Program Payroll at the end of Chapter 1, the user-defined identifiers listed below were used. Notice that the names were chosen to convey indications of their use. (The other identifiers in the program are predefined in Pascal.)

Identifier	How it is used
MaxHours	Maximum normal work hours
Overtime	Overtime pay rate factor
Payroll	The name of the program
PayRate	An employee's hourly pay rate
Hours	The number of hours an employee worked
Wages	Weekly wages for an employee
Total	Sum of weekly wages for all employees (total company payroll)
EmpNum	Employee identification number
Payfile	The output file (where the employee number, pay rate, hours, and wages for each employee are written)

The names we use to refer to things in our programs are totally meaningless to the computer. The computer will function just the same whether we refer to the value 3.14159265 as Pi or Cake, as long as we always call it the same thing. However, it is much easier for somebody to figure out how a program works if the names for things actually tell something about them. Whenever you have to make up a name for something in a program, you should pick one that will be meaningful to a human reader of the program.

Most Pascal compilers allow you to write names with upper- and lowercase letters. Usually they treat the uppercase and lowercase letters as if they were the same. Thus most compilers would consider the identifiers

DATAITEM1

dataitem1

DaTaItEm1

DataItem1

to be the same name. As you can see, the last of these forms is the easiest to read. This is our first encounter with writing style as an aspect of programming. We will mention other points of style as we talk more about Pascal. For example, you should be consistent throughout a program in your use of capitalization. Even though it makes no difference to the computer, a human reader of your program will find inconsistent capitalization to be very confusing.

Some compilers will restrict you to using only uppercase letters in writing your programs. If you are using one of these compilers, the good news is that you won't have to worry about capitalization. The bad news is that your programs will be a little more difficult to read.

T,M,V ⟵ In this book we will use both uppercase and lowercase letters in identifiers. If your compiler allows you to use both upper- and lowercase, we strongly urge you to do so.

Data Types

Data items are the physical symbols that represent information. A computer program operates on data (whether stored internally in memory, stored on disk or tape, or input from a terminal, card reader, or electrical sensor) and produces an output. When we write a program, the data is our "given" which we must translate into a more useful form.

In Pascal each data item must be of a specific type. The *data type* determines how the data items will be represented in the computer and what kinds of processing the computer will be able to perform on them. Usually, in Pascal, we have to define each type of data that we will use in our program. This means that before we can write any instructions for manipulating data of a particular type, we have to write a definition that tells the computer what form the data will take. This is analogous to defining technical terms before they are used when you are writing a paper.

Data Type The general form of a class of data items.

Fortunately, there are some types of data that are used so frequently that Pascal automatically defines them for us. We can use these data types without having to define them. We will use only these standard or built-in data types until Chapter 10, where we will show you how to define your own.

There are four simple types of data for which Pascal automatically defines the rules describing what the data items can look like and what you can and cannot do with them. Three of these data types are already familiar to you: *integer numbers, real numbers,* and *characters* (Char). The fourth type, *Boolean,* is so useful that it will soon become equally familiar to you.

Integer Integers are positive or negative whole numbers (no fractional part). They are made up of a sign and digits.

$$+22 \quad -16 \quad 1 \quad -426 \quad 0 \quad 4600$$

When the sign is omitted, positive is assumed. Commas are not allowed.

Theoretically there is no limit on the size of integers, but practical considerations and the limitations of computer hardware do place limits on how many digits an integer can have. Since this limit varies among machines, Pascal has a predefined identifier, *MaxInt,* whose value is set to the largest integer number that can be represented in that computer. If MaxInt were 32767, the range of integers allowed would be

$$-\text{MaxInt} \quad \text{through} \quad \text{MaxInt}$$

or

$$-32767 \quad \text{through} \quad 32767$$

T,M,V ⟵   MaxInt may be different for your machine, so you might print it to see how large it is. (This requires a Pascal program that you will be able to write by the end of this chapter.)

EmpNum, the identifier for the employee number in Program Payroll in Chapter 1, is of the Integer data type.

Real   Real numbers are decimal numbers. That is, they have an integer part and a fractional part, with a decimal point in between. They may also have an exponent, as in scientific notation. (In scientific notation a number is written as a decimal value multiplied by a power of 10 to indicate the actual position of the decimal point.) Instead of writing "3.504×10^{12}," however, we will write "$3.504E + 12$" to indicate the same exponent in Pascal. Some examples of real numbers are

$$127.54$$
$$0.57$$
$$193145.8423$$
$$1.74536E + 12$$

Real numbers will be given more thorough coverage in Chapter 8. There is one more thing that you should know about real numbers before then:

When writing real numbers in your program or inputting them as data, always use a decimal point with at least one digit on each side of it. If a number doesn't have a fractional part, put a zero to the right of the decimal point. If it doesn't have an integer part, put a zero to the left of the decimal point. (Note: Zero is thus written "0.0.")

Valid	Not valid
3.1415	.42
−111.011	16.
76.43	.2
0.43	.0
−1.0	0.
0.0	

In Program Payroll, the identifiers MaxHours, Overtime, PayRate, Hours, Wages, and Total are all Real because they are identifiers for things that may have decimal points.

Char   The character data type describes data consisting of one alphanumeric character. Alphanumeric characters include letters, digits, and special symbols:

'A'   'a'   '8'   '2'   '+'   '−'   '$'   '?'   '*'   ' '

Each machine has a set of alphanumeric characters that it can represent. This set is called the character set of the machine. (See Appendix J for some sample character sets.) Your machine may not support both upper- and lowercase letters. If not, you will have to use uppercase only. Notice that each character is enclosed in single quotes. The Pascal compiler needs the quotes to differentiate between the character data '8' or '+' and the integer 8 or the addition sign. Notice also that the blank, ' ', is a character.

You can't add '8' and '3', but you can compare data values of type Char. The character set of a machine is ordered in what is known as the collating sequence. Although this sequence varies from one machine to another, 'A' is always less than 'B', 'B' less than 'C', and so forth. Also, '1' is less than '2', '3' is less than '4', etc. None of the identifiers in Program Payroll is of type Char.

Boolean Boolean is a type with only two values: True and False. This type is associated with data created within a program and is used to represent the answers to questions. The importance of the type Boolean will become clearer when we discuss conditions and how decisions are made by the computer. The ability to choose alternative courses of action (selection) is an important part of a programming language. (See Chapter 4.)

Boolean data cannot be read in as data, as the other three types can, but it can be printed out.

The B in Boolean is capitalized because the data type is named after George Boole (1815–1864), an English mathematician who invented a system of logic using variables with only the two values True and False.

T,M,V ⟵

Data Storage

Memory Memory is divided into a large number of separate locations, each of which can hold a piece of data. Each memory location has an address that can be used to refer to it when data is stored in it or retrieved from it. We can visualize memory as a set of post office boxes, with the box numbers as the addresses used to designate particular locations. (See Figure 2-6.)

Figure 2-6
Memory

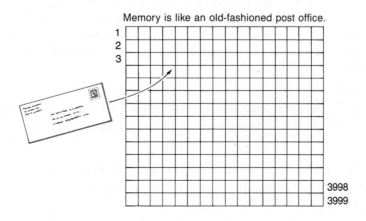

Memory is like an old-fashioned post office.

We could refer to memory locations by their addresses, as machine language programmers do. But how would you like to try to keep track of data stored in location 101101101? Or was it location 1011011001? Fortunately, higher-level languages such as Pascal offer an alternative.

In Pascal we can use identifiers as the names of memory locations. The computer keeps track of the address corresponding to each name. It is as if we could put only the names on our letters and the post office would look up the addresses. Of course this would require that everybody in the world have a different name; otherwise the post office wouldn't be able to figure out which address was whose. The same is true in Pascal—you must use each name to represent only one thing, except under special circumstances that we will consider in Chapters 6 and 7. For now, just remember that every name you make up for use in a Pascal program must be different from any of the other names you make up.

Identifiers can be used for both variable and constant names. In other words, an identifier can be the name of a memory location whose contents change or the name of a memory location whose contents never change.

In addition to variables and constants, the actual statements (instructions) of your program are also stored in various memory locations.

Variables A program operates on data. This data may be one of the simple types we have discussed: Integer, Real, Boolean, Char. Data is stored in memory. During execution of a program, different values may be stored in the same memory location at different times. Strictly speaking, the memory location is the *variable* and its contents are the value of the variable. The symbolic name that we assign to this memory location (variable) is the variable name or variable identifier.

Variable A location in memory, referenced by a variable name (identifier), where a data value can be stored (this value can be changed).

In practice, however, the variable name is referred to as the variable and its value is said to change. We will follow this convention in this text.

Variables must be declared in the *declaration* section of a Pascal program. (We discuss the declaration of variables in the program construction section of this chapter.) To declare a variable involves specifying both its name and its data type. This tells the compiler to name a memory location whose contents will be of a specific type.

Declaration A statement that associates an identifier with a process or object so that the user can refer to that process or object by name.

As a general rule, all identifiers in Pascal, including variables, must be declared or defined before use. This is why the declaration section comes before the main body of a Pascal program.

Pascal is known as a "strongly typed language." This means that only data values of the type specified in the declaration of the variable may be stored in that variable. The Pascal compiler will check to be sure that you haven't written any instructions that try to store a value of the wrong data type. If you have, the compiler will give you an error message usually something like "TYPE MISMATCH OF OP- ERANDS."

This is the syntax diagram of a variable declaration:

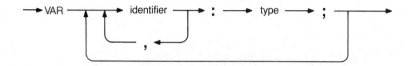

Notice that a : is used between the identifier and the data type in the declaration. These would be valid variable declarations:

```
VAR
    A, B : Integer;
    PayRate : Real;
    Ch : Char;
```

The reserved word VAR denotes the variable declarations. *Reserved words* are words that have special meaning in the Pascal language and hence cannot be used as identifiers. In this text we always write reserved words in capital letters to help distinguish them from identifiers.

Reserved Word A word that has special meaning in the Pascal language and cannot be used as an identifier.

Now look at the VAR section of Program Payroll from Chapter 1.

```
VAR
    PayRate,        (* Employee pay rate     *)
    Hours,          (* Hours worked          *)
    Wages,          (* Wages earned          *)
    Total:          (* Total company payroll *)
        Real;
    EmpNum:         (* Employee ID number    *)
        Integer;
    Payfile:        (* Company payroll file  *)
        Text;
```

This VAR section tells the compiler to set up locations in memory for four Real variables to be called PayRate, Hours, Wages, and Total and to set up one location for an Integer variable to be called EmpNum. (Type Text is explained in Chapter 3.)

Constants All numbers, integer and real, are constants. So are single characters and series of characters called strings.

16   32.3   'A'   'Howdy boys'

We can use these constants in our program, wherever appropriate, as part of expressions. (See the next section.) We can say, "Add 5 and 6 and put that value in the variable Sum." Any actual constant value stated in the program is called a *literal value* or sometimes simply a *literal.*

Literal Value	Any constant value written in a program.

Notice that the character literals and string literals are in single quotes. This is to differentiate between strings and identifiers. 'Amount' (in quotes) is the character string made up of the letters *A, m, o, u, n,* and *t* in that order. Amount (without the quotes) is an identifier, the name of a place in memory.

Although character literals and literal strings are put in quotes, literal Integers and Reals are not, because there is no chance that they will be confused with identifiers. Why? Because identifiers must start with a letter, and numbers must start with a digit or a plus or minus sign.

Instead of writing out every constant each time it appears, you can make your programs more readable by giving each constant a name and using those names throughout your program. Such constants are called *named constants* and are defined in the declaration section of your program. Using constant identifiers, or named constants, is just another way of representing the values of literals. In addition to making the program easier to read and making the meaning of the literal constant clearer, use of named constants makes it easier to change a program later on.

Named Constant	A location in memory, referenced by a constant name (identifier), where a data value is stored (this value cannot be changed).

This is the syntax diagram of the constant definition section:

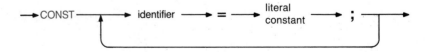

Notice that an = appears between the identifier and the literal (value) in the definition. These would be valid constant definitions:

```
CONST
    Stars = '********';
    Blank = ' ';
    Pi = 3.14159;
    InterestRate = 0.12;
    TaxRate = 0.001;
    Max = 20;
    Message = 'Error condition';
```

The named constant definitions (if there are any) come before the variable declarations.

Suppose you wrote a program to compute taxes. In several places you used the literal 0.05, which was the sales tax rate when you wrote the program. Now the rate has changed to 0.06. To change your program, you will have to go through and find every occurrence of the literal 0.05 and change it to 0.06. If the literal 0.05 is used for other purposes, such as computing some deductions, you will have to look at each place where 0.05 is used, figure out what it is used for, and decide whether it needs to be changed.

This process is much simpler if you use a named constant. Suppose you had defined a named constant called TaxRate as being equal to 0.05, and used it in every tax rate computation. To change your program, all you would have to do is change the declaration to make TaxRate equal 0.06. With this one modification you could correctly change all of the tax rate computations without affecting the other places where 0.05 is used.

Pascal allows us to declare constants with different names but the same value. If a value has different meanings in different parts of a program, it makes sense to define and use a constant with an appropriate name for each of those meanings.

Another reason for using named constants is that they are more reliable. If we have defined names for the constants, the Pascal compiler can tell if we make a typing mistake in using any of those names later on. A mistyped name simply will not have been defined, and the compiler will tell us so. On the other hand, the number 3.14149 is perfectly acceptable to the compiler, and even though we recognize that it's a mistyped version of Pi (3.14159), the compiler won't warn us that anything is wrong.

We strongly encourage you to use named constants rather than literal constants whenever the constant has some useful meaning associated with it. If you go back to Program Payroll in Chapter 1, you will see that named constants called MaxHours and Overtime are defined.

Assignment

The value of a variable is changed through an *assignment* statement.

Assignment The action that gives the value of an expression to a variable.

For example,

$$A := 10$$

assigns the value 10 to the variable A (puts the value 10 into the memory location called A). The syntax (form) of the assignment statement is

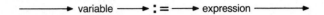

The semantics (meaning) of the assignment operator, := , is "is set equal to"; the value of the variable is set equal to the value of the expression. The previous value that the variable had is discarded and replaced by the value of the expression.

Only one variable can be on the left-hand side of an assignment statement. An assignment statement is *not* like a math equation such as $x + y = z + 4$; the expression (what is on the right-hand side of the :=) is evaluated, and that value is stored in the single variable on the left of the assignment operator. The value to be assigned to a variable must be of the same type as the variable. Given the declarations

```
VAR
   I, J :  Integer;
   Rate :  Real;
   Test :  Boolean;
   Ch   :  Char;
```

the following are valid assignments:

```
Rate := 0.36
Test := True
I := 2
Ch := 'B'
```

These are not valid assignments:

`I := 2.5`	I is Integer; 2.5 is Real.
`Ch := 3`	Ch is Char; 3 is an Integer constant.
`Test := 'A'`	Test is Boolean; 'A' is a character constant.
`Ch := 'Hello'`	Ch can hold only one character.
`Test := 'True'`	Test is Boolean; 'True' is a character string.

Variables keep their assigned values until they are changed by another assignment statement.

Expressions are made up of variables, constants, and operators. The following are all valid expressions:

```
I + 2
Rate - 6.0
4 - I
Rate
Test
I - J
```

The operators allowed in an expression depend on the data type of the constants and/or variables in the expression.

The arithmetic operators are

+	addition
−	subtraction
*	multiplication
/	division
DIV	integer division (no fractional part)
MOD	modulus (remainder from integer division)

V ↩

Since DIV and MOD are not operators you are familiar with, let's look at them more closely. Notice that they are only used with integers. When dividing one integer by another integer, you get an integer quotient and a remainder. DIV gives only the integer quotient; MOD gives only the remainder.

$$\begin{array}{r} 3 \\ 2\overline{)6} \\ 6 \\ \hline 0 \end{array} \Leftarrow 6 \text{ DIV } 2 \qquad\qquad \begin{array}{r} 3 \\ 2\overline{)7} \\ 6 \\ \hline 1 \end{array} \Leftarrow 7 \text{ DIV } 2$$
$$\;\Leftarrow 6 \text{ MOD } 2 \qquad\qquad\qquad \Leftarrow 7 \text{ MOD } 2$$

More examples:

Expression	Value
3 + 6	9
3 − 6	−3
2 * 3	6
8 DIV 2	4
8 DIV 8	1
8 DIV 9	0
8 DIV 7	1
8 MOD 8	0
8 MOD 9	8
8 MOD 7	1
0 MOD 7	0

Be careful; 7 MOD 0 and 7 DIV 0 will give an error, since the computer cannot divide by 0.

Since variables are allowed in expressions, the following are valid assignments:

```
I := J + 6
I := J DIV 2
J := I * 2
J := 6 MOD I
I := I + 1
J := J + I
```

Notice that the same variable can appear on both sides of the assignment operator. In the case of

$$J := J + I$$

the value in I and the value in J are first added together to get their sum and then this value is stored in J, replacing the previous value of J. The new value of J is thus the sum of J's old value and the value in I. This example points up the difference between assignment and mathematical equality. The mathematical equality

$$J = J + I$$

only makes sense if I is equal to zero. The assignment statement

$$J := J + I$$

makes sense, however, for *any* value of I.

Real values are added, subtracted, and multiplied just like Integer values. However, DIV and MOD have no meaning when applied to Real values. To divide with Real values, use the / operator.

If one operand is a Real and one is an Integer, the Integer value is converted into a Real value before the operation is performed. If you use / between two Integer operands, both are converted to Real values before the division is done. The result is a Real value. The conversion to Real values is just done temporarily for the purpose of a particular division (the conversion does not affect the values that are actually stored in the Integer variables).

Assigning Integer values to Real variables is valid because it is clear what you want to have done. Any Integer value can be exactly represented in Real form. For example, 2 can be 2.0, 42346 can be 42346.0. This is one of the rare exceptions to the fact that Pascal is a strongly typed language. You can actually assign a value of one type (Integer) to a variable of another type (Real).

However, you cannot assign a Real value to an Integer variable because it is not clear what you want done with the fractional part. If the Real value is 1.7, what happens to the .7? If something is ambiguous, it is illegal.

Given the declarations

```
VAR
  A, B : Integer;
  X : Real;
```

the following statements are valid:

Statement	Result
A := B + 2	B + 2 gives an Integer result that is stored in an Integer variable.
X := A + B	A + B gives an Integer result that is automatically converted to a Real, which can be stored in a Real variable.
X := A / B	A / B gives a Real result. No conversion is necessary.
X := 2 + 2.3	An Integer plus a Real gives a Real, which can be stored in a Real variable.

and the following statements are not valid:

Statement	Result
A := B + 2.0	An Integer plus a Real gives a Real, which cannot be stored in an Integer variable.
A := A / B	An Integer / an Integer gives a Real, which cannot be stored in an Integer variable.
A := X DIV B	The variables on either side of DIV must be Integer.
B := A + 2 / B	The / gives a Real result, which cannot be stored in an Integer variable.

The following chart summarizes what the resulting type will be, given the operator and the types of the operands.

	Type of operands			
Operator	*Real* *Real*	*Real* *Integer*	*Integer* *Real*	*Integer* *Integer*
+	Real	Real	Real	Integer
−	Real	Real	Real	Integer
*	Real	Real	Real	Integer
/	Real	Real	Real	Real
MOD	error	error	error	Integer
DIV	error	error	error	Integer

Remember that you can assign an Integer result to a Real variable, but you *cannot* assign a Real result to an Integer variable.

OUTPUT

Have you ever had the annoying experience of asking someone, "Do you know what time it is?" only to have the person smile smugly and say, "Yes, I do"? This is similar to the situation that currently exists between you and the computer. You now know enough Pascal syntax to be able to tell the computer to perform simple calculations, but the computer won't give you the answers unless you also tell it to write them out.

In Pascal we use a Write statement to write out the results of calculations. The Write statement takes the following form:

$$\longrightarrow \text{Write} \longrightarrow (\longrightarrow \text{parameter list} \longrightarrow) \longrightarrow$$

Here is an example of a Write statement:

```
Write('The answer is ', Result)
```

The Write statement is an example of a subprogram (recall our earlier discussion of the four basic Pascal structures: sequence, selection, loop, and subprogram). In

Pascal a subprogram can be of one of two types: a procedure or a function. *Write* is an example of a *procedure*.

Procedure A subprogram that is used by writing a statement consisting of the subprogram name, often followed by a parameter list.

Parameter lists are usually associated with subprograms. The *parameter list* provides a way of communicating with the subprogram. In the case of Write, the parameter list is simply a list of what you want printed. All the Write procedure does is to take the data that we give it and print it out.

Parameter List A mechanism for communicating with a subprogram. Data may be given to a subprogram and/or results received from the subprogram via its parameter list.

A parameter list can contain one or more expressions, separated by commas.

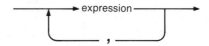

For example,

```
('Rate is ', Rate, ', and tax is ', Rate * Total)
```

When you use a Write statement, the computer temporarily puts your program on hold, starts the Write subprogram running, and gives it the data from the parameter list. When Write has finished printing the data, the computer goes back to your program and picks up where it left off.

The parameter list mechanism makes it possible for the same subprogram to work on many different sets of data. For example, you can have Write print out something different each time you use it simply by changing what you put in its parameter list.

We will see that there are many more subprograms available in Pascal, both procedures and functions (we'll see some functions in Part 2 of this chapter). In Chapters 6, 7, and 8 you'll learn to write subprograms of your own.

The following program segment uses Write statements to produce the output shown. (Note that numeric values appear as far to the right as possible within a fixed number of character positions in the output. They are thus said to be *right-justified* in a fixed fieldwidth. In the following, the fieldwidth is then assumed to be six character positions wide. We will explain this more fully in the next part of this chapter.) All of the items in the parameter list of a Write statement are printed on the same line.

Statements	What is printed (□ means blank)
I := 2;	
J := 6;	
Write(I);	□□□□□2
Write('I = ', I);	I□=□□□□□□2
Write('Sum = ', I + J);	Sum□=□□□□□□8
Write('ERROR MESSAGE');	ERROR□MESSAGE
Write('Error=', I);	Error=□□□□□2
Write('J:', J, 'I:', I);	J:□□□□□6I:□□□□□2

String constants may also be placed in the parameter list of a Write statement. Write prints string constants exactly as they appear in the parameter list, but *without* the quotes that you must use to enclose them. If you make the mistake of not putting quotes around a string, you will most likely get an error message, such as "UNDE-CLARED IDENTIFIER," from the Pascal compiler. You must also remember to put commas between each of the items (expressions or string constants) in the parameter list.

If you want to print a string that includes a single quote (an apostrophe), you must type two single quote marks with no spaces between them in the string. For example, a Write statement that prints the word *don't* would appear as

```
Write('don''t')
```

PROGRAM CONSTRUCTION

We can now collect the statements we have learned into a program. Pascal programs are composed of a heading, a declaration section, and a statement section. The outline looks like this:

I. Heading
II. Declarations
III. Statements

Here is an example of a program:

```
PROGRAM Example (Input, Output);

(* This is an example of a Pascal program. The first line is the
   heading, the declarations follow *)

CONST
   Freeze =  32;     (* The freezing point of water *)
   Boil   = 212;     (* The boiling  point of water *)
```

```
VAR
  Temp:                    (* Variable to hold the result of
                              averaging freeze and boil   *)
    Integer;

(* The executable statements begin here *)

BEGIN (* Example *)
  Write('Water freezes at ', Freeze);
  Write(' and boils at ', Boil, ' degrees.');
  Temp := (Freeze + Boil) DIV 2;
  Write('Halfway between is ', Temp, ' degrees.')
END.   (* Example *)
```

Notice the heading composed of the reserved word PROGRAM, followed by a programmer-chosen name for the program, followed by a list of the files used by the program. The files set up communication between your program and the outside world. (Files will be covered in Chapter 3.) Input is often your terminal keyboard and Output your terminal screen. This is the syntax diagram for a program heading:

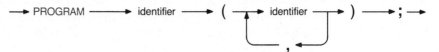

Next in the example program is a comment describing the program. Comments can appear anywhere in a program and are delimited by the (* *) pair. Some compil-

T,M,V ⟵ ers allow the use of { and } as substitutes for (* and *). The compiler ignores anything within these pairs.

The declaration section defines both the constants Freeze and Boil and the variable Temp. The declaration section gives information to the Pascal compiler for use in the translation phase. As a general rule, everything in Pascal must be defined before it is used.

The comments in the declaration section of the program are ignored by the Pascal compiler. They are there only for the benefit of human readers of the program. Pascal only needs to know the names and values of constants, or the names and data types of variables. A person reading the program, however, will find it much easier to understand what the program does if the meanings of the constants and variables are included. Thus it is a matter of good style, as well as consideration for other people who might one day have to figure out how the program works, to include comments that explain the significance of each declared name.

The statement section is the executable part of the program, set off with a BEGIN-END pair. It is this section that gets translated, and during the execution phase these translated instructions get executed. Program Example prints some messages about the freezing and boiling points of water and the average of the two.

Notice that the statements are separated by a semicolon (except before the END, where a semicolon isn't necessary). Semicolons are separators; they are not part of a statement. The Pascal program always ends with a period. (Comments following the period are ignored.)

Compound Statements

The executable statement section of a program is actually called a *compound state-ment.* This is the syntax diagram for a compound statement:

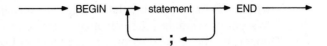

This is the syntax diagram for a statement:

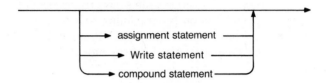

A statement can be empty (called the *null statement*) or it can be any of the state-ments we have seen, even another compound statement. This means that wherever a statement can be used, a compound statement can also be used. Later, when we introduce the syntax for branching and looping structures, you will see that this is very important.

You will have occasion to use compound statements often, especially as parts of other statements. The BEGIN-END pair delimits a compound statement. For this reason, there is no need to place a semicolon at the end of the last statement before the END. Leaving out a BEGIN-END pair can dramatically change the meaning as well as the execution of a program. This is why we always indent the statements inside a compound statement—the indentation makes a compound statement easy to spot in an otherwise long and complicated program.

Blocks

The declaration and statement sections comprise what is known as a *block.* The syntax diagram for a block is

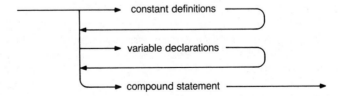

The declarations are optional, but if they are present they must appear after the constant definitions.

We can now define a program as a heading and a block (followed by a period).

```
──────► heading ──► ; ──► block ──► .
```

Program Formatting

Formatting involves determining the place on a line where a statement or declaration will begin and the places where extra blanks will be inserted for readability. As far as the compiler is concerned, Pascal statements are free format: they may appear anywhere on a line, and more than one may be on a line. The compiler only needs blanks to separate symbols and semicolons to separate statements. However, it is extremely important that your programs be readable, not only for your own sake, but also for the sake of anyone else who has to read them.

Just as an outline for an English paper has certain indentation rules to make it readable, Pascal programs have recommended indentation and formatting rules. Use Appendix G on programming style as a guide when writing your programs.

The following is a copy of Program Payroll that does not conform to any formatting standards. Need we say more?

```
PROGRAM Payroll (Input, Output, Payfile);   (* This program computes the
      wages for each employee and the total payroll for the company. *)
CONST MaxHours=40.00; (* Maximum normal work hours *)
Overtime=1.5; (* Overtime pay rate factor *)
VAR PayRate, (* Employee's pay rate *)
Hours,  (* Hours worked *)
Wages, (* Wages earned *)
Total (* Total company payroll *): Real;
EmpNum (* Employee ID number *): Integer;
Payfile (* Company payroll file *): Text;
PROCEDURE CalcPay (PayRate, (* Employee pay rate *)
Hours (* Hours worked *): Real;
VAR Wages (* Wages earned *): Real;
(* CalcPay computes wages from hours worked and the employee pay rate,
taking overtime into account *)
BEGIN (* CalcPay *)
IF Hours > MaxHours (* Check for Overtime *)THEN
Wages := (MaxHours*Payrate)+(Hours-MaxHours)*Payrate*Overtime
ELSE Wages := Hours*Payrate
END;   (* CalcPay *)
BEGIN (* Payroll *)
Rewrite(Payfile); (* Open file Payfile *)
Total := 0; Write('Enter employee number: ') ; (* prompting message *)
Readln(EmpNum); (* Read employee ID number *)
WHILE EmpNum <> 0 DO(* repeat until a zero ID # *)
BEGIN Write('Enter pay rate: '); (* Prompting message *)
Readln(Payrate); (* Read hourly pay rate *)
Write('Enter hour worked: '); (* Prompt *)
Readln(Hours);(* Read hours worked *)
CalcPay(Payrate, Hours, Wages); (* Compute Wages *)
Total := Total + Wages; (* Add wages to total *)
Writeln(Payfile, EmpNum, Payrate, Hours, Wages);
(* Put employee wage data in file Payfile *)
```

```
Write('Enter employee number: '); (* Prompt *)
Readln(EmpNum)
END; (* Print total payroll on screen *)
Writeln('Total payroll is ',Total:10:2)
END. (* Payroll *)
```

Problem Solving in Action

Your mother's birthday is coming up and you'd like to impress your Mom with your newly learned programming skills by having the computer wish her a Happy Birthday.

The problem to be solved here is not really how to write the greeting, but how to get the computer to do it. This problem can be approached in a variety of ways. Let's start by writing down the problem and the desired output:

Problem: Write a program to make the computer print out the message "Hi Mom! Happy Birthday!"

Output: Hi Mom! Happy Birthday!

The next step is to design the algorithm from which the program will be written. From the preceding description of the problem you should be able to tell that somewhere in your program you will need a statement that prints out the string constant 'Hi Mom! Happy Birthday!' Since this is all the program will have to do, the algorithm it will follow is only one line long:

Algorithm: Write 'Hi Mom! Happy Birthday!'

Now you can convert your algorithm into a complete Pascal program. The general form is

```
PROGRAM NameOfProgram (ListOfFiles);

(* General comments for the program. *)

declarations;

BEGIN  (* NameOfProgram *)

    statements

END.   (* NameOfProgram *)
```

To turn this general form into a real program, just fill in each of the details one at a time. First, you have to decide on a name for the program. This should be something that indicates what the program is used for. That is, you shouldn't just call it Herman. Let's call this program Birthday.

Next you have to decide what files the program will use. This is easier than it sounds. The only output will be to the terminal screen (or the printer, on a batch-processing system). The terminal screen is usually a special file called Output. Since

PSIA

there aren't any other files that your program will be dealing with, Output is all that has to be put in the list of files. The heading for this program can now be written:

```
PROGRAM Birthday (Output);
```

It is considered good style to include after the heading a comment that explains what the program does. It's also a good idea to put your name and the date on which you wrote the program into a comment, for the sake of posterity.

```
PROGRAM Birthday (Output);
(* This program prints a birthday greeting to my
Mom.

Programmer:  Your Name

Date Written: 4/17/86   *)
```

The next item in the general outline of a program is the declaration section. This is where you define any named constants or variables that you need in the program. How do you know what to put in the declaration section? When you design an algorithm, you will find yourself referring to constants and variables as you write the steps of the algorithm. Keep a list of the name of each variable or constant, its data type or value, and a note that explains how it is used. When you write the declaration section for the program, each constant in your list will become a constant declaration and each variable will become a variable declaration. For example, such a list for Program Example, which dealt with freezing and boiling temperatures, would look like this:

Quantities

Name	Value	Use
Freeze	32	The freezing point of water
Boil	212	The boiling point of water

Variables

Name	Data type	Use
Temp	Integer	Variable to hold the result of averaging freeze and boil

The resulting declaration section is

```
CONST
   Freeze = 32;    (* The freezing point of water. *)
   Boil   = 212;   (* The boiling point of water.  *)
```

PSIA

```
VAR
    Temp:              (* Variable to hold the result of
                          averaging freeze and boil.    *)
        Integer;
```

Because Program Birthday is so simple, it doesn't use any variables or quantities that need to be given names. So you don't have to write any declarations at all in this case.

The only thing left to be written is the statement section. To write the program statements, you simply go through the algorithm, translating it into Pascal statements according to the syntax diagrams. In the case of Program Birthday, the algorithm is just a single line that can easily be translated into a Pascal Write statement:

```
Write('Hi Mom! Happy Birthday!')
```

Now you can put this all together into a working Pascal program, like so:

```
PROGRAM Birthday (Output);

(* This program prints a birthday greeting to my
   Mom.

   Programmer:   Your Name

   Date Written: 4/17/86    *)

BEGIN  (* Birthday *)

    Write('Hi Mom! Happy Birthday!')

END.    (* Birthday *)
```

Voila! Your first Pascal program! But the work isn't over yet—you still have to enter the program on the computer, compile it, and run it. Getting that process straight can be time-consuming and frustrating, but keep at it! The fun is only just beginning!

SUMMARY

Writing a computer program involves a problem-solving phase and an implementation phase. We analyze the problem, using various strategies, and devise a workable algorithm. This algorithm is coded into a programming language and tested again. We repeat this process until we get a correct program solution.

The syntax (grammar) of the Pascal language is defined by syntax diagrams.

Identifiers are used in Pascal to name things, those that are predefined as well as those that are programmer-defined.

The basic predefined data types of Pascal are Integer, Real, Char, and Boolean. Variables and constants are defined to be of one of these types and occupy a place in memory. Variables can be assigned different values of their defined type in the program during execution. Constants may be either named or literal; their values cannot be changed during program execution.

Pascal includes sets of identifiers called reserved words and standard identifiers. You cannot define identifiers with the same names as are used for reserved words. You will not usually want to define identifiers with the same names as are used for standard identifiers, even though Pascal allows you to do so. Reserved words are listed in Appendix A, and standard identifiers in Appendix B.

T,M,V ⟵

There are three symbols in Pascal that are often confused: :, =, and := . The colon separates the variable name and its type in a variable declaration. The equal sign separates a constant name and its value in a constant definition. The assignment operator is used to change the value of a variable by assigning the value of an expression to that variable.

Write statements are used to display the output of a program. A Write statement will print the value of any expression in its parameter list. Write is an example of a procedure subprogram.

The general outline for a program is a heading followed by declarations, if any, and then statements. A program is formally defined as a heading and a block. A block is defined as constant definitions, variable declarations, and a compound statement. (The definition of a block will be expanded in later chapters.)

If you first write out the problem definition and the algorithm, the process of filling in the outline to make a working program will be much easier.

QUICK CHECK _____

1. You have just been given a large problem for which to write a program. You don't have any similar programs to work from, and you haven't worked on any problems similar to this one before. Which of the problem-solving methods might you apply to this situation? (pp. 38–41)

2. Use the following syntax diagram to decide whether your last name is a valid Pascal identifier.

IDENTIFIER

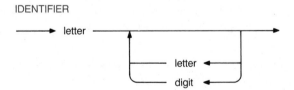

(pp. 44–47)

3. What form would a Pascal variable declaration take if it had one integer variable called Count, one real variable called Sum, and one character variable called Letter? (pp. 50–51)

4. Which of the following words are Pascal reserved words? (*Hint:* Look in Appendix A.)

BEGIN   PI   PROGRAM   INTEGER   MAXINT

(p. 51)

5. How would you write a Pascal constant declaration to give the name Pi to the value 3.14159? Would this declaration come before or after the variable declarations in a program? (pp. 52–53)

6. How would you write the following as a Pascal expression if the desired result were a real number? How would you write it if the desired result were an integer number?

$$\frac{9}{5}$$

(pp. 53–57)

7. What is the result of evaluating the following Pascal expression?

5 DIV 2

(pp. 53–57)

8. Write a Write statement to print out the title of this book (Introduction to Pascal and Structured Design). (pp. 57–59)

9. What will the following Write statement print out?

Write('The answer is ', 2 + 2)

(pp. 57–59)

10. What parts of the following Write statement are its parameters?

Write('For radius ', Radius, ' the diameter is ', Pi * 2 * Radius)

(pp. 57–59)

11. Fill in the blanks in the following Pascal program.

```
_____ Circle (Output);


_____
    Pi = 3.14159;        (* Ratio of circumference
                            to diameter            *)


____
    Circumference:       (* The computed circumference
                            of the circle          *)

    Real


____
    Circumference __ 2 * Pi * 7;
    Write _'The circumference of a circle of ',
           'radius 7 is '__
    Write _Circumference_


____
```

(pp. 59–61)

Answers
 1. Divide and conquer, or means-ends analysis.
 2. Unless your last name is hyphenated, it is probably a valid Pascal identifier.
 3. VAR
```
    Count:
      Integer;
    Sum:
      Real;
    Letter:
      Char;
```
 4. BEGIN, PROGRAM
 5. CONST
```
    Pi = 3.14159;   (* Comes before variable
                        declarations            *)
```
 6. 9 / 5 gives a real result; 9 DIV 5 gives an integer result.
 7. 2
 8. Write('Introduction to Pascal and Structured Design')
 9. The answer is   4
10. 'For radius '
    Radius
    ' the diameter is '
    Pi * 2 * Radius
11. PROGRAM Circle (Output);

```
    CONST
      Pi = 3.14159;        (* Ratio of circumference
                               to diameter              *)

    VAR
      Circumference:       (* The computed circumference
                               of the circle            *)

        Real;

    BEGIN
      Circumference := 2 * Pi * 7;
      Write ('The circumference of a circle of ',
             'radius 7 is ');
      Write (Circumference)
    END.
```

GOALS

■ *To be able to construct a specified Writeln statement.*

■ *To be able to use Write and Writeln together to produce output in a specified format.*

■ *To be able to use fieldwidth specifiers to produce output in a desired format.*

■ *To be able to construct expressions with multiple arithmetic operations in them.*

■ *To be able to use predefined Pascal function subprograms in expressions.*

■ *To be able to recognize examples of function usage.*

■ *To be able to design and write longer Pascal programs.*

The first part of this chapter brought you to the point of being able to write Pascal programs that perform simple computations and print out a single line. In this part we will expand your knowledge of Pascal syntax so that you can write programs that perform more complicated calculations and print multiple lines of output. We will also show how to arrange output to make it more readable.

THE WRITELN STATEMENT

In Part 1 of this chapter we did not consider the effect of having more than one Write statement in a program. If a program has multiple Write statements, all of the parameters of the successive Write statements are output on a single line. Thus, if the body of a program has the sequence of statements

```
I := 2;
J := 6;
Write(I);
Write('I = ', I);
Write('Sum = ', I + J);
Write('Error Message');
Write('Error#', I);
```

the output is actually

□□□□□2 I□=□□□□□□2 Sum□=□□□□□□8 Error□Message Error#□□□□□2

You can have output printed on different lines by using the *Writeln* statement.

The Writeln statement is similar to the Write statement (it is another example of a procedure subprogram), but it has the added feature of causing the *next* output to be printed on the next line. For example,

```
Write('Hi');
Write(' there,');
Write(' Lois Lane')
```

produces

```
Hi there, Lois Lane
```

whereas

```
Write('Hi');
Writeln(' there,');
Write(' Lois Lane')
```

produces

```
Hi there,
 Lois Lane
```

Another way to think of the Writeln statement is as a Write statement with an invisible extra parameter at the end of the parameter list which causes the terminal (or printer) to go to the start of the next line.

Here are some more examples:

Statements	Output produced
`Write('Hi there, ');`	
`Writeln('Lois Lane.');`	`Hi there, Lois Lane.`
`Write('Have you seen ');`	
`Write('Clark Kent?')`	`Have you seen Clark Kent?`
`Writeln('Hi there, ');`	`Hi there,`
`Writeln('Lois Lane.');`	`Lois Lane.`
`Writeln('Have you seen ');`	`Have you seen`
`Write('Clark Kent?')`	`Clark Kent?`
`Writeln('Hi there, ');`	
`Write('Lois Lane.');`	`Hi there,`
`Writeln(' Have you seen ');`	`Lois Lane. Have you seen`
`Write('Clark Kent?')`	`Clark Kent?`

What do you suppose the following will output?

```
Writeln('Hi there,');
Writeln;
Write('Lois Lane.');
```

Although it wouldn't make any sense to construct a Write statement without any parameters (because it wouldn't do anything), a Writeln without parameters still has a function to perform: It causes the terminal (or printer) to go to the start of the next line. Thus the output from this example would be

```
Hi there,

Lois Lane.
```

Whenever a Writeln with no parameters follows another Writeln, a blank line will be produced.

What if a Writeln with no parameters follows a Write?

```
Write('Hi there,');
Writeln;
Write('Clark Kent.');
```

The first Write statement causes the words "Hi there," to be printed. The Writeln then causes the terminal (or printer) to go to the next line, where the words "Clark Kent." are printed by the last Write statement, like so:

```
Hi there,
Clark Kent.
```

In fact, we could rewrite these three statements with just two statements:

```
Writeln('Hi there,');
Write('Clark Kent.');
```

In other words,

```
Write(parameter list);
Writeln;
```

is equivalent to

```
Writeln(parameter list);
```

THE APPEARANCE OF OUTPUT

Just as it is important to write programs neatly and clearly so that other people can understand them, it is also important that the output from a program be neatly arranged and easy to understand. Otherwise no one will want to look at it, and so the program will be essentially useless.

The first rule of designing the output from a program is to label anything that isn't self-explanatory. For example, if a program prints out the number 3.605551275, you would be hard pressed to guess what the number represents. Even if you knew that the number is the square root of 13, you still wouldn't know what information the number represents. It would be much more useful for the program to print out "A 13-square-mile plot of land is 3.605551275 miles on a side." This sentence tells the reader exactly what the significance of the output is.

Of course, not every number a program outputs should be part of an explanatory sentence. When a program is to output many numbers, it is often best to arrange them in columns, with a heading over each column that explains the significance of the numbers below it. Compare the readability of these two ways of organizing the same output information:

Method 1	Method 2	
	X	Square of X
The square of 1 is 1	1	1
The square of 2 is 4	2	4
The square of 3 is 9	3	9
The square of 4 is 16	4	16
The square of 5 is 25	5	25
The square of 6 is 36	6	36

The second method conveys the same information as the first method without repeating redundant information. It is also easier to locate a particular number in the neatly aligned columns. Arranging output to be neatly spaced and aligned is called *formatting* the output.

Formatting Output

There are two basic techniques for formatting output. To provide blank lines, successive Writeln statements with no parameters are used. To provide blank space within lines, groups of spaces enclosed in quotes are included in the parameter lists of Write and Writeln statements. For example, if we wanted to produce the following pattern of output:

```
    *   *   *   *   *   *   *   *   *

  *   *   *   *   *   *   *   *   *   *

  *   *   *   *   *   *   *   *   *
```

we would write the following Pascal statements:

```
      Writeln('   *   *   *   *   *   *   *   *   *');
      Writeln;
      Writeln(' *   *   *   *   *   *   *   *   *   *');
      Writeln;
      Writeln('   *   *   *   *   *   *   *   *   *');
```

All of the blanks and stars are enclosed in quotes so that they will be printed just as they are written in the program. The extra Writeln statements, with no parameters, provide the necessary blank lines between the rows of stars. Remember that if you intend for blanks in a Write or Writeln statement to be printed, they should be enclosed in quotes. For example,

will produce

```
**
```

Despite all of the apparent blanks between the two stars in the Writeln statement, the two stars are printed next to each other because the blanks are not enclosed by quotes.

Formatting Integer and Character Output

All of the formatting that we've looked at so far has been concerned with using blank space between items in our output. The items themselves have been formatted automatically. How this automatic formatting is done will vary from compiler to compiler. For example, in this book we use the convention that integer numbers are automatically formatted to be right-justified in a field that is six character positions wide.

To be able to completely control the format of the output, however, you also have to know how to format the items being printed. This is done by indicating how many *columns* you want a variable or constant to occupy in the printed output or on the terminal screen.

To indicate how many columns an output value should occupy, you print a : followed by an integer value after the variable or constant name. The integer following the : specifies how many columns (character positions) on the line the printed value of the variable or constant is to occupy.

The value of the variable or constant will be printed right-justified, with blanks filled in to the left to fill up the proper number of columns. Let's look at an example:

Ans = 33	Integer
Num = 7132	Integer
Ch = 'Z'	Char

Write statement parameters	Output (□ means blank)
1. (Ans:4, Num:5, Ch:3)	□□33□7132□□Z
	4 5 3
2. (Ans:2, Num:4, Ch:1)	337132Z
	2 4 1
3. (Ans:6, Ch:2, Num:5)	□□□□33□Z□7132
	6 2 5
4. (Ch:6, Num:4)	□□□□□Z7132
	6 4
5. (Ans:1, Num:5)	33□7132
	↑ 5
	1 automatically extended to fit the two-digit value

In (1) each of the values is specified to occupy enough columns so that there will be sufficient space separating them.

In (2) the values all run together because, for each value, the number of columns specified was just large enough to hold the value. This output is obviously not very readable. It would be better to make the number of columns larger than the actual number required to hold the printed value so that some space will be left between values.

In (3) there are extra blanks for readability, and in (4) there are not. In (5) the number of columns (the *fieldwidth*) is not large enough for the value in Ans. In this case, the fieldwidth is automatically extended so that all of the digits can be printed.

The automatic extension of the fieldwidth can be quite useful when you want a variable value to be printed in as few columns as possible. If the fieldwidth is specified as :1, the field will always be extended to just the number of places required to print the value. For example, if the variable Total has the value 149573,

```
Write('Total inventory is ', Total:1, ' widgets.')
```

will print

Total inventory is 149573 widgets.

If the value of Total is 6, the output will be

Total inventory is 6 widgets.

For a value of −1 in Total, the output is

Total inventory is −1 widgets.

You can also use fieldwidths with literal string constants:

Write statement parameters	Output (□ means blank)
1. ('The answer is ':16)	□□□The answer is 16 columns
2. (' ':5, 'X':4)	□□□□□□□□X 5 4 columns

In (1) three blanks are inserted at the left to make up the 16 character positions. In (2) the first five blanks come from ' ':5 and the next three are filled in to make 'X':4 cover four positions.

Up to now we have used only integer constants to specify the fieldwidth; sometimes it is advantageous to use integer variables and expressions. For example, the following program segment would plot a graph of an item's sales history.

```
JanuarySales := 5;
FebruarySales := 7;
MarchSales := 8;
AprilSales := 9;
MaySales := 10;
JuneSales := 9;

(* Print a star representing each month's sales. *)

Writeln('*':JanuarySales);
Writeln('*':FebruarySales);
Writeln('*':MarchSales);
Writeln('*':AprilSales);
Writeln('*':MaySales);
Writeln('*':JuneSales);
```

This program would print the following graph:

```
    *
     *
      *
       *
        *
       *
```

Problem Solving in Action

Problem: In the first part of this chapter you wrote a program to print a birthday greeting to your mother. Let's rewrite this program to make it a little fancier. We will use the same greeting, but now we will enclose it in a box of stars.

Output:

```
****************************************
*                                      *
*                                      *
*      Hi Mom!   Happy Birthday!       *
*                                      *
*                                      *
****************************************
```

Algorithm: The first step in figuring out the algorithm to print this greeting is to draw the output on graph paper, as in Figure 2-7.

Now we can see how many columns are taken up by each of the different parts of the output.

The leading blanks on each line can be printed by specifying that the first star on each line be printed in a field 16 columns wide. Because the star itself occupies only a

PSIA

*Figure 2-7
Graphing of
Output*

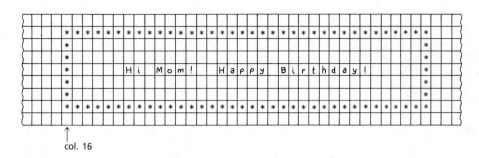

↑
col. 16

single column, the 15 blanks to the left of it will automatically be printed to fill the field out to the proper width. Similarly, by specifying appropriate fieldwidths for the other parts of the output, we can get many of the other blanks to be printed automatically. Our algorithm will thus look like this:

```
Writeln '*':16, '**********************************'
Writeln '*':16, '*':35
Writeln '*':16, '*':35
Writeln '*':16, '    Hi Mom!   Happy Birthday!     *'
Writeln '*':16, '*':35
Writeln '*':16, '*':35
Writeln '*':16, '**********************************'
```

Note that hardly any spaces are actually enclosed in quotes in this algorithm. The only spaces that are enclosed in quotes are in the greeting

```
'        Hi Mom!   Happy Birthday!      *'
```

We could have eliminated these too, by clever use of fieldwidth specifications, but it would hardly be worth the effort. When there are only a few spaces, it's best to write them out for the sake of readability.

We are now ready to write the program. To distinguish it from our Program Birthday, let's call this one Program ForMom. As with Program Birthday, there is no input, so the only file that we need to put into the list of files is Output. Here is the finished program:

```
PROGRAM ForMom (Output);

(* This program prints a fancy birthday
   greeting for my Mom.

   Programmer: Your Name

   Date Written: 4/19/86       *)
```

PSIA ▰▰▰▰▰▰

```
BEGIN (* ForMom *)
   Writeln('*':16,  '***********************************');
   Writeln('*':16,  '*':35);
   Writeln('*':16,  '*':35);
   Writeln('*':16,  '     Hi Mom!  Happy Birthday!      *');
   Writeln('*':16,  '*':35);
   Writeln('*':16,  '*':35);
   Writeln('*':16,  '***********************************')
END.  (* For Mom *)
```

Program ForMom, Written with a Procedure

If you compare Program Birthday with Program ForMom, you will notice that they both print exactly the same greeting. This is a simple example of a subtask that is common to two problems. Recall the building-block approach to problem solving: Look at existing problem solutions and combine what you can to help solve the current problem.

In Chapter 3 we will describe a method of designing programs that is based on the concept of modules. Modules are subtasks that can be designed and coded independently of each other. For example, the birthday greeting could be considered a (very small) module. One of the nice things about modules is that they can often be reused in other programs, via the building-block approach.

In Chapters 6 and 7 we will see that larger modules make very natural procedure subprograms (like Write and Writeln). For example, we could have rewritten Program Birthday as a procedure and then used it in Program ForMom to print out the actual greeting. Instead of writing

```
Writeln('*':16, '     Hi Mom!  Happy Birthday!      *');
```

we would then have written

```
Write('*':16, '       ');
Birthday;
Writeln('      *');
```

The statement Birthday; would cause the computer to put Program ForMom on hold and go execute Birthday, which would print the greeting. Execution would resume with the next statement in Program ForMom.

Not every module has to be a procedure, however. In this case, for example, it is actually easier just to rewrite the greeting from Birthday directly in Program For-

Mom. For larger problems, with more complicated subtasks, it will be much more appropriate to write modules as procedures. We will defer learning how to write subprograms until we have covered enough other material to make them useful.

Formatting Real Output

If you do not indicate how many columns a real value is to take up on output, the value will be printed in scientific (E) notation with one digit before the decimal point. Twenty-two columns is used by some systems as the default (assumed) value for the number of columns.

To indicate the number of columns to be used (the fieldwidth specification), you put a : followed by the number of columns (just as with integers) in a Write statement. A blank or a minus sign is always put before a real number and is included in the column count. The decimal point is also included in the count.

Here is an example. Remember, your machine may have a different range and use more or fewer digits for the exponent.

Value of I	Write statement	Output (□ means blank)
310.0	(I:10)	□3.10E+002
310.0	(I:9)	□3.1E+002
310.0	(I:12)	□3.1000E+002
310.0	(I:1)	□3.1E+002 (uses 9 columns)
0.0112	(I:10)	□1.12E−002
0.0112	(I:12)	□1.1200E−002
0.0112	(I:2)	□1.12E−002 (uses 10 columns)

With Reals, Pascal gives you a second option. If you specify a second : followed by an integer value, the output will be in decimal notation. The first number still specifies the total number of columns to be used; the second specifies the number of digits to print after the decimal point.

Value of I	Write statement	Output (□ means blank)
310.0	(I:10:2)	□□□□310.00
310.0	(I:10:5)	□310.00000
310.0	(I:9:5)	□310.00000 (uses 10 columns)
32.76	(I:8:3)	□□32.760
0.012	(I:8:3)	□□□□0.012
0.012	(I:8:2)	□□□□□0.01 (last digit not printed)

As with integers, the total number of columns is expanded if necessary, so no significant digits are lost. However, the number of columns for fractional digits will be limited by the second field specification. This would be useful, for example, if you wanted the output in dollars and cents.

MORE EXPRESSIONS

The expressions we've used so far have contained at most a single arithmetic operator. We will now see how to write more complicated expressions.

Precedence Rules

Expressions were defined as being made up of variables, constants, and operators. Our examples have shown constants and/or variables with one operator. Actually, expressions can be made up of many constants and/or variables and operators. For example,

$$I := I + J \text{ DIV } 2$$

is valid if I and J are Integer variables (I could also be Real). In an expression with more than one operator, it is not always clear in which order the operations are to be performed. Is I + J calculated first or is J DIV 2 calculated first? Pascal operators are ordered. This order is expressed in precedence rules.

* / DIV MOD	highest precedence
+ −	lowest precedence

So in the example above we divide J by 2 and then add I. We could change the order in which our example is evaluated by using parentheses. The statement

$$I := (I + J) \text{ DIV } 2$$

causes I and J to be added first and their sum divided by 2. (Here I and J must both be Integer.) Subexpressions in parentheses are evaluated first, and then the precedence of the operators is followed.

If we have the statement

$$A := (A + B) / A * 2$$

where A and B are Real variables, we evaluate the expression in the parentheses first. But do we divide the sum of A and B by the product of A and 2, or do we divide the sum of A and B by A and multiply this result by 2?

When there is more than one operator of the same precedence, we evaluate the expression from left to right. This means that in our example, after evaluating the overriding parentheses, we divide by A and multiply the result by 2.

Examples

```
10 DIV 2 * 3  = 15
10 MOD 3 − 4 DIV 2 = −1
5 * 2 / 4 * 2 = 5.0
5 * 2 / (4 * 2)  = 1.25
5 + 2 / (4 * 2)  = 5.25
```

These rules for defining how Pascal will evaluate an expression should not be new to you. They follow the way you would evaluate any arithmetic expression by hand.

Functions

The only type of subprogram that we have looked at so far is the procedure. Pascal also provides for a type of subprogram called a *function.*

Round, Trunc, and Sqrt are examples of the function type of subprogram. Functions are used in expressions in much the same way that arithmetic operators are. The name of the function is followed by a parameter list. For example, Sqrt(16) would cause the Sqrt function to compute the square root of 16. The value computed by a function simply takes its place in the expression, allowing further computation to be performed on it. For example, the expression

```
Sqrt(16) * 10
```

has a value of 40. First the Sqrt function is executed to compute the square root of 16, which is 4. Then the value 4 is multiplied by 10.

One of the distinguishing features of a function subprogram is that it computes a value, called the *function result* or just the *result,* and makes it available for use back in the expression that used the function. A function always returns exactly one result value for use in the expression—no more and no less. The Sqrt function can be given (or "passed") as a parameter either a Real value or an Integer value; however, its result is always a Real. On the other hand, the functions Trunc and Round take a Real parameter and return an Integer result value:

```
Round(3.7) = 4      rounds to nearest integer
Trunc(3.7) = 3      truncates decimal part
```

Where it is invalid to assign a Real to an Integer variable, we can use Round or Trunc to achieve an approximation. If J is an Integer variable, then

```
J := 16.3            is invalid
J := Round(16.3)     is valid
```

(The Real constant 16.3 used as a parameter for the Round function could just as easily have been a Real variable.) See Appendix B for a list of standard identifiers, including all of the functions and procedures that Pascal automatically provides for your use.

Problem Solving in Action

Problem: Write a program to calculate miles per gallon for a car, given the gallon amounts for some fillups and the starting and ending mileage. The starting mileage is 67,308.0, and the ending mileage is 68,750.7. During the period the car was filled up four times. The four amounts were 11.7, 14.3, 12.2, and 8.5 gallons. Compute miles per gallon for the car.

PSIA

Output: The quantities on which the calculations are based and the computed miles per gallon, all appropriately labeled.

Algorithm: If you were to do the computation by hand, you would add up the gallon amounts and then divide the sum into the mileage traveled. The mileage traveled is, of course, just the ending mileage minus the starting mileage. This is essentially the algorithm we will use in our program. Let's make all of the quantities named constants, however, so that it will be easier to change the program later.

```
Amt1 = 11.7
Amt2 = 14.3
Amt3 = 12.2
Amt4 = 8.5
StartMiles = 67308.0
EndMiles = 68750.7
MPG = EndMiles - StartMiles / Amt1 + Amt2 + Amt3 + Amt4
Writeln 'For the gallon amounts: '
Write Amt1:6:1, ',', Amt2:6:1, ',', Amt3:6:1, ',',
Writeln Amt4:6:1
Writeln
Writeln 'a starting mileage of ', StartMiles:8:1
Writeln 'and an ending mileage of ', EndMiles:8:1
Writeln
Writeln 'the mileage per gallon is ', MPG:7:2
```

From the algorithm we can write out our table of quantities and variables.

Quantities

Name	Value	Function
Amt1	11.7	Number of gallons for fillup 1
Amt2	14.3	Number of gallons for fillup 2
Amt3	12.2	Number of gallons for fillup 3
Amt4	8.5	Number of gallons for fillup 4
StartMiles	67308.0	Starting mileage
EndMiles	68750.7	Ending mileage

Variables

Name	Data type	Function
MPG	Real	Computed miles per gallon

We are now ready to write the program. Let's call it Mileage. The only file that we need to list in the heading is Output. We can take the declarations from the tables, and

PSIA ▬▬▬▬

the program statements can be easily translated from the algorithm. Here is the resulting program:

```
PROGRAM Mileage (Output);

(* This program computes miles per gallon given four
   amounts for gallons used and starting and ending
   mileages *)

CONST
   Amt1 = 11.7;        (* Number of gallons for fillup 1 *)
   Amt2 = 14.3;        (* Number of gallons for fillup 2 *)
   Amt3 = 12.2;        (* Number of gallons for fillup 3 *)
   Amt4 =  8.5;        (* Number of gallons for fillup 4 *)
   StartMiles = 67308.0;    (* Starting mileage         *)
   EndMiles   = 68750.7;    (* Ending mileage           *)

VAR
   MPG:                 (* Computed miles per gallon    *)
      Real;

BEGIN (* Mileage *)
   MPG := EndMiles - StartMiles / Amt1 + Amt2 + Amt3 + Amt4;
   Writeln('For the gallon amounts:');
   Write(Amt1:6:1, ',', Amt2:6:1, ',', Amt3:6:1, ',');
   Writeln(Amt4:6:1);
   Writeln;
   Writeln('a starting mileage of ', StartMiles:8:1);
   Writeln('and an ending mileage of ', EndMiles:8:1);
   Writeln;
   Writeln('the mileage per gallon is ', MPG:7:2)
END. (* Mileage *)
```

Testing and Debugging: Program Mileage is the longest program we've written so far. Now that our programs are becoming more complex, there will be more opportunity for them to have errors (bugs). The computer is a very literal device—it does exactly what we instruct it to do, which may not necessarily be what we intended. We can try to make sure that our program does what we want by tracing the execution of instructions before we run the program. This technique is known by many names: "playing computer," "desk checking," doing a "dry run," or doing a code "walk through."

A nonsense program is used below to illustrate the technique. Each line is numbered for reference purposes (the compiler does the same in order to refer to errors in specific lines). To check the execution, we keep track of the values of the program variables on the right-hand side. Variables with undefined values are indicated with a dash. When a variable is assigned a value, that value is listed in the appropriate column on the right.

PSIA ━━━━━━━━

| | | Value of | |
	A	B	C
1 PROGRAM Trace (Output);			
2 CONST			
3 X = 5;			
4 VAR			
5 A, B, C: Integer;	—	—	—
6 BEGIN (* Trace *)	—	—	—
7 B := 1;	—	1	—
8 C := X + B;	—	1	6
9 A := X + 4;	9	1	6
10 A := C;	6	1	6
11 B := C;	6	6	6
12 A := A + B + C;	18	6	6
13 C := C MOD X;	18	6	1
14 C := C * A;	18	6	18
15 A := A MOD B;	0	6	18
16 Writeln(A, B, C)	0	6	18
17 END. (* Trace *)			

Now that we've seen how this technique works, we can apply it to Program Mileage. We'll just list the statement section here:

Line	MPG
1 BEGIN (* Mileage *)	—
2 MPG := EndMiles – StartMiles /	—
3 Amt1 + Amt2 + Amt3 + Amt4;	63032.679
4 Writeln('For the gallon amounts: ');	63032.679
5 Write(Amt1:6:1, ',', Amt2:6:1, ',');	63032.679
6 Writeln(Amt3:6:1, ',', Amt4:6:1);	63032.679
7 Writeln;	63032.679
8 Writeln('a starting mileage of ',	63032.679
9 StartMiles:8:1);	63032.679
10 Writeln('and an ending mileage of ',	63032.679
11 EndMiles:8:1);	63032.679
12 Writeln;	63032.679
13 Writeln('the mileage per gallon is ',	63032.679
14 MPG:7:2)	63032.679
15 END. (* Mileage *)	63032.679

PSIA _____

There is obviously something wrong here—the MPG figure is way too big. The first statement in the program is the formula for calculating MPG. It is supposed to compute the difference between EndMiles and StartMiles and then sum the gallon values, finally dividing the sum into the difference. Calculating this value by hand, we get 30.89. Why is the program calculating 63032.679? According to the Pascal precedence rules of arithmetic, multiplications or divisions in an expression are calculated first, then additions and subtractions. The way we have written the formula for MPG, StartMiles is divided by Amt1 first. Then that value is subtracted from EndMiles. Finally, Amt2, Amt3, and Amt4 are added in. To get the program to calculate MPG correctly, we must put parentheses in the appropriate places, like so:

```
MPG := (EndMiles - StartMiles)/(Amt1 + Amt2 + Amt3 + Amt4);
```

This statement will cause the mileage difference to be computed first, then the amounts to be summed, and the division to be done last. The remaining statements all seem to work properly. The output from Program Mileage is

```
For the gallon amounts:
  11.7,   14.3,   12.2,   8.5

a starting mileage of   67308.0
and an ending mileage of   68750.7

the mileage per gallon is    30.89
```

This answer agrees with the one we calculated by hand. We have completed the problem-solving phase and converted our design into a Pascal program. We have traced the program and have an answer. We can now compile and run the program. If the program prints out the correct answer, we have finished.

It may seem redundant to calculate the answer by hand when you are writing a program to do the same task. In the MPG case it was redundant, since the program calculated the miles per gallon for a specific case. In Chapter 3 we will show you how to write programs for a general case that can be given specific values at run time. When you do this, it is important to have some hand-calculated answers to check against the program's output. Then you can run the program on other data and feel confident that its output is correct.

Checking the program's output against hand-calculated results is called *testing* the program. If your program produces results that do not match the hand-calculated ones, you must check both your program and your calculations, and correct whichever is in error.

PROGRAMS IN MEMORY

In the first part of this chapter we discussed the fact that each of the constants, variables, and translated statements in a program is stored in memory at run time. Now that we've seen some complete Pascal programs, we can take a closer look at how programs are kept in memory.

Figure 2-8 is a picture of Program Mileage as it appears in memory, after compilation. The CONST section of the program causes six memory locations to be assigned the names Amt1, Amt2, Amt3, Amt4, StartMiles, and EndMiles. It also causes the values 11.7, 14.3, 12.2, 8.5, 67308.0, and 68750.7 to be put into these locations.

The VAR section of the program causes the name MPG to be assigned to another memory location, but no value is stored in it. This place will be needed to hold the result of computing miles per gallon. The location named MPG is reserved for values of type Real.

The statements between BEGIN and END are actually translated into machine language instructions (binary numbers), but we have shown them as they are written in Pascal. After the translated version of the program is in memory, control of the computer is turned over to the first statement after the BEGIN. In other words, what the program says to do is actually done.

The first statement will cause the value 30.89293362 to be computed and stored in the location named MPG. The remainder of the statements print out various strings and values. The values that are printed are all fetched up from the appropriate locations as they are needed. Before these values are printed, the Writeln statements format them according to the fieldwidth specifications. This formatting process does *not* affect the actual values stored in the memory locations, but simply changes how they are printed.

SUMMARY

Output should be clear, understandable, and neatly arranged. Messages in the output can be used to describe the significance of values that are not self-explanatory. Blank lines and blank spaces within lines can be used to organize output and improve its appearance.

The Writeln statement may be used to produce output on multiple lines. Writeln statements without parameter lists may be used to generate blank lines in the output.

Fieldwidth specifications may be used in Write and Writeln statements to determine the appearance of values and constants in the output and to provide extra blank space in the output. The fieldwidth specification does *not* affect the values actually stored in memory, only their appearance in the output generated by a particular Write or Writeln statement.

Expressions may contain more than one operator. The order in which the operations are performed is determined by precedence rules. Multiplication and division operations are performed first; then addition and subtraction are performed. Multiple operations of the same

Figure 2-8
Translated Version
of Program
Mileage in
Memory

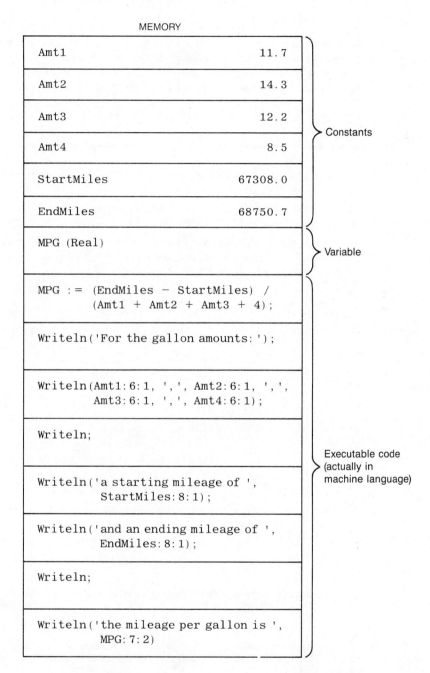

type are performed in left-to-right order. Parentheses can be used to override the precedence rules.

Pascal provides for two types of subprograms which differ primarily in the way in which they are called. Procedure subprograms are called by writing the name of the procedure (with its parameter list) as a Pascal statement. Function subprograms are called by writing the name of the function (with its parameter list) as part of an assignment statement. Pascal provides the predefined procedures and functions that are listed in Appendix B.

Tracing the execution of a program is a useful technique for finding bugs (errors) in the program before it is run on the computer. It is important to hand-calculate some results so that they can be compared to the output of the program when it is tested.

QUICK CHECK _____

1. Write a Writeln statement to print out the title of this book (Introduction to Pascal and Structured Design). (pp. 70–72)

2. How many Writeln statements (without parameters) would you have to insert after a Write('Hi') statement to cause a blank line to appear in the output? (pp. 70–72)

3. Assume a Real variable called Pay contains the amount 327.66101. What fieldwidth specification would you use with the variable to cause it to be printed as a dollars and cents amount with three leading blanks? (p. 79)

4. How would you write the following formula as a Pascal expression that produces a Real value as a result?

$$\frac{9}{5}C + 32$$

(pp. 80–81)

5. What Pascal functions can be used to convert a Real number into an Integer approximation of the number? (p. 81)

6. What part of the following Pascal expression is a call to a function?

$$77 \; DIV \; 11 \; + \; Abs\,(Temp) \; * \; MPG$$

(pp. 80–81)

7. What is the result of evaluating the expression

$$(1 \; + \; 2 \; * \; 2) \; DIV \; 1 \; + \; 1$$

(p. 81)

8. What are the steps involved in tracing a Pascal program with three variables called X, Y, and Z? (pp. 83–85)

Answers
1. Writeln('Introduction to Pascal and Structured Design')
2. Two Writeln statements are required after a Write statement to produce a blank line in the output.
3. Pay: 9: 2
4. 9 / 5 * C + 32
5. Trunc and Round 6. Abs(Temp) 7. The result is 6.
8. To the right of the program mark off a column for each of the variables. Begin executing the program statements by hand. Each time the value of a variable is changed, write the new value in its column, next to the current program statement.

EXAM PREPARATION EXERCISES _____

1. Mark the following as valid or invalid identifiers:

	Valid	Invalid
(a) `Item#1`	___	___
(b) `Data`	___	___
(c) `Y`	___	___
(d) `1Set`	___	___
(e) `Investment`	___	___
(f) `Bin-2`	___	___
(g) `Num5`	___	___
(h) `Sq Ft`	___	___

2. Given the syntax diagrams

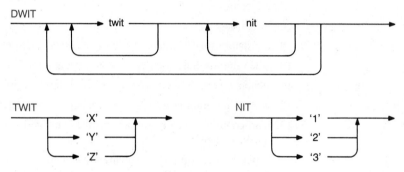

   mark the following as valid or invalid "dwits":

	Valid	Invalid
(a) XYZ	___	___
(b) 123	___	___
(c) X1	___	___
(d) 23Y	___	___
(e) XY12	___	___
(f) Y2Y	___	___
(g) ZY2	___	___
(h) XY23X1	___	___

3. Not formatting the program correctly will cause an error. (True or False?)

4. Mark the following as either valid or not valid.

	Valid	Invalid
(a) `X × Y = C`	___	___
(b) `Y : = Con`	___	___
(c) `CONST X = 10`	___	___
(d) `VAR X : Integer`	___	___
(e) `A : = B MOD C`	___	___

5. Match each of the following terms to the correct definition. There is only one correct answer for each.

_____ program	_____ variable
_____ algorithm	_____ constant
_____ compiler	_____ memory
_____ identifier	_____ syntax
_____ translation phase	_____ semantics
_____ execution phase	

1. a place in memory where a data value can be stored

2. a place in memory where a data value that cannot be changed is stored

3. the part of a computer that holds both program and data

4. an input device to a computer

5. the time spent planning a program

6. grammar rules

7. a looping structure

8. meaning

9. a program that translates assembly language instructions into machine code

10. when the machine code version of a program is being run

11. symbolic names made up of letters and digits beginning with a letter

12. when a program in a high-level language is translated into machine code

13. a program that takes a program written in a high-level language and translates it into machine code

14. a step-by-step outline for solving a problem

15. a sequence of instructions to a computer to perform a particular task

6. Compute the value of each expression if it is a legal expression. Indicate whether the value is Real or Integer. If the expression is not legal, indicate why.
   (a) `10 / 3 + 5 * 2`
   (b) `10 MOD 3 + 5 MOD 2`
   (c) `10 DIV 3 + 5 DIV 2`
   (d) `12.5 + (2.5 / (6.2 / 3.1))`
   (e) `-4 * (-5 + 6)`
   (f) `13 MOD 5 / 3`
   (g) `(10 / 3 MOD 2) / 3`

7. Evaluate the following expressions to find the result:
   (a) `Result := 15 MOD 4`
   (b) `Result := 7 DIV 3 + 2`
   (c) `Result := 2 + 7 * 5`
   (d) `Result := 45 DIV 8 * 4 + 2`
   (e) `Result := 17 + (21 MOD 6) * 2`
   (f) `Result := Sqr(4 * 2 + 2)`

8. Which of the following are reserved words and which are user-defined identifiers?

	Reserved	User-defined
(a) END	_____	_____
(b) SORT	_____	_____
(c) WRITEHI	_____	_____
(d) MOD	_____	_____
(e) THEEND	_____	_____

9. Reserved words can be used as variable names. (True or False?)

10. A block consists of an optional declarations part and a compound statement. (True or False?)

11. Trace the values of the variables in the following program. Use a ? if the value is undefined; repeat the value if it is the same.

```
                                                      A     B     C
PROGRAM Test3 (Input, Output);

CONST                                                ___   ___   ___
  N = 4;                                             ___   ___   ___

VAR                                                  ___   ___   ___
  A, B, C:                                           ___   ___   ___
    Integer;                                         ___   ___   ___

BEGIN                                                ___   ___   ___
  A := 5;                                            ___   ___   ___
  B := A * N;                                        ___   ___   ___
  C := A MOD N;                                      ___   ___   ___
  A := C;                                            ___   ___   ___
  B := A + C;                                        ___   ___   ___
  Writeln(A, B, C)                                   ___   ___   ___
END.
```

12. If A = 5 and B = 2, show what each of the following statements produces:

```
Writeln('A = ', A, ' B = ', B);
Writeln('Sum = ', A + B);
Writeln(A DIV B);
Writeln(B - A);
```

13. Name two things that contribute to the readability of programs.

14. Given the following program, determine what is printed.

```
PROGRAM Exercise (Output);

CONST
  Lbs = 10;

VAR
  Price, Cost:
    Integer;
  Ch:
    Char;

BEGIN
  Price := 30;
  Cost := Price * Lbs;
  Ch := 'A';
  Writeln('Cost is ');
  Writeln(Cost);
  Writeln('Price is ', Price, 'Cost is ', Cost);
  Write('Grade ', Ch, ' Costs ');
  Writeln(Cost)
END.
```

PREPROGRAMMING EXERCISES _____

1. Change the program in Exam Preparation Exercise 14 so that it prints the cost for 15 pounds.

2. Write the Pascal expressions that will compute both solutions from the quadratic formula. The formula is

$$\frac{-B \pm \sqrt{B^2 - 4AC}}{2A}$$

3. Input and run the following program. Information within parentheses is to be filled in by you. This information is called *program documentation*.

```
PROGRAM One (Output);

(*   Programming Assignment One          *)
(*   (your name)                         *)
(*   (date copied and run)               *)
(*   (description of the problem)        *)

CONST
  Debt = 300.0;          (* Original value owed    *)
  Paymt = 22.4;          (* Payment                *)
  Intr = 0.02;           (* Interest rate          *)

VAR
  Charg,                 (* Interest times debt    *)
  Reduc,                 (* Amount debt is reduced *)
  Remain:                (* Remaining balance      *)
    Real;

BEGIN
  Charg := Intr * Debt;
  Reduc := Paymt - Charg;
  Remain := Debt - Reduc;
  Writeln('Payment ', Paymt, ' Charge ',
          Charg, ' Balance owed ', Remain)
END.
```

4. Copy and run the following program. Fill in the comments by using the pattern shown in Exercise 3 above. Such information is entered for the benefit of someone reading the program.

```
PROGRAM Two (Output);

CONST
  TCost  = 600;
  Pounds = 10;
  Ounces = 11;
```

```
VAR
  TotOz,
  UCost:
    Real;

BEGIN
  TotOz := 16 * Pounds;
  TotOz := TotOz + Ounces;
  UCost := TCost / TotOz;
  Writeln('Cost per unit ', UCost)
END.
```

(Notice how hard it is to tell what the program does without the comments already in the code.)

PROGRAMMING PROBLEMS

1. Write a Pascal program that will print your initials in large block letters, with each of the block letters composed of the same character that it represents. The letters should be a minimum of seven printed lines in height and should appear all in a row. For example, if your initials are DOW, your program should print out

```
DDDDDDD        OOOOO      W         W
D      D       O     O     W         W
D       D      O       O    W         W
D       D      O       O    W    W    W
D       D      O       O    W   W W   W
D      D       O     O     W W     W W
DDDDDDD        OOOOO       WW       WW
```

Be sure to include appropriate comments in your program, choose meaningful identifier names, and use an indentation style similar to that in the example programs in this chapter.

2. Write a program that will print out the value of the predefined Pascal constant MaxInt and the value of −MaxInt. The output from your program should include messages that identify which value is MaxInt and which value is −MaxInt. Be sure to include appropriate comments in your program, choose meaningful identifier names, and use an indentation style similar to that in the example programs in this chapter.

3. Write a Pascal program that will convert a centigrade temperature to its Fahrenheit equivalent. The formula for this conversion is

$$\frac{9}{5}\text{Centigrade} + 32$$

In your program Centigrade should be a named constant so that its value can be changed easily. The program should print both the value of Centigrade and its Fahrenheit equivalent, with appropriate identifying messages. Your program should be properly commented, with meaningful identifier names and good indentation style.

- To be able to construct a Read or Readln statement to read in specified values.
- To be able to determine the contents of variables assigned values in a given Read or Readln statement.
- To be able to write proper prompting messages for a program that does interactive input/output.
- To know when batch input/output is appropriate and how it differs from interactive input/output.
- To be able to write programs that use Text files other than Input and Output.
- To be able to apply the top-down design methodology to solve a simple problem.
- To be able to take a top-down design and code it in Pascal, using self-documenting code.

3

Input and Design Methodology

A program needs data on which to operate. Until now, we have written all of the data values into the program itself, in literal and named constants. If this were the only way that we could provide data to a program, it would severely restrict what programs could do. We would have to rewrite the program each time we wanted to apply it to a different set of data. In this chapter we will look at ways of entering data into a program while it is running.

In the preceding chapters we have discussed general problem-solving strategies and how to write simple programs. For a simple problem, it is easy to choose a strategy, write the algorithm, and then code the program. As you encounter more complex problems, however, you will need to use a more organized approach to developing your algorithms. In the latter part of this chapter we will set aside Pascal particulars and look at a general methodology for developing algorithms: top-down design.

GETTING DATA INTO PROGRAMS

One of the biggest advantages of using a computer is being able to write a program that can be used with many different sets of data. This means, of course, that the data cannot be written directly into the program. The program and data must be kept separate until it is time to run the program. At that point, certain instructions in the program will cause the computer to place values from the data set into variables in the program. Once the values are stored in the variables, the program can go ahead and perform calculations with them.

Figure 3-1
Separating the
Data from the
Program

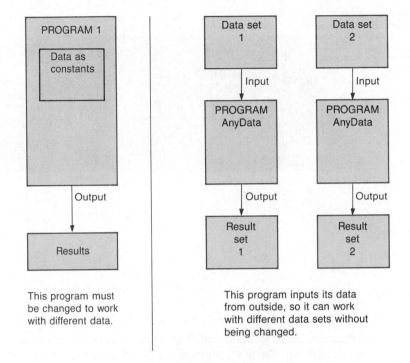

This program must
be changed to work
with different data.

This program inputs its data
from outside, so it can work
with different data sets without
being changed.

When the data set is separate from the program, you can change the values in the data set without having to change the program. (See Figure 3-1.) Whatever values you put into the data set will be the ones that the program will work with the next time it is executed. The process of placing values from an outside data set into variables in a program is called *input*. Recall the two input devices we mentioned in Chapter 1: the terminal keyboard and the card reader. The data set for the program may come from either of these (assuming your computer has both of them) or from a file on an auxiliary storage device such as a disk or tape.

How does the computer know which device or file has the data set for your program? You tell it where the data set is through commands that you issue when you run your program. What you are doing essentially is issuing a command to the computer to "run my program using the data set on file such and such." How the command is issued varies widely from system to system. For the time being, we will assume that all input will be from a terminal (for interactive systems) or card reader (for batch systems).

Read

In Pascal, one statement that causes the computer to get values from a data set and place them into variables is the Read statement. Its name comes from the idea that the computer is "reading" what we type into it. The syntax of the Read statement is

⟶ Read ⟶ (⟶ parameter list ⟶) ⟶

Unlike the parameter list for a Write statement, which can contain variables, constants, and expressions, the parameter list for a Read statement can contain only variables. This is because the Read parameter list specifies where input data values are to be placed, and only variables are allowed to have their values changed while the program is running. If there are multiple variables in the parameter list, they must be separated by commas; for example,

Read(Length, Width, Price)

The steps involved in executing the Read statement, where the parameters are Real or Integer variables, are as follows:

1. Get a number from the input data file or the terminal.
2. Store the number in memory in the first place named in the parameter list.
3. Is there another name still left in the parameter list? If so,

- Get a number.
- Store the number in the next place named in the parameter list.
- Repeat step 3.

If not, Read is completed.

How do you separate numbers on a data card or when you are typing them on the terminal? By putting blanks between them.

Just as with the assignment statement, you have to be careful that you don't try to input a Real value into an Integer variable. You can, however, read an Integer value into a Real variable.

Statement	Data	Contents after Read
(a) Read(X)	32	X = 32
(b) Read(A, B, C)	3 4 60	A = 3, B = 4, C = 60
(c) Read(D, E)	24 76	D = 24, E = 76
(d) Read(Y, Z)	46 32.4	Y = 46, Z = 32.4

NOTE: X, A, B, C, D, E, and Y are Integer variables, and Z is a Real variable.

How does the computer know which number to put into which variable? It simply takes the numbers in the order in which they are given and puts them into the variables on a first-come, first-served basis. That is, the first variable in the parameter list of the first Read statement in the program will get the first number typed in. If there is a second variable in the parameter list, it gets the second number typed. If more numbers are typed than there are variables in the parameter list, the computer will hold the extra numbers until it encounters the next Read statement. The first of those numbers then goes to the first variable in that Read statement. If there are extra values left when the program ends, the computer disregards them.

What is the difference between the statement Read(A) followed by the statement Read(B) and the statement Read(A, B)? Absolutely none. Using a list of variable identifiers is only a convenience for the programmer.

Readln

Pascal has a second input statement: Readln. Readln differs from Read in one major respect. After the variables in the parameter list have had values put into them, the Readln skips over any extra numbers on the line and goes to the start of the next line (or card). The extra numbers are simply discarded and are not read.

For example, if there are two integer data items on each line of input,

```
10 20
15 16
22 21
```

the following sets of statements are all equivalent:

(a) Read (A, B) ;
    Read (C, D) ;
    Read (E, F)

(b) Read (A) ;
    Read (B, C, D) ;
    Read (E, F)

(c) Read (A, B, C, D, E, F)

(d) Readln (A, B) ;
    Readln (C, D) ;
    Readln (E, F)

(e) Readln (A, B, C, D, E, F)

Variable	Value read
A	10
B	20
C	15
D	16
E	22
F	21

Note that (a) and (d) are the same except that one uses Read and the other Readln; so are (c) and (e). What happens if the Read statements in (b) are replaced by Readln statements? We run out of data and an error message occurs. Look what happens:

    Readln (A) ;   10 is stored in A (20 is skipped)
    Readln (B, C, D) ; 15 is stored in B
                        16 is stored in C
                        22 is stored in D (21 is skipped)

> `Readln(E, F)` There are no values to be put into E and F.

The second value on the first line of data (20) is not read because, after reading a value into A, the Readln(A) statement skips the rest of that line. The second value on the third line (21) is likewise skipped by the Readln(B, C, D) statement. In both cases, these numbers are leftovers on the input line after the Readln statements have finished putting values into the variables in their parameter lists.

The Reading Marker and ⟨eoln⟩

Before further exploring the effects of mixing Read and Readln statements, we must introduce the concept of the reading marker. The reading marker works somewhat like a bookmark, but instead of marking a place in a book, it keeps track of a place in a line of input. The reading marker is used to indicate the next character that has not yet been read. In other words, it marks the point in the input data where the computer will continue reading.

Read leaves the reading marker ready to begin with the first character following the last piece of data that was input. Readln inputs enough data to fill the variables in its parameter list and then moves the reading marker to the beginning of the next line. Each input line has an end-of-line character ⟨eoln⟩ to tell the computer where one line ends and the next begins. The Read and Readln will cross line boundaries ⟨eoln⟩ to find as many values as there are variables in their parameter lists.

Where does the ⟨eoln⟩ come from? What *is* it? The first question is easy. If you are working at a terminal, you generate an ⟨eoln⟩ yourself when you hit the return or new-line key. If you are using cards, the ⟨eoln⟩ character is automatically inserted after each card when the cards are read. The answer to the second question will vary from computer system to computer system. The ⟨eoln⟩ is a special nonprintable control character that a system recognizes. When your program is reading in values, the Read or Readln statement treats this character as a blank.

You can also generate an ⟨eoln⟩ by using a Writeln statement in your program. When you use a Writeln, you are actually outputting an ⟨eoln⟩ character directly after the variables in the parameter list have been written. The printer or screen goes to a new line when it recognizes this character.

Let's look at an example that uses the reading marker and ⟨eoln⟩. Given three lines of input data

> ```
> 123 456 789⟨eoln⟩
> 987 654 321⟨eoln⟩
> 888 777 666⟨eoln⟩
> ```

and given that A, B, C, and D are Integer variables, the following statements produce the results shown in the table below. The part of the input list printed in color is what has been read following execution of the statement. The reading marker, denoted by the shaded gray block, indicates the next character to be read.

Statements	Values read	Marker position after Read/Readln
(a) Read(A, B);	A = 123, B = 456	123 456 ▮789⟨eoln⟩ 987 654 321⟨eoln⟩ 888 777 666⟨eoln⟩
Read(C, D)	C = 789, D = 987	123 456 789⟨eoln⟩ 987 ▮654 321⟨eoln⟩ 888 777 666⟨eoln⟩
(b) Readln(A, B);	A = 123, B = 456	123 456 789⟨eoln⟩ ▮987 654 321⟨eoln⟩ 888 777 666⟨eoln⟩
Readln(C, D)	C = 987, D = 654	123 456 789⟨eoln⟩ 987 654 321⟨eoln⟩ ▮888 777 666⟨eoln⟩
(c) Read(A, B);	A = 123, B = 456	123 456▮789⟨eoln⟩ 987 654 321⟨eoln⟩ 888 777 666⟨eoln⟩
Readln(C, D)	C = 789, D = 987	123 456 789⟨eoln⟩ 987 654 321⟨eoln⟩ ▮888 777 666⟨eoln⟩
(d) Readln(A, B);	A = 123, B = 456	123 456 789⟨eoln⟩ ▮987 654 321⟨eoln⟩ 888 777 666⟨eoln⟩
Readln(C);	C = 987	123 456 789⟨eoln⟩ 987 654 321⟨eoln⟩ ▮888 777 666⟨eoln⟩
Readln(D)	D = 888	123 456 789⟨eoln⟩ 987 654 321⟨eoln⟩ 888 777 666⟨eoln⟩ ▮

Although we have used Integer data values in the above example, Real data values are read into Real variables exactly the same way.

Look back at Program Payroll in Chapter 1 and examine the Readln statements. EmpNum, PayRate, and Hours are each read in with a separate Readln. This implies that each data item is on a separate line.

Reading Character Data

Character data is treated differently from numeric data. Remember that a Char variable holds only *one* character. So when the program is reading values into variables declared to be of type Char, only one character is read.

Given the data   A10⟨eoln⟩
                                  BBB⟨eoln⟩
                                  999⟨eoln⟩

and given that X, Y, and Z are Char variables, the following Read and Readln statements produce the results indicated.

Statements	Values read	Marker position after Read/Readln
(a) Read(X, Y, Z)	X = 'A', Y = '1', Z = '0'	A10⟨eoln⟩ BBB⟨eoln⟩ 999⟨eoln⟩
(b) Readln(X);	X = 'A'	A10⟨eoln⟩ BBB⟨eoln⟩ 999⟨eoln⟩
Readln(Y);	Y = 'B'	A10⟨eoln⟩ BBB⟨eoln⟩ 999⟨eoln⟩
Read(Z)	Z = '9'	A10⟨eoln⟩ BBB⟨eoln⟩ 999⟨eoln⟩
(c) Readln(X, Y);	X = 'A', Y = '1'	A10⟨eoln⟩ BBB⟨eoln⟩ 999⟨eoln⟩
Readln(Z)	Z = 'B'	A10⟨eoln⟩ BBB⟨eoln⟩ 999⟨eoln⟩

Note that quotation marks are not needed around the character data values when they are input. It is only necessary to put quotes around character constants when you write them in programs, in order to differentiate them from identifiers or numeric constants. When data values are read in, there is no ambiguity. The type of the variable into which a value is to be stored determines how a value is interpreted when it is read.

Before the first Read or Readln in a program and after every Readln, the reading marker will be on the first character on a line (or card). After a Read, the marker indicates the first character following what was just read in. This can be a problem when you want the computer to read character data following a number. Because a number is usually followed by a space and a space is a character, the space will be read into the Char-type variable.

Look at what happens when numeric data and character data are mixed (Ch1 and Ch2 are Char variables, and P and Q are Integer variables). The data is

24 36 AB⟨eoln⟩

Statements	Values read	Marker position after Read/Readln
Read(P, Q);	P = 24, Q = 36	24 36 ▮AB⟨eoln⟩
Read(Ch1);	Ch1 = ' '	24 36 ▮AB⟨eoln⟩
Read(Ch2)	Ch2 = 'A'	24 36 A▮B⟨eoln⟩

It is important to remember that a Read involving a Char-type variable always reads only one character (whichever one the reading marker is on), and then advances the marker one character to the right. After the second Integer in the example is read, the marker is left at the space between the 6 and the A. Thus, when the computer goes to get a character to put into Ch1, it takes the blank and stores it in Ch1. This leaves the marker on the letter A, which consequently gets read into Ch2.

What if the desired result is to read the A into Ch1 and the B into Ch2? Somehow, we have to get rid of the blank between the 6 and the A. The way to get rid of the blank is to read it and then ignore it. We can do this in a couple of ways. One way is to declare another Char variable, Ch0, which is not used for any further computation, and then rewrite the input statements as follows:

Statements	Values read	Marker position after Read/Readln
Read(P, Q);	P = 24, Q = 36	24 36 ▮AB⟨eoln⟩
Read(Ch0);	Ch0 = ' '	24 36 ▮AB⟨eoln⟩
Read(Ch1);	Ch1 = 'A'	24 36 AB▮⟨eoln⟩
Read(Ch2)	Ch2 = 'B'	24 36 AB⟨eoln⟩

The other way to get rid of the blank between the 6 and the A is to read Ch1 twice in a row. The first time, the blank will be read into Ch1. The second read into Ch1 will read the A into Ch1, replacing the blank:

Statements	Values read	Marker position after Read/Readln
Read(P, Q);	P = 24, Q = 36	24 36 ▮AB⟨eoln⟩
Read(Ch1);	Ch1 = ' '	24 36 ▮AB⟨eoln⟩
Read(Ch1);	Ch1 = 'A'	24 36 A▮B⟨eoln⟩
Read(Ch2)	Ch2 = 'B'	24 36 AB⟨eoln⟩

Let's look at some more examples of mixing numeric and character input. We'll use the same data as before:

24 36 AB⟨eoln⟩

Statements	Values read	Marker position after Read/Readln
(a) Read(Ch1, Ch2)	Ch1 = '2', Ch2 = '4'	24 36 AB⟨eoln⟩
(b) Read(P, Q);	P = 24, Q = 36	24 36 AB⟨eoln⟩
Read(Ch1, Ch1);	Ch1 = ' ', Ch1 = 'A'	24 36 AB⟨eoln⟩
Read(Ch2, Ch2)	Ch2 = 'B', Ch2 = ' '	24 36 AB⟨eoln⟩

In (a), Ch1 holds a '2' and Ch2 holds a '4'. These are the characters '2' and '4', not the integers 2 and 4. Example (a) demonstrates that the Read statement can interpret the same data in two different ways, depending on the data type of the variable that's being filled. Example (b) shows that reading the ⟨eoln⟩ into a Char-type variable causes a blank to be stored in that variable.

More About Procedures and Parameters

One final note about Read and Readln: Just like Write and Writeln, Read and Readln are examples of procedure subprograms. Recall from Chapter 2 that a sub-program is simply a program that is available for you to use within other programs that you write. When your program tells the computer to go off and do the instructions in that subprogram, the program is said to be "calling" the subprogram. When the subprogram finishes up, the computer is said to "return" to your program. Parameters in the parameter list are said to be "passed" to the subprogram.

With the Write (or Writeln) procedure, variables, constants, and expressions can be passed to the subprogram. Read and Readln, however, accept only variables as parameters. This is because Read and Readln store values into their parameters when they return (and only variables can have values stored into them while the program is running). Read and Readln are thus said to "pass back" or "return" values through their parameters. The point to remember is that parameters can be used both for getting data into a procedure *and* for getting results back out.

The terms *procedure call* and *function call* will be used to distinguish between the calls for the two types of subprograms.

Interactive Input/Output

Recall from Chapter 1 that an interactive program is one in which the user communicates directly with the computer. Many of the programs that you write will be interactive in nature. There is a certain amount of etiquette involved in writing interactive programs. Mostly this involves providing clear instructions to the user for each item of data to be entered.

Before each data value is read by an interactive program, the program should print a message (via a Writeln statement) to the user explaining what is to be entered. Such messages are called *input prompts*. Without such messages, a user will have no idea of what to type into the program. A program that doesn't prompt for input values can be very frustrating to use, if it can be used at all. The program should also print out all of the data values typed in, so that the user can verify that they were entered correctly. Printing the input values is called *echo printing*. The following sample of a Pascal program segment and the output it generates shows proper use of prompts and echo printing. The interactive user input is shown in color. Although echo printing may seem redundant on a screen, it is crucial for the verification of input data.

```
Writeln('Enter the part number: ');
Readln(PartNumber);
Writeln('Enter the quantity of this part ordered: ');
Readln(Quantity);
Writeln('Enter the unit price for this part: ');
Readln(UnitPrice);
TotalPrice := UnitPrice * Quantity;
Writeln('Part ', PartNumber:6, ', quantity ',
        Quantity:6, ', at $', UnitPrice:7:2);
Writeln('each, will total $', TotalPrice:7:2);
```

Output:

```
Enter the part number:
4671
Enter the quantity of this part ordered:
10
Enter the unit price for this part:
27.25
Part   4671, quantity      10, at $  27.25
each, will total $ 272.50
```

The amount of information that you put into prompting messages will depend on the intended audience of the program. If you were writing this program for people unfamiliar with computers, you might write much more detailed messages; for example, "Type a four-digit part number, then press the key marked RETURN." If the program were intended for people who use computers all the time and would be using the program frequently, you could shorten the prompts to give a bare minimum of information, such as "Enter PN:" and "Enter Qty:" In programs for very experienced users, you can prompt for several values at once, then let them type all of the values on one input line:

```
Enter PN, Qty, Unit Price:
4176 10 27.25
```

In programs that request large amounts of data, this method saves the user keystrokes and time. However, this approach also makes it easier for the user to type values in the wrong order.

Beyond prompting for input, programs can interact with users in other ways. Often it is helpful to have a program print out some general instructions at the beginning ("Press RETURN after typing each data value."). When erroneous data is entered, a message that indicates the problem should be printed. For users who haven't worked much with computers, it is especially important that these messages be informative and friendly. For example

```
            ILLEGAL DATA VALUES!!!!!!!
```

is likely to upset such a user and doesn't provide any constructive information. Much better would be the message

```
That is not a valid part number. Part numbers must be four digits
long. Please reenter the number in its proper form:
```

Some computer systems may require you to code interactive programs a little differently than batch-oriented programs. For example, one common system requires you to put the filename "INPUT/" in the headings of interactive programs *T,M,V* ◁ and to put a Readln statement with no parameters before the first Read. You should check the manuals for your particular system to see if it has any special requirements.

Batch Input/Output

Although we will tend to use examples of interactive I/O in this text, many programs are written using batch I/O. Recall that in batch processing there is no interaction between the user and the computer during the actual processing. This method is often desirable when a program is to input or output large amounts of data. When many data values are to be read by a program, the usual practice is to prepare them ahead of time. This preparation may involve typing the values onto punch cards or into a disk file, which allows the user to go back and make changes or corrections as necessary before running the program.

When a program is designed to print lots of data, the output may be sent directly to a high-speed printer or another disk file. This permits the user to examine the data at leisure, after the program has been run. The next section discusses input and output with disk files.

Programs that are designed for batch processing do not need to print prompting messages for each input. It is still a good idea, however, to echo print each data value that is read. Echo printing permits the person reading the output to verify that the input values were prepared correctly. Because batch-oriented programs tend to print large amounts of data, their output often will be in the form of a table of columns with descriptive headings. We talked briefly about printing tables in Chapter 2 and will return to this topic in Chapter 5.

FILES OTHER THAN INPUT AND OUTPUT

In everything we've done so far, we've assumed that the input to our programs would come from the terminal keyboard (or card reader) and the output from our programs would go to the terminal screen (or printer). We've referred to the terminal keyboard and screen as "files" called Input and Output. Strictly speaking, the keyboard and screen aren't files—at least not in the same sense as the files into which we enter our programs. A true file is a named secondary memory area that holds a collection of information (such as the lines of a program that we have entered). The information in a file is usually stored on an auxiliary storage device, such as a disk (see Figure 3-2).

The reason we sometimes call Input and Output "files" is because we treat them just as we treat actual disk files. Our programs can write their output onto disk files in the same way that we've had them write output to the screen. Our programs can also read data from files in the same way that they read data from the keyboard.

Why would we want the output from a program to be written on a disk file? Because this gives us the option of looking at the output over and over again without having to run the program over and over. Most systems provide a command that allows you to display the contents of a file on your terminal screen. For example, if a file is called MPG.TXT, on many systems the following command will cause the contents of that file to be displayed on the screen:

Type MPG. TXT

Having output stored on a file will also permit another program to read the contents of the file as input. For example, Program Payroll from Chapter 1 writes its

Figure 3-2
A Typical Disk
Storage Unit

Control
Data

output to a file called Payfile, which can then be read by a program that prints out paychecks.

Why would we want to have a program read data from a file instead of the keyboard? If a program is to read a large quantity of data, it is easier to enter the data into a file with an editor than to type it directly into the program. With the editor we can go back and correct mistakes. Also, with the editor we do not have to enter the data all at once—we can take a break and come back later to enter more data. If we should want to rerun the program for some reason, having the data stored on a file will allow us to do so without having to reenter all of the data.

Using Files

If you want your program to make use of files other than Input and Output, you have to remember to do four things:

1. Put the names of the files in the program heading.
2. Declare the files in the VAR section.
3. Prepare each file for reading or writing with Reset or Rewrite statements (discussed later in this section).
4. Specify the name of the file to be used as the first parameter of each Read, Readln, Write, or Writeln statement.

Listing File Names in the Program Heading

Suppose we wanted Program Mileage from Chapter 2 to read data from a file and to write its output to a file. Let's call the files InMPG and OutMPG. We would then write the program heading like this:

```
PROGRAM Mileage (Output, InMPG, OutMPG);
```

Why do we need to list Output in the heading if all of the output from the program will be written on OutMPG? Because Pascal requires that Output be in the list in case any errors (such as attempting to divide something by zero) are encountered when the program is run. With an Output "file," error messages can be sent to the screen; otherwise there would be no way for the computer to notify us directly of any errors that occur. The file Input, however, does not need to be listed in the program heading.

There is one other comment we should make about putting the name of a file into the program heading. Pascal requires that file names be identifiers—that is, that they look just like Pascal variable names. Some systems, however, do not use the same format for file names. As we saw in the example of the Type command, on some systems a file might include a period in its name. The problem is how to reconcile two different formats for file names: the Pascal identifier format and the system format.

Unfortunately, there isn't a single good answer to this problem. Different systems solve it differently. On one system, for example, the names must be the same. On another system, you may be required to type a special command before you run your program. On yet another system, you may have to include a special nonstandard statement in your program to associate the name in the heading with the system name for a file. You will have to consult the manual for your particular system to *T,M,V* ↩ determine which of these methods it uses. Appendix I discusses special features of some of the more popular systems.

In this book we will use the ISO standard, which assumes that the file names used by the system are the same as the names we write in the program heading. Thus we will assume that if we put OutMPG in the program heading we can later use a system command such as

```
Type OutMPG
```

to display a copy of the output from the program on the screen.

Declaring Files in the VAR Section

The second thing we have to do in order to make our program work with files other than Input or Output is to declare the other files in the VAR section of the program. We do this in the same way that we declare any variable: We specify the name, followed by a colon, and then the data type for the name. What is the data type of a file? In a later chapter we will see that Pascal allows us to define files to be of many different data types. For now, however, we will use the standard type *Text,* which is in fact the data type of Input and Output. Input and Output do not need to be declared in the VAR section of a program because, like MaxInt, they are predefined in Pascal. For our example, we would declare files InMPG and OutMPG like this:

```
VAR
   InMPG,       (* Holds input mileages and gallons *)
   OutMPG:      (* Holds miles per gallon output    *)
      Text;
```

Preparing Files with Reset or Rewrite

The third thing that we must do to use files is to prepare the files we have declared for reading or writing. We prepare files for reading with the *Reset* statement and for writing with the *Rewrite* statement. In our example we will be writing to file OutMPG, so we must prepare it for writing as follows:

```
Rewrite(OutMPG);
```

Since we will be reading data from file InMPG, it must be prepared for reading with a Reset statement:

```
Reset(InMPG);
```

Both statements are examples of predefined procedure subprograms (notice the telltale parameters—the mark of a subprogram). Because these statements *prepare* files for reading or writing, they must be put in the program before any Read, Readln, Write, or Writeln statement that refers to the files. Usually it is a good idea to put them right after the first BEGIN so that the files will be prepared before the program does anything else.

```
(* End of declarations *)

BEGIN   (* Program *)

    (* Prepare files *)

    Reset(InMPG);
    Rewrite(OutMPG);

    (* Rest of program follows this *)
```

What exactly do Reset and Rewrite do? Reset gets a file ready for reading by setting the file reading marker to the first piece of data in the file. (Each input file has its own reading marker, which is independent from the reading marker for any other input file.) Reset also puts the file into *read mode.* (See Figure 3-3.) A file that is in read mode cannot be written to—that is, it can only be used to input data. If you try to use a read-mode file with Write or Writeln, you will get an error message when you run the program.

Rewrite gets a file ready for writing by placing the marker at the start of the file and putting the file into *write mode,* which erases whatever information (if any) the file previously contained. (See Figure 3-4.) A file that is in write mode cannot be used with Read or Readln. At any point in a program, you can change the mode of a file through the use of a Reset or Rewrite statement. Remember, however, that Rewrite erases the old contents of a file, and Reset always returns the file marker to

Figure 3-3
Effect of Reset
Operation

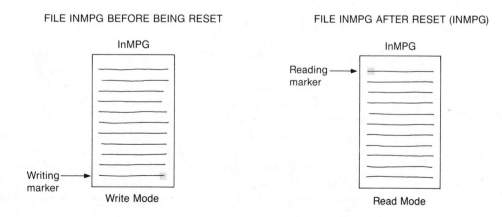

Figure 3-4
Effect of Rewrite
Operation

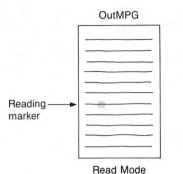
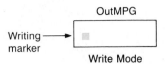

FILE OUTMPG BEFORE REWRITE

FILE OUTMPG AFTER REWRITE

OutMPG

OutMPG

Writing marker

Write Mode

Reading marker

Read Mode

the start of the file. Thus you *cannot*, for example, insert a new data value into a file by reading part way through the file, switching it to write mode with a Rewrite statement, and then writing the new data value at that point. The result would be a file with just the one new value in it, because the Rewrite statement would first erase the old contents of the file.

Pascal specifically forbids using Rewrite with Input, and attempting to do so will cause an error message. On many systems Reset(Input), Reset(Output), and Rewrite(Output) also produce error messages.

Specifying Files in Read, Readln, Write, and Writeln

There is only one more thing we have to do in order to use files other than Input or Output. Each Read, Readln, Write, or Writeln statement that uses a particular file must have the name of that file as its first parameter. For our example, this means that all of the Writeln statements that will output to OutMPG should look something like this:

```
Writeln(OutMPG, 'Miles Per Gallon is ', MPG:6:2);
```

Similarly, the program might contain a statement such as

```
Read(InMPG, Amt1, Amt2, Amt3, Amt4);
```

to instruct the computer to read data from the file InMPG.

What happens if you forget to specify the name of a file in a particular I/O statement? In that case, Write and Writeln statements will work just as they always have: They will write the contents of their parameter lists to Output (the terminal screen). Likewise, Read and Readln statements that don't have a file name as their first parameter will work as usual: They will fill the variables in their parameter lists with values obtained from Input (the terminal keyboard); however, if the identifier Input is not listed in the program heading, a syntax error will result.

Here is a sample program that reads its input from InMPG and writes its output to file OutMPG:

```
PROGRAM Mileage (Output, InMPG, OutMPG);

(* This program computes miles per gallon given four amounts
   for gallons used and starting and ending mileages for the
   entire period *)

VAR
    Amt1,           (* Number of gallons for fillup 1       *)
    Amt2,           (* Number of gallons for fillup 2       *)
    Amt3,           (* Number of gallons for fillup 3       *)
    Amt4,           (* Number of gallons for fillup 4       *)
    StartMiles,     (* Starting mileage                     *)
    EndMiles,       (* Ending mileage                       *)
    MPG:            (* Computed miles per gallon            *)
      Real;
    InMPG,          (* Holds gallon amounts and mileages    *)
    OutMPG:         (* Receives results of MPG computation  *)
      Text;

BEGIN (* Mileage *)
  (* Prepare files *)
  Reset(InMPG);
  Rewrite(OutMPG);
  (* Get data *)
  Read(InMPG, Amt1, Amt2, Amt3, Amt4);
  Read(InMPG, StartMiles, EndMiles);
  (* Compute miles per gallon *)
  MPG := (EndMiles - StartMiles) / (Amt1 + Amt2 + Amt3 + Amt4);
  (* Output results *)
  Writeln(OutMPG, 'For the gallon amounts:');
  Writeln(OutMPG, Amt1:6:1, ',', Amt2:6:1, ',', Amt3:6:1, ',',
          Amt4:6:1);
  Writeln(OutMPG);
  Writeln(OutMPG, 'a starting mileage of ', StartMiles:8:1);
  Writeln(OutMPG, 'and an ending mileage of ', EndMiles:8:1);
  Writeln(OutMPG);
  Writeln(OutMPG, 'the mileage per gallon is ', MPG:7:2)
END.    (* Mileage *)
```

In this program, the statement

```
                    Writeln(OutMPG);
```

has the same effect on OutMPG as

```
                    Writeln;
```

has on Output.

The Impact of Data Formats on Program Design

Specifying the input and output for a program involves much more than simply writing down lists of every data item that must be read or written by a program. For some programming problems you will be given exact formats for all of the input and output data. For other problems you may be able to design the input and output formats yourself.

Whenever you design the input and output formats for a program, take some time to examine the implications of those formats—they can have a substantial effect on the design of the program. For example, suppose you are writing a program that will read a student number and a letter grade. If you choose to arrange the data such that each line has a student number followed by a grade,

            9374123 B

the code to read a line of data will be something like

```
Read(StudentNum);
Read(Blank);        (* Read and discard the blank *)
Readln(Grade);
```

However, if you choose to put the grade first on the line, followed by the student number, a line of data will look like

            A 7715902

and the code required to read a line of data will be

```
Readln(Grade, StudentNum)
```

When you have to mix character and numeric data, it's easier to deal with characters followed by numbers than with numbers followed by characters. You will run into many other situations where the arrangement and format of input data (and output data) have a significant effect on how complicated the resulting program is. If you take the time to think ahead a little bit, you can save yourself a lot of work later on.

On the other hand, don't forget that most programs are written to be used by people. The formats of the input and output should help to make the program convenient and easy to use. Don't sacrifice ease of use just to save a few lines of code in the program.

TOP-DOWN DESIGN

In Chapters 1 and 2 we discussed the programming process and some strategies for solving problems. In this section we will put all these ideas together to form a methodology for developing programs. Recall that the programming process consists of a problem-solving phase and an implementation phase.

You were warned not to try to bypass the problem-solving phase even when a small problem did not seem to require it and you felt sure that you could write the program directly from the problem description. There are good reasons for going through the complete process. Even small problems have large numbers of details to be taken care of, and use of a methodical approach is the best way to ensure that nothing is forgotten.

The practice of applying the following methodology to small problems will prepare you to tackle larger programming problems that you cannot solve directly. As a by-product, your programs will be readable, understandable, easily debugged, and easily modified. We structure our approach to programming through a well-organized method or technique known as *top-down design.* Also called *stepwise refinement* and *modular programming,* this technique allows us to use the divide-and-conquer approach. Recall that with this approach a problem is divided into subproblems that can be handled more easily. After solving all the subproblems, we have a solution to the overall problem.

What we are doing in top-down design is working from the abstract (our description or specification of the problem) to the particular (our actual Pascal code).

If the problem description is a vaguely stated word problem, the first step is to create a *functional problem description*—a description that clearly states what the program is to do. In many cases creating a functional problem description requires further dialog between the person with the problem and the programmer.

Modules

We start by breaking the problem into a set of subproblems. Then each subproblem is divided into smaller subproblems. This process continues until each subproblem cannot be further divided. We are creating a hierarchical structure, also known as a *tree structure,* of problems and subproblems, called *functional modules.* Modules at one level can call on the services of modules at a lower level. These modules are the basic building blocks of our program.

The predefined procedures and functions, such as Write, Read, and Abs, are examples of modules that solve subproblems. The subproblems that they solve are so frequently encountered in programming that these procedures and functions have been permanently built into the Pascal programming language. Coding the modules of our design as subprograms is one way of building a Pascal program.

Once a problem has been divided into subproblems, modules, or segments, we can solve each module fairly independently of the others. For example, one module could read data values, another could print values after processing. Various processing modules might keep a cumulative total, keep a count of data values, detect error conditions, or do calculations.

Our design tree contains successive levels of refinement. (See Figure 3-5.) The top, or level 0, is our functional description of the problem; the lower levels are our successive refinements.

How do we divide the problem into modules? Well, let's think for a moment about how we human beings usually approach a big problem. We spend some time thinking about the problem in an overall sort of way, then we jot down the major steps. We then examine each of the major steps, filling in the details. If we don't know how to accomplish a specific task, we go on to the next one, planning to come back and take care of the one we skipped at some later time when we have more information.

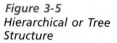

Figure 3-5
Hierarchical or Tree
Structure

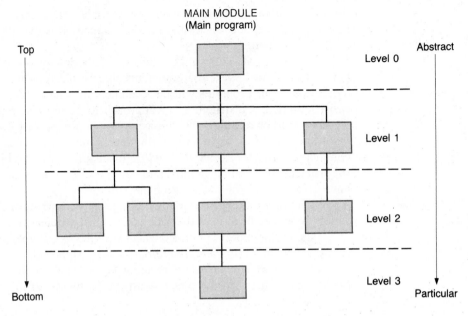

This is exactly how you should approach a programming problem. Think about how you would solve the problem by hand. Write down the major steps. This list of the major steps is your main module. Begin to develop the details of the major steps as level 1 modules. If you don't know how to do something, or feel yourself overwhelmed by details, just give the task a name and go on to the next one. That name can be expanded later as a lower-level module.

The process continues for as many levels as it takes to expand every task to the smallest details. This approach might be called the Procrastinator's Technique. If a task is cumbersome or difficult, put off the problem to a lower level—don't think about it today, think about it tomorrow. Of course tomorrow does come, but this whole process can then be applied to the troublesome subtasks. Eventually the whole problem is broken up into manageable units.

It may help you to pretend that you have a "smart friend" who can always solve the parts of a problem that are giving you trouble. Simply name these parts and set them aside for your smart friend to do. Once you have solved all of the parts that you know how to do, you can come back and look at one of the things you set aside. You will be amazed at how much simpler a task will look when you can concentrate entirely on it by itself. What previously gave you trouble will yield to your focused analysis, and you will have become your own smart friend. If, in solving this subproblem, you run up against another insurmountable task, set it aside for your smart friend to look at later.

Let's apply this design process to the pleasant task of planning a large party. A little thought reveals that there are two main tasks: inviting the people and actually preparing the food.

One approach to inviting the people would be to reach for the phone book and start calling your friends. However, you would soon be confused as to whom you reached, whose line was busy, and who had said what. A much better approach would be to make a list of those you wished to invite, then put the list aside and check it over the next day to see which of your friends you had forgotten.

Then, with this list in hand, you can go through and fill in the telephone numbers. Now you begin to call and mark down the responses. It may take a while to reach everyone, but you will know where you stand. Once you have an estimate of the number of people coming, you can start preparing the food.

Heaven help you if you just run in and start cooking! Without prior planning the job would be overwhelming. Instead, you can break down this task into planning the menu and preparing the food.

You can save a lot of time and effort in this task if you take advantage of what others have done by looking at suggested menus in cookbooks. (In programming we would look in the literature to see if algorithms already exist to solve this subproblem.) When choosing the menu, you can put off until later a careful examination of the recipes. The time to do that is when you are preparing the shopping list. (Defer details until later.)

The tree diagram in Figure 3-6 shows how the process has been broken down so far (not all of the level 2 modules are shown).

Note that each module expands a statement (task) listed at the level above. As humans we could probably take the level 2 modules and execute them from the description. For a computer program we would have to break them down into much finer detail. For example, "Write down names" would have to be at the following level of detail:

Do you have paper?
   No, get paper.
Do you have a pen?
   No, get a pen.
Pick up pen.
Put pen to paper.
(and so on. . . .)

Your top-down design for giving a party would be quite different if you had a great little delicatessen down the block and decided to let them cater your party.

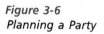

*Figure 3-6
Planning a Party*

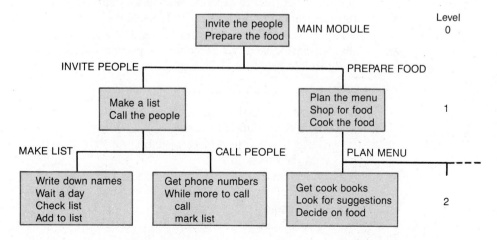

Then your main module would be

```
Invite the people
Call the delicatessen
```

No two top-down designs will be exactly alike. There is no set way of writing a design. Your design will reflect your own individual style. However, a good design will be modular, with tasks grouped into functional units.

Let's leave the social analogy now and look at the process applied to computer programming problems. Remember, the domain is new but the process is one you have done all your life.

The main module specifies the names of tasks. Each name of a task needs to be expanded at a lower level unless there is a one-to-one correspondence to a Pascal statement. This is true at each level. There will be as many modules at level 1 as there are names of tasks at level 0, and so on for each successive level.

The idea is to defer details. Push the actual code to as low a level as possible. When you don't have to worry about actual implementation, you can concentrate more on the functional divisions and algorithms. As you travel down the tree in your design, you make a series of design decisions. If a decision proves awkward or incorrect (and it will many times!), it is easy to backtrack (go back up the design tree to a higher-level module) and try something else. At least you don't have to scrap your whole design—only that small part you are working on. There may be many intermediate steps and trial solutions before you reach your final design.

The bulk of your time should be spent analyzing and designing your solution. Coding will then take very little time. If you also make sure that each module works by using test data for that module, your program should work when you put all the modules together. A little effort spent in testing each module can save a lot of effort spent in debugging your program.

Writing a top-down design is similar to writing an outline for an English paper. You can use English sentences or pseudocode (a mixture of English and Pascal control structures) to describe each task or subtask. The pseudocode control structures are similar to the looping and selection statements we will consider in Chapters 4 and 5. You will see examples of top-down designs using these statements when they are introduced. To demonstrate pseudocode, here is a main module for the fairly simple problem of finding the average of a list of numbers.

```
Initialize Sum and Count to zero
WHILE more data DO
   Get data (read in a piece of data)
   Add data to Sum
   Increment Count (add one to count)
Set Average to Sum / Count
Print Average
```

The WHILE-DO is the looping control structure, so the tasks

> Get data
> Add data to Sum
> Increment Count

are done over and over again until there is no more data (numbers in the list). Even though we haven't covered looping yet, the pseudocode for this algorithm is quite clear and understandable. This is one of the characteristics of an algorithm that has been well written in pseudocode: The algorithm is sufficiently clear that one doesn't have to be an experienced programmer to understand what it is doing.

Because this problem is such a simple one, we can code from this module (each statement can be directly translated into a Pascal statement). This example demonstrates pseudocode but doesn't really show off the beauty of top-down design: the reduction of problem complexity by the division of the problem into subproblems (modules) that can be handled more easily.

What are the advantages of a program produced from top-down design? It is easier to understand because it can be studied in functionally and logically organized pieces, it is easier to test, and it is easier to modify.

Your program should reflect your top-down design. Any changes in the design should be easy to make in the program. Someone reading your program should be able to see your decomposition of the problem and the structure of your solution.

Although writing new subprograms is one way of coding modules in our design, it is not the only way to code them. You can use the modular design technique even if you don't know anything about subprograms. In fact, modular design is a technique that is completely independent of the programming language. Should you ever need to write a program in FORTRAN, BASIC, COBOL, or Ada, you will still be able to use these techniques. In fact, as we saw with the example of planning a party, you can use this technique for solving problems in areas other than programming.

Methodology

The top-down design method can be broken down as follows:

1. Analyze the problem.
2. Write the main module.
3. Write the remaining modules.
4. Resequence and revise as necessary.

To implement a problem solution on the computer, you will start by analyzing and, if necessary, rewriting the problem statement. Analyzing the problem includes listing the input data, the desired output, and any assumptions you have made. You can then list the major steps in the computer solution. The list of major steps becomes the main module of the program. Each major step can then be given a closer examination and possibly be expanded to form an entire module with its own set of major steps. This expansion process is called *refinement.* As you refine your solution, you will discover that you need to define some variables and write some formulas. You should keep a list of all of the variables you need so that you can write their declarations when it's time to code the program. Let's take a closer look at each of the major steps in the top-down design methodology.

1. Analyze the Problem First you must understand the problem, rewriting it more clearly and completely if necessary. Understand what is given (Input) and what is required (Output). Specify the Input and Output formats. List assumptions you make (if any). Think. How would you solve the problem by hand? Are you familiar with any similar problems that have already been solved? Can you think of a good analogy? Develop an overall algorithm or general plan of attack. Keep your global view; don't get drawn into the lower-level details until you are ready to deal with them.

2. Write the Main Module You can use English or pseudocode to restate the problem in the main module. Use module names to divide the problem into functional areas. If the main module has more than 10 or 15 statements, you are at too low a level of detail. Introduce any control structures (such as selection or looping) that are needed at this point. Resequence logically if necessary. Postpone details to lower levels; you can always change the main module during further refinement.

Don't worry if you don't know how to solve an unwritten module at this point. Just pretend your smart friend has the answer, and postpone considering it until later refinements have been made. All you have to do in the main module is to give the names of lower-level modules that provide certain functions (solve certain tasks). Use meaningful module names.

3. Write the Remaining Modules There is no fixed number of levels. Modules at one level can specify more modules at lower levels. Each module must be complete, although it can reference unwritten modules. Do successive refinements by adding lower-level modules until each statement can be directly translated into a Pascal statement.

4. Resequence and Revise as Necessary Plan for change. Don't be afraid to start over. Several attempts and refinements may be necessary. Try to maintain clarity. Express yourself simply and directly.

We will use the following outline for our top-down designs. The sample problems following the next section show the use of this outline in a top-down design.

Problem statement

Discussion

Input description

Output description

Assumptions (if any)

Main module

Remaining modules by levels

"This was your first effort at TOP-DOWN design, wasn't it?"

Cartoon by M. LAD. TOPOLSKY

Documentation

As you create your top-down design, you are developing documentation for your program. Documentation consists of the written descriptions, specifications, development, and actual code of a program.

Good documentation helps users to read and understand a program and is invaluable when software is being modified (maintained). If you haven't looked at your program for six months and need to change it, you'll be happy that you documented it well. Of course, if someone else has to use and modify your program, documentation is indispensable.

Documentation external to the program includes specifications, development history, and top-down design. Internal documentation includes program formatting, comments, and self-documenting code. You can use the pseudocode from your top-down design as comments in your program.

The documentation we have discussed may be sufficient for the reader or maintainer of your programs. However, if your program will be used in a production environment, you must provide a user's manual as well.

Documentation should be kept up to date. Any changes made in a program should be indicated in all of the pertinent documentation.

Using *self-documenting code* will make your programs more readable.

> **Self-Documenting Code** A program containing meaningful identifiers as well as judiciously used clarifying comments.

Ideally, a Pascal program should be readable even by a nonprogrammer. Appendix G, Program Style, discusses some program documentation conventions.

Now let's look at a couple of sample problems that demonstrate top-down design methodology. Remember that it is important to go through all of the steps of the methodology so that you don't overlook anything in the development of a design.

Problem Solving in Action

Problem: Find the weighted average of three test scores. The data will be in the form of an integer test score followed by its associated weight, with each pair on a separate line.

Discussion: It is common to give different weights to tests in order to arrive at a student's grade in a course. For example, if two tests were worth 30 percent each and a final exam was worth 40 percent, we would take the first test grade and multiply it by 0.30, take the second test grade and multiply it by 0.30, and take the final and multiply it by 0.40. We would then add these three values to get a weighted average. We will use this "by-hand" algorithm to solve this problem.

Input: Three groups of data, each composed of

test score (Integer)   weight (Real)

Output: Print input data with headings (echo printing). Print the weighted average with explanation.

Assumptions: The three weights add up to 1.00, and the input data is correct (no error checking).

MAIN MODULE   Level 0

```
Get data
Print data
Find average
Print average
```

GET DATA   Level 1

```
Write 'Enter first test score and weight.'
Read Test1, Weight1
Write 'Enter second test score and weight.'
Read Test2, Weight2
Write 'Enter third test score and weight.'
Read Test3, Weight3
```

PRINT DATA

```
Print heading
Write Test1, Weight1
Write Test2, Weight2
Write Test3, Weight3
```

PSIA

FIND AVERAGE

> Ave = Test1 * Weight1 + Test2 * Weight2 + Test3 *
> Weight3

PRINT AVERAGE

> Write 'Weighted average = ', Ave

PRINT HEADING   Level 2

> Write 'Test Score   Weight'

Module Structure Chart:

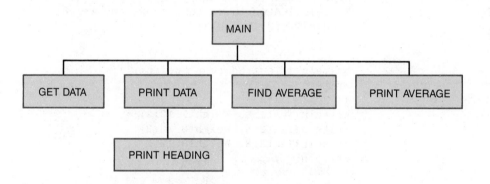

List of Variables from the Algorithm:

Variables

Name	Data type	Use
Test1	Integer	Score for first test
Test2	Integer	Score for second test
Test3	Integer	Score for third test
Weight1	Real	Weight for first test
Weight2	Real	Weight for second test
Weight3	Real	Weight for third test
Ave	Real	Weighted average of the tests

PSIA ▰▰▰▰

```pascal
PROGRAM TestAve (Input, Output);

(* Program to find the weighted average of three test scores *)

VAR
    Test1,          (* Score for first  test          *)
    Test2,          (* Score for second test          *)
    Test3:          (* Score for third  test          *)
       Integer;
    Weight1,        (* Weight for first  test         *)
    Weight2,        (* Weight for second test         *)
    Weight3,        (* Weight for third  test         *)
    Ave:            (* Weighted average of the tests *)
       Real;

BEGIN (* TestAve *)
  (* Get data *)
  Writeln('Enter first test score and weight.');
  Readln(Test1, Weight1);
  Writeln('Enter second test score and weight.');
  Readln(Test2, Weight2);
  Writeln('Enter third test score and weight.');
  Readln(Test3, Weight3);
  Writeln;
  (* Print heading *)
  Writeln(' Test Score    Weight ');
  Writeln;
  (* Print data *)
  Writeln(Test1:8, Weight1:12:2);
  Writeln(Test2:8, Weight2:12:2);
  Writeln(Test3:8, Weight3:12:2);
  Writeln;
  (* Find average *)
  Ave := Test1 * Weight1 + Test2 * Weight2 + Test3 * Weight3;
  (* Print average *)
  Writeln('Weighted average = ', Ave:7:2)
END.   (* TestAve *)
```

The program is designed for interactive data input from a terminal (notice the use of prompting messages). If when the program was run the user entered the input data

```
90   0.30
85   0.25
78   0.45
```

the dialog with the user would look like

PSIA

```
Enter first test score and weight.
90  0.30
Enter second test score and weight.
85  0.25
Enter third test score and weight.
78  0.45

 Test Score     Weight

      90          0.30
      85          0.25
      78          0.45

Weighted average =     83.35
```

Problem Solving in Action

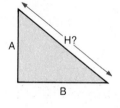

Problem: Determine the length of the hypotenuse of a right triangle given the lengths of the other two sides. The data will be in the form of two real numbers, one for each of the side lengths.

Discussion: You are probably familiar with the Pythagorean theorem, which states that the square of the hypotenuse of a right triangle is equal to the sum of the squares of the other two sides. Thus, to compute the length of the hypotenuse, you would square the lengths of the sides, sum the squares, and then find the square root of the sum. This is how you would solve the problem on a calculator. We will use the same technique in our computer solution.

Input: Two real numbers, one for each side of the triangle other than the hypotenuse.

Output:

 Print the input data with a message that identifies each number (echo printing).

 Print the length of the hypotenuse with an identifying message.

Assumptions: The two lengths are positive real numbers (no error checking).

MAIN MODULE   Level 0

```
Get data
Print data
Find length of hypotenuse
Print length of hypotenuse
```

PSIA

GET DATA   Level 1

> Write 'Enter the lengths of the two sides.'
> Read LengthOfA, LengthOfB

PRINT DATA

> Write 'Length of side A is ', LengthofA
> Write 'Length of side B is ', LengthOfB

FIND LENGTH OF HYPOTENUSE

> Compute SumOfSquares
> Hypotenuse = Sqrt(SumOfSquares)

PRINT LENGTH OF HYPOTENUSE

> Write 'The length of the hypotenuse is ', Hypotenuse

COMPUTE SUMOFSQUARES   Level 2

> SumOfSquares = Sqr(LengthOfA) + Sqr(LengthOfB)

Module Structure Chart:

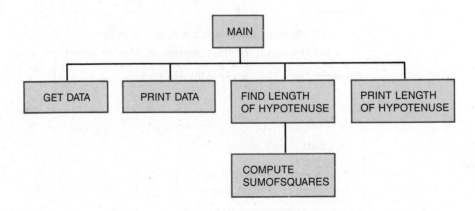

PSIA

List of Variables from the Algorithm:

Variables

Name	Data type	Use
LengthOfA	Real	Length of one of the sides
LengthOfB	Real	Length of the other side
SumOfSquares	Real	Sum of the squares of the two sides
Hypotenuse	Real	Length of the hypotenuse

```
PROGRAM Triangle (Input, Output);

(* This program finds the length of the hypotenuse of a
   right triangle, given the lengths of the other two sides *)

VAR
  LengthOfA,      (* Length of one of the sides     *)
  LengthOfB,      (* Length of the other side       *)
  SumOfSquares,   (* Sum of the squares of the sides *)
  Hypotenuse:     (* Length of the hypotenuse       *)
    Real;

BEGIN (* Triangle *)
  (* Get data *)
  Writeln('Enter the lengths of the two sides.');
  Readln(LengthOfA, LengthOfB);
  (* Print data *)
  Writeln;
  Writeln('The length of side A is ', LengthOfA: 7: 4);
  Writeln('The length of side B is ', LengthOfB: 7: 4);
  (* Compute sum of squares *)
  SumOfSquares := Sqr (LengthOfA) + Sqr (LengthOfB);
  (* Find length of hypotenuse *)
  Hypotenuse := Sqrt (SumOfSquares);
  (* Print length of hypotenuse *)
  Writeln('The length of the hypotenuse is ', Hypotenuse: 8: 4)
END.    (* Triangle *)
```

The data for this program is input: It is kept separate from the program and then is interactively read in when the program is executed. If when the program was run the user entered the input data

95.019   42.91

PSIA

the dialog with the user would look like

```
Enter the lengths of the two sides.
95.019   42.91

The length of side A is 95.0190
The length of side B is 42.9100
The length of the hypotenuse is 104.2587
```

TESTING AND DEBUGGING

An important part of implementing a program is testing it (checking the results). You should always try calculating a few data sets by hand and comparing your results with what the computer prints out. By now, you should be starting to realize that there is nothing magical about the computer. It is no more infallibly right than whoever is writing the instructions for it. So don't trust it to give you the correct answers until you've verified enough of them by hand to convince yourself that nothing is wrong.

From now on, at the end of each chapter you will find a section on testing and debugging. In these sections we will offer tips on how to test your programs and what to do if a program doesn't work the way you expected. However, don't wait until you've encountered a bug to read the testing and debugging sections. It's much easier to prevent bugs than it is to fix them.

Perhaps the two error messages most commonly encountered in testing programs that input data values are "OUT OF DATA ON FILE xxxxxx" (or "EOF ENCOUNTERED ON FILE xxxxxx") and "NUMERIC DATA EXPECTED". (The messages may be worded somewhat differently on your system.)

The "OUT OF DATA" error message indicates that the program has read all of the input data available on a file and that more data was required to fill variables in the parameter list of a Read (or Readln) statement. This may simply mean that the data file was improperly prepared so that it has fewer data values than the program needs.

If a program uses Readln statements to input a certain number of values from each line of data and the file has a greater number of values per line than the Readln statement does parameters, then the values that are skipped by the Readln statements may account for the program's running out of data prematurely.

Let's consider an example.

Data File   123 456 789⟨eoln⟩
                 987 654 321⟨eoln⟩

Code Segment   Readln(A, B);
                    Readln(C, D);
                    Readln(E, F);

The first two Readln statements in this example will exhaust the data in the file, leaving the third Readln statement with no data to read. In this case there are two possible corrections. Either the data file can be changed to have two values per line or the program can be changed to read three values from each line.

On the other hand, the cause of the "OUT OF DATA" error may be a Readln statement that should really be a Read statement. This can cause values to be inadvertently skipped when the program reads a data file that was prepared correctly.

The "NUMERIC DATA EXPECTED" error message will only occur when numeric and character data are mixed in the input. This error message indicates that a Read (or Readln) statement was supposed to read a value into a Real or Integer variable but the reading marker was positioned at the start of some character data.

Let's again look at an example.

Data   712 LAS

Code   Read(Num1, Num2)

If Num1 and Num2 are Integer variables, the value 712 will be read into Num1. This leaves the letters LAS, which cannot be read into Num2 as an integer value. In other words, a numeric value was expected at that point in the input but nonnumeric data was found instead.

You can cause this error to occur by entering some letters when a Pascal program prompts you to enter a number. (Try doing this—it's useful to know how your system will respond in such a situation, and it makes the experience a lot less startling the first time you do it accidentally.)

There are several possible sources of a "NUMERIC DATA EXPECTED" error message. The most frequent is just an error in the way in which the data was prepared or entered. Using the wrong variable name (which happens to be of the wrong data type) in a parameter list can also produce this message. Declaring a variable to be of the wrong data type is a variation of this problem. Lastly, using a Readln statement that reads the wrong number of values can cause values to be skipped so that the marker ends up positioned on the wrong type of input data.

When files other than Input and Output are used, the most frequent error is to forget to list the file name as the first parameter in a Read, Readln, Write, or Writeln statement. The usual effects of such an error are that the program unexpectedly requests data from the terminal, or that it prints on the screen output that should have been written into a file.

You will also get error messages if your program tries to input data from a file that is in write mode or output data to a file that is in read mode. This usually means either that the file was Reset when it should have been prepared with Rewrite (or vice versa) or that the wrong file name was used in a Read, Readln, Write, or Writeln statement.

By providing a framework that helps you organize and keep track of all of the details in designing and implementing a program, the top-down design method should help you to avoid these errors in the first place.

SUMMARY

Programs operate on data. Data and programs can be kept separate. (The same program can be run with many sets of input data.) The Read and Readln statements input data from a file or terminal and store the data in memory in the variables specified in their parameter lists.

The Read statement leaves the reading marker on the character immediately following whatever was just read. The Readln statement leaves the marker on the first character of the next line of data following what was just input. Both Read and Readln begin reading at the point indicated by the marker.

The end of a data line is indicated by the end-of-line character ⟨eoln⟩, which is a nonprintable control character. An end-of-line character is created each time you press the return key while entering data. The ⟨eoln⟩ is also automatically inserted after each card in batch-processing systems. Your program generates an ⟨eoln⟩ character each time a Writeln statement is executed.

Interactive programs prompt the user for each data entry and directly inform the user of any errors that occur. Designing an interactive dialog is an exercise in the art of communication.

Batch input/output is often used when large amounts of data are to be processed by a program. Batch processing allows the data to be prepared before the program is run, and permits the program to be run again with the same data in the event a problem arises during processing.

Files other than Input and Output are often used for batch processing and to permit the output from one program to be used as the input to another program. The four things you have to do to use these other files are (1) put the file names in the program heading; (2) declare the files in the VAR section; (3) prepare the files for reading or writing with Reset or Rewrite; and (4) use the name of the file as the first parameter in each Read, Readln, Write, or Writeln that uses that file.

Top-down design provides a method for breaking down problems into pieces that can be handled more easily. It can be thought of as a modular or building-block approach. If you do not know how to do a task, you give it a name and go on. Later you can come back and fill in the details. If you are overwhelmed by details, step back and look at just what you are trying to do. Write down those tasks to be developed later at a lower level, and go on.

Top-down design results in highly structured and readable programs. Careful attention to top-down design and program formatting and documentation is necessary in order to write "good" programs.

It is important to test a program and check its results against hand-calculated values in order to be sure that the program works correctly.

QUICK CHECK

1. Write a Pascal statement to input values into two variables called X and Y. (pp. 96–99)

2. Assume you have a program that contains three Readln statements, each with three variables in its parameter list. The data that is fed into the program consists of three lines of four values each. Which of the data values will be skipped by the program? (pp. 99–103)

3. What sort of message would you have a program print in order to prompt a novice computer user to input a social security number? How would you change the wording of the prompting message for an experienced user of computers? (pp. 103–105)

4. If a program is to input 1000 numbers, would interactive input be appropriate? (pp. 103–105)

5. What are the four things that you have to remember to do in order to use files other than Input and Output? (pp. 106–111)

6. According to the top-down design methodology, what is the first thing you should do when presented with a new problem? (pp. 117–118)

7. How many levels of refinement are there in a top-down design before you reach the point at which you can begin coding the program? (pp. 112–118)

Answers

1. Read(X, Y) or Readln(X, Y) 2. The last value on each line will be skipped. 3. For the novice user: Please type a nine-digit social security number, then press the key marked "RETURN." For the experienced user: Enter SSN. 4. No. Batch input is more appropriate for programs that input large amounts of data. 5. (1) Put the file names in the program heading. (2) Declare the files in the VAR section. (3) Use Reset or Rewrite to prepare each file. (4) Make sure that each I/O statement that will use a file has the name of the file as its first parameter. 6. Analyze the problem. 7. There is no fixed number of levels of refinement. You keep refining the solution through as many levels as necessary, until the steps are of about the same complexity as program statements.

EXAM PREPARATION EXERCISES

1. What is the main advantage of having a program input its data rather than writing all the data values as constants in the program?

2. For the Readln statement

```
Readln(E, F)
```

if the user enters the line of data

17   13   7   3

what will be the value of each variable and what will happen to any leftover data values in the input?

3. How is an ⟨eoln⟩ character entered from the terminal? How is it entered with cards? How can a program generate an ⟨eoln⟩ in its output, and what will this make the terminal do?

4. Real values can be read into Integer variables. (True or False?)

5. Spaces may be used to separate numeric data values that are being entered to a Pascal program. (True or False?)

6. Indicate whether or not each of the following code segments will always cause at least one entire line of input data to be skipped , regardless of the initial position of the reading marker.

(a) ```Read(A, B);```
   ```Read(C, D)```

(b) ```Readln;```
   ```Readln```

(c) ```Read;```
   ```Readln```

(d) ```Readln(A, B);```
   ```Readln```

(e) ```Read(A, B);```
   ```Readln;```
   ```Readln(C, D);```

(f) ```Readln(A, B);```
   ```Readln(C, D)```

7. Define the terms "input prompt" and "echo printing" as they apply to interactive input/output.

8. What is wrong with the following program if the desired effect is to read a value from a file called InData and write it to a file called OutData?

```
PROGRAM Copy (OutData, Output);

VAR
   InData:
      Text;
   A:
      Integer;

BEGIN (* Copy *)
   Rewrite(InData);
   Rewrite(OutData);
   Read(A);
   Write(OutData, A)
END.   (* Copy *)
```

9. Given the program in exercise 8, if file InData initially contains the value 144, what will it contain after the program is executed? If file OutData is initially empty, what will its contents be after the program is executed?

10. List three benefits of using top-down structured design in programming.
```

PREPROGRAMMING EXERCISES _____

1. Write a single Pascal Read statement that will input the following data values into the Real variables Length, Height, and Width.

   10.25   7.625   4.5⟨eoln⟩

2. If you were to change your answer to exercise 1 from a Read statement to Readln statements (without changing the parameter lists), would they have the same effect? If not, what would they do differently?

3. Write a pair of Readln statements that will input the first two data values on each of the following lines into the Real variables Length1, Height1, Length2, and Height2.

   10.25   7.625   4.5⟨eoln⟩
   8.5   11.0 0.0⟨eoln⟩

4. Write a series of statements that will input the first letter of each of the following names into the Char-type variables Chr1, Chr2, and Chr3.

   Pam⟨eoln⟩
   Ruth⟨eoln⟩
   Sue⟨eoln⟩

5. Write a set of variable declarations and a series of Readln statements to read the following lines of data into variables of the appropriate type. You may make up whatever variable names you like. Notice that the values are separated from one another by a single blank and that there are no blanks to the left of the first character on each line.

   A 100 2.78 g 14⟨eoln⟩
   207.98 w q 23.4 92⟨eoln⟩
   R 42 L 27 R 63⟨eoln⟩

6. Write a code segment for an interactive program to input values for a person's age, height, weight, and the initials of their first and last names. Assume that the person using the program is a novice computer user. How would you rewrite this code segment for an experienced user?

7. Fill in the blanks in the following program, which is to read four values from file DataIn and output them to file ResultsOut.

```
PROGRAM CopyFour  (_____,  _____. _____);

VAR
   Value1,
   Value2,
   Value3,
   Value4:
     Integer;

   _____,
   ResultsOut:
     _____;
```

```
BEGIN  (* CopyFour *)
      _____ (DataIn);
      _____ (ResultsOut);
   Read(_____, Value1, Value2, Value3, Value4);
   Writeln(_____, Value1, Value2, Value3, Value4);
END.   (* CopyFour *)
```

8. Rewrite the program in exercise 8 of the Exam Preparation Exercises so that it works correctly.

9. Use top-down design to write an algorithm for starting an automobile with a manual transmission and an automatic choke.

10. Use top-down design to write an algorithm for logging on to your particular computer system and entering and running a program. Your algorithm should be sufficiently simple and clear that a novice user could successfully follow it.

PROGRAMMING PROBLEMS

1. Write a top-down design and Pascal program to read an invoice number, quantity ordered, and unit price (all integers), and compute total price. The program should write out the invoice number, quantity, unit price, and total price with identifying phrases. The program should be properly indented, with appropriate comments and meaningful identifiers throughout. If you are using an interactive system, write the program to be run interactively, with informative prompts for each data value.

2. How tall is a rainbow? Because of the way light is refracted by water droplets, the angle between the level of your eye and the top of a rainbow is always the same. If you know the distance to the rainbow, you can multiply it by the tangent of that angle to find the height of the rainbow. The magic angle is 42.3333333 degrees. Pascal works in radians, however, so you will have to convert this angle to radians with the formula

$$\text{Radians} = \text{Degrees} \times \frac{\text{Pi}}{180}$$

(Pi is equal to 3.14159265.) Also, Pascal does not provide a tangent function. However, it is easy enough to compute the tangent with the sine and cosine functions that Pascal does provide. The formula for the tangent is simply

$$\text{Tangent} = \frac{\text{Sin(Radians)}}{\text{Cos(Radians)}}$$

If you multiply this number by the distance to the rainbow, you will get its height.
   Write a top-down design and a Pascal program to read a single real value, which is the distance to the rainbow, and compute the height of the rainbow. The program should print the distance to the rainbow and its height with phrases that identify which number is which. The program should be properly indented, with appropriate comments and

meaningful identifiers throughout. If you are using an interactive system, write the program so that it prompts the user for the input value.

3. You will sometimes see a second, fainter rainbow outside of a bright rainbow. This secondary rainbow has a magic angle of 52.25 degrees. Modify the program from exercise 2 so that it prints the height of both the main rainbow and the secondary rainbow (and the distance to the rainbows), with a phrase identifying each of the three numbers printed.

- To be able to construct a simple Boolean expression to evaluate a given condition.

- To be able to construct a complex Boolean expression to evaluate a given condition.

- To be able to construct an *IF-THEN-ELSE* statement to perform a specific task.

- To be able to construct an *IF-THEN* statement to perform a specific task.

- To be able to construct a set of nested *IF* statements to perform a specific task.

- To be able to test and debug a Pascal program with errors.

4

Selection

So far, the execution of statements in our programs has followed the statements' physical order. First the statement at the top of the program is executed, then the next statement, then the statement after that, and so on, until the statement at the bottom of the page is executed. (See Figure 4-1.) But what if we want the computer to execute either one statement *or* another statement depending on what has happened before? What if we want the computer to execute our statements in a logical order that is not the same as the physical order? To be able to do this we must have the capability to ask questions about what has happened so far in the execution of the program.

The IF statement is a statement that allows us to execute statements in a logical order that differs from their physical order. This statement allows us to ask a ques-

Figure 4-1
Sequential Control

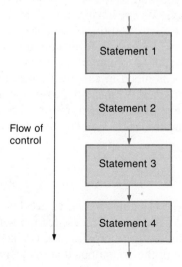

Flow of control

Statement 1

Statement 2

Statement 3

Statement 4

Figure 4-2
Selection
(Branching) Control
Structure

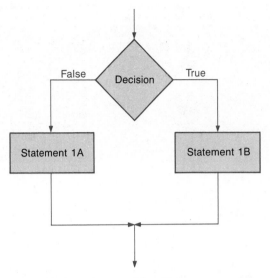

tion and then do one thing if the answer is yes (True) and another if the answer is
no (False). (See Figure 4-2.)

The first part of this chapter deals with how to ask questions, and the second
part deals with the IF statement itself.

CONDITIONS AND BOOLEAN EXPRESSIONS

To ask a question in Pascal, you make a statement. If the statement you make is true,
the answer to the question is yes. If the statement is not true, the answer to the
question is no. For example, if you wanted to ask, "Are we having spinach for dinner
tonight?" you would instead say, "We are having spinach for dinner tonight." If that
statement is true, the answer to the question is yes.

So, asking questions in Pascal amounts to making a statement (an assertion)
that may be either true or false. The computer checks the assertion against some
internal condition (the values contained in some variables, for instance) and sees
whether the assertion is true or false. We make our assertion in the form of a Boolean expression. The Boolean expression is then evaluated to either True or False,
giving us the answer to our question. But . . . what is a Boolean expression? How
do we evaluate one?

Boolean Expressions

Recall that the Boolean data type has only the two values True and False. In Pascal,
the assertions we make will take the form of an expression with a Boolean (True or
False) result, and are thus called *Boolean expressions*. Unlike the arithmetic operations we have seen so far, most of the operations that make up Boolean expressions

will seem unfamiliar to you. Actually, you have probably used these operations all of your life without knowing it.

A Boolean expression can be

1. A Boolean variable
2. An expression followed by a relational operator followed by an expression
3. A Boolean expression followed by a Boolean operator followed by a Boolean expression

Let's look at each of these in detail.

1. Boolean Variables A Boolean variable is a variable declared to be of type Boolean. This means the contents of this variable can be either True or False. Boolean variables differ from variables declared to be of type Integer, Real, or Char in that values cannot be read into them; they must be given a value within the program by an assignment statement. However, the values of Boolean variables and the Boolean constants True and False may be printed by Write or Writeln statements.

2. Relational Operators We can assign values to Boolean variables by setting them equal to the result of an expression followed by a relational operator followed by an expression.

```
VAR
  Test:
    Boolean;
  A,
  B:
    Integer;
       .
       .
       .
BEGIN
  Read(A, B);
  Test := A < B;
       .
       .
```

By comparing two values, we assert that a relationship (such as equality) exists between them. If the relationship really does exist, the assertion is True; otherwise, it is False. The relationships that we can check for in Pascal are

=	equal to
< >	not equal to
< =	less than or equal to
> =	greater than or equal to
>	greater than
<	less than

These symbols are called *relational operators* because, in Pascal, they cause the computer to perform operations that verify whether or not the indicated relationship exists between two values. For example, if X is 5 and Y is 10, the following expressions are all True:

$$X < Y$$
$$X <= Y$$
$$X <> Y$$
$$Y > X$$
$$Y >= X$$

If X is 'M' and Y is 'P', the expressions above are still true, because <, when referring to letters, means "comes before in the alphabet." Of course, we must be careful to compare things that are the same type—that is, numbers with numbers (Real or Integer) and characters with characters (Char). Comparing a value of type Char to a value of type Integer, for example, makes no sense and will result in an error message (even if the Char value is one of the digits '0' through '9').

The relational operators are not restricted to just comparing variables or constants. They can also be used to compare directly the results of arithmetic expressions. For example, we could compare the results of computing X + 3 and Y * 10:

Value of X	Value of Y	Expression	Result
12	2	X + 3 <= Y * 10	True
20	2	X + 3 <= Y * 10	False
7	1	X + 3 <> Y * 10	False
17	2	X + 3 = Y * 10	True
100	5	X + 3 > Y * 10	True

3. Boolean Operators   Relational operators compare things such as numbers and letters. Boolean operators are the special symbols AND, OR, and NOT, which are defined only for Boolean expressions. We can make more complex assertions by combining the relational operators with the Boolean operators. This allows us to make assertions such as "Final Score is greater than 90 AND Midterm Score is greater than 70." In Pascal, we would write such an expression as

```
(FinalScore > 90) AND (MidtermScore > 70)
```

In this case the AND requires *both* relationships to be True in order for the overall result to be True. If either or both of the relationships are False, AND will make the entire result False.

Look again at the example above. The computer first evaluates each of the relational operations (because they are enclosed in parentheses), giving two temporary Boolean results. These results are then combined by the AND operation to give another Boolean result.

The OR operation takes two Boolean values and combines them such that if *either* or *both* of them are True, the result is True. Both of the values must be False for the result to be False. This allows us to make assertions such as "Midterm Grade is equal to A OR Final Grade is equal to A." If either the Midterm Grade or the Final Grade is equal to A, the assertion is True. In Pascal this assertion would be written as

```
(MidtermGrade = 'A') OR (FinalGrade = 'A')
```

The AND and OR operators are like * or DIV in that they always appear between two expressions. The NOT operation, on the other hand, takes one Boolean value and gives its opposite as the result. Thus, if (Grade = 'A') is True, then NOT (Grade = 'A') is False. If (Grade = 'A') is False, then NOT (Grade = 'A') is True. NOT provides a convenient way of reversing the meaning of an assertion. For example,

```
NOT (Hours > 40)
```

is equivalent to writing

```
(Hours <= 40)
```

In some contexts the first form might be clearer, but in others the second one will make more sense. The following pairs of expressions are equivalent:

```
NOT (A = B)                    (A <> B)
NOT ((A = B) OR (A = C))       (A <> B) AND (A <> C)
NOT ((A = B) AND (C > D))      (A <> B) OR (C <= D)
```

Take a close look at these expressions and be sure you know why they are equivalent. It may help you to try evaluating them with some values for A, B, C, and D. You may notice a pattern in the way these expressions are written: The expression on the left is just the one to its right with a NOT added and the relational and Boolean operators reversed (for example, = instead of <>, OR instead of AND, and so on). This pattern of reversal is a handy one to know because it allows you to rewrite expressions in whichever form is easiest for somebody to read.

So far we have only shown the Boolean operators applied to results of comparisons, but they may also be applied directly to variables of type Boolean. For example, instead of writing

```
Z := (A < B) AND (C = D);
```

to assign a value to Boolean variable Z, we could use two intermediate Boolean variables, E and F:

```
E := A < B;
F := C = D;
Z := E AND F;
```

The following tables summarize the values that will be obtained by applying AND and OR to a pair of Boolean values (represented here by the Boolean variables X and Y).

Value of X	Value of Y	Value of (X AND Y)
True	True	True
True	False	False
False	True	False
False	False	False

Value of X	Value of Y	Value of (X OR Y)
True	True	True
True	False	True
False	True	True
False	False	False

The following table summarizes the results that will be obtained by applying the NOT operator to a Boolean value (represented by the Boolean variable X).

Value of X	Value of (NOT X)
True	False
False	True

Precedence of Operators

In Chapter 2 we discussed the precedence rules that Pascal follows in evaluating complex arithmetic expressions. These rules determine the order in which operations are performed. Pascal's precedence rules also cover the relational and Boolean operators. Relational operators have lower precedence than all other operators, including arithmetic and Boolean operators. The AND operator has the same precedence as multiplication and division; OR has the same precedence as addition and subtraction; NOT has higher precedence than any other operator. The following list shows the order of precedence for all of the operators that we've seen so far.

NOT	Highest precedence
* / DIV MOD AND	
+ − OR	
< <= = >= > <>	Lowest precedence

Operators on the same line in the above list have the same precedence. If there is more than one operator with the same precedence in an expression, the operators are evaluated left to right. Appendix D, Precedence of Operators, lists the order of precedence for all the operators in Pascal.

Parentheses can always be used to override the order of evaluation in an expression. The best rule to follow for deciding when to use parentheses is to use them when in doubt. The compiler will disregard unnecessary parentheses. If they make it easier for a human to understand the expression, they should be used.

One final comment about the use of parentheses: Pascal (like other programming languages) is very strict in its requirement that parentheses always be used in matched pairs. Whenever you write a complicated expression, always take a moment to go through and pair up all of the opening parentheses with their closing counterparts.

© 1977 United Feature Syndicate, Inc.

Writing Boolean Expressions

In most cases you will be able to figure out how to write a Boolean expression from the way it is stated in English or mathematical terms in an algorithm. There are, however, some tricky situations that you have to watch out for. Recall our earlier example of the Boolean expression

```
(MidtermGrade = 'A') OR (FinalGrade = 'A')
```

In English you would be tempted to write this expression as "MidtermGrade or FinalGrade equals A." In Pascal, however, you can't write the expression as you would in English. That is,

```
MidtermGrade OR FinalGrade = 'A'
```

won't work in Pascal, because MidtermGrade and FinalGrade are both of type *Char* and OR only works with *Boolean* values. You can't form the OR of two characters.

You might also be tempted to write the expression without any parentheses, which won't work either. Because OR has higher precedence than the relational operators, the expression

```
MidtermGrade = 'A' OR FinalGrade = 'A'
```

would be interpreted as

```
MidtermGrade = ('A' OR FinalGrade) = 'A'
```

which tells the computer to try to form the OR of 'A' and FinalGrade. Because OR only works on Boolean values, this expression will generate an error message (something like "TYPE CONFLICT OF OPERANDS").

In math books you might see notation such as

$$12 < Y < 24$$

which means "Y is between 12 and 24." This expression is also illegal in Pascal, because of the way it is evaluated. First the relation $12 < Y$ would be evaluated, giving a temporary Boolean result. The computer would then try to compare this Boolean value with the number 24, providing another opportunity for the "TYPE CONFLICT" error message to put in an appearance. To write this expression properly in Pascal you must use the AND operator:

```
(12 < Y)  AND  (Y < 24)
```

Relational Operators with Real and Boolean Data Types

The relational operators can be applied to any of the four basic data types, Integer, Real, Char, and Boolean. Up until now, we have limited our discussion to comparing Integer and Char variables and values.

Real numbers should not be compared for equality. Because small errors are likely to arise when calculations are performed on Real numbers, two Real numbers will very rarely be exactly equal. Thus you should test Real numbers for near equality. To do this, compute the difference between the two numbers and test to see if the result is less than some maximum allowable difference; for example,

```
Abs (R - S) < 0.00001
```

The formula $Abs(R - S)$ computes the difference between the two real variables R and S (Abs is the absolute value function). In the example, if the difference is less than 0.00001, the two numbers are considered close enough to be called equal. We will discuss this problem in more detail in Chapter 8.

You will only rarely make use of the fact that the relational operators also may be applied to Boolean values. However, there are some situations where it is handy to be able to test whether two Boolean variables are equal (or different). Pascal defines False to be less than True.

The Boolean Function Odd

Pascal provides a predefined Boolean function, called *Odd,* which takes an Integer operand and gives a result of True if the operand is odd (not evenly divisible by 2). For example,

```
Odd(3) = True
Odd(4) = False
```

SELECTION CONTROL STRUCTURES

Flow of Control

The order of execution of the statements in a program is called the *flow of control*. Think of the computer as being under the control of one program statement at a time. When a statement has been executed, control of the computer is turned over to the next statement (like a baton being passed in a relay race). Thus control (of the computer) is said to pass (or flow) from statement to statement.

Selection

The selection (or branching) control structure is used when an application requires that the computer choose between two or more possible actions.

The key to the concept of the selection control structure is that the computer must make a decision and then perform one of several possible actions. (See Figure 4-2.) The decision-making ability of the computer allows it to react to different circumstances in different ways.

Program Payroll from Chapter 1 provides an example of this selection process. The computer must decide whether or not a person has overtime pay. It does this by testing the assertion that the person has worked more than 40 hours against the value in the variable Hours. If that value is greater than 40, the assertion is True and the computer follows the instructions for computing overtime pay. If the value in Hours is less than or equal to 40, the assertion is False and the computer follows the instructions for computing only regular pay.

The IF Statement

The computer's ability to make decisions and execute different sequences of instructions is a key factor in its usefulness for solving practical problems. The Pascal structure that provides for branches in the flow of control is called an IF statement. With it, we can have the computer ask a question and choose a course of action: IF a certain condition exists, THEN perform one action, ELSE perform a different action. The condition that the computer checks is the validity of an assertion made by a Boolean expression.

The IF statement is called a *selection control structure* because it allows us to have the computer select one of two possible actions to perform. It is important to realize that the computer will actually perform only one of the two actions under any given set of circumstances. Nonetheless, we have to write *both* actions into our program. Why? Because, depending on the given circumstances, the computer will choose to execute *either* one action or the other. The IF statement provides a way for us to include both actions in our program and to give the computer a way of deciding which action to follow.

The IF-THEN-ELSE Form of IF Statement

Now let's look at how an IF statement is written in Pascal. Here is its syntax diagram:

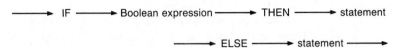

The following sample code fragment shows how you would write an IF statement in a program. This example demonstrates the general form of indentation that is used to help make the IF statement easier to read. It also shows the placement of a statement following an IF.

```
IF Boolean expression
   THEN
       statement 1A
   ELSE
       statement 1B;
statement 2
```

In terms of instructions to the computer, the above code fragment means "If the Boolean expression is True, execute statement 1A and then go on to execute statement 2. If the Boolean expression is False, execute statement 1B and then go on to execute statement 2." Figure 4-3 illustrates the flow of control of the IF-THEN-ELSE statement.

Figure 4-3
IF-THEN-ELSE
Structure
Diagram

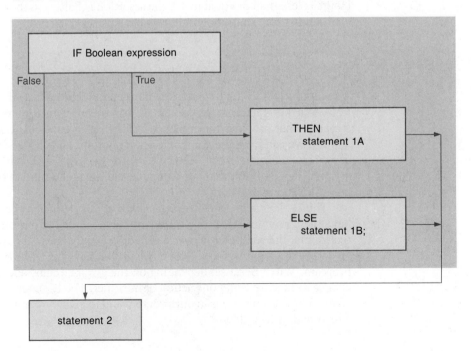

Figure 4-4
Flow of Control for
Division by Zero

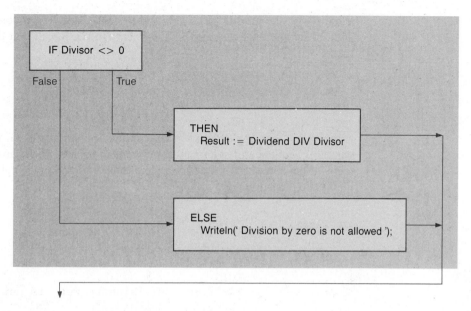

Such a statement might be used, for example, to check the divisor before the computer performs a division in order to make sure that it isn't zero. (Even computers can't divide something by zero.) If the divisor is zero, the computer should print out an error message instead of doing the division. The Pascal statements for this operation would look as follows:

```
IF Divisor <> 0
   THEN
      Result := Dividend DIV Divisor
   ELSE
      Writeln(' Division by zero is not allowed ');
```

Figure 4-4 illustrates the flow of control for this statement.

When the computer executes this statement, it first evaluates the Boolean expression "Divisor $<> 0$". If the value contained in the variable Divisor is not equal to zero, then the division is performed. If the value stored in Divisor is equal to zero, then the message "Division by zero is not allowed" is printed. In either case, execution continues with the statement that immediately follows the IF-THEN-ELSE structure.

Compound Statements

What if, when the divisor was equal to zero, we wanted to set the result of the division to MaxInt in addition to printing the error message? (MaxInt is as close to an infinite integer result as the computer can get.) We would need two statements in the same branch. So far, the syntax we've seen limits us to one statement in a branch.

What we really want is to be able to have the computer choose to execute one or another *sequence* of statements. This is easy to do. Recall that the compound statement

```
BEGIN
   Sequence of statements
END
```

is equivalent to a single Pascal statement. If you just put a BEGIN–END pair around whatever sequence of statements you want in each of the branches of the IF statement, the sequences of statements are each turned into single, compound statements. For example,

```
IF Divisor <> 0
   THEN
      Result : = Dividend DIV Divisor
   ELSE
      BEGIN
        Writeln(' Division by zero is not allowed ');
        Result : = MaxInt
      END;
```

If the value of Divisor is zero, then the computer will both print the error message and set the value of Result to MaxInt before continuing with whatever statement follows the END; . Compound statements can be used in both branches of an IF-THEN-ELSE; for example,

```
IF Divisor <> 0
   THEN
      BEGIN
        Result : = Dividend DIV Divisor;
        Writeln(' Division performed ')
      END
   ELSE
      BEGIN
        Writeln(' Division by zero is not allowed ');
        Result : = MaxInt
      END;
```

There is one seemingly peculiar rule of Pascal syntax that you should pay close attention to. There should be *no semicolon preceding the ELSE* in an IF-THEN-ELSE statement. Recall that the semicolon is used to separate statements from other statements. The ELSE is simply a continuation of a single IF-THEN-ELSE statement. If you do put in an extra semicolon, you will most likely get an error message saying that the ELSE is not expected. This is because, following the semicolon, Pascal will be looking for the start of a new statement—and there is no statement in Pascal that begins with an ELSE.

The IF-THEN Form of IF Statement

You will occasionally run into a situation where you would like one of the sequences of instructions in an IF statement to be empty. You might want to say, for example, "IF a certain condition exists, THEN perform some action; otherwise, don't do anything." Such an instruction can alternatively be thought of as requiring the computer to skip a sequence of instructions if a certain condition isn't met.

You could accomplish this simply by leaving the ELSE branch of an IF-THEN-ELSE statement empty (placing a semicolon immediately after ELSE). However, Pascal provides an easier way: It allows you to simply leave off the ELSE part entirely if you don't need it. The resulting statement is called an IF-THEN statement, and its syntax diagram is

$\longrightarrow$ IF $\longrightarrow$ Boolean expression $\longrightarrow$ THEN $\longrightarrow$ statement

The following example demonstrates how you would write an IF-THEN statement in a program. Note the indentation and the placement of a statement following the IF-THEN.

```
IF Boolean expression
    THEN
        statement 1;
statement 2;
```

These statements mean the following: If the Boolean expression is True, do statement 1 and then statement 2. If the Boolean expression is False, skip statement 1 and go directly to statement 2. Figure 4-5 illustrates the flow of control for an IF-THEN statement.

Just as with the IF-THEN-ELSE structure, the statement inside an IF-THEN may be compound. For example, let's say you are writing a program to compute income

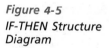

Figure 4-5
IF-THEN Structure
Diagram

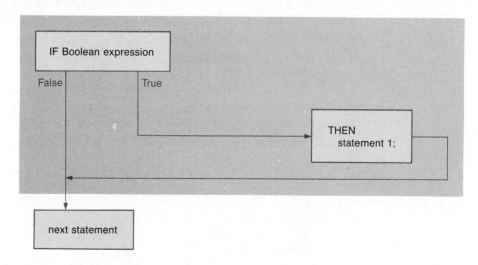

tax. One of the lines on the income tax form says, "Subtract line 23 from line 17 and enter result on line 24; if result is less than zero, enter zero and check box 24A." You can use an IF-THEN statement to do this in Pascal:

```
Result := Line17 - Line23;
IF Result < 0.0
   THEN
      BEGIN
         Writeln('Check box 24A');
         Result := 0.0
      END;
Line24 := Result;
```

This program fragment does exactly what the tax form said it should. It computes the result of subtracting line 23 from line 17. It then looks to see if the result is less than zero. If so, the fragment prints a message telling the user to check box 24A and then sets the result to zero. Finally, the calculated result (or zero, if the result is less than zero) is put into a variable called Line24.

Problem Solving in Action

Problem: Read in three integer numbers. If the first is negative, print the product of all three. Otherwise, print the sum of all three.

Discussion: If you were asked to do this by hand, you would take the three numbers and examine the first to decide what to do. If the first number was negative, you would multiply the three numbers together. If the first number was positive, you would add them up.

The process can be translated into a program directly. "Take the three numbers" will become a Read statement. We will use an IF-THEN-ELSE statement to "examine the first" and decide whether to multiply or add the numbers. Each branch of the IF-THEN-ELSE will have two steps in it. The first step will be to calculate the appropriate result. The second step will be to print the result and say whether the numbers were added or multiplied.

Input: Three integer numbers (Num1, Num2, Num3)

Output:

Input prompt message

Input (echo print)

Result of calculating the product or sum

MAIN MODULE   Level 0

```
Get Data
IF first number < 0
   THEN Calculate Product
   ELSE Calculate Sum
```

PSIA

GET DATA   Level 1

> Prompt for input
> Read Num1, Num2, Num3
> Echo print input data

CALCULATE PRODUCT

> Product = Num1 ∗ Num2 ∗ Num3
> Print 'The product is ', Product

CALCULATE SUM

> Sum = Num1 + Num2 + Num3
> Print 'The sum is ', Sum

Module Structure Chart:

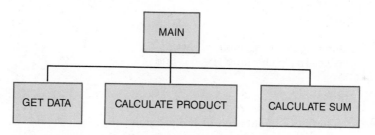

List of Variables from the Algorithm:

Name	Data type	Use
Num1	Integer	First number
Num2	Integer	Second number
Num3	Integer	Third number
Product	Integer	Result of multiplication
Sum	Integer	Result of addition

```
PROGRAM ProdSum (Input, Output);

(* This program reads three integer numbers and prints their product if
   the first number is negative.  If the first number is nonnegative,
   the sum of the three numbers is printed *)
```

PSIA

```
VAR
  Num1,           (* First   number              *)
  Num2,           (* Second number              *)
  Num3,           (* Third   number              *)
  Product,        (* Result of multiplication *)
  Sum:            (* Result of addition          *)
    Integer;

BEGIN (* ProdSum *)
  (* Get data *)
  Writeln('Enter three integer numbers: ');                    (* Prompt *)
  Readln(Num1, Num2, Num3);
  Write('For the numbers ');
  Write(Num1:1, ' ', Num2:1, ' ', Num3:1);                     (* Echo print *)
  IF Num1 < 0
    THEN
      BEGIN
        (* Calculate product *)
        Product := Num1 * Num2 * Num3;
        Writeln(' the product is ', Product:1)
      END
    ELSE
      BEGIN
        (* Calculate sum *)
        Sum := Num1 + Num2 + Num3;
        Writeln(' the sum is ', Sum:1)
      END
END.  (* ProdSum *)
```

Here is a sample run of the program:

```
Enter three integer numbers:
333 777 200
For the numbers 333 777 200 the sum is 1310
```

Here is another sample run of the program which demonstrates what happens when the first number is negative:

```
Enter three integer numbers:
-1 777 200
For the numbers -1 777 200 the product is -155400
```

This program will be examined in more detail in the Testing and Debugging section at the end of this chapter.

Nested IF Statements

There are no restrictions on what the statements in an IF statement can be. There-fore, an IF within an IF is okay. In fact, an IF within an IF within an IF . . . is legal. The limiting factor is that people cannot follow a structure if it gets too involved. Readability is one of the marks of a good program.

When we place an IF within an IF, we are creating what is called a *nested control structure.* The term *nesting* comes from an analogy to a set of mixing bowls that nest together, with smaller ones inside of larger ones. Here is an example of a problem that logically decomposes into a nested IF-THEN-ELSE structure.

```
IF today is Saturday or Sunday
   THEN
      IF it is raining
         THEN
            Sleep late
         ELSE
            Get up and go outside
   ELSE
      Go to work
```

In general, any problem that involves more than two alternative courses of action can be coded using nested IF statements. However, nested IF statements are not always the best choice for solving such problems. For example, in a problem involving printing out the name of a month given its number, there is no need for the ELSE branches and we can simply use a sequence of IF statements such as

```
IF Month = 1
   THEN
      Writeln('January');
IF Month = 2
   THEN
      Writeln('February');
IF Month = 3
   THEN
      Writeln('March');
         .
         .
```

This is simpler and shorter than writing the equivalent nested IF structure:

```
IF Month = 1
   THEN
      Writeln('January')
   ELSE
      IF Month = 2              (* Nested IF *)
         THEN
            Writeln('February')
         ELSE
            IF Month = 3         (* Nested IF *)
```

```
            THEN
                Writeln('March')
            ELSE
                IF Month = 4          (* Nested IF *)
                    .
                    .
```

The nested IF is particularly useful when one or more alternatives are dependent on the branch taken in another alternative. For example, before we try to print the name of the month, we should first check the data to be sure we have a valid month number:

```
IF (Month >= 1) AND (Month <= 12)
        THEN
            BEGIN
                IF Month = 1              (* Nested sequence of IFs *)
                    THEN
                        Writeln('January');
                IF Month = 2
                    .
                    .
            END
        ELSE
        Writeln('Month number is invalid.');
```

Whenever you encounter a problem in which some condition must be tested before another condition is tested, a nested IF structure will be appropriate.

The nested IF is also appropriate when a series of comparisons for consecutive ranges of values is to be performed. In the following Problem Solving in Action section, for example, the problem is to print different messages for different consecutive ranges of temperatures. We present two solutions for one of the modules, one using a sequence of IF statements and the other using a nested IF structure. Notice that the nested IF version uses fewer comparisons.

Problem Solving in Action

Problem: Read a temperature and print out what sport is appropriate for that temperature, using the following guidelines.

Sport	Temperature
swimming	> 85
tennis	$70 < temp <= 85$
golf	$32 < temp <= 70$
skiing	$10 < temp <= 32$
chinese checkers	$<= 10$

PSIA

Discussion: The temperature must be compared with the limits of each sport. When the proper range is found, the corresponding sport is printed. This comparison can be done with IF statements.

Input: Temperature, an Integer value

Output:

    Input prompt message
    Temperature (echo print)
    Appropriate sport

MAIN MODULE   Level 0

```
Get Temperature
Print Sport
```

GET TEMPERATURE   Level 1

```
Prompt for temperature value input
Read Temperature
```

PRINT SPORT

```
IF Temperature > 85
   THEN
      Write 'swimming'
IF Temperature <= 85 and > 70
   THEN
      Write 'tennis'
IF Temperature <= 70 and > 32
   THEN
      Write 'golf'
IF Temperature <= 32 and > 10
   THEN
      Write 'skiing'
IF Temperature <= 10
   THEN
      Write 'chinese checkers'
```

PSIA

Print Sport has five IF statements with a total of eight comparisons. However, this module can be coded as a set of nested IF statements. The middle IFs look as if they should have compound Boolean conditions; however, the structure of the IF-THEN-ELSE makes this unnecessary because you know that you wouldn't be executing the ELSE branch unless one of the conditions wasn't satisfied. Here is the rewritten algorithm for Print Sport:

PRINT SPORT

```
IF Temperature > 85
   THEN
      Write 'swimming'
ELSE IF Temperature > 70
   THEN
      Write 'tennis'
ELSE IF Temperature > 32
   THEN
      Write 'golf'
ELSE IF Temperature > 10
   THEN
      Write 'skiing'
ELSE
   Write 'chinese checkers'
```

Module Structure Chart:

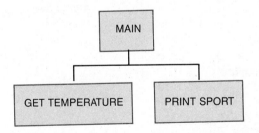

Since this algorithm has only one variable, we won't bother with the list of variables. From now on, to save space, we will omit the list of constants and variables from the Problem Solving in Action sections. We recommend, however, that you continue the practice of writing out these lists as you design your own algorithms. The lists will save you considerable effort when you are writing the declarations for your programs.

PSIA ▬▬▬▬▬

```pascal
Program Sport (Input, Output);

(* This program outputs an appropriate
   sport for a given temperature *)

VAR
   Temperature:        (* The outside temperature *)
      Integer;

BEGIN (* Sport *)
  (* Get Temperature *)
  Writeln('Enter the outside temperature:');
  Readln(Temperature);
  Writeln('For a temperature of ', Temperature:1);
  Write('the appropriate sport is ');
  (* Print Sport *)
  IF Temperature > 85
    THEN
      Writeln('swimming.')
  ELSE IF Temperature > 70
    THEN
      Writeln('tennis.')
  ELSE IF Temperature > 32
    THEN
      Writeln('golf.')
  ELSE IF Temperature > 10
    THEN
      Writeln('skiing.')
  ELSE
    Writeln('chinese checkers.')
END.   (* Sport *)
```

Here is a sample run of Program Sport:

```
Enter the outside temperature:
-30
For a temperature of -30
the appropriate sport is chinese checkers.
```

Here is another sample run:

```
Enter the outside temperature:
52
For a temperature of 52
the appropriate sport is golf.
```

PSIA ▰▰▰▰▰

Figure 4-6 shows how the flow of control works in this example.

Figure 4-6
Flow of Control in
Module Print Sport

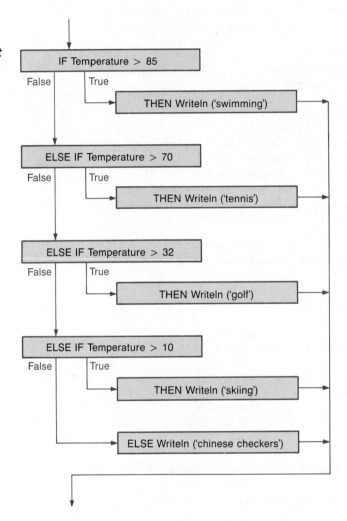

In the preceding problem the nested IF version of the solution had only four relational operators, whereas the other solution had eight relational operators. Thus the nested IF solution is the more efficient of the two: It uses fewer operations to accomplish the same function.

As fast as modern computers are, many applications require so much computation that inefficient algorithms can waste many hours of computer time that could otherwise be put to productive use. You should always be on the lookout for ways to make your programs more efficient, as long as doing so does not make them difficult for a human reader to understand. It is usually better to sacrifice a little efficiency for the sake of more readable programs. In the following Problem Solving in Action section we have chosen for our solution a nested IF structure that is easily understood although somewhat inefficient.

Problem Solving in Action

Problem: Many universities send warning notices to freshmen who are in danger of failing a class. You are to calculate the average of three test grades and print out the student ID number, the average, and whether or not the student is passing. Passing is a 60-point average or better. If the student is passing but with less than a 70 average, indicate that he or she is marginal.

Discussion: To calculate the average we will have to read in the three test scores, add them up, and divide by 3.

To print the appropriate message we will have to determine whether the average is above or below 60. If it is above 60, we will have to determine if it is between 60 and 70.

In doing this calculation by hand, you would probably notice if a test grade was negative and question it. If the semantics of your data imply that the values should be positive, then your program should test to be sure they are. Here we will test to make sure each grade is positive and use a Boolean variable to report the result of the test.

Input: Student ID (Integer) followed by three test grades (Integer).

Output:

Prompt for input

Input (echo print)

Message containing student ID, passing/failing, average grade, possible marginal indication, or error message if any of the test scores are negative

MAIN MODULE   Level 0

```
Get Data
Test Data
IF DataOK
   THEN
       Calculate Average
       Print Message
   ELSE
       Print 'Invalid data' Message
```

GET DATA   Level 1

```
Print Prompt
Read StudentID, Test1, Test2, Test3
Print StudentID, Test1, Test2, Test3
```

PSIA

TEST DATA

```
IF (Test1 < 0) OR (Test2 < 0) OR (Test3 < 0)
  THEN
    DataOK is False
  ELSE
    DataOK is True
```

CALCULATE AVERAGE

```
Average = (Test1 + Test2 + Test3) / 3
```

PRINT MESSAGE

```
Print StudentID, Average
IF Average >= 60
  THEN
    Print 'Passing'
    IF Average < 70
      Print ' but marginal'
  ELSE
    Print 'Failing'
```

Module Structure Chart:

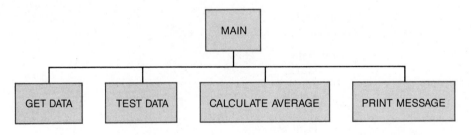

```
PROGRAM Notices (Input, Output);

(* This program determines a student's average based on three
   test scores, and the student's passing/failing status *)

VAR
  Average:      (* Average of three test scores    *)
    Real;
  StudentID,    (* Student's identification number *)
```

PSIA ◢▬▬▬▬▬▬▬

```
   Test1,           (* Score for first  test            *)
   Test2,           (* Score for second test            *)
   Test3:           (* Score for third  test            *)
      Integer;
   DataOK:          (* Will be true if data are correct *)
      Boolean;

BEGIN  (* Notices *)
  (* Get Data *)
  Writeln('Enter a Student ID and three test scores:');
  Readln(StudentID, Test1, Test2, Test3);
  Writeln('Student Number: ', StudentID:1, ' Test Scores: ',
          Test1:1, ', ', Test2:1, ', ', Test3:1);
  (* Test Data *)
  IF (Test1 < 0) OR (Test2 < 0) OR (Test3 < 0)
    THEN
      DataOK := False
    ELSE
      DataOK := True;
  IF DataOK
    THEN
      BEGIN
        (* Calculate Average *)
        Average := (Test1 + Test2 + Test3) / 3.0;
        (* Print Message *)
        Write('Average score is ', Average:4:2, ' -- ');
        IF Average >= 60.0
          THEN                                  (* Print passing message *)
            BEGIN
              Write('Passing');
              IF Average < 70.0
                THEN
                  Writeln(' but marginal.')
                ELSE
                  Writeln('.')
            END
          ELSE                                  (* Print failing message *)
            Writeln('Failing.')
      END
    ELSE                                        (* Data are invalid *)
      Writeln('Invalid data:  Score(s) less than zero.')
END.  (* Notices *)
```

Here is a sample run of the program:

```
Enter a Student ID and three test scores:
9483681 73 62 68
Student Number: 9483681 Test Scores: 73, 62, 68
Average score is 67.67 — Passing but marginal.
```

PSIA ▬▬▬▬▬

Here is a sample run with invalid data:

```
Enter a Student ID and three test scores:
9483681 73 -10 62
Student Number: 9483681 Test Scores: 73, -10, 62
Invalid Data: Score(s) less than zero.
```

As we said before, the branching structure in our solution to this problem is not as efficient as it might be. We assigned a value to DataOK in one statement before testing it in the next. We could have done this another way. We could simply have said

```
DataOK := NOT ((Test1 < 0) OR (Test2 < 0) OR (Test3 < 0))
```

In fact, we could reduce the code even more. How about

```
IF (Test1 >= 0) AND (Test2 >= 0) AND (Test3 >= 0)
```

in place of IF DataOK? To convince yourself that these two variations do work, try them by hand with some test data. If these shorter statements will do the same thing, why did we use the longer form in the program? Because the longer form expresses more clearly what we are doing. The computer will perform the task correctly whichever way we write it, so we chose the way that is easiest for a person to understand, even if it is a little less efficient.

In Program Notices the test scores were tested to be sure they were positive. This type of data checking is important. If you know that something must always be true about your data, put a test in your program to make sure that the input data is valid.

There are four IF-THEN-ELSE statements in Program Notices. To test each branch, take the following sets of values for Test1, Test2, and Test3 and hand-calculate what happens.

100	100	100
60	60	60
50	50	50
-50	50	50

The first set is valid and gives an average of 100, which is passing and not marginal. The second set is valid and gives an average of 60, which is passing but marginal. The third set gives an average of 50, which is failing. The fourth set has an invalid test grade, and an error message would be printed.

When IF statements are nested, there is sometimes confusion about the IF-ELSE pairings: To which IF does an ELSE belong? For example, suppose we change slightly the problem definition for Program Notices. If a student's average is 70 or greater, print nothing. If it is between 60 and 70, print "Passing but marginal"; if it is below 60, print "Failing."

Coding this slight change gives an IF-THEN-ELSE nested within an IF-THEN as follows.

```
IF Average < 70.0
   THEN
      IF Average < 60.0
         THEN
            Writeln('Failing')
         ELSE
            Writeln('Passing but marginal')
```

How do we know that "Passing but marginal" will be written when the average is between 60 and 70 and not when the average is 70 or above? In other words, how do we know to which IF an ELSE belongs? The rule is that an ELSE is paired with the closest preceding IF. In this example we formatted the code to reflect this pairing. However, formatting does not affect the execution of the code. If the ELSE had been lined up with the first THEN, it still would have belonged to the second IF.

Suppose we had written the third IF-THEN-ELSE statement in Program Notices like this:

```
IF Average >= 60.0
   THEN
      BEGIN
         Write('Passing');
         IF Average < 70.0
            THEN
               Writeln('but marginal')
      END
   ELSE
      Writeln('Failing')
```

A compound statement is needed in the THEN branch because we want to execute two statements in that branch. However, even if we removed one of the statements, the Write('Passing') statement, we would still need the BEGIN-END pair. Why? Because we want the ELSE branch as part of the first IF statement, not the second. The BEGIN-END pair around the nested IF statement indicates that the nested IF statement is complete, so the ELSE is matched up with the outside IF statement.

TESTING AND DEBUGGING

In Chapter 1 we discussed the problem-solving phase and the implementation phase of computer programming. Both phases have testing as an integral part. Let's apply testing at both phases to the problem for which Program ProdSum was developed earlier in this chapter.

Testing at the problem-solving phase involves looking at each level of our top-down design and saying, "If the levels below this one are expanded correctly, will this level do what needs to be done?"

In this case, if (1) Get Data correctly inputs three values, (2) Calculate Product correctly multiplies the three numbers together and prints the result, and (3) Calculate Sum correctly adds the three numbers and prints the result, then the main program is correct.

The next step is to examine each module at level 1 and ask the question "If the level 2 modules are assumed to be correct, will this module do what it is supposed to do?" In this example there are no level 2 modules, so the level 1 modules must be complete. Note that there is no code in the top-down design. We could just as easily translate the design into FORTRAN (another widely used high-level language) as. into Pascal.

Get Data reads in three values, Num1, Num2, and Num3. (The next refinement is actually coding this instruction. Whether or not it is coded correctly is *not* the problem at this phase; that is determined in the implementation phase.)

Calculate Product assigns to variable Product the result of multiplying the contents of Num1, Num2, and Num3. That is what the product means, so this step is correct and the calculated product is printed.

Calculate Sum assigns to the variable Sum the result of adding Num1, Num2, and Num3. This is what the sum means, so this step is correct and the calculated sum is printed.

Once the algorithm has been desk-checked, the translation of the top-down design into a programming language can begin.

Testing at the implementation phase is done at several different points. After the coding has been done, you should go over your code carefully, checking to make sure that the top-down design has been faithfully reproduced. The code is then entered at the terminal (or punched on cards). At this stage you should take some actual values and hand-calculate what the output should be by doing a code walk-through. In a later testing phase, you can use these same values as input and check the results.

In Chapter 1 we also discussed the compilation phase and execution phase. The program you have coded is now ready for the compilation phase. The Pascal compiler takes the program coded in Pascal and translates it into a language that the machine you are using can execute.

There are two distinct outputs from the compilation phase: a listing of the program with error messages (if any) and the translated version of the program ready to be executed (if there are no errors). See Appendix F, Compiler Error Messages, for an example of error messages in a program listing.

Now the translated version of your program is ready to be executed. At this stage the tasks you wanted done are finally done; that is, a line is read, a value is tested, and so on.

You are now in the debugging phase. This is where you locate and correct all errors (called bugs) in your program. Errors are of two types: syntactic or semantic. Syntactic errors are errors in Pascal syntax and are usually caught by the compiler. Semantic errors are errors that give you the wrong answer; these are more difficult

Figure 4-7
Programming
Process

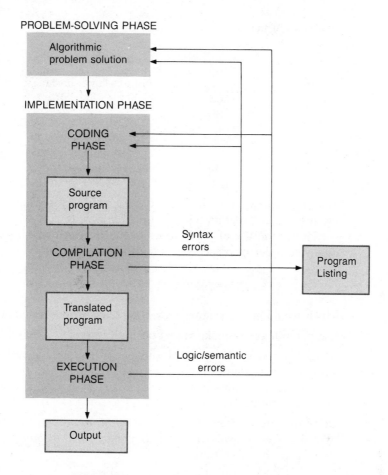

to locate and usually surface at execution time. The error may be an undetected bug in your top-down design or a keying error that created a syntactically correct but meaningless statement.

Figure 4-7 pictures the programming process we have just discussed. The figure indicates where syntax and semantic errors occur and at which phase they can be corrected.

Testing and Debugging Hints

1. Echo print all input data. This way you know your input data is what you thought it was.

2. Test for bad data in your program. If a data value must be positive, put an IF statement in to test the value. If the value is negative, an error message should be printed; otherwise, processing should continue. For example, Program Sport should have the following statement inserted after the first Writeln

(the echo print):

```
IF  (Temperature > 120)  OR  (Temperature < -25)
    THEN
        Writeln('Temperature data is in error.')
    ELSE
        BEGIN
            (* balance of program *)
                .
                .
                .
        END
```

This IF statement tests the limits of reasonable temperatures and only executes the rest of the program if the data is reasonable.

Notice the use of parentheses in the IF statement. If parentheses weren't used, the order of precedence would impose

```
Temperature > (120 OR Temperature) < -25
```

which would give a syntax error. This leads to the next hint.

3. Use parentheses to make your Boolean expressions clear and correct.

4. Be sure that the opening and closing parentheses match each other properly. To verify that parentheses are properly paired, start with the innermost pair and draw a line connecting them. Do the same for the others, working your way out to the outermost pair.

5. Don't use $=<$ to mean *less than or equal to;* only the symbol $<=$ will work. Likewise, $=>$ is invalid as a form of *greater than or equal to;* you must use $>=$ to indicate this operation.

6. Remember that semicolons *separate* statements.

   An IF-THEN-ELSE is one statement. A semicolon before the ELSE would tell the translator that it had reached the end of an IF-THEN statement. The translator would then expect the next word, ELSE, to begin a new statement. Since ELSE is not the first word in any statement and is a reserved word, an error would occur.

   Always check each IF-THEN-ELSE to be sure that you do not have a semicolon before the ELSE.

7. Check your declarations to be sure each variable name used has been declared.

8. Be sure that each identifier is only declared once. If you find any declared more than once, check the program to be sure you haven't used the same name for two different things. Make sure that you haven't misspelled any names.

9. Take sample data values and try them by hand as we did for Program Notices. (More on this in Chapter 5.)

10. If an answer produced by your program does not agree with the value you calculated by hand, try the following suggestions.
    (a) Redo your arithmetic.
    (b) Recheck your input data.

(c) Go carefully over the section of code that does the calculation. If you are in doubt about the order in which the operations are performed, insert clarifying parentheses.

(d) Check for Integer overflow. The value of an Integer variable may have exceeded MaxInt during calculations. Many systems will give you an error message if this happens; however, some will not.

(e) Check the conditions in branching statements to be sure that the correct branch is taken under all circumstances.

SUMMARY

Chapter 4 has described a way of asking questions about the execution of a program as it runs. A Boolean expression is evaluated and is assigned the value True if the expression is true or False if the expression is not true.

The IF statement allows you to take different paths through a program, based on the value of a Boolean expression. The IF-THEN-ELSE allows you to choose between two courses of action. The IF-THEN allows you to choose whether or not to take a particular course of action.

The branches of an IF-THEN or IF-THEN-ELSE can be any statement—simple or compound. They can even be (or include) another IF statement.

QUICK CHECK

1. How would you write a Pascal expression that compares the variable Letter to the constant 'Z' and returns True if Letter is less than 'Z'? (pp. 136–142)

2. How would you write a Pascal expression that returns True if Letter is between 'A' and 'Z', inclusive? (pp. 136–142)

3. What kind of statement would you use to make a Pascal program print out "Is a letter" if the value in Letter is between 'A' and 'Z', inclusive, and print out "Is not a letter" if the value in Letter is not in that range? (pp. 143–146)

4. What kind of statement would you use to make a Pascal program print out "Is a Letter" only if the value in Letter is between 'A' and 'Z', inclusive? (pp. 147–148)

5. On a telephone each of the digits 2 through 9 has a segment of the alphabet associated with it. What kind of control structure would you use to decide which segment a given letter falls into and to print out the corresponding digit? (pp. 151–152)

6. Assume that you've written a program to print out the corresponding phone digit, given a letter of the alphabet. Everything seems to work right except that you can't get the digit '5' to print out—all of the letters that should cause it to be printed produce '6' as the result. What steps would you take to find and fix this bug? (pp. 161–165)

Answers
1. Letter < 'Z' 2. (Letter >= 'A') AND (Letter <= 'Z') 3. An IF-THEN-ELSE statement 4. An IF-THEN statement 5. A nested IF statement 6. Go carefully over the section of code that should print out '5'. Check the branching condition and the output statement for that section. Try some sample values by hand.

EXAM PREPARATION EXERCISES

1. Given the following values for Boolean variables X, Y, and Z, evaluate the Boolean expressions and answer T if the result is True or F if the result is False.

X = True, Y = False, Z = True

(a) (X AND Y) OR (X AND Z)

(b) (X OR NOT Y) AND (NOT X OR Z)

(c) X OR Y AND Z

(d) NOT (X OR Y) AND Z

2. Given the following values for variables I, J, K, and L, add whatever parentheses are necessary to the expressions below so that they will evaluate to True.

I = 10, J = 19, K = True, L = False

(a) I = J OR K

(b) I >= J OR I <= J AND K

(c) NOT K OR K

(d) NOT L AND L

3. What will the following program segment write in a case where
   (a) Height exceeds MinHeight and Weight exceeds MinWeight
   (b) Height is less than MinHeight and Weight is less than MinWeight

```
IF Height >= MinHeight
  THEN
    IF Weight >= MinWeight
      THEN
        Writeln('Eligible to serve')
      ELSE
        Writeln('Too light to serve')
  ELSE
    IF Weight >= MinWeight
      THEN
        Writeln('Too short to serve')
      ELSE
        Writeln('Too short and too light to serve')
```

4. Match each Boolean expression in the left column with the Boolean expression in the right column that tests for the same condition.

(a) (X < Y) AND (Y < Z)

(b) (X > Y) AND (Y >= Z)

(c) (X <> Y) OR (Y = Z)

(d) (X = Y) OR (Y <= Z)

(e) (X = Y) AND (Y = Z)

(1) NOT (X <> Y) AND (Y = Z)

(2) NOT ((X <= Y) OR (Y < Z))

(3) ((Y < Z) OR (Y = Z)) OR (X = Y)

(4) NOT (X >= Y) AND NOT (Y >= Z)

(5) NOT ((X = Y) AND (Y <> Z))

5. The following expressions make sense, but are invalid according to Pascal syntax rules. Rewrite them as valid Pascal Boolean expressions.

(a) X < Y <= Z

(b) X, Y, and Z are greater than 0

(c) X is equal to neither Y nor Z

(d) X = Y and Z

6. For each of the following problems, decide which of the branching statements (IF-THEN-ELSE or IF-THEN) is most appropriate.

   (a) Students who are candidates for admission to a college submit their SAT scores. If a student's score is equal to or above a certain minimum value, then a letter of acceptance is printed for the student. Otherwise, a rejection notice is sent.

(b) For employees who have more than 40 hours of work in a week, overtime pay must be calculated and added to their regular pay.

(c) In solving a quadratic equation, whenever the value of the discriminant is negative, the computer should print out a message that notes that the roots are imaginary.

(d) In a computer-controlled sawmill, if the cross section of a log is greater than certain dimensions, the saw is adjusted to cut 4″ × 8″ beams; otherwise, it is adjusted to cut 2″ × 4″ studs.

7. What is the cause of the error message "ELSE NOT EXPECTED" when the following segment of Pascal code is run?

```
IF Mileage < 24.0
   THEN
      Writeln('Gas guzzler.');
   ELSE
      Writeln('Fuel efficient.');
```

8. The following segment of Pascal code is supposed to print "Type AB" when both TypeA and TypeB (Boolean variables) are True, and print "Type O" when both variables are False. Instead, "Type O" is printed whenever just one of the variables is False. Insert a BEGIN-END pair to make the code segment work as it should.

```
IF TypeA OR TypeB
   THEN
      IF TypeA AND TypeB
         THEN
            Writeln('Type AB')
   ELSE
      Writeln('Type O');
```

9. The following nested IF structure has five possible branches that may be taken depending on the values read into the character variables A, B, and C. To test the proper execution of the structure, five sets of data are needed, each set causing a different branch to be taken. Write a list of five such test data sets.

```
Read(A, B, C);
IF A = B
   THEN
      IF B = C
         THEN
            Writeln('All initials are the same.')
         ELSE
            Writeln('First two are the same.')
   ELSE IF B = C
      THEN
         Writeln('Last two are the same.')
   ELSE IF A = C
      THEN
         Writeln('First and last are the same.')
      ELSE
         Writeln('All initials are different.')
```

	A =	B =	C =
Test data set 1:	A = ____	B = ____	C = ____
Test data set 2:	A = ____	B = ____	C = ____
Test data set 3:	A = ____	B = ____	C = ____
Test data set 4:	A = ____	B = ____	C = ____
Test data set 5:	A = ____	B = ____	C = ____

10. If X and Y are Boolean variables, do the following two expressions test the same condition?

    (a) X <> Y

    (b) (X OR Y) AND NOT (X AND Y)

PREPROGRAMMING EXERCISES

1. Write a statement containing a comparison that sets the Boolean variable Available to True if NumberOrdered is less than or equal to NumberOnHand minus Number-Reserved.

2. Declare Eligible to be a Boolean variable. Assign it the value True.

3. Write a statement containing a Boolean expression that assigns True to the Boolean variable Candidate if SATScore is greater than or equal to 1100, GPA is not less than 2.5, and Age is greater than 15. Candidate should be False otherwise.

4. Given the declarations

```
                    VAR
                      LeftPage:
                        Boolean;
                      PageNumber:
                        Integer;
```

   write a statement that sets LeftPage to True if PageNumber is even.

5. Write an IF statement (or IF statements) that will assign to the variable Biggest the greatest value contained in variables I, J, and K. Assume the three values are distinct.

6. Rewrite the following IF-THEN-ELSE statement, using two IF-THEN statements instead.

```
IF Year MOD 4 = 0
   THEN
      Writeln(Year, ' is a leap year.')
   ELSE
      BEGIN
         Year := Year + 4 - Year MOD 4;
         Writeln(Year, ' is the next leap year.')
      END
```

7. Write an IF-THEN-ELSE statement that assigns to the variable Largest the greatest value contained in the variables A, B, and C. Assume the three values are distinct.

8. Simplify the following program segment so that fewer comparisons are necessary.

```
                         IF Age > 64
                            THEN
                               Write('Social Security');
                         IF Age < 18
                            THEN
                               Write('Exempt');
                         IF (Age >= 18) AND (Age < 65)
                            THEN
                               Write('Taxable');
```

9. Correct the syntax errors in the following program.

```
        PROGRAM Exercise (Input, Output)

CONST
   A = 10
   B = 5
   C = 6

VAR
   D;
   E;
   F:
      Integer

BEGIN
   Read(D, E  F)
   IF (D > A)
      THEN
         D = A + D;
      ELSE
         D = A
   E := D + F
   Write('This program does not make sense,
      E, F  D)
END;
```

10. Cross out any unnecessary semicolons in the following Pascal program segment.

```
        BEGIN;
           (* This is a nonsense program. *);
        A := 10;
        IF A > 0;
           THEN;
              IF A < 20;
                 THEN;
                    Writeln('A is in range');
                 ELSE;
                    BEGIN;
                       Writeln('A is too high');
                       A := 10;
                    END;
```

```
                              ELSE;
                                IF  A  =  0;
                                  THEN;
                                     Writeln('A is null');
                                  ELSE;
                                     BEGIN;
                                        Writeln('A is too low');
                                        A  :  =  10;
                                     END;
                    END.
```

PROGRAMMING PROBLEMS

1. Write a top-down design and a Pascal program that will input a single letter and print out the corresponding digit on the telephone. The digits and letters on a telephone are associated as follows:

$$2 = ABC, \quad 3 = DEF, \quad 4 = GHI, \quad 5 = JKL,$$
$$6 = MNO, \quad 7 = PRS, \quad 8 = TUV, \quad 9 = WXY$$

There is no digit corresponding to either Q or Z. For these letters your program should print a message indicating that they do not exist on a telephone dial.

If you are using an interactive system, the program might operate as follows:

```
Enter a single letter and I will tell you what the corresponding
digit is on the telephone.
R
The digit 7 corresponds to the letter R on the telephone.
```

Here is another example:

```
Enter a single letter and I will tell you what the corresponding
digit is on the telephone.
Q
There is no digit on the telephone that corresponds to Q.
```

Your program should print a message indicating that there is no matching digit for any nonalphabetic character that the user enters.

On systems that use both uppercase and lowercase letters, the program needs to recognize only uppercase letters; the lowercase letters can be included with the invalid characters.

If you are using an interactive system, prompt the user with an informative message for the input value.

Your program should echo print the input letter as part of the output. Use proper indentation, with appropriate comments and meaningful identifiers throughout the program.

2. People who deal with historical dates use a number called the Julian Day in calculating the number of days between two events. The Julian Day is the number of days that have elapsed since January 1, 4713 B.C. For example, the Julian Day for October 16, 1956 is

2435763. Formulas exist for computing the Julian Day from a given date and vice versa. One very simple formula computes the day of the week from a given Julian Day. The formula is

```
DayOfTheWeek = (JulianDay + 1) MOD 7
```

This formula will give a result of 0 for Sunday, 1 for Monday, and so on up to 6 for Saturday. For Julian Day 2435763, the result of this formula would be 2 (a Tuesday). Your job is to write a top-down design and a Pascal program that will input a Julian Day, compute the day of the week using the above formula, and then print out the name of the day that corresponds to that number. Be sure to echo print the input data and to use proper indentation and sufficient comments.

On an interactive system, the execution of the program might look as follows:

```
Enter a Julian Day Number:
2451545
Julian day number 2451545 is a Saturday.
```

3. The date for any Easter Sunday can be computed as follows (all variables are of type Integer):

Let A be Year MOD 19

Let B be Year MOD 4

Let C be Year MOD 7

Let D be (19 * A + 24) MOD 30

Let E be (2 * B + 4 * C + 6 * D + 5) MOD 7

Then the date for Easter Sunday is March (22 + D + E). Note that this formula can give a date in April. Write a program that will input the year and output the date of Easter Sunday for that year, with the proper month name and day number in that month. Echo print the input as part of the output; for example,

```
Enter the year (example 1988):
1985
Easter is Sunday, April 7 in 1985.
```

- To be able to construct syntactically correct WHILE loops.
- To be able to construct count-controlled loops with a WHILE statement.
- To be able to construct event-controlled loops with a WHILE statement.
- To be able to use EOF to control the inputting of data.
- To be able to use EOLN to control the inputting of character data.
- To be able to construct counting loops with a WHILE statement.
- To be able to construct summing loops with a WHILE statement.
- To be able to use flags to control the execution of a WHILE loop.
- To be able to write the invariant conditions for a loop from a problem specification.
- To be able to choose the proper type of loop for a given problem.
- To be able to construct a correct WHILE loop of which another WHILE loop is a part.
- To be able to format output neatly using column headings.
- To be able to choose data sets to test a program comprehensively.

5

Looping

Chapter 4 introduced the concept that the flow of control in a program could differ from the physical order of the statements. The physical order is the order in which the statements appear in a program; the order in which we want the statements to be executed is called the *logical order.*

Use of the IF statement was presented as a way of making the logical order differ from the physical order. IF a condition (or set of conditions) is True, THEN one statement is executed; ELSE a different statement is executed. In the abbreviated IF-THEN form, no statement is executed if the condition (or set of conditions) is False.

The IF statement is a branching control structure. Looping control structures give us another way to make the logical order different from the physical order: A loop executes the same statement (simple or compound) over and over, as long as a condition (or set of conditions) is met.

In this chapter we will discuss various types of loops and how they may be constructed using the Pascal WHILE statement. We will also discuss loops that contain other loops (called *nested loops*) and the printing of headings and columns on output tables.

WHILE STATEMENT

The WHILE statement tests a condition just as the IF statement does.

```
WHILE Boolean expression DO
    statement1;
```

Figure 5-1
WHILE Structure
Diagram

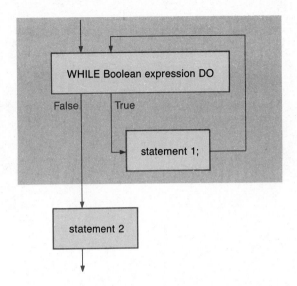

means "If the Boolean expression is True, execute statement 1. After the execution of statement 1, go back and test the Boolean expression again." This process continues until the Boolean expression becomes False. At that time statement 1 (which could be a compound statement) is skipped, and execution continues with the first statement following the loop. What if the Boolean expression is False to begin with? Then the effect is much like that of an IF-THEN statement when the condition is False: Statement 1 is never executed, and execution continues with the first statement following the loop. Statement 1 is often called the body of the loop. Figure 5-1 illustrates the flow of control of the WHILE statement.

The syntax diagram for the WHILE statement is

——————→ WHILE ——————→ Boolean expression ——————→ DO ——————→ statement ——————→

At first glance you might think that IF and WHILE are alike. They do have similarities, but a careful examination shows their fundamental differences. (See Figure 5-2.) In the IF structure, statement 1 may be either skipped or executed

Figure 5-2
Comparison of IF
and WHILE

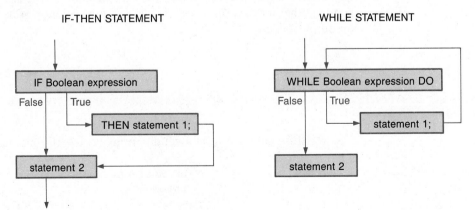

exactly once. In the WHILE structure, statement 1 may be either skipped or executed over and over any number of times. Thus, if the Boolean expression is initially False, the WHILE will act much like an IF-THEN. If the Boolean expression is True, however, the WHILE may behave very differently.

In the WHILE, flow of control returns to a test of the Boolean expression after each execution of statement 1; in the IF, it does not. The IF is used to *choose* a course of action. The WHILE is used to *repeat* a course of action.

Note that in each case statement 1 can be a compound statement: a series of statements enclosed by a BEGIN-END pair. You will almost always use WHILE loops of the following form:

```
WHILE Boolean expression DO
    BEGIN
        series of statements
    END
```

This structure will cause the entire series of statements to be repeated (assuming the Boolean expression is True).

LOOPS USING THE WHILE STATEMENT

Since the concept of looping is fundamental to programming, we will now spend some time looking at typical types of loops and how to implement them with the Pascal WHILE statement. When you are analyzing problems and doing top-down design, you will see these looping situations come up again and again.

Each time the body of a loop is executed, we say that a pass has been made through the loop. This pass is also called an *iteration* of the loop.

Iteration An individual pass through, or repetition of, the body of a loop.

When the last pass has been made through a loop and the flow of control proceeds to the first statement following the loop, the program is said to have *exited the loop*.

Loop Exit The point in the execution of a loop when repetition of the body ends and control passes to the first statement following the loop.

The condition that causes a loop to be exited is called the *termination condition*. In the case of the WHILE loop, the *termination condition* is simply that the Boolean expression in the WHILE statement is evaluated and found to equal False.

Termination Condition The condition that causes a loop to be exited.

In solving problems, you will encounter two major types of loops: those that repeat a known number of times (*count-controlled loops*) and those that repeat until something happens within the loop body to signal that the looping process should cease (*event-controlled loops*).

Count-Controlled Loop A loop that executes a known number of times.

Event-Controlled Loop A loop that terminates when something happens inside of the loop body to signal that the loop should be exited.

If you are making an angel-food cake according to a recipe that says, "Beat the mix 300 strokes," then you are executing a count-controlled loop. If, however, you are making a pie crust according to a recipe that says, "Cut with a pastry blender until the mixture resembles coarse meal," then you are executing an event-controlled loop.

Count-Controlled Loops

A count-controlled loop is a loop that executes a specified number of times. It makes use of a variable called the *loop control variable* (sometimes abbreviated LCV). There are three parts to a count-controlled loop: initializing the LCV, testing the LCV, and incrementing the LCV. The following code segment uses the WHILE statement to do the testing:

```
Count := 1;              (* Initialization *)
WHILE Count <= 10 DO     (* Test           *)
   BEGIN
      .
      .
      .
      Count := Count + 1 (* Incrementation *)
   END
```

Count is the loop control variable. It is set to 1 outside of the loop. The WHILE statement tests the expression Count <= 10 and executes the compound statement as long as the expression is True. The last statement in the compound statement increments Count by adding 1 to it. You will use statements of the form

```
variable := variable + 1
```

many times in programming. Placing such a statement in the body of a loop causes the value of the variable to be incremented repeatedly by 1. Each time the statement is executed, 1 is added to the previous value of the variable and this result replaces the old value. Variables that are used in this way are therefore called *counters*. The loop control variable of a count-controlled loop is always a counter.

Notice that a WHILE statement always tests for the termination condition first. If the condition is False to begin with, the body of the loop is never executed. It is the programmer's responsibility to see that the condition to be tested is set correctly (initialized) before the WHILE statement begins.

```
Count := 1;  ←——————————————— variable Count must be initialized
WHILE Count <= 10 DO
   BEGIN
             .
             .
             .
      Count := Count + 1 ←——————— Count must be incremented (changed)
   END
```

The programmer must also make sure the condition is changed within the loop so that it will become False at some point; otherwise the loop will never be exited. A loop whose termination condition never becomes False is called an *infinite loop* because, unless there is some intervention from outside of the program, the loop will execute forever. If your program goes on running for much longer than you expect it to, chances are that you have an infinite loop. In that case, you may have to issue an operating system command to stop the program. (On many systems this is accomplished by pressing Control-C. Other common ways of stopping a program include pressing the Break key and pressing Control-T followed by Return. Check the manual for your system to see which method it uses.)

T,M,V ↩

How many times will the loop in the example above be executed—9 or 10? To determine the number of times, look at what the loop control variable is initialized to and then look at the test to see what its final value will be. In this case Count, the loop control variable, is initialized to 1. The test indicates that the loop body will be executed as long as Count is less than or equal to 10. That is, the loop body will be executed for each value of Count up through 10 and will be skipped when Count becomes 11. If Count starts out at 1 and runs up to 10, this means the loop body will be executed 10 times. If we had wanted the loop to execute 11 times, we could have either initialized Count to 0 or changed the test to "Count <= 11". We have to be careful not to change both or we'll end up with a loop that executes 12 times!

Event-Controlled Loops

There are several kinds of event-controlled loops: sentinel controlled, EOF controlled, EOLN controlled, and flag controlled. The common factor in all of these loops is that the termination condition depends on some event occurring during execution of the loop body.

Sentinel-Controlled Loops Loops are often used to read in and process long lists of data. Each time the loop body is executed, a new piece of data is read and then processed. There is a problem with this process, however: How does the program decide when to stop the read-process cycle and exit the loop?

One common solution to this problem involves the use of a special data value called a *sentinel* value. This value, which the program must watch for, is a signal that there is no more data to be processed. In other words, the reading of the sentinel value is the event controlling the looping process. The process continues as long as the data value read is *not* the sentinel. The loop is exited when the sentinel is recognized.

A sentinel value must be chosen with care. It cannot be a normal data value. A sentinel value must be something that could never be an actual data value. For example, if a program reads calendar dates, we could use February 31 as a sentinel value. Such a loop might take the following form:

```
WHILE NOT ((Month = 2) AND (Day = 31)) DO
   BEGIN
            .                            (* Get a date *)
            .                            (* Process it *)
   END
```

There is a problem in this loop. Look closely at the termination condition. What are the values of Month and Day prior to the first pass through the loop? They are undefined. Somehow we must give initial values to these variables. We could always assign some arbitrary values to them, but then there is the danger that the arbitrary values could accidentally be processed. Also, it is inefficient to initialize variables with values that are never supposed to be used.

The Priming Read with Sentinel-Controlled Loops   The solution to this problem is to read the first set of data values *before* entering the loop. This will initialize the variables with real data values prior to the loop-termination test. Such a Read is called a *priming Read* because the idea is similar to that of priming a pump by pouring in a bucket of water when the pump is first started. Let's add the priming Read to the loop and see how it looks:

```
(* Get a date *)
WHILE NOT ((Month = 2) AND (Day = 31)) DO
   BEGIN
            .                            (* Get a date *)
            .                            (* Process it *)
   END
```

There is still a problem here. Notice that the first thing done inside of the loop is to get a date. Presumably values will be read for Month and Day, but that will cause the initial values for Month and Day to be overwritten. Thus the first date in the data list will never be processed.

What we really want to do when we enter the loop is to immediately process the data that we've already read into Month and Day. So, we need to do the processing first. But then where in the loop do we get the next data set to be processed from the data list? We do this *last*. Just before the end of the loop body, where the computer would go back up to the top of the loop and check the termination condition, we read the next data set. Thus the termination test can be applied to the next data set before it gets processed. Let's see how this would look:

```
Writeln('Enter month and day: ');
Read(Month, Day);
  WHILE NOT ((Month = 2) AND (Day = 31)) DO
    BEGIN
                              (* Process the date *)
        .
        .
        Writeln('Enter month and day: ');
        Read(Month, Day)
    END
```

This segment will work just fine. The first data set is read in, and if it is not the sentinel, it gets processed. At the end of the loop, the next data set is read in. Then we go back to the top of the loop, and if the new data set is not the sentinel, it gets processed just like the first one did. When the sentinel value is read, the WHILE expression becomes False, and execution continues with the statement immediately following the loop. Therefore the sentinel is not processed.

A few last thoughts about sentinel values. Many times the problem will dictate which value can be a sentinel. For example, if the problem does not allow data values of zero, then the sentinel value should be zero. Sometimes there will be no single value that is invalid, but rather a combination of values that is invalid. The combination of February and 31, as a day of the month, is one such example. Sometimes a range of values will be the sentinel (negative numbers, for example). Sometimes there will not be any data values that are invalid for a problem. In that case you may have to require that the data set for each loop iteration contain an extra value whose only purpose is to signal whether or not any more data follows. For example, in the following data set, the second value on each line is used to indicate whether or not there is additional data. If the value is 0, there is no more data, and if it is 1, another line of data follows.

Data values	Sentinel values
10	1
0	1
−5	1
8	1
−1	1
47	0

What happens if you forget to enter the sentinel value? If the input to the program is being entered interactively from a terminal, the loop will simply be executed again, causing another prompt for input. At that point, you will be able to enter the sentinel value. If the input to the program is from a file or cards (batch data entry), there isn't an opportunity to add the sentinel value while the program is running. When the data has all been read from the file, the loop will execute one more time and try to read another value from the file. Since there isn't any data left on the file, the program will halt and an error message will be printed by the system.

When the last data set has been read from a file, we say that the computer has reached the end of the file (abbreviated EOF). Thus, if you forget to include the sentinel value as the last piece of data in a file, you may get an error message something like "TRIED TO READ PAST EOF." In the next section you will see that Pascal provides a way to use EOF as a sentinel value.

EOF Loops EOF is a built-in Boolean function provided in Pascal to determine whether the last data value has been read. EOF becomes True when the next character to be read is the special end-of-file character ⟨eof⟩. It follows the last end-of-line ⟨eoln⟩ character. (See Chapter 3.) You do not have to worry about putting the ⟨eof⟩ character after your data. The system does it automatically.

Example data file   ⟨value⟩⟨value⟩⟨value⟩...⟨eoln⟩
⟨value⟩⟨value⟩⟨value⟩...⟨eoln⟩
⟨value⟩⟨value⟩⟨value⟩...⟨eoln⟩
⟨value⟩⟨value⟩⟨value⟩...⟨eoln⟩
⟨eof⟩

We use the EOF function to control loops where data will be read in but we do not know in advance how many sets of data values there will be. An example of the code for such a loop follows.

```
WHILE NOT EOF DO
    BEGIN
        Readln(Value1, Value2, Value3, ...);
          .
          .
          .
    END
```

(Notice that since EOF is True if there is no more data, you must use NOT EOF to control your loop.)

The Readln leaves the marker ready to read the character at the beginning of each new line. When the data has all been read in, the next character will be the ⟨eof⟩ character.

In order to use a Readln we must know how our data is organized on each line. There are times when this is not the case and a Read statement must be used. But look what happens if we simply replace the Readln with a Read:

```
WHILE NOT EOF DO
    BEGIN
        Read(Value);
          .
          .
          .
    END
```

Sample data   24 36 37⟨eoln⟩
⟨eof⟩

Operation	Value	Marker position after indicated operation
Before loop	Value = ?	▮24 36 37⟨eoln⟩ ⟨eof⟩
After first pass through the loop	Value = 24	24▮36 37⟨eoln⟩ ⟨eof⟩
After second pass through the loop	Value = 36	24 36▮37⟨eoln⟩ ⟨eof⟩
After third pass through the loop	Value = 37	24 36 37▮⟨eoln⟩ ⟨eof⟩

Notice that the input marker is left on the ⟨eoln⟩. EOF will return False because the file is not empty (the ⟨eoln⟩ character is still to be read). The loop is executed again. Since there is no more data, an error message such as "TRIED TO READ PAST EOF" will result. Note the subtle difference between a file that is empty and a file that is simply out of data. Unless the marker is on the ⟨eof⟩ character, a file is not truly empty. (The ⟨eoln⟩ can still be read as a blank.)

There are several ways to get around this problem. Since it is caused by using Read with numeric data, the simplest way is to avoid using the combination of Read with numeric data and EOF-controlled loops: Readln can be used instead. If you must use Read with numeric data, use a sentinel-controlled loop instead of an EOF-controlled loop. If you can't use either of these alternatives, then you will have to write your program to read all of the data as characters and convert them into numeric values. Believe it or not, you will be able to do this by the time you read Chapter 15.

EOLN Loops   EOLN is a Boolean function provided in Pascal to determine if the last character in a line of input has been read. EOLN becomes True when the next character to be read is the ⟨eoln⟩ character. This function is used to control a loop that will process character data.

The following EOLN loop will read and print all of the characters on a line:

```
WHILE NOT EOLN DO
   BEGIN
      Read(Character);
      Write(Character)
   END
```

This loop will continue until the next character to be read is the ⟨eoln⟩ character. At that time EOLN will become True, NOT EOLN will become False, and the loop will not be executed. Since characters are always read one at a time, a priming Read is not necessary. In fact, if you used a priming Read, the last character of input data would not get processed. After the last character was read, EOLN would become True, and the body of the loop would not be executed to process that last character.

EOF and EOLN may also be used with files other than Input. If a file has previously been set to read mode with the Reset procedure, you can test for EOF or EOLN on that file by specifying the name of the file as a parameter:

```
EOF (Filename)
EOLN (Filename)
```

In all of our discussions of ⟨eof⟩ and ⟨eoln⟩ we have talked about them as if they were explicit characters. This is not true in some systems. However, whatever technique a system uses to separate lines (cards) and files, the functions EOF and EOLN operate as described.

Flag-Controlled Loops   A *flag* is a Boolean variable that is used to control the logical flow of a program. We can set a Boolean variable to True before a WHILE, and then when we wish to stop executing the loop we set it to False. That is, a Boolean variable is used to record whether or not the event that controls the process has occurred. For example, the following segment of code would cause the reading and summing of values to continue until the data contained a negative value. (The variables in the code segment are all of type Integer, except Positive, which is the Boolean flag variable.)

```
Sum : = 0;
Positive : = True;                      (* Initialize flag *)
WHILE Positive DO
  BEGIN
    Read(Number);
    IF Number < 0                       (* Test input value *)
      THEN
        Positive : = False      (* Set flag if event occurred *)
      ELSE
        Sum : = Sum + Number
  END
```

Note that sentinel-controlled loops can be coded with flags. In fact, the above code is using a negative value as a sentinel.

We are not limited to initializing flags to True. We can also initialize them to False. We must then use the NOT operation in the WHILE expression, and set the flag to True when the event occurs. Compare the preceding code segment with the one that follows (both segments perform the same task).

```
Sum : = 0;
Negative : = False;                     (* Initialize flag *)
WHILE NOT Negative DO
  BEGIN
    Read(Number);
    IF Number < 0                       (* Test input value *)
      THEN
        Negative : = True       (* Set flag if event occurred *)
      ELSE
        Sum : = Sum + Number
  END
```

As a last example, let's look at the looping structure in Program Payroll in Chapter 1. This is a sentinel-controlled loop in which a zero employee number (EmpNum) is used to stop the reading and processing cycle. It could have been coded using a flag as follows. (MoreData is a Boolean variable; the other variables are of type Integer.)

```
Readln(EmpNum);
MoreData := EmpNum <> 0;        (* MoreData is True if EmpNum <> 0 *)
WHILE MoreData DO
   BEGIN
      .

      .
      Readln(EmpNum);           (* Get the next employee number *)
      MoreData := EmpNum <> 0   (* And update the flag accordingly *)
   END
   .

   .
```

Looping Subtasks

So far we have looked primarily at ways to use loops to affect the flow of control in our programs. But looping by itself does nothing. The loop body must perform a task in order for the loop to be useful. In this section we'll look at some subtasks that are frequently used in loops.

Counting Loops   The loop in the following example includes a counter variable; however, the loop is *not* a count-controlled loop. In a count-controlled loop a counter variable is used *and* the ending condition for the loop depends on the value of the counter. As the following example demonstrates, there are other uses for a counter besides just controlling execution of the loop.

A common subtask is to keep track of how many times a loop is executed, even though this count is not used to control execution of the loop. For example, the following program fragment reads, counts, and prints characters until a period is encountered. (Character is of type Char; Count is of type Integer.)

```
Count := 0;                        (* Initialize counter *)
Read(Character);                (* Read the first character *)
WHILE Character <> '.' DO
   BEGIN
      Write(Character);
      Count := Count + 1;          (* Increment counter *)
      Read(Character)           (* Get the next character *)
   END
```

The loop continues until a period character is read. At the termination of the loop, Count contains the number of characters written, one less than the number read. Note that if a period is the first character, nothing is printed and Count contains a zero—as it should. A priming Read is used because this loop is sentinel controlled. Even though it is reading single characters, it is not an EOLN-controlled loop.

The counter variable in the preceding example is called an *iteration counter* because its value is equal to the number of iterations through the loop.

Iteration Counter A counter variable that is incremented for each iteration of a loop.

Notice that according to our definition the control variable of a count-controlled loop can be thought of as an iteration counter. However, as we have just seen, not all iteration counters are loop control variables.

Summing Loops If you know how many data values you have (say 10) and want to sum them, the following code will work. Note that this loop is also count controlled.

```
Sum : = 0;                                  (* Initialize the sum *)
Count : = 1;                         (* Initialize the control variable *)
WHILE Count <= 10 DO
   BEGIN
      Read(Number);                         (* Input a value *)
      Sum : = Sum + Number;              (* Add the value to sum *)
      Count : = Count + 1           (* Increment control variable *)
   END
```

When this fragment has been executed, Sum will contain the sum of the 10 values read, Count will contain 11, and Number will contain the last number read.

In this example the loop control variable is being incremented by 1 each time through the loop. For each new value of Count, there is a new value for Number. Does this mean we can decrement Count by 1 and get the previous value of Number? No! Because Count is a counter being incremented by 1, its previous value is known. Once a new value has been read into Number, the previous value is gone forever unless we've saved it in another variable. We will see how to do this in the next section.

Let's look at another example. We want to count and sum the first 10 even numbers in a set of data. This problem looks quite a bit like the last one except that we need to test each number to see if it is even or odd. If it is odd, we do nothing. If it is even, we increment the counter and add the value to our sum. In the following code segment, all of the variables are of type Integer.

```
Count : = 1;                               (* Initialize the LCV *)
Sum : = 0;                                 (* Initialize sum *)
WHILE Count <= 10 DO
   BEGIN
      Read(Number);                        (* Get the next value *)
      IF (Number MOD 2) = 0           (* Test to see if value is even *)
         THEN
            BEGIN
               Count : = Count + 1;        (* Increment counter *)
               Sum : = Sum + Number        (* Add value to sum *)
            END
   END
```

In this example there is no relation between the value of the loop control variable and the number of times that the loop is executed. Count is only incremented when an even number is read. The counter in this example is called an *event counter* because it is incremented only when a certain event occurs. The counter in the previous example was an iteration counter because it was incremented during each iteration of the loop.

Event Counter A counter variable that is incremented each time a particular event occurs.

Keeping Track of a Previous Value Let's look at the case in which we want to count how many numbers there are in a set of Integer data and to print out that count and the last two data values. We will use a negative value as a sentinel.

Remembering the last two values involves remembering the current value and the previous one. When a value that is not the sentinel is read, the current value will become the previous value and the value just read will become the new current value. When the sentinel is read, reading will be finished. (Positive is a Boolean variable in the following code segment. The other variables are of type Integer.)

```
Positive := True;                              (* Initialize flag *)
Count := 1;                                  (* Initialize counter *)
Read(Current);                          (*Initialize current value *)
WHILE Positive DO
  BEGIN
    Read(Next);                                (* Get next value *)
    IF Next < 0                         (* Test for sentinel value *)
      THEN
        Positive := False         (* Set flag if sentinel was read *)
      ELSE
        BEGIN
          Count := Count + 1;              (* Increment counter *)
          Previous := Current;    (* Set next to last value read *)
          Current := Next              (* Set last value read *)
        END
  END;
Writeln(Count:1, ' values were read.');
Writeln('The last value read was ', Current:1);
Writeln('and the next to last was ', Previous:1)
```

Study this routine carefully. There will be many times when you will need to keep track of the last value read in addition to the current value. By the way, what will happen if there are no data values? Right; "TRIED TO READ PAST EOF". What will happen if there is only one data value in addition to the sentinel? Previous will be undefined.

HOW TO DESIGN LOOPS

It's one thing to understand how a loop works when you look at it and something else again to be able to design a loop that solves a given problem. In this section we will look at how to design loops.

Designing a loop is essentially a matter of determining what conditions must exist at the start of each pass through the loop in order for it to work correctly. The key feature of these conditions is that they are true at the start of every iteration of that loop. Because they are always true at the beginning of every iteration, the conditions are called the *loop invariant*. If we take the time to determine the loop invariant, the task of designing the loop can be greatly simplified.

Loop Invariant Those conditions that must exist at the start of each iteration of a particular loop in order for the loop to execute properly.

At first glance, you might think that the loop invariant is simply the condition in the WHILE statement that determines whether the loop body will be executed. Although this condition is certainly part of the loop invariant, it is not all of it. The conditions that make up the invariant must also take into consideration such things as the allowable ranges of particular variables, how counters and sums are updated, and so on.

Here is an example of an invariant condition: If a problem requires us to sum up the first 10 odd integers that are input, the variable that keeps the count of odd integers must start at 0 and can range upward to 10. If the counter goes outside this range, there is something wrong with the design of the loop.

Another invariant condition this problem requires is that the value in the counter be equal to the number of odd numbers that have been input. This may seem obvious, but consider its implications: The counter must be initialized to 0 (no odd numbers have been read at first) and must be incremented each time an odd number is input (*not* each time the loop is executed). Now we know that the algorithm for the loop must contain at least the following steps:

```
Initialize OddCount to 0
WHILE OddCount is less than or equal to 10
  BEGIN
      .
      .
      IF Number is odd,
          THEN increment OddCount
      .
      .
  END
```

We can then translate this algorithm into the following Pascal statements:

```
OddCount := 0;        (* Initialize *)
WHILE OddCount <= 10 DO
    BEGIN
        .
        .
        IF Odd(Number)
            THEN
                OddCount := OddCount + 1;
        .
        .
    END
```

Is this code segment sufficient for the loop to execute properly? Not quite; another condition that we must add to the invariant is that a new value must be available for input at the start of each iteration. If the input is to come from a terminal, a value will always be available for the asking. However, to ensure that it is a *new* value for each iteration, there must be a statement in the loop that will read one new value during each iteration. The required Read statement must be inserted prior to the IF statement, because the IF statement tests the new value. Here is the revised loop invariant:

1. The value of the counter can range from 0 to 10, inclusive.
2. The value of the counter must be equal to the number of odd numbers that have been input.
3. A new value must be available for input at the start of each iteration.

The revised algorithm is

```
Initialize OddCount to 0
WHILE OddCount is less than or equal to 10
    BEGIN
        Read Number
        IF Number is odd,
            THEN increment OddCount
    END
```

and the revised Pascal loop is as follows:

```
OddCount := 0;        (* Initialize *)
WHILE OddCount <= 10 DO
    BEGIN
        Read(Number);
        IF Odd(Number)
            THEN
                OddCount := OddCount + 1;
    END
```

This program fragment is sufficient to accomplish what the problem required. However, it is still not complete. To make this a well-written code segment, we should add a Writeln statement before the Read to prompt the user to enter a number.

Determining the Loop Invariant

As you can see, writing down the loop invariant is a good way to bring to light all of the things that must be done for a loop to work properly. Once the essential operations have been determined, we can go back and add nonessential operations that enhance the code or perform extra tasks.

How do we determine all of the conditions that make up the loop invariant? This isn't always easy to do, and even experienced programmers occasionally miss one or more of the invariant conditions when they design a loop. There is, however, a set of questions that will help us get started on the right track:

1. What is the condition that ends the loop?
2. How should the condition be initialized and updated?
3. What is the process being repeated?
4. How should the process be initialized and updated?

Designing a loop can be divided into two tasks: designing the control flow and designing the processing that takes place in the loop. The first two questions will help us to design the parts of the loop that control its execution. The last two questions will help us to design the processing that takes place within the loop body. Let's take a closer look at each of these design tasks and its corresponding pair of questions.

Designing the Flow of Control for a Loop

We will begin by looking at the ending condition for the loop. The most important issue in loop design is deciding what will make the loop stop. If the ending condition isn't well thought out, the potential exists for infinite loops and other bugs. So our first question when starting to design a loop should be

What is the condition that ends the loop?

Another way of putting this is "What condition must become *True* in order for the loop to *end?*" This question can usually be answered through a close examination of the problem statement. Here are some examples:

Key phrase in problem statement	Ending condition
"Sum the 365 daily temperatures"	The loop ends when a counter reaches 366 (count controlled)
"Process all the data on the file"	The loop ends when EOF is encountered during reading. (EOF loop)
"Until 10 odd integers have been read"	The loop ends when 10 odd numbers have been input. (event counter)
"The end of data is indicated by a negative test score"	The loop ends when a negative input value is encountered. (sentinel controlled)

Once we have determined the ending condition for the loop, we can write the part of the invariant that will become the condition in the WHILE statement. Essentially, the invariant is just the opposite of the ending condition. This is because the condition in the WHILE statement must become *False* in order for the loop to *end*. We write the corresponding condition in the invariant to express the fact that it must be *True* in order for the loop to be *executed*.

Examples   TempCount must be less than or equal to 365.

EOF must be false at the start of an iteration.

OddCount must be less than or equal to 10.

TestScore must not equal the sentinel value.

You can see that these examples are the exact opposites of the ending conditions. All of the invariant conditions are statements about what must be *True* at the start of an iteration in order for the iteration to be executed correctly.

Just determining the proper ending condition isn't enough to ensure that the loop ends—or that it even gets executed. We must also include statements that make sure the loop gets started correctly and that cause the loop to reach the ending condition. The next question to ask is

How should the condition be initialized and updated?

The answer to this question depends on the type of ending condition. Let's look at some examples.

Sentinel-Controlled   A priming Read may be the only initialization required in a sentinel-controlled loop. If the source of input is a file other than Input or Output, a Reset may also be required to prepare the file for reading. To update the condition, a new value is read at the end of each iteration. For example,

A new value must be input for processing prior to the start of each iteration. (This implies a priming Read before the first iteration, and an update Read at the end of each iteration.)

The file must be prepared for input (Reset).

EOF- or EOLN-Controlled   There will not usually be any initialization required with EOF- and EOLN-controlled loops (except to Reset a file other than Input). The status of the EOF and EOLN functions is updated every time a value is input. If the loop doesn't read any data, however, it will never reach EOF or EOLN, so the loop invariant must include a condition that requires the loop to keep reading data. For example,

At the start of each iteration the input marker must have been previously positioned on a new value. (This implies that a value must be available for input at the start of the first iteration.)

Iteration Counter and Event Counter   The counter variable must be given an initial value. In a count-controlled loop this initial value will usually be 1. If the counter variable is counting events within the loop, it will usually be initialized to 0. If the process requires the counter to run through a specific range of values, the initial value will be the lowest value in that range.

The update operation in a counting loop requires that the value of the counter be increased by 1 for each iteration or event. (Occasionally you will encounter a problem that requires a counter to count from some value *down* to a lower value. In this case the initial value will be the greater value, and the counter will be decremented by 1 for each iteration or event.) Example invariant conditions:

TempCount must be equal to the number of the iteration that is about to be executed. (Implies initialization to 1, and incrementation by 1 for each iteration.)

OddCount must be equal to the number of odd integers that have been input. (Implies initialization to 0, and incrementation by 1 each time an odd integer is input.)

Flag-Controlled The Boolean flag variable must be initialized to True or False, as appropriate. Example invariant conditions:

Found must be equal to False at the start of each iteration.

Positive must be equal to True at the start of each iteration.

The update operation is somewhat different in a flag-controlled loop than in the other loops. The flag variable essentially remains unchanged until it is time for the loop to end. Some condition within the process being repeated will be detected and cause an assignment statement to change the value of the flag. Since the update depends on the process, we have to design the process before we can design the update operation for a flag-controlled loop.

Designing the Process Within the Loop

Once the looping structure itself has been determined, the details of the process can be filled in. The definition of the problem may require the process to sum up data values or to keep a count of data values that satisfy some test. Summing and counting are operations we've seen in the examples.

In designing the process we must first decide what has to be accomplished by a single iteration. We ignore the loop, assuming for a moment that the process is only going to execute once. What tasks must the process perform? In other words,

What is the process being repeated?

To answer this question, we must take another look at the problem statement; for example,

Count the number of integers on file HowMany.

This statement tells us that the process to be repeated is a counting operation. Here's another example:

Read a stock price for each business day in a week, and compute the average price.

We can immediately tell that in this case part of the process involves reading a data value. We have to conclude from our knowledge of how an average is computed that the process will also involve summing the data values.

Reading, counting, and summing are operations that are frequently used in looping processes. Another common loop process involves reading data, performing a calculation, and writing out the result. There are many other operations that can appear in looping processes—those mentioned here are only the simplest examples. We'll look at some other processes later on.

After we have determined the basic operations to be performed, we can then design the parts of the process that are necessitated by the loop. When a process is placed in a loop body, we often have to add some steps to take into account the fact that it will execute more than once. This part of the design typically involves initializing certain variables before the loop is entered and then reinitializing or updating variables prior to each subsequent pass through the loop. Thus we must ask,

How should the process be initialized and updated?

How this is done will depend on what kind of process is involved. If the process is a summing operation, it involves initializing to 0 and updating by adding data values to the sum. This can be expressed by an invariant of the form

> At the start of each iteration, Sum must be equal to the total of all StockPrice values that have been input.

This condition implies that before any StockPrice values have been input, Sum is equal to 0.

A similar sort of invariant can be used to describe event-counting operations:

> At the start of each iteration, Count must be equal to the number of events that have occurred.

Sometimes the process within a loop will require several different sums and counts to be performed. Each of these will have its own invariant condition, which simply means that you will have more statements to initialize variables, more statements to add up sums, and more statements to increment counting variables. Just deal with each summing or counting operation by itself: First write the invariant for the specific operation; then you can write the initialization statement, followed by the summing or incrementing statement. When you've done this for a particular summing or counting operation, you can go on to the next one.

Problem Solving in Action

Problem: File Income contains a set of income amounts. Each amount is preceded by the letter 'F' for female or the letter 'M' for male. Compute the average income for females and the average income for males.

Discussion: This problem decomposes into three main steps. First we must go through the data, counting and summing separately for each sex. Then we can compute the averages. Finally, we print the results.

The first step is the most difficult by far. It will involve a loop with several subtasks. We'll use our four questions to develop these in detail.

What is the ending condition for the loop? The ending condition is EOF on file

PSIA

Income, so the loop invariant is

EOF on file Income must be false at the start of each iteration.

which results in the WHILE statement

WHILE NOT EOF on file Income, DO

How should the ending condition be initialized and updated?

The file must be prepared for reading.

A new sex and amount must be available for input at the start of each iteration.

The resulting algorithm is

```
Prepare file Income for reading
WHILE NOT EOF on file Income, DO
    Readln Sex and Amount from Income
    .
    .      ( Process being repeated )
```

What is the process being repeated? From our knowledge of how to compute an average, we know that we have to count the number of amounts and divide this number into the sum of the amounts. Because we have to do this for both males and females, the process consists of four parts: counting the females and summing their income and counting the males and summing their income. We will develop each of these in turn.

How must the process be initialized and updated?

At the start of each iteration, FemaleCount must be equal to the number of females that have been found in the input.

At the start of each iteration, FemaleSum must be equal to the total of all female income amounts that have been found in the input.

The revised algorithm is

```
Initialize FemaleCount to 0
Initialize FemaleSum to 0
Prepare file Income for reading
WHILE NOT EOF on file Income, DO
    Readln Sex and Amount from Income
    IF Sex is Female
        THEN
            Increment FemaleCount
            Add Amount to FemaleSum
```

The other part of the process (counting males and summing their income) adds the following conditions to the invariant:

PSIA ▰▰▰▰▰▰

> At the start of each iteration, MaleCount must be equal to the number of males (nonfemales) that have been found in the input.

> At the start of each iteration, MaleSum must be equal to the total of all male (nonfemale) income amounts that have been found in the input.

These conditions can be met by adding an ELSE to the IF statement in the process. Now we have enough information to write the entire algorithm.

Input: A file, Income, of income amounts, with one amount per line. Each amount is preceded by a letter (either F for female or M for male). The letter is the first character on each input line and is followed by a blank, which separates the letter from the amount.

Output: The number of females and their average income, and the number of males and their average income.

Assumptions: There is at least one male and one female among all of the data sets. The only gender codes on the file are 'M' and 'F'—any other codes will be counted as 'M'.

MAIN   Level 0

```
Separately Count Females and Males and Sum Incomes
Compute Average Incomes
Output Results
```

SEPARATELY COUNT FEMALES AND MALES AND SUM INCOMES   Level 1

```
Initialize Ending Condition
Initialize Process
WHILE NOT EOF on file Income, DO
    Update Ending Condition
    Update Process
```

COMPUTE AVERAGE INCOMES

```
Set FemaleAverage to FemaleSum / FemaleCount
Set MaleAverage to MaleSum / MaleCount
```

OUTPUT RESULTS

```
Write FemaleCount and FemaleAverage
Write MaleCount and MaleAverage
```

PSIA

INITIALIZE END CONDITION   Level 2

```
Reset Income
```

INITIALIZE PROCESS

```
Initialize FemaleCount to 0
Initialize FemaleSum to 0
Initialize MaleCount to 0
Initialize MaleSum to 0
```

UPDATE END CONDITION

```
Readln Sex and Amount from Income
```

UPDATE PROCESS

```
IF Sex is Female
   THEN
      Increment FemaleCount
      Add Amount to FemaleSum
   ELSE
      Increment MaleCount
      Add Amount to MaleSum
```

Module Structure Chart:

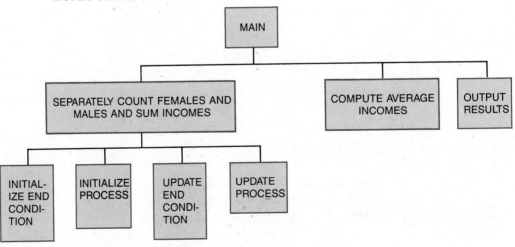

PSIA ▰▰▰▰▰

Now we can write the program:

```
PROGRAM Incomes (Income, Output);

(* This program reads a file of income amounts that are classified by
   sex, and computes the average income for each sex *)

VAR
   Income:            (* File of income amounts          *)
     Text;
   Sex:               (* Coded 'F' = female, 'M' = male  *)
     Char;
   FemaleCount,       (* Number of female income amounts *)
   MaleCount:         (* Number of male income amounts   *)
     Integer;
   Amount,            (* Amount of income for a person   *)
   FemaleSum,         (* Total of female income amounts  *)
   MaleSum,           (* Total of male income amounts    *)
   FemaleAverage,     (* Average female income           *)
   MaleAverage:       (* Average male income             *)
     Real;

BEGIN (* Incomes *)
   (* Separately count females and males and sum incomes *)
   (* Initialize ending condition *)
   Reset(Income);                                  (* Prepare file for reading *)
   (* Initialize process *)
   FemaleCount := 0;                               (* Initialize FemaleCount *)
   FemaleSum := 0.0;                               (* Initialize FemaleSum *)
   MaleCount := 0;                                 (* Initialize MaleCount *)
   MaleSum := 0.0;                                 (* Initialize MaleSum *)
   WHILE NOT EOF(Income) DO
     BEGIN
       (* Update ending condition *)
       Readln(Income, Sex, Amount);               (* Get next Amount *)
       (* Update process *)
       IF Sex = 'F'
         THEN
           BEGIN
             FemaleCount := FemaleCount + 1; (* Increment Female Count *)
             FemaleSum := FemaleSum + Amount    (* Sum Female Amount *)
           END
         ELSE
           BEGIN
             MaleCount := MaleCount + 1;        (* Increment Male Count *)
             MaleSum := MaleSum + Amount        (* Sum Male Amount *)
           END
     END;
```

PSIA

```
(* Compute average incomes *)
FemaleAverage : = FemaleSum / FemaleCount;
MaleAverage : = MaleSum / MaleCount;
(* Output results *)
Writeln('For ', FemaleCount:1, ' females, the average income is ',
        FemaleAverage:9:2);
Writeln('For ', MaleCount:1, ' males, the average income is ',
        MaleAverage:9:2)
END.   (* Incomes *)
```

Testing: With an EOF-controlled loop, the obvious test cases are a file with data and an empty file. We should also look carefully to see if there is a case that could cause the computer to read all of the data without reaching the ⟨eof⟩ mark.

We should test input values of both 'F' and 'M' for the sex. We should also try some other values. (In this case, any value other than 'F' will be treated as an 'M'.)

When a loop includes counting or summing subtasks, it is important to test some typical data (so we can compare the results with our hand-calculated values) and some atypical data (to see how the process behaves). An atypical data set for testing a counting operation is an empty file, which should result in a count of 0. Any other result for the count indicates an error. For a summing operation, atypical data might include negative or zero values.

Program Incomes is not designed to handle either empty files or negative income values. An empty file will cause both FemaleCount and MaleCount to equal 0 at the end of the loop. Although this is correct, the statements that compute average income will then cause the program to crash because they will be dividing by 0. A negative income is simply treated like any other value, even though it is probably an error. To correct these problems we should insert IF-THEN-ELSE statements to test for the error conditions at the appropriate points in the program. When an error is detected, the program should print an error message instead of carrying out the usual computation. This prevents a crash and permits the program to keep running.

A program that can recover from erroneous inputs and keep running is said to be *robust.*

We've postponed our discussion of loop invariants for flag-controlled loops because the ending-condition invariants and the process invariants for these loops are often related. Now that we've covered both of these kinds of invariant conditions, we are ready to go back and consider the design of flag-controlled loops. Let's do this in the context of another sample problem.

(145)	150.4
Pm	Sm
61	62
237.0482	(244)
Np	Pu
93	94

Problem Solving in Action

Problem: The radioactive isotope plutonium-235 has a half life of 26 minutes. The half-life is the time that it takes for half of the isotope to decay. Thus, after 26 minutes only half of the isotope will be left. After another 26 minutes, only half of this half, or one-quarter of the original amount, will be left. Your job is to write a program that will determine how long (to the nearest half-life time) it takes plutonium-235 to decay

PSIA ▬▬▬▬

to the point at which only a specified percentage is left. The percentage is a real value input by the user.

Discussion: The way to do this problem by hand is to start with 100 percent (representing the full amount of pure plutonium-235) and repeatedly divide this number by 2 until it is less than the specified percentage. The number of times that you divide by 2 is the number of half-life times required for the isotope to decay to that percentage. If you multiply the number of half-life times by 26 (the time for one half-life), you will get the total time required for the decay to occur.

Our solution to this problem is called a *simulation.* We are designing an algorithm that models the behavior of physical materials and processes. Simulation is one of the most valuable computer applications. Through simulation we can carry out experiments that would be too expensive (or dangerous) to perform with real materials.

We can easily break this problem into three parts: Get Data, Division Loop, and Print Results. Both the Input and Output sections will be quite simple.

For the loop we will use a flag-controlled loop that will execute until the remaining percentage is less than the specified remaining percentage.

What is the ending condition for the loop? The loop will execute until the control flag becomes true. We can restate this as an invariant:

At the start of each iteration, flag SmallEnough must be False.

How should the ending condition be initialized and updated? The invariant for the ending condition implies that flag SmallEnough should be initialized to False. In order to determine how the flag should be updated, we must first look at the process being repeated.

What is the process being repeated? The number of half-life times is incremented for each iteration of the loop. The percentage of plutonium remaining is divided by 2 for each iteration of the loop. The resulting percentage is compared against the value input by the user. If the remaining percentage is less than or equal to the input value, flag SmallEnough should be set to True. We can now write the invariant for updating the control flag:

Flag SmallEnough must be False only if the percentage of plutonium-235 remaining (the value in Pu235Left) is greater than the specified amount (the value in Percentage).

Notice that this invariant changes the interpretation of how the loop control flag should be initialized. Rather than simply initialize the flag to False, we must check first to be sure that the value input by the user (the specified percentage) isn't greater than or equal to 100. If it is, then the flag should be initialized to True; otherwise, it can be set to False.

How should the process be initialized and updated? The invariant for this consists of two conditions:

The number of half-life times (HalfLives) must equal the number of loop iterations at the start of each iteration. (Implies initialization to 0 and incrementation by 1.)

The value of Pu235Left must be equal to 100 percent divided by 2, HalfLives times. (Implies initialization to 100, and division by 2 on each iteration.)

PSIA ▰▰▰▰▰

Input: A real number, representing the percentage of plutonium-235 that is to remain.

Output:
    The time required for the isotope to decay to the specified percentage
    The number of half-life times
    The percentage remaining

Assumptions: None.

MAIN MODULE   Level 0

```
Get Data
Division Loop
Print Results
```

GET DATA   Level 1

```
Writeln 'What is the desired remaining percentage?'
Readln Percentage
```

DIVISION LOOP

```
Initialize Process
Initialize Ending Condition
WHILE NOT SmallEnough DO
    Update Process
    Update Ending Condition
```

PRINT RESULTS

```
Set DecayTime to HLTime * HalfLives
Writeln 'After ', DecayTime:1, ' minutes, plutonium-235 ',
  'has passed through '
Writeln HalfLives:1, ' half-life times.'
Writeln 'The percentage remaining is then ', Pu235Left:8:4,
  '%, which is less than'
Writeln 'or equal to the specified value of ',
  Percent:8:4, '%.'
```

INITIALIZE PROCESS   Level 2

```
Set Pu235Left to 100
Set HalfLives to 0
```

PSIA

INITIALIZE ENDING CONDITION

```
IF Percentage >= Pu235Left
    THEN
        Set SmallEnough to True
    ELSE
        Set SmallEnough to False
```

UPDATE PROCESS

```
Set Pu235Left to Pu235Left / 2.0
Increment HalfLives
```

UPDATE ENDING CONDITION

```
IF Pu235Left < = Percentage
    THEN
        Set SmallEnough to True
```

Module Structure Chart:

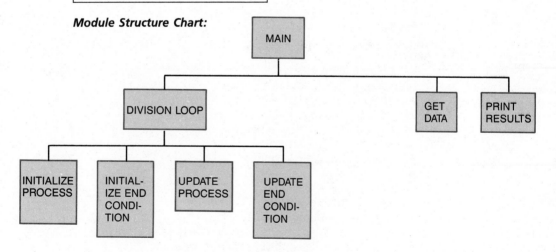

We can now write the program:

```
PROGRAM HalfLife (Input, Output);

(* This program determines the time required for plutonium-235
   to decay below a specified percentage *)

CONST
  HLTime = 26;        (* Half-life time for Pu-235 in minutes   *)
```

PSIA ▬▬▬▬▬

```
VAR
  HalfLives,            (* Number of half-life periods          *)
  DecayTime:            (* Time for decay to specified percentage *)
    Integer;
  Percentage,           (* Percentage specified by user          *)
  Pu235Left:            (* Percentage Pu-235 left after decay    *)
    Real;
  SmallEnough:          (* Loop control flag                     *)
    Boolean;

BEGIN (* HalfLife *)
  (* Get data *)
  Writeln('What is the desired remaining percentage?');
  Readln(Percentage);
  (* Division loop *)
  (* Initialize process *)
  Pu235Left := 100;              (* Initialize Pu-235 percentage *)
  HalfLives := 0;                       (* Initialize HalfLives *)
  (* Initialize ending condition *)
  IF Percentage >= Pu235Left
    THEN
      SmallEnough := True
    ELSE
      SmallEnough := False;
  WHILE NOT SmallEnough DO
    BEGIN
      (* Update process *)
      Pu235Left := Pu235Left / 2.0;
      HalfLives := HalfLives + 1;
      (* Update ending condition *)
      IF Pu235Left <= Percentage
        THEN
          SmallEnough := True
    END;
  (* Print results *)
  DecayTime := HLTime * HalfLives;
  Writeln('After ',DecayTime:1,
          ' minutes, plutonium-235 has passed through ');
  Writeln(HalfLives:1, ' half-life times.');
  Writeln('The percentage remaining is then ', Pu235Left:8:4,
          '%, which is less than');
  Writeln('or equal to the specified value of ', Percentage:8:4, '%.')
END.  (* HalfLife *)
```

Testing: The valid range of values for percentages is 0 through 100. Therefore we should test Program HalfLife on data values for the extremes of this range (0 and 100), some out-of-range values (negative and greater than 100), and some typical values.

PSIA

Notice that there are three decision points in the code. An alternative approach to testing Program HalfLife is to try the cases where percentage is less than, equal to, and greater than 100. We should also check cases where SmallEnough is initially True and initially False. And we should try to find cases that cause the flag to be set to False after one pass through the loop, several passes, or not at all (infinite loop).

Program HalfLife does not check for negative input values. Furthermore, an input percentage of zero will cause the loop to execute infinitely. To make this program more robust, an error-checking IF-THEN-ELSE statement should be added to prevent trying to process negative and zero values.

The following is another sample problem in loop design. In this case we will design a count-controlled loop that finds the minimum and maximum values in a data set.

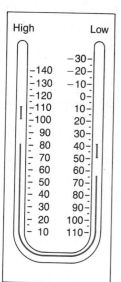

Problem Solving in Action

Problem: Take hourly outdoor temperature readings for one 24-hour period. Find the day's high and low temperatures from this data.

Discussion: This is easy to do by hand. We simply scan the list, looking for the highest and lowest values. How can we simulate this process in an algorithm? Well, let's look a little more carefully at what we are actually doing.

To find the largest number in a list of numbers, we compare the first number with the second and remember which one is larger. This number is then compared with the third one. The larger number is again remembered and compared with the fourth. This process continues until we run out of numbers on our list. The one we remember is the largest.

We use the same process to find the smallest number, only we remember the smaller number instead of the larger one. Now that we understand the process in detail, we can design an algorithm for it.

What is the ending condition? How should it be initialized and updated? Because there will be exactly 24 values on the list, we can use a counter to control the loop. Here are the invariant conditions:

At the start of each iteration, Hour must be greater than or equal to 1 and less than or equal to 24.

At the start of each iteration, Hour must be equal to the number of iterations that have been executed.

What is the process being repeated? How should it be initialized and updated? The process reads a value, echo prints it, and checks to see if it should replace the current high or low value. The real problem is how to initialize the process. What values should the first number be compared to? The variables High and Low must be given starting values, and we must be able to change these starting values immedi-

PSIA

ately. So we will set High to the lowest negative number possible (−MaxInt), and we will set Low to the highest positive number possible (MaxInt). Therefore the first temperature read in will be lower than Low and higher than High and will replace the values in each. The invariant condition that guarantees this is

> Before any values have been input, High must be equal to the lowest integer possible, and Low must be equal to the highest integer possible.

The following invariant conditions ensure that the process is updated correctly:

> Prior to the start of each iteration, the input marker must have advanced to a new temperature value.

> At the start of each iteration, High must be equal to the highest temperature value that has been input.

> At the start of each iteration, Low must be equal to the lowest temperature value that has been input.

Input: 24 Integer numbers representing hourly temperatures.

Output:

> The temperatures (echo print)
> The day's high temperature
> The day's low temperature

Assumptions: At least 24 Integer numbers will be input before EOF is reached. None of the data values is equal to MaxInt or −MaxInt.

MAIN MODULE   Level 0

```
Initialize Process
Initialize Loop Ending Condition
WHILE Hours <= NumHrs DO
    Update Process
    Update Loop Ending Condition
Print
```

INITIALIZE PROCESS   Level 1

```
Set High to Lowest Integer
Set Low to Highest Integer
```

INITIALIZE LOOP ENDING CONDITION

```
Initialize Hour to 1
```

PSIA ▬▬▬▬

UPDATE PROCESS

```
Get Temp
Echo Print Temp
Smallest So Far?
Largest So Far?
```

UPDATE LOOP ENDING CONDITION

```
Increment Hour
```

PRINT

```
Writeln 'High temperature is ', High
Writeln 'Low temperature is ', Low
```

SMALLEST SO FAR?   Level 2

```
IF Temp < Low
    THEN Set Low to Temp
```

LARGEST SO FAR?

```
IF Temp > High
    THEN Set High to Temp
```

Module Structure Chart:

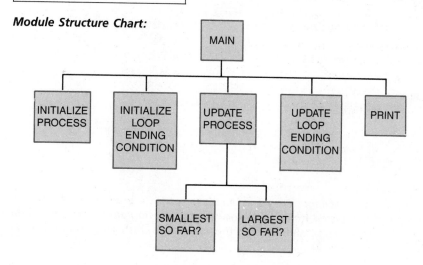

PSIA ▬▬▬▬▬

```
PROGRAM TempStat (Input, Output);

(* This program calculates the high and low temperature
   from 24 hourly temperature readings *)

CONST
   NumHrs = 24;          (* Number of hours in time period        *)

VAR
   Temp,                 (* An hourly temperature reading         *)
   High,                 (* Highest temperature seen so far       *)
   Low,                  (* Lowest  temperature seen so far       *)
   Hour:                 (* Loop control variable for hours in a day *)
      Integer;

BEGIN (* TempStat *)
   (* Initialize process *)
   High := -MaxInt;          (* Initialize High to impossibly low value  *)
   Low  :=  MaxInt;          (* Initialize Low to impossibly high value *)
   (* Initialize loop ending condition *)
   Hour := 1;
   WHILE Hour <= NumHrs DO
      BEGIN
         (* Update process *)
         Read(Temp);                (* Get an hourly temperature *)
         Writeln(Temp:6);           (* Echo print the input value *)
         (* Smallest so far? *)
         IF Temp < Low
            THEN
               Low := Temp;
         (* Largest so far? *)
         IF Temp > High
            THEN
               High := Temp;
         (* Update loop ending condition *)
         Hour := Hour + 1
      END;
   (* Print *)
   Writeln;
   Writeln('High temperature is ', High:1);
   Writeln('Low temperature is ', Low:1)
END.   (* TempStat *)
```

Testing: Program TempStat reads 24 integer values. The WHILE statement can be tested for correct execution by entering data sets with 23 and 24 values in them. The first set should cause the program to crash. If the program doesn't crash, there must be

PSIA

an error in the loop that is causing too few values to be read. If the program encounters EOF and crashes on the set with 24 values, we know that it's trying to read too many values.

We should try data sets that present the high and low temperatures in different orders. For example, we should try one set with the lowest temperature as the first value, and another set with it as the last value. We should do the same for the highest temperature. We should also try a data set where the temperature goes up and down several times, and another where the temperatures are all the same. Finally, we should test the program on some typical sets of data and check the output with results we've determined by hand. For example, given the data

```
45  47  47  47  50  50  55  60  70  70  72  75
75  75  75  74  74  73  70  70  69  67  65  50
```

the output would look like this:

```
45
47
47
47
50
50
55
60
70
70
72
75
75
75
75
74
74
73
70
70
69
67
65
50

High temperature is 75
Low  temperature is 45
```

What would happen if we made the two IF-THEN statements into one IF-THEN-ELSE statement, as shown below?

```
IF Temp < Low
    THEN
        Low : = Temp
    ELSE
        IF Temp > High
            THEN
                High : = Temp
```

At first glance the single statement looks more efficient. Why should you ask if Temp is larger than High if you know it is lower than Low? Logically we shouldn't have to; however, because of the way High and Low are initialized, if we didn't we would get the wrong answer if the highest temperature was the first value read in.

In this chapter's Preprogramming Exercises you will be asked to redo Program TempStat using another initialization scheme that removes this data-dependent bug. (Hint: Use a priming Read and set High and Low to that first value.)

NESTED LOGIC

Chapter 4 described nested IF statements. Both the WHILE and IF statements contain statements and are themselves statements. So the body of a WHILE statement or the branch of an IF statement can contain other WHILE and/or IF statements. Remember that any statement can be replaced with a compound statement. This nesting can be extended to create complex control structures.

Of course, if control structures become too complex, a program will be difficult to understand, debug, and maintain. In the next chapter we will look at a way of keeping this kind of complexity under control.

How could we extend the previous algorithm to calculate daily temperature statistics for a year? We'd simply put a count-controlled loop around the body of Program TempStat.

```
WHILE more days DO
    WHILE more data DO
        Get Temp
        Smallest so far?
        Largest so far?
    Print
```

The two loops would be coded as follows. Note that we are assuming it is not a leap year!

```
Day := 1;                    (* Initialize outer loop counter *)
WHILE Day <= 365 DO
  BEGIN
     .
     .

     Hour := 1;              (* Initialize inner loop counter *)
     WHILE Hour <= 24 DO
       BEGIN
          .
          .

          Hour := Hour + 1   (* Increment inner loop counter *)
       END;
     .
     .

     Day := Day + 1          (* Increment outer loop counter *)
  END
```

Notice that each loop has a counter that is initialized to 1 and is incremented at the end of the loop. This is a useful pattern.

Let's take a closer look at the general pattern of a nested loop. The pattern looks as follows, where OutCount is the counter for the outer loop, InCount is the counter for the inner loop, and Limit1 and Limit2 are the number of times each loop is to be executed:

```
OutCount := 1;                   (* Initialize outer loop counter *)
WHILE OutCount <= Limit1 DO
  BEGIN
     .
     .

     InCount := 1;               (* Initialize inner loop counter *)
     WHILE InCount <= Limit2 DO
       BEGIN
          .
          .

          InCount := InCount + 1   (* Increment inner loop counter *)
       END
     OutCount := OutCount + 1     (* Increment outer loop counter *)
END
```

Although both of these loops are count-controlled loops, the same pattern can be used with any type of loop. The following program fragment shows an example of an EOLN loop nested within an EOF loop where characters are read and printed. The number of lines in the input is printed at the end. (The numbers to the right of the code will be used in the trace of the program that follows.)

```
LineCount := 0;                                  1
WHILE NOT EOF DO                                 2
   BEGIN
      WHILE NOT EOLN DO                          3
         BEGIN
            Read(Character);                     4
            Write(Character);                    5
         END;
      Readln;                                    6
      LineCount := LineCount + 1;                7
      Writeln                                    8
   END;
Writeln(LineCount:1, ' lines read.')             9
```

Data T□⟨eoln⟩
D2⟨eoln⟩
⟨eof⟩

NOTE: There are two characters on the first line: a 'T' and a blank.

Figure 5-3
Code Walkthrough

Statement	Variables		Expressions		Output
	LineCount (Integer)	Character (Char)	EOLN	EOF	
1.1	0	—	—	—	—
2.1	0	—	—	F	—
3.1	0	—	F	—	—
4.1	0	T	—	—	—
5.1	0	T	—	—	T
3.2	0	T	F	—	—
4.2	0	□	—	—	—
5.2	0	□	—	—	□
3.3	0	□	T	—	—
6.1	0	□	—	—	—
7.1	1	□	—	—	—
8.1	1	□	—	—	⟨eoln⟩
2.2	1	□	—	F	—
3.4	1	□	F	—	—
4.3	1	D	—	—	—
5.3	1	D	—	—	D
3.5	1	D	F	—	—
4.4	1	2	—	—	—
5.4	1	2	—	—	2
3.6	1	2	T	—	—
6.2	1	2	—	—	—
7.2	2	2	—	—	—
8.2	2	2	—	—	⟨eoln⟩
2.3	2	2	—	T	—
9.1	2	2	—	—	2 lines read

Output T□⟨eoln⟩
D2⟨eoln⟩
2 lines read.

Notice that there are two WHILE loops: an EOLN loop within an EOF loop.

Let's look at exactly what happens at execution time with a specific set of data values. We will need to keep track of the contents of the variables Character and LineCount, as well as the results of the Boolean EOLN and EOF expressions. In order to do so, we'll need some kind of simple notation system. The system we will use is to number each line, omitting the BEGINs and ENDs, as above. As we go through the program, we will then indicate the first time line 1 is executed by 1.1, the second by 1.2, and so on. (See Figure 5-3.) We will use a box to stand for a blank, and the iterations of the loops will be enclosed by a brace on the left.

This technique, called a code walkthrough, is similar to what we did in Chapter 3 when we traced program variables. It is an extremely useful technique for debugging a program. We are using it here to point out several interesting things.

Since LineCount and Character are variables, their values remain the same until explicitly changed. This is indicated by the repeating values. The values of the Boolean expressions EOLN and EOF, however, exist only when the test is made. This is indicated by a dash in that column at all times except when the test is made.

The data itself is made up of two lines of characters, each with two characters. Notice two things: A blank (□) is a character, and whereas the 2 in the data is a character, the number 1 in statement 7 is an integer 1 and can be added to LineCount. Although the 1 and 2 both look like numbers to us, they are represented in memory in two entirely different ways. How does the computer know which we mean? Because we tell it. Statement 7 is an arithmetic assignment statement which adds a 1 to the Integer variable LineCount. Since Character is of type Char, the 2 read into Character is character data.

Designing Nested Loops

To design a nested loop structure, we begin by designing the outermost loop as usual. When we reach the point at which it's time to design the process being repeated, the outermost loop will include the nested loop. We can then design the nested loop just as we would any other loop. This process can be repeated for any number of levels of nesting.

For example, suppose we would like to extend our radioactive decay program to read a series of percentages and then compute and print the decay time for each one. The series of percentages will be ended by a percentage that is less than or equal to zero.

What is the ending condition for the loop? A sentinel value of 0 or less is input. Invariant:

The input must be greater than 0 at the start of each iteration.

How should the ending condition be initialized and updated? Invariant:

A new value must be input prior to the start of each iteration. (Implies a priming Read.)

What is the process being repeated? The process is the computation of the decay time required for plutonium-235 to reach a given percentage. This computation involves another loop, which we've already designed.

Now we can write the algorithm:

```
GET DATA
Writeln 'What is the desired remaining percentage?'
Writeln '(Enter 0 or less to stop this program.)'
Read Percentage
OUTER LOOP
WHILE Percentage > 0 DO
     DIVISION LOOP
     Set Pu235Left to 100
     Set HalfLives to 0
     IF Percentage > = Pu235Left
       THEN
          Set SmallEnough to True
       ELSE
          Set SmallEnough to False
     WHILE NotSmallEnough DO
          Set Pu235Left to Pu235Left / 2.0
          Increment HalfLives
          IF Pu235Left < = Percentage
            THEN
               Set SmallEnough to True
     PRINT RESULTS
     Set DecayTime to HLTime * HalfLives
     Writeln 'After ', DecayTime:1, ' minutes, plutonium-235 ',
       'has passed through'
     Writeln HalfLives:1, ' half-life times.'
     Writeln 'The percentage remaining is then ', Pu235Left:8:4, '% ',
     Writeln ' which is less than or equal to the specified value of '
     Writeln Percent:8:4, '%.'

     Writeln 'What is the desired remaining percentage?'
     Writeln '(Enter 0 or less to stop this program.)'
     Read Percentage
END
```

Printing Headings and Columns

Programs that use loops, especially those that use nested loops, often produce large amounts of output. To be useful, this output must be organized in some way, typically in columns of values with headings. Write and Writeln, combined with specified fieldwidths, can be used to align headings and columns of numbers.

The first step is to decide exactly what is to be printed. Returning to the temperature-data problem, we will illustrate the process by setting up the Writeln state-

Figure 5-4
Output Formatting

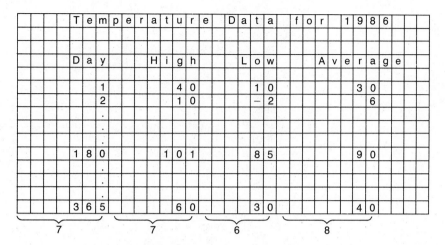

ments to create a table with a year's worth of daily high, low, and average temperatures. The table should contain a heading describing what is in the table, column
headings describing what values are being printed, and the values themselves.

The next step is to take a pencil and paper and make a sketch of how the table
might look. Line up headings and put in some actual values. Graph paper is useful
here. After several tries, you might come up with the layout in Figure 5-4. Notice
that we have added two columns to the original output from the temperature data
problem, one that shows to which day of the year the corresponding temperatures
refer and another that shows the average temperature for each day. Once you have
the headings and data lined up the way you want them, you need to mark off the
number of character positions associated with each heading or data value.

The table heading takes up 25 character positions. If we wanted four blanks at
the left end of this line, we would use a fieldwidth specification of ":29." To position
the column headings, we count the number of characters in each heading, including
any spaces to the left. These values will be the fieldwidth specifications for the
column headings. In our example, these are ":7," ":7," ":6," and ":10," respectively. To line up the values in each column under the column headings, count the
number of character positions from the end of the previous column to the last
character position in the column whose fieldwidth is being determined. This count
becomes the fieldwidth—in this case, ":7," ":7," ":6," and ":8," respectively.

The following program segment shows the Writeln statements to print the table
we have designed.

```
(* Print table heading *)
Writeln('Temperature Data for 1986':29);
Writeln;
Writeln;
(* Print column headings *)
Writeln('Day':7, 'High':7, 'Low':6, 'Average':10);
(* Initialize outer loop ending condition *)
Day := 1;
```

```
WHILE Day <= 365 DO
  BEGIN
    (* Outer loop processing *)
    (* Initialize inner loop process *)
    High : = -MaxInt;
    Low : = MaxInt;
    Sum : = 0;
    (* Initialize inner loop ending condition *)
    Hour : = 1;
    WHILE Hour <= NumHrs DO
      BEGIN
        (* Inner loop process *)
        Read(Temp);
        Sum : = Sum + Temp;
        IF Temp < Low
          THEN
            Low : = Temp;
        IF Temp > High
          THEN
            High : = Temp;
        (* Update inner loop ending condition *)
        Hour : = Hour + 1
      END;
    Average : = Sum DIV NumHrs;
    Writeln(Day: 7, High: 7, Low: 6, Average: 8);
    (* Update outer loop ending condition *)
    Day : = Day + 1
  END;
```

Problem Solving in Action

Problem: The Mill Hollow Boring and Bearing Company occasionally has to ship products outside of its delivery area. They have asked you to write a program that will print shipping invoices. They only need to print one invoice at a time, but an invoice may have several items on it.

The input will be a series of data sets, one set per item, each set on a separate line. Each data set contains the quantity of an item shipped, a description of the item, and the unit price for the item. End of data is indicated by an item quantity of 0 or less in a data set. After the last data set is processed, the total number of items and the total amount should be output.

Discussion: We will assume that some other program prints the shipping labels. This program will simply read each line of data and print out the quantity, description, unit price, and amount for the given number of units. Running sums of the quantity and amount values must be kept. There will be two loops in this program: a sentinel-controlled loop to control the reading of data sets and a count-controlled loop to read and print the string of 30 characters in the item description.

PSIA ▰▰▰▰▰▰▰▰

Outer Loop Invariants: The value of Quantity must be greater than 0 at the start of each iteration (implies priming Read). The input marker must have advanced to a new line of data prior to the start of each iteration. TotalUnits must equal the sum of the quantities that have been read and printed so far. TotalAmount must equal the sum of the computed Amount values. A line of output must be printed for each line of input with an item quantity greater than 0.

Inner Loop Invariants: At the start of each iteration, the loop control counter will equal the number of the loop iteration that is about to be executed. One character will be input and printed during each iteration.

Here is a sample design for the table that will be output. From it we can determine the appropriate fieldwidths for aligning headings with columns of values.

```
            Mill Hollow Boring and Bearing Company
                   128 East Southwest Street
            North Old Newgate, New Hampshire   01010


                      Shipping Invoice

Quantity            Description              Price      Amount

   9999    XXXXXXXXXXXXXXXXXXXXXXXXXXXXXX   99999.99   9999999.99
   9999    XXXXXXXXXXXXXXXXXXXXXXXXXXXXXX   99999.99   9999999.99

Total Units Ordered: 99999999            Total:   9999999.99
```

Input: Each line of input will contain the quantity shipped of an item (Integer), followed by a blank, followed by a 30-character description of the item, followed by another blank, then the unit price for the item (Real). The end of data is indicated by a data set with a quantity of items shipped that equals 0 or less.

Output: An invoice with four columns of information: number of items shipped, description of each item, unit price of each item, and the billing amount for the given number of items. Each column will have an appropriate heading, as should the overall invoice. After the last item has been printed, the total number of units shipped and the total amount for the invoice will be printed.

MAIN MODULE   Level 0

```
Initialize Process
Initialize Ending Condition
IF Quantity > 0
  THEN
    Print Headings
WHILE Quantity > 0 DO
  Update Process
  Update Ending Condition
Print Totals
```

PSIA

INITIALIZE PROCESS
Level 1

> Initialize Total Units to 0
> Initialize Total Amount to 0.0

INITIALIZE ENDING CONDITION

> Read Quantity

PRINT HEADINGS

> Writeln 'Mill Hollow Boring and Bearing Company':50
> Writeln '128 East Southwest Street':43
> Writeln 'North Old Newgate, New Hampshire 01010':50
> Writeln
> Writeln 'Shipping Invoice':38
> Writeln
> Writeln 'Quantity', 'Description':22, 'Price':19,
>   'Amount':11
> Writeln

UPDATE PROCESS

> Write Quantity:6
> Read and Print Description
> Readln Price
> Write Price:10:2
> Set Amount to Quantity * Price
> Writeln Amount:12:2
> Set TotalUnits to TotalUnits + Quantity
> Set TotalAmount to TotalAmount + Amount

UPDATE ENDING CONDITION

> Read Quantity

PRINT TOTALS

> Writeln
> Writeln 'Total Units Ordered: ', TotalUnits:8,
>   'Total:':21, TotalAmount:12:2

PSIA ⟋⟍⟍⟍⟍⟍⟍⟍⟍

READ AND PRINT DESCRIPTION   Level 2

```
Read Blank
Write ' ':4
Set Counter to 1
WHILE Counter <= DescrLength DO
    Read Character
    Write Character
    Increment Counter
```

Module Structure Chart:

Here is the program:

```
PROGRAM Invoice (Input, Output);

(* This program prints a shipping invoice given data for
   quantities, item descriptions, and unit prices *)

CONST
    DescrLength = 30;        (* Characters in an item description    *)

VAR
    Quantity,               (* Number of items ordered             *)
    TotalUnits,             (* Total items for invoice             *)
    Counter:                (* Loop control for printing description *)
        Integer;
    Price,                  (* Unit price for an item              *)
    Amount,                 (* Amount for Quantity of items        *)
    TotalAmount:            (* Total amount for invoice            *)
        Real;
    Blank,                  (* Dummy variable to hold extra blanks *)
    Character:              (* Holds one character of description  *)
        Char;
```

PSIA ▰▰▰▰▰

```pascal
BEGIN (* Invoice *)
  (* Initialize process *)
  TotalUnits := 0;
  TotalAmount := 0.0;
  (* Initialize ending condition *)
  Read(Quantity);
  IF Quantity > 0                  (* End of data signalled by Quantity <= 0 *)
    THEN                                              (* Print headings *)
      BEGIN
        Writeln('Mill Hollow Boring and Bearing Company':50);
        Writeln('128 East Southwest Street':43);
        Writeln('North Old Newgate, New Hampshire  01010':50);
        Writeln;
        Writeln('Shipping Invoice':38);
        Writeln;
        Writeln('Quantity', 'Description':22, 'Price':19, 'Amount':11);
        Writeln
      END;
  WHILE Quantity > 0 DO
    BEGIN
      (* Update process *)
      Write(Quantity:6);
      (* Read and print description *)
      Read(Blank);                          (* Discard extra blank *)
      Write(' ':4);
      Counter := 1;                              (* Initialize LCV *)
      WHILE Counter <= DescrLength DO
        BEGIN
          Read(Character);                                (* Process *)
          Write(Character);
          Counter := Counter + 1                    (* Update LCV *)
        END;
      Readln(Price);
      Write(Price:10:2);
      Amount := Quantity * Price;
      Writeln(Amount:12:2);
      TotalUnits := TotalUnits + Quantity;
      TotalAmount := TotalAmount + Amount;
      (* Update ending condition *)
      Read(Quantity)
    END;
  (* Print totals *)
  Writeln;
  Writeln('Total Units Ordered: ', TotalUnits:8, ' Total:':21,
          TotalAmount:12:2)
END.   (* Invoice *)
```

Testing: Because Program Invoice is so complex, we will discuss testing for it both here and in the Testing and Debugging section. Here we will look at the important points to watch for in testing data sets with typical values.

The output from this program, given valid test data, is an invoice consisting of three sections. The first section is the company name and address and the column headings. Carefully examine this section of the output for spelling mistakes, proper centering of the name and address, and correct spacing of the column headings.

The second section is the list of items being shipped. There should be one line in this section for each line of input. Check that the first and last lines of data were processed correctly—it is in these lines that errors in loop control most often appear. Make sure that the columns of numbers are correctly aligned under the appropriate headings. Compare the output in the Amount column with your hand-calculated results.

The third section of the output consists of the totals. Look for spelling and spacing errors, and compare the printed values against your hand-calculated results.

TESTING AND DEBUGGING

We will use Program Invoice for our discussion of testing. The purpose of testing a program is not so much to show that it works as to see if there is any way to break the program.

Testing The process of executing a program with the intention of finding errors.

One way to break Program Invoice should be immediately apparent: As with any sentinel-controlled loop, omitting the sentinel value from the data will cause problems. The only way to deal with this problem is to write good documentation so that the user won't forget to put the sentinel at the end of the data.

What other ways are there to break the program? Another obvious way is to enter an item description that is too long. The marker would still be in the middle of character data when the program tried to read the value for Price. Solving this problem requires some techniques we haven't covered yet. For now the best solution is again to document the potential problem.

One more way to break Program Invoice is to give a negative value for a price. This error is easy to eliminate. An IF statement in the outer loop can test for a negative price, print an error message, and skip to the statement that updates the ending condition.

To further test Program Invoice we would make up some data sets, run them through the program, and compare the output to our hand-calculated results. The program's execution should be checked with valid data, invalid data, and marginally valid data. The latter involves testing the program with data that is at or near any limits the program might have. For example, we could test Program Invoice with an item description exactly 30 characters long, or we could test Program HalfLife with percentages near 0 and 100.

We should also test a program with a series of different data sets that cause each branch in the code to be separately tested. If we design our test data to do this, it will not only tell us whether a bug exists but also help us pinpoint the bug. For Program Invoice this means we should try at least one data set in which the first quantity is 0, to verify that the program actually skips printing the headings in that case. For Program Incomes this would involve testing data sets for both females and males, to see that both cases work properly.

Testing a program can be as challenging as writing it in the first place. To really successfully test a program you must step back, take a fresh look at what you have written, and then attack it in every way you can imagine to try to make it fail. This isn't always easy to do, but it's necessary if a program is to be considered reliable. (A reliable program is one that works consistently and without errors.)

Testing and Debugging Hints

1. Plan your test data carefully to test all sections of your program.

2. Beware of infinite loops. An infinite loop is a loop in which the expression in the WHILE statement never becomes False. The symptom is that the program doesn't stop. If you are at a terminal, your program just keeps going and doesn't terminate. If you are on a system that monitors the amount of time a program is taking and stops it if it goes too long, a message such as "Time limit exceeded" could be output.

   If an infinite loop occurs, check your logic and the syntax of your loops. Check to be sure there is no semicolon immediately after the DO in the WHILE loop. This will cause an infinite loop in most cases. In a count-controlled loop, make sure the control variable has been incremented within the loop. In a flag-controlled loop, make sure the flag is eventually changed.

3. Avoid using Read with numeric data and EOF-controlled loops. Use Readln instead. If you must use Read with numeric data, use a sentinel-controlled loop instead of an EOF-controlled loop.

4. Check the loop-termination conditions carefully and be sure that something in the loops causes them to be met. Especially watch for values that go one iteration too long or too short.

5. Trace the execution of the loop by hand with a code walkthrough. Simulate the first few passes and the last few passes very carefully to see how the loop really behaves. Remember to carry out the process exactly as the computer would—which is not necessarily how you thought you told the computer to do it.

6. Write out the loop invariant—the consistent, predictable part of its behavior for each iteration. Look for patterns that the invariant will establish. Are they just what you wanted?

7. If all else fails, use debug Writeln statements. Debug Writeln statements are Writeln statements inserted in a program to aid in debugging. They provide an

output message indicating the flow of execution in the program. They are also useful for reporting the value of variables at a certain point in the program.

For example, if you wanted to know the value of variable Sum at a certain point in a program, you could insert the statement

```
Writeln('Sum = ', Sum:1)
```

at that point. If this debug Writeln statement is in a loop, you will get as many values of Sum as there were executions of the body of the loop.

After you have debugged your program, you can remove the debug Writeln statements.

8. An ounce of prevention is worth a pound of debugging. Use the four questions, write the loop invariants, and design your loops correctly to begin with. This may seem like extra work, but it really pays off in the long run.

SUMMARY

The WHILE statement is a looping construct that allows the program to repeat a statement as long as an expression is True. When the expression is False, the statement is skipped, and execution continues with the first statement following the loop.

With WHILE you can construct several distinct types of loops that you will use again and again. These types of loops fall into two categories: count-controlled loops and event-controlled loops.

Count-controlled loops are loops in which a statement is repeated a specified number of times. You initialize a variable to be used as a counter immediately before the WHILE statement. (This variable is often called the LCV for loop control variable.) The control variable is tested against the limit in the expression of the WHILE. The last statement in the WHILE loop's compound statement must increment the control variable.

Event-controlled loops continue execution until something inside the loop body signals that the looping process should cease. Event-controlled loops include those that test for EOF, EOLN, a sentinel value in the data, or a change in a flag variable.

EOF loops are loops that continue to input (and process) data values until there is no more data. To implement them with a WHILE statement, the expression NOT EOF must be used, since EOF becomes True when there are no more data values.

EOLN loops are used to input (and process) character data until there are no more characters on a line.

Sentinel-controlled loops are input loops that use a data value not in the possible range of valid data values as a signal to stop reading.

A flag is a variable that is set in one part of the program and tested in another to control the logical flow. In a flag-controlled WHILE loop, a flag is set before the WHILE, tested in the expression, and changed somewhere in the body of the loop.

Counting is a looping suboperation which keeps track of how many times the loop is repeated or how many times some event occurs. This count can be used in computations and/or to control the loop.

A counter is a variable that is used for counting. It may be a loop control counter in a count-controlled loop, an iteration counter in a counting loop, or an event counter that counts the number of times a particular condition occurs in a loop.

Summing is a looping suboperation in which a running sum is kept. It is like counting in that a variable is initialized outside the loop. The summing operation, however, adds up unknown values, whereas the counting operation adds a constant (1) to the counter each time.

A loop invariant is a set of conditions that specify what must be true at the start of each iteration of a loop in order for it to work properly. Writing out the loop invariant is a good way to begin the process of designing a loop.

All output should be annotated and placed on the page so as to make reading easy. Large amounts of output are often easier to read if presented as a table of columns, with a heading for each column. Tables can be printed quite easily through the use of fieldwidth specifiers.

Testing is the art of trying to break a program to find any bugs or weaknesses it might have. After you have coded a solution in Pascal (or any other language) and the syntax bugs have been removed, you must run your program on carefully chosen sets of test data to test it thoroughly.

QUICK CHECK _____

1. How would you write a WHILE statement that will loop until the value of a Boolean variable Done becomes True? (pp. 173–175)

2. What are the three parts of a count-controlled loop? (pp. 176–177)

3. Is it with Read or Readln that you must be careful in writing an EOF-controlled loop? (pp. 180–182)

4. Should you use a priming Read with an EOLN-controlled loop that is reading data of type Char? (pp. 178–181)

5. What is the difference between a loop with a counting operation and a count-controlled loop? (pp. 183–184)

6. What is the difference between a summing operation in a loop and a counting operation in a loop? (pp. 184–185)

7. In general, how would you code a sentinel-controlled loop using a flag variable? (pp. 182–183)

8. What kind of loop is the following invariant most likely associated with? (pp. 186–191)

   Day may range from 1 to 365 and must indicate the number of the iteration that is about to be executed.

9. What kind of loop would you choose to write in a program that is to read the closing price of a stock for each day of the week? (pp. 186–191)

10. How would you extend the loop in Question 9 to make it read 52 weeks' worth of prices? (pp. 209–210)

11. Fill in the fieldwidths for the following Writeln so as to roughly center the output under the headings. Assume that the values are up to three digits long. (pp. 210–212)

    ```
    Writeln('Day':8, 'Temperature':15);   (* Heading *)
    Writeln(Day:_____, Temp:_____);
    ```

12. How would you test a program that is supposed to separately count the number of females and males in a data set? (Females are represented by 'F's in the data, males are represented by 'M's.) (pp. 217–218)

Answers

1. WHILE NOT Done DO 2. Initialization, testing, and incrementation 3. You must be careful when using Read on numeric data with an EOF-controlled loop. 4. No 5. The counter in a count-controlled loop appears in the Boolean expression that controls the loop. In a loop with a counting operation, the counter simply counts certain events within the loop. 6. A counting operation in a loop increments the counter by a fixed value. A summing operation in a loop adds unknown values to the total. 7. Check for the sentinel value within the loop and set a flag to True when the sentinel is read in. The Boolean expression in the WHILE statement then checks this flag. 8. A count-controlled loop 9. Since there are five days in a business week, you would use a count-controlled loop that runs from 1 to 5. 10. Nest the original loop inside of a count-controlled loop that runs from 1 to 52. 11. Writeln (Day: 8, Temp: 11) 12. Run the program with a data set in which the number of females is different from the number of males. Run it again with a data set that has only females, and again with a set that has only males. Finally, run it with a data set that has some illegal values (other letters).

EXAM PREPARATION EXERCISES _____

1. What does the following loop print out? (Number is of type Integer.)

```
Number := 1;
WHILE Number < 11 DO
   BEGIN
      Number := Number + 1;
      Writeln (Number: 7)
   END
```

2. Merely by rearranging the order of the statements (not changing how any of them are written), make the loop in exercise 1 print the numbers from 1 to 10.

3. When the following code is executed, how many iterations of the loop will be performed?

```
Number := 2;
Done := False;
WHILE NOT Done DO
   BEGIN
      Number := Number * 2;
      IF Number > 64
         THEN
            Done := True
   END
```

4. Does the following program segment need a priming Read? If not, explain why. If so, add the Read in the proper place. (Letter is of type Char.)

```
WHILE NOT EOF DO
   BEGIN
      WHILE NOT EOLN DO
         BEGIN
            Read (Letter);
            Write (Letter)
         END;
      Readln;
      Writeln
   END
```

5. Write the invariant conditions for the following loop. (Sum and Count are of type Integer.)

```
Sum  := 0;
Count  := 0;
WHILE Count < 22 DO
    BEGIN
        Sum  := Sum + Count;
        Count  := Count + 1
    END
```

6. What sentinel value might you choose for a program that will read telephone numbers as integers?

7. (a) What are the contents of Sum and Number at the end of execution of the following program?

```
PROGRAM Pretest (Input, Output);

CONST
   N = 8;

VAR
   I, Sum, Number:
      Integer;
   Flag:
      Boolean;

BEGIN (* Pretest *)
   Sum := 0;
   I := 1;
   Flag := False;
   WHILE (I <= N) AND NOT Flag DO
      BEGIN
         Read(Number);
         IF Number > 0
            THEN
               Sum := Sum + Number
            ELSE
               IF Number = 0
                  THEN
                     Flag := True;
         I := I + 1
      END;
   Writeln('End of test. ', Sum:1, ' ', Number:1)
END.   (* Pretest *)
```

Assume this data: 5   6   −3   7   −4   0   5   8   9

(b) Does this data fully test the program? Explain your answer.

8. Write the invariant for an EOF-controlled loop that reads numeric values, counts them, sums them, and sums the squares of the values. (Each input line contains exactly one value.)

9. Give three different ways of changing the following loop so that it executes 20 times instead of 19 times. Which of the three changes will make the value of Count range from 1 to 20?

```
Count : = 1;
WHILE Count < 20 DO
    Count : = Count + 1;
```

10. The following program segment is supposed to read and print all of the input data, character by character. Will it work? If not, what does it do wrong and how can it be fixed?

```
Read(Character);
WHILE NOT EOF DO
    BEGIN
        Read(Character);
        WHILE NOT EOLN DO
            BEGIN
                Write(Character);
                Read(Character)
            END;
        Writeln
    END
```

PREPROGRAMMING EXERCISES _____

1. Write a program segment that sets a Boolean variable Danger to True and stops reading in data if Pressure (a Real variable being read in) exceeds 510.0. Use Danger as a flag to control the loop.

2. Write a program segment that counts the number of times the integer 28 occurs in a file of 100 integers.

3. Write a program segment that reads a file of grades for a class (any size) and finds the class average.

4. (a) Write statements to create the following headings:

   ```
              Sales
   Week1      Week2      Week3
   ```

   (b) Write a statement to print values lined up under each week. The values are stored in the Integer variables Week1, Week2, and Week3. The last digit of each number should fall under the '1', '2', or '3' of its column heading.

5. Write a program segment to read in integers and then count and print out the number of positive integers and the number of negative integers. If a value is zero, it should not be counted. The process should continue until EOF becomes True.

6. Write a program segment that adds up the even integers from 16 to 26 inclusive.

7. Rewrite Program TempStat, presented earlier, using a different initialization scheme. One temperature should be read before the loop and all values (except Hour) initialized to the first temperature. Trace your program to be sure it works.

8. Write a program segment that prints out the sequence of all the hour and minute combinations in a day, starting with 1:00 A.M. and ending with 12:59 A.M.

9. Rewrite the code segment for exercise 8 so that it prints the times in ten-minute intervals, arranged as a table of six columns with 24 rows.

10. (a) Make the appropriate changes to Program Incomes, presented earlier, so that it will print error messages when negative income values are input and then go on with processing any remaining data. The erroneous data set should not be included in any of the calculations. Thoroughly test the modified program with data sets of your own design.

    (b) Change Program Incomes so that it does not crash when there isn't any data on the input file. It should, however, print an appropriate error message. Test the revised program with data sets of your own design.

11. Make appropriate additions to Program HalfLife, presented earlier, to prevent it from trying to compute the number of half-lives for negative or zero percentages. It should print an appropriate error message when such an input is encountered. Test the revised program with data sets of your own design.

PROGRAMMING PROBLEMS

1. Write a top-down design and a Pascal program that will input an integer and a character. The output will be a diamond composed of the character and extending the width specified by the integer. For example, if the integer is 11 and the character is *, the diamond will look like

```
         *
        ***
       *****
      *******
     *********
    ***********
     *********
      *******
       *****
        ***
         *
```

If the integer entered is an even number, it should be rounded up to the next highest odd number. Your program should use meaningful variable names, proper indentation, and appropriate comments, and if it is interactive, it should provide good prompting messages.

2. Suppose you are putting together some music tapes for a party. You have arranged a list of songs in the order in which you want to play them. However, you would like to leave empty as little as possible of the 45 minutes' worth of tape on each side of a cassette. Thus you want to figure out the total time for a group of songs and see how well they will fit on a cassette. Write a top-down design and a Pascal program that will help you do this. The program will input a reference number and a time for each song, until it encounters a reference number of 0. The times should each be entered in the form of minutes and seconds (two integer values). For example, if song number 4 takes 7 minutes and 42 seconds to play, the data entered for that song would be 4, 7, and 42.

The program should echo print the data for each song and the current running total of the time. The last data set (reference number 0) should not be added to the total time. After all of the data has been read, the program should print a message indicating the difference between the total and 45 minutes (the playing time for one side of a cassette).

If you are writing this program for a batch system, the output should be in the form of a table with columns and headings. For example;

Song number	Song Time Minutes	Seconds	Total Time Minutes	Seconds
------	-------	-------	-------	-------
1	5	10	5	10
2	7	42	12	52
5	4	19	17	11
3	4	33	21	44
4	10	27	32	11
6	8	55	41	6
0	0	1	41	6

```
There are 3 minutes and 54 seconds of tape left.
```

On an interactive system the output will have prompting messages interspersed with the results. For example,

```
Enter the song number:
1
Enter the number of minutes:
5
Enter the number of seconds:
10
Song number 1, 5 minutes and 10 seconds.
Total time is 5 minutes and 10 seconds.
For the next song,
Enter the song number:
      .
      .
      .
```

Your program should use meaningful variable names, proper indentation, and appropriate comments, and if it is interactive, it should provide good prompting messages. It should discard any invalid data sets (such as negative numbers) and print an error message indicating that the data set has been discarded and what was wrong with it.

3. Using top-down design, write a program that will print out the approximate number of words in a file of text. For our purposes, the approximate number of words will be equal to the number of gaps following words. A gap is defined as one or more spaces in a row. Thus, a sequence of spaces counts as just one gap. The ⟨eoln⟩ character is also counted as a gap. Conveniently, when ⟨eoln⟩ is read into a variable of type Char, the value that gets stored in the variable is a space. Anything other than a space or ⟨eoln⟩ is considered to be part of a word. For example, there are 19 words in the following hint, according to our definitions. (*Hint:* Only count a space as a gap if the previous character read is something other than a space.)

Thoroughly test your program with data sets of your own design. Your program should echo print the data.

GOALS

To be able to write a program that uses procedures to reflect the structure of your top-down design.

To be able to write a module of your own design as a procedure.

To be able to correctly define a procedure to do a specified task.

To be able to invoke that procedure correctly.

To be able to use formal and actual parameters correctly.

To be able to define and use local variables correctly.

To be able to write a program that uses multiple calls to a single procedure.

6

Procedures

You have been using procedures and functions since the Write statement was introduced in Chapter 2. By now you should be quite comfortable with the idea of calling these subprograms to perform some task in a program. So far, we have not considered how the procedures and functions are created. Creating procedures and functions is the topic of this chapter and the two that follow.

You might wonder why we've waited until now to look at this topic. The reason lies in the major purpose behind using subprograms: We write our own procedures and functions to help organize and simplify large and complex programs. Until now our programs have been relatively small and simple, so we haven't needed to write subprograms. Now that we've covered three of the basic control structures, sequence, branch, and loop, we are ready to introduce the last of the basic control structures, subprograms, so we can begin writing larger and more complex programs.

TOP-DOWN STRUCTURED DESIGN WITH PROCEDURES

Let's look at the top-down design to write a program segment that processes six data lines, each containing five values. The output is to be the sum of the five values in each data set along with the number of the data line.

Problem Solving in Action

Problem: Write a program that processes six data lines, each of which contains five integer values. The number of the data line and the sum of the five values on the line should be printed out for each line.

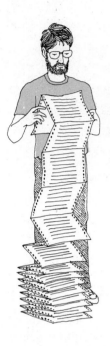

PSIA

Discussion: The input is in terms of data sets. We must read five values from a line, sum them, and print out the data set number and the sum. A count-controlled summing loop will work for this. The invariant for this loop is that ValueCount must be equal to the number of the iteration that is about to be executed and must be in the range of 1 through 5. Also, Sum must be equal to the total of all the data values that have been read from this line, and a new value must be available for input at the start of each iteration.

We have to repeat this process for each of the six data sets. Nesting the above solution for one data set within a count-controlled loop allows us to repeat the process for all six data sets. The invariant for this loop is that DataSetNumber must be equal to the number of the iteration that is about to be executed and must be in the range of 1 through 6. Also, the marker must have advanced to the start of a new line of data prior to the beginning of each iteration.

Input: Six sets of data with five integer values in each set.

Output: Six lines of output, each line containing the number of the data line, the five input values (echo printed), and the sum of the five values.

Assumptions: None.

MAIN MODULE   Level 0

```
Initialize DataSetNumber to 1
WHILE DataSetNumber <= 6 DO
   Print Data Set Number
   Print and Process Data Set
   Update Process
   Increment DataSetNumber
```

PRINT DATA SET NUMBER   Level 1

```
Write 'Data set number ', DataSetNumber:1, ' is '
```

PRINT AND PROCESS DATA SET

```
Initialize ValueCount to 1
Initialize Sum to 0
WHILE ValueCount <= 5 DO
   Read Number
   Write Number:1, ', '
   Add Number to Sum
   Increment ValueCount
```

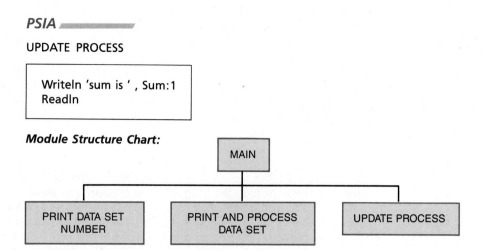

PSIA

UPDATE PROCESS

> Writeln 'sum is ' , Sum:1
> Readln

Module Structure Chart:

```
                    ┌──────────┐
                    │   MAIN   │
                    └──────────┘
        ┌──────────────────┼──────────────────┐
┌───────────────┐  ┌───────────────┐  ┌───────────────┐
│ PRINT DATA SET │  │PRINT AND PROCESS│  │UPDATE PROCESS │
│    NUMBER      │  │   DATA SET     │  │               │
└───────────────┘  └───────────────┘  └───────────────┘
```

At this point we are ready to write the complete Pascal program. We can write the declarations and code from our algorithm.

```pascal
PROGRAM Exercise (Input, Output);

(* This program reads 6 data sets of 5 integer values and prints the
   number of each data set, the values in each data set, and the sum of
   the values in each data set.  Each data set is entered as a single
   line of input *)

VAR
  DataSetNumber,      (* Outer loop control variable                *)
  ValueCount,         (* Inner loop control variable                *)
  Number,             (* Variable into which data values are read *)
  Sum:                (* Holds the sum of values in a data set      *)
     Integer;

BEGIN (* Exercise *)
  (* Initialize outer loop control variable *)
  DataSetNumber := 1;
  (* Outer loop *)
  WHILE DataSetNumber <= 6 DO
    BEGIN
      (* Print data set number *)
      Write('Data set number ', DataSetNumber:1, ' is ');
      (* Print and process data set *)
      ValueCount := 1;                        (* Initialize inner LCV *)
      Sum := 0;                    (* Initialize inner loop process *)
      WHILE ValueCount <= 5 DO
        BEGIN
          Read(Number);                        (* Update process *)
          Write(Number:1, ', ');
          Sum := Sum + Number;
          ValueCount := ValueCount + 1          (* Update LCV *)
        END;
```

PSIA ▬▬▬▬

```
(* Update process *)
Writeln('sum is ', Sum:1);                          (* Print result *)
Readln;                                       (* Go to next data set *)
(* Update outer loop control variable *)
DataSetNumber := DataSetNumber + 1
END
END.   (* Exercise *)
```

Testing: .To test this program, we would simply make up six data sets of five values each, run them through the program, and compare the output with our hand-calculated results. It would be a good idea to make some of the data sets sum to zero or to negative values. Finally, when the program is executed, we should observe its behavior to be sure it doesn't try to read one too many or too few data values or data sets. If it tries to read too many values, an "OUT OF DATA" error message will result. If the program reads too few values, either the sums will be wrong (if less than five values are read per data set) or fewer than six sums will be printed (if the outer loop isn't executing six times).

If we gave this code to someone and asked for a description of the program, the person might say something like "Well, you have a counting loop and then another counting loop—no, the second one is summing too—." The beautiful explanatory top-down structure is no longer readily apparent. Wouldn't it be nice if the main program could be written as shown below?

```
BEGIN
   DataSetNumber := 1;                         (* Initialize LCV *)
   WHILE DataSetNumber <= 6 DO
     BEGIN
       Write('Data set numbers ', DataSetNumber:1, ' is ');

       Print and Process Data Set;

       Update Process;

       DataSetNumber := DataSetNumber + 1        (* Update LCV *)
     END
END.
```

The structure is now evident in the code: Six data sets are being processed. We have preserved the top-down design in our main program, thus making it more readable and understandable. If we had procedures named "Print and Process Data

Set" and "Update Process," we could actually write the main program in the preceding form, simply calling each procedure in the same way that we call other procedures like Read and Write. The code would then clearly describe the solution to the problem.

Whenever use of a procedure could simplify the code, it's time to define a new procedure subprogram. This is actually quite simple to do in Pascal. Basically, a procedure looks just like a program except that the PROGRAM heading is replaced by a PROCEDURE heading, and the last END in the procedure has a semicolon following it instead of a period.

A PROGRAM heading names a program and lists the files from which it gets input and to which it sends output. Similarly, a PROCEDURE heading names a procedure and lists the variables (parameters) that serve as its input and output. Just like any other identifier in Pascal, the name of a procedure is not allowed to include blanks. Thus we will have to write the names of our new procedures as Print AndProcessDataSet and UpdateProcess.

Let's look at how we can rewrite Program Exercise using procedures with these names. The body of the main program will be

```
BEGIN  (* Exercise *)
  DataSetNumber := 1;                                    (* Initialize LCV *)
  WHILE DataSetNumber <= 6 DO
    BEGIN
      Write('Data set number ', DataSetNumber:1, ' is ');

      PrintAndProcessDataSet(Sum);

      UpdateProcess(Sum);

      DataSetNumber := DataSetNumber + 1                 (* Update LCV *)
    END
END.   (* Exercise *)
```

This program segment is now very similar to the main module of our top-down design. The calls to PrintAndProcessDataSet and UpdateProcess include the variable Sum as a parameter. In the case of PrintAndProcessDataSet, this parameter provides the means for the procedure to return the sum of the data values that it reads. We've seen this mechanism before: When calling Read, we put variables in its parameter list to allow it to return values. The only difference is that the value returned by PrintAndProcessDataSet is one that is calculated, rather than being an input value. In the case of procedure UpdateProcess, the parameter provides a way for the program to give a value to the procedure. This is the same as passing a value to Write. The parameter mechanism can be used either to pass data to a procedure or to receive data from a procedure (or for both purposes at once).

Let's look at how PrintAndProcessDataSet is written. Most of this code should look familiar to you, but look carefully at the PROCEDURE heading and the last END.

```
PROCEDURE PrintAndProcessDataSet (VAR Total:
                                       Integer);


(* This procedure reads a data set of five values,
   echo prints, and then returns the sum of the
   values *)


VAR
   ValueCount,        (* Loop control variable *)
   Number:            (* Holds an input value  *)
     Integer;

BEGIN (* PrintAndProcessDataSet *)
   ValueCount := 1;                         (* Initialize LCV *)
   Total := 0;                       (* Initialize loop process *)
   WHILE ValueCount <= 5 DO
     BEGIN
       Read(Number);                   (* Update loop process *)
       Write(Number:1 ', ');
       Total := Total + Number;
       ValueCount := ValueCount + 1        (* Update LCV *)
     END
END;   (* PrintAndProcessDataSet *)
```

This segment is called a *procedure declaration.* Notice that the last END in a procedure declaration is followed by a semicolon. Since this is a declaration, it will appear in the declaration section of the program that uses it (Exercise, in this case). Just like any other declaration, a procedure declaration ends with a semicolon. Even though a procedure looks a lot like a program, it is important to remember that only a program ends with a period.

Take another look at the PROCEDURE heading. Between the parentheses you'll see some code that looks very much like a variable declaration. This code is called a *formal parameter declaration.* Procedure PrintAndProcessDataSet declares one formal parameter, called Total, of type Integer.

Notice that the name of the formal parameter does not have to be the same as the parameter in the call to the procedure. We'll see why the parameter names can differ when we take a closer look at the declaration and use of parameters later, but first let's see how the procedures and the program body get put together to form a complete program.

```
PROGRAM Exercise (Input, Output);

(* This program reads 6 data sets of 5 integer values and prints the
   number of each data set, the values in each data set, and the sum of
   the values in each data set.  Each data set is entered as a single
   line of input *)

VAR
  DataSetNumber,        (* Outer loop control variable          *)
  Sum:                  (* Holds the sum of values in a data set *)
    Integer;

(*********************************************************************)

PROCEDURE PrintAndProcessDataSet (VAR Total:
                                      Integer);

(* This procedure reads a data set of 5 values, echo prints, and
   then returns the sum of the values *)

VAR
  ValueCount,        (* Loop control variable *)
  Number:            (* Holds an input value  *)
    Integer;

BEGIN (* PrintAndProcessDataSet *)
  ValueCount := 1;                              (* Initialize inner LCV *)
  Total := 0;                          (* Initialize inner loop process *)
  WHILE ValueCount <= 5 DO
    BEGIN
      Read(Number);                                  (* Update process *)
      Write(Number:1, ', ');
      Total := Total + Number;
      ValueCount := ValueCount + 1                       (* Update LCV *)
    END
END;   (* PrintAndProcessDataSet *)

(*********************************************************************)

PROCEDURE UpdateProcess (VAR Total:
                             Integer);

(* This procedure prints the sum of the values in a data set, and calls
   Readln to go to the next set of data values *)

BEGIN (* UpdateProcess *)
  Writeln('sum is ', Sum:1);                           (* Print Result *)
  Readln                                           (* Go to next data set *)
END;   (* UpdateProcess *)

(*********************************************************************)
```

```
BEGIN  (* Exercise *)
   DataSetNumber := 1;                              (* Initialize LCV *)
   WHILE DataSetNumber <= 6 DO
      BEGIN
         Write('Data set number ', DataSetNumber:1, ' is ');
         PrintAndProcessDataSet(Sum);
         UpdateProcess(Sum);
         DataSetNumber := DataSetNumber + 1          (* Update LCV *)
      END
END.   (* Exercise *)
```

AN OVERVIEW OF USER-DEFINED PROCEDURES

Now that we've seen an example of how a procedure is declared, let's look briefly and informally at some of the more important points of procedure construction and use. This overview will provide the background for more formal discussion later in the chapter.

Flow of Control in Procedure Calls

Notice that procedures are declared physically before the main program or level 0 module. Thus the physical order is different from the logical order. What then is the logical order in which these statements are executed? In the case of our example program, execution starts with the statement following the BEGIN with the (* Exercise *) comment next to it. What makes this BEGIN special? It is paired with the last END in the program, the END with the period after it. During compilation the procedure and the program get translated in the order in which they physically appear. When the program is executed, however, control is transferred to the first statement in the main program and the program proceeds in logical sequence. Figure 6-1 illustrates this physical versus logical ordering of procedures.

When the name of a procedure is encountered as a statement, logical control is passed to the first statement following the first BEGIN in the procedure (the first statement in the procedure body). Therefore the logical order of the Program Exercise with procedures is identical to the logical order of our original version. The difference is that the structure of the top-down design is maintained in the coding of the second version. The semantics of the problem solution itself are clearly reflected in the code for the main program. As our problems get more complex, this clarity of design will become increasingly important.

When to Use Procedures

A program may have any number of procedures declared in it. For example, in Program Exercise we could have coded the first module in our design (Print Data Set Number) as a procedure and declared it before PrintAndProcessDataSet in the procedure declarations section of the program. We didn't do so because the code for

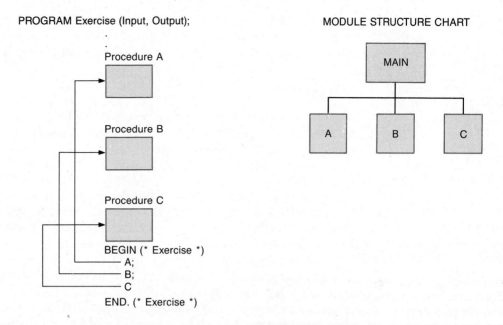

*Figure 6-1
Physical versus
Logical Order of
Procedures*

this module is only a single line. Turning it into a procedure would only complicate the overall program—which entirely defeats the purpose of using subprograms.

In general, any module can be coded as a subprogram (procedure or function). The decision to code a module as a subprogram should be based on whether or not the overall program will be easier to understand as a result. There are other factors that can affect this decision, but for now this is the simplest heuristic (strategy) to use.

Procedures and Blocks

Remember that a program was defined as a PROGRAM heading and a block. We can expand our definition of a block from Chapter 2 to include procedures. This is our expanded syntax diagram for a block:

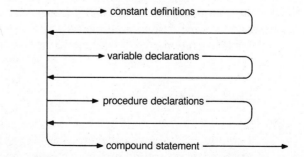

By definition, a program can contain procedures. A procedure is defined as a PROCEDURE heading and a block. Therefore, we can declare a procedure within a procedure within a procedure. . . . We will not consider nesting of procedures until Chapter 7. It is mentioned here only to show that even very complicated top-down designs can be coded without losing the structure of the problem.

Parameters

Let's take another look at the parameters in the PROCEDURE heading. These *formal parameters* represent the way the main program and procedures (or procedures and other procedures) communicate. Through them, the main program can input (pass) values to a procedure to use in its processing, and the procedure can output (return) results to the program.

The procedure PrintAndProcessDataSet reads, prints, and sums values. The main program does not care what values are read, only what their sum is. Therefore it tells the procedure where to leave the sum by giving it the location (the variable Sum) when it turns control over to the procedure.

The parameters in the program's call to a procedure are said to be the *actual parameters,* as opposed to the formal parameters that are listed in the PROCEDURE heading. The fact that in Program Exercise the actual parameter is named Sum and the formal parameter in each procedure is named Total makes no difference. The procedures are prepared to receive Integer variables, and the program provides one called Sum each time it calls a procedure.

In a sense, the formal parameter Total is just a convenient place holder in the procedure declaration. When the procedure is called with Sum as its actual parameter, all of the references to Total in the procedure will *actually* be made to Sum (hence the name actual parameter). If the procedure were to be called again with a different variable as an actual parameter, all the references to Total would actually refer to that other variable until the procedure returned control to the main program. (Parameters will be discussed in greater detail later in this chapter.)

It is only because actual and formal parameters can have different names that we can call a procedure with different actual parameters. If you're wondering why we would want to be able to use a procedure with different actual parameters, just consider the Read procedure—it would be pretty useless if we always had to use exactly the same names in its parameter list every time we called it.

This brings up another advantage of using subprograms. Once a subprogram has been declared, we can call it from many places in the program (or from other subprograms). Use of multiple calls can save a great deal of effort in coding many problem solutions. We'll take another look at this topic toward the end of the chapter.

An Analogy

Before we formally define all the terms we have been using, let's leave the world of computing and draw an analogy from the world of entertainment. There is going to be a big concert on Friday night, and since no programming assignments are due on Saturday, you decide to go. When you get to the box office, you find that you have to fill out a form with your ticket request. The form has places where you are to write in the number and type of seats you would like and the performance date. The form also has places where the reservation clerk will fill in your seat numbers and the price of the tickets. You write down that you want two balcony seats for Friday night's performance and hand the form to the clerk. You wait patiently while the clerk goes off to check (on her computer terminal) to see whether seats are available and to calculate what the cost will be if they are. Five minutes later she comes back to the window and hands the form back to you. You see from what she has written on it that you have your balcony seats and the price is $30. You pay the clerk and then go on about your business.

This everyday happening illustrates how procedure calls work. The clerk is like a procedure. You, acting as the main program, have her do some work for you. To do her job she must have some information: which seats you would like and for which night you want the tickets. These are her input parameters. You then wait until she completes her task. You expect her to return some information to you: the availability of the tickets and their price. These are the clerk's output parameters. Once she gives you this information (and the tickets), you can go on about your business.

The clerk does this task all day long with different input values. Each ticket order activates the same process. The purchaser waits until the clerk returns with output information based on the purchaser's specific input.

The form containing the information that gets passed between you and the clerk is analogous to the actual parameters of a procedure call. The spaces on the form represent variables in the main program. When you hand the form to the clerk, some of the places contain information and some are empty. The clerk has the form in her hand while she is doing her job, so she can write information in the blank spaces. (She could also change what you have written, but in this case she doesn't.)

When a program calls a procedure, the program allows the procedure to access the variables listed in the actual parameter list. While the procedure is executing, it can access the values in those variables and even change them. When the procedure finishes, the program goes on about its business, making use of whatever new information the procedure left in the variables.

The formal parameter list is the set of shorthand or slang terms the clerk uses to describe the items on the ticket order form. For example, she may think in terms of "shows," "blocks," "reservations," and "receipts." These are her terms (formal parameters) for what the order form calls "performance date," "group of seats desired," "group of seats reserved," and "total price" (the actual parameters).

How does a procedure know which actual parameters go with which formal parameters? Consider how the clerk does this matching. She doesn't waste time reading the names on the form every time somebody hands her a ticket order; she just knows that the first item is the performance date (show), the second is the group of seats desired (block), and so on. In other words, she only pays attention to the position of each item in the parameter list. This is how actual parameters get matched to formal parameters: They are matched by their relative positions in the two parameter lists.

Now that we have covered procedures intuitively through an example, a brief informal discussion, and an analogy, we will formally define the terms we have been using.

PROCEDURE DECLARATIONS

A procedure is defined as a heading and a block. The heading has the following form:

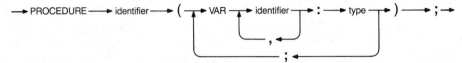

This is a simplified version of the complete syntax diagram for a procedure heading. We will expand this definition in Chapter 7.

The identifiers listed in the heading (the parameter list) are the formal parameters of the procedure. They are the "input" to the procedure (a list of variables that the procedure needs to use) and the "output" from the procedure (a list of variables that the procedure is to calculate or read in for the calling program). A variable (parameter) is listed only once in the heading, even if it is both an input and an output parameter. Within the body of the procedure, these parameters are treated like any other variable. Notice that the type of each parameter is given in the formal parameter list.

As in a program, other variables that are not parameters may also be declared in procedures. These variables will be discussed shortly.

Procedures are declared in a program after the variable declarations and before the main body. This means that procedures must physically appear in the program before the place where they are called; otherwise a compiler error will result. If one procedure is called by another, the procedure being called must be declared before the one that calls it. This is just another example of having to define something before we use it.

Why don't we have to declare Read and Write? Because they are predefined by Pascal. This means that Pascal automatically declares and defines them for every program. Appendix B lists all of the identifiers that are predefined in Pascal, including predefined procedures.

PROCEDURE CALL (INVOCATION)

To call (or *invoke*) a procedure we use the name of the procedure as a statement in the main program or the body of another procedure, with the variables it is to use in parentheses following the name. This is the syntax diagram of a *procedure call:*

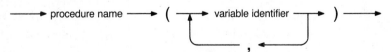

A *procedure call* in a program results in the execution of the body of the called procedure. Control then flows to the program statement following the call. In our ticket clerk analogy, once the purchaser gets back the necessary information, he or she goes on to other things.

| **Procedure Call** | A statement that transfers control to a procedure. In Pascal this statement is the name of the procedure followed by a list of actual parameters. |

Execution of a procedure proceeds until the last END in the procedure is reached, at which point execution of the main program resumes with the statement immediately following the procedure call. This is called the *return,* because the flow of control returns to the point from which the procedure was called. Barring bugs such as infinite loops in a procedure, there should be a return for every call that is executed in a program.

Naming Procedures

When you choose a name for a procedure, keep in mind how calls to it will look. A procedure call is written as a statement. It should therefore sound like it is doing something. For this reason, it is a good idea to choose a name that is a verb or has a verb as part of it. For example, the statement

```
Mean(First, Second, Third, Average)
```

has no verb to explain its use. Adding the verb "Compute" makes the name sound much more like an action:

```
ComputeMean(First, Second, Third, Average)
```

You might even want to throw in the word "Of," to make it read a little more smoothly:

```
ComputeMeanOf(First, Second, Third, Average)
```

When you are picking a name for a procedure, write down sample calls with different names until you come up with one that sounds good and tells someone reading the program exactly what the procedure does.

PARAMETERS

The variables given to a procedure in the call are called actual parameters. The procedure is written using variable names called formal parameters, listed in its heading.

| **Formal Parameter** | A variable declared in a procedure heading. |

| **Actual Parameter** | A variable listed in the call to a procedure. |

When a procedure is executed, it uses the variables (actual parameters) given to it in the procedure call. How is this done? Remember that a variable identifier is assigned a location in memory. When a procedure is invoked, a list of the locations, in the order in which they appear in the actual parameter list, is given to the procedure.

Let's look at another analogy. Suppose you are doing volunteer work at the local library. The librarian asks you to compile some information that has been requested and hands you a slip of paper with the call numbers for the books you will need. You then go into the book stacks and get the books yourself.

In this analogy you are playing the part of the procedure. To do your job, you need some information from the librarian, who is playing the part of the main program. Instead of giving you the information directly, the librarian simply gives you the locations of the information in the library. The library represents the data area in memory for the main program. You must go into the library and retrieve the information yourself. Likewise, the main program gives locations of data values to the procedure, and the procedure then accesses the main program's data area for the information it needs.

It is important to keep in mind that it is the *locations* of the actual parameters and not their values that are passed to the procedure. There is only one copy of the information, which is used by both the program (or calling procedure) and the procedure being called. When the procedure is called, the actual and formal parameters are matched by position and become synonyms for the same location in memory. Whatever value is left in one of those locations by the procedure is the value that will be found there by the program after the return. Therefore, you must be careful about how you use the formal parameters inside the procedure. Any change that a procedure makes to its formal parameters will affect the actual parameters back in the main program.

These formal parameters are called *variable* or VAR *parameters,* hence the similarity in appearance to a VAR declaration in the main program. The name stems from the fact that the corresponding actual parameters may have their values changed by the procedure when it is called. In Chapter 7 we will look at a second type of parameter, a *value parameter,* through which only a copy of the value of the actual parameter is given to the procedure. Because only the value (not the address) of the actual parameter is passed to a formal value parameter, the procedure cannot change the value of the actual parameter.

When the procedure returns control to the program, the link between the actual and formal parameters is broken. They are synonymous only during a particular call to the procedure. Each call causes a positional matchup to occur between the two parameter lists involved. When control returns to the statement following the call, the matchup is dissolved. The only evidence that it ever occurred is that some of the values in the actual parameter variables may now be different than they were before the procedure was called. (See Figure 6-2.)

Each actual parameter must have the same data type as the formal parameter in the same position. Also, there must be the same number of actual parameters in a call as there are formal parameters in the procedure heading. Notice how the two parameter lists match up in the following example (the data type of each of the actual parameters is what you would assume from its name):

PROCEDURE ShowMatch (VAR Num1:Real; VAR Num2:Integer; VAR Letter:Char);

ShowMatch(RealVariable,   IntegerVariable,   CharVariable);

Each parameter in this example is matched to the parameter in the same position in the opposite list. It is essential that the actual parameters agree in type with what is specified for the matching formal parameters. The data type that the procedure expects to find must be what is actually there. This will become increasingly important later as we work with more complex data types. If the matched parameters are not of the same data type, a compiler error message such as "TYPE MIS-MATCH OF OPERANDS" will occur.

Figure 6-2
The Temporary
Nature of
Parameter
Matching in a
Procedure Call

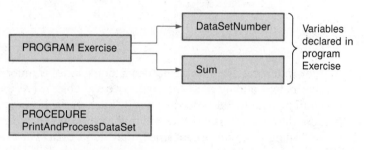

When flow of control is in program Exercise, DataSetNumber and Sum can be accessed as shown by the arrows

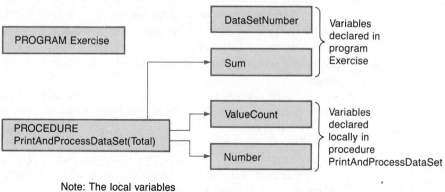

When flow of control is in procedure PrintAndProcessDataSet, the procedure can access the three variables indicated by the arrows.

Note: The local variables exist only when flow of control is inside the procedure.

It is up to the programmer to make sure that the formal and actual parameter lists match up semantically, as well as syntactically. For example, suppose the call in Program Exercise to PrintAndProcessDataSet were

```
PrintAndProcessDataSet(DataSetNumber);
```

The parameter lists would match up in type and number of parameters, so no syntax error would be signaled. However, the output would be incorrect because the parameter list would contain the wrong variable. Similarly, if the parameter list for a procedure contains two formal parameters of the same data type, we must be careful that the actual parameters are in the right order. If they are in the wrong order, no syntax error will result—but the answers we get will be wrong.

LOCAL VARIABLES

In PrintAndProcessDataSet we needed a loop control counter and a place to read in a value before adding it to the sum. Two variables were thus defined in a VAR declaration within the procedure itself. Such variables are called *local variables* because they are accessible only within the block in which they are declared. As far as the calling program is concerned, they don't exist. For example, if you tried to print the contents of Number from the main program, a compile time error such as "UNDEFINED IDENTIFIER" would occur.

The values of local variables are destroyed when the procedure returns control to the calling program. So, every call to a procedure is independent of every other call to that same procedure. Every time the procedure is called, its local variables start out with their values undefined. What this means is that local variables must be initialized each time within the procedure itself.

In our concert ticket reservation analogy, a scratch pad used by the clerk to figure the price of your tickets would be the equivalent of local variables. The fact that the local variables are not saved between calls to the procedure might be simulated by having the clerk throw away the top sheet from the pad after each ticket order.

Because the values of local variables are destroyed upon the return from the procedure containing them, local variables cannot be used to store values between calls to a procedure. If a procedure calculates a value that is to be used in a later call to the same procedure, the value must be passed back to the calling program through a parameter. The next time the procedure is called, the program can pass that value back into the procedure. The program's data storage area is the only safe place to store values between procedure calls.

The following code segment illustrates each of the parts of the procedure declaration and calling mechanism that we have discussed.

```
PROGRAM Terms (Input, Output);              (* Program parameters — files *)

VAR                                    (* Main program variable declarations *)
  Global1,
  Global2:
    Integer;
  Global3:
    Real;

PROCEDURE One (VAR Position1,          (* Procedure declaration with *)
                   Position2:          (* three formal parameters    *)
                     Integer;
                   VAR Position3:
                     Real);

VAR                                            (* Local variables *)
  Local1,
  Local2:
    Integer;

BEGIN (* One *)
  .                                    (* Body of procedure One *)
  .
END;   (* One *)

BEGIN (* Terms *)
  .                                    (* Body of Program Terms *)
  .
  One(Global1, Global2, Global3);      (* Procedure call to One with *)
  .                                    (* three actual parameters    *)
  .
END.   (* Terms *)
```

MULTIPLE CALLS TO THE SAME PROCEDURE

At the start of this chapter we said that procedures are used as a way of making a program reflect its top-down design. There is a second major reason for using procedures. If there is a task that must be done in more than one place in a program, we can avoid repetitive coding by writing it as a procedure and then calling it wherever we need it. Let's look at an example that illustrates this use of procedures.

Problem Solving in Action

Problem: A new regional sales manager for the Greenley Department Stores has just come into town. He wants to see department by department comparisons of the two Greenley stores in town. These comparisons are to be generated monthly in the form

PSIA ▬▬▬

of bar graphs for use as a management tool. The daily sales for each department are kept on each store's accounting files. Data on each store is stored in the form

    Department ID number

    Number of business days for the department

    Daily sales for day 1

    Daily sales for day 2

    .

    .

    Daily sales for last day in period

    Department ID number

    Number of business days for the department

    Daily sales for day 1

    .

    .

The bar graph to be printed is of the form

```
Bar Graph Comparing Departments of Store#1 and Store#2

Store   Sales in 1,000s of dollars

 #    0         5        10        15        20        25
      |.........|.........|.........|.........|.........|
      Dept 1030
 1    ***********************
      Dept 1030
 2    *******************************************

      Dept 1210
 1    *****************************************************
      Dept 1210
 2    ********************************************

      Dept 2040
 1    *************************************************
      Dept 2040
 2    *********************************
```

As you can see from the bar graph, each star represents $500 in sales. No stars are printed if a department's sales are less than or equal to $250.

Discussion: Reading the input data from both files is straightforward. We need to Reset the files (let's call them Store1 and Store2) and read a department ID number, the number of business days, and the following daily sales for that department. After processing each department, we can read the data for the next department, continuing until we run out of departments (EOF is encountered). Since the process is the same

PSIA ━━━

for reading Store1 and reading Store2, we can use one procedure for reading both files. All we have to do is pass the file name as a parameter to the procedure. We want total sales for each department, so this procedure will have to sum the daily sales for a department as they are read. A procedure can be used to print the output heading. Another procedure can be used to print out each department's sales for the month in graphic form.

There will be three loops in this program, one in the main program, one in the procedure that gets the data, and another in the procedure that prints the bar graph. The loop invariant for the main program is that EOF must be False on *both* Store1 and Store2 at the start of each iteration, and that a new department's sales values must be available for input. One graph for each store must be printed for each iteration of this loop that is completed.

The loop invariant for the GetData procedure requires an iteration counter that ranges from 1 to the number of days for the department. Also, a summing operation is needed to total up the sales for the period.

At first glance it might seem that the invariant for the PrintData procedure is like that for any counting loop. However, let's look at how we would do this process by hand. Suppose we wanted to print a bar for the value 1850. We would first make sure the number was greater than 250, then print a star and subtract 500 from the original value. We would check again to see if the new value was greater than 250, then print a star and subtract 500. This process would repeat until the resulting value was less than or equal to 250. Thus, our loop invariant will require a counter that will be decremented by 500 for each iteration, with a termination value of 250 or less. A star will be printed for each iteration of the loop.

Input: Two data files (Store1, Store2), each containing

> DeptID—department ID number (Integer)
> NumDays—number of business days (Integer)
> Sales—daily sales (Real)

repeated for each department.

Output: Bar graph showing total sales for each department

Assumptions:

> Each file is in order by department IDs.
> There are the same departments in each store.
> There is one piece of data per line of input.

MAIN MODULE   Level 0

```
PrintHeader
WHILE NOT EOF(Store1) AND NOT EOF(Store2) DO
    GetData for Store1
    PrintData for Store1 dept.
    GetData for Store2
    PrintData for Store2 dept.
```

PSIA

PRINTHEADER   Level 1

```
Writeln title
Writeln heading
Writeln bar graph scale
```

GETDATA (Input: DataFile; Output: DeptID, DeptSales)

```
Readln DeptID
Readln NumDays
Initialize DeptSales to 0
Initialize Days (LCV) to 1
WHILE Days <= NumDays DO
   Readln Sales
   Add Sales to DeptSales
   Increment Days
```

PRINTDATA (Input: DeptID, StoreNum, DeptSales)

```
Writeln DeptID
Write StoreNum
WHILE DeptSales > 250 DO
   Write '*'
   Decrement DeptSales by $500
Writeln
```

To develop this top-down design we had to make several passes through the design process, and several mistakes had to be fixed in order to arrive at the design you see here. So don't get discouraged if you don't come up with a perfect top-down design on the first try every time.

Module Structure Chart:

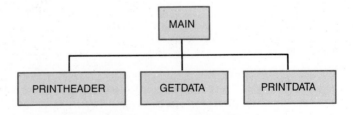

The following Pascal program parallels our design.

PSIA ━━━━━━━

```
PROGRAM Graph (Store1, Store2, Output);

(* This program generates bar graphs of monthly sales by department for
   two Greenley department stores, permitting department by department
   comparison of sales *)

VAR
   StoreNum,      (* Store ID number              *)
   ID:            (* Department ID number         *)
      Integer;
   Sales1,        (* Department sales for store 1 *)
   Sales2:        (* Department sales for store 2 *)
      Real;
   Store1,        (* Accounting file for store 1  *)
   Store2:        (* Accounting file for store 2  *)
      Text;

(**********************************************************************)

PROCEDURE PrintHeader;

(* This procedure prints the title for the bar chart, a heading,
   and the numeric scale for the chart *)

BEGIN (* PrintHeader *)
   Writeln('Bar Graph Comparing Departments of Store#1 and Store#2');
   Writeln;
   Writeln('Store  Sales in 1,000s of dollars');
   Writeln('  #    0         5        10        15        20        25');
   Writeln('       |.........|.........|.........|.........|.........|');
END;   (* PrintHeader *)

(**********************************************************************)

PROCEDURE GetData (VAR DataFile:    (* Input accounting file *)
                        Text;
                   VAR DeptID:       (* Department number     *)
                        Integer;
                   VAR DeptSales:    (* Dept's monthly sales  *)
                        Real);

(* This procedure takes an input accounting file as a parameter, reads
   the department ID number and number of days of sales from that file,
   then reads one sales figure for each of those days, computing a total
   sales figure for the month.  This figure is returned in DeptSales *)
```

PSIA ▬▬▬▬▬

```
VAR
  NumDays,        (* Number of business days in the month    *)
  Day:            (* The LCV for a loop reading daily sales *)
    Integer;
  Sale:           (* One day's sales for the department       *)
    Real;

BEGIN (* GetData *)
  Readln(DataFile, DeptID, Numdays);      (* Get ID and number of days *)
  DeptSales := 0.0;                              (* Initialize process *)
  Day := 1;                                          (* Initialize LCV *)
  WHILE Day <= NumDays DO
    BEGIN
      Readln(DataFile, Sale);                       (* Update process *)
      DeptSales := DeptSales + Sale;
      Day := Day + 1                                    (* Update LCV *)
    END
END;   (* GetData *)


(**********************************************************************)


PROCEDURE PrintData (VAR DeptID,        (* Department ID number     *)
                         StoreNum:      (* Store number             *)
                           Integer;
                         VAR DeptSales: (* Total sales for the dept. *)
                           Real);

(* This procedure prints the department ID number, the store number,
   and a bar graph of the sales for the department.  The bar graph
   is printed at a scale of one mark per $500 *)

BEGIN (* PrintData *)
  Writeln('      Dept ', DeptID:1);                    (* Print ID *)
  Write(StoreNum:3, ' ':4);               (* Print store number *)
  WHILE DeptSales > 250 DO
    BEGIN
      Write('*');                       (* Print '*' for each $500 *)
      DeptSales := DeptSales - 500                      (* Update LCV *)
    END;
  Writeln                                       (* Go to a new line *)
END;   (* PrintData *)


(**********************************************************************)


BEGIN (* Graph *)
  Reset(Store1);
  Reset(Store2);
  PrintHeader;
```

PSIA ▬▬▬▬

```
WHILE NOT EOF(Store1) and NOT EOF(Store2) DO          (* For each dept *)
  BEGIN
    Writeln;
    StoreNum := 1;                                     (* Process Store 1 *)
    GetData(Store1, ID, Sales1);
    PrintData(ID, StoreNum, Sales1);
    StoreNum := 2;                                     (* Process Store 2 *)
    GetData(Store2, ID, Sales2);
    PrintData(ID, StoreNum, Sales2)
  END
END.   (* Graph *)
```

Testing: This program should be tested both with data files that contain the same number of data sets and with data files that contain different numbers of data sets for the two stores. The case where one or both of the files are empty should be tested. The test data should include a set that generates a monthly sales figure of $0 and one that generates more than $25,000 in sales. The program should also be tested to see what it does with negative days, negative sales, and mismatched department IDs. This series of tests will reveal that, if this program were really being written for a department store, we would have to add several checks for invalid data.

The main program of Graph not only reflects our top-down design, but calls both GetData and PrintData twice. The result is a program that is shorter and more readable than one in which the code for each procedure is repeated.

TESTING AND DEBUGGING ▬▬▬▬▬▬▬

The combination of the formal parameters defined in a procedure and all the actual parameters that are passed to the procedure by the main program constitutes an *interface* between the procedure and the program. The errors that occur with the use of procedures are usually due to an incorrect interface between the main program and a procedure (or between two procedures, in the case of one procedure calling another). This section shows how to design these interfaces in order to avoid bugs.

For each module listed in the main program, make a list of the following items:

1. What information (data values) the main program has that the procedure needs.
2. What information (data values) the procedure will produce that the main program will need later.

The identifiers used to reference the values in (1) and (2) become the variables in the actual parameter lists in calls to the procedure. The formal parameter list for the procedure should contain variables of the same type in the same order. Often the identifiers used to reference items in the two lists will be the same. This makes it easier for humans to read the code. However, the items are actually matched up by their positions in the formal and actual parameter lists, not by spelling.

The actual parameters are declared, along with all of the other variables for the program, in the VAR section of the main program. The formal parameters are declared in the procedure heading. All other variables that the procedure needs to use are local and must be declared in the VAR section of the procedure itself.

This process may be repeated for all the modules at the second level, then at the third level, and so on. At each new level, the interface to a module is defined as part of the module above it in the module structure chart. We'll take a closer look at the design of nested procedures in the next chapter.

Testing and Debugging Hints

1. Follow the documentation guidelines carefully (see Appendix G) when writing procedures. As your programs get more complex, it becomes increasingly important to adhere to the documentation and formatting standards. Label the main BEGIN-END pair of each procedure with the procedure name. Even if the procedure name seems to define the process being done, describe that process in comments. Use comments to explain the purposes of all of the formal parameters and local variables in a procedure.

2. Be sure to put a semicolon after the procedure heading. Be sure that the last END in the procedure has a semicolon after it—not a period.

3. Be sure the formal parameter list gives the type of each parameter.

4. Be sure the actual parameter lists of all calls to the procedure match the formal parameter list in number and order of items and types of variables.

5. Be sure to repeat the keyword VAR for each type of formal parameter (see the syntax diagram). In the next chapter we'll discuss what happens if you omit the keyword VAR in a formal parameter list.

SUMMARY

Pascal allows programs to be written in functional modules. Therefore the structure of a program can parallel its top-down design even when the program is very complicated. To make your main program (what is between the BEGIN-END. pair) look exactly like Level 0 of your top-down design, you simply write each functional module as a procedure. The main program then executes the procedures in logical sequence.

Communication between the calling program and the procedure is handled through the use of two lists of identifiers: the formal parameter list (which includes the type of each identifier), which is in the PROCEDURE heading, and the actual parameter list, which is in the calling statement. The identifiers in these lists must agree in number, position, and type.

Part of the top-down design process involves determining what data must be given to the lower-level module and what information must be received back. The module interfaces defined become the formal and actual parameter lists, and the module name becomes the name of the procedure. A call to the procedure is accomplished by writing the procedure's name as a statement, with the appropriate actual parameters enclosed in parentheses.

In addition to having variables defined in its formal parameter list, a procedure may have local variables declared within it. These variables are accessible only within the block in which they are declared. Local variables must be initialized each time the procedure containing them is called, because their values are destroyed when the procedure returns.

Procedures may be called from more than one place in a program and from other procedures. The positional matching mechanism allows the use of different variables as actual parameters to the same procedure. Multiple calls to a procedure, from different places and with different actual parameters, can be used to greatly simplify the coding of many complex programs.

QUICK CHECK _____

1. If a design has one level 0 module and three level 1 modules, how many procedures is it likely to have? (pp. 234–235)

2. Where in a program are procedures declared? (p. 238)

3. How does the syntax of a procedure differ from the syntax of a program? (pp. 232, 238)

4. What would a call to a procedure with the heading

```
PROCEDURE QuickCheck (VAR Size:
                            Integer;
                      VAR Area:
                            Real;
                      VAR Initial:
                            Char);
```

look like if the actual parameters were the variables Radius (a Real), Number (an Integer), and Letter (a Char)? (pp. 238–242)

5. How is the matchup between the formal and actual parameters in question 4 made? When during execution does the matchup take place, and how long does it last? What is actually passed from the program to the procedure through this mechanism? (pp. 239–242)

6. Where in a procedure are local variables defined, and what are their initial values equal to? (pp. 242–243)

7. What is one way that a procedure can be used to simplify the coding of an algorithm? (pp. 243–249)

Answers:
1. Three 2. In the declaration section, just before the main program body. 3. A procedure begins with a PROCEDURE heading rather than a PROGRAM heading, and ends with an "END;" instead of an "END." 4. SelfCheck(Number, Radius, Letter) 5. The matchup is done on the basis of the parameters' positions in each list each time the procedure is called and lasts until the procedure returns. The locations of the actual parameters are passed to the procedure. 6. In the declaration section of the procedure. Their initial values are undefined. 7. The coding may be simplified if it's possible to call the procedure from more than one place in the program.

EXAM PREPARATION EXERCISES _____

1. Define the following:

   procedure call   actual parameter

   parameter list   variable (or VAR) parameter

   positional matching   local variable

   formal parameter

2. A variable called Widgets is stored in memory location 13571. When the statements

   ```
   Widgets := 23;
   Drop(Widgets);
   ```

   are executed, what information is passed to the formal VAR parameter in procedure Drop?

3. Assume that, in exercise 2, the formal parameter for procedure Drop is called Clunkers. After the procedure performs the assignment

   ```
   Clunkers := 77;
   ```

   what is the value in Widgets? in Clunkers?

4. Identify the following items in the program fragment shown below.

   procedure heading   formal parameters

   actual parameters   procedure call

   local variables   procedure body

   ```
   PROGRAM Fragment (Input, Output);

   VAR
      Formal1,
      Formal2,
      Formal3:
         Boolean;

   PROCEDURE Test (VAR Actual1,
                       Actual2,
                       Actual3:
                          Boolean);

   VAR
      Test1,
      Test2:
         Integer;

   BEGIN
          .
          .
   END;
   ```

```
BEGIN
       .
       .
   Test(Formal1, Formal3, Formal2);
   Test(Formal2, Formal1, Formal3);
       .
       .
END.
```

5. For the program in exercise 4, fill in the following tables to show the matching that takes place between the actual and formal parameter lists in each of the two calls to procedure Test.

First Call to Test		Second Call to Test	
Formal	Actual	Formal	Actual
1. _____	_____	1. _____	_____
2. _____	_____	2. _____	_____
3. _____	_____	3. _____	_____

6. Show what is printed by the following program.

```
PROGRAM PreExam (Input, Output);

CONST
   Ten = 10;
VAR
   A,
   B,
   C:
       Integer;

PROCEDURE Test (VAR Z,
                    X,
                    A:
                        Integer);
BEGIN (* Test *)
   Readln(Z, X, A);
   A := Z * X + A
END;   (* Test *)

BEGIN (* PreExam *)
   Test(A, B, C);
   B := B + Ten;
   Writeln('The answers are ', B, C, A, Ten)
END.   (* PreExam *)
```

Use these data items: 3   2   4

7. Number the marked statements in the following program to show the order in which they will be executed (the logical order of execution).

```
PROGRAM Execute (Input, Output);

VAR
  Number1,
  Number2:
    Integer;

PROCEDURE Logical (VAR Value1,
                       Value2:
                           Integer);

VAR
  Value3:
    Integer;

BEGIN (* Logical *)
____    Readln(Value3, Value1);
____    Value2 := Value1 + 10
END;    (* Logical *)

BEGIN (* Execute *)
____    Writeln('Exercise');
____    Logical(Number1, Number2);
____    Writeln(Number1:6, Number2:6)
END.    (* Execute *)
```

8. How many of the marked statements in the preceding program are *not* procedure calls?

9. What would be the result if the last Writeln statement of the program in exercise 7 were changed to

```
Writeln(Value1:6, Value2:6)
```

10. If the program in exercise 7 were run with the data items 10   15, what would be the values of each of the variables just prior to the execution of the last statement in the program?

Number1 = _____   Number2 = _____   Value3 = _____

PREPROGRAMMING EXERCISES _____

1. Write the procedure heading for a procedure called Max that accepts a pair of integers and returns the greater of the two. Use comments to identify the parameters as input, output, or both.

2. Given the procedure heading

```
        PROCEDURE Halve (VAR FirstNumber,    (* Input/Output *)
                             SecondNumber:   (* Input/Output *)
                             Integer);
```

write the remainder of the procedure so that when it returns, the values that were originally in FirstNumber and SecondNumber have been replaced with half their original values.

3. Write a procedure named Increment, with one variable parameter of type Integer, that adds 15 to the value received in the parameter and returns the new value to the calling program.

4. (a) Write a procedure that reads in data values of type Integer (HeartRate) until a normal heart rate (between 60 and 80) is read or EOF becomes True. The procedure should return a parameter called Normal that contains True if a normal heart rate is read or False if ⟨eof⟩ is encountered.
   (b) Write the invoking statement for your procedure. Use the same variable names as in the procedure.

5. Given the procedure

```
            PROCEDURE Rotate (VAR FirstValue,
                                  SecondValue,
                                  ThirdValue:
                                      Integer);
            VAR
              Temp:
                 Integer;

            BEGIN
              Temp := FirstValue;
              FirstValue := SecondValue;
              SecondValue := ThirdValue;
              ThirdValue := Temp
            END;
```

   (a) Add appropriate comments to the procedure that will tell a reader what the procedure does and the purpose of each of the parameters and variables.
   (b) Write a program that reads three values, echo prints them, calls procedure Rotate with the three values as parameters, and then prints the parameters after the procedure returns.

6. Modify the procedure in exercise 5 to perform the same sort of operation on four values. Modify the program you wrote for part (b) of exercise 5 to work with the new version of this procedure.

7. Write a procedure that returns the first nonblank character it encounters on file Input. Call the procedure SkipBlanks.

8. Write a procedure that skips all characters on file Input until a blank is encountered. Call the procedure SkipToBlank.

9. Modify the procedure in exercise 8 so that it returns the number of characters that were skipped.

PROGRAMMING PROBLEMS

1. This problem involves rewriting the program developed for Programming Problem 3 in Chapter 5, using procedures. If you did Preprogramming Exercises 7 and 8 in this chapter, this problem should be very easy.

   Develop a top-down design and write a Pascal program to determine the number of words typed in as input. For the sake of simplicity, we will define a word to be any sequence of characters without blanks. Blanks are used to separate words (note that EOLN is quite conveniently represented by a blank when it is read as a character). Words may be separated by any number of blanks. A word may be any length from a single character to an entire line of characters. If you are writing the program for a batch system, then it should echo print the input. On an interactive system you do not need to echo print for this program.

   For example, for the following data the program would indicate that 26 words were entered.

   ```
   This isn't exactly an example of gOOd english, but it
   does demonstrate that a wOrd is just a se@uence of
   characters    withOu+ any blank$. ##### .......
   ```

   Hint: One way of solving this problem involves using a procedure that reads sequences of nonblank characters and another that reads sequences of blanks.

   Now that your programs are becoming more complex, it is even more important that you use good indentation, meaningful identifiers, plenty of comments, and good style.

2. Develop a top-down design and write a Pascal program to play the children's game "rock, paper, scissors." In this game, two people simultaneously choose either rock, paper, or scissors. Whether or not one wins depends not only on what one chooses, but also on what one's opponent chooses. The rules are as follows:

   Paper covers rock; paper wins.

   Scissors cut paper; scissors win.

   Rock breaks scissors; rock wins.

   All matching combinations are ties.

   The input to the program will be on two files, Player1 and Player2. Each line of a file contains one of the letters R, P, and S (for rock, paper, and scissors, respectively). Corresponding lines in the two files represent one play by the two players. The series of plays ends when ⟨eof⟩ is reached on one or both of the files.

   The program should print out each play and who the winner is. At the end of the game, the program should print the number of plays won by each player and the number of ties, and declare an overall winner.

   As always, use plenty of comments, good documentation and coding style, and meaningful identifiers throughout this program. It's up to you to decide which of your design modules should be coded as procedures to make the program easier to understand.

3. Develop a top-down design and write a Pascal program to print a calendar for a year, given the year and the day of the week that January 1 falls on. It may help to think of this task as printing 12 calendars, one for each month, given the day of the week that a month

starts on and the number of days in the month. Each successive month starts on the day of the week that follows the last day of the preceding month. Days of the week should be numbered 0 through 6 for Sunday through Saturday. Don't forget that years that are divisible by four are leap years. Here is a sample run for an interactive system:

```
What year do you want a calendar for?
1985
What day of the week does January 1 fall on?
(Enter 0 for Sunday, 1 for Monday, etc.)
2
        1985

     January

  S  M  T  W  T  F  S
  ─────────────────────
        1  2  3  4  5
  6  7  8  9 10 11 12
 13 14 15 16 17 18 19
 20 21 22 23 24 25 26
 27 28 29 30 31


     February

  S  M  T  W  T  F  S
  ─────────────────────
                 1  2
  3  4  5  6  7  8  9
 10 11 12 13 14 15 16
 17 18 19 20 21 22 23
 24 25 26 27 28


 . . . . . . . . . . . . . . . . . . .
 . . . . . . . . . . . . . . . . . . .
 . . . . . . . . . . . . . . . . . . .


     December

  S  M  T  W  T  F  S
  ─────────────────────
  1  2  3  4  5  6  7
  8  9 10 11 12 13 14
 15 16 17 18 19 20 21
 22 23 24 25 26 27 28
 29 30 31
```

In writing your program, be sure to use good indentation, meaningful identifiers, plenty of comments, and good style.

■ *To be able to do the following tasks, given a Pascal program with procedures:*
   determine whether each parameter is a VAR or value parameter
   determine whether a variable is being referenced globally
   determine which variables are local variables
   determine which variables are defined in each block.

■ *To be able to do the following tasks, given a top-down design of a problem:*
   determine what the formal and actual parameter lists should be for each module
   determine which formal parameters should be VAR parameters and which should be value parameters
   determine what local variables should be declared for each module
   code the program correctly.

■ *To be able to determine the scope of each variable in a program.*

■ *To be able to determine the contents of variables during execution of a program with procedures.*

■ *To understand and be able to avoid undesirable side effects.*

7

Value Parameters and Nested Scope

Chapter 6 introduced procedures and VAR parameters. We saw that when VAR parameters are used care must be taken to avoid unintentionally changing the value of an actual parameter. Because the location of an actual parameter is passed to a VAR parameter, any changes that a procedure makes to a VAR parameter are made directly to the corresponding actual parameter.

This chapter will introduce another kind of parameter in which the *value* of the actual parameter is what is transmitted to the formal parameter. Formal parameters of this type are, reasonably enough, called *value parameters.* When a procedure changes a value parameter, the actual parameter does not change. Using value parameters thus helps us to avoid unintentional changes to actual parameters.

This chapter will also examine the Pascal rules by which a procedure may access identifiers that are declared outside of its own block.

VAR/VALUE PARAMETERS

We saw in Chapter 6 that with the VAR parameter, the *location* of an actual parameter is passed to the corresponding formal parameter. (VAR parameters are sometimes said to be *passed by address,* because a memory address is passed to the formal parameter. VAR parameters are also said to be *passed by reference,* because statements in the procedure can directly refer to the actual parameter.) With a *value* parameter, on the other hand, a *copy* of the value of the actual parameter is passed to the formal parameter. (We say that this kind of parameter is *passed by value.*) Because the procedure doesn't know the location of an actual parameter that is passed by value, it cannot change the contents of the actual parameter.

The different types of parameters can be a little confusing. The following table summarizes each of the types we've seen.

Parameter type	Usage
Actual	Appears in a procedure call statement. May be passed to either a formal VAR or a formal value parameter.
Formal VAR	Appears in a procedure heading. Receives the address of the actual parameter in the corresponding position of the procedure call.
Formal value	Appears in a procedure heading. Receives a copy of the value stored in the actual parameter in the corresponding position of the procedure call.

As you can see, there are really only three kinds of parameters that we have to work with. There are now two kinds of formal parameters: VAR and value. VAR and value parameters can be freely mixed. That is, a single procedure heading can contain both VAR and value parameters. We'll get to the syntax for value parameters shortly, but first let's look at how and why they are used.

Value Parameter Semantics

When a parameter is passed by value, the procedure only works with a copy of the value of the actual parameter. The actual parameter is thus protected from any changes that a procedure might try to make to it. If a procedure does contain a statement that changes a value parameter, only the copy of the actual parameter is changed, not the original.

When a procedure returns, the values stored in its formal parameters are erased. Thus the program or procedure that made the call never sees any of the changes that were made to the formal value parameters. Value parameters are very much like local variables in this respect in that the values stored in local variables by a procedure are destroyed when the procedure returns. The difference between the two is that the values of local variables are undefined when a procedure starts to execute, whereas formal value parameters are automatically set equal to the corresponding actual parameters.

Because the contents of value parameters are destroyed when the procedure returns, they cannot be used to return information to the calling procedure or program. What good are parameters that information can't come back through? First of all, not all parameters are used to return results. Some are used only for inputting values to a procedure. Value parameters are perfect for this task. If you want to return a result, of course, you should use a VAR parameter. In our ticket clerk analogy, we would use value parameters to pass the request to the clerk and VAR parameters to get the seat assignments and price back.

Interface Design

We return now to the issue of interface design, which was discussed briefly in Chapter 6. Recall that the combination of the formal parameters and actual parameters constitutes an interface between the calling program and the procedure being called.

In Chapter 6 we saw that to design this interface we must write down all of the things the calling program has that the procedure needs, and all of the things the procedure computes that the program needs. This list of all the values that get passed back and forth can be directly coded as the formal and actual parameters (the interface).

In Chapter 6, however, all of the formal parameters were VAR parameters. How do we fit value parameters into the interface design process? Consider that the things to be passed back and forth can be divided into three types:

1. Those the program has that the procedure needs.

2. Those the procedure computes that must be returned to the program.

3. Those the program has that the procedure needs, but that the procedure also changes and must return to the program.

These three categories can be called *needs, returns,* and *needs/returns* (alternatively, they are sometimes called *in, out,* and *in/out*). Now, when we create our list of the things that get passed between the program and the procedure, we will mark each item in the list with one of these classifications. Any item that can be classified purely as a need should be coded as a formal value parameter. Items in the remaining two classes (returns and needs/returns) will be the formal VAR parameters.

There are exceptions to this rule. Pascal requires that all files that are passed as parameters be passed as VAR parameters. The reason for this exception has to do with the way parameters and files are implemented, and the fact that the values in a file are not stored in main memory. We will see one more exception in Chapter 11.

Why do we need to bother with the two types of formal parameters? Why not just use VAR parameters all the time? There are three reasons for using value parameters: (1) They prevent unwanted side effects in the program; (2) they make the interface design clear to someone reading the program; and (3) their actual parameters can be expressions.

Let's go over each of these reasons. First of all, what is a *side effect?* Let's look at an example. Suppose you included the following statement in a Pascal program:

```
Writeln(Variable);
```

What you expect is that the call to Writeln will print the value of the variable. But what if Writeln also *changes* the value of the variable? This is an example of an unexpected and unwanted side effect. Side effects are often caused by a combination of VAR parameters and careless coding in a procedure; somewhere in the procedure, an assignment statement stores a temporary result in one of the VAR parameters, accidentally changing the value of an actual parameter back in the program. The use of value parameters avoids this type of side effect by preventing the change to the formal parameter from reaching the actual parameter.

Appropriate use of VAR and value parameters helps anyone reading a program to know which actual parameters might be subject to change and which will not be changed. Such information can be a great help in debugging.

In Chapter 6 we were restricted to using only variables as actual parameters. This was because VAR parameters must be passed the location of a variable, which the procedure may subsequently assign a new value to. Since value parameters are only passed copies of the values of their actual parameters, anything that has a value may be passed to a value parameter. This includes constants, variables, and even expressions. An expression is simply evaluated and a copy of the result is placed in the corresponding value parameter. Also, just as an Integer value may be assigned to a Real variable, an Integer value may be passed to a value parameter of type Real (this is not allowed with VAR parameters).

If these three reasons make you wonder why you would ever want to use VAR parameters, just keep in mind that sometimes a procedure has to return results. All of the returned results must be passed back through VAR parameters. However, the remaining formal parameters should be value parameters.

Value Parameter Syntax

Value parameters are distinguished from VAR parameters by not having the keyword VAR before the identifier in the formal parameter list. The syntax diagram for a procedure heading is expanded to the following form.

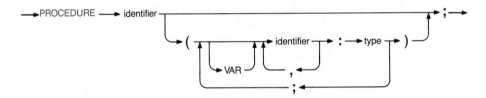

Let's look at an example of a procedure heading with a mixture of VAR and value parameter declarations:

```
PROCEDURE Example (VAR Parameter1:        (* A VAR parameter          *)
                       Integer;
                   Parameter2,            (* Two value parameters      *)
                   Parameter3:            (* of type Real              *)
                       Real;
                   VAR Parameter4:        (* Another VAR parameter     *)
                       Real;
                   Parameter5:            (* A value parameter         *)
                       Boolean;
                   Parameter6:            (* A value parameter         *)
                       Char);
```

As you can see, value parameter declarations are like VAR parameter declarations except that the keyword VAR is omitted. Since there is no Pascal keyword to make it easy to spot the value parameters, it's important to use an indentation style that will make them obvious in the code.

The following problem illustrates the interface design process and the use of value and VAR parameters.

Problem Solving in Action

Problem: Write a program that reads names in the form

Mary   Brown
Sam   Green

and prints them out in the form

Brown, M.
Green, S.

The input may contain any number of blanks preceding the first name and between the first and last names. Each person's name is on a separate line of input.

Discussion: This would be an easy task to do by hand. We would read the two names and write down the second one, followed by a comma. We would then go back and write down the first letter of the first name, followed by a period. This is basically how we will program the problem. The hard part is trying to simulate "reading the two names." The program will have to read one character at a time, then examine it and decide what to do with it.

Let's analyze this process by going character by character through the input by hand, moving from left to right. The first character will be either a blank or a letter. If it is a blank, we skip over it and get another character. If it is a letter, we need to save it, since it is the first initial.

Once we have the first initial, we are not interested in the rest of the first name. So we must continue to read until we reach the last name. How do we recognize the beginning of the last name? Well, it is the first letter after the blank(s) following the first name. Once we find the last name, we continue reading and printing each character until we find a blank. Then we print a comma followed by a blank and the initial of the first name, which we saved, followed by a period.

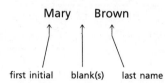

Mary   Brown

first initial   blank(s)   last name

Now that we have analyzed the problem, we can do our top-down design.

Input: A series of names, with one person's name (first and last) on each line of input in the form

First   Last

where there may be any number of blanks preceding the first name and one or more blanks between the two names.

Output: A corresponding series of lines of the form

Last, F.

Assumptions: Middle names are not present in the input.

PSIA ▰▰▰▰▰▰▱

MAIN MODULE   Level 0

```
WHILE NOT EOF DO
   GetInitial
   PrintLast
   PrintInitial
```

GETINITIAL   (Returns: Initial)   Level 1

```
SkipBlanks
SaveInitial
```

PRINTLAST

```
FindLast
Print
```

PRINTINITIAL

```
Writeln', ', Initial, '.'
```

SKIPBLANKS   (Returns: First nonblank letter)   Level 2

```
GetCh
WHILE Ch = blank
   GetCh
```

SAVEINITIAL

```
Initial  Ch
```

FINDLAST   (Returns: First character of last name)

```
SkipFirst
SkipBlanks
```

PSIA

PRINT (Needs: First character of last name)

```
WHILE Ch <> blank DO
    Write(Ch)
    GetCh
```

SKIPFIRST   Level 3

```
WHILE Ch <> blank
    GetCh
```

GETCH

```
Read(Ch)
```

This design goes to four levels. From the design we can see that SaveInitial, Print-Initial, and GetCh are only one line of code each. Let's not make them procedures but instead put each line of code in the level above.

Module Structure Chart:

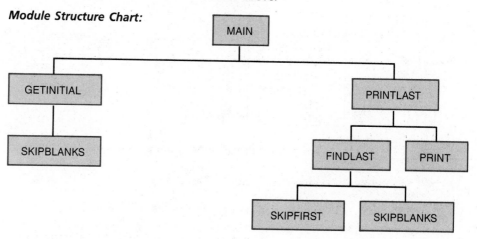

Before coding this problem, we need to spell out clearly the module or procedure interfaces.

MAIN MODULE: Calls GetInitial and PrintLast. Must receive back from GetInitial the first letter of the first name (actual parameter). No parameters are passed between Main and PrintLast.

GETINITIAL: Is called by Main. Calls SkipBlanks. Must return the first letter of the first name (formal VAR parameter) to Main. Must receive back from SkipBlanks the first nonblank character (actual parameter).

PSIA

PRINTLAST: Is called by Main. Calls FindLast and Print. Returns nothing to main (no formal parameters). Must receive the first character of the last name from FindLast (actual parameter). Must pass the first character of the last name to Print (actual parameter).

FINDLAST: Is called by PrintLast. Returns the first character of the last name to PrintLast (formal VAR parameter). Calls SkipFirst and SkipBlanks. No parameters are passed between FindLast and SkipFirst. Receives the first character of the last name from SkipBlanks (actual parameter).

SKIPFIRST: Is called by FindLast. Just reads until a blank is found, so needs nothing and returns nothing (no formal parameters).

SKIPBLANKS: Is called by GetInitial and FindLast. Returns the first nonblank character it reads to the calling procedure (formal VAR parameter).

PRINT: Is called by PrintLast. Needs the first character of the last name from PrintLast (formal value parameter). Returns nothing.

Now we can begin to code our program. Does the physical order of the procedures matter? Yes, a procedure must be declared before it is used or referenced by another procedure. Therefore, the lowest-level modules should be declared first. Within this constraint, however, it improves readability to put the modules in logical order. For example, a lower-level module that is only called by one higher-level module may be nested within the calling module. A good ordering here would be

```
SkipBlanks
GetInitial
PrintLast
    FindLast
        SkipFirst
    Print
```

The following Pascal program parallels our design.

```pascal
PROGRAM Transpose (Input, Output);

(* This program reformats names to be in the form of last name, comma,
   blank, first initial, period.  The input is in the form of first
   name, blanks, last name with one person's name per input line *)


CONST
   Blank = ' ';        (* Name separator character *)


VAR
   Initial:            (* Holds first initial       *)
      Char;

(************************************************************************)
```

PSIA ▬▬▬▬▬

```
PROCEDURE SkipBlanks (VAR Ch:          (* Returns first nonblank input *)
                                  Char);

(* Reads characters from Input until a nonblank is found *)

BEGIN (* SkipBlanks *)
  Read(Ch);
  WHILE Ch = Blank DO
    Read(Ch)
END;   (* SkipBlanks *)


(************************************************************************)


PROCEDURE GetInitial (VAR Initial:     (* Returns first initial *)
                                  Char);

(* Returns the first letter in the first name *)

VAR
  Ch:       (* Holds letter returned by SkipBlanks *)
    Char;

BEGIN (* GetInitial *)
  SkipBlanks(Ch);
  Initial := Ch
END;   (* GetInitial *)


(************************************************************************)


PROCEDURE PrintLast;

(* Skips the rest of the first name, then prints the person's
   last name on Output *)

VAR
  Ch:      (* Holds first letter of last name *)
    Char;


(************************************************************************)


PROCEDURE FindLast (VAR Ch:      (* Returns first char of last name *)
                               Char);

(* Scans Input for the first letter of a person's last name by
   skipping the nonblank characters in the first name, then skipping
   the blanks between the first and last names *)


(************************************************************************)
```

PSIA ▬▬▬▬▬▬

```
PROCEDURE SkipFirst;

(* Skips over characters remaining in a person's first name by
   reading characters from Input until a blank is found *)

VAR
   Ch:        (* Holds a character from the first name *)
     Char;

BEGIN (* SkipFirst *)
  Read(Ch);
  WHILE Ch <> Blank DO
    Read(Ch)
END;   (* SkipFirst *)

(*********************************************************************)

BEGIN (* FindLast *)
  SkipFirst;
  SkipBlanks(Ch)
END;   (* FindLast *)

(*********************************************************************)

PROCEDURE Print (Ch:    (* Receives first character of last name *)
                   Char);

(* Prints a person's last name by printing the input parameter and
   then reading and printing from Input to Output until a blank is
   read *)

BEGIN (* Print *)
  WHILE Ch <> Blank do
    BEGIN
      Write(Ch);
      IF NOT EOLN
        THEN
          Read(Ch)
        ELSE
          Ch := Blank
    END
END;   (* Print *)

(*********************************************************************)
```

PSIA

```
BEGIN (* PrintLast *)
  FindLast(Ch);
  Print(Ch)
END;    (* PrintLast *)


(****************************************************************)

BEGIN (* Transpose *)
  WHILE NOT EOF DO
    BEGIN
      GetInitial(Initial);
      PrintLast;
      Writeln(', ', Initial, '.');                  (* Print Initial *)
      Readln
    END
END.    (* Transpose *)
```

Testing: The test data for Program Transpose should include names of different lengths, ranging from a single character to many characters. Some of the names should be preceded by one or more blanks, and the number of blanks separating the two names should be varied. It would also be instructive to try the program with some invalid data, such as a line with no names, one name, more than two names, and so on.

Notice that Program Transpose has several procedures nested within procedures: SkipFirst is nested in FindLast, and Print and FindLast are nested in PrintLast. Nesting is a matter of style in this program, and more will be said about nesting procedures later in this chapter. The important thing to observe at this point is how the pattern of a block is repeated at each level of nesting.

This problem is actually too simple to need such an involved structure. For example, some of the procedures have only two lines of code between BEGIN and END. We could just as easily have written these statements directly in place of the call to those procedures. However, we've set the problem up this way to illustrate such concepts as interface design, nesting of procedures, and multiple calls to a procedure (SkipBlanks).

This is not to say that you should never write a procedure with as few as two statements in it. In some cases your decomposition of a problem will make a two-line procedure quite appropriate. When deciding whether to code a module directly in the next higher level or as a procedure, simply ask yourself the following question: Which way will make the overall program easier to read, understand, and modify later? With experience you will develop your own set of guidelines for making this decision. For example, if a two-line module is to be called from several places in the program, it should be coded as a procedure.

In Program Transpose a specific style is followed in the comments next to the formal parameters to aid users in distinguishing how each parameter is used. The comments next to the formal VAR parameters all begin with the word "Returns." The comment next to the single formal value parameter begins with the word "Receives." If any of the formal VAR parameters had been used to get the value of an actual parameter and then change the actual parameter's contents, their comments would have started with "Receives/returns." These comments can be written from the needs/returns lists developed during the interface design process. Here is another example:

```
PROCEDURE Example (    Ch:      (* Receives ...                  *)
                    Char;
              VAR Num1,        (* Receives/returns ...           *)
                    Num2,        (* Receives/returns ...           *)
                    Sum:         (* Returns ...                    *)
                    Integer);
```

Comments in the form of rows of asterisks were used in Program Transpose to make each procedure stand out from the surrounding code. Each procedure also had its own block of introductory comments, just like those at the start of a program. It's important to put as much care into documenting each procedure as you would into documenting a program.

Well-designed and well-documented procedures can often be reused directly in other programs. For example, skipping blanks is a common operation in processing character data. Whenever you encounter this subproblem, you should be able to directly use procedure SkipBlanks from Program Transpose. Many programmers keep a library of such procedures that they use over and over again. In fact, there are even companies that sell collections of procedures for various applications (statistical analysis, business, graphics, etc.).

Well-documented procedures can make it easy for you to code solutions developed with the building-block approach to problem solving discussed in Chapter 2.

LOCAL VERSUS GLOBAL DECLARATIONS

As we saw in Chapter 6, local variables are those variables defined in the VAR section of a procedure (not to be confused with VAR parameters). These are variables that the procedure needs for itself, such as counter variables.

In Program Transpose, GetInitial needed a place to read a character into, so a local variable Ch was defined. Procedure PrintLast also needed a place to read a character into, so a local variable called Ch was defined there also. The fact that both used the same identifier causes no problems because, as we saw in Chapter 6, local variables can be accessed only by statements within the block in which they are defined.

GetInitial is *outside* of the block defined by PrintLast. Thus, statements in GetInitial cannot access anything declared in the block defined by PrintLast. The opposite is also true: PrintLast is outside of GetInitial's block, so statements within PrintLast cannot access anything declared in GetInitial. To each of these procedures, it's as if the other procedure's local variables didn't even exist. Thus they can both use the same local variable name without any confusion.

The same access rules apply to any of the declarations or definitions that may appear in a block: Constants and procedures may be accessed only in the block in which they are defined or declared. Thus they are called local constants and local procedures, respectively.

So much for local declarations. What are *global* declarations? Any variable, constant, or procedure declared in the *main program* is global and may be referenced at any point following its declaration (including points within procedures). In Program Transpose, Blank is a global constant. It is defined in the main program and used in SkipBlanks, SkipFirst, and Print. SkipBlanks is a global procedure. It is defined in the main program and used in GetInitial and FindLast. GetInitial and PrintLast are also global procedures, but they are used only by the main program. There is one global variable declared in Program Transpose, but it is only accessed by the main program.

Global Any identifier declared in the main program is said to be global because it is accessible to everything that follows it.

When a procedure contains a local identifier with the same name as a global identifier, the local identifier takes precedence within the procedure. This principle is called *name precedence*.

Name Precedence A local identifier in a procedure takes precedence over a global identifier with the same spelling in any references that the procedure makes to that identifier.

Let's look at another example of local and global declarations.

```
PROGRAM Example (Input, Output);
CONST
   A = 17;

VAR
   B,     (* A global variable      *)
   C:     (* Another global variable *)
      Integer;

PROCEDURE One (C:        (* Prevents access to global C *)
               Real);
```

```
            VAR
              B:          (* Prevents access to global B *)
                Real;

            BEGIN (* One *)
              B := 2.3;
              Writeln('A = ', A:1);
              Writeln('B = ', B:3:1);
              Writeln('C = ', C:3:1)
            END;    (* One *)

            BEGIN (* Example *)
              B := 4;
              C := 6;
              One(42.0)
            END.    (* Example *)
```

In this example, procedure One accesses global constant A, but defines its own local variables B and C. Thus the output would be

```
    A = 17
    B = 2.3
    C = 42.0
```

Local variable B takes precedence over global variable B, effectively hiding the global B from the statements in procedure One. Formal parameter C also blocks access to global variable C from within the procedure. Formal parameters act just like local variables in this respect.

SCOPE RULES

Now that we've looked intuitively at the rules that define how a statement may access identifiers declared outside of its block, we can formally define the access rules. If we were to list all of the places from which a global identifier would be accessed, we would be describing that identifier's *scope of access,* often just referred to as its *scope.* The access rules are thus called *scope rules.*

Scope Rules The rules that determine where in a program a given identifier may be accessed.

The Pascal scope rules are a little more complicated than the preceding examples because they must take into account what happens when procedures are nested within other procedures. When procedures are nested, we refer to anything that is declared in a block containing a nested procedure as being *nonlocal* to that procedure. (Global identifiers are nonlocal with respect to all blocks other than the main program.) If a procedure accesses any identifier declared outside of its own block, we call this access a *nonlocal access.*

Nonlocal Any identifier declared outside of a given block is said to be nonlocal with respect to that block.

The actual scope rules are as follows:

1. The scope of an identifier includes all of the statements following its definition, within the block containing the definition. This includes nested blocks, except as noted in rule 2.

2. The scope of an identifier does not extend to any nested block that contains a locally defined identifier with the same spelling.

3. The scope of a formal parameter is identical to the scope of a local variable in the same procedure.

Let's look at Program Transpose in terms of the blocks it defines and see just what these rules mean. Figure 7-1 shows the headings and declarations in Program Transpose, with the resulting scopes of access indicated by boxes.

In Figure 7-1 (page 274), anything inside a box can refer to anything whose box includes that box, but anything outside of a box can't refer to anything inside that box. Thus a statement in procedure SkipFirst could access any identifier declared in SkipFirst, FindLast, PrintLast, or the main program. A statement in SkipFirst could *not* access identifiers declared in Print, GetInitial, or SkipBlanks, because to do so it would have to enter their boxes from outside.

Notice that the formal parameters for a procedure are inside the procedure's box, but the procedure name itself is outside of the box. If the name of the procedure were also inside the box, the program could never call the procedure.

Imagine the walls of the boxes in Figure 7-1 as two-way mirrors with the reflective side on the outer surfaces and the see-through side on the inner surfaces. If you stood in the box for FindLast, you would be able to see out through all of the surrounding boxes to the declarations of the main program (and anything in between). However, you would not be able to see into any other boxes, because their mirrored outer surfaces would block your view. Likewise, if someone were standing in a box that was outside of yours (such as Print), they wouldn't be able to see anything in your box. Furthermore, if there were a box inside your box (such as SkipFirst), you would only see its mirrored surface, but somebody inside the Skip-First box would be able to look out and see everything declared in your box. Because of this analogy, the term *visible* is often used in describing a scope of access. For example, we might say that Blank is visible throughout the program, meaning that it can be accessed from anywhere in the program.

Figure 7-1 does not tell the whole story of the scope of access in Program Transpose. The figure only represents scope rules 1 and 3. We must also keep the name precedence of rule 2 in mind. For example, a variable called Ch is defined in six different places in Program Transpose. Because of name precedence, the scope of

Figure 7-1
Scope Diagram for
Program Transpose

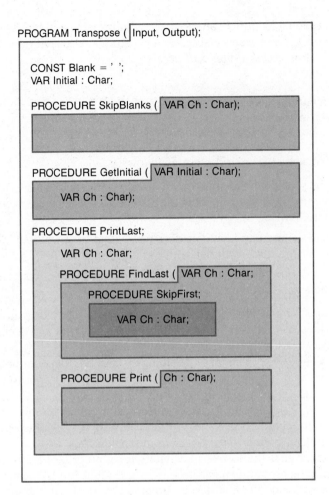

each of those variables is restricted to the procedure in which it is defined—all of the nested procedures redefine Ch locally.

Name precedence is implemented by the compiler as follows. When a statement refers to an identifier, the compiler first checks the declarations in the procedure containing the statement. If the identifier isn't declared there, the compiler goes outside of the procedure. If procedures are nested, the compiler works its way outward through each level of nesting until it finds an identifier with the same spelling. If there are any identifiers with the same name declared at a level that is even further out, they are never reached.

If the compiler searches all the way out to the declarations in the main program and still can't find an identifier with the same name, a compiler error message such as "UNDECLARED IDENTIFIER" will result.

Such a message most likely indicates a misspelling or that the identifier was not declared. However, this message may also indicate that the nesting of procedures is such that the scope of the identifier doesn't include the block where the error occurred. Or it might be that the identifier was not declared before the reference to it.

Here is another example to demonstrate the scope rules.

```
PROGRAM Example (Input, Output);

VAR
  A1:      (* One global variable     *)
     Integer;
  A2:      (* Another global variable *)
     Boolean;

(****************************************************************)

PROCEDURE Block3 (    A1:      (* Prevents access to global A1 *)
                      Integer;
              VAR B2:      (* Has same scope as C1 and D2   *)
                      Boolean);

VAR
  C1,       (* A variable local to Block3         *)
  D2:       (* Another variable local to Block3 *)
     Integer;

BEGIN (* Block3 *)
  .
  .
END;  (* Block3 *)

(****************************************************************)

PROCEDURE Block1;
VAR
  A1,       (* Prevents access to global A1              *)
  B2:       (* Local to Block1, no conflict with B2 in Block3 *)
     Integer;

(****************************************************************)

PROCEDURE Block2;

VAR
  C1,       (* Local to Block2, no conflict with C1 in Block3 *)
  B2:       (* Prevents nonlocal access to B2 in Block1, no
               conflict with B2 in Block3 *)
     Integer;

BEGIN (* Block2 *)
  .
  .
END;  (* Block2 *)

(****************************************************************)
```

```
BEGIN (* Block1 *)
  .

  .

  .

END;   (* Block1 *)

(*****************************************************************)

BEGIN (* Example *)
  .

  .

  .

END.   (* Example *)
```

Figure 7-2 shows the scope diagram for Program Example.

Another way to document the scope of identifiers is with a table showing which identifiers may be accessed by statements in each procedure. Across the top of the table we will write the name of each procedure, including the main program. Down the side of the table we will list all of the identifiers, grouped according to where they are declared. In the table body, an asterisk indicates that statements in the

Figure 7-2
Scope Diagram for
Program Example

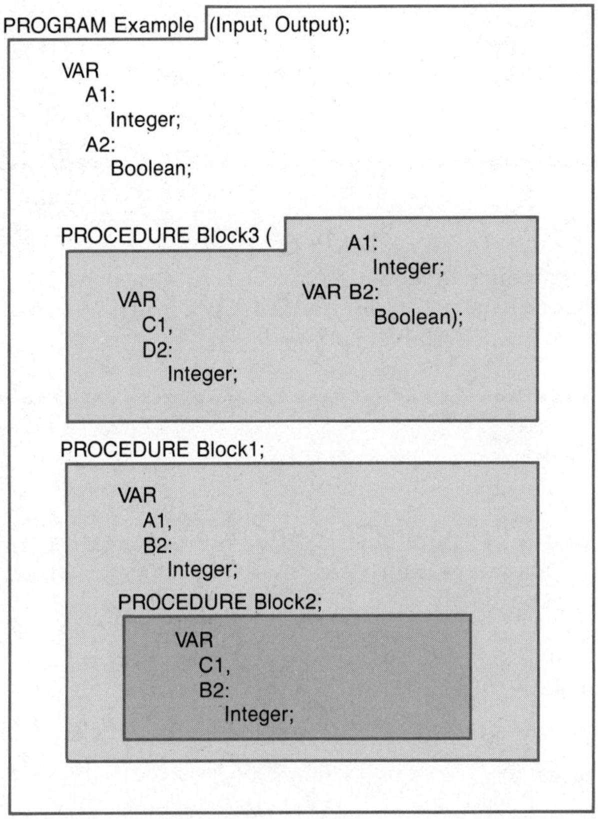

procedure named in the column heading are allowed to refer to the identifier listed in the left-hand column. For Program Example, such a table would look like this:

| | Procedure | | | |
Identifier	Example	Block3	Block1	Block2
Example				
A1	* ·			
A2	*	*	*	*
Block3	*	*	*	*
A1		*		
B2		*		
C1		*		
D2		*		
Block1	*		*	*
A1			*	*
B2			*	
Block2			*	*
C1				*
B2				*

Remember that the scope rules also apply to procedure names and constants. You may notice from this table that the scope rules allow a statement in a procedure to call that procedure. This process, called *recursion,* will be discussed in Chapter 8 and again in Chapter 17.

SIDE EFFECTS

If a procedure can directly access variables in the blocks surrounding it, you may wonder why we bother with parameter lists. You may be tempted to just skip designing the interface for a procedure and write the procedure using references to nonlocal variables. *Don't!* The use of nonlocal variable references is a very poor programming practice which can lead to program bugs that are extremely hard to locate. These bugs usually take the form of unwanted side effects.

Earlier in this chapter we mentioned that we use value parameters to minimize side effects, but what exactly is a side effect?

> **Side Effect** Any effect of one module on another module that is not a part of the explicitly defined interface between them.

A module is a procedure, a function, or the main program. The interface to a procedure is defined by its needs/returns list, which becomes the parameter list in the procedure heading.

Figure 7-3
Side Effects

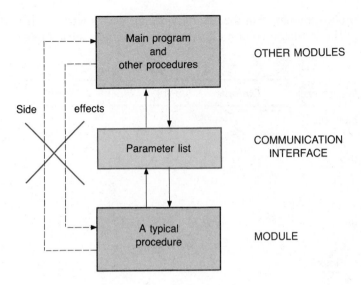

When a procedure accesses information stored outside of its own block in a manner other than through its parameters, the potential exists for unwanted side effects. For example, a bug in the procedure might cause the procedure to change the value of a global variable in an unexpected way, causing an error to occur in the main program.

It's also possible for unwanted side effects to occur if a formal VAR parameter is used where a value parameter will suffice. For example, if the VAR parameter is used as a loop control variable, the value of the actual parameter will be unintentionally changed, and the calculations that take place after the procedure returns may then produce erroneous results.

The symptoms of a side-effect bug are very misleading, because the trouble appears to be caused by one part of the program when it is really being caused by something that happens in another part of the program. This is what makes side-effect bugs so hard to find.

However, if procedures only access nonlocal variables through their parameter lists, and all needs-only parameters are value parameters, then each procedure is essentially isolated from what happens in other parts of the program and there won't be any side effects. In short, the actions of one procedure should not have side effects elsewhere in the program. The only external effect that a procedure should have is to transfer information through the well-defined interface of the parameter list. (See Figure 7-3.)

When a procedure is isolated from what happens in the rest of the program, it can be treated as an independent module. Procedures that have this kind of independence can be reused easily in other programs. Thus, if you carefully design the interface for every procedure that you write, you will soon have a large library of useful procedures that can be applied to many problems.

Here is a short example of a program that runs but produces incorrect results because of side effects.

```
PROGRAM Trouble (Input, Output);

(* This is an example of poor programming style, which
   causes a bug when the program is executed *)

VAR
   Ct:         (* Supposed to count input lines, but does it? *)
      Integer;
   Ch:         (* Holds one input character                 *)
      Char;


(**************************************************************************)

PROCEDURE Charct;

(* Counts the number of characters in a
   line of input and prints the count *)

BEGIN (* Charct *)
   Ct := 0;                                              (* Side effect *)
   WHILE NOT EOLN DO
     BEGIN
       Read(Ch);                          (* Global variable access *)
       Ct := Ct + 1                                      (* Side effect *)
     END;
   Readln;
   Writeln(Ct:1, ' characters on this line.')        (* Global access *)
END;   (* Charct *)


(**************************************************************************)

BEGIN (* Trouble *)
   Ct := 0;
   WHILE NOT EOF DO
     BEGIN
       Ct := Ct + 1;
       Charct
     END;
   Writeln(Ct:1, ' lines of input processed.')
END.   (* Trouble *)
```

Program Trouble is supposed to count and print the number of characters on each line of input. After the last line has been processed, it should print the number of lines. Strangely enough, each time the program is run, it reports that the number of lines of input is the same as the number of characters in the last line of input.

If a local variable Ct is declared in procedure Charct, the program will work correctly. There will be no conflict between the local Ct and the global Ct, because they are separate variables visible only to the blocks in which they are local. Ch, of course, should be declared locally in the procedure, since it is used only in the procedure.

Global Constants

Contrary to what you might think, it is acceptable to reference named constants globally. Because the values of global constants cannot be changed while the program is running, no side effects will occur.

There are two advantages to globally referencing constants: ease of change and consistency. If we have to change the value of a constant at a later date, it's easier to just change one global definition than to change a local definition in every procedure. By defining a constant in only one place, we also ensure that all of the parts of the program that reference it will use exactly the same value.

This is not to say that you should define *all* constants globally. If a constant is only needed in one procedure, then it should be defined locally within that procedure.

Here is the best rule for knowing where to define constants: A constant should be declared in the lowest-level block that contains all of the references to the constant. Quite often this ends up being the program declaration block.

DESIGNING PROGRAMS WITH NESTING

In Program Graph in Chapter 6 there was no nesting of procedures. We could just as easily have written Program Transpose without nesting procedures, had we not wanted to use the program to illustrate scope rules. Whether or not you nest your procedures is a matter of style and what your top-down design calls for. It is perfectly all right to list all your procedures sequentially without nesting, as long as you declare each procedure before you call it.

Nesting can sometimes make changing a program more difficult. For example, if we decided that we wanted another procedure in Program Transpose to call Skip-First, we might have to rewrite our program—because SkipFirst is nested in FindLast which is nested in PrintLast. The scope rules prevent a procedure at the same level as PrintLast from calling the nested SkipFirst.

If you think that you may want to call a procedure from more than one place, don't nest it. If one procedure is an integral part of another and has no functional meaning in any other context, nest it.

One advantage of nesting is that it makes your program follow more closely your top-down design. Another advantage is that, if a procedure has nested within it all of the procedures it will need to use, then it will be completely independent and can easily be reused in other programs. For example, to reuse GetInitial from Program Transpose in another program, we would also have to copy SkipBlanks into the new program. If SkipBlanks had been nested inside of GetInitial, we could simply copy SkipBlanks as part of GetInitial—knowing that GetInitial constitutes a complete, self-contained unit.

The disadvantage of strict application of nesting is that it may cause us to unnecessarily duplicate some code. For example, if SkipBlanks were nested inside of GetInitial, then FindLast could not call it. We would then have to nest a second copy of SkipBlanks inside of FindLast. This would make FindLast a complete, self-contained unit, but it would also waste program memory space in the computer.

We can compromise between strict nesting and straight line declarations of procedures by nesting those procedures that will be used only in the context of another procedure, while globally declaring those procedures that are widely used. The documentation for each globally declared procedure should include a list of all the procedures that make use of it. In the documentation for procedures that call the global procedure, it should be noted that the global procedure is necessary for proper execution.

It should also be noted that the module structure chart for a design only specifies how modules are called by other modules. The chart does not indicate whether the called modules are nested or declared globally. For example, Figure 7-4 shows the module structure chart for Program Transpose.

It would appear from studying this chart that SkipBlanks is declared twice in the program. However, we know that this isn't the case. There is another style of chart, called a *module nesting chart,* that depicts the nesting structure of modules and shows calls between them. Figure 7-5 shows a module nesting chart for Program Transpose.

Figure 7-4
Module Structure
Chart for Program
Transpose

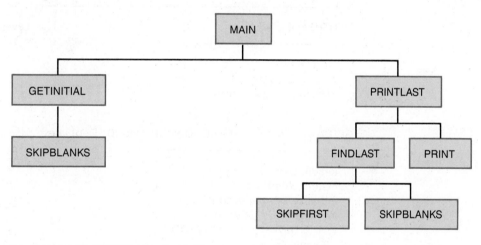

Figure 7-5
Module Nesting
Chart for Program
Transpose

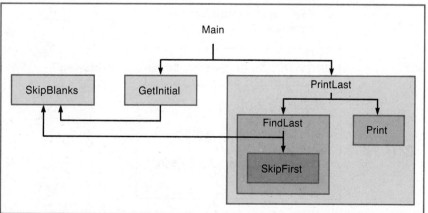

TESTING AND DEBUGGING

In Chapter 6 we wrote Program Graph using only VAR parameters. We also made several assumptions: Each file is in order by department IDs, there are the same departments in each store, and there is one piece of data per input line. What if there is an error in the data files? We have not paid too much attention to data error checking (also called *data validation*) in our programs, yet errors do occur. Let's redo our design for Program Graph to make use of value parameters where appropriate, and add some data validation. Here is our old design for Program Graph.

MAIN MODULE   Level 0

```
PrintHeader
WHILE NOT EOF(Store1) AND NOT EOF(Store2) DO
   GetData for Store1
   PrintData for Store1 dept.
   GetData for Store2
   PrintData for Store2 dept.
```

PRINTHEADER   Level 1

```
Writeln title
Writeln heading
Writeln bar graph scale
```

GETDATA   (Input: DataFile; Output: DeptID, DeptSales)

```
Readln DeptID
Readln NumDays
Initialize DeptSales to 0
Initialize Days (LCV) to 1
WHILE Days <= NumDays DO
   Readln Sales
   Add Sales to DeptSales
   Increment Days
```

PRINTDATA   (Input: DeptID, StoreNum, DeptSales)

```
Writeln DeptID
Write StoreNum
WHILE DeptSales > 250 DO
   Write '*'
   Decrement DeptSales by $500
Writeln
```

We can check for mismatched department IDs in the main program. To do this we will have to call GetData for both stores before we call PrintData. We will have to keep the returned IDs in separate variables, and compare their values after the second call to GetData. We can check for too few data values by inserting tests for EOF in procedure GetData. We can also add to the main program a test that will tell us if the two files do not have the same number of data sets.

From the old design it's easy to see that all the parameters for procedure PrintData can be value parameters. The use of value parameters will allow us to pass the store number as a literal constant in the calls to that procedure. It would also appear that the first parameter for procedure GetData could be a value parameter; however, DataFile is a parameter of type Text. Recall that files must be passed as VAR parameters.

Here is our new design. (We have replaced the Input and Output designations used for parameters in Chapter 6 with our new classification of parameters as Needs, Needs/Returns, or Returns.)

MAIN MODULE   Level 0

```
PrintHeader
WHILE NOT EOF(Store1) AND NOT EOF(Store2) DO
   GetData for Store1
   GetData for Store2
   IF ID1 <> ID2
     THEN
        Writeln 'Data error: Department IDs don''t match.'
     ELSE
        PrintData for Store1 dept.
        PrintData for Store2 dept.
IF EOF(Store1) <> EOF(Store2)
   THEN
     IF EOF(Store1)
     THEN
        Writeln 'Ran out of data for Store 1 before Store 2.'
     ELSE
        Writeln 'Ran out of data for Store 2 before Store 1.'
```

PRINTHEADER   Level 1

```
Writeln title
Writeln heading
Writeln bar graph scale
```

GETDATA   (Needs/Returns: DataFile; Returns: DeptID, DeptSales)

```
Readln DeptID from Data File
IF EOF(DataFile)
  THEN
    Writeln 'Data error: No data following dept. ID'
  ELSE
    Readln NumDays from Data File
    Initialize DeptSales to 0
    Initialize Days (LCV) to 1
    WHILE Days <= NumDays DO
      IF EOF(DataFile)
        THEN
          Writeln 'Data error: Ran out of data in mid-set.'
          Set Days to NumDays + 1 (end condition)
        . ELSE
          Readln Sales from Data File
          Add Sales to DeptSales
          Increment Days
```

PRINTDATA   (Needs: DeptID, StoreNum, DeptSales)

```
Writeln DeptID
Write StoreNum
WHILE DeptSales > 250 DO
  Write '*'
  Decrement DeptSales by $500
Writeln
```

The following Pascal program parallels our new design.

```
PROGRAM Graph (Store1, Store2, Output);

(* This program generates bar graphs of monthly sales by department for
   two Greenley department stores, permitting department by department
   comparison of sales *)

VAR
  ID1,            (* Department ID number for store 1 *)
  ID2:            (* Department ID number for store 2 *)
    Integer;
  Sales1,         (* Department sales for store 1      *)
  Sales2:         (* Department sales for store 2      *)
    Real;
  Store1,         (* Accounting file for store 1      *)
  Store2:         (* Accounting file for store 2      *)
    Text;

(********************************************************************)
```

```
PROCEDURE PrintHeader;

(* This procedure prints the title for the bar chart, a heading,
   and the numeric scale for the chart *)

BEGIN (* PrintHeader *)
  Writeln('Bar Graph Comparing Departments of Store#1 and Store#2');
  Writeln;
  Writeln('Store  Sales in 1,000s of dollars');
  Writeln(' #    0         5         10        15        20        25');
  Writeln('         |.........|.........|.........|.........|.........|')
END;   (* PrintHeader *)

(*****************************************************************************)

PROCEDURE GetData (VAR DataFile:        (* Receives/returns acct. file *)
                         Text;
                     VAR DeptID:          (* Returns dept. number        *)
                         Integer;
                     VAR DeptSales:       (* Returns monthly sales       *)
                         Real);

(* This procedure takes an input accounting file as a parameter, reads
   the department ID number and number of days of sales from that file,
   then reads one sales figure for each of those days, computing a total
   sales figure for the month.  This figure is returned in DeptSales *)

VAR
  NumDays,        (* Number of business days in the month  *)
  Day:            (* The LCV for a loop reading daily sales *)
    Integer;
  Sale:           (* One day's sales for the department    *)
    Real;

BEGIN (* GetData *)
  Readln(DataFile, DeptID);                      (* Get department ID *)
  IF EOF(DataFile)                               (* Data validation test *)
    THEN
      Writeln('Data error: No data following dept. ID.')
    ELSE
      BEGIN
        Readln(DataFile, Numdays);               (* Get number of days *)
        DeptSales := 0.0;                        (* Initialize process *)
        Day := 1;                                (* Initialize LCV *)
```

```
                WHILE Day <= NumDays DO
                  BEGIN
                    IF EOF(DataFile)                        (* Data validation test *)
                      THEN
                        BEGIN
                          Writeln('Data error: Ran out of data in mid-set.');
                          Day := NumDays + 1          (* Set loop end condition *)
                        END
                      ELSE
                        BEGIN
                          Readln(DataFile, Sale);           (* Update process *)
                          DeptSales := DeptSales + Sale;
                          Day := Day + 1                      (* Update LCV *)
                        END
                  END
            END
END;   (* GetData *)


(****************************************************************************)


PROCEDURE PrintData (DeptID,              (* Receives dept. ID number   *)
                     StoreNum:            (* Receives store number      *)
                       Integer;
                     DeptSales:           (* Receives total dept. sales *)
                       Real);

(* This procedure prints the department ID number, the store number,
   and a bar graph of the sales for the department.  The bar graph
   is printed at a scale of one mark per $500 *)

BEGIN (* PrintData *)
  Writeln('      Dept ', DeptID:1);                        (* Print ID *)
  Write(StoreNum:3, ' ':4);                      (* Print store number *)
  WHILE DeptSales > 250 DO
    BEGIN
      Write('*');                       (* Print '*' for each $500 *)
      DeptSales := DeptSales - 500               (* Update LCV *)
    END;
  Writeln                               (* Go to a new line *)
END;   (* PrintData *)


(****************************************************************************)


BEGIN (* Graph *)
  Reset(Store1);
  Reset(Store2);
  PrintHeader;
```

```
        WHILE NOT EOF(Store1) AND NOT EOF(Store2) DO        (* For each dept. *)
          BEGIN
            Writeln;
            GetData(Store1, ID1, Sales1);
            GetData(Store2, ID2, Sales2);
            IF ID1 <> ID2                                   (* Data validation test *)
              THEN
                Writeln('Data error: Department IDs don''t match.')
              ELSE
                BEGIN
                  PrintData(ID1, 1, Sales1);
                  PrintData(ID2, 2, Sales2);
                END
          END;
        IF EOF(Store1) <> EOF(Store2)
          THEN
            IF EOF(Store1)
              THEN
                Writeln('Ran out of data for Store 1 before Store 2.')
              ELSE
                Writeln('Ran out of data for Store 2 before Store 1.')
      END.   (* Graph *)
```

If either file ends prematurely or the department IDs are not the same for both stores, then an error message is printed. (More data validation could be added to this program—this is just an example.) It's important to note that each of the error messages in Program Graph describes the exact error that caused the message to be printed. This is a good programming practice to follow, because it aids the user of the program in determining what is wrong with the data. (Imagine how hard this would be if all of the error messages just said "Data error.")

We took advantage of the fact that a value parameter can have an expression for an actual parameter by using a constant in the call to PrintData. If we used a constant as the actual parameter for a VAR parameter, a compile-time error such as "ACTUAL PARAMETER MUST BE A VARIABLE" would result. A VAR parameter must have the address of a variable.

Many program bugs are the result of unintentional side effects. If you reference global variables only through the parameter list of your procedures, you will save yourself a lot of headaches during the debugging phase. Confusing and spurious effects of procedures will be avoided.

Stubs and Drivers

One of the advantages of a modular design is that we can begin to test the design long before the code has been written for all of the modules. How can we do this? By writing little dummy procedures called *stubs* for the modules that haven't been implemented yet. A stub will usually just consist of a Writeln statement that prints a message to the effect that "Procedure such-and-such just got called." Even though the stub doesn't do anything, it allows us to determine whether the stub was called at the right time by the program or calling procedure.

A stub can also be used to print the set of values that were passed to it in its parameters. This output tells us whether or not the part of the program that has been implemented is doing its job properly. Sometimes the stub will assign new values to its VAR parameters to simulate data being read or results being computed. This gives the rest of the program something to keep working on. Because we can choose the values that are returned by the stub, we have better control over the conditions of the test run.

Here is a stub that simulates procedure Print in Program Transpose.

```
PROCEDURE Print (Ch:     (* Receives first character of last name *)
                    Char);

(* Stub for procedure Print in Program Transpose *)

BEGIN (* Print *)
  Writeln('Print was called with Ch = ', Ch);
END;   (* Print *)
```

Here is a stub that simulates a call to SkipBlanks by returning an arbitrarily chosen character.

```
PROCEDURE SkipBlanks (VAR Ch:     (* Returns first nonblank input *)
                          Char);

(* Stub for procedure SkipBlanks in Program Transpose *)

BEGIN (* SkipBlanks *)
  Writeln('SkipBlanks was called here. Returning ''X''.');
  Ch := 'X'
END;   (* SkipBlanks *)
```

Each of these stubs is simpler than the procedure it simulates. This will usually be the case, since the object of using stubs is to provide a simple, predictable environment for testing the other parts of the program.

If you are having trouble debugging a particular procedure, you may want to test it in complete isolation. In that case, you would substitute stubs for all of the procedures that it calls. In addition, you would replace the program or procedure that calls it with a dummy program, called a *driver*. A driver is a stripped-down program that has just the bare minimum in definitions required to call the procedure being tested. By surrounding a procedure with a driver and stubs, you gain complete control of the conditions under which it executes. This allows you to try out different situations and combinations until a pattern that pinpoints the bug emerges.

Stub A dummy procedure or function that assists in testing part of a program. A stub has the same name and interface as a procedure or function that would actually be called by the part of the program being tested, but is usually much simpler.

Driver A simple main program that is used to call a procedure or function being tested. The use of a driver permits direct control of the testing process.

For example, the following program is a driver for procedure GetInitial in Program Transpose. A stub that simulates SkipBlanks is also used in this example.

```
PROGRAM GetInitialDriver (Output);

(* Provides an environment for testing procedure
   GetInitial in isolation from Program Transpose *)

VAR
  Initial:          (* Parameter to GetInitial *)
    Char;

(*******************************************************************)

PROCEDURE SkipBlanks (VAR Ch:          (* Returns first nonblank input *)
                          Char);

(* Stub for procedure SkipBlanks in Program Transpose *)

BEGIN (* SkipBlanks *)
  Writeln('SkipBlanks was called here.  Returning ''X''.');
  Ch := 'X'
END;   (* SkipBlanks *)

(*******************************************************************)

PROCEDURE GetInitial (VAR Initial:     (* Returns first initial *)
                          Char);

(* Returns the first letter in the first name *)

VAR
  Ch:             (* Holds letter returned by SkipBlanks *)
    Char;

BEGIN (* GetInitial *)
  SkipBlanks(Ch);
  Initial := Ch
END;   (* GetInitial *)

(*******************************************************************)

BEGIN (* GetInitialDriver *)
  Initial := 'Z';
  GetInitial(Initial);
  Writeln('GetInitial returned ', Initial)
END.   (* GetInitialDriver *)
```

Stubs and drivers are also used in *team programming*. When a project is too big for a single programmer to complete in a reasonable amount of time, it may be assigned to a team of programmers. The programmers develop the overall design and the interfaces between the modules (parameter lists). Each programmer then designs and codes one or more of the modules, and uses drivers and stubs to test the code. When all of the modules have been coded and tested, they are assembled into what should be a working program.

For team programming to work, it is essential that all of the module interfaces be explicitly defined and that the coded modules adhere strictly to the specifications for those interfaces. Obviously global variable references must be carefully avoided in a team programming situation, since it is impossible for everyone in a large team to know how everyone else is using every variable.

There is even one school of thought that says that global variables are so troublesome in a team programming situation that they should not even be allowed by the programming language. (There is another school of thought that says that they can be useful so long as they are extremely well documented.) Pascal does allow global variables, but there is a trick we can use to completely avoid them. The trick is to simply turn the main module into a procedure and have no other modules nested within it. The main module procedure must be the last procedure declared in the program. The structure of the program will then be as follows. Notice that the only statement in the body of the main program is a call to procedure Main.

```
PROGRAM NoGlobals (Input, Output);

(* Note: No VAR section here *)

PROCEDURE One  (...
              .

PROCEDURE N  (...
              .
              .

PROCEDURE Main;
VAR
              .

BEGIN (* Main *)
              .
                           (* Main module *)
              .
END;   (* Main *)

BEGIN (* NoGlobals *)
  Main
END.   (* NoGlobals *)
```

Testing and Debugging Hints

1. Make sure that variables used as actual parameters to a procedure are declared in the block where the procedure call is made.

2. Declare each procedure before any calls are made to it. (Don't call a procedure that hasn't been previously declared.)

3. When using formal and actual parameters, be aware that they are matched by position in the parameter list and their types must be the same.

   There is one exception to the rule that actual and formal parameters have to match data types exactly: If the formal parameter is a *value* parameter of type Real, the actual parameter may be either Real or Integer. (This is the same rule that allows us to assign Integer values to Real variables.)

4. Remember that a VAR parameter requires a variable as an actual parameter, whereas a value parameter can have any expression that supplies a value of the same data type (or in some cases even another data type, as noted in the preceding hint) as an actual parameter.

5. Use value parameters unless a value must be returned. VAR parameters can change the value of an actual parameter; value parameters cannot.

6. Carefully define the interface and the parameter list to eliminate side effects. Variables used only in a procedure should be declared as local variables. *Do not* reference nonlocal variables directly from inside a procedure.

7. Watch out for misspellings in local declarations. If you intend to use a local name that is the same as a global name, a misspelling in the local declaration will wreak havoc. The Pascal compiler won't complain, but instead will cause every reference to the local name to be to the global name instead.

8. Remember that the same identifier cannot be used in both the formal parameter list and the local declarations of a procedure.

9. Be sure the keyword VAR precedes each VAR parameter in the formal parameter list. A series of VAR parameters of the same data type may be separated by commas and preceded by a single VAR. When the keyword VAR is not used, the parameter is a value parameter. For example, given the parameter list

```
PROCEDURE One (    A,              (* value *)
                   B:              (* value *)
                      Integer;
               VAR C:              (* VAR   *)
                      Boolean;
                   D:              (* value *)
                      Boolean;
                   E,              (* value *)
                   F:              (* value *)
                      Real;
               VAR G,              (* VAR   *)
                   H:              (* VAR   *)
                      Integer);
```

C, G, H are VAR parameters, and A, B, D, E, F are value parameters.

10. Keep the scope rules in mind when arranging the order and nesting structure of procedures in a program. For example, given the structure

```
PROGRAM A

    PROCEDURE B

        VAR X: Integer;

    PROCEDURE C

    PROCEDURE D
```

procedures B and C can be called from within program A, but procedure D cannot be called from within A. Procedure B cannot call procedures C or D. Procedures B, C, and D may be called from within procedure C or procedure D.

11. If necessary, use debug Writeln statements to indicate when a procedure is called and if it is executing correctly. The values of the variables in the actual parameter list can be printed immediately before (to show the values of the input parameters) and immediately after (to show the values of the output parameters) the call to the procedure. You may want to use debug Writeln statements in the procedure itself to indicate every time it is called.

SUMMARY

Pascal has two types of formal parameters: VAR and value. VAR parameters have the word VAR before them in the formal parameter list. Value parameters do not have the word VAR before them. Parameters that return values from a procedure should be VAR parameters. All others should be value parameters. This minimizes side effects, since only a copy of the value of an actual parameter is passed to a value parameter and thus the original value cannot be changed.

Anything declared in the main program is visible to all procedures and is called *global.* Anything that is declared outside of a procedure that is visible from within that procedure is called *nonlocal* with respect to that procedure. This may include declarations in blocks in which the procedure is nested (if any). It is not good programming practice to reference nonlocal variables directly. All communication between the modules of a program should be done through the use of formal and actual parameter lists.

The use of global constants, on the other hand, is considered to be an acceptable programming practice, because it adds consistency and makes a program easier to change while avoiding the pitfalls of side effects.

The scope of a declaration refers to the parts of the program from which it is visible. The scope rules say that an identifier is visible to all statements between its definition and the end of its block, except those in nested blocks that declare an identifier with the same name. The formal parameters of a procedure have the same scope as would local variables declared in the procedure.

Stubs and drivers can be used to test procedures in isolation from the rest of a program. They are particularly useful in the context of team programming projects.

QUICK CHECK _____

1. (a) What distinguishes a variable parameter from a value parameter in a procedure heading? (p. 262)
   (b) How can you tell if a variable reference inside a procedure is local or global? (pp. 270–272)
   (c) Where are local variables defined in a procedure? (pp. 270–272)
   (d) When does the scope of an identifier not include a nested block? (pp. 272–274)

2. Assume that you are designing a program and you realize you will need a procedure that reads a given number of real values and returns their average. The number of values is in an integer variable called DataPoints, declared in the program.
   (a) How many parameters will there be in the actual and formal parameter lists, and what will their data type(s) be? (pp. 260–262)
   (b) Which of the formal parameters should be VAR and which should be value? (pp. 260–262)
   (c) What local variables, if any, will be required in the procedure? (pp. 260–262)

3. A program declares a variable called Framistats and a procedure called Fumble. Inside of Fumble, another procedure called Drop is declared. Inside of Drop, a variable, again called Framistats, is declared. Which version of Framistats would be accessed by the program, by Fumble, and by Drop? (pp. 270–274)

4. What is the difference between the kinds of information that are passed to VAR and value parameters? Which parameter protects the actual parameter from being changed by the procedure? (pp. 259–260)

5. Why is it a good idea to use value parameters whenever possible? Why is it a good idea to avoid directly accessing global variables? (pp. 277–280)

Answers
1. (a) A value parameter is not preceded by VAR in a procedure heading. (b) If the variable is not defined in either the VAR section of the procedure or its formal parameter list, then the reference is global. (c) Local variables are declared in the VAR declaration section of the procedure. (d) When the nested block declares an identifier with the same name. 2. (a) There will be two parameters: an Integer containing the number of values to be read and a Real containing the average. (b) The Integer should be a value parameter. The Real should be a VAR parameter. (c) Local variables will be needed for an input value, the sum, and the count of the values. 3. The program and Fumble access the Framistats declared by the program. Drop accesses its own version of Framistats. 4. VAR parameters receive locations of actual parameters. Value parameters get copies of the values in the actual parameters, thus protecting the actual parameters from change. 5. Both using value parameters and not accessing global variables directly will minimize side effects. Value parameters can also be passed expressions.

EXAM PREPARATION EXERCISES _____

1. Using a VAR parameter (passing by reference), a procedure can obtain the initial value of an actual parameter as well as change the value of the actual parameter in the calling program. (True or False?)

2. Using a value parameter, the value of a variable can be passed to a procedure and used for computation there, without any modification to the value of the variable in the main program. (True or False?)

3. A particular procedure can be a nested block relative to the program that contains it, and an enclosing block to any procedures declared within it. (True or False?)

4. Identifiers declared at the beginning of a block are accessible to all executable statements that are part of that block, including statements belonging to nested blocks (assuming the nested blocks don't have local identifiers with the same names). (True or False?)

5. If we declare a local variable in a procedure with the same name as a variable in an enclosing block, no confusion will result because references to variables in procedures are first interpreted as references to local variables. (True or False?)

6. Define the following:

value parameter   nonlocal access
variable parameter   scope
local variable   side effects
global variable   name precedence

7. Given the block structure

```
PROGRAM ScopeRules (Input, Output);
VAR
  A,
  B:
    Integer;

PROCEDURE Block1;
VAR
  A1,
  B1:
    Integer;

  PROCEDURE Block2;
  VAR
    A,
    A2,
    B2:
      Integer;
  BEGIN (* Block2 *)
     .
     .
  END;   (* Block2 *)

BEGIN (* Block1 *)
   .
   .
END;   (* Block1 *)

PROCEDURE Block3;
VAR
  A3,
  B3:
    Integer;
```

```
           BEGIN  (* Block3 *)
               .

           END;   (* Block3 *)

           BEGIN  (* ScopeRules *)
               .

           END.   (* ScopeRules *)
```

(a) A and B are global variables, accessible to all parts of Program ScopeRules, including procedure Block2. (True or False?)
(b) Since ScopeRules is the outermost block, statements in its body can reference all variables declared in inner blocks, including procedure Block2. (True or False?)
(c) Since procedure Block2 is the innermost block, its local variables can be accessed by all other blocks. (True or False?)
(d) Variable A1 is global with respect to procedure Block2. (True or False?)
(e) Variable B2 is local to procedure Block1. (True or False?)
(f) The statement A1 := A would be legal in procedure Block1. (True or False?)
(g) The statement A3 := A1 would be legal in procedure Block3. (True or False?)
(h) Variables A2 and B2 are not defined in any of the outer blocks. (True or False?)
(i) The statement A := B2 in procedure Block2 would assign the value of B2 to the local variable A, and the global A would not be affected. (True or False?)
(j) Variables A1 and B1 are global with respect to procedure Block2, local to procedure Block1, and not defined for the program outer block. (True or False?)

8. Draw a scope diagram for the block structure in exercise 7.

9. Read the following program containing procedure Change. Fill in the values of all variables before and after the procedure is called. Then fill in the values of all variables after the return to the main program. (Let "u" indicate an undefined value.)

```
           PROGRAM Sample (Input, Output);
           VAR
             A,
             B:
                Integer;

           PROCEDURE Change (    X:
                                    Integer;
                               VAR Y:
                                    Integer),
           VAR
             B:
                Integer;
           BEGIN (* Change *)
             B := X;
             Y := Y + B;
             X := Y
           END; (* Change *)
```

```
BEGIN (* Sample *)
  A := 10;
  B := 7;
  Change(A, B);
  Writeln(A:6, B:6)
END.  (* Sample *)
```

Variables in Sample just before Change is called.

A _____

B _____

Variables in Change when it is first called.

X _____

Y _____

B _____

Variables in Sample after return from Change.

A _____

B _____

10. Write the output produced by execution of the following program. (This program is not intended to make any sense, only to test your knowledge of scope rules and side effects.)

```
PROGRAM ScopeOut (Input, Output);
VAR
    A,
    B,
    C:
      Integer;

PROCEDURE One (    X,
                   Y:
                       Integer;
                 VAR Z:
                       Integer);
VAR
    A:
      Integer;
BEGIN (* One *)
  A := 1;
  B := 7;
  X := Y;
  Z := A + X
END;  (* One *)
```

```
BEGIN  (* ScopeOut *)
  A := 4;
  B := 5;
  C := 12;
  One(A, B, C);
  Writeln(A, B, C)
END.   (* ScopeOut *)
```

PREPROGRAMMING EXERCISES _____

1. (a) Write a procedure that returns the sum of the squares of three numbers (Integers) and returns a Boolean variable equal to True if all three numbers are positive or False otherwise. Use VAR and value parameters as required.
   (b) Write the calling statement for your procedure if the three numbers are stored in A, B, and C.

2. Write a procedure that will read in a specified number of Real values and return their average. A call to this procedure might look like

   ```
   GetMeanOf ( 5, Mean);
   ```

   where the first parameter specifies the number of values to be read and the second parameter receives the result.

3. Write a procedure that will compute the distance between two points on a plane, given their coordinates. If one of the points is located at (X1, Y1) and the other is located at (X2, Y2), the formula for the distance is

   $$\text{Sqrt}(\text{Sqr}(X2 - X1) + \text{Sqr}(Y2 - Y1))$$

   All of the parameters to this procedure should be of type Real.

4. Given the following procedure body, write a heading that declares VAR and value parameters as necessary. (*Hint:* Make a list of all the identifiers in the procedure and notice which ones aren't declared locally.)

   ```
   VAR
     Sales1,
     Sales2:
       Real;

   BEGIN  (* GetAverage *)
     Writeln('Department ', DeptNum:1);    (* Needs *)
     Readln(Sales1, Sales2);
     Writeln('has weekly sales of ', Sales1:5:2,
             ' and ', Sales2:5:2);
     AvgSales := (Sales1 + Sales2)/2.0;  (* Returns *)
     Writeln('for an average of ', AvgSales:5:2)
   END;   (* GetAverage *)
   ```

5. Write a procedure heading, given the following list.

RocketSimulation

Needs	Thrust (Real)
Needs/Returns	Weight (Real)
Needs	TimeStep (Integer)
Needs	TotalTime (Integer)
Returns	Velocity (Real)
Returns	OutOfFuel (Boolean)

6. Write a procedure that will be passed three parameters: Hours, Minutes, and ElapsedTime. ElapsedTime is an Integer number of minutes to be added to the starting time passed in through Hours and Minutes. The resulting new time will be returned through Hours and Minutes. For example:

Before Call to AddTime	After Call to AddTime
Hours = 12	Hours = 16
Minutes = 44	Minutes = 2
ElapsedTime = 198	ElapsedTime = 198

7. Write a program called Acronym that will read a series of words from a line of input and print out the acronym formed by the first letters of the words. If you reuse the procedures developed for Program Transpose in this chapter, you shouldn't have to write any procedures of your own. Example I/O:

Input:

United Nations International Children's Emergency Fund

Output:

UNICEF

8. Rewrite Program Acronym in exercise 7 as a procedure that can be called to print the acronym formed by the words in one line of input. Write a program that calls procedure Acronym for each line of input on a file until EOF is reached. (*Hint:* The primary change to Program Acronym will be to replace its program heading with a procedure heading.)

9. The following program was written with very poor style. Global variable references were used in place of parameters. Rewrite it without global variable references, using good programming style.

```
PROGRAM SideEffects(Input, Output);
VAR A,B,C: Integer;
PROCEDURE MashGlobals;
VAR Temp: Integer;
BEGIN
  Temp: =A+B;
  A: =B+C;
  B: =Temp
END;
```

```
        BEGIN
          Readln(A,B,C);
          MashGlobals;
          Writeln('A= ',A:1, ' B= ',B:1, ' C= ',C:1)
        END.
```

10. Rewrite Program Graph from this chapter, adding data validation tests for negative sales, sales greater than $20,000, and department IDs not in order.

PROGRAMMING PROBLEMS _____

1. Write a top-down design and a Pascal program with procedures that will help you balance your checking account. The program should let you enter the initial balance for the month, followed by a series of transactions. For each transaction entered, the program should echo print the transaction data, the current balance for the account, and the total service charges. Service charges are $0.10 for a deposit and $0.15 for a check. If the balance drops below $500 at any point during the month, a service charge of $5 will be assessed for the month. If the balance drops below $50, the program should print a warning message. If the balance becomes negative, an additional service charge of $10 should be assessed for each check until the balance becomes positive again.

   A transaction will take the form of a letter, followed by a blank and a real number. If the letter is a "C," then the number is the amount of a check. If the letter is a "D," then the number is the amount of a deposit. The last transaction will consist of the letter "E," with no number following it. A sample run, on an interactive system, might look like this:

```
Enter the beginning balance:
879.46
Enter a transaction:
C 400.00
Transaction: Check in amount of $400.00
Current balance: $479.46
Service charge: Check − $0.15
Service charge: Below $500 − $5.00
Total service charges: $5.15

Enter a transaction:
D 100.00
Transaction: Deposit in amount of $100.00
Current balance: $579.46
Service charge: Deposit − $0.10
Total service charges: $5.25

Enter a transaction:
E
Transaction: End
Current balance: $579.46
Total service charges: $5.25

Final balance: $574.21
```

As usual, your program should use good style, proper indentation, meaningful identifiers, and appropriate comments. Also, be sure to check for data errors such as invalid transaction codes or negative amounts.

2. In this problem you will design and implement a Roman numeral calculator. Most people are unaware that the subtractive Roman numeral notation commonly in use today (such as IV meaning 4) was only rarely used during the time of the Roman Republic and Empire. For ease of calculation, the Romans most frequently used a purely additive notation in which a number was simply the sum of its digits (4 equals IIII in this notation). Each number starts with the digit of highest value and ends with the one of smallest value. This is the notation we will use in this problem.

Your program will input two Roman numbers and an arithmetic operator and print out the result of the operation, also as a Roman number. The values of the Roman digits are as follows:

I	1
V	5
X	10
L	50
C	100
D	500
M	1000

Thus, the number MDCCCCLXXXVIIII represents 1989. The arithmetic operators that your program should recognize in the input are +, −, *, and /. These should perform the Pascal operations of integer addition, subtraction, multiplication, and division.

One way of approaching this problem is to convert the Roman numbers into integers, perform the required operation, and then convert the result back into a Roman number for printing. The following might be a sample run of the program, for an interactive system:

```
Enter the first number:
MCCXXVI
The first number is 1226
Enter the second number:
LXVIIII
The second number is 69
Enter the desired arithmetic operation:
+
The sum of MCCXXVI and LXVIIII is MCCLXXXXV (1295)
```

Your program should use good style, appropriate comments, meaningful identifiers, and proper indentation and avoid side effects. It should also check for errors in the input, such as illegal digits or arithmetic operators, and take appropriate actions when these are found. You may also have the program check to be sure that the numbers are in purely additive form—digits are followed only by digits of the same or lower value.

3. Develop a top-down design and write a program to produce a bar chart of gourmet popcorn production for a cooperative farm group on a farm-by-farm basis. The input to the program will be a series of data sets, one per line, with each set representing the production for one farm. The output will be a bar chart that identifies each farm and displays its production in pints of corn per acre.

Each data set will consist of the name of a farm, followed by a comma and a space, then a Real number representing acres planted, then a space, then an Integer number representing pint jars of popcorn produced.

The output will be a single line for each farm, with the name of the farm starting in the first column on a line and the bar chart starting in column 30. Each mark in the bar chart will represent 250 jars of popcorn per acre. The production goal for the year is 5000 jars per acre; a vertical bar should appear in the chart for farms with lower production, or a special mark for farms with production greater than or equal to 5000 jars per acre. For example, given the input file

```
Orville's Acres,  114.8  43801
Hoffman's Hills,  77.2  36229
Jiffy Quick Farm,  89.4  24812
Jolly Good Plantation,  183.2  104570
Organically Grown Inc.,  45.5  14683
```

the output would be

```
               Pop Co-Op
                          Production in
Farm Name                 Thousands of
                          Pint Jars per Acre
                            1   2   3   4   5   6
                          ---|---|---|---|---|---|
Orville's Acres           ***************        |
Hoffman's Hills           ******************     |
Jiffy Quick Farm          ***********            |
Jolly Good Plantation     *********************#***
Organically Grown Inc.    *************          |
```

This problem should decompose neatly into several procedures. As usual, your program should be written with good programming style, plenty of comments, and no global variable references. Your program should be able to handle data errors (such as a farm name longer than 29 characters) without crashing.

- *To be able to determine where it is appropriate to use a function.*
- *To be able to design and code a function for a specific task.*
- *To be able to invoke a function properly.*
- *To understand how real numbers are represented in the computer.*
- *To understand how the limited numeric precision of the computer can affect calculations.*
- *To know what a recursive call is.*

8

Functions, Precision, and Recursion

In the last two chapters we examined the procedure type of subprogram. In this chapter we will look at the other type of subprogram: the *function*. The main difference between procedures and functions is the way in which they are called. A procedure call is a statement in a program, whereas a function call is part of an expression. We can often simplify the coding of complex expressions by defining our own functions, which is especially helpful when the expression is to be used repeatedly within a program.

Because functions are often used for numerical computations, this chapter is also a good place to look at the limitations of the computer in doing calculations. We will look at a few ways in which these limitations can cause numerical errors to occur and at how such errors can be avoided.

FUNCTIONS

Everything we have said about procedures is also true about functions. Functions are used mainly in situations where we wish to return only one value as a result and that result is to be used directly in an expression.

For example, suppose that in a particular problem we have three data sets with two values each and we need to find the average of the greater of the two values in each set. To do this, we must determine the greater value for each data set, sum those values, then divide by three. If we code this algorithm directly, we have

```
    IF Set1Value1 > Set1Value2
      THEN
        Temp1 : = Set1Value1
      ELSE
        Temp1 : = Set1Value2;
    IF Set2Value1 > Set2Value2
      THEN
        Temp2 : = Set2Value1
      ELSE
        Temp2 : = Set2Value2;
    IF Set3Value1 > Set3Value2
      THEN
        Temp3 : = Set3Value1
      ELSE
        Temp3 : = Set3Value2;
    Average : = (Temp1 + Temp2 + Temp3) / 3.0;
```

If we had a function called Max that returned the greater of two values passed to it, the following expression would then accomplish the same purpose as the program fragment above.

```
    Average : = (Max (Set1Value1, Set1Value2) +
                 Max (Set2Value1, Set2Value2) +
                 Max (Set3Value1, Set3Value2)) / 3.0
```

The following is a *function definition* for Max.

```
FUNCTION Max (Num1,       (* Receives first value   *)
              Num2:       (* Receives second value  *)
                Real):
                Real;     (* Returns a Real result *)

(* This function returns the maximum of its two inputs *)

BEGIN (* Max *)
  IF Num1 > Num2
    THEN
      Max : = Num1
    ELSE
      Max : = Num2
END;  (* Max *)
```

The first thing you probably noticed about the function definition is that it looks a lot like a procedure definition except that the heading begins with the word FUNC-TION instead of the word PROCEDURE. If you look at the heading a little more closely, you will notice something else: The formal parameter list is followed by a colon (:) and then the name of a data type.

A function returns one value. That value is returned not through a parameter but through the name of the function. The data type at the end of the function heading defines the type of result value that the function will return. This type will often be referred to as the *function type,* although a more proper term is *function result type.*

Function Result Type The data type of the result value returned by a function.

You may also have noticed that function Max has statements that assign values to the function name. It is through these assignments that the result value gets passed back to the point where the function was called. The function name is a special variable. A value that is assigned to the function name will be returned as the result. (See Figure 8-1.) If, in a function, more than one value is assigned to its name, only the last value assigned before the function returns will get passed back as the result.

You cannot use a function name exactly as you would use a variable. Only when the function name appears to the left of a := is it like a variable. If you use the function name in an expression, it is a call to the function. (This means you can't assign temporary values to the function name and then use them later on.) When a function is called from within itself, it is said to be making a *recursive call.* We will return to the topic of recursion later on in the chapter. For the time being, you should avoid using the function name in an expression within the function itself.

Keep in mind that expressions can be used in many places in addition to assignment statements. They can appear in IF statements, in WHILE statements, as actual

Figure 8-1

Assigning a Value to the Function Name Transmits the Results Back to the Expression That Called the Function

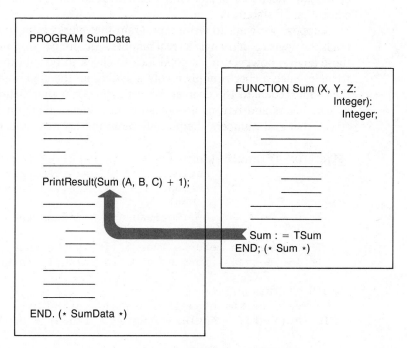

```
PROGRAM SumData
    _____
    _____
    _____
    ____
    _____
    _____
    _____
    ____

    PrintResult(Sum (A, B, C) + 1);
    _____
    _____
    _____
    _____
    _____

    END. (* SumData *)
```

```
FUNCTION Sum (X, Y, Z:
                    Integer):
                    Integer;
    _____
    _____
    _____
    _____
    _____
    _____

    Sum : = TSum
    END; (* Sum *)
```

parameters in calls to subprograms that have value parameters, and so on. A function can be used in _any_ expression.

The syntax diagram for the function heading is

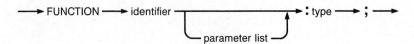

The parameter list is the same as for a procedure:

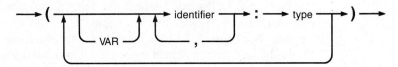

Except for the keyword FUNCTION and the function result type, the function heading is just like a procedure heading.

Boolean Functions

Functions are not restricted to returning numerical results. For example, they can also be used to evaluate a condition and return a Boolean result. Boolean functions can be quite useful when a branch or a loop depends on some complex condition. Rather than code the condition directly into the controlling expression of an IF or WHILE statement, we can use a call to a Boolean function to form the controlling expression. Let's look at an example of a Boolean function and how it can be used to control an IF statement.

Suppose we want to write a program that works with triangles. The program reads the angles of a triangle as real numbers. Before performing any calculations on those angles, however, it's a good idea to check to be sure that they really form a triangle. Such a check simply involves adding up the angles and checking to see if their sum is equal to 180 degrees. We can write a function that takes the three angles as parameters and returns a Boolean result. Such a function would look like this (recall that real numbers should only be tested for _near_ equality):

```
FUNCTION Triangle (Angle1,         (* Receives first angle      *)
                   Angle2,         (* Receives second angle     *)
                   Angle3:         (* Receives third angle       *)
                     Real):
                   Boolean;  (* Returns True if a triangle *)

(* This function returns True if its three input values add up
     to 180 degrees, forming a valid triangle; otherwise, False *)

BEGIN (* Triangle *)
   (* Test for sum of angles "equal" to 180.0 *)
   IF Abs(Angle1 + Angle2 + Angle3 - 180.0) < 0.00000001
     THEN
       Triangle := True
```

```
        ELSE
            Triangle := False
    END;  (* Triangle *)
```

The following program fragment shows how function Triangle might be called:

```
Readln(AngleA, AngleB, AngleC);
IF Triangle(AngleA, AngleB, AngleC)        (* function call *)
    THEN
        Writeln('The three angles form a valid triangle.')
    ELSE
        Writeln('Those angles do not form a triangle.');
```

The expression in the IF statement is much easier to understand than it would be if the condition were coded directly into the IF statement. When a conditional test is at all complicated, a Boolean function is in order.

Function Interface Design and Side Effects

The interface to a function can be designed in much the same way as is the interface to a procedure. We simply write down a list of all of the things the function needs and what it must return. Since functions are designed to be used where a single value is to be returned, however, there should only be one item labeled "returns" in the list. Everything else in the list should be labeled "needs," and there shouldn't be any "needs/returns" type of parameters.

The sending back or changing of more than one value in a function call is an unwanted side effect of a function and should be avoided. If your interface design calls for multiple values to be returned, or for the values of actual parameters to be changed, then you should use a procedure instead of a function.

Because formal VAR parameters allow their corresponding actual parameters to be changed, they are a potential source of side effects. Therefore, a good rule of thumb is never to use VAR parameters in the formal parameter list of a function. Use value parameters exclusively in function definitions. The one exception to this rule is the case where a file is to be passed to a function. Pascal only allows a file to be passed to a formal VAR parameter. When a file is passed to a function, however, the only operations that should be performed on it are tests such as EOF and EOLN. A function should not be used to perform input or output operations, because such operations are considered to be side effects of the function.

There is an extra advantage to using only value parameters in a function definition: Constants and expressions can then be passed as actual parameters to the function. For example, function Triangle can be called in the following manner using literals and an expression:

```
IF Triangle(30.0, 60.0, 30.0 + 60.0)
    THEN
        Writeln('A 30-60-90 angle combination forms a triangle.')
    ELSE
        Writeln('Something is very wrong.')
```

When to Use Functions

There aren't any formal rules for when to use a procedure and when to use a function, but here are a few guidelines:

1. If there is more than one output from your module, do not use a function.
2. If there is only one output from the module and it is a Boolean value, a function is probably called for.
3. If there is only one output and that value is to be used immediately in an expression, a function is probably called for.
4. When in doubt, use a procedure. Any function can be recoded as a procedure with the function name becoming an output parameter of the procedure.
5. If both a procedure and a function are acceptable, use the one you feel more comfortable with.

Functions were included in Pascal to provide a way to simulate mathematical operations called functions. Pascal provides a set of built-in commonly used mathematical functions. A list of these appears in Appendix B.

Problem Solving in Action

Problem: Determine how many possible words there are of a given length. By "word" we simply mean any combination of letters of a given length. This calculation is simple to make, but it will demonstrate nicely how we can use functions in solving problems.

Discussion: Let's look at how we would solve this problem by hand. If we were interested in single-letter words, there would be only 26 possibilities—each of the letters in the alphabet. If we were interested in two-letter words, for each of the 26 possible first letters there would be 26 possible second letters. This means that there would be 26 times 26 possible combinations ($26 \times 26 = 676$). For three-letter words there would be 26 times 26 times 26 possible combinations, and so on.

If the number of letters is N, then there will be 26^N combinations (that is, 26 to the power N).

We can rough out our design at this point. There will be a module that gets data from the user, a module that computes 26^N, and, lastly, a module that prints this value out.

We'll use the most straightforward method of computing 26^N: simply multiplying 26 by itself N times. Because the number of iterations is known, a count-controlled loop is appropriate. The loop will count down to 0 from the initial value of the exponent. For each iteration of the loop, 26 will be multiplied by the previous product. This operation is similar to summing, but involves multiplication instead of addition.

Input: An integer number, entered by the user, specifying the number of characters in a word.

Output: The number of possible words of the length specified by the user, assuming a 26-character alphabet.

PSIA _____

MAIN MODULE   Level 0

> Get Number of Characters
> Compute 26^N
> Print Number of Possible Words

GET NUMBER OF CHARACTERS   Level 1

> Writeln 'How many characters are in a word?'
> Read CharCount from Input

COMPUTE 26^N (Needs: Exponent, Returns: 26^N)

> Initialize Result to 1
> WHILE Exponent > 0 DO
>   Result := Result * 26
>   Decrement Exponent
> Return Result through function name

PRINT NUMBER OF POSSIBLE WORDS

> Writeln 'There are ', WordCount:1, ' possible ',
>   CharCount:1, ' character words.'

Module Structure Chart:

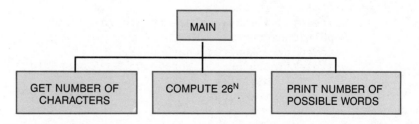

Compute 26^N will be implemented as a function (called Power26) that has one Integer parameter and returns an Integer result. We are now ready to code this design.

```
PROGRAM PossibleWords (Input, Output);

(* This program computes the number of possible combinations
   of N letters, where N is a number entered by the user.  An
   alphabet of 26 characters is assumed *)
```

PSIA ▰▰▰▰▰▰▰

```
VAR
  CharCount,          (* The number of letters in a word *)
  WordCount:          (* The number of possible words    *)
    Integer;


(*************************************************************************)


FUNCTION Power26 (Exponent:          (* The power to which 26 is raised *)
                    Integer):
                      Integer;

(* This function raises 26 to a specific power *)

VAR
  Count,              (* Keeps track of how many times 26
                          has been multiplied by itself   *)
  Result:             (* Holds intermediate powers of 26 *)
    Integer;

BEGIN  (* Power26 *)
  Result := 1;
  WHILE Exponent > 0 DO
    BEGIN
      Result := Result * 26;
      Exponent := Exponent - 1
    END;
  Power26 := Result
END;   (* Power26 *)


(*************************************************************************)


BEGIN  (* PossibleWords *)
  Writeln('How many characters are in a word?');
  Readln(CharCount);
  WordCount := Power26(CharCount);
  Writeln('There are ', WordCount:1, ' possible ', CharCount:1,
          ' character words.')
END.   (* PossibleWords *)
```

Testing: This program should be tested with input values that include negative numbers and 0. It should also be tested with some very large input values (such as MaxInt). A sample run of this program would appear as follows:

```
How many characters are in a word?
5
There are 11881376 possible 5 character words.
```

▰▰▰▰▰▰▰▰▰▰▰▰▰▰▰▰▰▰▰▰▰▰▰▰▰▰▰▰▰▰▰▰▰▰▰▰▰▰

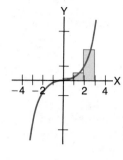

Let's look at another problem that will make good use of functions. This problem is taken from calculus and uses a technique called numerical integration, which amounts to finding the area under a curve on a graph.

Problem Solving in Action

Problem: Numerically integrate the function X^3 over a range specified by the user. In other words, given a pair of real numbers, find the area under the graph of X^3 between those two numbers. (See Figure 8-2.)

Discussion: We will compute an approximation to this area. If we divide the area under the curve into equal narrow rectangular strips, the sum of the areas of these rectangles (Divisions) will be close to the actual area under the curve. (See Figure 8-3.) The narrower we make the rectangles, the more accurate our approximation should be.

We'll let the user enter the low and high values for the function, as well as the number of rectangles into which the area will be subdivided. The width of a rectangle will then be

$$(\text{High} - \text{Low}) / \text{Divisions}$$

The height of a rectangle will be equal to the value of X^3 when X is at the horizontal midpoint of the rectangle. The area of a rectangle is equal to its height times its width. Since the leftmost rectangle will have its midpoint at

$$(\text{Low} + \text{Width} / 2.0)$$

Figure 8-2
Integral of X^3 Between 0 and 3

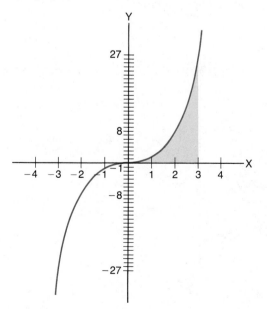

Figure 8-3
Approximation of Area Under a Curve

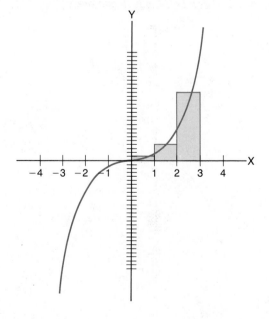

its area will be equal to the following (see Figure 8-5):

$$(Low + Width / 2.0)^3 * Width$$

The second rectangle will have its left edge at the point where X equals

$$Low + Width$$

and its area will be equal to the following (see Figure 8-5):

$$(Low + Width + Width / 2.0)^3 * Width$$

The left edge of each rectangle is at a point that is Width greater than the left edge of the rectangle to its right. Thus we can step through the rectangles by having a loop that is controlled by a counter starting at Divisions and counting down to zero. This loop will contain a second counter (*not* the loop control variable) that starts at Low and counts by steps of Width up to (High − Width). The reason for the two counters is that the second counter must be a Real, and it is poor programming technique to have a loop control variable be a Real variable. (More on this subject later in this chapter.) For each iteration of this loop, we'll compute the area of the corresponding rectangle and add this value to the total area under the curve.

We'll want a function to compute the area of a rectangle, given the position of its left edge and its width. Let's also make X^3 a separate function called Funct. That way, we can substitute other functions in its place without changing the rest of the design. Our program can then be quickly converted to numerically integrate any single variable function.

Figure 8-4
Area of the Left-Most Rectangle

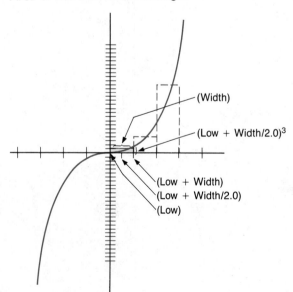

Figure 8-5
Area of the Second Rectangle

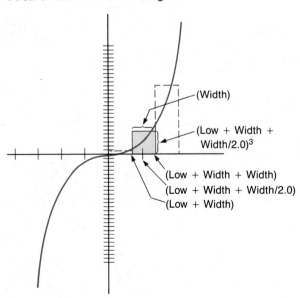

PSIA ▰▰▰▰▰▰▰

Here is our design:

MAIN MODULE   Level 0

```
Get Data
Width  ⟵  (High − Low) / Divisions
Initialize Area to 0.0
Initialize LeftEdge to Low
WHILE Divisions > 0 DO
  Area  ⟵  Area + RectArea(LeftEdge, Width);
  LeftEdge  ⟵  LeftEdge + Width;
  Divisions  ⟵  Divisions − 1
Print Result
```

RECTAREA   (Receives LeftEdge, Width: Real;   Level 1
                Returns Area: Real)

```
RectArea  ⟵  Funct(LeftEdge + Width / 2.0) ∗ Width
```

GETDATA   (Returns Low, High: Real; Divisions: Integer)

```
Prompt for Low and High
Readln Low and High
Prompt for Divisions
Readln Divisions
Echo print input data
```

FUNCT   (Receives X: Real; Returns XCubed: Real)   Level 2

```
Funct  ⟵  X ∗ X ∗ X
```

Module Structure Chart:

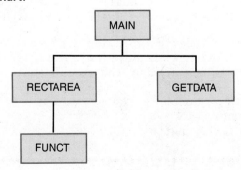

PSIA ▰▰▰▰▰▰

Program Integrate implements our design. Notice that procedures and functions can be mixed together in the declaration section of a program.

```
PROGRAM Integrate (Input, Output);

(* This program takes as input three Real values.  These are the
   Low, High values for the range of a function to be numerically
   integrated and the number of slices to be used in approximating
   the integral of the function.  As written, this program
   integrates the function X cubed.  However, any single variable
   function may be substituted for the function named Funct *)


VAR
   Low,            (* Lowest value in range to be integrated  *)
   High,           (* Highest value in range to be integrated *)
   Width,          (* Computed width of a rectangular slice   *)
   LeftEdge,       (* Left edge point in a rectangular slice  *)
   Area:           (* Total area under the curve              *)
     Real;
   Divisions:      (* Number of slices to divide the range by *)
     Integer;

(****************************************************************)


FUNCTION RectArea (LeftEdge,      (* Left edge point of rectangle *)
                   Width:         (* Width of rectangle           *)
                   Real):
                   Real;          (* Returns area of rectangle    *)

(* This function computes the area of a rectangle that is Width
   wide, and whose height is given by the value computed by Funct
   on the midpoint of the rectangle's range *)

(****************************************************************)


FUNCTION Funct (X:             (* Receives value to be cubed *)
                Real):
                Real;          (* Returns X cubed            *)

(* This function computes X cubed.  You may replace this
   function with any single variable function that is to
   be integrated by the rest of this program *)

BEGIN (* Funct *)
   Funct := X * X * X
END;  (* Funct *)


(****************************************************************)
```

PSIA ━━━━━━━━━

```
BEGIN  (* RectArea *)
  RectArea := Funct(LeftEdge + Width / 2.0) * Width
END;   (* RectArea *)


(***********************************************************************)


PROCEDURE GetData (VAR Low,          (* Returns bottom of range *)
                       High:         (* Returns top of range    *)
                       Real;
                   VAR Divisions:    (* Returns division factor *)
                       Integer);

(* This procedure prompts for input of Low, High and Divisions
   values and returns the three values input to the program *)

BEGIN  (* GetData *)
  Writeln('Enter Low and High values of integration range (Real).');
  Readln(Low, High);
  Writeln('Enter the number of divisions to use (Integer).');
  Readln(Divisions);
  Writeln('The integral of X cubed over the range ', Low:10:7);
  Writeln('to ', High:10:7, ' with ', Divisions:1,
          ' subdivisions of the range, ')
END;   (* GetData *)


(***********************************************************************)


BEGIN  (* Integrate *)
  GetData(Low, High, Divisions);                     (* Get Data *)
  Width := (High - Low) / Divisions;         (* Compute slice width *)
  Area := 0.0;
  LeftEdge := Low;
  (* Calculate and sum area of each slice *)
  WHILE Divisions > 0 DO
    BEGIN
      Area := Area + RectArea(LeftEdge, Width);
      LeftEdge := LeftEdge + Width;
      Divisions := Divisions - 1
    END;
  (* Print Result *)
  Writeln('is equal to ', Area:10:7)
END.   (* Integrate *)
```

PSIA ▰▰▰▰▰

Testing: This program should be tested with sets of data that include positive, negative, and zero values. It is especially important to try input values of 0 and 1 for the number of divisions. The results from the program should be compared against values calculated by hand using the same algorithm, and against the true value of the integral of X^3, which is given by the formula

$$1 / 4 * (High^4 - Low^4)$$

MORE ON REAL NUMBERS

We have used real numbers off and on since they were introduced in Chapter 2, but we have not actually examined them in depth. Real numbers have some special properties when we use them on the computer. Thus far we've pretty much ignored these properties; now it's time to consider them in detail.

Representation of Real Numbers

Let's assume we have a computer where each word (location) in memory is divided up into a sign plus five decimal digits. This means that when a variable or constant is defined, the cell or location assigned to it consists of five digits and a sign. When an Integer variable or constant is defined, the interpretation of the number stored in that place is quite straightforward. When a Real variable or constant is defined, the number stored there has both a whole number part and a fractional part. It must be coded in some way to represent both parts.

Let's see what such coded numbers might look like and what this coding does to arithmetic values within our programs, beginning with integers. The range of the numbers we can represent with five digits is −99,999 to +99,999:

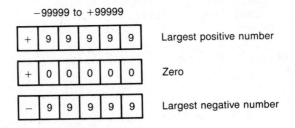

−99999 to +99999

| + | 9 | 9 | 9 | 9 | 9 | Largest positive number

| + | 0 | 0 | 0 | 0 | 0 | Zero

| − | 9 | 9 | 9 | 9 | 9 | Largest negative number

Our *precision* (the number of digits we can represent) is five digits, and each number within that range can be represented exactly.

What happens if we allow one of those digits (the left-most one, for example) to represent an exponent?

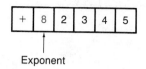

Then +82345 represents the number $+2345 * 10^8$. The range of numbers we can now represent is much larger:

$$-9999 * 10^9 \quad \text{to} \quad 9999 * 10^9$$

or

$$-9,999,000,000,000 \quad \text{to} \quad +9,999,000,000,000$$

However, our precision is now only four digits. That is, we can represent only four significant nonzero digits of the number itself. Any four-digit number can be represented exactly in our system, but what happens to larger numbers? The four left-most digits are represented correctly, and the balance of the digits are assumed to be 0. The right-most digits, or least significant digits, are lost. Figure 8-6 shows what happens.

Note that 1,000,000 can be represented exactly, but −4,932,416 cannot. Since this coding scheme limits us to four *significant* (nonzero) *digits*, the digits that cannot be represented are assumed to be zero.

To extend our coding scheme to represent real numbers, we need to be able to represent negative exponents. For example:

$$4394 * 10^{-2} = 43.94$$

or

$$22 * 10^{-4} = .0022$$

Since our scheme does not allow for a sign for the exponent, we shall have to change the scheme slightly. We will let the sign that we have be the sign of the exponent and

Figure 8-6
Coding Using
Positive Exponents

NUMBER	POWER OF TEN NOTATION	CODED REPRESENTATION						VALUE
		Sign	Exp					
+99,999	$+9999 * 10^1$	+	1	9	9	9	9	+99,990
		Sign	Exp					
−999,999	$-9999 * 10^2$	−	2	9	9	9	9	−999,900
		Sign	Exp					
+1,000,000	$+1000 * 10^3$	+	3	1	0	0	0	+1,000,000
		Sign	Exp					
−4,932,416	$-4932 * 10^3$	−	3	4	9	3	2	+4,932,000

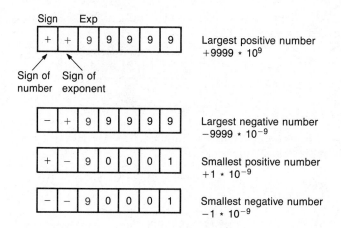

Figure 8-7
*Coding Using
Positive and
Negative
Exponents*

add a sign to the far left to represent the sign of the number itself. (See Figure 8-7.)

All of the numbers between 9999×10^{-9} and 9999×10^{9} can now be represented accurately to four digits. Adding negative exponents to our scheme has allowed us to represent fractional numbers.

Figure 8-8 shows how we would encode some real numbers.

Note that our precision is still only four digits. The numbers 0.1032, 5.406, and 1,000,000 can be represented exactly. However, the number 476.0321, with seven significant digits, is represented as 476.0; the "321" cannot be represented.

Most modern computers do not use decimal arithmetic. However, real numbers are encoded in binary machines through a scheme similar to the one outlined here, the only difference being that binary digits are used instead of decimal digits.

All computers limit the precision (number of significant digits) of a real number. In our representation we have used only five digits in order to simplify the examples, and some computers really are limited to only 4 or 5 digits of precision. However, a more typical system will have about 10 to 15 significant digits in its representation.

Figure 8-8
*Coding of Some
Real Numbers*

NUMBER	POWER OF TEN NOTATION	CODED REPRESENTATION						VALUE
		Sign	Exp					
0.1032	$1032 * 10^{-4}$	+	–	4	1	0	3	2	0.1032
−5.4060	$-5406 * 10^{-3}$	–	–	3	5	4	0	6	−5.406
−0.003	$-3000 * 10^{-6}$	–	–	6	3	0	0	0	−0.0030
476.0321	$4760 * 10^{-1}$	+	–	1	4	7	6	0	476.0
1,000,000	$1000 * 10^{3}$	+	+	3	1	0	0	0	1,000,000

Arithmetic with Real Numbers

When we use integer arithmetic, our results are exact. Real arithmetic, however, cannot be exact. Let's examine the situation by adding three real numbers X, Y, and Z together, using our coding scheme.

First we will add X to Y and then add Z to the result. Next we will add Y to Z and then add X to that result. The associative law of arithmetic says that the two answers should be the same—but are they?

We will continue our scheme of coding four significant digits and an exponent. Let's use the following allowable values for X, Y, and Z:

$$X = -1324 * 10^3 \qquad Y = 1325 * 10^3 \qquad Z = 5424 * 10^0$$

Here is the result of adding Z to the sum of X and Y:

$$
\begin{array}{lll}
(X) & -1324 * 10^3 & \\
(Y) & \underline{1325 * 10^3} & \\
 & 1 * 10^3 = 1000 * 10^0 &
\end{array}
$$

$$
\begin{array}{lll}
(X + Y) & 1000 * 10^0 & \\
(Z) & \underline{5424 * 10^0} & \\
 & 6424 * 10^0 & \longleftarrow \quad (X + Y) + Z
\end{array}
$$

Here is the result of adding X to the sum of Y and Z:

$$
\begin{array}{lll}
(Y) & 1325000 * 10^0 & \\
(Z) & \underline{5424 * 10^0} & \\
 & 1330424 * 10^0 = 1330 * 10^3 & \text{(truncated to four digits)}
\end{array}
$$

$$
\begin{array}{lll}
(Y + Z) & 1330 * 10^3 & \\
(X) & \underline{-1324 * 10^3} & \\
 & 6 * 10^3 = 6000 * 10^0 & \longleftarrow \quad X + (Y + Z)
\end{array}
$$

These answers are the same in the thousands place but are different thereafter. The error behind this discrepancy is called *representational error*. Adding Y to Z gives a number with seven significant digits, but only four digits can be stored.

It is because of representational errors that it is unwise to use a real number as a loop control variable. Since precision may be lost in calculations involving real numbers, it is very difficult to predict when (or even *if*) a loop control variable of type Real will become equal to the termination value. A count-controlled loop with a control variable of type Real may behave in an unpredictable fashion.

It is also because of representational errors that we said in Chapter 4 that you should never compare real numbers for exact equality. Two real numbers will rarely be exactly equal, and thus they should only be compared for near equality. If the difference between the two numbers is less than some acceptable small value, they can be considered equal for the purposes of the given problem.

How Pascal Implements Real Numbers

Now let's formally define some of the terms we used informally in the previous section.

Real Number	A number that has a whole and a fractional part and no imaginary part.

The type Real is limited to the *range* and precision defined in a specific implementation of Pascal, for the number of digits used to represent the exponent and the number of digits used for the number itself (called the *mantissa*) will vary from

T,M,V, ⇦ machine to machine.

Range	The interval within which values must fall, specified in terms of the largest and smallest allowable values.
Significant Digits	Those digits from the first nonzero digit on the left to the last nonzero digit on the right (plus any zero digits that are exact).
Precision	Maximum number of significant digits.
Representational Error	Arithmetic error caused by the fact that the precision of the true result of arithmetic operations is greater than the precision of the machine.

Real is a standard type in Pascal. When you declare a variable to be of type Real, the value stored in that place is interpreted as a *floating point number* (the name given to real numbers represented according to the scheme described in the preceding section). That is, the left-most part of the memory location is assumed to contain the exponent and the number itself is assumed to be in the balance of the location. The system is called floating point representation because the number of significant digits is fixed and the decimal point floats (is moved to different positions as necessary). In our coding scheme example, every number is stored as four digits, with the left-most one being nonzero and the exponent adjusted accordingly. 1,000,000 was stored as

+	+	3	1	0	0	0

and 0.1032 was stored as

+	−	4	1	0	3	2

This allowed for the maximum precision possible.

There are two ways of expressing real numbers in Pascal, whether they are constants or data. One way is by using a decimal point; the other way is by using power of 10 notation. Since many terminals cannot do superscripts, an E is used before the exponent. The syntax diagram is shown below.

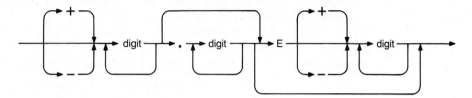

Valid reals	Invalid reals	
1.1	.032	(no digit before '.')
55E5	1.	(no digit after '.')
56.3E+01	5.E−32	(no digit after '.')
1000.0E42	1000	(no 'E' or '.')
21E − 36	21.0E	(no digit after 'E')

In addition to representational errors, there are two other problems to watch out for in real arithmetic: underflow and overflow.

Underflow is the condition that arises when the value of a calculation is too small to be represented. Any value too small to be represented is set to 0.0.

Going back to our decimal representation, let's look at a calculation involving very small numbers:

$$\begin{array}{r} 4210 * 10^{-8} \\ *\quad 2000 * 10^{-8} \\ \hline 8420000 * 10^{-16} = 8420 * 10^{-13} \end{array}$$

This value cannot be represented in our scheme, because an exponent of -13 is too large. Our maximum is -9. Therefore the result of this calculation is set to 0.0. Obviously any answer depending on this calculation will not be exact.

Overflow is a more serious problem, because there is no logical recourse when it occurs. For example, the results of the calculation.

$$\begin{array}{r} 9999 * 10^{9} \\ *\quad 1000 * 10^{9} \\ \hline 9999000 * 10^{18} = 9999 * 10^{21} \end{array}$$

cannot be stored, so what should we do? To be consistent with our response to underflow, we could set the result to $9999 * 10^9$ (the maximum representable value in this case). Yet this seems intuitively wrong. The alternative is to stop with an error message.

Since Pascal does not define what should happen in the case of overflow, different compilers solve the problem in different ways. You might try to cause an overflow with your compiler and see what happens. Some systems will print a run-time error message such as "ARITHMETIC OVERFLOW". On other systems you will simply get an answer that is equal to the largest number that can be represented.

We have been discussing problems with real numbers, but integer numbers can also overflow both negatively and positively. To see how your compiler handles the situation, you should try adding 1 to MaxInt and -1 to $-$MaxInt. On one system, adding 1 to MaxInt sets the result to -0!

Another type of error that can occur with real numbers is called cancellation error. A cancellation error is a form of representational error that occurs when numbers of widely differing sizes are added or subtracted. Let's look at an example:

$$(1 + .00001234) - 1 = .00001234$$

The laws of arithmetic say this equation should be true. But is it, if the computer does the arithmetic?

$$
\begin{array}{r}
100000000 * 10^{-8} \\
+ \quad\quad 1234 * 10^{-8} \\
\hline
100001234 * 10^{-8}
\end{array}
$$

To four digits, the sum is $1000 * 10^{-3}$. Now the computer subtracts 1:

$$
\begin{array}{r}
1000 * 10^{-3} \\
- \quad 1000 * 10^{-3} \\
\hline
0
\end{array}
$$

The result is 0, not .00001234.

Sometimes you can avoid adding two real numbers that are very different in size by carefully arranging the calculations in a program. For example, suppose a problem requires that many small real numbers be added to a large real number. The result will be more accurate if the program first sums the smaller numbers and then adds the sum to the large number, for the sum itself will be a larger number and can be added to the large real number with greater accuracy.

Practical Implications of Limited Precision

All of this discussion of representational, overflow, underflow, and cancellation errors may seem purely academic. In fact, these errors have serious practical implications in many problems.

Consider the numerical integration problem presented earlier in this chapter. The user specifies the low and high values of the range to be integrated, as well as the number of subdivisions to be used in computing the result. The more subdivisions that are used, the more accurate the result should be, since the rectangles will be narrower and thus more closely approximate the shape of the area under the curve. This would seem to indicate that we can get very precise results by using a very large number of subdivisions. In fact, there is a point beyond which an increase in the number of subdivisions will *decrease* the precision of the results. If we specify too many subdivisions, the area of an individual rectangle will become so small that the computer can no longer represent its value accurately. Adding up all of those inaccurate values will produce a total area that has an even greater error.

Numerical integration may seem somewhat removed from real-world problems, so we close this section with three examples that illustrate how limited precision can have disastrous effects.

During the Mercury space program, several of the spacecraft splashed down a considerable distance from their computed landing points. This delayed the recovery of the spacecraft and the astronaut, putting both in some danger. The problem was eventually traced to an imprecise representation of the Earth's rotation period in the program that calculated the landing point.

As part of the construction of a hydroelectric dam, a long set of high-tension cables had to be constructed to link the dam to the nearest power distribution point. The cables were to be several miles long, and each one was to be a continuous unit (because of the high power output from the dam, shorter cables couldn't be spliced together). The cables were constructed at great expense and strung between the two points. However, it turned out that they were too short, so another set had to be manufactured. The problem was traced to errors of precision in calculating the length of the catenary curve (the curve that a cable forms when hanging between two points).

An audit of a bank turned up a mysterious account with a large amount of money in it. The account was traced to an unscrupulous programmer who had used limited precision to his advantage. The bank computed interest on its accounts to a precision of a tenth of a cent. The tenths of cents were not added to the customers' accounts, so the programmer had the extra tenths for all of the accounts summed and then deposited in an account in his name. Since the bank had thousands of accounts, these tiny amounts added up to a large amount of money. However, because the rest of the bank's programs did not use as much precision in their calculations, the scheme went undetected for many months.

The moral of this discussion is twofold. (1) The results of Real calculations often will not be what you expect, and these errors can have serious consequences. (2) If you are working with very large numbers or very small numbers, you need more information than this book provides and should consult a numerical methods text.

RECURSION

When we introduced functions at the start of this chapter, we cautioned against using the name of the function in an expression inside of the function itself. A situation in which a function calls itself is referred to as a *recursive call.*

Recursive Call   A subprogram call in which the subprogram being called is the same as the one making the call.

The word *recursive* means "having the characteristic of coming up again, or repeating." In this case, a subprogram call is being repeated by the subprogram itself.

In the function Power26 in Program PossibleWords, we used the local variable Result instead of just using the identifier Power26 to hold the intermediate powers of 26. On the surface this extra variable looks redundant, but it is necessary because Power26 is a function name, not a variable name. If Power26 had been used in an expression, the logical order of execution would have caused control to be turned over to Power26 again. This would have been an unwanted recursive call.

Recursion is a very powerful feature of Pascal and will be used in more advanced work. But until you understand how to use recursion effectively, you must not use the name of a function in an expression within the body of that function; you must define and use a local variable to hold temporary results and set the name of the function to the value of the local variable before the function is exited. This is why we used the local variable Result. If the function name will never appear in an expression in the body of the function, you don't need a local variable such as Result. Note that the function name may appear any number of times on the *left*-hand side of assignment statements in the body of the function.

For those of you whose curiosity has been piqued, we include one recursive example here. (Recursion is dealt with in more depth in Chapter 17.) Pascal does not have an exponentiation operator, so let's write a function to calculate

$$X^n$$

where X and n are both nonzero, positive integers. The formula is

$$X^n = \underbrace{X * X * X * \cdots * X}_{n \text{ times}}$$

Another way of writing this relationship would be

$$X^n = X * \underbrace{(X * X * \cdots * X)}_{(n-1) \text{ times}}$$

If we know what X^{n-1} is, we can calculate X^n, since $X^n = X(X^{n-1})$. In like manner we can reduce X^{n-1} further:

$$X^n = X * (X * \underbrace{(X * \cdots * X))}_{(n-2) \text{ times}}$$

If we know what X^{n-2} is, we can calculate X^{n-1} and thus calculate X^n, since $X^n = X(X(X^{n-2}))$. We can continue this process until the innermost expression becomes X^1. We know what X^1 is; it's X.

We express this reasoning in the following recursive function Power, which has two parameters, X and N.

```
FUNCTION Power (X,             (* Base number            *)
                    N:         (* Power to raise base to *)
               Integer):
                    Integer;   (* Returns X to N power    *)

(* This function recursively computes X to the N power *)
```

```
BEGIN  (* Power *)
  IF  N = 1
    THEN
      Power  := X
    ELSE
      Power  := X * Power (X,  N − 1)              (* Recursive call *)
END;    (* Power *)
```

Each call to function Power passes the actual parameters to the version being called. The value of X will be the same for each version of Power, but the value for N will decrease by 1 for each call until N − 1 becomes 1. The call to function Power where N is 1 stops the calling chain, because Power can now be given a value. Power is assigned the value X, which is passed back to the version of function Power that made the last call. The value of Power for that version can then be calculated and passed back to the version that made that call. This process continues until the value of Power can be passed back to the original call.

Let's see what a call to Power with X = 2 and N = 3 does. The statement

$$\text{Num} := \text{Power}\,(2, 3)$$

in the body of the program assigns the value returned by the call to the variable Num. The value returned by Power and assigned to Num should be 8 (2 to the third power, or 2 * 2 * 2).

For illustrative purposes let's assume that each call to Power creates a complete new version of Power. Each box in Figure 8-9 represents the code for Power listed

Figure 8-9
Recursion in
Power(2, 3)

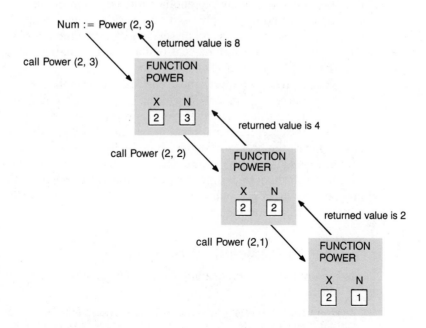

above, along with the values of the actual parameters for that version. Use the figure and the code to convince yourself that the Power function does what it is supposed to do. Each version of Power gets its parameters from the function call in the version above it in the diagram. There is no confusion as to which N is being used because N is a formal parameter.

If you find this example not only crystal clear but obvious, go ahead and use recursion. It is a powerful technique. If you don't really feel comfortable with recursion, don't worry. Understanding recursion is not one of the goals of this chapter. We have covered it here so that you can avoid accidentally using it and can recognize the effects of unwanted recursion. The accidental use of recursion usually results in a condition called *infinite recursion,* which is the recursive equivalent of an infinite loop.

Infinite Recursion The situation in which a subprogram calls itself over and over without end.

In actuality, recursive calls can't go on forever. Each time a subprogram calls itself, a little more of the computer's memory space is used up to store the old values of the variables. Eventually, all of the memory space will be used up and an error message such as "RUN-TIME STACK OVERFLOW" will be printed.

TESTING AND DEBUGGING

Because functions are simply another form of subprogram, the same testing and debugging techniques that are used for procedures may be applied to functions. For example, we can use stubs and drivers to test a function in isolation from the rest of the program. The only difference is that an expression, rather than a procedure call, must be used in a driver to call the function.

When a problem requires the use of real numbers that are very large, very small, or very precise, it is important to keep in mind the limitations of the particular system you are using. When testing a program that performs Real calculations, determine the acceptable margin of error beforehand and then design your test data to try to push the program beyond those limits. Carefully check the accuracy of the computed results. (Keep in mind when you "hand calculate" the correct results that a pocket calculator may have less precision than your computer system.) If the program produces acceptable results when given worst-case data, it will probably perform correctly on typical data.

Testing and Debugging Hints

1. Be sure the function heading includes the data type that will be assigned to the function name.
2. Don't forget to assign a value to the function name before the function returns. Make sure that the value assigned is of the correct type.

3. Don't use the function name in an expression within the function declaration unless you are deliberately writing a recursive function. If you do this by mistake, a syntax error such as "PARAMETER LIST EXPECTED" will probably occur. If, however, the function has no *formal* parameters and you use the function name in an expression in the function declaration, a run-time error such as "STACK OVERFLOW" will occur.

4. Remember that a function call must be part of an expression. Functions cannot be called like procedures.

5. In general, don't use VAR parameters in the formal parameter list of a function declaration. However, a VAR parameter must be used when a file is to be passed to a formal parameter.

6. Don't directly compare Real values for equality. Instead, check them for near equality. The tolerance for near equality will depend on the particular problem you are solving.

7. Use integers if you are dealing with whole numbers only. Any integer can be represented exactly by the computer, as long as it is within the range $-$MaxInt to MaxInt. Also, on most machines, integer arithmetic is faster.

8. Be aware of representational, cancellation, overflow, and underflow errors. If possible, try to arrange calculations in your program to keep real numbers from becoming too large or too small.

9. Be aware of the precision limit of the system you are using. Avoid calculations in which numbers that are of very different magnitudes are added or subtracted.

SUMMARY

Pascal provides two kinds of subprograms for us to use: procedures and functions. A function is called from within an expression, and returns a single result value which is then used in the evaluation of the expression. In order for the result value to be returned, it must be assigned to the function name within the function declaration.

The function heading differs from a procedure heading in that it begins with the keyword FUNCTION and ends with a colon (:) and a data type. The data type specifies the type of the function result.

All of the scope rules, as well as the rules about VAR and value parameters, apply to both procedures and functions. However, it is considered a poor programming practice to use VAR parameters in a function declaration, because doing so increases the potential for side effects.

Real numbers are represented in the computer by a mantissa and an exponent. This permits the use of numbers that are much larger or smaller than those that can be represented with the type Integer. The type Real also allows us to perform calculations on numbers with fractional parts.

Representational errors can affect the accuracy of a program's computations. When using real numbers, keep in mind that if two numbers are too different in size from each other, adding or subtracting them may give inaccurate results.

Keep in mind that the computer has a limited range of numbers that it can represent. If a program tries to compute a value that is too large or too small, an error message will probably result when the program executes.

Recursion provides an alternative to looping as a way to cause statements to be repeated. However, unless you fully understand how to use recursion, you may prefer to avoid it for now. We will return to the topic of recursion in Chapter 17.

QUICK CHECK

1. For each of the following, decide whether a function or a procedure is the most appropriate implementation. (p. 308)
   (a) Selecting the larger of two values for further processing in an expression.
   (b) Printing a paycheck.
   (c) Computing the area of a hexagon.
   (d) Testing whether an input value is valid and returning True if it is.
   (e) Computing the two roots of a quadratic equation.

2. What would the heading for a function called Min look like, if it has two Integer parameters called Num1 and Num2 and returns an Integer result? (pp. 303–307)

3. What would a call to Min look like, if the actual parameters are a variable called Deductions and the literal 2000? (pp. 303–307)

4. Why is it inappropriate to use a variable of type Real as a loop control variable? (pp. 316–319)

5. If a computer has four digits of precision, what would be the result of the following addition operation? (pp. 319–322)

$$400400.000 + 199.9$$

6. What is a recursive call? (pp. 323–326)

Answers
1. (a) function (b) procedure (c) function (d) function (e) procedure
2. `FUNCTION Min  (Num1,`
                `Num2:`
                    `Integer):`
                      `Integer;`
3. `Result := Min(Deductions, 2000)`   4. Because representational errors can cause the loop termination condition to be evaluated with unpredictable results.   5. 400500.000 (Actually, 4.005E+5)   6. A subprogram call to itself.

EXAM PREPARATION EXERCISES

1. A function call is always a component of an expression, but a procedure call is always a statement in itself. (True or False?)

2. Both procedures and functions must have a result type. (True or False?)

3. VAR parameters in the formal parameter list of a function are considered bad style. (True or False?)

4. Given the function heading

```
FUNCTION HighTaxBracket (Inc,
                         Ded:
                           Integer):
                             Boolean;
```

is the following statement a legal call to the function, if Income and Deductions are of type Integer?

```
IF HighTaxBracket(Income, Deductions)
   THEN
      Writeln(' Upper Class');
```

5. If a system supports 10 digits of precision for real numbers, what will be the results of the following computations?

   (a) 1.4E+12 + 100.0

   (b) 4.2E−8 + 100.0

   (c) 3.2E−5 + 3.2E+5

6. Given the code segment

```
Sum := 0;            (* Sum is of type Integer *)
WHILE NOT EOF DO
  BEGIN
    Readln(Amount)
    Sum := Sum + Round(Amount);
  END;
Writeln(Sum: 6);
```

and the input data

$$0.5 \quad 0.5 \quad 0.5 \quad 0.5 \quad 0.5 \quad 0.5 \quad 0.5 \quad \langle EOF \rangle$$

what will the output be? Is this value much different from the sum of the input values?

7. Rewrite the code segment in exercise 6 so that the value printed is the integer value that is closest to the actual sum of the input data.

8. Define the following terms:

recursion	mantissa
result type	exponent
representation error	significant digits
overflow	

9. Identify all of the syntax errors in the following function declaration.

```
FUNCTION Errors: Boolean;
                (A: Boolean,
                 B: Integer)
BEGIN  (* Errors *)
   Errors := A AND NOT B
END;   (* Errors *)
```

10. Explain why it is a poor programming practice to use formal VAR parameters in a function declaration.

PREPROGRAMMING EXERCISES

1. Write the heading for a function called Epsilon that returns a Real result, given two Real parameters called High and Low.

2. Write the heading for a function called Equal that returns a Boolean result, given three Real parameters called Num1, Num2, and Difference.

3. Using the heading you wrote for Exercise 2 above, write a function that returns True if the difference between Num1 and Num2 is less than the value in Difference, and returns False otherwise.

4. Write a heading for a function called EOForEOLN that has no parameters and returns a Boolean result.

5. Given the function heading

```
FUNCTION Hypotenuse (Side1,
                     Side2:
                         Real):
                         Real;
```

write the body of the function to return the length of the hypotenuse of a right triangle. The lengths of the other two sides are passed to the function through the formal parameters. The formula for the hypotenuse is

$$Sqrt(Sqr(Side1) + Sqr(Side2))$$

6. Write the complete function heading for the following function body, which compares EOF on two files that are passed as parameters and returns True if both files have the same status.

```
BEGIN  (* SameStatus *)
  SameStatus := EOF(File1) = EOF(File2)
END;   (* SameStatus *)
```

7. Write a function called CompassHeading that returns the sum of its four Real parameters: TrueCourse, WindCorrAngle, Variance, and Deviation.

8. Write a function called P5 that returns the fifth power of its Real parameter.

9. Write a function called Min that returns the smallest of its three Integer parameters.

10. Write a function called Postage that returns the cost of mailing a package, given the weight of the package in pounds and ounces, and a cost per ounce.

PROGRAMMING PROBLEMS

1. If a principal amount (P) is placed in a savings account for which the interest is compounded Q times per year, then the amount of interest earned after N years will be given by the following formula (*I* is the decimal interest rate):

$$Amount = P * (1 + I / Q)^{N*Q}$$

Write a Pascal program that will input the values for P, I, Q, and N and output the interest earned for each year up through year N. You should use a function to compute the amount of interest. Your program should appropriately prompt the user, label output values, and have good style.

2. The distance to the landing point of a projectile that is launched at an angle Angle (in radians) with an initial velocity of Velocity (in feet per second), ignoring air resistance, is given by the formula

$$\text{Distance} = (\text{Sqr(Velocity)} * \text{Sin}(2 * \text{Angle})) / 32.2$$

Write a Pascal program that implements a game in which the user first enters the distance to a target. The user then enters the angle and velocity for launching a projectile. If the projectile comes within a tenth of one percent of the distance to the target, the user wins the game. If the projectile doesn't come close enough, the user is told how far the projectile went and is allowed to try again. If, after five tries, there isn't a winning input, then the user loses the game.

In order to simplify input for the user, your program should allow the angle to be input in degrees. The formula for converting degrees to radians is

$$\text{Radians} = \text{Degrees} * 3.14159265 / 180.0$$

Each of the formulas in this problem should be implemented as a Pascal function in your program. Your program should appropriately prompt the user for input, label output values, and have good programming style.

3. Write a program that will compute the number of days between two dates. One way of doing this is to have the program compute the Julian day number for each of the dates and subtract one from the other. The Julian day number is the number of days that have elapsed since noon on January 1, 4713 B.C. The following algorithm may be used to calculate the Julian day number.

Given Year (an integer, such as 1987), Month (an integer between 1 and 12 inclusive), and Day (an integer in the range of 1 through 31), if Month is 1 or 2, then subtract 1 from Year and add 12 to Month.

If the date comes from the Gregorian calendar (later than October 15, 1582), then compute an intermediate result with the following formula (otherwise let IntRes1 equal 0):

$$\text{IntRes1} = 2 - \text{Year DIV 100} + \text{Year DIV 400}$$

Compute a second intermediate result with the formula

$$\text{IntRes2} = \text{Trunc}(365.25 * \text{Year})$$

Compute a third intermediate result with the formula

$$\text{IntRes3} = \text{Trunc}(30.6001 * (\text{Month} + 1))$$

Finally, the Julian day number is computed with the formula

$$\text{JulianDay} = \text{IntRes1} + \text{IntRes2} + \text{IntRes3} + \text{Day} + 1720994.5$$

Your program should make appropriate use of functions in solving this problem. These formulas require nine significant digits and thus might not be computable on some systems.

As usual, your program should prompt for input (the two dates) if it is to be run interactively. You should use good style and plenty of comments.

- To understand the difference between atomic and composite data types.
- To be able to declare a variable of a set type.
- To be able to write set expressions.
- To be able to write relational expressions with sets.
- To be able to write a REPEAT statement to solve a given problem.
- To be able to write a FOR statement to solve a given problem.
- To be able to write a CASE statement to solve a given problem.
- To be able to write an IF-THEN-ELSE statement, using a set and the IN operator, that will prevent execution of a CASE statement with an invalid selector value.

9

Sets and Additional Control Structures

In the preceding chapters we introduced Pascal statements for the control structures sequence, selection, loop, and subprogram (procedure and function). In the cases of selection and subprogram, we introduced more than one way of implementing these structures. For example, a selection may be implemented by either an IF-THEN statement or an IF-THEN-ELSE statement. The IF-THEN is actually sufficient to implement any selection structure. However, Pascal provides the IF-THEN-ELSE as a matter of convenience because the two-way branch is a structure that is frequently used in programming.

This chapter will introduce three new Pascal statements which, like the IF-THEN-ELSE, are not essential to programming but are very convenient in many situations. One of these Pascal statements, the CASE statement, makes it easier to write selection structures with many branches. The other two statements, FOR and REPEAT, make it easier to program certain types of looping structures.

First, however, we will introduce a new data type called a *set* that is often used in conjunction with the CASE statement. This is the first new data type we've seen since Chapter 3, and the first of many user-defined data types that we will see. (Integer, Real, Char, Boolean, and Text are all predefined by Pascal.) In fact, the remaining chapters in this book will be largely devoted to introducing additional user-defined data types.

SETS

A declaration associates an identifier with a process or object. The processes are procedures and functions. The objects have primarily been variables and constants of type Char, Integer, Real, or Boolean. Since each of these objects has had a single value, it has been logical to think of an identifier as being a synonym for its value.

The objects, however, do not have to be single values. For example, a Text file can be considered as an object that contains any number of values.

In this chapter we will introduce a new data type that allows us to associate an identifier with a collection of values. That is, an object of this type will not be a single value but a *set* of values. In fact, such an object is called a *set*. Because a set is composed of multiple values, it is called a *composite data type*. Integer, Real, Char, and Boolean are referred to as *atomic data types*. (We will introduce additional atomic data types in Chapter 10.)

Composite Data Type A data type that allows a collection of values to be associated with an identifier of that type.

Atomic Data Type A data type that allows only a single value to be associated with an identifier of that type.

In mathematics a set is a collection, group, or class of items. Pascal sets are just the same, with the restrictions that (1) the items or values of a set must all be of the same atomic data type and (2) they must not be real numbers. Real numbers are not allowed in sets because of the problems associated with representational errors, which we saw in Chapter 8.

In mathematics a set may be of any size; however, Pascal compilers impose a limit on the number of values a set can have. The manual for your compiler should specify what this limit is. Appendix I includes information on limits of several of the *T,M,V,* ↩ most widely used Pascal compilers.

Set An unordered collection of distinct values (components) chosen from the possible values of a single atomic data type (other than Real) called the component or base type.

There are three special types of sets that are important: *subsets,* which are sets that are contained within another set, the *universal set,* which is a set that contains all the values of the base type, and the *empty set,* which contains no values at all.

Subset A set X is a subset of the set Y if each element of X is an element of Y. If there is at least one element of Y that is not in X, then X is called a *proper subset* of Y.

Empty Set The set with no members at all.

Universal Set The set containing all of the values of the component type.

The following syntax diagram illustrates how to define a variable of a set data type.

VAR ⟶ identifier list ⟶ **:** ⟶ SET OF data type

For example,

```
VAR
    SetOne,
    SetTwo:
        SET OF 'A'..'Z';
    SetThree:
        SET OF 1..12;
```

creates set variables called SetOne, SetTwo, and SetThree, where the components of the first two sets may be any of the uppercase letters of the alphabet, and the components of the third set may be any of the integers in the range 1 through 12. 'A'..'Z' is shorthand for the characters A and Z and all the letters in between. Similarly, 1..12 is shorthand for the numbers 1 and 12 and all of the integers in between. We will look at this shorthand in detail in the next chapter.

SetOne and SetTwo are variables that can contain no, one, or any combination of capital letters. The capital letters constitute the component, or base, type of the set. It is the fact that we can choose the base type of a set that makes the set a user-defined data type. Each time we define a set variable with a different base type, we are also defining a new data type.

Like all variables, SetOne and SetTwo do not start out with any letters in them. They are undefined until values are put into them. Think of a set as an Easter egg basket. The basket has been designed for the purpose of holding Easter eggs. There are no eggs in it, however, until you actually put some into the basket.

We use the assignment statement to put values into a set. We can assign the value of one set variable to another. However, the two set variables must be of the same data type; that is, they must have the same base type. We can also assign the value of a set literal to a set variable. A set literal is specified by a list of literals of the base type, enclosed in square brackets. For example,

```
SetOne := ['A', 'E', 'I', 'O', 'U']
```

assigns the set literal containing the letters A, E, I, O, and U to the set variable SetOne.

A set literal may also include ranges of values of the base type. For example,

```
SetOne := ['A'..'D']
```

would assign the letters A, B, C, and D to SetOne. This notation may be combined with lists of literal values to form set literals. For example,

```
SetOne := ['E'..'M', 'A', 'S'..'V', 'Z']
```

assigns the letters E through M, A, S through V, and Z to variable SetOne.

To create a set containing only the letter P, the following statement can be used.

```
SetTwo := ['P']
```

To define a set with no components (the empty set), we use

```
SetOne := []
```

Note that after the preceding assignment, the set variable SetOne is *not undefined.* It is a set with no components in it; it is an *empty* set. To create a set with all the possible values in it (the universal set), we use a set literal containing all of the values in the base type. For example,

```
SetTwo := ['A'..'Z']
```

In all of these cases, we are assigning a set on the right-hand side of the assignment statement to a set on the left-hand side. The brackets are used to indicate that the components listed inside are members of a set.

In addition to defining set variables and assigning set literals to set variables, we may also assign the results of set expressions to set variables. There are three operations defined on sets: union, intersection, and difference.

+ (Union): The union of two set variables is a set made up of those components which are in either or both of the set variables.

* (Intersection): The intersection of two set variables is a set made up of those components occurring in both set variables.

− (Difference): The difference between two set variables is a set made up of those elements in the first set variable that are not in the second.

The following code segment illustrates the three set operations.

Statement	*Resulting Set*
SetOne := ['P', 'Q'];	['P', 'Q']
SetTwo := SetOne + ['R','S'];	['P','Q','R','S']
SetOne := SetOne − SetTwo;	[]
SetOne := SetOne + ['A','B'];	['A','B']
SetOne := SetOne + ['A','S'];	['A','B','S']
SetTwo := SetOne * SetTwo;	['S']

To add a value to a set, use the union operator:

```
SetOne := SetOne + ['Q']
```

To delete a value from a set, use the difference operator:

```
SetOne := SetOne − ['Q']
```

Adding a value that is already in a set has no effect; deleting a value that is not in a set has no effect.

We can assign SetOne to be vowels and SetTwo to be consonants using the following code fragment.

```
SetTwo := ['A'..'Z'];              (* Universal set *)
SetOne := ['A','E','I','O','U'];
SetTwo := SetTwo - SetOne;
```

This is certainly easier than listing every consonant.

We can also perform conditional tests on sets. The relational operators (=, <>, <=, >=, <, >) have the following meaning when applied to two sets.

Expression	*Returns True If*
`SetOne = SetTwo`	SetOne and SetTwo are identical.
`SetOne <> SetTwo`	there is at least one value in SetOne not in SetTwo or there is at least one value in SetTwo not in SetOne.
`SetOne <= SetTwo`	SetOne is a subset of SetTwo.
`SetOne < SetTwo`	SetOne is a proper subset of SetTwo—there is at least one value in SetTwo not in SetOne.
`SetOne >= SetTwo`	SetTwo is a subset of SetOne.
`SetOne > SetTwo`	SetTwo is a proper subset of SetOne—there is at least one value in SetOne not in SetTwo.

Given the assignments

```
SetOne := ['A', 'B', 'C', 'D'];
SetTwo := ['C', 'D']
```

the following expressions will be evaluated as shown.

Expression	*Result*
`SetOne = SetTwo`	False
`SetOne >= SetTwo`	True
`SetOne > SetTwo`	True
`SetTwo >= SetOne`	False
`SetTwo > SetOne`	False
`SetTwo <= SetOne`	True
`SetTwo < SetOne`	True

There is one more conditional operator that may be applied between a value of the component type and a set. The IN operator tests whether the component is a member of a set. For example,

```
value IN SetOne
```

returns True if the value is in SetOne and False if the value is not in SetOne.

The IN operator makes it very convenient for us to write certain kinds of conditional tests. Suppose we are writing a program that counts the vowels in a file. One way of testing a letter to see if it's a vowel would be

```
IF (Letter = 'A') OR (Letter = 'E') OR (Letter = 'I') OR
   (Letter = 'O') OR (Letter = 'U')
   THEN
      (* Vowel *)
```

With the IN operator and a set composed of the vowel letters, this test can be reduced to

```
IF Letter IN ['A', 'E', 'I', 'O', 'U']
   THEN
      (* Vowel *)
```

The IN operator has the same precedence as the other relational operators. Recall that the relational operators are lower in precedence than other operators. When used with sets, the +, *, and − operators have the same precedence as when they are used with integers or reals.

The following problem demonstrates the use of sets and the IN operator.

Problem Solving in Action

Problem: Read and print alphanumeric characters from file Data. When the entire file has been read, print a summary table showing the percentage of uppercase letters, the percentage of lowercase letters, the percentage of decimal digits, the percentage of blanks, and the percentage of end-of-sentence punctuation marks in the data file ('?', '!', '.').

Discussion: Doing this task by hand would be tedious, but quite straightforward. We would set up five places to make hash marks, one for each of the categories of symbols to be counted. We would then take the text character by character, determining which category each character was in, and making a hash mark in the appropriate place.

We can look at a character and tell immediately which category to hash mark. We will simulate this by using sets with the IN operator. We can ask if each character is in the set of uppercase letters, the set of lowercase letters, the set of digits, the set of blanks, or the set of punctuation marks.

PSIA ▰▰▰▰▰▰▰

Input: Text on file Data

Output: A copy of the text on file Data and a table giving the name of each category and what percent the category represents

Assumptions: None

MAIN MODULE   Level 0

```
WHILE NOT EOF
    WHILE NOT EOLN
        Read a character
        Write a character
        Increment proper counter
    Readln
    Writeln
Calculate and print percentages
```

Note that we have to skip over the end-of-line markers; otherwise they would be counted as blanks.

INCREMENT PROPER COUNTER   Level 1

```
IF Character IN set of uppercase letters
    Increment Uppercase Counter
ELSE IF Character IN set of lowercase letters
    Increment Lowercase Counter
ELSE IF Character IN set of digits
    Increment Digit Counter
ELSE IF Character is a blank
    Increment Blank Counter
ELSE IF Character IN set of punctuation
    Increment Punctuation Counter
```

At this point we realize that the instructions do not indicate whether the percentages are to be taken of the total number of characters read, including those that do not fit any of the categories, or of the total number of characters that fall into the five categories. We will assume that all characters should be counted. We will thus need to add to this module one more ELSE statement where we increment a counter (called LeftOverCounter) for all characters that do not fall into the five categories.

PSIA ▰▰▰▰▰

CALCULATE AND PRINT PERCENTAGES

> Writeln
> Total ⟵ sum of 6 counters
> Writeln 'Percentage of uppercase letters: ',
>   UppercaseCounter / Total * 100
> Writeln 'Percentage of lowercase letters: ',
>   LowercaseCounter / Total * 100
> Writeln 'Percentage of decimal digits: ',
>   DigitCounter / Total * 100
> Writeln 'Percentage of blanks: ',
>   BlankCounter / Total * 100
> Writeln 'Percentage of end-of-sentence punctuation: ',
>   PunctuationCounter / Total * 100

Module Structure Chart:

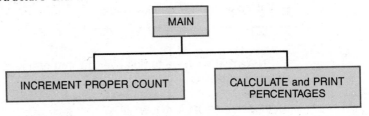

```
PROGRAM CategoryCount (Output, Data);

(* File Data is echo printed on Output.  A table is printed to show the
   percent of characters in the file that belong to five categories:
   uppercase letters, lowercase letters, decimal digits, blanks, and
   end-of-sentence punctuation marks.  ASSUMPTION: Percents are based on
   total number of characters in the file *)


VAR
    UppercaseCounter,        (* Number of uppercase letters *)
    LowercaseCounter,        (* Number of lowercase letters *)
    DigitCounter,            (* Number of digits            *)
    BlankCounter,            (* Number of blanks            *)
    PunctuationCounter,      (* Number of punctuation marks *)
    LeftOverCounter:         (* Number of other characters  *)
        Integer;
    Data:                    (* Input text file             *)
        Text;
    Character:               (* Current input character     *)
        Char;


(*************************************************************************)
```

PSIA ▬▬▬▬

```
PROCEDURE IncrementProperCount
    (VAR UppercaseCounter,          (* Receives/returns count    *)
         LowercaseCounter,          (* Receives/returns count    *)
         DigitCounter,              (* Receives/returns count    *)
         BlankCounter,              (* Receives/returns count    *)
         PunctuationCounter,        (* Receives/returns count    *)
         LeftOverCounter:           (* Receives/returns count    *)
            Integer;
         Character:                 (* Receives current character *)
            Char);

(* The proper counter is incremented for each character *)

BEGIN (* IncrementProperCount *)
   IF Character IN ['A'..'Z']
     THEN
         UppercaseCounter := UppercaseCounter + 1
     ELSE IF Character IN ['a'..'z']
       THEN
         LowercaseCounter := LowercaseCounter + 1
     ELSE IF Character IN ['0'..'9']
       THEN
         DigitCounter := DigitCounter + 1
     ELSE IF Character IN [' ']
       THEN
         BlankCounter := BlankCounter + 1
     ELSE IF Character IN ['.', '?', '!']
       THEN
         PunctuationCounter := PunctuationCounter + 1
     ELSE
         LeftOverCounter := LeftOverCounter + 1
END;   (* IncrementProperCount *)


(*******************************************************************)


PROCEDURE CalculatePrint (UppercaseCounter,       (* Receives count *)
                          LowercaseCounter,       (* Receives count *)
                          DigitCounter,           (* Receives count *)
                          BlankCounter,           (* Receives count *)
                          PunctuationCounter,     (* Receives count *)
                          LeftOverCounter:        (* Receives count *)
                             Integer);

(* The total number of characters is calculated and the
   percentage of each category of characters is printed *)

VAR
  Total:          (* Total number of characters in file *)
     Integer;
```

PSIA

```
BEGIN (* CalculatePrint *)
  Writeln;
  Total := UppercaseCounter + LowercaseCounter + DigitCounter +
           BlankCounter + PunctuationCounter + LeftOverCounter;
  Writeln('Percentage of uppercase letters: ',
          UppercaseCounter / Total * 100:5:2);
  Writeln('Percentage of lowercase letters: ',
          LowercaseCounter / Total * 100:5:2);
  Writeln('Percentage of decimal digits: ',
          DigitCounter / Total * 100:5:2);
  Writeln('Percentage of blanks: ',
          BlankCounter / Total * 100:5:2);
  Writeln('Percentage of end-of-sentence punctuation: ',
          PunctuationCounter / Total * 100:5:2)
END;   (* CalculatePrint *)


(*************************************************************************)


BEGIN (* CategoryCount *)
  Reset(Data);
  (* Initialize counters to zero *)
  UppercaseCounter := 0;
  LowercaseCounter := 0;
  DigitCounter := 0;
  BlankCounter := 0;
  PunctuationCounter := 0;
  LeftOverCounter := 0;

  WHILE NOT EOF(Data) DO
    BEGIN
      WHILE NOT EOLN(Data) DO
        BEGIN
          Read(Data, Character);
          Write(Character);
          IncrementProperCount(UppercaseCounter, LowercaseCounter,
                               DigitCounter, BlankCounter,
                               PunctuationCounter, LeftOverCounter,
                               Character);
        END;
      Readln(Data);
      Writeln
    END;
  CalculatePrint(UppercaseCounter, LowercaseCounter, DigitCounter,
                 BlankCounter, PunctuationCounter, LeftOverCounter)
END.   (* CategoryCount *)
```

PSIA

Testing: To be thoroughly tested, Program CategoryCount must be run with all possible combinations of the categories of characters we are counting. Listed below is the minimum set of cases that must be tested.

1. All of the categories of characters are present.
2. Four of the categories are present; one is not. (This alone will require five test runs.)
3. Only characters that fall into one of the five categories are present.
4. Other characters are present.

The percentages listed below came from a run in which the data file was an earlier version of the section of this text beginning with the title Sets and ending with the program itself. The file included all the word processing commands embedded in the text. For obvious reasons, we are showing only the percentages, not the echo print of the input!

Output from Program CategoryCount:

```
Percentage of uppercase letters: 2.05
Percentage of lowercase letters: 22.32
Percentage of decimal digits: 0.05
Percentage of blanks: 7.03
Percentage of end-of-sentence punctuation: 68.27
```

In Program CategoryCount we needed to use only literal sets—those written in the body of the program. A set variable is used in the problem at the end of the chapter.

ADDITIONAL CONTROL STRUCTURES

REPEAT Statement

The REPEAT statement is a looping control structure in which the loop condition is tested at the end of the loop. This format guarantees that the loop will be executed at least once. The syntax diagram for the REPEAT-UNTIL is

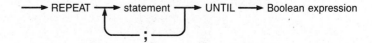

This is how you would write a REPEAT statement:

```
REPEAT
    statement1;
    statement2;
       .
       .
UNTIL Boolean expression
```

The segment means "Keep executing the statements between the REPEAT and the UNTIL as long as the expression is False. When the expression becomes True, exit the loop."

Because UNTIL delimits the statement, a BEGIN-END pair is not necessary for the body of the loop.

Let's take a WHILE loop and a REPEAT loop that do the same task and compare them. The task is to find the first numeric character in a file of data.

WHILE solution:
```
Read (Data, Character);
WHILE Character NOT IN ['0'..'9'] DO
    Read(Data, Character);
```

REPEAT solution:
```
REPEAT
    Read(Data, Character)
UNTIL Character IN ['0'..'9']
```

The WHILE solution requires a priming Read so that Character will have a value before the loop is entered. The REPEAT solution does not require a priming Read because the statements within the loop are executed before the expression is evaluated.

Let's take a look at another example. REPEAT loops are especially useful for data validation. Suppose we want to write a program that reads test scores interactively. A score must be in the range of 0 to 100. We have already written a Boolean function called Valid that returns True if its parameter is within this range. The following loops will then ensure that the input value is in the acceptable range.

WHILE solution:
```
Writeln('Enter a test score.');
Readln(Score);
WHILE NOT Valid(Score) DO
    BEGIN
        Writeln('Invalid score.  Scores must be ',
                'in the range of 0 through 100.');
        Writeln('Enter a test score.');
        Readln(Score)
    END
```

REPEAT solution:
```
REPEAT
    Writeln('Enter a test score.');
    Readln(Score);
```

```
     IF NOT Valid(Score)
        THEN
           Writeln('Invalid score.  Scores must be ',
                   'in the range of 0 through 100. ')
     UNTIL Valid(Score)
```

The expressions controlling the loops are complements of each other. The WHILE continues looping as long as the expression is True; the REPEAT continues looping as long as the expression is False.

Because the WHILE statement tests the loop condition before executing the body of the loop, it is called a *pretest loop*. The REPEAT statement does the opposite and is thus known as a *posttest loop*.

The REPEAT can be used to implement a count-controlled loop if we know in advance that the loop will always be executed at least once. Use of the WHILE and REPEAT statements to implement a count-controlled loop is shown below.

```
          Counter : = 1;
          WHILE Counter  <= N DO
             BEGIN

                 .

                Counter : = Counter + 1
             END;

          Counter : = 1;
          REPEAT

                 .

             Counter : = Counter + 1
          UNTIL Counter > N
```

Figure 9-1 compares the flow of control in the WHILE and REPEAT loops.

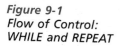

Figure 9-1
Flow of Control:
WHILE and REPEAT

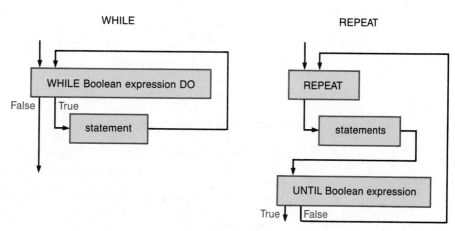

It is important to keep in mind that the WHILE statement uses the expression to decide when to *keep* looping and the REPEAT statement uses the expression to decide when to *stop* looping. To transform a loop using one statement into an equivalent loop using the other statement, the expressions must be complemented. Complementing an expression means turning it into its opposite. When an expression is True, its complement must be False; when an expression is False, its complement must be True.

The following list shows some common looping conditions along with their complements.

Expression	*Complement*
`NOT EOF`	`EOF`
`Character IN ['a'..'z']`	`NOT (Character IN ['a'..'z'])`
`I >= N`	`I < N`
`(I < N) AND NOT FOUND`	`(I >= N) OR FOUND`

After we look at the last looping construct, the FOR statement, we will consider some guidelines for determining when it is appropriate to use each type of loop.

FOR Statement

The FOR statement is designed to simplify the writing of count-controlled loops. The statement

```
FOR Count := 1 TO N DO
    statement;
```

means "Set the loop control variable Count to 1. If N is less than 1, do not enter the loop. Otherwise, execute the statement and increment I by 1. Stop the loop when it has been executed with Count equal to N." This statement is functionally equivalent to the following WHILE Loop.

```
Count := 1;
WHILE Count <= N DO
  BEGIN
    statement;
    Count := Count + 1
  END;
```

The syntax diagram for the FOR statement is

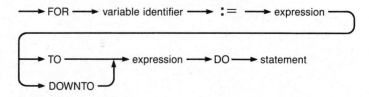

Just as in the WHILE Loop, the statement in the FOR loop may be a compound statement. If the DOWNTO version is used, the loop control variable is decremented by 1 for each iteration instead of being incremented by 1. The following two loops will execute the same number of times.

```
FOR Count : = 1 TO Limit DO
   statement;

FOR Count : = Limit DOWNTO 1 DO
   statement;
```

FOR statements are very convenient, and many programmers tend to overuse them. Be warned: FOR loops are not general-purpose loops. They are designed exclusively for count-controlled loops. To use them intelligently, you should know and remember the following facts about FOR loops:

1. The loop control variable (LCV) may not be changed within the loop. Its value may be used, but not changed. That is, the LCV may appear in an expression but not on the left-hand side of an assignment statement.

2. The LCV is incremented or decremented by 1 automatically. If you need to increment or decrement by another value, you should use a WHILE or REPEAT loop.

3. The LCV is undefined at the end of the loop. If, in a statement following the FOR loop, you try to use the LCV in an expression, the effects will vary from compiler to compiler. You may get a run-time error message, or you may simply get erroneous results. You might expect the LCV to be the final value plus 1, but it is not. It is undefined. For example,

```
FOR Count : = 0 TO 10 DO
   BEGIN
      Cube : = Count * Count * Count;
      Writeln(Count:1, ' ', Cube:1)
   END;
Writeln(Count:1)
```

would first print a table of the cubes of the numbers 0 through 10. Then either an error message or an unexpected value would be printed, not the number 11.

4. When you use a FOR statement in a procedure or function, the LCV must be declared as a local variable within the same procedure or function.

5. The loop is executed with the LCV at the initial value, the final value, and all values in between. If the initial value is greater than the final value, the FOR statement is not executed. If the initial value is equal to the final value, the FOR statement is executed once.

6. You cannot put an additional termination condition in the loop. The heading must be exactly like the following:

```
FOR name : = initial value TO final value DO
```

or

```
FOR name := initial value DOWNTO final value DO
```

where name must be a variable and initial value and final value can be any valid expressions (variables and/or constants and operators).

The initial and final values of the FOR loop may be expressions of any atomic data type except Real (because of the representational errors associated with Reals). Thus, in addition to Integer values, a FOR loop can be used with Char or Boolean values. For example, the following loop prints the alphabet.

```
FOR Letter := 'A' TO 'Z' DO
    Write(Letter);
Writeln;
```

Just like WHILE loops, REPEAT and FOR loops may be nested. For example, the nested FOR structure

```
FOR Endletter := 'A' TO 'G' DO
    BEGIN
        FOR PrintedLetter := 'A' TO EndLetter DO
            Write(PrintedLetter);
        Writeln;
    END;
```

prints the following triangle of letters.

```
A
AB
ABC
ABCD
ABCDE
ABCDEF
ABCDEFG
```

Guidelines for Choosing a Looping Statement

Here are some guidelines to help you decide when it is appropriate to use each of the three Pascal looping statements.

1. If the loop is a simple count-controlled loop, use a FOR statement. If the loop is controlled by a counter and an event, or if the loop must count by a value other than 1 or −1, then a FOR loop is inappropriate. Use a WHILE or REPEAT loop instead.

2. If the loop is an event-controlled loop and the body of the loop will always be executed at least once, a REPEAT statement is appropriate.

3. If the loop is an event-controlled loop and nothing is known about the first execution, use a WHILE statement.

4. If both a WHILE and a REPEAT are appropriate, use the one that better reflects the semantics of the loop. That is, if the problem is stated in terms of when to continue looping, use a WHILE statement. If the problem is stated in terms of when to stop looping, use a REPEAT statement.

5. When in doubt, use a WHILE statement.

CASE Statement

The CASE statement is a selection control structure that allows you to list several alternative courses of action and choose one to be executed at run time. The selection is done by matching up the value of an expression (case selector) with a label attached to a course of action. For example, the statement

```
CASE I OF
    1   :   statement1;
    2   :   statement2;
    3,4 :   statement3
END;   (* Case *)
statement4
```

means "If I is a 1, execute statement1 and continue with statement4. If I is a 2, execute statement2 and continue with statement4. If I is a 3 or a 4, execute statement3 and continue with statement4."

The syntax diagram for the CASE statement is

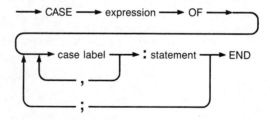

where a case label is a literal or named constant of any atomic type except Real. (We will expand the definition of case label in the next chapter.) The expression is called the *case selector,* and the list of labels is called the *case label list.*

Case Selector The expression or variable whose value determines which case label list is selected (cannot be Real).

Case Label List A list of values of the same type as the case selector, appearing in the body of the CASE statement.

In the example, I is the case selector and

$$1$$
$$2$$
$$3, 4$$

are case label lists. Each case label value should appear just once in a given CASE statement. If a value appears more than once as a label in a CASE statement, a compiler error will result.

The following program fragment would print the appropriate comment based on a student's grade.

```
CASE Grade OF
  'A', 'B' : Write('Good Work');
  'C'      : Write('Average Work');
  'D', 'F' : Write('Poor Work')
END (* Case *)
```

Grade is the CASE selector, and 'A', 'B', 'C', 'D', and 'F' are the values in the case label lists. If Grade contains an 'A' or a 'B', "Good work" will be printed. If Grade contains a 'C', "Average Work" will be printed. If Grade contains a 'D' or an 'F', "Poor Work" will be printed.

What if we wish to execute more than one statement in a course of action? For example, we might also want to keep a count of students who are doing poor work. Recall that we may use a compound statement in any place where a single statement may be used. The following program fragment contains a compound statement to not only write out a message but also keep a count of how many times we have done so.

```
CASE Grade OF
  'A', 'B' : Write('Good Work');
  'C'      : Write('Average Work');
  'D', 'F' :
    BEGIN
      Write('Poor Work');
      NumberInTrouble := NumberInTrouble + 1
    END
END (* Case *)
```

What happens if Grade does not contain one of these five letters? The result is undefined. We cannot predict what will happen. The ISO standard for Pascal states that this is an error condition. Many Pascal implementations will thus print a run-time error message. However, some Pascal implementations just skip the entire statement if there is no match between the selector and a label. There are also some compilers that have implemented an OTHERWISE clause to the CASE statement to handle this problem.

T,M,V ⬑

There is a way to make the result of an invalid case selector value predictable. We can use the IN operator to check to be sure that the case selector is one of the values in a case label list. For example, we can make sure that Grade is an allowed value with the following check.

```
If Grade IN ['A', 'B', 'C', 'D', 'F']
   THEN
       CASE Grade OF
                   .
                   .
       END (* Case *)
   ELSE
       Writeln('Grade is not a legal letter grade.')
```

This technique cannot be used when the list of labels does not form a valid base type for a set. For example, if the number of labels exceeds the number of set elements allowed by your Pascal compiler, you won't be able to write a set literal containing those labels. In that case, you will have to use a series of equality tests (one per case label) and OR operations in the IF-THEN-ELSE statement that precedes the CASE. As an example, suppose a problem requires 288 different branches based on 1000 possible values for the case selector. Most compilers will not support 1000 elements in a set. In such a situation the following IF-THEN-ELSE could be used.

```
IF (Select = 1) OR (Select = 2) OR (Select = 3) OR
                  .
                  .
   (Select = 1000)
   THEN
     CASE Select OF
        1,2,3,4,5      :    statement1;
        6,7,8,9,10     :    statement2;
                  .
                  .
        998,999,1000 :    statement288
     END (* Case *)
   ELSE
     statement289;
```

Of course, in this situation it would have been much simpler to write the IF-THEN-ELSE as

```
IF (Select >= 1) AND (Select <= 1000)
   THEN
       CASE Select OF
                   .
                   .
```

In fact, the CASE statement itself could be replaced with a series of nested IF-THEN-ELSE statements. Nested IF statements may always be used in place of a CASE statement. If you start to write a CASE statement and discover that each label list is a continuous range of values, a nested IF-THEN-ELSE structure is probably called for. Thus, the preceding example could be rewritten

```
IF (Select >= 1) AND (Select <= 1000)
  THEN
  IF (Select >= 1) AND (Select <= 5)
    THEN
       statement1
  ELSE IF (Select >= 6) AND (Select <= 10)
    THEN
       statement2

          .
          .
          .

  ELSE
     statement288
  ELSE
     statement289
```

Keep in mind that Pascal provides the CASE statement as a matter of convenience. Whenever it is convenient to use the CASE statement, do so. However, don't feel obligated to try to fit every multi-way branch into a CASE statement. Some multi-way branches are easier to code as nested IF statements.

Here is a summary of the three new control structures that we have looked at in this chapter.

REPEAT statement: A looping control statement in which the expression is evaluated at the end of the loop, guaranteeing at least one execution of the loop. The loop continues as long as the expression is False.

FOR statement: A looping control statement with predefined initial and final values for the loop control variable, and automatic incrementing (or decrementing) of the loop control variable. If the ending value is greater (smaller) than the initial value, the loop is not executed.

CASE statement: A selection control structure that provides for multi-way selection of different courses of action. It is less general than a nested IF-THEN-ELSE structure, but is often more convenient to use.

The following problem illustrates the use of the FOR and REPEAT control structures, along with data type Set.

Problem Solving in Action

Problem: It is time to assign final letter grades in a large history class. At the moment the grades are in the form of numeric averages ranging from 0 to 100. Every grade below 60 is an automatic F. However, the exact cutoff for the other letter grades may vary slightly.

To determine the cutoff for the various letter grades, it is useful to see a list of the numeric grades with an indication of whether any student has a given numeric grade.

PSIA ▬▬▬▬

We will print a list of numeric grades between 60 and 100 and mark those that actually occur with an asterisk.

Discussion: We are not interested in how many people have a particular grade, only whether a grade exists in a set of grades. The clue to the solution lies in the expression "set of grades." We can create a set variable to contain numbers from 60 to 100. As we read in a grade, we can test to see if it is between 60 and 100. If it is, we can put it into the set.

When we have read in all the grades, we can print out all the values that are in the set. Since there is no direct way to print the values from a set, we will have to use a loop that goes from 60 to 100, asking if the loop control variable is IN the set.

Input: Integer grades, one per line, read from the terminal.

Output: The numbers from 60 to 100, listed one per line. (Asterisks will mark those numbers for which there is a grade.)

Assumptions: None

MAIN MODULE   Level 0

```
REPEAT
   Read Grade
   IF Grade between 60 and 100
      THEN
         SetOfGrades := SetOfGrades + [Grade]
UNTIL no more grades
Print numbers
```

The REPEAT loop is appropriate for the main looping structure. We want to keep reading and processing values until we reach the end of the list of numbers. A REPEAT-UNTIL end-of-file will accomplish this.

PRINT NUMBERS   Level 1

```
FOR Counter going from 60 to 100
   Write Counter
   IF Counter IN SetOfGrades
      Write '*'
   Writeln
```

We need to print the numbers 60 and 100 and all those in between. This is exactly what the FOR loop is designed to do.

Even though the program is not a long one, ideally the printing module should be made a procedure. However, we have not yet studied the mechanism that will allow us to define the set as a formal parameter of a procedure, and we do not want to access

PSIA

the set globally. So we will have to code this program without using a procedure. In the next chapter we will study the mechanism that will allow us to use sets as parameters.

Module Structure Chart:

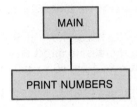

Program Gradelist implements our algorithm.

```
PROGRAM GradeList (Input, Output);

(* The numbers between 60 and 100 are printed. Numbers that correspond
   to a grade in the input file are marked with an asterisk *)

VAR
  SetOfGrades:          (* Keeps track of actual grades    *)
    SET OF 60..100;
  Counter,              (* Loop control variable           *)
  Grade:                (* Numeric grade between 0 and 100 *)
    Integer;

BEGIN (* GradeList *)
  (* Initialize SetOfGrades to empty *)
  SetOfGrades := [];
  (* Read and add grades to SetOfGrades *)
  REPEAT
    Readln(Grade);                                (* Get a grade *)
    IF (Grade >= 60) AND (Grade <= 100)       (* Check if in range *)
      THEN
        SetOfGrades := SetOfGrades + [Grade]      (* Add it to set *)
  UNTIL EOF;
  (* Print Numbers *)
  FOR Counter := 60 TO 100 DO
    BEGIN
      Write(Counter:3);                           (* Print number *)
      IF Counter IN SetOfGrades          (* Test for set membership *)
        THEN
          Write(' *');                             (* Mark number *)
      Writeln
    END
END. (* GradeList *)
```

PSIA ▰▰▰▰▰

Testing: To test this program we need to use the following types of data.

Data that includes values less than 60
Data that includes values more than 100
Data that includes one or more values of 60
Data that includes one or more values of 100
Data that includes single values between 60 and 100
Data that includes duplicate values between 60 and 100
Data that does not include some values between 60 and 100

The following data was used to test the program. The input specification called for one value per line, but here we have listed multiple values on a line in order to conserve space.

```
66 67 88 99 100 44 33 77 67 81 88 99 77 67 68 87 97 99 95 86
84 79 68 66 77 98 80 56 67 76 87 67 66 78 76 75 78 86 65 67
91 89 90 56 77 67 74 76 78 60
```

Here is the output produced from the input data. (Again, we have printed it here in four columns to save space.)

60 *	70	80 *	90 *
61	71	81 *	91 *
62	72	82	92
63	73	83	93
64	74 *	84 *	94
65 *	75 *	85	95 *
66 *	76 *	86 *	96
67 *	77 *	87 *	97 *
68 *	78 *	88 *	98 *
69	79 *	89 *	99 *
			100 *

The following scheme for assigning letter grades makes use of the natural breaks that occur in the distribution of the averages. Having the grades listed in this form makes the natural breaks obvious.

Grades between 60 and 68: 'D'
Grades between 74 and 81: 'C'
Grades between 84 and 91: 'B'
Grades 95 and above: 'A'

TESTING AND DEBUGGING

The same testing techniques we've used with WHILE loops apply to REPEAT and FOR loops. There are, however, a few additional considerations with REPEAT and FOR loops.

The special consideration with a REPEAT loop is that it will always execute at least once. Thus you should always try some data sets that will show the result of executing a REPEAT loop the minimal number of times.

With a data-dependent FOR loop, it is important to test for proper results from the program when the FOR loop executes zero times. This occurs when the starting value is greater than the ending value (or less than the ending value, in the case of the DOWNTO form of the FOR loop). Thus, if the starting and/or ending values of a FOR loop depend on the input data, you should test the program with at least one data set that will cause the loop to be skipped.

When a program contains a CASE statement, it should be tested with enough different data sets to make sure that each case branch is selected and executed correctly. The program should also be tested to see how it behaves when the case selector contains a value that is not in any of the case label lists.

If a program uses a variable of type set, you should try to find data values that will cause a value that is outside of the base type to be assigned to the set variable. For example, if a SET OF 'A'..'Z' is defined in the program, be sure to try some data values such as '?' and '8' to see if the program catches those values before trying to perform set operations with them.

Testing and Debugging Hints

1. The size of a set (the total number of values that can be in the set) is limited in Pascal. Check the manuals for your particular compiler for this limitation.

2. Initialize set variables before using them.

3. Do not attempt to print sets directly. Test elements for set membership and print each element that is a member.

4. Brackets are used to denote set literals, but are not used in the declaration of set variables. The set variable Letter may be defined as a SET OF 'A'..'Z', but the statement

```
Letter : = Letter + 'A'
```

is not valid because 'A' is not a set. Using brackets around the 'A' makes it a set literal with the letter 'A' in it. Therefore

```
Letter : = Letter + ['A']
```

is a valid statement.

5. All of the set operators except IN have two sets as their operands. The IN operator has a base type value as its first operand and a set as its second operand. Thus, if Letter is declared as a SET OF 'A'..'Z', the following are valid comparisons.

```
['A'] = Letter  (* Tests equality of two sets *)
'A' IN Letter   (* No brackets needed around 'A' because first
                   operand must be of base type *)
```

6. Remember that the standard operators +, −, and * have different meanings when used with sets.

7. Keep in mind that the REPEAT loop is a posttest loop. The expression is evaluated after the first iteration of the loop. If there is a possibility that the loop should be skipped entirely, use a WHILE statement.

8. Remember that the FOR statement is a special-purpose loop. The FOR loop is a count-controlled loop in which the initial value and the final value are listed in the statement itself. The increment is always 1 for the TO version and −1 for the DOWNTO version.

9. The loop control variable for the FOR statement must be a local variable when the FOR statement is used within a procedure or a function.

10. Reread the warnings in the FOR statement sections.

11. The case label lists are made up of values, not variables. They may, however, include named constants.

12. If there is a possibility that the case selector might not be one of the values in a case label list, test it for set membership with an IF-THEN-ELSE before executing the CASE statement.

13. The type of the case selector must be the same as the type of the values in the case label lists.

14. Double check long CASE statements to make sure that you haven't skipped any branches.

15. Always include the comment (* Case *) after the END of a CASE statement. This helps eliminate confusion if you must later track down an error involving a mismatched BEGIN-END pair.

SUMMARY

An identifier declared to be of an atomic data type (such as Integer, Real, Boolean, or Char) can hold only a single value. An identifier declared to be of a composite type (such as Set or Text) may represent multiple values.

A set is a collection of values and is hence a composite data type. We can create a set, put values into it with the union operator, and remove values from it with the difference operator. We can determine whether a value is in the set with the IN operator. These operations are very useful for checking the value of a case selector prior to execution of a CASE statement. They are also useful for processing text data.

The REPEAT is a general-purpose looping statement. It is like the WHILE loop except that its loop test occurs at the end of the loop. Pascal also provides a special-purpose looping statement, the FOR statement, to be used exclusively for count-controlled loops. The loop control variable of the FOR statement may be of any atomic data type except Real.

The CASE statement is a multi-way selection statement. It allows the program to choose among a set of alternatives. The CASE can always be simulated using nested IF-THEN-ELSE statements. However, if CASE can be used, it makes the code shorter and more self-documenting. CASE cannot be used with Real values as labels.

The FOR, REPEAT, and CASE statements are the ice cream and cake of Pascal. We can live without them, but they are very nice to have.

QUICK CHECK _____

1. What distinguishes an atomic data type from a composite data type? (pp. 333–334)

2. Write the declaration for a set variable called Digits, whose base type is the characters '0' through '9'. (pp. 334–335)

3. Write an expression that will assign all of the characters '0' through '4', and '6' through '9' (all of the digits except '5') to the set variable Digits. *Hint:* Use the set difference operator. (pp. 335–337)

4. How would you test to see whether the set variable Numbers is a proper subset of the set variable Digits? (pp. 337–338)

5. You have decided to rewrite a WHILE statement in a program as a REPEAT statement. The condition in the WHILE is (Day < 1) OR (Day > 31). Write the UNTIL portion of the REPEAT statement. (pp. 343–346)

6. A certain problem requires a simple count-controlled loop that starts at 10 and counts down to 1. Write the FOR statement that will do this. (pp. 346–348)

7. Write a CASE statement that, given an Integer selector called Name, will print your first name if Name = 1, your middle name if Name = 2, and your last name if Name = 3. (pp. 349–352)

8. Modify the code segment for the preceding question so that it prints an error message if the value in Name is not 1, 2, or 3. (pp. 349–352)

Answers
1. An atomic type associates one value with an identifier. A composite type may associate multiple values with an identifier.
2. `VAR Digits: SET OF '0'..'9'`
3. `Digits := ['0'..'9'] - ['5']`
4. `IF Numbers < Digits`
5. `UNTIL (Day >= 1) AND (Day <= 31)`
6. `FOR Count := 10 DOWNTO 1 DO`
7.
```
CASE Name OF
    1 : Writeln('Mary');
    2 : Writeln('Lynn');
    3 : Writeln('Smith')
END (* Case *)
```
8.
```
IF Name IN [1,2,3]
    THEN
        CASE Name OF
            1 : Writeln('Mary');
          2 : Writeln('Lynn');
            3 : Writeln('Smith')
        END; (* Case *)
    ELSE
        Writeln('Invalid name selector.')
```

EXAM PREPARATION EXERCISES _____

1. Define the following terms:

   composite type
   case selector
   case label
   posttest loop

2. Is the following a valid declaration of a set variable? Explain your answer.

$$\text{VAR Digits : ['0'..'9']}$$

3. Determine whether each of the following set expressions is valid or invalid. Assume that the variable Digits is declared as a SET OF '0'..'9'.

	Valid	Invalid
(a) 'A' IN Digits	_____	_____
(b) ['X','Y','Z'] >= ['N'..'Y']	_____	_____
(c) Digits / ['1']	_____	_____
(d) Digits * ['1']	_____	_____
(e) ['1'] + ['2'] + ['3'] = ['1'..'3']	_____	_____
(f) ['1'..'9'] > ['0'..'9'] − ['3'..'7']	_____	_____
(g) 4 IN Digits	_____	_____

4. Given the declarations and assignments

```
VAR
    Digits,
    Odds,
    Evens:
        SET OF '0'..'9'

Digits := ['0'..'9'];
Odds := ['1','3','5','7','9'];
Evens := ['2','4','6','8'];
```

   evaluate the expressions

	Result
(a) Digits + ['1']	_____
(b) Digits * ['1']	_____
(c) Digits − ['1']	_____
(d) ['1'] + ['2'] + ['3'] <= Digits	_____
(e) ['1'..'9'] > Digits − ['3'..'7']	_____
(f) Digits − Odds = Evens	_____
(g) Digits > Odds + Evens	_____
(h) Odds * Digits	_____
(i) Odds − Evens	_____
(j) Odds * Evens * Digits > []	_____

5. When a WHILE loop is converted into a REPEAT loop, the ending condition of the REPEAT loop is the complement of the ending condition of the WHILE loop. (True or False?)

6. A REPEAT loop does not require a BEGIN-END pair surrounding the loop body because REPEAT and UNTIL serve as the delimiters of the loop. (True or False?)

7. Is the following a valid FOR statement? Assume that Initial is a variable of type Char. Explain your answer.

```
        FOR Initial := 'Z' DOWNTO 'A' DO
            Write(Initial:2)
```

8. (a) The value of the LCV may be changed within a FOR loop. (True or False?)
   (b) The LCV of a FOR loop within a procedure must be declared locally. (True or False?)
   (c) It is impossible to write an infinite loop using only the FOR statement. (True or False?)
   (d) The FOR loop is a general-purpose loop because any WHILE loop can be rewritten as a FOR loop. (True or False?)

9. What will be printed by the following program fragment?

```
        FOR ROW := 1 TO 10 DO
            BEGIN
                FOR Col := 1 TO 10 - Row DO
                    Write('*');
                Write(' ':Row*2-1);
                FOR Col := 1 TO 10 - Row DO
                    Write('*');
                Writeln;
            END
```

10. A case selector may be any expression that results in a value of type Integer, Real, or Boolean. (True or False?)

11. The values in case label lists may appear in any order, but duplicate labels are not allowed within a given CASE statement. (True or False?)

12. All possible values for the case selector must be included among the case label lists for a given CASE statement. (True or False?)

PREPROGRAMMING EXERCISES _____

1. Rewrite the following using set notation:
   (a) (0 < I) AND (I < 25)
   (b) (Ch = 'A') OR (Ch = 'J') OR (Ch = 'K')
   (c) (X = 1) OR (X > 50) AND (X <= 100)

2. (a) Define three set variables called SetA, SetB, and SetC that can contain any of the uppercase alphabetic characters.
   (b) Assign 'A'..'N' to SetA.
   (c) Assign 'K'..'Z' to SetB.
   (d) Show the contents of SetC after the following operations.

Result

```
SetC : = SetA + Set B       _____
SetC : = SetA − SetB        _____
SetC : = SetA * SetB        _____
SetC : = SetB − SetA        _____
```

(e) Evaluate the following expressions.

Result

```
SetA <> SetB            _____
SetA <= SetB            _____
SetA * SetB > SetA      _____
SetA + SetB >= SetA     _____
```

3. Write a program segment that reads and sums until it has summed 10 data values or until a negative value is read, whichever comes first. Use a REPEAT loop for your solution.

4. Write a procedure called GetYesOrNo that returns a single character value equal to either 'Y' or 'N'. The procedure should read the value from Input and test to see whether it is one of the two acceptable responses. If the response is not 'Y' or 'N', the procedure should print an appropriate error message, prompt for another input, and again read a character. The procedure should not return until it has read a valid response. Use a REPEAT loop for your solution.

5. Rewrite the following WHILE loop using a REPEAT loop.

```
Response : = 'Y';
WHILE Response <> 'N' DO
    BEGIN
        Writeln('Enter Y for Yes, N for No');
        GetYesOrNo(Response);
        Write('Valid response.')
    END;
```

6. Rewrite the following code segment using a WHILE loop.

```
IF NOT EOF
    THEN
        REPEAT
            Read(Ch);
            Writeln(Ch)
        UNTIL EOF
```

7. Rewrite the following code segment using a FOR loop.

```
Sum : = 0;
Count : = 1;
WHILE Count <= 1000 DO
    BEGIN
        Sum : = Sum + Count;
        Count : = Count + 1
    END;
```

8. Write a function that accepts two Integer parameters, called Base and Exponent, and returns Base raised to the Exponent power. Use a FOR loop in your solution.

9. Write a CASE statement that does the following:

> If the value of Grade is
> 'A',   add 4 to Sum
> 'B',   add 3 to Sum
> 'C',   add 2 to Sum
> 'D',   add 1 to Sum
> 'F',   print 'Student is on probation'

10. Modify the code for Exercise 9 so that an error message is printed if Grade does not equal one of the five possible grades.

PROGRAMMING PROBLEMS _____

1. Develop a top-down design and write a Pascal program that will input a two-letter abbreviation for one of the 50 states and print out the full name of the state. If the abbreviation isn't valid, the program should print an error message and again ask for an abbreviation. The names of the 50 states and their abbreviations are

State	Abbreviation	State	Abbreviation
Alabama	AL	Montana	MT
Alaska	AK	Nebraska	NE
Arizona	AZ	Nevada	NV
Arkansas	AR	New Hampshire	NH
California	CA	New Jersey	NJ
Colorado	CO	New Mexico	NM
Connecticut	CT	New York	NY
Delaware	DE	North Carolina	NC
Florida	FL	North Dakota	ND
Georgia	GA	Ohio	OH
Hawaii	HI	Oklahoma	OK
Idaho	ID	Oregon	OR
Illinois	IL	Pennsylvania	PA
Indiana	IN	Rhode Island	RI
Iowa	IA	South Carolina	SC
Kansas	KS	South Dakota	SD
Kentucky	KY	Tennessee	TN
Louisiana	LA	Texas	TX
Maine	ME	Utah	UT
Maryland	MD	Vermont	VT
Massachusetts	MA	Virginia	VA
Michigan	MI	Washington	WA
Minnesota	MN	West Virginia	WV
Mississippi	MS	Wisconsin	WI
Missouri	MO	Wyoming	WY

Hint: Use nested CASE statements, where the outer case statement uses the first letter of the abbreviation as its selector.

2. Write a top-down design and a Pascal program that reads a date in numeric form and prints it in English. For example:

```
Enter a date in the form mm dd yy.
10  27  42
October twenty seventh, nineteen hundred and forty two.
```

Here is another example:

```
Enter a date in the form mm dd yy.
12  10  10
December tenth, nineteen hundred and ten.
```

The program should work for any date in the twentieth century and should print an error message for any invalid date, such as 2 29 83 (1983 wasn't a leap year).

3. Write a top-down design and a Pascal program that will convert letters of the alphabet into their corresponding digits on the telephone. The program should repeatedly let the user enter letters until a Q or a Z is entered (Q and Z are the two letters that are not on the telephone). An error message should be printed for any nonalphabetic character that is entered.

The letters and digits on the telephone have the following correspondence.

ABC = 2	DEF = 3	GHI = 4
JKL = 5	MNO = 6	PRS = 7
TUV = 8	WXY = 9	

Here is an example:

```
Enter a letter.
P
The letter P corresponds to 7 on the telephone.
Enter a letter.
A
The letter A corresponds to 2 on the telephone.
Enter a letter.
S
The letter S corresponds to 7 on the telephone.
Enter a letter.
C
The letter C corresponds to 2 on the telephone.
Enter a letter.
A
The letter A corresponds to 2 on the telephone.
Enter a letter.
L
The letter L corresponds to 5 on the telephone.
Enter a letter.
2
Invalid letter, enter Q or Z to quit.
Enter a letter.
Z
Quit.
```

- To be able to use the functions Ord, Succ, and Pred with ordinal data types.
- To be able to define and use an enumerated data type.
- To be able to define and use a subrange data type.
- To be able to distinguish an anonymous user-defined type from a named user-defined type.
- To be able to tell whether two data types are compatible.
- To be able to tell whether an expression is assignment compatible with a given variable.
- To be able to use the FOR and CASE statements with user-defined enumerated data types.

10

Simple Data Types

In Chapter 2 we defined a data type as the general form of a class of data items. In this chapter we will give a fuller, more formal definition of data type. The built-in data types Integer, Real, Char, and Boolean will be reviewed in terms of the expanded definition.

There are times when these built-in data types cannot adequately represent all the data in a program. Pascal has a mechanism for letting us create new data types. That is, we can define new data types ourselves. In this chapter we will examine this very useful feature in detail.

DATA TYPES

Data Type A formal description of the set of values (called the domain) that a variable or constant of that type can have and of the basic set of operations that can be applied to values of that type.

Let's examine the data types Integer, Real, Boolean, and Char in light of this new definition. For each of these data types, how is the set of values described and what basic operations are defined?

The formal description of Integer values and the allowable operations of the Integer data type come from mathematics; the operations are +, −, /, ∗, MOD, and DIV. The same is true for Reals except that the operations DIV and MOD are, of course, excluded. In Chapter 4 we defined the set of values that a Boolean variable can have (True, False) and the set of operations allowed on these values (AND, OR, and NOT). These definitions come from an area of mathematics known as Boolean algebra.

The description of the values of type Char will vary from machine to machine, for the values of type Char are the alphanumeric characters in the character set of the particular machine. There are three character sets that are widely used: CDC-Scientific, ASCII, and EBCDIC.

The tables in Appendix J show the ordering of the characters in these character sets. The ordering is called the *collating sequence* of the character set. Although the ordering of the characters is different in each of these character sets, it is comforting to note that the letters are ordered in relation to each other and the numbers are ordered in relation to each other in the way that we would expect them to be. That is, 'A' < 'B' < 'C' . . . and '1' < '2' < '3' . . . .

However, numbers come before letters in the ASCII character set and after letters in the EBCDIC and CDC-Scientific character sets. Furthermore, lowercase letters precede uppercase letters in EBCDIC, come after uppercase letters in ASCII, and are not included at all in CDC-Scientific.

No common operations are associated with characters, so we haven't defined any (yet).

The four built-in data types have two properties in common. Each is made up of indivisible, or atomic, elements, and each is ordered. Data types with these properties are called *scalar data types*.

Scalar Data Types Data types in which the set of values is ordered and each value is atomic (indivisible).

When we say that a value is atomic, we mean that it has no component parts that can be accessed independently. It is a value, stored in a place in memory. For example, a single character is atomic; it is an indivisible value of the Char data type. However, the literal string 'Good Morning' is not atomic; it is composed of 12 scalar values of the Char data type.

When we say that a set of values is ordered, we mean that the standard relational operators can be applied to the values. That is, for any two values Data1 and Data2 of the same scalar data type, the following expressions are legal.

```
Data1 < Data2
Data1 > Data2
Data1 = Data2
Data1 <= Data2
Data1 >= Data2
Data1 <> Data2
```

In addition, for any particular values of Data1 and Data2, exactly one of the first three expressions above is True. If Data1 and Data2 are Reals or Integers, the meaning of the relational operators is the standard mathematical meaning.

If Data1 and Data2 are character variables, the relational operators refer to the relative positions of the two characters in the collating sequence of the character set. For example, if Data1 contains 'j' and Data2 contains 'C', Data1 < Data2 would be True in the EBCDIC character set and False in the ASCII character set.

Since Boolean is a scalar data type, it is ordered—False is defined to come before True. Admittedly this is not very useful, but it is consistent.

Three of the built-in data types have an additional property: Each value (except the first) has a unique predecessor, and each value (except the last) has a unique successor. Scalar data types that have this property are called *ordinal data types*.

Ordinal Data Types Data types in which each value (except the first) has a unique predecessor and each value (except the last) has a unique successor.

Of the standard data types only type Real is not ordinal. Real numbers are not ordinal because a Real value has no unique predecessor or successor. If one more digit of precision is added, the predecessor and successor change. That is, 0.0501 is the predecessor of 0.0502 (four digits precision), but 0.05019 is the predecessor of 0.05020 (five digits precision).

Ord, Pred, and Succ Functions

Ord, Pred, and Succ are three additional operations on ordinal data types, based on the ordinal properties. Pascal provides these operations as built-in functions.

Ord An operation that returns the position of a value in the ordering of an ordinal data type.

The Ord operation is done by the Pascal function Ord, which takes as a parameter an ordinal value and returns an Integer that represents the parameter's place in the ordering of the data type. If the parameter is of type Char, the result represents the parameter's place in the collating sequence of the particular character set. The first position in the collating sequence is 0, not 1 as we might expect.

If the parameter is of type Integer, the result will be the integer itself, because each integer represents its own place in the ordering. If the parameter is of type Boolean, the result will be either a 0 (False) or a 1 (True).

Ord can be used to convert a digit that is read in *character* form to its *numeric* equivalent. Since the digits '0' to '9' are consecutive in each of the common character sets, subtracting Ord('0') from the Ord of any digit in character form gives the digit in numeric form. We can think of Ord('0') as being a constant that, when subtracted from the Ord of a digit in character form, gives the digit in numeric form. That is,

```
Ord('0') - Ord('0') = 0
Ord('1') - Ord('0') = 1
Ord('2') - Ord('0') = 2
```

For example, in ASCII,

```
Ord('0')  =  48
Ord('2')  =  50
Ord('2')  -  Ord('0')  =  50  -  48  =  2
```

Note that Ord(2) is always 2, but Ord('2') will be different in each character set.

Pred An operation that returns the unique predecessor of a value of an ordinal data type.

This operation is done by the Pascal function Pred, which takes as a parameter an ordinal value and returns the value of its immediate predecessor. A run-time error occurs if the parameter is the first value in the data type. That is, the expression Pred(Data) where Data is $-$MaxInt would cause an error.

Succ An operation that returns the unique successor of a value of an ordinal data type.

This operation is performed by the Pascal function Succ, which takes as a parameter an ordinal value and returns the value of its immediate successor. If the parameter is the last element in the data type, a run-time error occurs.

Examples of these three operations are shown in the table.

Operation	Result	Character Set
Ord('B')	2	CDC
Ord('B')	66	ASCII
Ord('B')	194	EBCDIC
Ord(23)	23	
Ord(−21)	−21	
Ord(False)	0	
Ord(True)	1	
Succ('B')	'C'	all sets
Succ(2)	3	
Succ('2')	'3'	all sets
Succ(−33)	−32	
Pred(−32)	−33	
Pred(0)	−1	
Pred('A')	@	ASCII
Pred('A')	nonprinting character	EBCDIC
Pred('A')	':'	CDC
Pred(−MaxInt)	error message	

Chr Function

An additional operation, called Chr, can be defined on values of type Char.

Chr An operation that takes an ordinal position and returns the character in that position.

Function Chr implements the operation Chr in Pascal. It takes as its parameter an Integer ordinal position and returns the corresponding character. Chr is the inverse of the Ord operation on Char values. To convert a single-digit number into its character representation, we use

```
Chr(number + Ord('0'))
```

Theoretically, one way to print out the collating sequence of the characters in a particular machine would be to print the Chr of the loop control variable in a FOR loop going from 0 to the number of characters minus 1.

The following program implements this simple algorithm.

```
PROGRAM Order (Output);

(* The character set is printed in order *)

CONST
  NumChar = 256;  (* Put in the number of characters in the set *)

VAR
  Counter:
    Integer;

BEGIN (* Order *)
  FOR Counter := 0 TO NumChar - 1 DO
    Writeln(Counter, CHR(Counter):3)
END.   (* Order *)
```

The counter has to run from 0 to the number of characters minus 1 because the first ordinal position is 0, not 1, as mentioned earlier.

This simple little program, which demonstrates the Chr operation, works well in theory. However, in practice, it works as planned only on machines using the CDC-Scientific set. With the EBCDIC and ASCII sets, not all the characters are printable. Some of these nonprintable characters are used to control the screen and/or the printer.

Another example of the use of Chr and Ord is shown below in function Upper, which converts lowercase ASCII letters to uppercase. It uses the fact that in ASCII each lowercase letter is exactly 32 positions beyond the corresponding uppercase letter. Notice that this function *will not* work with the other two character sets.

```
FUNCTION Upper (Ch : Char) : Char;

(* Converts lowercase ASCII letters to upper-
   case. All other characters are unchanged.
   Uses the fact that lowercase ASCII letters
   are 32 positions beyond uppercase letters *)

CONST
   Shift = 32;

BEGIN
   IF (Ch >= 'a') AND (Ch <= 'z')
      THEN              (* CH is a lowercase letter *)
         Upper : = Chr (Ord (Ch) - Shift)
      ELSE
         Upper : = Ch
END;
```

The moral of the last two examples is that you must be familiar with the character set of the machine you are using.

USER-DEFINED SCALAR DATA TYPES

The concept of a data type is fundamental to all programming languages. One of the strengths of the Pascal language is that it allows users to create new data types by means of a *type definition*. The declaration section of a Pascal program can include a TYPE section immediately before the VAR section. In the TYPE section the user describes the set of possible values in a new data type and gives the set a name (a type identifier).

Type Definition A definition of a data type in the TYPE declaration of a block, with the type identifier to the left of the equal sign and the description of the set of values to the right.

```
TYPE
   Days = (Sunday, Monday, Tuesday, Wednesday,
            Thursday, Friday, Saturday);
   Scores = 0..100;
   WeekDays = Monday..Friday;
```

These examples illustrate the two ways to define new scalar data types. One way is to list the set of literal values that are allowed in the data type (Days). The other way is to define a data type to be a consecutive subset of an already defined data type (Scores, WeekDays).

Once a new data type has been defined, its identifier can be used anywhere the standard types are used: in the VAR section, in formal parameter lists, and in function definitions. In fact, a type identifier can be used later in the TYPE section.

The simplified version of the syntax diagram of the TYPE section is shown below. The TYPE section comes between the CONST section and the VAR section.

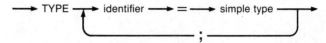

A simple type can be one of the following:

1. Another type identifier (Char, Integer, Real, and Boolean are also type identifiers)

2. An enumerated type

3. A subrange type

Figure 10-1 shows where the TYPE section goes in a program. Now let's examine in detail how to define enumerated types and subrange types.

Enumerated Data Types

There are several ways to describe the set of values that make up a data type. One way is to reference a well-defined existing set of values. Char, Integer, and Real were defined in this way.

Figure 10-1
Syntax Diagram
Showing Placement
of TYPE

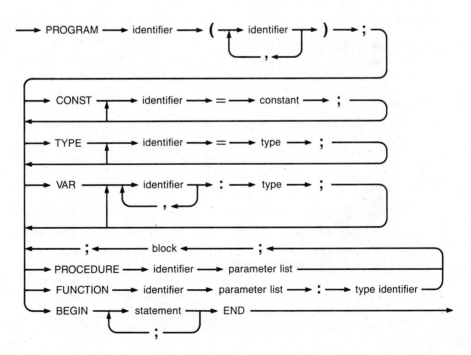

Another way to define this set (the domain) is to list all the literal values that a variable of that type can have. The Boolean data type was defined this way. It has two values: True and False.

Pascal allows the user to define new ordinal types by listing (enumerating) the literal values that make up the type. These literal values must be legal Pascal identifiers. The identifiers are separated by a comma, and the entire set is enclosed in parentheses. Data types defined this way are called *enumerated data types*.

Enumerated Data Type An ordered set of literal values (identifiers) defined as a data type in a program.

The syntax diagram for an enumerated type is given below.

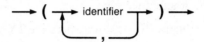

The built-in type Boolean is an enumerated type defined as

```
TYPE
    Boolean = (False, True)
```

An enumerated type made up of some animal names is defined below.

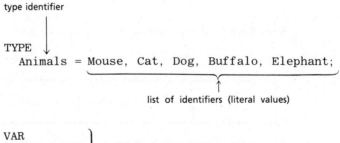

Mouse is now a literal in the data type Animals. Notice that Mouse is not a variable name. Mouse is one of the *values* that the variables Stray and Pet can contain.

The assignment statement

```
Stray := Elephant
```

does not assign to Stray the character string 'Elephant'; nor does it assign to Stray the contents of a variable named Elephant. It assigns the value Elephant, which is one of the values that make up the data type Animals.

It is very important to understand the distinction between the TYPE section and the VAR section. A type definition in the TYPE section describes the set of values in a data type. That is, it describes what values variables and constants of that type can contain. No variables of that type exist until they are declared in the VAR section. We can think of a TYPE definition as creating a pattern and a VAR declaration as making something from that pattern.

In Pascal, enumerated types are ordinal. The ordering is defined by the order in which the identifiers are listed in the TYPE declaration. Applying relational operators to variables of an enumerated type is like applying relational operators to variables of type Char. The relation being tested is "comes before" or "comes after" in the ordering of the set of values.

Since enumerated types are ordinal, the Pred, Succ, and Ord operations are defined on values of enumerated types. Remember, however, that the Ord of the first identifier listed in an enumerated type is 0, not 1. Following are a few examples *T,M,V* ⇦ of these operations applied to our Animals data type.

Operation	*Result*	
Pred(Cat)	Mouse	
Pred(Elephant)	Buffalo	
Pred(Mouse)	error	(doesn't exist)
Succ(Mouse)	Cat	
Succ(Cat)	Dog	
Ord(Mouse)	0	
Ord(Buffalo)	3	
Ord(Elephant)	4	

Since Mouse, Cat, and so on are literals, they can be used in the label list of a CASE statement.

```
CASE Pet OF
   Mouse : Write('Set trap.');
   Dog,
   Cat : Write('Pet.');
   Buffalo,
   Elephant : Write('Run!')
END;   (* Case *)
```

Enumerated types can be used in FOR loops as well. For example, we can process each animal in turn with the following FOR loop.

```
FOR Pet := Mouse TO Elephant DO ..
```

Likewise, we can set up a WHILE loop, using the Succ function to increment the loop counter.

```
Pet := Mouse;
WHILE Pet <= Buffalo DO
  BEGIN
    (* Process Pet *)
    Pet := Succ(Pet)
  END;
(* Process Pet which is now Elephant *)
```

The last value (Pet = Elephant) must be processed outside of the loop, because trying to take the Succ of Elephant at the end of the loop would cause an error. When we are working with enumerated types, the FOR loop is a better choice than the WHILE loop.

The identifiers that make up an enumerated type must follow the rules for identifiers. For example,

```
Vowel = ('A', 'E', 'I', 'O', 'U')
```

is not legal for two reasons. First, the items are not identifiers. An identifier cannot begin with a special character, a single quote in this case. Second, 'A', 'E', 'I', 'O', and 'U' are literals in the built-in data type Char, and it is not legal to redefine them as literals in type Vowel.

```
Starch = (Corn, Rice, Potato, Bean);
Grain = (Wheat, Corn, Rye, Barley, Sorghum);
```

Type Starch and type Grain are legal by themselves, but together they are not. Identifiers must be unique. Corn cannot be defined twice.

```
Places = (1st, 2nd, 3rd);
```

Type Places is not legal, because identifiers cannot begin with a number. Identifiers must begin with a letter.

How can we input values for enumerated types? In standard Pascal, we cannot do so directly. We have to input values indirectly by reading a number or a letter code and then translating it to one of the user-defined values in our program. For example, the following program fragment reads in an animal represented by its first letter and converts it to one of the values in Animals.

```
Read(Character);
IF Character = 'M'
  THEN Pet := Mouse
  ELSE IF Character = 'C'
    THEN Pet := Cat
  ELSE IF Character = 'D'
    THEN Pet := Dog
  ELSE IF Character = 'B'
    THEN
      BEGIN
        Pet := Buffalo;
        Writeln('Are you sure?')
      END
```

```
        ELSE IF Character = 'E'
          THEN
            BEGIN
              Pet := Elephant;
              Writeln('You must be kidding!')
            END;
```

Constants or variables of enumerated data types cannot be printed directly either. Printing must be done indirectly by using a nested IF or a CASE statement to print the character string associated with the value we wish to print.

```
        CASE Pet OF
          Mouse : Write('Mouse');
                      .
                      .
          Elephant : Write('Elephant')
        END;   (* Case *)
```

Boolean values are the exception to the rule; they may be printed.

Why should we go to this much trouble? Why not just use a single letter as a code? We use enumerated data types to make our programs more readable. In Chapter 3 we discussed self-documenting code; using enumerated data types is a major way to make code self-documenting. We will demonstrate this in the following problem.

Problem Solving in Action

Problem: Play the children's game "rock, paper, and scissors."

In this game, two people simultaneously choose either rock, paper, or scissors. Whether a player wins or loses depends not only on that player's choice but also on the opponent's. The rules are as follows:

Rock breaks scissors; rock wins.

Paper covers rock; paper wins.

Scissors cuts paper; scissors wins.

All matching combinations are ties.

The overall winner is the player who wins the most individual games.

Discussion: We will assume that everyone has played this game and understands it. (If not, ask a sister, brother, child or see Chapter 6, Programming Problem 2.) Therefore, our discussion will center on how to simulate the game in a program.

For input, we will have to use alphanumeric characters to stand for rock, paper, and scissors. We can input 'R', 'P', and 'S' and convert the letters to a user-defined data type made up of the literals Rock, Paper, and Scissors.

Each player will create a file composed of a series of the letters 'R', 'P', and 'S', representing a series of individual games. The letters will be read, one from each file, and converted into the appropriate literals. Let's call each literal a play. The plays will be compared, and a winner will be determined. The number of games won will be

PSIA

incremented for the winning player. The game will be over when there are no more plays (the files are empty).

Input: A series of letters representing player A's plays (FileA, one per line) and a series of letters representing player B's plays (FileB, one per line), with each play indicated by an 'R', 'P', or 'S'

Output:

A game number, followed by which player won that game

The total number of games won by each player

The overall winner

Assumptions: The game is over when one of the files runs out of plays.

MAIN MODULE   Level 0

```
WHILE more games DO
   Get Play
   IF Plays are legal
      THEN
         Process play
      ELSE
         Write an error message
Print Big Winner
```

GET PLAYS   Level 1

```
Read PlayerA's play from FileA (CharForA)
Read PlayerB's play from FileB (CharForB)
Legal ⟵── (CharForA IN ['R', 'P', 'S'])
            AND (CharForB IN ['R', 'P', 'S'])
IF Legal
   THEN
      PlayerA ⟵── Convert (CharForA)
      PlayerB ⟵── Convert (CharForB)
```

PSIA

PROCESS PLAYS

```
IF PlayerA = PlayerB
   THEN
      Writeln 'Game number ' GameNumber ' is a tie.'
   ELSE IF (PlayerA = Paper) AND (PlayerB = Rock)
      THEN
         PlayerAWins
   ELSE IF (PlayerA = Scissors) AND (PlayerB = Paper)
      THEN
         PlayerAWins
   ELSE IF (PlayerA = Rock) AND (PlayerB = Scissors)
      THEN
         PlayerAWins
   ELSE
      PlayerBWins
```

PRINT BIG WINNER

```
Writeln 'Player A has won ' WinsForA ' games.'
Writeln 'Player B has won ' WinsForB ' games.'
IF WinsForA > WinsForB
   THEN
      Writeln 'Player A has won the most games'
   ELSE IF WinsForB > WinsForA
      THEN
         Writeln 'Player B has won the most games'
   ELSE
      Writeln 'Player A and Player B have tied.'
```

CONVERT   Level 2

```
CASE Character OF
   'R' : Convert ⟵ Rock
   'P' : Convert ⟵ Paper
   'S' : Convert ⟵ Scissors
```

PLAYERAWINS

```
Writeln 'Player A has won game number ' GameNumber
WinsForA ⟵ WinsForA + 1
```

PSIA ▰▰▰▰▰

PLAYERBWINS

```
Writeln 'Player B has won game number ' GameNumber
WinsForB ⟵ WinsForB + 1
```

Now we are ready to code the simulation of the game. We must remember to initialize our counters. Speaking of counters, we have assumed that we know the game number for each game, yet nowhere have we kept track of the game number. We need to add a counter in our loop in the main module.

MAIN MODULE

```
Initialize counters
GameNumber ⟵ 0
WHILE more games DO
    GameNumber ⟵ GameNumber + 1
    Get Plays
    IF Plays are legal
        THEN
            Process Plays
        ELSE
            Write an error message
Print Big Winner
```

Module Structure Chart:

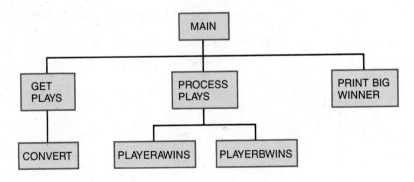

```
PROGRAM Game (FileA, FileB, Output);

(* This program simulates the children's game 'rock, paper, and
   scissors.'  Each game consists of inputs from two players,
   coming from FileA and FileB.  A winner is determined for each
   individual game, and for the games overall. *)
```

PSIA ▬▬▬▬▬

```
TYPE
  PlayType = (Rock, Paper, Scissors);

VAR
  PlayerA,                  (* Player A's play        *)
  PlayerB:                  (* Player B's play        *)
    PlayType;
  WinsForA,                 (* Number of games A wins *)
  WinsForB,                 (* Number of games B wins *)
  GameNumber:               (* Number of games played *)
    Integer;
  FileA,                    (* Player A's plays       *)
  FileB:                    (* Player B's plays       *)
    Text;
  Legal:                    (* True if play is legal  *)
    Boolean;

(**********************************************************************)

PROCEDURE PlayerAWins (     GameNumber:  (* Receives game number      *)
                           Integer;
                       VAR WinsForA:     (* Receives/returns win count *)
                           Integer);

(* Message that Player A has won the current game is written
   and Player A's total is updated *)

BEGIN  (* PlayerAWins *)
  Writeln('Player A has won game number ', GameNumber:1);
  WinsForA := WinsForA + 1
END;   (* PlayerAWins *)

(**********************************************************************)

PROCEDURE PlayerBWins (     GameNumber:  (* Receives game number      *)
                           Integer;
                       VAR WinsForB:     (* Receives/returns win count *)
                           Integer);

(* Message that Player B has won the current game is written
   and Player B's total is updated *)

BEGIN  (* PlayerBWins *)
  Writeln('Player B has won game number ', GameNumber:1);
  WinsForB := WinsForB + 1
END;   (* PlayerBWins *)

(**********************************************************************)
```

PSIA▬▬▬▬▬

```
PROCEDURE ProcessPlays (     GameNumber:   (* Receives game number       *)
                             Integer;
                             PlayerA,       (* Receives A's play           *)
                             PlayerB:       (* Receives B's play           *)
                             PlayType;
                         VAR WinsForA,       (* Receives/returns A's win count *)
                             WinsForB:       (* Receives/returns B's win count *)
                             Integer);
```

(* ProcessPlays determines the winning play. If there is a tie, a
   message is written. Otherwise the number of wins of the winning
   player is incremented. *)

```
BEGIN (* ProcessPlays *)
  IF PlayerA = PlayerB
    THEN
       Writeln('Game Number ', GameNumber:1, ' is a tie.')
    ELSE IF (PlayerA = Paper) AND (PlayerB = Rock)
      THEN
         PlayerAWins(GameNumber, WinsForA)
    ELSE IF (PlayerA = Scissors) AND (PlayerB = Paper)
      THEN
         PlayerAWins(GameNumber, WinsForA)
    ELSE IF (PlayerA = Rock) AND (PlayerB = Scissors)
      THEN
         PlayerAWins(GameNumber, WinsForA)
    ELSE
       PlayerBWins(GameNumber, WinsForB)
END;   (* ProcessPlays *)
```

(***)

```
PROCEDURE GetPlays (VAR PlayerA,        (* Returns A's play               *)
                        PlayerB:        (* Returns B's play               *)
                        PlayType;
                    VAR Legal:          (* Returns True if both plays legal *)
                        Boolean);
```

(* PlayerA's play is read from FileA, PlayerB's play is read from
   FileB. If both plays are legal, Legal is set to True and both
   plays are converted to corresponding values of PlayType. Else
   Legal is False and PlayerA and PlayerB are undefined. FileA
   and FileB are accessed globally. *)

```
VAR
  CharForA,                 (* PlayerA's input *)
  CharForB:                 (* PlayerB's input *)
   Char;
```

(***)

PSIA

```
FUNCTION Convert (Character:              (* Receives play character *)
                     Char): PlayType;     (* Returns play literal    *)

(* Converts character into associated value in PlayType *)

BEGIN  (* Convert *)
  CASE Character OF
    'R' : Convert := Rock;
    'P' : Convert := Paper;
    'S' : Convert := Scissors
  END  (* Case *)
END;   (* Convert *)

(*********************************************************************)

BEGIN  (* GetPlays *)
  Readln(FileA, CharForA);
  Readln(FileB, CharForB);
  Legal := (CharForA IN ['R', 'P', 'S']) AND
           (CharForB IN ['R', 'P', 'S']);
  IF Legal
    THEN
      BEGIN
        PlayerA := Convert(CharForA);
        PlayerB := Convert(CharForB)
      END
END;   (* GetPlays *)

(*********************************************************************)

PROCEDURE PrintBigWinner (WinsForA,        (* Receives A's win count *)
                          WinsForB:        (* Receives B's win count *)
                               Integer);

(* Number of wins for each player and the overall winner are printed *)

BEGIN  (* PrintBigWinner *)
  Writeln('Player A has won ', WinsForA:1, ' games.');
  Writeln('Player B has won ', WinsForB:1, ' games.');
  (* Determine and print winner *)
  IF WinsForA > WinsForB
    THEN
      Writeln('Player A has won the most games.')
    ELSE IF WinsForB > WinsForA
      THEN
        Writeln('Player B has won the most games.')
    ELSE
      Writeln('Player A and Player B have tied.')
END;   (* PrintBigWinner *)

(*********************************************************************)
```

PSIA ◢▬▬▬

```
BEGIN (* Game *)
  Reset(FileA);
  Reset(FileB);
  WinsForA := 0;
  WinsForB := 0;
  GameNumber := 0;
  (* Play a series of games and keep track of who wins *)
  WHILE NOT EOF(FileA) AND NOT EOF(FileB) DO
    BEGIN
      GameNumber := GameNumber + 1;
      GetPlay(PlayerA, PlayerB, Legal);
      IF Legal
        THEN
          ProcessPlay(GameNumber, PlayerA, PlayerB, WinsForA, WinsForB)
        ELSE
          Writeln('Game Number ', GameNumber:1,
                  ' contained an illegal play.')
    END;
  (* Print overall winner *)
  PrintBigWinner(WinsForA, WinsForB)
END.   (* Game *)
```

Testing: Program Game was tested with the following files. They are listed side by side so that you can see the pairs that made up each game. Note that each combination of 'R', 'S', and 'P' has been used at least once. In addition, there is an error in each file.

FileA	FileB
R	R
S	S
S	S
R	S
R	P
P	P
P	P
R	S
S	T
A	P
P	S
P	R
S	P
R	S
R	S
P	P
S	R

PSIA ━━━━━━━━━

Output from the screen:

```
Game Number 1 is a tie.
Game Number 2 is a tie.
Game Number 3 is a tie.
Player A has won game number 4
Player B has won game number 5
Game Number 6 is a tie.
Game Number 7 is a tie.
Player A has won game number 8
Game Number 9 contained an illegal play.
Game Number 10 contained an illegal play.
Player B has won game number 11
Player A has won game number 12
Player A has won game number 13
Player A has won game number 14
Player A has won game number 15
Game Number 16 is a tie.
Player B has won game number 17
Player A has won 6 games.
Player B has won 3 games.
Player A has won the most games.
```

An examination of the output shows it to be correct. Player A did win 6 games, and Player B did win 3 games. Player A did win the most games. This one set of test data is not enough to allow us to declare the program completely tested, however. It should be run with test data where Player B wins, where Player A and Player B tie, where FileA is longer than FileB, and where FileB is longer than FileA.

Subrange Types

Pascal allows the programmer to define a new data type, called a *subrange type,* to be a subrange of an existing ordinal data type. The existing ordinal type, called the host or base type, can be either an enumerated type or one of the built-in ordinal types.

The subrange is defined by listing the lowest value in the subrange and the highest value in the subrange, with two periods between them. Lowest and highest refer to the ordering of the host type. The first value (lowest) must come before (or be equal to) the second value (highest) in the ordering of the host type.

Subrange Type A data type composed of a specified range of any ordinal type.

The syntax diagram for a subrange type is

where the value can be a named constant or a literal. Notice that no spaces are allowed between the periods.

The following are some examples of subrange types and the values they include.

Subrange type	Values included	Host type
Num = 5..10;	5, 6, 7, 8, 9, 10	Integer
Letter = 'A'..'D';	'A', 'B', 'C', 'D'	Char
Domestic = Mouse..Dog;	Mouse, Cat, Dog	Animals
Wild = Buffalo..Elephant;	Buffalo, Elephant	Animals

Notice that enumerated types are enclosed in parentheses, but subrange types are not.

```
TYPE
    Weather = (Rain, Fog, Hail, Sleet, Humid,
                   Cold, Hot, Dry);
    WetWeather = Rain..Sleet;
```

Subrange types improve the readability of a program. Telling readers the range of values a variable can take improves their understanding of the variables used in the program. Perhaps even more importantly, subrange types allow us to take advantage of *automatic range-checking* in our program. Not all languages have this feature; Pascal does.

Automatic Range-Checking The automatic detection of the assignment of an out-of-range value to a variable.

Automatic range-checking works as follows: When a value is assigned to a variable, the system checks to see whether that value is within the specified range. If it is not, the run-time error message "VALUE OUT OF RANGE" is printed. This feature can be invaluable during debugging. For example, if we tried to store 'F' in a variable of type Letter (defined above to be 'A'..'D'), we would get an error message.

Automatic range-checking can be extremely useful when we know the bounds of a variable. If a counter should never get larger than 100, we create a subrange 0..100. If a variable of that subrange is incremented one time too many and becomes 101, we will know it immediately.

Although we could let range-checking take care of checking for invalid input data values, such a tactic is bad programming practice. If an out-of-range value is detected, an error message is printed and the program crashes. Although crashing might be acceptable in student programs, it should be prevented if at all possible in a program being run in industry.

A much better practice is to do your own range-checking by putting checks on invalid data in the form of statements in a program. This practice allows the user to

Figure 10-2
Program Outline
with TYPE Section

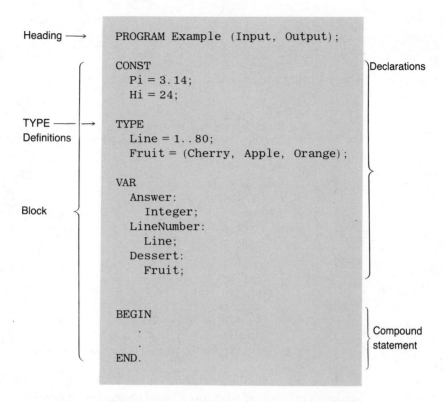

```
Heading ⟶        PROGRAM Example (Input, Output);

                 CONST                                        ⎫Declarations
                    Pi = 3.14;
                    Hi = 24;

TYPE ──┐──⟶       TYPE
Definitions          Line = 1..80;
                     Fruit = (Cherry, Apple, Orange);

                 VAR
                    Answer:
                       Integer;
Block                LineNumber:
                       Line;
                    Dessert:
                       Fruit;


                 BEGIN                                         ⎫Compound
                     .                                         ⎬statement
                     .
                 END.
```

decide what should be done when invalid data is encountered. In some cases the program can take corrective measures and then continue the processing. Some of the specifics of this approach will be discussed in the Testing and Debugging section.

Figure 10-2 shows a program outline with both an enumerated type Fruit and a subrange type Line. Remember that procedures and functions can have their own declaration sections, which can themselves contain TYPE definitions. The same scope rules that apply to variables also apply to type identifiers.

Anonymous and Named Data Types

New data types defined in the TYPE section are called *named types* because the definition is given a name, the type identifier. Variables of these new data types are declared in the VAR section by placing the type identifier next to the variable, with a colon in between.

Named Type A type defined in the TYPE section of a program.

Variables of enumerated and subrange types can also be declared by placing the type definition to the right of the colon following the variable in the VAR section. A type defined this way is called an *anonymous type* because it does not have a type identifier (a name) associated with it.

Anonymous Type A type defined in the VAR section of a program.

The following two examples are equivalent:

```
TYPE
    CounterType = 0..100;
    Coins = (Nickel, Dime, Quarter, HalfDollar);

VAR
    Counter:
        CounterType;
    Change:
        Coins;
```

and

```
VAR
    Counter:
        0..100;
    Change:
        (Nickel, Dime, Quarter, HalfDollar);
```

If we can create these data types in the VAR section, why do we need the TYPE section? *Only named types are allowed on the formal parameter list of a function or procedure.* Subrange and enumerated type definitions are not allowed in the formal parameter list of a function or a procedure. Variables that are anonymously typed cannot be actual parameters to procedures or functions.

The use of anonymous typing is not a good programming practice. A type definition describes what something can look like; we do not actually have the thing itself until a variable of that type has been declared. Defining a type and declaring a variable of that type are two distinct operations and should be kept separate. To mix them is bad style.

In addition, named types, like named constants, make a program more readable, more understandable, and more modifiable.

TYPE COMPATIBILITY

We have mentioned numerous times that Pascal is a strongly typed language; values of one data type cannot be put into a variable of a different data type. Strong typing is based on a relationship among data types called *compatibility*. Two data types are said to be *type compatible* if they have the same definition, if they have the same type identifier, if one is a subrange of the other, or if both are subranges of the same host type.

Type Compatible Implies that the types have the same type definition or type identifier, that they are subranges of the same host type, or that one is a subrange of the other.

The compiler checks whether both sides of an assignment statement are type compatible. If they are not, a compile-time syntax error message is generated. The only assignment allowed between noncompatible types is the assignment of an Integer expression to a Real variable. This is allowed because any Integer value can be represented exactly in Real form.

The compiler also checks whether formal and actual parameters of procedures and functions are type compatible. For VAR parameters, the restriction is even more stringent: Formal and actual parameters must have the *same* type identifier.

At run time an additional constraint is put on assignment statements. They must be *assignment compatible*. The actual values being stored during execution of the program must be within the range of values of the variables into which they are being stored (if the variables are a subrange).

Assignment Compatible Implies that the types are compatible and the value being stored in a variable is within the subrange of that variable.

An assignment compatibility error is determined at run time and causes a "VALUE OUT OF RANGE" error message.

Actual value parameters must be assignment compatible with their associated formal value parameters, since a copy of the value of the actual parameter is stored where the procedure or function can access it and the type of the storage place is the type of the formal parameter.

Let's look at the declaration section of a program and some possible statements and determine which are legal and which are not.

```
TYPE
   ColorType = (Red, Yellow, Blue, Green,
                Orange, Pink, Purple);
   Primary = Red..Blue;

VAR
   Paint,
   Color:
     ColorType;
   PColor:
     Primary;
```

```
PROCEDURE Mix (    Color1,
                   Color2:
                       Primary;
              VAR Result:
                       ColorType);

     .
     .
PROCEDURE Spray (    Color:
                        Green..Purple;    (* Illegal *)
                     NewColor:
                        (Black, White));  (* Illegal *)

     .
     .
BEGIN (* Main *)
     .
     .
  PColor := Color;
     .
     .
  Mix(Paint, Color, PColor);            (* Illegal *)
     .
     .
  Mix(Paint, Color, Paint);
END.   (* Main *)
```

The heading for procedure Mix is legal. The parameters are all defined using named data types.

The heading for procedure Spray is not legal. Only named types can be used in the formal parameter list. A type cannot be defined in the formal parameter list of a procedure or function.

The assignment statement

```
          PColor := Color;
```

is legal, since a value in a subrange type is still considered to be in the original type. However, if the value in Color is not in the subrange Primary, a run-time error will occur.

The procedure call

```
          Mix(Paint, Color, PColor);
```

is not legal. PColor (actual parameter) is of type Primary, and Result (formal parameter) is of type ColorType. Actual VAR parameters must have the same type identifier as their corresponding formal VAR parameters.

The procedure call

```
          Mix(Paint, Color, Paint);
```

is legal. Paint and Color are of type ColorType and Color1 and Color2 are of type Primary, but this is allowed because they are value parameters. There would be a run-time error, however, if Paint or Color contained values outside of the subrange Primary.

SETS AND ADDITIONAL CONTROL STRUCTURES REVISITED

Now that we have defined ordinal types, we can expand some definitions from Chapter 9.

The values that make up a set can be of any ordinal type. The shorthand notation we used to define the values in a set is, of course, subrange notation. We used this notation to restrict the number of values in the set. Some systems allow a set of type Char, but some restrict the size of a set to less than the number of characters in the character set. No system allows a set of type Integer; it is much too large!

In Chapter 9 we were unable to make module Print Numbers a procedure. We could not use a set as a parameter because we did not know how to give a type a name. We were using anonymous typing to define SetOfGrades. Now that we know better, we can use the following declaration.

```
TYPE
  GradeRange = 60..100;
  SetType = SET OF GradeRange;

VAR
  SetOfGrades:
    SetType
```

The loop control variable, the initial value, and the final value in a FOR loop can be of any ordinal type. The operation we described as incrementing the loop control variable by 1 can be restated as "take the successor of." The operation we described as decrementing the loop control variable by 1 can be restated as "take the predecessor of."

The FOR loop is especially useful for looping through an enumerated type. If a WHILE or REPEAT statement is used, the last (or the first) value has to be processed outside of the loop in order to avoid taking the Succ of the last (or the Pred of the first) value in the enumerated type.

The items in the case label list can be the values or named constants in any ordinal data type. In the following problem a data type made up of the months of the year is used as the type of the case selector and case label lists.

Problem Solving in Action

Problem: Everyone has at least one friend who *always* remembers everyone's birthday. Each year when we receive appropriate greetings on our birthday from this friend, we promise to do better about remembering the birthdays of others.

Let's write a program that will print the names of those friends with a birthday in a given month.

Discussion: To solve this problem by hand, we would turn our calendar to the month in question and list the names written there. That is exactly what our program will do: recognize which month is being requested and call a procedure that writes out the information for that month. The information for each month will be represented as a series of Write statements.

Three months begin with J: January, June, and July. Two months begin with M: March and May. Two months begin with A: April and August. The rest have unique first letters. The months with unique first letters can be recognized by reading only the first character of the input. April, August, and January can be recognized by reading only the first two characters. June, July, March, and May require three characters to distinguish them.

Input: A month entered from the keyboard (Month), with first letter capitalized

Output: The names (and birthdays) of all friends with a birthday in Month

Assumptions: None

MAIN MODULE   Level 0

```
Get Month
CASE Month OF
    January    : PrintJanuary
    February   : PrintFebruary
    March      : PrintMarch
    April      : PrintApril
    May        : PrintMay
    June       : PrintJune
    July       : PrintJuly
    August     : PrintAugust
    September  : PrintSeptember
    October    : PrintOctober
    November   : PrintNovember
    December   : PrintDecember
```

PSIA ▰▰▰▰▰▰▰

GET MONTH   Level 1

```
Read FirstCharacter, SecondCharacter,
     ThirdCharacter
CASE FirstCharacter OF
  F : Month ⟵ February
  S : Month ⟵ September
  O : Month ⟵ October
  N : Month ⟵ November
  D : Month ⟵ December
  J : JCheck
  A : ACheck
  M : MCheck
```

PRINT JANUARY

.
.
.

PRINT DECEMBER

JCHECK   Level 2

```
IF SecondCharacter is an 'a'
  THEN
     Month ⟵ January
  ELSE IF ThirdCharacter is an 'l'
  THEN
     Month ⟵ July
  ELSE
     Month ⟵ June
```

ACHECK

```
IF SecondCharacter is a 'p'
  THEN
     Month ⟵ April
  ELSE
     Month ⟵ August
```

PSIA

MCHECK

```
IF ThirdCharacter is an 'r'
   THEN
      Month ⟵ March
   ELSE
      Month ⟵ May
```

The print procedures are composed of Writeln statements that print all the information for the month. In order to test the program, we coded all the print procedures to print one line stating that the month has been printed.

A procedure or function that only states that the subprogram has been called is known as a *stub*. Stubs are used in testing the top levels of a program before the lower modules have been completely coded.

Module Structure Chart:

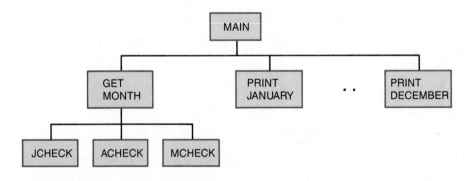

```
PROGRAM BirthdayReminder (Input, Output);

(* This program takes a month as input and prints the
   list of birthdays associated with that month *)

TYPE
   Months = (January, February, March, April, May, June,
             July, August, September, October, November, December);

VAR
   Month:
      Months;


(*******************************************************************)


PROCEDURE GetMonth (VAR Month:
                         Months);
```

PSIA ▰▰▰▰▰▰▰▰

```
(* The user is prompted to enter a month. Only the
   characters needed to determine the month are read *)

VAR
  FirstCharacter,
  SecondCharacter,
  ThirdCharacter:
    Char;

(*********************************************************************)

PROCEDURE JCheck (VAR Month:
                        Months;
                      SecondCharacter,
                      ThirdCharacter:
                        Char);

(* Determines which month beginning with J *)

BEGIN (* JCheck *)
  IF SecondCharacter = 'a'
    THEN
      Month := January
    ELSE IF ThirdCharacter = 'l'
      THEN
        Month := July
    ELSE
      Month := June
END;  (* JCheck *)

(*********************************************************************)

PROCEDURE ACheck (VAR Month:
                        Months;
                      SecondCharacter:
                        Char);

(* Determines which month beginning with A *)

BEGIN (* ACheck *)
  IF SecondCharacter = 'p'
    THEN
      Month := April
    ELSE
      Month := August
END;  (* ACheck *)

(*********************************************************************)
```

PSIA

```
PROCEDURE MCheck (VAR Month:
                          Months;
                      ThirdCharacter:
                          Char);

  (* Determines which month beginning with M *)

  BEGIN (* MCheck *)
    IF ThirdCharacter = 'r'
      THEN
        Month := March
      ELSE
        Month := May
  END;   (* MCheck *)


(**********************************************************************)

BEGIN (* GetMonth *)
  Write('Please enter month, capitalizing first letter.');
  Writeln(' Hit return.');
  Readln(FirstCharacter, SecondCharacter, ThirdCharacter);
  CASE FirstCharacter OF
    'F' : Month := February;
    'S' : Month := September;
    'O' : Month := October;
    'N' : Month := November;
    'D' : Month := December;
    'J' : JCheck(Month, SecondCharacter, ThirdCharacter);
    'A' : ACheck(Month, SecondCharacter);
    'M' : MCheck(Month, ThirdCharacter)
  END (* Case *)
END;   (* GetMonth *)


(**********************************************************************)

PROCEDURE PrintJanuary;

BEGIN (* PrintJanuary *)
  Writeln('January printed')
END;   (* PrintJanuary *)


(**********************************************************************)

PROCEDURE PrintFebruary;

BEGIN (* PrintFebruary *)
  Writeln('February printed')
END;   (* PrintFebruary *)


(**********************************************************************)
```

PSIA ◢▬▬▬▬▬

```
PROCEDURE PrintMarch;

BEGIN (* PrintMarch *)
  Writeln('March printed')
END;   (* PrintMarch *)


(******************************************************************)


PROCEDURE PrintApril;

BEGIN (* PrintApril *)
  Writeln('April printed')
END;   (* PrintApril *)


(******************************************************************)


PROCEDURE PrintMay;

BEGIN (* PrintMay *)
  Writeln('May printed')
END;   (* PrintMay *)


(******************************************************************)


PROCEDURE PrintJune;

BEGIN (* PrintJune *)
  Writeln('June printed')
END;   (* PrintJune *)


(******************************************************************)


PROCEDURE PrintJuly;

BEGIN (* PrintJuly *)
  Writeln('July printed')
END;   (* PrintJuly *)


(******************************************************************)


PROCEDURE PrintAugust;

BEGIN (* PrintAugust *)
  Writeln('August printed')
END;   (* PrintAugust *)


(******************************************************************)
```

PSIA ━━━━━━━

```
PROCEDURE PrintSeptember;

BEGIN (* PrintSeptember *)
  Writeln('September printed')
END;   (* PrintSeptember *)


(**********************************************************************)

PROCEDURE PrintOctober;

BEGIN (* PrintOctober *)
  Writeln('October printed')
END;   (* PrintOctober *)


(**********************************************************************)


PROCEDURE PrintNovember;

BEGIN (* PrintNovember *)
  Writeln('November printed')
END;   (* PrintNovember *)


(**********************************************************************)

PROCEDURE PrintDecember;

BEGIN (* PrintDecember *)
  Writeln('December printed')
END;   (* PrintDecember *)


(**********************************************************************)

BEGIN (* BirthdayReminder *)
  GetMonth(Month);
  CASE Month OF
    January   : PrintJanuary;
    February  : PrintFebruary;
    March     : PrintMarch;
    April     : PrintApril;
    May       : PrintMay;
    June      : PrintJune;
    July      : PrintJuly;
    August    : PrintAugust;
    September : PrintSeptember;
    October   : PrintOctober;
    November  : PrintNovember;
    December  : PrintDecember
  END (* Case *)
END.  (* BirthdayReminder *)
```

PSIA

Testing: In order to test this program, we ran it twelve times. For each run a different month was used as input. On each run, the appropriate print procedure was called and the corresponding message was printed.

The program is still not finished. If you want to use this program, you will have to create the Writelns to print the data for your friends. The abbreviated print procedures (the stubs) we used to test the rest of the program show that each print procedure is called correctly.

We will have more to say about testing this program in the Testing and Debugging Section.

Program BirthdayReminder uses an enumerated data type in a way that illustrates a principle of good style called *control abstraction.*

Control Abstraction The separation of the logical properties of a control structure from its implementation.

The logic that is expressed in the CASE statement in the main module is clear, uncluttered, and self-documenting. The details of how the input characters are converted into a value of the data type Months are hidden down at a lower level.

If the details of how a solution is implemented are pushed down to as low a level as possible, the implementation can be changed without affecting higher-level routines. To demonstrate the usefulness of this principle, procedure GetMonth will be completely rewritten in Chapter 12, and the program will be run without changing any of the other procedures.

TESTING AND DEBUGGING

Several times in this book we have had our programs test for invalid data and write an error message if an invalid data value was detected. Writing an error message is certainly necessary, but it is only the first step. We must decide what action the program should take next. The approach that should be taken will differ depending on whether the program is being run in a batch environment or in an interactive environment.

In a batch environment the program has no interaction with the person entering the data. The data has been put on a file, and the program reads the data from that file. Therefore, the program should try to adjust for the bad data items if at all possible.

If the invalid data item is not essential, the program can skip the bad item and continue with the processing. For example, if a program averaging test grades encounters a negative test score, it would be appropriate for it simply to skip the negative score altogether. The program must make sure, of course, that the number of tests does not include that one. Or, if an educated guess can be made as to the probable value of the bad data item, the item can be set to that value and processing continued.

In either event a message should be written stating that an invalid data item was encountered and outlining the steps that were taken. Such messages form what is called an exception report.

If the data item is essential and no guess is possible, processing should be terminated. A message should be written giving as much information as possible about the invalid data item.

In an interactive environment the program has the opportunity to interact with the person entering the data. The program can prompt the user to supply another value. The program might provide a definition of the limits on the input values as an aid to the user. Another possibility is for the program to ask the person at the keyboard what to do. The user could be given a list of actions and asked to choose among them.

The problem itself and the severity of the error should determine what action is taken in any error condition.

These suggestions on how to handle bad data assume that the program recognizes that a bad data item has been entered. There are two ways to approach error detection: passively and actively.

Passive error detection refers to leaving it to the system to detect errors. This may seem easier, but the problem is that control of the processing is lost when an error does occur. An example of passive error detection would be to use a subrange of 0..100 for exam scores. If a negative score was read, the program would crash with an ''OUT OF RANGE'' error message.

Active error detection involves checking for possible errors in the program itself and determining an appropriate action in light of a problem. An example of active error detection would be to use type Integer for the exam scores and have the program test each score as it is read in to make sure that it is between 0 and 100.

Program BirthdayReminder uses passive error detection. If the input is typed incorrectly, the program crashes. Let's rewrite Procedure GetMonth to incorporate active error detection.

The first character that is read must be checked to see whether it is in the set of possible first letters. If it is not, the CASE statement must be skipped. If the first character is an 'A', 'J', or 'M', the second or third character (or both) must be checked.

The first character should be checked where it is read, in the main body of GetMonth. The second and/or the third character should be checked in the procedure that uses it. Procedures JCheck, ACheck, and MCheck will need an extra parameter to let GetMonth know whether an error has occurred.

If an error has occurred and it is not possible to determine which month is meant, procedure GetMonth must notify the user and request another input. This implies that the CASE statement must be in a loop that continues until a month has been recognized.

This scheme will not check the spelling of each month. It will only check to see that there are enough correct letters to recognize a month.

```
PROCEDURE GetMonth (VAR Month:
                         Months);

(* The user is prompted to enter a month. Only the characters
   needed to determine the month are read.  If the month cannot be
   recognized, the user is prompted to reenter the month *)

VAR
  FirstCharacter,
  SecondCharacter,
  ThirdCharacter:
    Char;
  Error:
    Boolean;

(***************************************************************)

  PROCEDURE JCheck (VAR Month:
                          Months;
                          SecondCharacter,
                          ThirdCharacter:
                          Char;
                    VAR Error:
                          Boolean);

  (* If SecondCharacter and ThirdCharacter are legal, Error is False and
     Month is determined.  ELSE Error is True and Month is undefined. *)

  BEGIN (* JCheck *)
    Error := NOT (SecondCharacter IN ['a', 'u'])
             OR NOT (ThirdCharacter IN ['l', 'n']);
    IF NOT Error
      THEN
        IF SecondCharacter = 'a'
          THEN
            Month := January
          ELSE IF ThirdCharacter = 'l'
            THEN
              Month := July
          ELSE
            Month := June
  END;  (* JCheck *)

(***************************************************************)
```

```
PROCEDURE ACheck (VAR Month:
                          Months;
                      SecondCharacter:
                          Char;
                  VAR Error:
                          Boolean);

(* If SecondCharacter is legal, Error is False and Month is
   determined.  ELSE Error is True and Month is undefined. *)

BEGIN (* ACheck *)
  Error := NOT (SecondCharacter IN ['p', 'u']);
  IF NOT Error
    THEN
      IF SecondCharacter = 'p'
        THEN
          Month := April
        ELSE
          Month := August
END;   (* ACheck *)


(***********************************************************************)

PROCEDURE MCheck (VAR Month:
                          Months;
                      ThirdCharacter:
                          Char;
                  VAR Error:
                          Boolean);

(* If ThirdCharacter is legal, Error is False and Month is determined.
   ELSE Error is True and Month is undefined. *)

BEGIN (* MCheck *)
  Error := NOT (ThirdCharacter IN ['r', 'y']);
  IF NOT Error
    THEN
      IF ThirdCharacter = 'r'
        THEN
          Month := March
        ELSE
          Month := May
END;   (* MCheck *)


(***********************************************************************)
```

```
BEGIN (* GetMonth *)
  REPEAT
    Write('Please enter month, capitalizing first letter.');
    Writeln(' Hit return.');
    Readln(FirstCharacter, SecondCharacter, ThirdCharacter);
    Error := NOT (FirstCharacter IN
            ['F', 'S', 'O', 'N', 'D', 'J', 'A', 'M']);
    IF NOT Error
      THEN
        CASE FirstCharacter OF
          'F' : Month := February;
          'S' : Month := September;
          'O' : Month := October;
          'N' : Month := November;
          'D' : Month := December;
          'J' : JCheck(Month, SecondCharacter, ThirdCharacter, Error);
          'A' : ACheck(Month, SecondCharacter, Error);
          'M' : MCheck(Month, ThirdCharacter, Error)
        END; (* Case *)
    IF Error
      THEN
        Writeln('Unable to determine which month is wanted.');
  UNTIL NOT Error
END;  (* GetMonth *)
```

Testing and Debugging Hints

1. Use a subrange type if you know the bounds on the values of a variable and including a value outside of that range would be a fatal error.

2. Use enumerated types to make your programs more readable, understandable, and modifiable.

3. Do not use anonymous typing. Define data types in the TYPE section and declare the variables of that type in the VAR section.

4. Enumerated types are in parentheses; subrange types are not.

5. Variables cannot be used in the declaration sections of a program. Information in the CONST, TYPE, and VAR sections is used by the computer at compile time. Variables do not get values until execution time. So defining a subrange type 1..N makes no sense unless N is defined in the CONST section.

6. Use the same type identifier for formal and actual parameters. VAR parameters must have the same type identifier for both formal and actual parameters. Value parameters must have formal and actual parameters that are type compatible. Type definitions may not appear on a parameter list.

7. Do not apply Succ to the last element of a type or Pred to the first.

8. Do not use variables of an enumerated type in I/O operations.

9. Routines that rely on a particular character set's collating sequence may not run on another machine.

SUMMARY

A data type is a set of values together with the operations that can be applied to them. There are four standard simple types in Pascal: Integer, Real, Char, and Boolean. The sets of values and operations for Integers, Reals, and Booleans come from mathematics. The set of values for type Char is defined by the specific character set of a machine.

Types Integer, Char, and Boolean are called ordinal types because they have the ordinal property that a unique successor and a unique predecessor exist for all but the first and last items in the set of values. Ordinal data types have three additional operations defined on them: Pred, Succ, and Ord.

Pascal allows the user to define additional ordinal data types. An enumerated data type is created by listing the constant identifiers that make up the set of values of that type. The operations automatically defined on enumerated types are the relational operators, Pred, Succ, and Ord.

A subrange type is made up of a continuous subset of an existing ordinal type. The operations defined on the subrange type are the same as those defined on the host data type.

User-defined data types are extremely useful in the writing of clear, self-documenting programs.

QUICK CHECK

1. What is the result of each of these three functions? (pp. 367–368)

$$Ord(23) \qquad Succ('J') \qquad Pred(True)$$

2. Define an enumerated data type called AutoMakes, consisting of the names of five of your favorite car manufacturers. (pp. 370–375)

3. Define a subrange type called Digits, consisting of the characters '0' through '9'. (pp. 383–385)

4. Why is the use of anonymous data types considered to be a poor programming practice? (pp. 385–386)

5. Given the following two data type definitions, decide whether the types are type compatible. (pp. 386–389)

```
TYPE
    Colors = (Infrared, Red, Orange, Yellow,
              Green, Blue, Indigo, Violet,
              Ultraviolet);
    Visible = Red..Violet;
```

6. If RoomNumber is a variable of type 1..500, is the following expression assignment compatible with RoomNumber? (pp. 386–389)

$$Pred(RoomNumber\ DIV\ 500)$$

7. Write a FOR statement that will "count" from Red to Violet, using a control variable of type Visible, as defined in question 5. Call the control variable Rainbow. (p. 389)

Answers

1. 23, 'K', False 2. TYPE AutoMakes = (Saab, Jaguar, AMC, Chevrolet, Ford);
3. TYPE Digits = '0'..'9'; 4. Because anonymous types cannot be passed as parameters to procedures and functions. 5. They are type compatible because one is a subrange of the other. 6. The expression is not assignment compatible because the only two values it may have (1 and 0) are outside of the subrange allowed by RoomNumber. 7. FOR Rainbow := Red TO Violet DO statement;

EXAM PREPARATION EXERCISES _____

1. Where does the formal description for the set of values for each of the standard data types come from?

2. Distinguish between a scalar data type and an ordinal data type.

3. List the operations defined on all ordinal data types.

4. Given the type declaration

   ```
   TYPE
       Members = (Smith, Jones, Grant, White);
   ```

   the expression Jones > Grant would be _____.

5. Scalar data types are ordered so that every variable must be less than, equal to, or greater than any other variable of that type. (True or False?)

6. Fill in the table based on the following definitions.

   ```
   TYPE
       Perfume = (Poison, DiorEssence, ChanelNo5, Coty);
   ```

Operation	Result
Ord(Poison)	_____
Succ(Coty)	_____
Pred(ChanelNo5)	_____

7. The type of the predeclared ordinal function Ord must be Integer, since it returns the internal integer representation of a character. (True or False?)

8. Automatic range-checking should always be used to test input data for values that are out of range. (True or False?)

9. Only named data types can be formal VAR parameters, but anonymous data types can be actual VAR parameters. (True or False?)

10. When are two types *type compatible?*

11. Are assignment compatibility errors determined at compile time or at run time?

12. Active error detection leaves error hunting to Pascal, whereas passive error detection requires that the programmer do the error hunting. (True or False?)

13. *Control abstraction* makes changes in the form of data easier to implement. (True or False?)

PREPROGRAMMING EXERCISES _____

1. Define an enumerated type for the local area high schools.

2. Define an enumerated type for the National Football Conference.

3. Define a subrange of the teams in Exercise 2 for the Eastern Division, Western Division, and Central Division. Did you have to redefine the order of the teams in order to define these subranges?

4. Define a subrange type made up of the uppercase letters.

5. Define a subrange type made up of the single-digit numbers.

6. Define a subrange type made up of the numerals '0' to '9'.

7. Define an enumerated type for the days of the week.

8. Write the print procedures for Program BirthdayReminder for your friends and family.

9. Rewrite Program GradeList using a procedure to do the printing.

PROGRAMMING PROBLEMS _____

1. Read in the sides of a triangle and determine whether the triangle is an isosceles triangle (two sides are equal), an equilateral triangle (three sides are equal), or a scalene triangle (no sides are equal). Use an enumerated data type (Isosceles, Equilateral, Scalene).

   The sides of the triangle are to be entered as integer values, three per line. For each set of sides, print out the kind of triangle or an error message saying that the three sides do not make a triangle. (For a triangle to exist, any two sides together must be longer than the remaining side.) Continue analyzing triangles until < eof > .

2. Expand Program BirthdayReminder to read in a month and a date. The data should be converted into a value in the enumerated type (FirstWeek, SecondWeek, ThirdWeek, FourthWeek) using the following formula.

Dates 1–7:	FirstWeek
Dates 8–14:	SecondWeek
Dates 15–21:	ThirdWeek
Dates 22+:	FourthWeek

   Each monthly print procedure should take the week as a parameter and print the following message heading:

   ```
   'Reminders for the ' (first, second, third, fourth)
   'week of ' (January..) ' are: '
   ```

3. Rewrite Programming Problem 1 from Chapter 9 using the Succ function to increment the loops.

4. Read in a real number character by character, convert the number to its numeric form, and print the result in E-notation. Your algorithm should convert the whole number part to an integer and the fractional part to an integer and combine the two integers as follows:

   $$\text{Result} \longleftarrow \text{Whole number} + (\text{Fraction}/(10^{\text{number of digits in fraction}}))$$

For example, 34.216 would be converted into 34 + (216/1000). You may assume that the number has at least one digit on either side of the decimal point.

5. The program that plays the rock, paper, and scissors, takes its input from two files. Rewrite the program using interactive input. The main module should be as follows:

```
REPEAT
    Get command
    IF Continue
        Play Game
UNTIL Stop
```

Command should be an enumerated type (Continue, Stop). In the Get Command module the first player should be prompted to enter a C for Continue or an S for Stop. If the first player wishes to continue, ask the second player. Command should be Continue if both players enter a C and Stop otherwise.

If both players wish to continue, the first player and then the second player should be prompted to enter a play.

- To be able to define a one-dimensional array for a given problem.
- To be able to choose appropriate index and component types for a one-dimensional array.
- To be able to assign a value to an individual component of an array.
- To be able to access a value that is stored in an individual component of an array.
- To be able to fill an array with data and process the data in the array.
- To be able to apply subarray processing to a given problem.
- To be able to use parallel arrays.
- To be able to define and use an array with index values that have semantic content.

11

One-Dimensional Arrays

In the last chapter we examined the concept of a data type and looked at the mechanism in Pascal that allows us to define ordinal data types. In this chapter we will expand the definition of a data type to include structured data types, which are organized collections of components given a single name.

There are times when it is necessary to show relationships among different variables or to store and reference variables as a group. This is very difficult to do if each variable must be named individually. For example, if a set of values must be printed in reverse order, all of the values must be read and saved before the last value can be accessed and printed. If the number of values is unknown, there is no way to set up individual variables into which to store each value. A *one-dimensional array* is a structured data type that can be used to solve this problem easily.

In this chapter we will discuss structured data types in general, solve a problem that requires one (a one-dimensional array), and then examine the array data type in great detail.

STRUCTURED DATA TYPES

In Chapter 9 we introduced the concept of using an identifier to name a collection of values. A data type that is a collection of values of a simpler type is called a *composite type* because it is composed of other types. There are two kinds of composite types: structured and unstructured.

A set is an unstructured composite type. The values in a set are not organized with respect to one another. The only relationship that values in a set share is that they are members of the same set: they are eggs in the same Easter basket. We cannot access the values in a set individually; we can only ask if a specific value is in the set. The set is the only unstructured composite type in Pascal.

On the other hand, a *structured data type* is a composite data type made up of an *organized* collection of components of some other data type. Not only is the collection given a name, but each component can be accessed individually by specifying its position within the organized collection.

> **Structured Data Type** A collection of components whose organization is characterized by the method used to access individual components. The allowable operations on a structured data type are the storage and retrieval of individual components.

Just as compound statements (structured statements) are composed of other statements organized sequentially, structured types are organized compositions of other types.

Structured types are always built out of simpler types. Simple scalar types, both built-in and user-defined, are the building blocks for structured types. Scalar types can be thought of as atomic or primitive types (indivisible units), and the structured types can be thought of as being composed of these atomic types. (See Figure 11-1.)

The particular accessing method used to store and retrieve individual components of a structured data type will depend on how the components are structured. For one-dimensional arrays (the subject of this chapter) the accessing operations are based on an index or subscript that indicates which component within the collection of components is to be stored or retrieved.

In Chapter 13 we will extend the concept of a one-dimensional array to two dimensions. That is, we will use a table with rows and columns. The accessing will be done with a pair of indices, one for the row and one for the column.

In Chapter 14 we will look at the record data type in which the accessing is done through a named field of the record. In Chapter 15 the remaining built-in data types of Pascal will be covered. However, at the lowest level, each component must be a simple scalar type.

We will begin our discussion of arrays by looking at a problem that requires one.

*Figure 11-1
Atomic (Simple)
and Composite
Types*

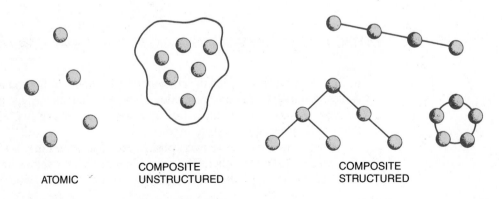

ATOMIC

COMPOSITE
UNSTRUCTURED

COMPOSITE
STRUCTURED

Problem Solving in Action

Problem: A file contains two lists of positive integer numbers, separated by a negative number. These two lists of numbers should be identical. Write a program to compare the lists and print out any pairs of numbers that are not the same. The number of integers on each list is unknown. The only information available is that there will be no more than 500 on each list.

Discussion: If the lists of numbers were on different files, the solution would be easy. Pairs of numbers could be read, one number from each file, and compared. Since the lists are on the same file, the first list will have to be read and stored, one number at a time, until the negative number is read. Then the second list can be read, one number at a time, and these numbers compared with the numbers in the first list which we have saved.

This implies that not only will we have to save the numbers in the first list, but we will have to be able to access them in the same order in which they were read. That is, numbers in corresponding positions in the two lists must be compared.

If we were doing this checking by hand, we would write the numbers from the first list on a pad of paper, one per line. The line number would correspond to the number's position in the list. That is, the first number would be on the first line, the second number would be on the second line, and so on. The first number in the second list would be compared to the number on the first line. The second number in the second list would be compared to the number on the second line.

This algorithm would work if there were some way to relate a variable's name to its position in the list. We might do something like naming the variables for the first list FirstList1, FirstList2, FirstList3, . . . if only there weren't so many!

The solution to this naming problem is to use a structured data type called a one-dimensional array. A one-dimensional array is a structured collection of values from which we can access the first value, the second value, and so on. An array variable named FirstList can be defined with 500 places. Each individual place in the array can be accessed by specifying which of the 500 places we want at any particular time.

We will first look at how to use an array in this specific problem. In the next section we will look carefully at the syntax and semantics of the array data type.

There are two steps to defining an array variable FirstList. The first step is to describe in the TYPE section what the array should look like. The second step is to declare such an array variable in the VAR section.

```
CONST
    MaxNumber = 500;        (* Maximum number *) ⎫
                                                  ⎪
TYPE                                              ⎬  describe
    IndexRange = 1..MaxNumber;                    ⎪  structure
    ListType = ARRAY[IndexRange] OF Integer;      ⎭

VAR
    FirstList:                                        create one
        ListType;
```

The array type ListType is described in the TYPE section by using the keyword ARRAY followed by a subrange type in brackets. This subrange type specifies the number of places that are to be associated with this array type—500, in this case. The "OF

Integer" indicates that each of the 500 places may contain an integer number. That is, the type of each of the individual values that will be stored in the array will be Integer.

To access any of the places in the array variable FirstList, we give the variable name followed by a number in brackets (for example, FirstList[1], FirstList[2]). This number, called the index, specifies which one of the 500 places we want. The index may be a constant, a variable, or an expression.

Now we can complete the top-down design and program for our problem.

Input: A file containing two lists of positive integer numbers (Data). The lists are separated by a negative integer and are of equal length.

Output: The statement that the lists are identical, or a list of the pairs of values that do not correspond

Data Structures: A one-dimensional array to hold the first list of numbers (FirstList) (Figure 11-2)

Remember: ListType is a *pattern;* FirstList is a *variable made from that pattern.*

MAIN MODULE   Level 0

Read First List
AllOk is set to True
Compare lists
IF AllOk
   Print 'The two lists are identical.'

When procedure ReadFirstList is run, the first number will be stored in FirstList[1]; the second, in FirstList[2]; the third, in FirstList[3]. This implies that we will need a counter to keep track of which number is being read. When the negative number is encountered, the counter will tell us how many of the 500 places set aside were actu-

Figure 11-2
One-Dimensional
Array Data
Structure

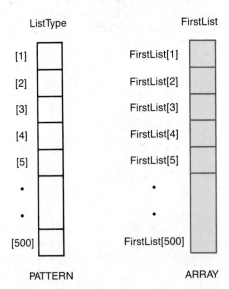

PSIA

ally needed. We can use this value (call it Length) to control the reading and comparing loop in the Compare List module.

READ FIRST LIST   Level 1

```
Initialize Counter to 0
Read a Number
WHILE Number >= zero
    Counter ⟵— Counter + 1
    FirstList[Counter] ⟵— Number
    Read a Number
Length ⟵— Counter
```

COMPARE LISTS

```
FOR Counter going from 1 to Length
    Read Number from second list
    IF numbers not the same
        AllOk ⟵— False
        Print both numbers
```

NUMBERS NOT THE SAME   Level 2

```
Number <> FirstList[Counter]
```

PRINT BOTH NUMBERS

```
Writeln FirstList[Counter], Number
```

Module Structure Chart:

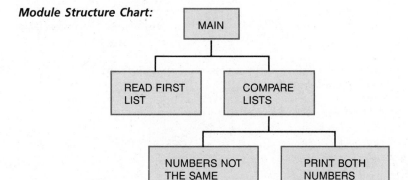

Since the last two modules are only one line each, they will be coded in module Compare Lists.

PSIA ▰▰▰▰▰▰▰

```
PROGRAM CheckLists (Data, Output);

(* There are two lists of integers on file Data, separated by a negative
   integer.  These two lists are compared.  If they are identical, a
   message is printed.  If not, nonmatching pairs are printed.
   Assumption:  Lists are of equal length. *)

CONST
  MaxNumber = 500;   (* Maximum in each list *)

TYPE
  IndexRange = 1..MaxNumber;
  ListType = ARRAY[IndexRange] OF Integer;

VAR
  FirstList:        (* Holds first list            *)
    ListType;
  AllOk:            (* True if lists are identical *)
    Boolean;
  Length:           (* Length of first list        *)
    IndexRange;
  Data:             (* Data file                   *)
    Text;

(*****************************************************************************)

PROCEDURE ReadFirstList(VAR FirstList:       (* Returns filled FirstList *)
                            ListType;
                        VAR Length:          (* Returns number of values *)
                            IndexRange;
                        VAR Data:
                            Text);           (* Data file                *)

(* The first list is read into FirstList. A count of the number of
   values in the list is kept and returned in Length. *)

VAR
  Counter:          (* Loop control variable    *)
    0..MaxNumber;
  Number:           (* Variable used for reading *)
    Integer;
```

PSIA ▬▬▬▬▬▬

```pascal
BEGIN (* ReadFirstList *)
  Counter := 0;
  Read(Data, Number);
  WHILE Number >= 0 DO
    BEGIN
      Counter := Counter + 1;
      FirstList[Counter] := Number;
      Read(Data, Number)
    END;
  Length := Counter
END;   (* ReadFirstList *)
```

(***)

```pascal
PROCEDURE CompareLists(VAR AllOK:          (* Returns True if lists match *)
                           Boolean;
                       FirstList:      (* First list of numbers      *)
                           ListType;
                       Length:         (* Length of list             *)
                           Integer;
                       VAR Data:       (* Data file                  *)
                           Text);
```

(* Read second list and compare to values in FirstList.
   Lists are assumed to be the same length. *)

```pascal
VAR
  Counter,      (* Loop control counter *)
  Number:
    Integer;

BEGIN (* CompareLists *)
  FOR Counter := 1 TO Length DO
    BEGIN
      Read(Data, Number);
      If Number <> FirstList[Counter]
        THEN
          BEGIN
            AllOk := False;
            Writeln(FirstList[Counter]:4, Number:4)
          END
    END
END;   (* CompareLists *)
```

(***)

PSIA

```
BEGIN (* CheckLists *)
   Reset(Data);
   ReadFirstList(FirstList, Length, Data);
   AllOk := True;
   CompareLists(AllOk, FirstList, Length, Data);
   IF AllOk
      THEN
         Writeln('The two lists are identical.')
END.    (* CheckLists *)
```

Testing: The program was run with two sets of data, one in which the two lists were identical and one in which there were errors. The data and the results from each are shown below.

Data Set One:	Data Set Two:
21	21
32	32
76	76
22	22
21	21
−4	−4
21	21
32	32
76	176
22	12
21	21

Output:

```
The two lists are identical.
```

Output

```
76 176
22 12
```

ONE-DIMENSIONAL ARRAYS

Now that we have demonstrated how useful one-dimensional arrays can be, we will describe how they are defined and how individual components are accessed and then show some examples of defining and accessing a variety of different arrays.

Defining Arrays

A one-dimensional array is a structured collection of components whose individual components can be accessed by their position within the collection.

> **One-Dimensional Array** A structured collection of components of the same type, given a single name. Each component is accessed by an index that indicates the component's position within the collection.

One-dimensional array data types are defined in the TYPE section of a program. Variables of that type are declared in the VAR section of the program. The syntax diagram describing how a one-dimensional array data type is defined is shown in Figure 11-3.

The index type gives the range of index values. It is used by the compiler to determine how many components there are going to be in this array type and how each individual component will be accessed. The index type can be Char, Boolean, an enumerated type, or a subrange type.

The component type describes the type of the components themselves and follows the keyword OF. Thus the component type describes what will be stored in each component of the array. For now we will assume that the component types are atomic. In subsequent chapters we will define arrays in which the component type is a composite type.

Once a one-dimensional data structure has been defined in the TYPE section, any number of variables of that type can be declared in the VAR section. An array variable can be treated as a unit when it is passed as a parameter, and yet each component can be accessed separately. For example, in Program CheckLists the array variable FirstList was passed as a unit to procedures ReadFirstList and CompareLists. Within each procedure the individual components of FirstList were accessed. In fact, each component is itself a variable of the component type.

Figure 11-3
Syntax Diagram of a One-Dimensional Array

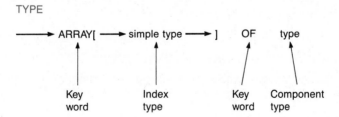

Accessing Individual Components

To access the array variable as a unit, we simply give the array name. To access an individual component, we list the name of the array variable, followed by an expression that specifies which individual component is to be accessed. The syntax diagram for accessing a particular component within the array is given below.

$$\longrightarrow \text{variable identifier} \longrightarrow [\longrightarrow \text{expression} \longrightarrow]$$

The expression used to access a particular component must result in a value of the index type. We can treat the component being accessed just like any simple variable reference. We can assign it a value, read a value into it, write its contents, pass it as a parameter, and use it in an expression. Take, for example, the following two statements from Program CheckLists.

```
FirstList[Counter] := Number
IF Number <> FirstList[Counter]
```

In the first statement an integer number is being stored into the array variable FirstList. If Counter is 1, the number is being stored in the first place in the array. If Counter is 2, the number is being stored in the second place in the array. If Counter has a value that is not within the index type, an error occurs. For example, if the first list of numbers read by Program CheckLists had 501 numbers in it, Counter would be 501. Trying to access FirstList[Counter] when Counter contains 501 would cause a run-time error.

In the second statement the contents of a particular place in the array is being retrieved and compared with the value in Number. The place in the array is again indicated by the value of Counter. If Counter is 1, the value in the first place is being retrieved. If Counter is 2, the value in the second place is being retrieved.

Figure 11-4 shows the indexing expression as a constant, a variable, and a more complex expression.

Examples of Defining and Accessing Arrays

We will now look in detail at some specific examples of defining, declaring, and accessing arrays.

```
CONST
   NumStudents = 25;

TYPE
   NumGrades = 1..NumStudents;
   GradeType = ARRAY[NumGrades] OF Char;

VAR
   Grades :
      GradeType;
   Counter:
      NumGrades;
   OneGrade:
      Char;
```

Figure 11-4
Index as a
Constant, a
Variable, and an
Expression

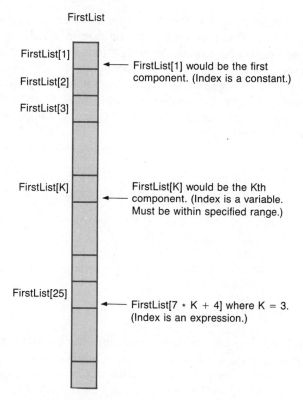

FirstList

FirstList[1] — FirstList[1] would be the first
component. (Index is a constant.)

FirstList[2]

FirstList[3]

FirstList[K] — FirstList[K] would be the Kth
component. (Index is a variable.
Must be within specified range.)

FirstList[25] — FirstList[7 * K + 4] where K = 3.
(Index is an expression.)

GradeType is a pattern for an array with 25 components, each of which can contain a character. Each component in this pattern can be accessed by its position in the group of 25. Grades is an array variable of GradeType. Each component of Grade is a Char variable, just like OneGrade or any other Char variable we have used before. Figure 11-5 illustrates these relationships.

Figure 11-5
Array Pattern,
Array Variable, and
Array Component

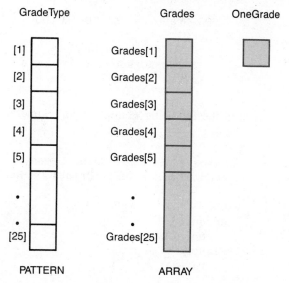

GradeType   Grades   OneGrade

[1]   Grades[1]

[2]   Grades[2]

[3]   Grades[3]

[4]   Grades[4]

[5]   Grades[5]

•   •

•   •

[25]   Grades[25]

PATTERN   ARRAY

In our examples so far, the index type has been a subrange of the integers beginning with 1. This corresponds to the case in which we want to access the components by their position in the array—that is, the first, the second, the third, and so on until the last. This is the most common way of thinking about an array. In fact, some programming languages only allow the index type to be a subrange of the integers beginning with 1. However, Pascal is much more flexible. The index type can be any subrange or named ordinal type. The next example shows an array where the indices are letters.

```
TYPE
   LetterGrades = 'A'..'D';
   GradeCount = ARRAY[LetterGrades] OF Integer;

VAR
   Class1Grades:
      GradeCount;
   Class2Grades:
      GradeCount;
   Grade:
      LetterGrades;
```

GradeCount is a pattern for an array with four components, each of which can contain an Integer value. Class1Grades and Class2Grades are two array variables of this type. The components in Class1Grades can be accessed by Class1Grades['A'], Class1Grades['B'], Class1Grades['C'], and Class1Grades['D']. The components in Class2Grades can be accessed by Class2Grades['A'], Class2Grades['B'], Class2Grades['C'], and Class2Grades['D']. See Figure 11-6.

If Class1Grades['A'] is used as a counter to tally the number of As in Class1, Class1Grades['B'] is used as a counter to tally the number of Bs in Class1, and so on, the following code fragment will set the counters (components) to 0.

Figure 11-6

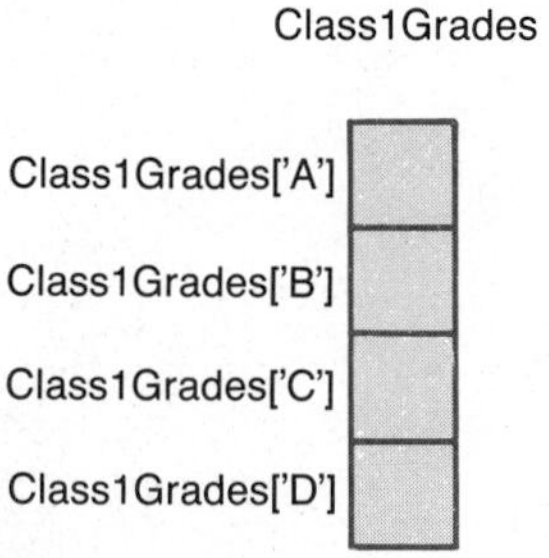

Class1Grades

Class1Grades['A']

Class1Grades['B']

Class1Grades['C']

Class1Grades['D']

```
FOR Grade := 'A' TO 'D' DO
   BEGIN
      Class1Grades[Grade] := 0;
      Class2Grades[Grade] := 0
   END
```

The index type in the following example is an enumerated type.

```
TYPE
   Drink = (Orange, Cola, Lemon);
   AmountType = ARRAY[Drink] OF Real;

VAR
   Amount:
      AmountType;
   Flavor:
      Drink;
```

Figure 11-7

Amount

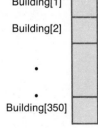

Amount[Orange]

Amount[Cola]

Amount[Lemon]

AmountType creates a pattern for a group of three Real components representing dollar sales figures. Amount is an array variable of this type. Amount has three components. (See Figure 11-7.) The following code will print the values in the array.

```
FOR Flavor := Orange TO Lemon DO
    Writeln(Amount[Flavor]);
```

The next example is a little more complex. The component type is a subrange type.

```
CONST
  BuildingSize = 350;
  MaxPeople = 5;

TYPE
  Occupant = 0..MaxPeople;
  NumRooms = 1..BuildingSize;
  Rooms = ARRAY[NumRooms] OF Occupant;

VAR
  Building:
    Rooms;
  TotalNumber:
    Integer;
  Counter:
    NumRooms;
```

Figure 11-8

Building

Building[1]

Building[2]

•

•

Building[350]

Type Rooms is a pattern for a group of 350 components. The component type of Rooms is a subrange type called Occupant. Building is an array variable of type Rooms. Each component in Building can contain an integer between 0 and 5. (See Figure 11-8.) If values have been read into the array, then the following code will sum the number of occupants in the building.

```
TotalNumber := 0;
FOR Counter := 1 TO BuildingSize DO
    TotalNumber := TotalNumber +
                       Building[Counter];
```

Note that the named constants BuildingSize and MaxPeople are used in defining the type Rooms. Changes can be made much more easily if constants are used in this manner. If BuildingSize changes from 350 to 400, only the CONST section needs to be changed. If the literal value 350 were used in place of BuildingSize, at least two statements would have to be changed and probably many more throughout the program in which this fragment is embedded.

Notice that each of the array structures is shown with the name of the array variable on top. This is to emphasize that the array variable is a structure with a name. An array variable can be assigned as a whole to another array variable of the same type. For example,

```
Class1Grades := Class2Grades
```

is a legal assignment statement. Array variables can be passed as a complete structure to a procedure or function.

Notice also that each individual component in each structure is shown with its name: the name of the array variable followed by an index. This setup emphasizes that each component in an array variable is itself a variable of the component type and can be explicitly accessed.

Figure 11-9 shows four of these arrays with some sample contents.

When working with arrays, we use a variable to help us find the variable we are looking for. This can be confusing; let's take another look.

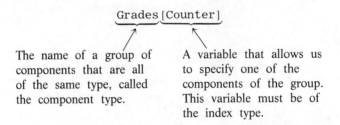

Grades is an array variable; Grades[Counter] is a Char variable. The expression that determines which of the components we want to access can be a constant, a simple variable (as in the above example), or a complex expression. When the expression is evaluated, the value must be within the range of the index type.

Figure 11-9
Array Variables
with Sample
Contents

Grades		Class1Grades	
Grades[1]	'A'	Class1Grades['A']	24
Grades[2]	'F'	Class1Grades['B']	16
Grades[3]	'C'	Class1Grades['C']	12
•		Class1Grades['D']	3
•			
•			
Grades[25]	'B'		

Amount		Building	
Amount[Orange]	112.4	Building[1]	1
Amount[Cola]	36.5	Building[2]	3
Amount[Lemon]	3.7	Building[3]	5
		•	
		•	
		Building [350]	4

PROCESSING AN ARRAY

Assume these declarations in the main program.

```
CONST
   NumStudents = 10;

TYPE
   Grades = 'A'..'F';
   RangeOfStudents = 1..NumStudents;
   StudentType = ARRAY[RangeOfStudents] OF Grades;

VAR
   Students:
      StudentType;
   IDNumber:
      RangeOfStudents;
```

The array variable Students is pictured in Figure 11-10. Values are shown for each of the components, which implies that some processing of the array has already taken place. Following are some simple examples showing how the array may be used.

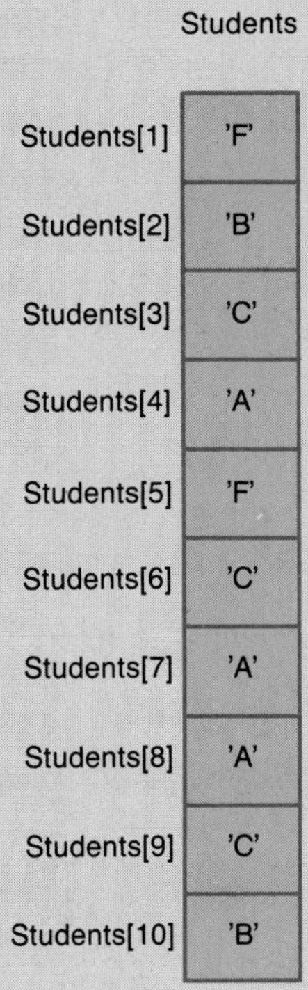

Figure 11-10
Array Variable Students with Values

Students

Students[1]	'F'
Students[2]	'B'
Students[3]	'C'
Students[4]	'A'
Students[5]	'F'
Students[6]	'C'
Students[7]	'A'
Students[8]	'A'
Students[9]	'C'
Students[10]	'B'

Statement	Result
`Read(Students[2]);`	Assigns the next character in file Input to the component in the array variable Students indexed by 2.
`Students[4] := 'A';`	Assigns the character 'A' to the component in the array variable Students indexed by 4.
`IDNumber := 6;`	Assigns 6 to the index variable IDNumber.
`Students[IDNumber] := 'C';`	Assigns the character 'C' to the component of the array variable Students indexed by ID-Number (that is, by 6).
`FOR IDNumber := 1 TO NumStudents DO` `  Write(Students[IDNumber]);`	Loops through the array variable Students, printing each component. In this case, the output would be FBCAFCAACB

`FOR IDNumber := 1 TO NumStudents DO`
`  Writeln('Student ', IDNumber:1,`
`         ' Grade ', Student[IDNumber]);`
	Loops through the array variable Students, printing each component in a more readable form. IDNumber is used as the index, but it also has semantic content—it is the student's identification number. The output would be
	
	Student 1 Grade F
	Student 2 Grade B
	.
	
	Student 10 Grade B

USING ARRAYS IN PROGRAMS

There are three types of array processing that come up so frequently that we will say a word about them before introducing them in a problem. These are using only part of the defined array (a subarray), using two arrays in parallel (parallel arrays), and using for the index type values that have specific meaning within the problem.

Subarray Processing

The size of an array in storage is established at compile time. Thus the number of locations for an array must be known in advance. Since the exact number of components to be put into the array is often dependent on the data itself, we have to define the array variable to be as big as the maximum size it might ever need to be.

As values are put into the components of the array, we can keep a count of how many there are. Then we can use this count when we are processing the array. This way we process only those places in the array that have values stored in them. Any remaining places are not processed.

For example, if there are 250 students in a class, a program to do a statistical analysis of the grades on a test would have to set aside 250 locations to hold the test grades. However, some students would surely be absent on the day of the test. So in the processing the number of test grades would be counted, and that number, rather than 250, would be used to control the processing of the array.

We often call the number of actual data values in an array the *length* of the array. Procedures and functions that have array parameters should also have the length passed as a parameter. We did this in Program CheckLists at the beginning of this chapter.

```
PROCEDURE ReadFirstList (VAR FirstList:
                             ListType;
                    VAR Length:
                             IndexRange;
                    VAR Data:
                             Text);
```

Parallel Arrays

In many problems there are several pieces of information that go together. For example, we might have social security numbers and grades for a particular group of students. We can set up one Integer array for the social security number and one Char array for the grades. We can then access the components in the arrays in parallel. A particular social security number goes with a particular grade because they have the same position in their respective arrays (that is, they have the same *index value*).

In Figure 11-11, the grade in Grade[1] is the grade for the student whose social security number is in SSNum[1], the grade in Grade[2] is the grade for the student whose social security number is in SSNum[2], and so on.

Figure 11-11
Parallel Arrays

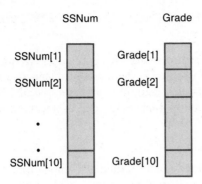

Indices with Semantic Content

In some problems the index has meaning beyond simple position (that is, the index has *semantic content*). For example, the employees in a company might be given identification numbers ranging from 100 to 500. If a one-dimensional array variable of salary figures were defined as

```
TYPE
    IDNumbers = 100..500;
    Salaries = ARRAY[IDNumbers] OF Real;

VAR
    Salary: Salaries;
```

the index of a specific salary would be the employee identification number of the person making that salary. That is, Salary[201] would be the salary for the employee whose company identification number is 201.

In order to give you more practice with both problem solving and the use of one-dimensional arrays, we will end this chapter with two case studies that involve the types of processing we outlined in this section.

Problem Solving in Action

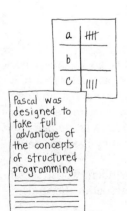

Pascal was designed to take full advantage of the concepts of structured programming.

Problem: Count the frequency of occurrence of certain characters in a sample of text. The characters we are interested in will be input from the keyboard. The text will be on a file.

Discussion: To do this by hand, we would probably make a list of the characters whose frequency we wanted to count. Then we would start processing the text character by character. We would take each character in the text and check to see whether it was on our list of characters. If it was on the list, we would make a hash mark beside it.

This algorithm can be used directly in a program. The list of characters whose frequency we wish to count can be read into an array of type Char. This is analogous to making a list of the characters. To see whether or not a character is on the list, we can then scan the list of characters, comparing the character we are looking for with the ones on the list.

PSIA ━━━━━

To simulate making a hash mark, we use a second array that is the same size as the one containing the characters. This second array will be of type Integer. If we find the character on our list, we will add 1 (make a hash mark) to the component in the second array that has the same index. For example, if the first character on our list is an 'A,' then each time we find an 'A' the first slot in the integer array will be incremented by 1.

Input:

A list of the characters to be counted; one per line on Input. (The character # ends the list.)

Text to be processed character by character (on file Data)

Output: The characters to be counted and their frequency

Data Structures:

A one-dimensional array of type Char to hold the characters being counted (CharList)

A one-dimensional array of type Integer to hold the corresponding frequencies (FreqList)

MAIN MODULE   Level 0

```
Reset Data
Get CharList
Set FreqList to 0
WHILE more characters DO
    Get a Character
    Scan list for Character
    IF Found
        Increment FreqList
Print CharList and FreqList
```

GET CHARLIST   Level 1

```
Counter ⟵ 0
Read a Character
WHILE Character <> # DO
    Counter ⟵ Counter +1
    CharList[Counter] ⟵ Character
    Read a Character
Length ⟵ Counter
```

Since we don't know how many characters will be on the list to be counted, the array we define will have to be large enough to hold all the characters in the character set of the machine minus 1. (Since we are using # as a signal value, we assume that it is not to be counted.)

When all of CharList has been read, the value of Counter will be the length of the array with data in it. That is, when the list is searched for a character, only those components between CharList[1]..CharList[Length] need be examined. This is another example of subarray processing. Note that Counter is being used both as a counter and as an index.

SET FREQLIST TO 0

```
FOR Index going from 1 to Length
    FreqList[Index] ⟵— 0
```

GET A CHARACTER

```
Read Character from file Data
```

SCAN LIST

```
Found ⟵— False
Index ⟵— 0
WHILE NOT found AND more components in list
    Index ⟵— Index + 1
    IF Character = CharList[Index]
        Found ⟵— True
```

If Found is True, the value of Index says where in array CharList the character was found.

INCREMENT FREQLIST

```
FreqList[Index] ⟵— FreqList[Index] + 1
```

PRINT CHARLIST AND FREQLIST

```
FOR Index going from 1 to Length
    Writeln CharList[Index],' occurred ', FreqList[Index]:3,
    ' times. '
```

Since Get a Character and Increment FreqList are only one simple statement each, they will be coded directly in the main module. Let's look at the interfaces of the other procedures.

PSIA

Procedure	Needs	Returns	Comments
GetCharList		CharList Length	Length will be last value of Index.
ZeroFreqList	FreqList Length	FreqList	
ScanList	CharList Length Character	Found Index	If Found is True, Index gives place found.
Print	FreqList CharList Length		

Remember that any variables in the Returns column must be VAR parameters. Those listed only in the Needs column should be value parameters. The exception is when you have a *large* data structure that is an input parameter only. In that case, storing a copy of the data structure might take up more memory space than is available. Thus, in procedure Print the parameter FreqList should be VAR. This exception will be discussed later in this chapter.

Module Structure Chart:

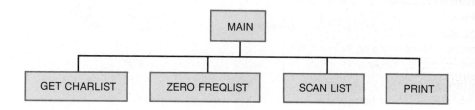

```
PROGRAM CharCount (Input, Data, Output);

(* Program to count the frequency of occurrence of specified
   characters in text *)

CONST
   MaxLength = 255;   (* Maximum number of different characters *)
   EndOfList = '#';

TYPE
   IndexRange = 1..MaxLength;
   IndexCount = 0..MaxLength;
   ListType = ARRAY[IndexRange] OF Char;
   CountType = ARRAY[IndexRange] OF Integer;
```

PSIA ▱▱▱▱▱▱

```
VAR
  CharList:          (* Characters to be counted       *)
    ListType;
  FreqList:          (* Frequency counts               *)
    CountType;
  Length:            (* Number of characters to count  *)
    IndexCount;
  Found:             (* True if character found on list *)
    Boolean;
  Data:              (* Text to be counted on file Data *)
    Text;
  Character:         (* Temporary character            *)
    Char;
  Index:             (* Returns position of character  *)
    IndexCount;

(*************************************************************************)

PROCEDURE GetCharList (VAR CharList:     (* Returns list of characters *)
                            ListType;
                       VAR Length:       (* Returns length of list     *)
                            IndexCount);

(* Characters are read from Input and stored in CharList until the
   EndOfList character is read.  Length is the number of characters in
   the list.  The Char constant EndOfList is accessed globally.
   Assumption: There are no duplicate characters *)

VAR
  Counter:       (* Loop control counter *)
    Integer;
  Character:     (* Used for reading     *)
    Char;

BEGIN  (* GetCharList *)
  Counter := 0;
  Readln(Character);
  WHILE Character <> EndOfList DO
    BEGIN
      Counter := Counter + 1;
      CharList[Counter] := Character;
      Readln(Character)
    END;
  Length := Counter
END;  (* GetCharList *)

(*************************************************************************)
```

PSIA ═══════════

```
PROCEDURE ZeroFreqList (VAR FreqList:        (* Returns zeroed list      *)
                                 CountType;
                             Length:          (* Receives length of list *)
                                 IndexCount);

(* The first Length positions of FreqList are set to 0 *)

VAR
  Index:              (* Loop control counter *)
    IndexRange;

BEGIN (* ZeroFreqList *)
  FOR Index : = 1 TO Length DO
    FreqList[Index]  : = 0
END;   (* ZeroFreqList *)


(************************************************************************)

PROCEDURE ScanList (      CharList:        (* Receives list of chars       *)
                              ListType;
                          Length:          (* Receives length of char list *)
                              IndexCount;
                          Character:       (* Receives input character     *)
                              Char;
                      VAR Index:           (* Returns index of match        *)
                              IndexCount;
                      VAR Found:           (* Returns False if no match     *)
                              Boolean);

(* CharList is searched for Character.  If Found is True, Index is where
   Character is found in CharList.  If Found is False, Character is not
   in CharList and Index is undefined. *)

BEGIN (* ScanList *)
  Found : = False;
  Index : = 0;
  WHILE (Index < Length) AND NOT Found DO
    BEGIN
      Index : = Index + 1;
      IF Character = CharList[Index]
        THEN
          Found : = True
    END
END;   (* ScanList *)


(************************************************************************)
```

PSIA ▬▬▬▬

```
PROCEDURE Print (VAR FreqList:           (* Receives table of char counts  *)
                        CountType;
                     CharList:            (* Receives list of chars counted *)
                        ListType;
                     Length:              (* Receives length of lists       *)
                        IndexCount);

(* Character list with associated frequencies is printed *)

VAR
  Index:
    IndexRange;

BEGIN (* Print *)
  FOR Index := 1 TO Length DO
    Writeln(CharList[Index], ' occurred ',
            FreqList[Index]:3, ' times. ')
END;  (* Print *)

(********************************************************************)

BEGIN (* CharCount *)
  Reset(Data);
  GetCharList(CharList, Length);
  ZeroFreqList(FreqList, Length);
  (* Count occurrences of desired characters in text on Data *)
  WHILE NOT EOF(Data) DO
    BEGIN
      WHILE NOT EOLN(Data) DO
        BEGIN
          Read(Data, Character);
          ScanList(CharList, Length, Character, Index, Found);
          IF Found
            THEN
              FreqList[Index] := FreqList[Index] + 1
        END;
      Readln(Data)
    END;
  Print(FreqList, CharList, Length)
END.  (* CharCount *)
```

Let's do a partial code walk-through of this program with the following data. The characters to be counted are

a   e   i   o   u

PSIA ━━━━━━━

and the text is

> Roses are red,
> violets are blue.
> If I can learn Pascal,
> so can you.

The contents of the data structures after procedures GetCharList and ZeroFreqList are executed are as follows:

CharList[1] is 'a'	FreqList[1] is 0	Length is 5
CharList[2] is 'e'	FreqList[2] is 0	
CharList[3] is 'i'	FreqList[3] is 0	
CharList[4] is 'o'	FreqList[4] is 0	
CharList[5] is 'u'	FreqList[5] is 0	

We will assume that the control structures of the reading loops in the main program are correct and look at the three inner statements:

1. `Read (Data, Character)`
2. `ScanList (CharList, Length, Character, Index, Found)`
3. `IF Found`
   `THEN`
   `FreqList [Index] := FreqList [Index] + 1`

The following table shows the partial walk-through. The number to the left of the period refers to one of the three statements listed above, and the number to the right of the period refers to the number of times the statement has been executed.

Statement	Character	Index	Found	FreqList
1.1	R	?	?	
2.1	R	?	False	
3.1	R	?	False	
1.2	o	?	False	
2.2	o	4	True	
3.2	o	4	True	FreqList[4] is 1
1.3	s	4	True	
2.3	s	?	False	
3.3	s	?	False	
1.4	e	?	False	
2.4	e	2	True	
3.4	e	2	True	FreqList[2] is 1
.				
.				
1.9	e	?	False	
2.9	e	2	True	
3.9	e	2	True	FreqList[2] is 2

PSIA

The output from the program using this data would be as follows:

```
a occurred   7 times.
e occurred   7 times.
i occurred   1 times.
o occurred   4 times.
u occurred   2 times.
```

At first glance the output does not seem right. If you count the characters by hand you come up with three occurrences of 'i'. Note, however, that two of the occurrences are of 'I', not 'i'. If we want to count uppercase letters and lowercase letters to be the same, we have to convert one of them. (The algorithm for converting ASCII lowercase letters to uppercase letters was given in Chapter 10.)

Testing: If the machine we are using does not recognize one of the characters that is input, a run-time error message such as "ILLEGAL CHARACTER IN TEXT" will result. There is no way to test for this, since the error occurs when we are trying to read a character.

The test data for this program should include cases in which (1) there are no characters to be counted, (2) there is no text to count, and (3) both files contain input data with a variable number of lines.

Program CharCount is the implementation of an algorithm that not only uses parallel arrays and subarray processing but parallels the way a human would do the problem by hand. There is nothing wrong with this solution except that we are not taking advantage of all the information we have. Let's change the problem statement slightly and approach the solution from another angle, this time keeping in mind the features of Pascal.

Problem Solving in Action

Problem: Count the frequency of occurrence of *all* the characters in a sample of text.

Discussion: Pascal already has a built-in list of all the characters it recognizes. They are the values of type Char. Pascal also allows us to use any ordinal type as an index type. So instead of searching a list of characters for a value and counting the frequency in a parallel array, we will let Pascal do all that for us. How? By using the characters themselves as the indices into the frequency list.

In Chapter 10 we mentioned that the ASCII and EBCDIC character sets have non-printing characters. We need to set up our frequency array to count only those characters that are printable. Fortunately, the printing characters are all grouped together, so we can define a subrange of the characters to be our index type.

We will use MinChar and MaxChar to represent the first and last values in the index range. (MinChar and MaxChar have to be set in the CONST section; they are not built-in identifiers.)

A	⊬⊬⊬
B	II
⋮	
Z	I
a	⊬⊬⊬ I
b	III
⋮	
3	II
1	III
⋮	
9	II

Pascal was designed to take full advantage of the concepts of structured programming.

PSIA

```
TYPE
   Frequency = ARRAY[MinChar..MaxChar] OF Integer
```

	CDC	*ASCII*	*EBCDIC*
MinChar	':'	' '	' '
MaxChar	';'	'~'	'9'

Freq[MinChar] would be the counter for colons in CDC and blanks in ASCII and EBCDIC.

Freq[MaxChar] would be the counter for semicolons in CDC, ~s in ASCII, and 9s in EBCDIC.

Freq[Character] would be the counter for whatever character Character contained.

Let's look at how this problem is simplified by the fact that the index itself has meaning.

Input: A file of text (Data)

Output: Each printable character in the character set, followed by the number of times it occurred

Data Structures: An array of frequencies (Freq) indexed by the characters being counted

MAIN MODULE   Level 0

```
Zero FreqCount
WHILE more characters DO
   WHILE NOT EOLN DO
      Read Character from Data
      Increment FreqCount[Character] by 1
   Readln Data
PRINT characters and frequencies
```

ZERO FREQCOUNT   Level 1

```
FOR Index from MinChar to MaxChar DO
   Initialize FreqCount[Index] to 0
```

PRINT CHARACTERS AND FREQUENCIES

```
FOR Index from MinChar to MaxChar DO
   Writeln Index:2, ' OCCURRED ', FreqCount[Index]:3, ' TIMES'
```

PSIA

Module Structure Chart:

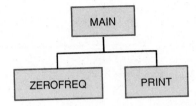

```
PROGRAM CountAll (Data, Output);

(* Program to count frequency of occurrence of characters in text.
   Choose one of the 3 following lines depending on the character
   set of the machine being used. *)

CONST
  MinChar = ' ';   MaxChar = '~';      (* ASCII   *)
(*MinChar = ' ';   MaxChar = '9'; *)   (* EBCDIC *)
(*MinChar = ':';   MaxChar = ';'; *)   (* CDC     *)

TYPE
   IndexRange = MinChar..MaxChar;
   CountType = ARRAY[IndexRange] OF Integer;

VAR
  FreqCount:
    CountType;
  Character:
    IndexRange;
  Data:
    Text;

(***********************************************************************)

PROCEDURE ZeroFreqCount (VAR FreqCount: (* Returns zeroed table *)
                                 CountType);

(* Puts zeroes in all elements of the character counting array *)

VAR
  Index:
    IndexRange

BEGIN (* ZeroFreqCount *)
  FOR Index := MinChar TO MaxChar DO
    FreqCount[Index] := 0
END;  (* ZeroFreqCount *)

(***********************************************************************)
```

PSIA

```
PROCEDURE Print (FreqCount:      (* Receives table of char counts *)
                    CountType);

(* Prints each character and the number of times it occurred *)

VAR
   Index;
     IndexRange;

BEGIN (* Print *)
   FOR Index : = MinChar TO MaxChar DO
     IF FreqCount[Index] <> 0
       THEN
           Writeln(Index:2, ' OCCURRED ', FreqCount[Index]:3, ' TIMES')
END;    (* Print *)


(*************************************************************************)

BEGIN (* CountAll *)
   Reset(Data);
   ZeroFreqCount(FreqCount);                              (* Zero counters *)
   (* Keep reading and counting until no more characters *)
   WHILE NOT EOF(Data) DO
     BEGIN
       Read(Data, Character);
       FreqCount[Character] : = FreqCount[Character] + 1;
       IF EOLN(Data)
         THEN
             Readln(Data)
     END;
   Print(FreqCount)
END.    (* CountAll *)
```

See how much simpler the solution becomes when we take advantage of the fact that the character itself can be the index to its own frequency counter? In Programming Problem 1 at the end of this chapter you will be asked to modify this program to handle the case in which we are interested in counting a specified subset of the characters (as we were in the previous problem).

Using the same input file as was used in the previous problem,

```
                    Roses are red,
                    violets are blue.
                    If I can learn Pascal,
                    so can you.
```

we get the following output from Program CountAll.

PSIA ▰▰▰▰

```
  OCCURRED  10  TIMES
, OCCURRED   2  TIMES
. OCCURRED   2  TIMES
I OCCURRED   2  TIMES
P OCCURRED   1  TIMES
R OCCURRED   1  TIMES
a OCCURRED   7  TIMES
b OCCURRED   1  TIMES
c OCCURRED   3  TIMES
d OCCURRED   1  TIMES
e OCCURRED   7  TIMES
f OCCURRED   1  TIMES
i OCCURRED   1  TIMES
l OCCURRED   4  TIMES
n OCCURRED   3  TIMES
o OCCURRED   4  TIMES
r OCCURRED   4  TIMES
s OCCURRED   5  TIMES
t OCCURRED   1  TIMES
u OCCURRED   2  TIMES
v OCCURRED   1  TIMES
y OCCURRED   1  TIMES
```

Testing: Two things must be tested in this program: whether it counts the characters correctly and whether it can handle files of varying numbers of lines.

To adequately test whether this program counts characters correctly, we would have to create a data file that contains all of the printable characters at least once and some of them more than once.

In order to make sure that the program would run correctly on files that have varying numbers of lines, we would have to test the program on an empty file, a file with one line, and a file with more than one line.

We ran Programs CharCount and CountAll using part of this chapter as data (23,040 characters, including text processing characters) to show you that they do indeed work correctly on large files.

Output from Program CharCount:

```
a occurred 1152 times.
e occurred 1708 times.
i occurred 719 times.
o occurred 862 times.
u occurred 444 times.
```

Output from Program CountAll:

(We show the output in two columns to save space.)

	OCCURRED	4624 TIMES
"	OCCURRED	2 TIMES
#	OCCURRED	4 TIMES
'	OCCURRED	78 TIMES
(	OCCURRED	106 TIMES
)	OCCURRED	106 TIMES
*	OCCURRED	538 TIMES
+	OCCURRED	9 TIMES
,	OCCURRED	85 TIMES
−	OCCURRED	109 TIMES
.	OCCURRED	181 TIMES
0	OCCURRED	18 TIMES
1	OCCURRED	54 TIMES
2	OCCURRED	30 TIMES
3	OCCURRED	18 TIMES
4	OCCURRED	14 TIMES
5	OCCURRED	8 TIMES
6	OCCURRED	2 TIMES
7	OCCURRED	5 TIMES
9	OCCURRED	6 TIMES
:	OCCURRED	77 TIMES
;	OCCURRED	82 TIMES
<	OCCURRED	16 TIMES
=	OCCURRED	50 TIMES
>	OCCURRED	3 TIMES
?	OCCURRED	10 TIMES
@	OCCURRED	6 TIMES
A	OCCURRED	90 TIMES
B	OCCURRED	26 TIMES
C	OCCURRED	283 TIMES
D	OCCURRED	99 TIMES
E	OCCURRED	172 TIMES
F	OCCURRED	131 TIMES
G	OCCURRED	40 TIMES
H	OCCURRED	27 TIMES
I	OCCURRED	191 TIMES
L	OCCURRED	167 TIMES
M	OCCURRED	70 TIMES
N	OCCURRED	84 TIMES
O	OCCURRED	112 TIMES
P	OCCURRED	62 TIMES
Q	OCCURRED	4 TIMES
R	OCCURRED	182 TIMES
S	OCCURRED	80 TIMES
T	OCCURRED	165 TIMES
U	OCCURRED	46 TIMES
V	OCCURRED	24 TIMES
W	OCCURRED	24 TIMES
X	OCCURRED	1 TIMES
Y	OCCURRED	13 TIMES
Z	OCCURRED	14 TIMES
[	OCCURRED	48 TIMES
]	OCCURRED	48 TIMES
_	OCCURRED	334 TIMES
a	OCCURRED	1152 TIMES
b	OCCURRED	145 TIMES
c	OCCURRED	520 TIMES
d	OCCURRED	394 TIMES
e	OCCURRED	1708 TIMES
f	OCCURRED	259 TIMES
g	OCCURRED	211 TIMES
h	OCCURRED	636 TIMES
i	OCCURRED	719 TIMES
j	OCCURRED	12 TIMES
k	OCCURRED	38 TIMES
l	OCCURRED	409 TIMES
m	OCCURRED	241 TIMES
n	OCCURRED	922 TIMES
o	OCCURRED	862 TIMES
p	OCCURRED	247 TIMES
q	OCCURRED	85 TIMES
r	OCCURRED	1058 TIMES
s	OCCURRED	763 TIMES
t	OCCURRED	1280 TIMES
u	OCCURRED	444 TIMES
v	OCCURRED	72 TIMES
w	OCCURRED	163 TIMES
x	OCCURRED	109 TIMES
y	OCCURRED	176 TIMES
z	OCCURRED	7 TIMES
|	OCCURRED	56 TIMES
~	OCCURRED	3 TIMES

Program CountAll is not only simpler, but it gives more information and executes faster! The moral is to take advantage of the features of the language you are using.

SPECIAL NOTE ON PASSING ARRAYS AS PARAMETERS

The data type of a variable (including an array variable) that is used as a formal parameter must be a named data type. For example,

```
PROCEDURE Pass(VAR List:
                    ARRAY[1..20] OF Integer)
```

would be illegal, whereas

```
PROCEDURE Pass(VAR List:
                    ListType)
```

would be legal provided Procedure Pass is within the scope of the type identifier ListType.

In Chapter 7 we said that there would be one more exception to the rule of always using value parameters for input-only parameters. Large arrays are this exception. It is a good idea to pass large data structures as VAR parameters even if they are not output parameters. Remember that copies of value parameters are stored in their corresponding formal parameters. Therefore, when an array is passed as a value parameter, the entire array is copied into its corresponding formal parameter. Not only is extra space required to hold the copy, but the copying itself takes a lot of time. Thus, passing large arrays as VAR parameters saves both memory and time.

Of course, this method can lead to inadvertent errors if the values are changed within the procedure. You must be very careful to make sure that this does not happen. In the case of the passing of large data structures, the practical concerns of memory and time efficiency override stylistic issues.

TESTING AND DEBUGGING

Finally, we should add a word of caution about the choice of looping structure to use when processing arrays.

The most common error that you will encounter in processing arrays is the message "ARRAY INDEX OUT OF BOUNDS". This means that your program attempted to access a component of an array using an index value that is outside the range of indexes for which the array is defined.

For example, given the declarations

```
TYPE
    Index = 1..100;
    Table = ARRAY[Index] OF Char;
```

```
VAR
   Counter:
      Integer;
   Line:
      Table;
```

the following FOR statement would print the contents of array Line and then cause the program to crash with the "ARRAY INDEX OUT OF BOUNDS" error message.

```
FOR Counter := 1 TO 101 DO
   Write (Line [Counter]);
```

This example is trivial to debug, but you won't always use a simple FOR statement in accessing arrays. Suppose we were to read data into array Line in another part of the program. We would use a WHILE statement that reads to EOLN:

```
Counter := 0;
WHILE NOT EOLN DO
   BEGIN
      Counter := Counter + 1;
      Read (Line [Counter])
   END
```

This seems reasonable enough, but what if the input contains a line with more than 100 characters? After the one-hundredth character is read, the loop continues to execute and on the next iteration the program crashes because the array index is out of bounds.

The moral is: when processing arrays, give special attention to the design of loop termination conditions. Always ask yourself if there is any possibility that the loop could keep running after the last array component has been processed.

Whenever you see the "ARRAY INDEX OUT OF BOUNDS" error message, a good first suspicion is a loop that fails to terminate properly. A second point to check is any array access involving an index that is based on input data or a calculation. When an array index is input as data, then a data validation check is an absolute necessity.

Testing and Debugging Hints

1. Be consistent when using arrays. Arrays are described in the TYPE section; variables that conform to that type are declared in the VAR section. Values are stored into the individual components of an array variable during execution of the program. These three actions—describing, declaring, using—must all be consistent.

2. Components of arrays are variables. The individual components of an array are themselves variables of the component type. When values are stored into an array, these values must be of the component type; otherwise, a type-conflict error will occur.

3. Indices must be within the index range. When an individual component in an array is accessed, the index must be within the index range. Attempting to access a component in the array that doesn't exist will cause an index-out-of-range error.

4. The size of an array must be determined at compile time. Often the size of an array must be decided upon before we know how big the array needs to be— that is, before we know how much data we actually have. This means that an array must be declared to be as large as it could ever possibly be within the context of the particular problem. When values are read into the array, they are counted. Only the components that have data in them are later processed. The number of components being used is often called the length of the array.

5. Pass the length as well as the array to procedures and functions when subarray processing is to take place within them.

SUMMARY

In addition to being able to create user-defined atomic and unstructured composite data types, we can create structured composite data types. A structured data type is a type in which a name is given to a structured group of components. The group can be accessed as a whole, or each individual component can be accessed separately.

The array data type gives a name to a sequential group of components. Each component can be accessed by its relative position within the group. Each component of the array is a variable of the component type. To access a particular component, we give the name of the array and an index that specifies which one of the group we want.

The index must be of the index type. The index type can be any named ordinal type except Integer. Therefore, the components in an array can be accessed sequentially by stepping through the values of the index type.

QUICK CHECK

1. Define an array data type called Quiz that will contain 12 components indexed by the integers 21 through 32. The component type is Boolean. (pp. 414–420)

2. If an array is to hold the number of correct answers given by students to each question on a 20-question True/False quiz, what data types should be used for the indices and components of the array? (pp. 414–420)

3. Given the definitions

```
CONST
  MaxLength = 30

TYPE
  IndexRange = 1..MaxLength
  NameString = ARRAY[IndexRange] OF Char;

VAR
  FirstName:
    NameString;
```

write an assignment statement that will store 'A' in the first component of array FirstName. (pp. 416–420)

4. Given the declarations in question 3, write a Writeln statement that will print the value of the fourteenth component of array FirstName. (pp. 416–420)

5. Given the declarations in question 3, write a FOR statement that will fill array FirstName with blanks. (pp. 421–422)

6. Given the declarations in question 3 and the following program fragment that reads characters into array FirstName until a blank is encountered, write a FOR statement that will print out the portion of the array that is filled with input data. (pp. 423–432)

```
Length := 0;
REPEAT
  Read(Letter);
  IF Letter <> ' '
    THEN
      BEGIN
        Length := Length + 1;
        FirstName[Length] := Letter
      END
UNTIL Letter = ' ';
```

7. Define two parallel arrays indexed by the integers 1 through 100. One of the arrays will contain student numbers (type Integer); the other will consist of values of the enumerated type defined by

```
TYPE
  Gender = (Female, Male);
```

(pp. 423–432).

8. Define an array data type in which the index values represent the musical notes A through G (excluding sharps and flats) and the component type is Real. (pp. 424, 432–437)

Answers
1. TYPE
```
Quiz = ARRAY[21..32] OF Boolean;
```
2. The index type is 1..20; the component type is Integer.
3. `FirstName[1] := 'A';`
4. `Writeln(FirstName[14]);`
5. FOR LCV := 1 TO MaxLength DO
```
   FirstName[LCV] := ' ';
```
6. FOR LCV := 1 TO Length DO
```
   Write(FirstName[LCV]);
```
7. TYPE
```
   Gender = (Female, Male);
   Index = 1..100;
   Students = ARRAY[Index] OF Integer;
   Genders = ARRAY[Index] OF Gender;
```
```
VAR
   Number:       (* Student numbers for 100 students *)
     Students;
   Sex:          (* Gender for the same 100 students *)
     Genders;
```
8. TYPE
```
   NoteRange = 'A'..'G'
   Notes = Array[NoteRange] OF Real
```

EXAM PREPARATION EXERCISES _____

1. Every component in an array must have the same type, which is fixed at compile time, but the type of the indices may vary during execution. (True or False?)

2. Both the indices and the components must be an ordinal type. (True or False?)

3. Write a code fragment to do the following tasks:
   (a) Define a subrange data type ScoreRange to be from 0 to 100.
   (b) Define an array data type StudentScores of length MaxLength. The components are of type ScoreRange.
   (c) Declare an array variable QuizOne to be of type StudentScores.

4. Write a code fragment to do the following tasks:
   (a) Define an enumerated type BirdType made up of bird names.
   (b) Define an integer array data type SitingType indexed by BirdType.
   (c) Declare an array variable Sitings of type SitingType.

5. Given the declarations

```
CONST
   MaxLength = 100;

TYPE
   Colors = (blue, green, gold, orange, purple,
             red, white, black)
   Range = 1..MaxLength;
   RainbowType = ARRAY[Range] OF Colors;
   CountType = ARRAY[Colors] OF Integer;
```

```
VAR
  Count:
    CountType;
  Rainbow:
    RainbowType;
```

answer the following questions:
(a) How many variables are there of type Colors?
(b) How many Integer variables are there?
(c) What is the index type of the array variable Count?
(d) What is the index type of the array variable Rainbow?
(e) How many components are there in the array variable Count?
(f) How many components are there in the array variable Rainbow?

6. Using the declarations in exercise 5, write code fragments to do the following tasks:
(a) Initialize Count to all zeros.
(b) Initialize Rainbow to all white.
(c) Count the number of times green appears in Rainbow.
(d) Print the value in Count indexed by blue.
(e) Sum the values in Count.

7. Declare array variables for each of the following situations. Be sure to use good style.
(a) A 24-component Real array for which the index goes from 1 to 24.
(b) A 24-component Integer array for which the index goes from 24 to 47.
(c) A 26-component Boolean array for which the index goes from 'A' to 'Z'.
(d) A 10-component Char array for which the index goes from -10 to -1.

PREPROGRAMMING EXERCISES _____

Use the following declarations in exercises 1–8. You may declare any other variables that you need.

```
CONST
  MaxLength = 100;

TYPE
  IndexType = 1..MaxLength;
  FailType = ARRAY[IndexType] OF Boolean;
  PassType = ARRAY[IndexType] OF Boolean;
  ScoreType = ARRAY[IndexType] OF Integer;

VAR
  Failing:
    FailType;
  Passing:
    PassType;
  Grade:
    Integer;
  Length:
    IndexType;
```

1. Write a Pascal procedure that will initialize Failing to False. Pass Length and Failing as parameters.

2. Write a Pascal procedure that has Failing, Score, and Length as parameters. Set Failing to True wherever the parallel value of Score is less than 60.

3. Write a Pascal procedure that has Passing, Score, and Length as parameters. Set Passing to True wherever the parallel value of Score is greater than or equal to 60.

4. Write a Pascal function TalleyPass that takes Passing and Length as parameters and returns the number of components in Passing that are True.

5. Write a Pascal function Error that takes Passing, Failing, and Length as parameters. Error is True if any parallel components are the same.

6. Write a Pascal procedure that takes Score, Passing, Grade, and Length as parameters. The procedure should set Passing to True wherever the parallel value of Score is greater than Grade.

7. Write a Pascal function that takes Grade, Length, and Score as parameters. The function should return the number of values in Score that are greater than or equal to Grade.

8. Write a Pascal procedure that takes Score and Length as parameters and reverses the order of the components in Score. That is, Score[1] goes into Score[Length], Score[2] goes into Score[Length − 1], and so on.

PROGRAMMING PROBLEMS _____

1. Modify Program CountAll so that its output is the same as Program CharCount. That is, print the frequency of occurrence of a specified list of characters.

2. The local baseball team is computerizing its records. You are to write a program that computes batting averages. There are 20 players on the team, identified by the numbers 1 through 20. Their batting records are coded on a file as follows. Each line contains four numbers: the player's identification number and the number of hits, walks, and outs he or she made in a particular game.

Example:

3   2   1   1

The above example indicates that during one game player number 3 was at bat 4 times and made 2 hits, 1 walk, and 1 out. For each player there are several records on the file. Each player's batting average is computed by adding the player's total number of hits and dividing by the total number of times at bat. A walk does not count as either a hit or a time at bat when batting average is being calculated.

You are to print a table showing each player's identification number, batting average, and number of walks.

3. One of the local banks is gearing up for a big advertising campaign and would like to see how long its customers are waiting for service at drive-in windows. Several employees have been asked to keep accurate records for the 24-hour drive-in service. The collected

information, which will be read from a file, will consist of the time when the customer arrived in hours, minutes, and seconds, the time when the customer was actually served, and the ID number of the teller.

Write a program that does the following:

1. Reads in the wait data.
2. Computes the wait time in seconds.
3. Calculates the mean, standard deviation (the sum of the differences between each value and the average divided by the number of values), and range.
4. Prints a single-page summary showing the values calculated in 3.

Input:

The first data line or card contains a title.

The remaining lines or cards each contain a teller ID, an arrival time, and a service time. The times are broken up into hours, minutes, and seconds according to a 24-hour clock.

Processing:

Calculate the mean and the standard deviation and locate the shortest wait time and the longest wait time for any number of records up to 100.

Output:

The input data (echo print)

The title

The following values, all properly labeled: number of records, mean, standard deviation, and range (minimum and maximum)

4. Your history professor has so many students in her class that she has trouble determining how well the class does on exams. She has found out that you are a computer whiz and has asked you to write a program to do some simple statistical analyses on exam scores, in return for which she will not flunk you even though you failed on the first quiz. You, of course, cheerfully agree. Your program must work for any size class up to 100 ($0 < N < 100$).

Write and test a computer program that does the following:

1. Reads the test grades from file Data.
2. Calculates the class mean, standard deviation, and percentage of the test scores falling in the ranges <10, 10–19, 20–29, 30–39, . . . , 80–89, and ≥90.
3. Prints a single-page summary showing the mean and standard deviation, as well as a histogram showing the percentage distribution of test scores. This page will be formatted so that it can be torn off as a complete one-page report.

Input:

The first data line or card contains the number of exams to be analyzed and an alphanumeric title for the report.

The remaining lines or cards have 10 test scores on each line or card until the last, and 1 to 10 scores on the last. The scores are all integers.

Output:

1. The input data as they are read
2. An analysis report consisting of the title that was read from data, the number of scores, the mean, the standard deviation (labeled), and the histogram. The report should begin at the top of a new page.

5. A small postal system ships packages within your state. Acceptance of parcels is subject to the following constraints:

   1. Parcels are not to exceed a weight of 50 pounds.
   2. Parcels are not to exceed 3 feet in length, width, or depth and may not have a combined length and girth exceeding 6 feet. (The girth of a package is the circumference of the package around its two smallest sides; mathematically the formula is

$$\text{Girth} = 2 * (S1 + S2 + S3 - \text{Largest})$$

   where Largest is the largest of the three parcel dimensions, S1, S2, and S3.)

Your program should process a transaction file containing one entry for each box mailed during the week. Each entry contains a transaction number, followed by the weight of the box, followed by its dimensions (in no particular order). The program should print the transaction number, weight, and postal charge for all accepted packages, and the transaction number and weight for all rejected packages. At the end of the report, you must print the number of packages processed and the number rejected.

Input:

Parcel Post table—weight and cost (show 25 values). This table should be stored in two one-dimensional arrays. The postal cost of each parcel can then be determined by first searching the Weight array and then using the corresponding element in the Cost array. If a package weight falls between two weight categories in the table, your program should use the cost for the higher weight.

Transaction file—transaction number, weight, and three dimensions for an arbitrary number of transactions. Assume that all weights are whole numbers and that all dimensions are given to the nearest inch.

Output:

First line—appropriate headings

Next N records—transaction number, whether accepted or rejected, weight, and cost

Last line—number of packages processed, number of packages rejected

6. The final exam in your psychology class is to be 30 multiple-choice questions. Your instructor says that if you write the program to grade the finals you won't have to take it. You, of course, accept.

Input:

The first data line or card contains the key to the exam. The correct answers are the first 30 characters; they are followed by an integer number that says how many students took the exam (call it N).

The next N lines or cards contain student answers in the first 30 character positions followed by the student's name in the next 10 character positions.

Output:

For each student, the student's name, followed by the number of correct answers, followed by "PASS" if the number correct is 60 percent or better or "FAIL" otherwise.

■ To be able to search an array for a component with a given value.

■ To be able to sort the components of an array into ascending or descending order.

■ To be able to insert a value into an ordered list.

■ To be able to search an ordered list for a given value using the binary search algorithm.

■ To be able to define and use arrays that contain character strings.

12

Applied Arrays

Chapter 11 introduced the concept of a one-dimensional array, a data structure composed of a collection of components (also called elements) of the same type given a single name. Each individual component is accessed by an index. There are two types associated with each component: the type of the component itself (that is, what can be stored there) and the type of the index expression which specifies the particular component in the collection.

There are some common algorithms that are applied over and over again in many different contexts to data stored in a one-dimensional array. In this chapter we will examine some of these algorithms and write the Pascal code to implement them as general-purpose procedures.

We will also consider the *packed array,* a special kind of one-dimensional array that is used to process alphabetic information like words or names. A packed array will be used to rewrite procedure GetMonth in Program BirthdayReminder, as promised in Chapter 10.

We will conclude with a problem in which several of the general-purpose procedures developed in this chapter are used to process a list of names.

ALGORITHMS ON LISTS

In Program CharCount in Chapter 11, we used two one-dimensional arrays: one to hold a list of characters and another to hold a list of counters. In Program CountAll in Chapter 11, we used a single one-dimensional array to hold a list of counters in which the array index represented the letter being counted. In general, a one-dimensional array is the structure to use to represent a list.

Chapter 2 outlined heuristics or strategies to use in solving problems. One of the most useful of these is pattern recognition—many times you will find that a problem or subproblem is similar to one you've already done. The algorithms that we will examine in this chapter will provide you with patterns you should look for when solving problems that involve processing lists. When you recognize that your processing involves one of these common tasks, you won't have to design the algorithm or write the code. You can turn back to this chapter and adapt the procedures written here.

Sequential Search in an Unordered List

In Program CharCount we had a procedure ScanList that searched through an array of characters looking for a particular one. We called this procedure ScanList because if we were to do the task by hand we would scan the list of characters looking for the one we wanted. Scanning a list to find a particular value is part of many everyday tasks. We scan the TV section to see what time a program comes on. We scan newspaper ads to see if certain shoes are on sale.

We will recode procedure ScanList as a general-purpose sequential search procedure that can be used in other programs. To make it more general, we will replace the problem-dependent variable names with general ones. The following definitions are assumed to be in the block that will enclose this procedure (usually the main program).

```
CONST
  MaxLength = (* maximum possible number of components needed *)

TYPE
  ItemType = (* some scalar type *)
  ListType = ARRAY[1..MaxLength] OF ItemType;
```

This general-purpose search procedure will need five parameters:

1. the array to be searched
2. the length of the list
3. the item being searched for
4. a flag telling whether or not the search was successful
5. the index indicating where the item was located (if found)

The array to be searched is made up of components of type ItemType. The array itself is of type ListType.

We will call the array being searched List and the item being searched for Item. Length, Found, and Index will serve the same purposes here as they did in procedure ScanList. That is, Length is the number of components in the List, Found tells whether the item is in the List, and Index gives the location of Item if it is in the List.

You will note that the two output parameters Index and Found are redundant. Index would be sufficient, because the calling routine could check to see if Index was greater than Length. If it was, then Item was not found. However, we will keep this redundancy for clarity.

```
PROCEDURE Search (      List:           (* Array to be searched       *)
                        ListType;
                        Item:           (* Value being searched for    *)
                        ItemType;
                        Length:         (* Size of the list            *)
                        Integer;
                   VAR Index:           (* Location of value if found *)
                        Integer;
                   VAR Found:           (* True if value is found      *)
                        Boolean);

(* List is searched for Item. If Item is found, Found is True and Index
   gives the location. Otherwise, Found is False and Index is Length +
   1. *)

BEGIN (* Search *)
  Found : = False;
  Index : = 0;
  WHILE (Index <= Length) AND NOT Found DO
    BEGIN
      Index : = Index + 1
      IF Item = List[Index]
        THEN
          Found : = True
    END
END;    (* Search *)
```

This procedure will now search an array of any type (ItemType) for a value of that type (See Figure 12-1.) We can use this generalized sequential search procedure in any program requiring an array search.

Notice that this algorithm finds the first occurrence of the item being searched for. How could we modify the algorithm to find the last occurrence? We would initialize Index to Length and decrement Index each time through the loop, stopping when we found the item we wanted or when Index became 0.

Before we leave this search algorithm, let's introduce a variation that will make the program more efficient, although logically a little more complex.

The condition on the WHILE loop is a compound condition: We want to stop either when we find the value we are searching for or when we run out of values to check. If we insert the value we are searching for into List[Length+1], we guarantee that we will always find the value we are searching for. The condition Index < = Length, which sees if there are values left to check, can then be eliminated. (See Figure 12-2.)

Eliminating a condition saves the machine time that would be required to test the condition. In this case, the condition being eliminated controlled a WHILE loop, so we save the machine time required to test it during every iteration of the loop.

Figure 12-1
Generalized
Sequential Search

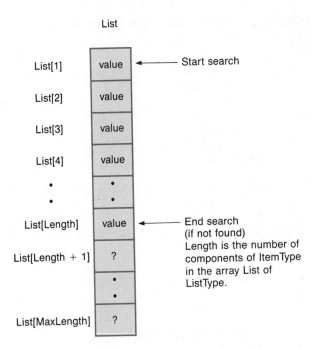

List

List[1]	value	◄—— Start search
List[2]	value	
List[3]	value	
List[4]	value	
•	•	
•	•	
List[Length]	value	◄—— End search (if not found) Length is the number of components of ItemType in the array List of ListType.
List[Length + 1]	?	
•	•	
List[MaxLength]	?	

Figure 12-2
Generalized
Sequential Search
with Item in
Position Length
Plus One

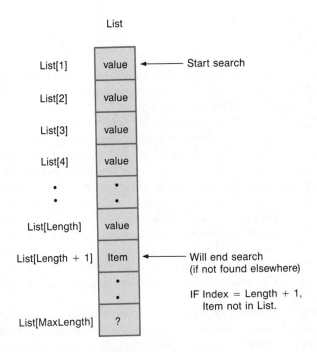

List

List[1]	value	◄—— Start search
List[2]	value	
List[3]	value	
List[4]	value	
•	•	
•	•	
List[Length]	value	
List[Length + 1]	Item	◄—— Will end search (if not found elsewhere)
•	•	IF Index = Length + 1, Item not in List.
List[MaxLength]	?	

By storing the value being searched for in List[Length+1], we are making the assumption that the length of List will always be less than MaxLength. This assumption should be included in the procedure documentation.

After the loop, Found can be set by checking to see if Index = Length + 1. Procedure Search2 incorporates these changes.

```
PROCEDURE Search2 (      List:          (* Array to be searched        *)
                            ListType;
                         Item:          (* Value being searched for     *)
                            ItemType;
                         Length:        (* Size of the list             *)
                            Integer;
                     VAR Index:         (* Location of value if found   *)
                            Integer;
                     VAR Found:         (* True if value is found        *)
                            Boolean);

(* Item is inserted into List[Length+1]. List is searched for Item. If
   Item is found somewhere other than in List[Length+1], Found is True
   and Index says where. Otherwise, Found is False and Index is Length +
   1. Assumption: Length is less than MaxLength. *)

BEGIN (* Search2 *)
  Found := False;
  Index := 0;
  List[Length+1] := Item;
  (* Search List for Item *)
  WHILE NOT Found DO
    BEGIN
      Index := Index + 1;
      IF Item = List[Index]
        THEN
          Found := True
    END;
  Found := Index <> Length + 1
END;   (* Search2 *)
```

Sorting

Another task commonly performed on lists is ordering the components in the list. For example, we might have a list of stock numbers that we want to put in either ascending or descending order. Or we might have a list of words that we want to put in alphabetical order.

Arranging values in order is known as *sorting*. In Chapter 10 we discussed the ordering inherent in any ordinal type. Because of this ordering, we can compare and sort, in ascending or descending order, values of any ordinal type.

If you were given a sheet of paper with a column of 20 numbers on it and were asked to write the numbers in ascending order, you would probably

1. Look for the smallest number.
2. Write it on the paper in a second column.
3. Cross the number off the original list.
4. Repeat the process, always looking for the smallest number remaining on the original list.
5. Stop when all the numbers had been crossed off the original list.

We could implement this algorithm directly in Pascal, but we would need two arrays: the original one and a second one into which to move the components in order. If our list of numbers is very large, the need for two arrays could prove to be a problem. We might not have enough memory for two copies of a large list.

It is also difficult to "cross off" an array component. We would have to simulate this by using some dummy value like MaxInt. That is, we would have to set the value of the "crossed off" variable to something that would not interfere with the processing of the rest of the components.

A slight variation on this by-hand algorithm, however, will allow us to sort the components in place. *In place* means that we will not have to use a second array. Instead of moving a component to a second array and crossing it off the original list, we can put that value in its proper place in the original array by having it swap places with the component that is there.

If our array is called List and contains Length values, we can state the algorithm as follows:

```
FOR Counter = 1 TO Length
    Find Minimum in List[Counter]..List[Length]
    Swap Minimum with List[Counter]
```

Figure 12-3 illustrates how this algorithm works.

This sort, known as straight selection, belongs to a class of sorts called exchange or interchange sorts. There are many types of sorting algorithms. Exchange sorts are characterized by the exchanging of pairs of array components until the array is sorted. Exchanging the contents of two variables—two components in an array—requires use of a temporary variable so that no values are lost. (See Figure 12-4.)

Figure 12-3
Straight Selection
Exchange Sort

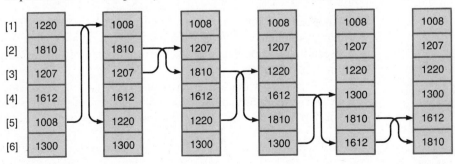

Figure 12-4
Exchanging the
Contents of Two
Places

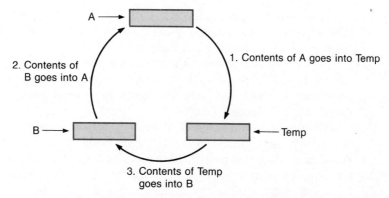

Two parameters are needed for the exchange sorting procedure: the list to be sorted and the length of the list. As in the search procedure, we will assume that a type called ListType has been defined. The code for this sorting algorithm is

```
PROCEDURE ExSort (VAR List:          (* Array to be searched              *)
                         ListType;
                      Length:        (* Number of elements in the array *)
                         Integer);

(* An unordered list with Length values is taken as input.  The same
   list with the components in ascending order is returned. *)

VAR
  Temp:           (* Temporary variable     *)
     ItemType;
  PassCount,      (* Loop control variable   *)
  PlaceCount,     (* Loop control variable   *)
  MinIndex:       (* Index of minimum so far *)
     Integer;

BEGIN (* ExSort *)
  FOR PassCount := 1 TO Length - 1 DO
     (* List[1]..List[PassCount-1] is already sorted and
        contains the PassCount - 1 smallest items *)
     BEGIN
       MinIndex := PassCount;
       (* Find the index of the smallest component
           in List[PassCount]..List[Length] *)
       FOR PlaceCount := PassCount + 1 TO Length DO
         IF List[PlaceCount] < List[MinIndex]
           THEN
              MinIndex := PlaceCount;
       (* Swap List[MinIndex] and List[PassCount] *)
       Temp := List[MinIndex];
       List[MinIndex] := List[PassCount];
       List[PassCount] := Temp
     END
  END;   (* ExSort *)
```

Note that the outer loop runs from 1 to Length − 1. Since the last value, (List[Length]), is in its proper place if the rest of the array is sorted, the loop does not need to be executed when PassCount = Length.

Note also that each time through the inner loop we are looking for the minimum value in the rest of the array (List[PassCount]..List[Length]). Therefore MinIndex is initialized to PassCount and the inner loop runs from PlaceCount equal to PassCount + 1 through Length.

The third point to note is that we may swap a component with itself. We could avoid such an unnecessary swap by checking to see if MinIndex is equal to PassCount. Since this comparison would have to be made during each iteration of the loop, it is more efficient not to check for this possibility and just to swap something with itself occasionally. If the components we were sorting were much more complex than simple numbers, we might reconsider this decision.

This algorithm sorts the components into ascending order. To sort them into descending order, we would need to look for the maximum value in each iteration instead of the minimum value. Simply changing the relational operator in the inner loop from < to > will effect this change. MinIndex, of course, would no longer be a meaningful identifier and should be changed to MaxIndex.

Sequential Search in a Sorted List

When we are searching for an item in an unordered list, we don't know that the item is *not* in the list until we have compared it to every item in the list. If the list we are searching is ordered, we know that an item is not there when we pass the place in the list where the item would be if it were in the list. For example, if a list contains the values

7
11
13
76
98
102

and we are looking for 12, we need only compare 12 with 7, 11, and 13 to know that 12 is not in the list.

If, at any comparison, the item we are searching for is greater than the one we are comparing it to in the list, we increment our counter and compare our item with the next one in the list. If our item is equal to the one we are comparing it to in the list, we have found the one we are looking for. If our item is less than the one we are comparing it to in the list, then we know that our item is not in the list. In either of the last two cases, we stop looking, since the item is no longer greater than the current component in the list.

```
Stop  ←—— False
WHILE NOT Stop AND more places to look
   IF Item > current component in List
      THEN increment current place
      ELSE Stop  ←—— True
Found ←—— Item = current component
```

We can make this algorithm more efficient by removing the compound condition (AND more places to look) as we did in Search2. We will store Item in List[Length+1]. Stop will be set to True if Item is less than or equal to the value in the current place in the list. On exit from the loop we can set Found to be True if Item is equal to the current component and the current place is not Length + 1.

```
Stop  ←—— False
WHILE NOT Stop
   IF Item > current component in List
      THEN increment current place
      ELSE Stop  ←—— True
Found ←—— (current place < > Length + 1)
            AND Item = current component
```

This search procedure will need the same parameters as the previous one. We must add the assumption that the list is sorted.

```
PROCEDURE SearchOrd (    List:          (* Array to be searched       *)
                           ListType;
                         Item:          (* Value to be found          *)
                           ItemType;
                         Length:        (* Number of values in array  *)
                           Integer;
                     VAR Index:         (* Location of value if found *)
                           Integer;
                     VAR Found:         (* True if value is found      *)
                           Boolean);

(* List is searched for an occurrence of Item. If Item is found, Found
   is True and Index is the place in List where Item occurs. Otherwise,
   Found is False. Assumptions: List is sorted in ascending order;
   Length is less than MaxLength *)

VAR
   Stop:           (* True when search terminates *)
     Boolean;
```

```
BEGIN (* SearchOrd *)
   Index := 1;
   Stop := False;
   List[Length+1] := Item;
   (* Exit loop when value is found or not there *)
   WHILE NOT Stop DO
      (* Item is not in List[1]..List[Index-1] *)
    IF Item > List[Index]
       (* Item is not in List[1]..List[Index] *)
      THEN
         Index := Index + 1
      ELSE
         (* Item is either found or not there *)
         Stop := True;
   (* Determine whether Item was found or not there *)
   Found := (Index <> Length + 1) AND (Item = List[Index])
END; (* SearchOrd *)
```

Both of our search algorithms take on the average the same number of comparisons to find an item in a list. The advantage of the second algorithm is that we find out sooner if an item is *not* there. Thus the second algorithm is slightly more efficient. However, it only works on a sorted list.

Inserting into an Ordered List

What happens if we want to put additional values into an already sorted list? We can always store the new value at List[Length+1], increment Length, and sort the array again. Such a solution, however, is a very inefficient way to solve the problem.

If we were inserting a value by hand into a list sorted in ascending order, we would probably write the new value out to the side and draw a line showing where it belongs. How would we know where it belongs? We would scan the list until we found a value greater than the one we were inserting. The new value should go in the list just before the value that was greater than the new one.

We can do something very similar in our procedure. We can find the proper place in the list using the by-hand algorithm. Instead of writing the value to the side with an arrow showing where it belongs, we will have to shift all the values larger than the new one down one place in the array to make space for the new value. The main algorithm is expressed as follows, where Item is the value being inserted.

```
WHILE place not found AND more places to look
   IF Item > current component in List
      THEN increment current place
      ELSE place found
Shift List down
Insert Item
Increment Length
```

The algorithm for Shift List Down is

$$
\begin{aligned}
\text{List[Length+1]} &\longleftarrow \text{List[Length]} \\
\text{List[Length]} &\longleftarrow \text{List[Length}-1\text{]} \\
&\quad\vdots \\
\text{Length[Index+1]} &\longleftarrow \text{List[Index]}
\end{aligned}
$$

A DOWNTO version of the FOR loop can be used to shift the components in the list down one position. Insert Item and Increment Length can be coded directly. This algorithm is illustrated in Figure 12-5.

There is something very familiar about the WHILE loop in our algorithm. It is logically exactly like the WHILE loop in SearchOrd! In SearchOrd we leave the loop either when we find Item or when we determine that it is not there. We determine that Item is not there when we pass the place in the list where Item belongs.

This is exactly what we need to do here. We can use SearchOrd to find the insertion place for us. On return from SearchOrd, if Found is False, Index is the place in List where Item should be inserted. What do we do if Found is True? We can either insert a second copy or skip the insertion, as we choose, as long as the procedure documentation clearly states what is being done. Inserting a second copy seems more reasonable. Therefore Index will be the insertion point whether or not Item exists in the list.

Figure 12-5
Inserting in an
Ordered List

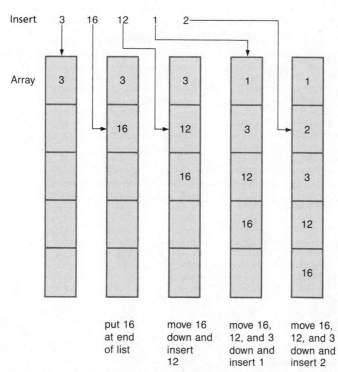

This procedure will need three parameters: the list, the number of components in the list, and the item being inserted. Again, we will use the same variable names, List, Item, and Length. Only this time List and Length must be VAR parameters because they are changed each time the procedure is invoked.

```
PROCEDURE Insert (VAR List:             (* Array to be changed        *)
                        ListType;
                  VAR Length:           (* Number of values in array *)
                        Integer;
                      Item:             (* Value to be inserted       *)
                        ItemType);

(* Item is inserted into its proper place in the sorted list List.
   Assumption: Length is less than MaxLength. If a match occurs,
   Item will be inserted before the one that is there *)


VAR
   PlaceFound:   (* True if value is found   *)
     Boolean;
   Index,        (* Current position in List *)
   Count:        (* Loop control variable    *)
     Integer;


(***********************************************************************)

PROCEDURE SearchOrd (     List:         (* Array to be searched        *)
                            ListType;
                          Item:         (* Value to be found           *)
                            ItemType;
                          Length:       (* Number of values in array   *)
                            Integer;
                      VAR Index:        (* Location of value if found *)
                            Integer;
                      VAR Found:        (* True if value is found      *)
                            Boolean);

(* List is searched for an occurrence of Item. If Item is found,
   Found is true and Index is the place in the List where Item
   occurs. Otherwise, Found is False and Index is where Item
   belongs. Assumption: List is sorted in ascending order. *)


VAR
   Stop:         (* True when search terminates *)
     Boolean;

BEGIN   (* SearchOrd *)
   Index := 1;
   Stop := False;
   List[Length+1] := Item;
   (* Exit loop when value is found or not there *)
```

```
        WHILE NOT Stop DO          (* Item is not in List[1]..List[Index-1] *)
          IF Item > List[Index]
            THEN                    (* Item is not in List[1]..List[Index] *)
              Index := Index + 1
            ELSE                    (* Item is either found or not there *)
              Stop := True;
          (* Determine whether Item was found or not there *)
          Found := (Index <> Length + 1) AND (Item = List [Index])
        END;     (* SearchOrd *)


      (****************************************************************)

  BEGIN  (* Insert *)
    SearchOrd(List, Item, Length, Index, PlaceFound);
    (* Shift List[Index]..List[Length] down one *)
    FOR Count := Length DOWNTO Index DO
      List[Count+1] := List[Count];
    (* Insert Item *)
    List[Index] := Item;
    (* Increment Length *)
    Length := Length + 1
  END;   (* Insert *)
```

Notice that this procedure will work even if the list is empty. When the list is empty, SearchOrd stores Item in List[1], where it is immediately found. On return from SearchOrd, Index is 1. Since Index is greater than the value of Length (which is 0), the FOR loop is not executed. Item is stored in the first position in List, and Length is set to 1.

This algorithm also works if Item is larger than any component in the list. When this happens, Index is Length + 1 and Item is stored properly.

This algorithm can be used as the basis for another sorting algorithm called an *insertion sort*. Values can be inserted one at a time into a list that was originally empty. An insertion sort is a good sort to use when input data needs to be sorted. Each value can be put into its proper place as it is read.

Binary Search in an Ordered List

There is a second search algorithm on a sorted list that is considerably faster both for finding an item in a list and for determining that an item is not in the list. This algorithm is called a *binary search*.

A binary search is based on the principle of successive approximation. It involves dividing the list in half (dividing by 2—that's why it's called *binary* search) and determining if the item is in the upper or lower half of the list. This is done repeatedly until the item is found or it is determined that the item is not in the list.

This method is analogous to the way we look up words in a dictionary: We compare the word we're looking for with a word on the page that we turn to. As a point of reference, we usually look at the first word on the right-hand page of the dictionary.

Figure 12-6
Binary Search

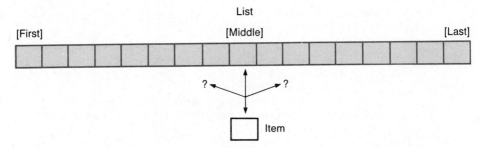

If the word we're looking for comes before this word alphabetically, we continue our search with the left-hand section of the dictionary. Otherwise, we continue with the right-hand section of the dictionary. We do this repeatedly until we find our word. If it is not there, we realize that either we have misspelled the word or our dictionary isn't complete.

The algorithm for a binary search is given below. The list of values is called List, and the value being looked for is called Item. (See Figure 12-6.)

1. Compare Item to List[Middle]. If Item = List[Middle], then we have found it. If Item < List[Middle], then Item is in the first half of the List if it is in the list at all. If Item > List [Middle], then Item is in the second half of the List if it is in the list at all.

2. Redefine List to be that half of List that Item will be in (if it is there) and repeat the process in step 1.

3. Stop when we have found Item or know it isn't there. We know that Item isn't there when there is nowhere else to look and we still have not found it.

This algorithm makes intuitive sense. With each comparison, at best we find the item for which we are searching; at worst we eliminate one half of the remaining List from consideration.

We need to keep track of the index of the first possible place to look (First) and the last possible place to look (Last). This means that at any one time we are looking for our item in List[First]..List[Last]. When this procedure is initialized, First is set to 1 and Last is set to the length of List.

This procedure will need the same five parameters as the two previous search procedures needed: the list, the item, the length of the list, a Boolean flag that tells whether or not the item is in the list (Found), and the index of the position of the item within the list (if it is there).

```
PROCEDURE BinSearch (    List:         (* Array to be searched       *)
                           ListType;
                         Item:         (* Value to be found           *)
                           ItemType;
                         Length:       (* Number of values in array   *)
                           Integer;
                    VAR  Index:        (* Location of value if found  *)
                           Integer;
                    VAR  Found:        (* True if value is found       *)
                           Boolean);
```

```
(* List is searched for an occurrence of Item. If Item is found, Found
   is True and Index gives the location of Item within List. Otherwise,
   Found is False and Index is undefined *)

VAR
  First,          (* Bound on list *)
  Last,           (* Bound on list *)
  Middle:         (* Middle index  *)
    Integer;

BEGIN (* BinSearch *)
  First := 1;
  Last  := Length;
  Found := False;
  WHILE (Last >= First) AND NOT Found DO
    BEGIN
      Middle := (First + Last) DIV 2;
      IF Item < List[Middle]
        (* Item is not in List[Middle]..List[Last] *)
        THEN
          Last := Middle - 1
        ELSE
          IF Item > List[Middle]
            (* Item is not in List[First]..List[Middle] *)
            THEN
              First := Middle + 1
            ELSE
              Found := True
    END;
  Index := Middle
END;   (* BinSearch *)
```

Let's do a code walk-through of this algorithm. (See Figure 12-7, page 464.) The value being searched for is 24. Figure 12-7a shows the values of First, Last, and Middle during the first iteration. In this iteration 24 is compared with 103, the value in List[Middle]. Since 24 is less than 103, Last becomes Middle − 1 and First stays the same. Figure 12-7b shows the situation during the second iteration. This time 24 is compared with 72, the value in List[Middle]. Since 24 is less than 72, Last becomes Middle − 1 and First again stays the same.

In the third iteration (Figure 12-7c), Middle and First are both 1. The value 24 is compared with 12, the value in List[Middle]. Since 24 is greater than 12, First becomes Middle + 1. In the fourth iteration (Figure 12-7d), First, Last, and Middle are all the same. Again 24 is compared with the value in List[Middle]. Since 24 is less than 64, Last becomes Middle − 1. This makes Last less than First, and the process stops. Found is False.

The binary search algorithm is the most complex algorithm that we have examined so far. The table shows First, Last, Middle, and List[Middle] for searches for 106, 400, and 406 respectively, using the same data as in the previous example. Go over the results shown in this table carefully; be sure you thoroughly understand this algorithm.

Figure 12-7
Code Walk-
Through of
Procedure
BinSearch. Item
is 24.

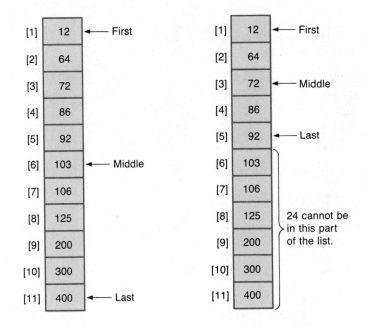

(a) First iteration
24 < 103

(b) Second iteration
24 < 72

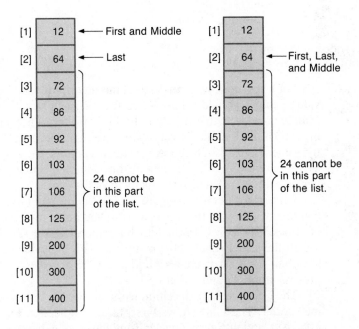

(c) Third iteration
24 > 12

(d) Fourth iteration
24 < 64, Last becomes < First

Item	First	Last	Middle	List[Middle]	Termination of loop
106	1	11	6	103	
	7	11	9	200	
	7	8	7	106	Found = True
400	1	11	6	103	
	7	11	9	200	
	10	11	10	300	
	11	11	11	400	
					Found = True
406	1	11	6	103	
	7	11	9	200	
	10	11	10	300	
	11	11	11	400	
	12	11			Last < First
					Found = False

You will notice that the loop never executed more than four times. It will never execute more than four times in a list of eleven components. This is because the list is being cut in half each time through the loop. The table below compares a sequential search and a binary search in terms of the average number of iterations of the loop needed to find an item in a list.

Length of list	Average number of iterations	
	Sequential search	Binary search
10	5.5	2.9
100	50.5	5.8
1000	500.5	9.0
10,000	5000.5	12.4

If the binary search algorithm is so much faster, why don't we use it all the time? The binary search is certainly faster in terms of the number of times through the loop. But notice that more computations are being done within the loop in a binary search than in the other search algorithms. This means that if the number of components in the list is small (say under 20), the sequential search algorithms are faster, because they do less work at each iteration. As the number of components in the list increases, the binary search algorithm becomes relatively more efficient. Remember, however, that both the sequential search in an ordered list and the binary search require the list to be sorted, and sorting itself takes time.

Keep three factors in mind when you are deciding which search algorithm to use:

1. the length of the list to be searched
2. whether or not the list is already ordered
3. the number of times the list is to be searched

Let's now turn our attention to a special kind of array which is useful when working with alphabetic data.

WORKING WITH WORDS

Some structured data types have an option called the packed option. The choice of this option is indicated by inserting the keyword PACKED before the keyword indicating the structured data type (for example, the word ARRAY). The Packed option tells the computer to put as many components as possible into each place in memory. Since the size of memory cells varies from machine to machine, the amount of memory space saved by packing will vary. However, using the Packed option with an array of characters is useful even if no memory is saved. When we define a packed array of characters, we have what is called a *string* or string variable. Strings are extremely useful in working with alphabetic information.

String A collection of characters that is interpreted as a single data item; a packed character array.

In the declarations

```
CONST
   StringLength = 10;
TYPE
   IndexRange = 1..StringLength
   String = PACKED ARRAY[IndexRange] OF Char;
VAR
   Word1,
   Word2,
   Word3,
   Word4:
      String;
```

Word1, Word2, Word3, and Word4 are string variables. Yes, they are still arrays, and each position in the array can be accessed separately. However, string variables can also be printed as a unit (that is, without using a loop), and two of them can be compared if they are of the same type. We do, however, have to read characters into strings one character at a time.

Since a string variable is an array, its length is fixed by its type definition. We cannot store more characters in a string than its length allows. If the value to be stored is shorter than the length of the string, it may be necessary to use padding blanks (assign the blank character to the unused array components). Given the above declarations, the following are examples of valid and invalid assignment statements.

Statement	Status	Reason
Word1 : = 'Tremendous'	Valid	Exactly 10 characters
Word2 : = 'Big'	Invalid	Less than 10 characters
Word3 : = 'Infinitesimal'	Invalid	More than 10 characters
Word4 : = 'Small '	Valid	Exactly 10 characters (padded with blanks)

Like unpacked arrays, string variables of the same type can be assigned to one another. After the assignment

$$Word1 \; := \; Word4$$

Word1 contains 'Small   '.

The relational operators ($=, <>, <=, >=, <, >$) may be applied to strings of the same type. Strings are ordered according to the collating sequence of the character set. When two strings are compared, the characters of each string are compared one by one from left to right. The first unequal pair of characters determines the order. For example, given that Word1 and Word4 both now contain 'Small   ', the following expressions would return the results indicated:

Statement	Result
Word1 <> Word4	False (They are equal.)
Word4 <= 'Tremendous'	True ('S' comes before 'T'.)
Word1 = 'Tremendous'	False (They are not equal.)
'Big ' < Word1	True ('B' comes before 'S'.)
Word1 = 'SMALL '	False ('M' <> 'm')

The preceding results would be the same with any character set. However, different character sets give different results if uppercase and lowercase letters are intermixed or the words are padded with blanks. Uppercase letters come before lowercase letters in ASCII and after lowercase letters in EBCDIC. Blanks come before all letters in ASCII and EBCDIC but after letters in CDC-Scientific.

Strings (packed arrays of characters) give us the best of both worlds. We can treat them as simple variables when printing or comparing them, yet we can access each component separately if need be. For example, if we want to set Word1 to all blanks, we can assign a constant defined as ten blanks to Word1 or we can set each character to a blank in a loop.

```
CONST
   Blanks = '          ';
   .
   .
   .
   Word1 := Blanks;                (* As a unit *)

   FOR Count := 1 TO 10 DO         (* In a loop *)
      Word1[Count] := ' ';
```

468 _____ *12 Applied Arrays*

The following program, which reads in characters and writes them out again, gives an example of declaring and using strings.

```
PROGRAM ReadWrite (Input, Output);

(* This program reads in 15 characters, stores them in a string, and
   prints the string *)

CONST
    Heading = 'Good Morning,';            (* Define a string constant *)

TYPE
    IndexRange = 1..15;
    String15 = PACKED ARRAY[IndexRange] OF Char; (* Define a string type *)

VAR
    Count:            (* Index into the string      *)
       Integer;
    Character:        (* Holds one character         *)
       Char;
    Message:          (* Declare a string variable *)
       String15;

BEGIN   (* ReadWrite *)
    Writeln(Heading);                                (* String constant *)
    Writeln('Input message with exactly 15 characters.');
    (* Input message *)
    FOR Count := 1 TO 15 DO
      BEGIN
        Read(Character);
        Message[Count] := Character
      END;
    (* Output message *)
    Write(' The message is: ');
    Writeln(Message)                                 (* String variable *)
END.    (* ReadWrite *)
```

NOTE: String variable Message can be printed directly by using the array variable name without subscripts.

Given the input data

        Have a nice day

the output from the program would be

```
Good morning,
Input message with exactly 15 characters.
 The message is: Have a nice day
```

Notice that in the reading loop we read each character into a character variable Character rather than reading directly into Message[Count]. Although standard Pascal does not allow a component of a packed structure to be passed as a variable parameter, we can read directly into one component of a packed array. We chose not to do so for clarity.

T,M,V ⇦ Before we leave the topic of strings, we should caution that some implementations of Pascal have a built-in data type called String. Check Appendix I to see if your Pascal compiler is one of them. If it is, you should read the documentation on strings for your compiler.

Problem Solving in Action

Problem: Rewrite procedure GetMonth from Chapter 10 using an entirely different algorithm. Without changing any of the rest of Program BirthdayReminder, rerun the program.

Discussion: In Chapter 10 we developed Program BirthdayReminder, which took a month entered from the terminal and printed a list of all friends having birthdays that month. The characters in the month were read one at a time until the program recognized which month had been keyed in. Once the month was recognized, the rest of the characters in the name of the month were ignored (that is, not read in).

Now that we know how to use strings, we can read the entire month into a string variable and process the name of the month as a whole word rather than decoding it character by character.

We will have an array of strings that contains the months of the year. The month that is entered at the terminal will be read into a string variable. Procedure Search will be used to search the array for the input string. If it is found, Index will be used to access a parallel array containing the enumerated data type months.

That is, we will convert the months in string form to the equivalent months in the enumerated data type by using parallel arrays, one containing strings and the other containing the enumerated equivalents. If the string is not found, an error message can be issued and the user prompted to reenter the month.

Data Structures:

An array of strings containing the months of the year

An array containing the enumerated data type made up of the months of the year

The two arrays would look like Figure 12.8:

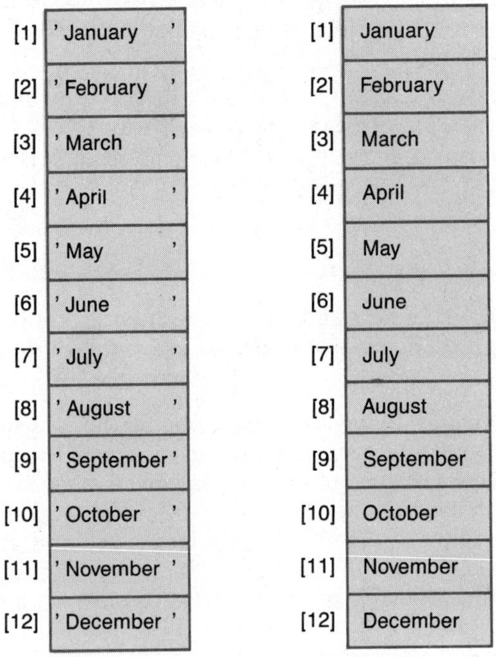

Figure 12-8
Data Structures for
Program GetMonth.

[1]	' January '
[2]	' February '
[3]	' March '
[4]	' April '
[5]	' May '
[6]	' June '
[7]	' July '
[8]	' August '
[9]	' September '
[10]	' October '
[11]	' November '
[12]	' December '

[1]	January
[2]	February
[3]	March
[4]	April
[5]	May
[6]	June
[7]	July
[8]	August
[9]	September
[10]	October
[11]	November
[12]	December

Although these two arrays look the same written on paper, they are quite different in the program. One contains the months in character form; the other contains the months in the form of an enumerated data type.

Let's call the string representation of a month SMonth and the enumerated version Month, as it is called in Program BirthdayReminder. The array of strings can be called SMonthAry and the parallel array MonthAry.

The algorithm for GetMonth using this structure is as follows:

GET MONTH   Level 1

```
REPEAT
  Get SMonth
  Search(SMonthAry, SMonth, 12, Index, Found)
  IF Found
    THEN
      Month ⟵ MonthAry[Index]
    ELSE
      Write error message
UNTIL Found
```

PSIA ▬▬▬▬

GET SMONTH   Level 2

```
SMonth ⟵— all blanks
Count ⟵— 0
WHILE NOT EOLN AND (Count < 9)
    Count ⟵— Count + 1
    Read(Character)
    SMonth[Count] ⟵— Character
```

Now we can code the new procedure GetMonth. We must remember to initialize the arrays SMonthAry and MonthAry.

```
PROCEDURE GetMonth (VAR Month:        (* Returns month in enumerated form *)
                         Months);

(* The user is prompted to enter a month. If the month is valid, the
   corresponding user-defined month is returned. Otherwise the user is
   prompted to try again *)

TYPE
    String9 = PACKED ARRAY[1..9] OF Char;
    MonthsInCharForm = ARRAY[1..12] OF String9;
    MonthsInEnumForm = ARRAY[1..12] OF Months;
    ListType = MonthsInCharForm;
    ItemType = String9;

VAR
    SMonth:                (* Input month in string form            *)
        String9;
    MonthAry:              (* Table of months in enumerated form    *)
        MonthsInEnumForm;
    SMonthAry:             (* Parallel table of months in string format *)
        MonthsInCharForm;

(************************************************************************)

PROCEDURE GetSMonth (VAR SMonth:        (* Input month string *)
                              String9);

(* Reads in a month in character form *)

VAR
    Count:                (* Loop control variable *)
        Integer;
```

PSIA ▰▰▰▰▰▰

```
BEGIN (* GetSMonth *)
  Count : = 0;
  SMonth := '             ';
  Writeln('Please enter month, capitalizing first letter.');
  WHILE NOT EOLN AND (Count < 9) DO
    BEGIN
      Count : = Count + 1;
      Read(SMonth[Count])
    END;
  (* Skip over <eoln> in case the input is in error.
     Otherwise an infinite loop would occur. *)
  Readln
END;   (* GetSMonth *)
```

(***)

```
PROCEDURE Initialize (VAR SMonthAry:               (* Table of strings     *)
                           MonthsInCharForm;
                      VAR MonthAry:                (* Table of enum.values *)
                           MonthsInEnumForm);
  BEGIN (* Initialize *)
    SMonthAry[1]  : = 'January   ';
    SMonthAry[2]  : = 'February  ';
    SMonthAry[3]  : = 'March     ';
    SMonthAry[4]  : = 'April     ';
    SMonthAry[5]  : = 'May       ';
    SMonthAry[6]  : = 'June      ';
    SMonthAry[7]  : = 'July      ';
    SMonthAry[8]  : = 'August    ';
    SMonthAry[9]  : = 'September';
    SMonthAry[10] : = 'October   ';
    SMonthAry[11] : = 'November  ';
    SMonthAry[12] : = 'December  ';
    MonthAry[1]  : = January;
    MonthAry[2]  : = February;
    MonthAry[3]  : = March;
    MonthAry[4]  : = April;
    MonthAry[5]  : = May;
    MonthAry[6]  : = June;
    MonthAry[7]  : = July;
    MonthAry[8]  : = August;
    MonthAry[9]  : = September;
    MonthAry[10] : = October;
    MonthAry[11] : = November;
    MonthAry[12] : = December;
  END;   (* Initialize *)
```

(***)

PSIA

```
BEGIN (* GetMonth *)
  Initialize(SMonthAry, MonthAry);
  REPEAT
    GetSMonth(SMonth);
    Search(SMonthAry, SMonth, 12, Index, Found);
    IF Found
      THEN
        Month := MonthAry[Index]
      ELSE
        Writeln('Month is misspelled.')
  UNTIL Found
END;  (* GetMonth *)
```

Because Program BirthdayReminder is so long, we will not repeat it here. However, we guarantee that this procedure GetMonth was substituted for the one in Chapter 10 and the program was rerun.

Problem Solving in Action

Problem: You are the grader for a U.S. government class. The teacher has asked you to prepare two lists: one of those students who have taken the exam and the other of those students who have missed it. The catch is that he wants the lists before the exam is over.

Since you have a portable personal computer, you decide to write an interactive program that will take each student's name as the student enters the exam room, mark that the student is present on a list of students, and print the lists of absentees and attendees for your teacher.

Discussion: How would you do this by hand? You would stand at the door with a list of the students in the class. As each student came in, you would take his or her name and check it off the list. When all the students had entered, you would go through the names, making a list of those whose names were checked off and a list of those whose names were not checked off.

This by-hand algorithm should do quite nicely as a model for your program. Rather than stand by the door, you will have the computer by the door. As each student enters the room, you will enter his or her last name at the keyboard. Your program will scan the list of students for that student's name and mark that the student is present. When the last student has entered, you can enter a special name, perhaps ENDDATA, that will signal to the program to print the two lists.

How can "mark that the student is present" be simulated? By having an array that will be accessed in parallel with the array of names. The component type of this second array will be the data type made up of the two values Present and Absent. This array will be initialized to Absent; when a name is found in the list of students, the corresponding position in the second array will be set to Present.

PSIA

You will have to prepare in advance the list of students in the class. That should be easy. You already have a roster for the class. The only problem is that the roster is ordered by social security number. If you enter the names directly from the roster, they will not be in alphabetical order. Does that matter?

Yes, in this case it does matter. The size of the class is 200, and you expect the teacher to use the program several times each semester. (He has a portable computer as well.) The size of the list to be searched and the frequency with which the program will be used suggest that a binary search should be used. Remember, a binary search is faster for a list of this size, but it requires that the list be in sorted form. You decide to go ahead and create the file with the names of the students in order by social security number. The first thing the program will do is read in the names of the students from this file and sort them. All of the names can be input at once and sorted using procedure ExSort, or each name can be put into its proper place as it is read using procedure Insert. You decide to take the second approach.

Input:

A list of the students in the class (file Roster)

Each student's name as he or she enters the room (Input)

Output:

A list of those students taking the exam

A list of those students who are absent

Data Structures:

A one-dimensional array of names (Students)

A one-dimensional array of "checks" (Attendance)

A temporary string to read names into (Name)

Figure 12-9 pictures the data structures used in this program.

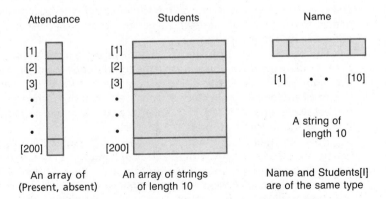

Figure 12-9
Data Structures for
Program Exam

PSIA ▬▬▬▬▬

MAIN   Level 0

```
Get Class Roster
Check in Students
Print List(s)
```

GET CLASS ROSTER   Level 1

```
WHILE more names on roster DO
   Get Name
   Insert Name into list of students
```

CHECK IN STUDENTS

```
WHILE more students DO
   Get Name
   Process Name
```

Level 1 control structures are as follows:

```
'more names on roster'     EOF(Roster)
'more students'            Name <> 'ENDDATA    '
```

The decision to use a signal string to end the data will require that Check In Students be rewritten using a priming Read. Name must have a value on entering the loop. A prompt to the student should also be included. Therefore, Check In Students becomes

CHECK IN STUDENTS

```
Write 'Enter last name'
Get Name
WHILE more students DO
   Process Name
   Write 'Enter last name'
   Get Name
```

PSIA

GET NAME   Level 2

```
Name ⟵ BLANKS
Count ⟵ 0
WHILE NOT EOLN AND Count < 10
    Count ⟵ Count + 1
    Read Character
    Name[Count] ⟵ Character
```

INSERT NAME

For Insert Name you can use procedure Insert, which we wrote earlier.

PROCESS NAME

```
Binary Search Students for Name
IF Found
    THEN
        Attendance[Index] ⟵ Present
    ELSE
        Writeln 'Name not on list.'
```

PRINT   Level 1

```
Writeln 'The following students are
        taking the exam.'
PrintList(Present)
Writeln 'The following students have
        missed the exam.'
PrintList(Absent)
```

PRINTLIST (FLAG)   Level 2

```
FOR Count going from 1 to Length
    IF Attendance[Count] = Flag
        THEN Writeln Students[Count]
```

At this point, you need to go back over the top-down design and test it. Have you forgotten anything? Yes, you will need to initialize the array Attendance to all Absent. Anything else? No. The design is ready to be coded.

PSIA

INITIALIZE ATTENDANCE   Level 1

FOR Count going from 1 to number of students
    Attendance[Count] ⟵ Absent

Module Structure Chart:

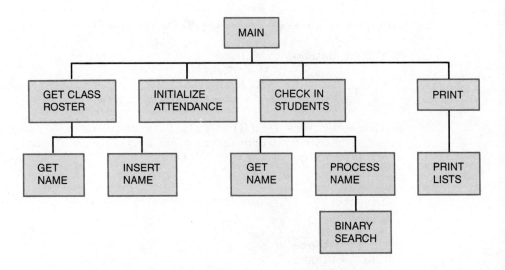

```
PROGRAM Exam (Input, Output, Roster);

(* Program Exam compares students who come to take an exam against
   a class roster.  The list of students who took the exam and the
   list of students who missed the exam are printed *)

CONST
  NumStudents = 200;          (* Maximum number of students *)
  Blanks = '          ';      (* Empty name string          *)
  EndData = 'EndData   ';     (* Sentinel value name        *)
  StringLength = 10;          (* Size of name strings       *)

TYPE
  NameString = PACKED ARRAY[1..StringLength] OF Char;
  AttendanceType = (Absent, Present);
  ItemType = NameString;
  ListType = ARRAY[1..NumStudents] OF ItemType;
  CheckType = ARRAY[1..NumStudents] OF AttendanceType;
```

PSIA ▰▰▰▰

```
VAR
  Students:          (* An array of strings       *)
    ListType;
  Attendance:        (* Array of 'check marks'     *)
    CheckType;
  Length,            (* Number of students there *)
  Count:             (* Loop control variable      *)
    Integer;
  Roster:            (* Input file                 *)
    Text;
```

(***)

```
PROCEDURE GetName (VAR Data:          (* Input file                *)
                        Text;
                   VAR Name:          (* Returns one name from file *)
                        NameString);
```

(* Characters are read from file Data and stored in Name until either
   EOLN(Data) or 10 characters have been read. Assumption: Names
   will be unique within 10 letters. *)

```
VAR
  Character:        (* Temporary character *)
    Char;

BEGIN (* GetName *)
  Name := Blanks;
  Count := 0;
  (* Read characters until EOLN or 10 characters read *)
  WHILE NOT EOLN(Data) AND (Count < 10) DO
    BEGIN
      Count := Count + 1;
      Read(Data, Character);
      Name[Count] := Character
    END;
  Readln(Data)
END;   (* GetName *)
```

(***)

```
PROCEDURE Insert (VAR List:          (* List to be changed          *)
                       ListType;
                  VAR Length:        (* Number of elements in List *)
                       Integer;
                  Item:              (* Item to be inserted         *)
                       ItemType);
```

(* Item is inserted into its proper place in the sorted list List.
   Assumption: Length is less than MaxLength. If a match occurs,
   Item will be inserted before the one that is there. *)

```
                PSIA
        VAR
          PlaceFound:
            Boolean;
          Index,              (* Current position in List *)
          Count:              (* Loop control variable    *)
            Integer;


        (***********************************************************************)


        PROCEDURE SearchOrd (     List:          (* List to be searched        *)
                                    ListType;
                                  Item:          (* Item to be found            *)
                                    ItemType;
                                  Length:        (* Number of elements in List *)
                                    Integer;
                              VAR Index:         (* Location of Item if found   *)
                                    Integer;
                              VAR Found:         (* True if Item is found       *)
                                    Boolean);

        (* List is searched for an occurrence of Item.  If Item is found,
           Found is True and Index is the place in List where Item occurs.
           Otherwise, Found is False and Index is where Item belongs.
           Assumption:  List is sorted in ascending order. *)

        VAR
          Stop:               (* True at end of search *)
            Boolean;

        BEGIN (* SearchOrd *)
          Index := 1;
          Stop := False;
          List[Length+1] := Item;
          (* Exit loop when value is found or not there *)
          WHILE NOT Stop DO
            (* Item is not in List[1]..List[Index-1] *)
            IF Item > List[Index]
              (* Item is not in List[1]..List[Index] *)
              THEN
                Index := Index + 1
              ELSE
                (* Item is either found or not there *)
                Stop := True;
          (* Determine whether Item was found or not there *)
          Found := (Index <> Length + 1)
        END;   (* SearchOrd *)


        (***********************************************************************)
```

PSIA ▬▬▬▬

```
BEGIN  (* Insert *)
  SearchOrd(List, Item, Length, Index, PlaceFound);
  (* Shift List[Index]..List[Length] down one *)
  FOR Count := Length DOWNTO Index DO
    List[Count+1] := List[Count];
  (* Insert Item *)
  List[Index] := Item;
  (* Increment Length *)
  Length := Length + 1
END;   (* Insert *)


(*****************************************************************************)

PROCEDURE BinSearch (     List:            (* Array to be searched         *)
                            ListType;
                          Item:            (* Item to be found             *)
                            ItemType;
                          Length:          (* Number of elements in List *)
                            Integer;
                      VAR Index:           (* Location of Item if found    *)
                            Integer;
                      VAR Found:           (* True if Item is found        *)
                            Boolean);

(* List is searched for an occurrence of Item.  If Item is found, Found
   is True and Index gives the location of Item within List.
   Otherwise, Found is False and Index is undefined. *)

VAR
  First,          (* Bound on list *)
  Last,           (* Bound on list *)
  Middle:         (* Middle index  *)
    Integer;

BEGIN (* BinSearch *)
  First := 1;
  Last := Length;
  Found := False;
  WHILE (Last >= First) AND NOT Found DO
    BEGIN
      Middle := (First + Last) DIV 2;
      IF Item < List[Middle]
        (* Item is not in List[Middle]..List[Last] *)
        THEN
          Last := Middle - 1
        ELSE
          IF Item > List[Middle]
            (* Item is not in List[First]..List[Middle] *)
```

PSIA ▰▰▰▰▰▰▰▰

```
                THEN
                   First := Middle + 1
                ELSE
                   Found := True
         END;
       Index := Middle
   END;   (* BinSearch *)


(*******************************************************************)

PROCEDURE ProcessName (     Students:      (* List of students       *)
                              ListType;
                            Length:        (* Number of elements in List *)
                              Integer;
                            Name:          (* Input student name      *)
                              NameString;
                        VAR Attendance:    (* List of check marks     *)
                              CheckType);
```

(* If Name is in Students, then corresponding position in Attendance is
   set to Present. Otherwise, error message is printed. Procedure
   BinSearch is called to do the search. Procedure accesses global
   constant EndData. *)

```
VAR
  Index:       (* Location of student name if found *)
    Integer;
  Found:       (* True if student is on roster     *)
    Boolean;

BEGIN (* ProcessName *)
  IF Name <> EndData
    THEN
      BEGIN
        BinSearch(Students, Name, Length, Index, Found);
        IF Found
          THEN
            Attendance[Index] := Present
          ELSE
            Writeln('Name not on list.')
      END
END;   (* ProcessName *)


(*******************************************************************)
```

PSIA ▰▰▰▰▰▰

```
PROCEDURE Print (Students:        (* List of students        *)
                    ListType;
                 Attendance:       (* List of check marks      *)
                    CheckType;
                 Length:           (* Number of elements in lists *)
                    Integer);
```

(* The names of those taking the exam are printed. The names of those
   absent are printed. *)

```
VAR
  Flag:                    (* Controls which list to print *)
    AttendanceType;
```

(***)

```
PROCEDURE PrintList (Flag:                   (* Type of list to print *)
                       AttendanceType);
```

(* If Flag is Absent the students who are absent are printed.
   If Flag is Present the students who are present are printed. *)

```
VAR
  Count:          (* Loop control variable *)
    Integer;

BEGIN (* PrintList *)
  FOR Count := 1 TO Length DO
    IF Attendance[Count] = Flag
      THEN
        Writeln(Students[Count])
END;  (* PrintList *)
```

(***)

```
BEGIN (* Print *)
  Writeln('The following students are taking the exam.');
  PrintList(Present);
  Writeln('The following students have missed the exam.');
  PrintList(Absent)
END;  (* Print *)
```

(***)

```
PROCEDURE InitializeAttendance (VAR Attendance: (* List of check marks *)
                                  CheckType);
```

(* The array which records attendance is initialized to Absent. *)

PSIA ▰▰▰▰▰▰▰

```pascal
VAR
  Count:            (* Loop control variable *)
    Integer;

BEGIN (* InitializeAttendance *)
  FOR Count := 1 TO NumStudents DO
    Attendance[Count] := Absent
END;   (* InitializeAttendance *)

(*****************************************************************************)

PROCEDURE CheckInStudents (    Students:        (* List of students    *)
                               ListType;
                               Length:          (* Number of elements   *)
                               Integer;
                           VAR Attendance:      (* List of check marks  *)
                               CheckType);

(* Student names are entered at the keyboard and passed to
   procedure ProcessName *)

VAR
  Name:               (* Name of student checking in *)
    NameString;

BEGIN (* CheckInStudents *)
  Write('Enter last name ');
  GetName(Input, Name);
  Writeln;
  WHILE Name <> EndData DO
    BEGIN
      ProcessName(Students, Length, Name, Attendance);
      Write('Enter last name ');
      GetName(Input, Name);
      Writeln
    END
END;   (* CheckInStudents *)

(*****************************************************************************)

PROCEDURE GetClassRoster (VAR Students:    (* List of students    *)
                              ListType;
                          VAR Length:       (* Number of elements *)
                              Integer;
                          VAR Roster:       (* Roster data file   *)
                              Text);

(* The class roster is read from file Roster. *)
```

PSIA ▰▰▰▰▰▰

```
VAR
  Name:                    (* An input student name *)
    NameString;

BEGIN (* GetClassRoster *)
  (* Input names of students in the class *)
  WHILE NOT EOF(Roster) DO
    BEGIN
      GetName(Roster, Name);
      Insert(Students, Length, Name)
    END
END;   (* GetClassRoster *)

(****************************************************************************)

BEGIN (* Exam *)
  Reset(Roster);
  Length := 0;
  InitializeAttendance(Attendance);
  GetClassRoster(Students, Length, Roster);
  CheckInStudents(Students, Length, Attendance);
  Print(Students, Attendance, Length)
END.  (* Exam *)
```

Testing: The program must be tested with names that are more than 10 characters, exactly 10 characters, and less than 10 characters. Names from the terminal must be spelled incorrectly as well as correctly. The following test data was used.

On roster:

```
Dale
MacDonald
Weems
Vitek
Westby
Smith
Jamison
Jones
Kirshen
NameLongerThanTenCharacters
Gleason
Thompson
Ripley
Lilly
```

PSIA

Copy of the screen during the run:

```
Enter last name  Weems
Enter last name  Dale
Enter last name  McDonald
Name not on list.
Enter last name  MacDonald
Enter last name  Vitek
Enter last name  Jamison
Enter last name  Westby
Enter last name  NameLongerThanTenCharacters
Enter last name  Gleason
Enter last name  EndData
The following students are taking the exam.
Dale
Gleason
Jamison
NameLonger
MacDonald
Vitek
Weems
Westby
The following students have missed the exam.
Jones
Kirshen
Lilly
Ripley
Smith
Thompson
```

By assuming that all students have a unique last name, we have simplified the problem considerably. Programming problem 2 is a similar problem where you must account for both first and last names.

TESTING AND DEBUGGING

In this chapter we have discussed and coded six general-purpose procedures: three sequential searches, a binary search, an exchange sort, and an insertion into an ordered list (which can also be used as a sort). We have used three of these procedures in programs that have been tested. We need to test the other three procedures.

A procedure can be desk checked in isolation. In order to test the actual code by running it, we must embed the procedure in a driver program. This program should read in data, call the procedure, and print out the results. Following is the algorithm for a driver to test procedure Search:

```
Get List of components
WHILE more items
  Get Item
  Search(List, Item, Length, Index, Found)
  IF Found
    THEN
      Print Item, ' found at index position ', Index
    ELSE
      Print Item, ' not found in list'
```

The driver would have to be run with several sets of test data in order to thoroughly test procedure Search. The minimum set of lists of components would be

1. A list of no components
2. A list of one component
3. A list of MaxLength components
4. A list of more than one but less than MaxLength

The minimum set of items being searched for would be

1. Item in List[1]
2. Item in List[Length]
3. Item between List[1] and List[Length]
4. Item < List[1]
5. Item > List[Length]
6. Item between List[1] and List[Length] but not there

Since ItemType can be any data type that the relational operators can be applied to, procedure Search should be tested with components of several different types.

We will leave the coding of this driver program and the creating of the test data as an exercise. (See Programming Problem 5.) Procedures Search2 and ExSort should be tested in like manner.

At the beginning of this section we said that three of the procedures had been tested in programs. However, in order to make sure that they stand up as general-purpose procedures, they should be subjected to the same rigorous testing that we have proposed for Search, Search2, and ExSort.

In two of the search procedures (Search2 and SearchOrd), we stored the value being searched for in List[Length+1]. Written into the documentation was the assumption that Length would be less than MaxLength (the number of places in the array). This leaves the calling module with the responsibility for checking that Length is not equal to MaxLength.

Another way to approach this possible error condition would be to add an error flag to the formal parameter list of these two procedures and have the procedures themselves check to make sure Length is not equal to MaxLength. If Length were found to be equal to MaxLength, the error flag would be set to True and the search terminated.

Either way of handling the problem is acceptable. The important point is that it must be clearly stated whether the calling routine or the procedure is to check for the error condition. If the assumption listed in the procedure documentation is that the condition will not occur, then the calling module must make sure that the procedure is not called with Length equal to MaxLength. The assumption is a form of contract between the procedure and the calling module. Such an assumption is called a *precondition* of the procedure.

Testing and Debugging Hints

1. Review the Testing and Debugging Hints for Chapter 11. They apply to all one-dimensional arrays, including strings.

2. Only strings of the same type can be compared.

3. Don't attempt to store more characters than there are components in a packed array.

4. Passing components of a packed structure as VAR parameters is not allowed.

5. General-purpose procedures and functions should be tested outside the context of a particular program, using a driver.

6. Test data should be chosen carefully to test all end conditions and some in the middle. End conditions are those that reach the limits of the structure used to store them. For example, in a one-dimensional array there should be test data items in which the number of components is 0, 1, and MaxLength (MaxLength $-$ 1 in the case of Search2), as well as between 1 and MaxLength.

SUMMARY

This chapter has provided practice in working with one-dimensional arrays. Algorithms that search and sort data stored in an array have been examined, and procedures have been written to implement these algorithms. These procedures can be used again and again in different contexts because they have been written in a general fashion.

The components in the array are of type ItemType. ItemType can be defined to be any ordinal data type or a packed array of characters.

Pascal has an option called the packed option that can be applied to data structures such as arrays. PACKED ARRAYS of Char, called strings, can be printed directly and compared. Strings are very useful in working with alphabetic data. Since strings can be compared, our general-purpose procedures can be used with arrays of strings.

QUICK CHECK _____

1. In a search of an unordered array of 1000 values, what will be the average number of loop iterations required to find a value? What is the maximum number of iterations that may be required to find a value? (pp. 450–453)

2. The following program fragment sorts a list into descending order. Change it to sort in ascending order. (pp. 453–456)

```
FOR PassCount := 1 TO Length - 1 DO
  BEGIN
    MinIndex := PassCount;
    FOR PlaceCount := PassCount + 1 TO Length DO
      IF List[PlaceCount] < List[MinIndex]
        THEN
          MinIndex := PlaceCount;
    Temp := List[MinIndex];                    (* Swap *)
    List[MinIndex] := List[PassCount];
    List[PassCount] := Temp
  END
```

3. Describe how the list insertion operation could be used to build a sorted list from unordered input data. (pp. 458–461)

4. Describe the basic principle behind the binary search algorithm. (pp. 461–465)

5. Define an array data type that will hold a string of 15 characters. Define an array variable of this type, and write an assignment statement that initializes the variable to all blanks. (pp. 466–467)

Answers
1. The average number is 500 iterations. The maximum is 1000 iterations. 2. The only required change is to replace the $<$ symbol in the inner loop with a $>$. As a matter of good style, however, the name MinIndex should be changed to MaxIndex. 3. The list is initialized with a length of 0. Each time a data value is read, the insert operation is called to add the value to the list in its correct position. When all of the data has been read, it will be stored in order in the array. 4. The binary search takes advantage of the fact that an array is sorted by looking at an element in the middle of the array and deciding whether the sought-after element precedes or follows the midpoint. The search is then repeated on the appropriate half, quarter, eighth, and so on of the array until the element is located.
5. TYPE
```
    Index15 = 1..15;
      String15 = PACKED ARRAY[Index15] OF Char;

  VAR
    Name:
      String15;

  Name := '               ';   (* 15 blanks *)
```

EXAM PREPARATION EXERCISES _____

1. Design an appropriate data structure for each of the following problems.
   (a) A record store sells classical records (A), jazz records (B), rock records (C), and other records (D). Sales receipts are kept in the following format.

   > Code (1 character, either A, B, C, or D)
   >
   > Amount (amount of sale)

   The owner of the store wants to total the amount of sales for each record category.
   (b) A payroll master file is made up of the following data:

   > IDNumber (five-digit number)
   >
   > Rate (hourly rate of pay)
   >
   > Dependents (number of dependents)

   (c) A transaction file is made up each month of the following data:

   > IDNumber (five-digit number)
   >
   > Hours (number of hours worked)

   The payroll file is ordered; the transaction file is not. Payroll checks are to be issued.

2. Sketch an algorithm for processing the data structures in exercises 1(a) and 1(b). Your answer should read like the Discussion section of Problem Solving in Action. You are not being asked for a top-down design.

3. Given the declarations

   ```
   CONST
     NameLength = 20;
     WordLength = 10;

   TYPE
     NameIndex = 1..NameLength;
     WordIndex = 1..WordLength;
     NameType = PACKED ARRAY[NameIndex] OF Char;
     WordType = PACKED ARRAY[WordIndex] OF Char;

   VAR
     FirstName,
     LastName:
       NameType;
     Word:
       WordType;
     Flag:
       Boolean;
   ```

   Mark the following statements valid or invalid.

Statement	Valid	Invalid

(a) FOR I := 1 TO NameLength DO   _____   _____
    Write(FirstName[I])

(b) Write(LastName)   _____   _____

(c) IF FirstName = LastName   _____   _____
    THEN
        Flag := True

(d) FOR I := 1 TO WordLength DO   _____   _____
    Read(Word[I])

(e) Read(Word)   _____   _____

(f) IF Word = FirstName   _____   _____
    THEN
        Flag := False

(g) IF FirstName[1] = Word[1]   _____   _____
    THEN
        Flag := True

4. (a) Define a data type NameType to be a string of NameLength.
   (b) Define a data type PersonType to be an array of PeopleLength of NameType.
   (c) Declare an array variable People to be of type PersonType.

5. (a) Define a data type CarType to be an enumerated type made up of the names of cars.
   (b) Define a data type Inventory to be an array of MaxNumber of CarType.
   (c) Declare an array variable Cars of type Inventory.

6. Given the declarations

```
CONST
    NameLength = 20;
    NumberOfBooks = 200;
    TitleLength = 30;

TYPE
    TitleIndex = 1..TitleLength;
    NameIndex = 1..NameLength;
    BooksOutIndex = 1..NumberOfBooks;
    BookName = PACKED ARRAY[TitleIndex] OF Char;
    PersonName = PACKED ARRAY[NameIndex] OF Char;
    BookType = ARRAY[BooksOutIndex] OF BookName;
    PersonType = ARRAY[BooksOutIndex] OF PersonName;

VAR
    Books:
        BookType;
    Borrower:
        PersonType;
    BookIn:
        BookName;
    Name:
        PersonName;
```

Mark the following statements valid or invalid.

Statement	Valid	Invalid
(a) `Write(BookIn)`	_____	_____
(b) `Read(BookIn)`	_____	_____
(c) `FOR I := 1 TO NameLength DO` `Write(BookIn)`	_____	_____
(d) `FOR I := 1 TO NumberOfBooks DO` `Writeln(Books[I])`	_____	_____

(e) `FOR I := 1 TO NumberOfBooks DO`
    `IF BookIn = Books[I]`
        `THEN`
            `Writeln(BookIn, Borrower[I])`
	_____	_____

(f) `IF BookIn = Name`
    `THEN`
        `Writeln('Error')`
	_____	_____

7. Write code fragments to do the following tasks, using the declarations given in exercise 6. Assume that the books listed in Books have been borrowed by the person listed in the corresponding position of Borrower.
   (a) Write a code fragment to print each book borrowed by Name.
   (b) Write a code fragment to count the number of books borrowed by Name.
   (c) Write a code fragment to count the number of copies of BookIn that have been borrowed.
   (d) Write a code fragment to count the number of copies of BookIn that have been borrowed by Name.

PREPROGRAMMING EXERCISES _____

1. Write a Pascal function Index that searches an Integer array List for an Integer value Item and returns the place in the array where Item is found. There are Length values in List. If Item is not in the array, Index should be set to 0.

2. Write a Pascal procedure that takes as input two Integer arrays (A and B) of length Length. This procedure should return as output the product of those components of B for which the corresponding components of A are negative.

3. Write a Pascal function Found that searches a Real array List for a Real value greater than the value of Item. If such a value is found, the function returns True; otherwise, it returns False. The number of components in List is passed as a parameter.

4. Rewrite SearchOrd to give it an additional formal parameter OverFlow. If Length is equal to MaxLength, OverFlow is True, an appropriate error message is printed, and the search is not made. Otherwise, OverFlow is False. MaxLength may be accessed globally. Change the documentation to reflect this change.

5. Write a Pascal procedure that searches a list List of length Length for Item. If Item is found, it is deleted and the list is compacted (that is, all the components below Item are moved up one place). Length is adjusted appropriately. Item is of type ItemType.

6. Write a Pascal procedure that removes all occurrences of Item in a list List of length Length. Adjust Length appropriately. Item is of type ItemType.

7. Write a Pascal procedure that initializes the Boolean array Present to False. MaxLength, the number of components in the array, may be accessed globally.

8. Write a Pascal procedure that takes two parallel arrays, Present (Boolean) and Score (Real), as parameters. This procedure should store a zero in each position of Score for which True is in the parallel position of Present. Pass Length as a parameter.

9. Write a Pascal function that returns the sum of the product of parallel components in two integer arrays Data and Weight. Pass Length as a parameter.

10. Modify procedure BinSearch so that Index is where Item should be inserted when Found is False.

11. Modify procedure Insert so that it uses procedure BinSearch rather than procedure Search-Ord to find the insertion point.

PROGRAMMING PROBLEMS _____

1. A company wants to know the percentages of total sales and total expenses attributable to each salesperson. Each salesperson has a data line or card giving the salesperson's last name (maximum of 20 characters), followed by a comma, followed by the salesperson's first name (maximum of 10 characters). The next line or card contains the salesperson's total sales (Integer) and expenses (Real).

   Write a program that produces a report with a header line containing the total sales and total expenses. Following this header line should be a table with each salesperson's first name, last name, percentage of total sales, and percentage of total expenses.

2. Only authorized shareholders are allowed to attend a stockholders' meeting. Write a program to read a person's name from the terminal, check it against a list of shareholders, and print a message saying whether or not the person may attend the meeting.

   The list of shareholders is on file Data in the following format: first name (maximum 10 characters), blank, last name (maximum 20 characters). Use EOF to stop reading the file. The maximum number of shareholders is 1000.

   The user should be prompted to enter his or her name in the same format as is used for the data on the file. If the name does not appear on the list, the program should repeat the instructions on how to enter the name and then tell the user to try again. A message saying that the person may not enter should be printed only after he or she has been given a second chance to enter the name.

   The prompt to the user should include the message that a Q should be entered to end the program.

3. Enhance the program in problem 2 as follows:

   1. Print a report showing how many stockholders there were at the time of the meeting, how many were present at the meeting, and how many people who tried to enter were denied permission to attend.

   2. Follow this summary report with a list of the names of the stockholders, with either 'Present' or 'Absent' after each name.

4. The local bank in Programming Problem 3, Chapter 11, was so successful with its advertising campaign that the parent bank decided to collect data on waiting times from banks all over the state and run a contest. However, this time they decided to assign frustration levels to wait times as follows:

Wait time	Frustration level
Wait $< =$ (mean $-$ standard deviation)	'Amazed'
(Mean $-$ standard deviation) $<$ Wait $<$ Mean	'Pleased'
Mean $< =$ Wait $<$ (mean $+$ standard deviation)	'Calm'
(Mean $+$ standard deviation) $< =$ Wait $<$ (Mean $+$ 2 $*$ standard deviation)	'Irritated'
(Mean $+$ 2 $*$ standard deviation) $< =$ Wait	'Berserk'

where Mean is the mean waiting time and Wait is the wait time. Calculate frustration levels for each recorded wait.

Input: Same as in Programming Problem 3, Chapter 11, except that two digits have been added to the teller ID number to indicate at which bank the teller is located.

Output: Same as for problem 3, Chapter 11, plus

1. A bar graph (histogram) showing frustration level distribution.
2. A table sorted by three-digit ID number showing (a) ID number, (b) wait time, and (c) frustration level.

5. Complete the driver program described in the Testing and Debugging Section. Use it to thoroughly test procedures Search, Search2, and ExSort. Choose your test data carefully, making sure that all cases are tested.

- To be able to define a two-dimensional array data type.
- To be able to access a component of a two-dimensional array variable.
- To be able to initialize a two-dimensional array.
- To be able to sum the rows of a two-dimensional array.
- To be able to sum the columns of a two-dimensional array.
- To be able to print the values in a two-dimensional array.
- To be able to define a two-dimensional array data type using the array-of-arrays form of definition.
- To be able to define a multidimensional array data type.
- To be able to process a multidimensional array variable.
- To be able to choose an appropriate array data structure for a given problem.

13

Multidimensional Arrays

The basic elements of programming include the following:

1. Problem solving and algorithm design (top-down design methodology)
2. Statement structures (sequence, selection, iteration, procedure)
3. Data structures
4. A programming language with which to test the algorithms (Pascal).

We have demonstrated that there is much more to programming than merely knowing the syntax and semantics of a programming language. In addition to understanding design methodology and ways to structure statements and programs, it is important to understand the way data is structured.

Data structures play an important role in the design process. The data structure chosen directly affects the design, since it determines the algorithms used to process the data. The data structure we have been discussing in the two previous chapters is the one-dimensional array. The ability to reference a group of data objects by one name simplifies the design of many algorithms.

In many problems, however, the relationship represented in data is more complex than a simple list of items. In this chapter we will examine a data structure called a *two-dimensional array,* which can be used to represent data that lends itself to presentation in table form.

Two-dimensional arrays are useful for representing games like chess, tic-tac-toe, or Scrabble. Several of the programming exercises involve writing procedures to simulate moves in a game. They are also useful in graphics, where the screen is thought of as a two-dimensional array.

The concept of a two-dimensional array (a table) will then be extended to that of a structure called a multidimensional array (which cannot easily be visualized).

TWO-DIMENSIONAL ARRAYS

Just as a one-dimensional array is the data structure used to represent a list, a two-dimensional array is a data structure used to represent a table with rows and columns, provided each item in the table is of the same data type.

A component in a two-dimensional array is accessed by giving what corresponds to the row and column numbers of the item in a table. This is actually a familiar task. Think of a street map as a table. If you want to find a street on a map, you first look up the street name on the back of the map to find the coordinates of the street. The coordinates are usually a letter and a number. The letter tells you what row to look on, and the number tells you what column to look under. You will find the street you are looking for where the row and column meet.

Two-Dimensional Array A collection of components, all of the same type, structured in two dimensions. Each component is accessed by a pair of indices which represent the component's position within each dimension.

Figure 13-1 shows a two-dimensional array that has 100 rows and 9 columns. The rows are accessed by an integer ranging from 1 to 100; the columns are accessed by an uppercase letter ranging from A to I. Each individual component is accessed by a row-column pair, with the row a number in the range 1..100 and the column a letter in the range A..I.

A two-dimensional array is defined in exactly the same way as a one-dimensional array, except that two index types must be described rather than only one. The two index types are listed within brackets, with a comma between them. The syntax diagram for the relevant portion of the TYPE section is shown below, along with an example.

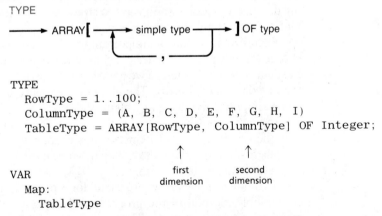

```
TYPE
    RowType = 1..100;
    ColumnType = (A, B, C, D, E, F, G, H, I)
    TableType = ARRAY[RowType, ColumnType] OF Integer;
                                ↑              ↑
                              first         second
VAR                         dimension      dimension
    Map:
        TableType
```

To access a component in a two-dimensional array we have to use expressions that state where the component lies on each dimension. There are two ways to list these expressions. One way is to put each expression in brackets beside the name of

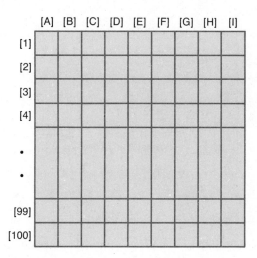

Figure 13-1
A Two-Dimensional Array

the array variable (Map[1][A]). The other way is to list the two expressions in one pair of brackets, with a comma between them (Map[1, A]). The syntax diagram for these two methods is shown below, with an example of each.

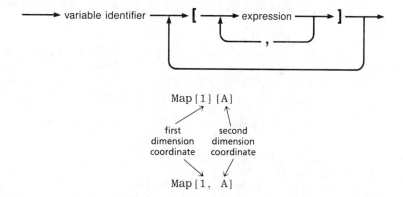

The second form (Map[1, A]), called the abbreviated form, is more commonly used.

Let's look now at some examples.

```
TYPE
   Weeks = 1..52;
   Days  = 1..7;
   YearType = ARRAY[Weeks, Days] OF Integer;

VAR
   Year:
      YearType;
```

Figure 13-2
Array Variable Year

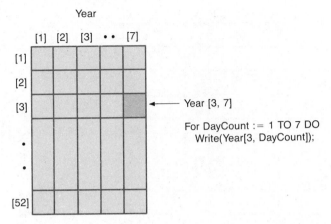

YearType is a two-dimensional array with 364 components. We can think of it as a table with 52 rows and 7 columns. The contents of each place in the table (each component) can be any Integer value. Year is an array variable of type YearType. Year[3, 7] would refer to the Integer value in the third row and the seventh column.

If the data represented high temperatures for each day in a year, Year[3, 7] would be the temperature for the seventh day of the third week. The code fragment shown in Figure 13-2 would print the temperature values for the third week.

Another representation of the same data might be as follows:

```
TYPE
    Days = (Monday, Tuesday, Wednesday, Thursday,
            Friday, Saturday, Sunday);
    Weeks = 1..52;
    YearType = ARRAY[Weeks, Days] OF Integer;

VAR
    Year:
        YearType;
```

Here, Year would have the same number of rows and columns, but the second component would be accessed differently. The second dimension would be accessed by an expression of type Days. Year[3, Sunday] would correspond to the same component as Year[3, 7] in the first example. If DayCount were of type Days and WeekCount of type Integer, the code fragment shown in Figure 13-3 would set the entire array to 0.

Shown below is a code fragment that defines a third two-dimensional array structure that has the same number of rows and columns as the previous ones but different index types and component types.

```
TYPE
    NumberRange = -2..49;
    LetterRange = 'a'..'g';
    DataType = ARRAY[NumberRange, LetterRange] OF Char;
```

Figure 13-3
Array Variable Year
(alternate form)

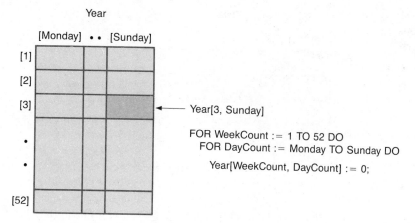

FOR WeekCount := 1 TO 52 DO
  FOR DayCount := Monday TO Sunday DO
    Year[WeekCount, DayCount] := 0;

Figure 13-4
Array Variable
Data

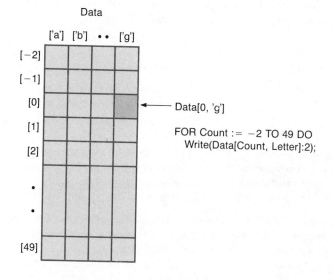

FOR Count := −2 TO 49 DO
  Write(Data[Count, Letter]:2);

```
VAR
  Data:
    DataType;
```

In this case, the accessing expression for the row would have to be in the subrange −2..49, and the accessing expression for the column would have to be in the subrange 'a'..'g'. Each component can be any character in the character set of the machine. The code fragment shown in Figure 13-4 would print the column whose index is Letter.

If the index types were listed in reverse order, the rows and columns would be reversed. That is, if

```
DataType = ARRAY[LetterRange, NumberRange] OF Char;
```

Figure 13-5
Array Variable
Data (second
definition)

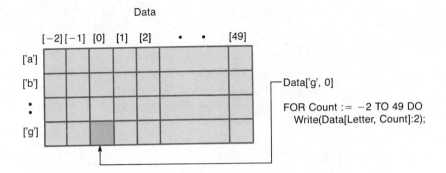

Data

[−2] [−1] [0] [1] [2] • • [49]

['a']

['b']

⋮

['g']

┌─Data['g', 0]

FOR Count := −2 TO 49 DO
  Write(Data[Letter, Count]:2);

then the array Data of type DataType would look as shown in Figure 13-5. The code fragment would print the row whose index is Letter.

To visualize a two-dimensional array, we will let the first dimension define the rows and the second dimension define the columns.

Problem Solving in Action

Problem: There has just been a hotly contested city council election. Let's do an analysis of the votes for the four candidates by precinct. We would like to know how many votes each candidate received in each precinct, how many total votes each candidate received, and how many total votes were cast in each precinct.

Discussion: The data is available in the form of a pair of numbers for each vote. The first number is the precinct number; the second number is the place on the ballot of the candidate for whom the vote was cast.

If we were doing the analysis by hand, our first task would be to go through the data, counting how many people in each precinct voted for each candidate. We would probably create a table with precincts down the side and candidates across the top. Each vote would be recorded as a hash mark in the appropriate column and row (Figure 13-6).

Figure 13-6

Precinct	Smith	Jones	Adams	Smiley
1	~~////~~ //	//	~~////~~ ~~////~~ //	~~////~~
2	~~////~~ ~~////~~ //	//	~~////~~	///
3	//	~~////~~ ///	~~////~~ ~~////~~ ~~////~~	///
4	~~////~~	~~////~~ ///	~~////~~ ~~////~~	//

PSIA

When all of the votes had been recorded, a sum of each column would tell us how many votes each candidate received. A sum of each row would tell us how many people voted in each precinct.

As is so often the case, this by-hand algorithm can be used directly in our program. A two-dimensional array can be created where each component will be a counter for the number of votes for that candidate in that precinct. That is, the array indexed by [2, 1] would be the counter for the votes for Smith in precinct 2.

Input:

Precinct number, ballot position of candidate (available on file Vote, one vote per line)

Candidate names, entered from the terminal (to be used for printing the output)

Output:

A table showing how many votes each candidate received in each precinct

The total number of votes for each candidate

The total number of votes in each precinct

Data Structures:

A two-dimensional array Votes, where the rows represent precincts and the columns represent candidates

A one-dimensional array of strings containing the names of the candidates (to be used for printing) (Figure 13-7)

Figure 13-7

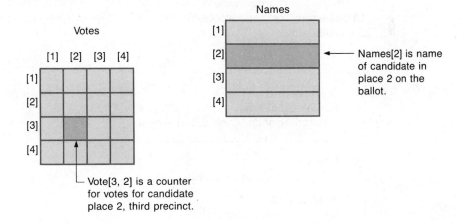

Vote[3, 2] is a counter for votes for candidate place 2, third precinct.

Names[2] is name of candidate in place 2 on the ballot.

PSIA ▬▬▬▬▬

MAIN MODULE   Level 0

```
Get Candidate Names
Set Votes to Zero
WHILE more votes
   Read Precinct, Candidate
   Votes[Precinct, Candidate] ◀—— Votes[Precinct, Candidate] + 1
Print Table (of votes)
Print Totals per Candidate
Print Totals per Precinct
```

GET CANDIDATE NAMES   Level 1

```
Writeln 'Enter the names of the candidates,
        one name per line, in the order in which
        they appear on the ballot.'
FOR Count going from 1 to the number of candidates
   Get a Name
   Candidates[Count] ◀—— Name
```

Note that each candidate's name is being stored in the slot in the array that corresponds to his or her position on the ballot. This will be very useful when the totals are being printed. That is, the index has semantic content. It represents the candidate's place on the ballot.

In the last chapter there was a procedure GetName which read in a string of up to 10 characters from the console. We can use a similar procedure to read in the names of the candidates.

SET VOTES TO ZERO

```
FOR all precincts
   FOR all candidates
      Votes[Precincts, Candidates] ◀—— 0
```

PRINT TABLE

```
FOR all candidates
   Write Names[Candidates]:12
FOR all precincts
   FOR all candidates
      Write Votes[Precincts, Candidates]:12
   Writeln
```

PSIA

PRINT TOTALS PER CANDIDATE

```
(* Calculate column sums *)
FOR all candidates
    Total ⟵ 0
    FOR all precincts
        Total ⟵ Total + Votes[Precincts, Candidates]
    Writeln 'Total votes for ', Names[Candidates:12], Total:3
```

PRINT TOTALS PER PRECINCT

```
(* Calculate row sums *)
FOR all precincts
    Total ⟵ 0
    FOR all candidates
        Total ⟵ Total + Votes[Precincts, Candidates]
    Writeln 'Total votes for precinct', Precincts:3, ':', Total:3
```

The program for this algorithm follows.

```
PROGRAM Election (Input, Output, Report, Vote);

(* Votes represented by precinct number and ballot position are read
   from file Vote and tallied.  Sums per precinct and per candidate
   are calculated.  All totals are printed *)

CONST
  NumberOfPrecincts = 4;
  NumberOfCandidates = 4;

TYPE
  PrecinctRange = 1..NumberOfPrecincts;
  CandidateRange = 1..NumberOfCandidates;
  String10 = PACKED ARRAY[1..10] OF Char;
  VoteCount = ARRAY[PrecinctRange, CandidateRange] OF Integer;
  NameType = ARRAY[CandidateRange] OF String10;
```

PSIA ▬▬▬

```
VAR
  Votes:              (* Totals for precincts versus candidates *)
    VoteCount;
  Vote,               (* Input file of precincts and candidates *)
  Report:             (* Output file receiving summaries        *)
    Text;
  Names:              (* Array of candidate names               *)
    NameType;
  Candidate:          (* Candidate number input from file Vote *)
    CandidateRange;
  Precinct:           (* Precinct number input from file Vote  *)
    PrecinctRange;

(***************************************************************************)

PROCEDURE GetAName (VAR Name:              (* Name typed in *)
                        String10);

(* A name of up to 10 letters is read from the terminal *)

VAR
  Count:         (* Loop counter                *)
    Integer;
  Character:     (* Used for reading a character *)
    Char;

BEGIN  (* GetAName *)
  Count : = 0;
  Name : = '          ';
  WHILE NOT EOLN AND (Count < 10) DO
    BEGIN
      Count : = Count + 1;
      Read(Character);
      Name[Count] : = Character
    END;
  Readln
END;    (* GetAName *)

(***************************************************************************)

PROCEDURE GetNames (VAR Names:             (* Array of candidate names *)
                        NameType);

(* Reads in a list of candidate names *)
```

PSIA ═══════════

```
VAR
  Name:                   (* Name read from terminal *)
    String10;
  Candidates:             (* Loop counter                *)
    CandidateRange;

BEGIN (* GetNames *)
  Writeln('Enter the names of the candidates one per line, ',
          'in the order they appear on the ballot.');
  FOR Candidates := 1 TO NumberOfCandidates DO
    BEGIN
      GetAName(Name);
      Names[Candidates] := Name
    END
END;   (* GetNames *)

(*********************************************************************)

PROCEDURE ZeroVotes (VAR Votes:           (* Array of totals *)
                         VoteCount);

(* Array Votes is set to all zero *)

VAR
  Precincts:              (* Loop counter *)
    PrecinctRange;
  Candidates:             (* Loop counter *)
    CandidateRange;

BEGIN (* ZeroVotes *)
  FOR Precincts := 1 TO NumberOfPrecincts DO
    FOR Candidates := 1 TO NumberOfCandidates DO
      Votes[Precincts, Candidates] := 0
END;   (* ZeroVotes *)

(*********************************************************************)

PROCEDURE PrintTable (Votes:              (* Array of totals        *)
                         VoteCount;
                      Names:              (* Array of candidate names *)
                         NameType);

(* Votes are printed *)

VAR
  Precincts:              (* Loop counter *)
    PrecinctRange;
  Candidates:             (* Loop counter *)
    CandidateRange;
```

PSIA

```
BEGIN (* PrintTable *)
  (* Set up headings *)
  Write(Report, ' ':17);
  FOR Candidates := 1 TO NumberOfCandidates DO
    Write(Report, Names[Candidates]:12);
  Writeln(Report);
  (* Print by row *)
  FOR Precincts := 1 TO NumberOfPrecincts DO
    BEGIN
      Write(Report, 'Precinct', Precincts:4);
      FOR Candidates := 1 TO NumberOfCandidates DO
        Write(Report, Votes[Precincts, Candidates]:12);
      Writeln(Report)
    END;
  Writeln(Report)
END;   (* PrintTable *)


(*****************************************************************)


PROCEDURE PrintPerCandidate (Votes:          (* Array of totals        *)
                                  VoteCount;
                             Names:          (* Array of candidate names *)
                                  NameType);


(* Votes per person are summed and printed *)


VAR
  Candidates:          (* Loop counter                *)
    CandidateRange;
  Precincts:           (* Loop counter                *)
    PrecinctRange;
  Total:               (* Total votes for each candidate *)
    Integer;

BEGIN (* PrintPerCandidate *)
  FOR Candidates := 1 TO NumberOfCandidates DO
    BEGIN
      Total := 0;
      (* Sum columns *)
      FOR Precincts := 1 TO NumberOfPrecincts DO
        Total := Total + Votes[Precincts, Candidates];
      Writeln(Report, 'Total votes for ', Names[Candidates]:12, Total:3)
    END
END;   (* PrintPerCandidate *)


(*****************************************************************)
```

PSIA

```
PROCEDURE PrintPerPrecinct (Votes:                (* Array of totals *)
                                VoteCount);

(* Votes per precinct are summed and printed *)

VAR
   Candidates:                (* Loop counter                *)
     CandidateRange;
   Precincts:                 (* Loop counter                *)
     PrecinctRange;
   Total:                     (* Total votes for each precinct *)
     Integer;

BEGIN (* PrintPerPrecinct *)
   FOR Precincts := 1 TO NumberOfPrecincts DO
     BEGIN
       Total := 0;
       (* Sum rows *)
       FOR Candidates := 1 TO NumberOfCandidates DO
         Total := Total + Votes[Precincts, Candidates];
       Writeln(Report, 'Total votes for precinct',
             Precincts:3, ':', Total:3)
     END
END;   (* PrintPerPrecinct *)


(******************************************************************)


BEGIN (* Election *)
  Rewrite(Report);
  Reset(Vote);
  GetNames(Names);                          (* Get candidates names *)
  ZeroVotes(Votes);                         (* Zero out counters *)
  (* Read and tally votes *)
  WHILE NOT EOF(Vote) DO
    BEGIN
      Readln(Vote, Precinct, Candidate);
      Votes[Precinct, Candidate] := Votes[Precinct, Candidate] + 1
    END;
  PrintTable(Votes,Names);
  PrintPerCandidate(Votes,Names);
  PrintPerPrecinct(Votes)
END.   (* Election *)
```

Testing: This program was run with the data listed on the next page. (We have listed it in three columns to save space.) The names of the candidates entered from the console were Smith, Jones, Adams, and Smiley. In this data set, there is at least one

PSIA

vote for each candidate in each precinct. Exam Preparation Exercise 1 asks you to outline a complete testing strategy for this program.

Input data:

```
1 1    3 1    3 3
1 1    4 3    4 4
1 2    3 4    4 4
1 2    3 2    4 3
1 3    3 3    4 4
1 4    2 1    4 4
2 2    2 3    4 1
2 2    4 3    4 2
2 3    4 4    2 4
2 1    3 2    4 4
```

The output, which was written on file Report, is listed below.

		Jones	Smith	Adams	Smiley
Precinct	1	2	2	1	1
Precinct	2	2	2	2	1
Precinct	3	1	2	2	1
Precinct	4	1	1	3	6

```
Total votes for Jones          6
Total votes for Smith          7
Total votes for Adams          8
Total votes for Smiley         9
Total votes for precinct   1:  6
Total votes for precinct   2:  7
Total votes for precinct   3:  6
Total votes for precinct   4: 11
```

MORE ON ARRAY PROCESSING

In Program Election we visualized the data as a table where the rows represented precincts and the columns represented candidates. The definition of the array Votes was as follows:

```
CONST
   NumberOfPrecincts = 4;
   NumberOfCandidates = 4;
```

```
TYPE
  PrecinctRange = 1..NumberOfPrecincts;
  CandidateRange = 1..NumberOfCandidates;
  VoteCount = ARRAY[PrecinctRange, CandidatesRange] OF Integer;

VAR
  Votes:
    VoteCount;
```

In four of the procedures in the program, the elements in the table Votes were examined in a systematic fashion. In procedure ZeroVotes, each element of the array was initialized to 0. In procedure PrintPerPrecinct, the rows of the table (representing votes in the same precinct for the different candidates) were summed and printed. In procedure PrintPerCandidate, the columns of the table (representing votes for the same candidate in the different precincts) were summed and printed. In procedure PrintTable, the table of votes was printed.

These four procedures represent tasks that are performed very frequently on data in a table (that is, data represented in a two-dimensional array):

1. Initialize the table to all zeroes (or some special value).
2. Sum the rows.
3. Sum the columns.
4. Print the table.

We will look at each of these tasks in detail. First, we will rewrite the data definition using more general identifiers such as Row and Column rather than problem-dependent identifiers. Then we will abstract the processing from the election problem and look at the algorithms in terms of generalized table processing.

```
CONST
  NumberOfRows = 4;
  NumberOfColumns = 4;


TYPE
  RowRange = 1..NumberOfRows;
  ColumnRange = 1..NumberOfColumns;
  TableType = ARRAY[RowRange, ColumnRange] OF Integer;


VAR
  Table:
    TableType;
  RowLength,              (* Data in 1..RowLength *)
  Rows:
    RowRange;
  ColumnLength,           (* Data in 1..ColumnLength *)
  Columns:
    ColumnRange;
```

Initialize the Table

Initializing the table requires that each element in the table be accessed in a systematic manner and set to some special value, usually 0. In procedure ZeroVotes, the elements in the table were set to 0, one row at a time. Following is the code that implemented this task, with Precincts replaced by the general identifier Row and Candidates replaced by the general identifier Column.

```
FOR Row := 1 TO NumberOfRows DO
   FOR Column := 1 TO NumberOfColumns DO
      Table[Row, Column] := 0;
```

Row was held at 1 while Column went from 1 to NumberOfColumns. Therefore the first row was initialized to 0 as follows:

```
Table[1, 1]  [1, 2]  [1, 3]  [1, 4]
```

Then Row was incremented to 2, and the second row was set to 0 as follows:

```
Table[2, 1]  [2, 2]  [2, 3]  [2, 4]
```

When Row was incremented to 3, the third row was set to 0; when Row was incremented to 4, the fourth row was set to 0.

This task is recoded below as a general-purpose procedure with four parameters:

1. The name of the table (Table)
2. The number of rows (NumberOfRows)
3. The number of columns (NumberOfColumns)
4. The value to which the components in the table must be initialized (Item).

```
PROCEDURE InitializeTable (VAR Table:
                              TableType;
                           NumberOfRows,
                           NumberOfColumns:
                              Integer;
                           Item:
                              ItemType);

(* Table[1,1] .. Table[1,NumberOfColumns] is set to Item.
   Table[2,1] .. Table[2,NumberOfColumns] is set to Item.
   Process continues until entire array is set to Item. *)

VAR
  Row,
  Column:
    Integer;
```

```
BEGIN (* InitializeTable *)
  FOR Row := 1 TO NumberOfRows DO
    FOR Column := 1 TO NumberOfColumns DO
      Table[Row, Column] := Item
END;  (* InitializeTable *)
```

Add procedure Initialize to your set of general-purpose procedures. You can use this procedure whenever you need to initialize a two-dimensional array with integer indices.

Sum the Rows

In procedure PrintPerPrecinct, each row was summed and printed. The code is repeated below, with general identifiers substituted for the problem-dependent ones.

```
FOR Row := 1 TO RowLength DO
  BEGIN
    Total := 0;
    FOR Column := 1 TO ColumnLength DO
      Total := Total + Table[Row, Column];
    Writeln('Row sum: ', Total)
  END;
```

Again two loops are required: the outer loop controls the rows, the inner loop controls the columns. Note that we have the loops run from 1 to RowLength and ColumnLength, not NumberOfRows and NumberOfColumns. This is analogous to using Length rather than MaxLength when processing a one-dimensional array. That is, we are doing subarray processing. Figure 13-8 illustrates processing by row.

Figure 13-8
Partial Table
Processing by Row

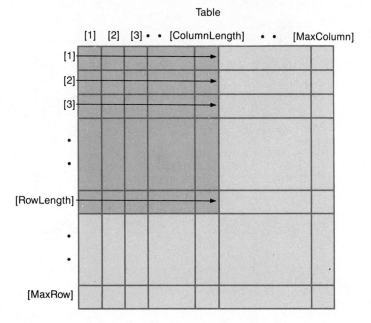

Sum the Columns

In procedure PrintPerCandidate, on the other hand, each column is summed and printed. The code to perform this task is given below, with general identifiers substituted. Again we have generalized the code to sum only the columns that contain valid data.

```
FOR Column : = 1 TO ColumnLength DO
  BEGIN
    Total := 0;
    FOR Row := 1 TO RowLength DO
      Total := Total + Table[Row, Column];
    Writeln('Column sum : ', Total)
  END;
```

In contrast to those in procedures ZeroVotes and PrintPerPrecinct, the elements in procedure PrintPerCandidate are accessed by column. That is, the outer loop controls the column and the inner loop controls the rows. Therefore all the components in the first column are accessed (summed) before the outer loop index changes and the components in the second column are accessed. Figure 13-9 illustrates accessing by column.

Figure 13-9
Partial Table
Processing by
Column

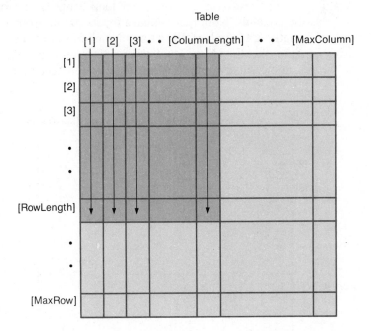

Print the Table

An examination of the code in procedure PrintTable (repeated below with generic identifiers) shows that this is another case of row processing, just like procedures ZeroVotes and PrintPerPrecinct.

```
FOR Row := 1 TO RowLength DO
    BEGIN
        FOR Column := 1 TO ColumnLength DO
            (* Write each column value in a row *)
    END;
```

Almost all processing involving data stored in a two-dimensional array (as a table) will fall into one of these two categories: processing by row or processing by column. Although in our examples the index type on both dimensions has been Integer, this need not be the case. The pattern of operation of the loops will be the same *no matter what types the indices are.*

The looping patterns for row processing and column processing are so useful that they are summarized below. To make the patterns more general, we have used MinRow..MaxRow for the index type of the first dimension (row) and MinColumn..MaxColumn for the index type of the second dimension (column). Note that row processing has the row as the outer loop; column processing has the column as the outer loop.

Column Processing:

```
FOR Column := MinColumn TO MaxColumn DO
    FOR Row := MinRow TO MaxRow DO
        BEGIN
            (* Whatever processing is required *)
        END;
```

Row Processing:

```
FOR Row := MinRow TO MaxRow DO
    FOR Column := MinColumn TO MaxColumn DO
        BEGIN
            (* Whatever processing is required *)
        END;
```

Problem Solving in Action

Problem: Management would like to see the patterns in absenteeism across each department for a week. The absentee figures are kept on file Absent. Each data line contains the daily figures for departments A through F.

Management wants the figures in the form of a table showing the number of employees absent in each department each day and the percentage difference (+ or −) from each department's weekly average. In addition, they want a summary of ab-

PSIA ▰▰▰▰▰▰

senteeism across the entire company for a week. This summary is to be in the form of a bar chart showing what percentage of the total absences occurred on each day of the week.

Discussion: Each data line contains the daily absentee figures for every department. The figures must be read in and stored in a table (which is exactly what we would do if we were doing the task by hand). Once the table has been created, the average absentee rate can be calculated for each department. The table and the averages can be used to calculate the percentage difference.

The first step then is to decide what the table that holds the input data should look like. The departments can be columns and the days can be rows or the other way around. There are only six departments now, but the company is growing. It would be better to make the days of the week the columns and the departments the rows. That way the program can be altered to run again later with more departments simply by adding a row. Rows can be added to a table easily; adding columns can cause a problem with printing since the width of a print line or screen is fixed.

As the data is read, it can be stored into an array having the structure shown in Figure 13-10.

Finding the average for each department requires row processing; we sum the rows and divide by 5. Comparing each day's figures to the average also requires row processing. Finally, printing the table requires row processing. Actually we can calculate the percentage differences while we are printing the table.

To compile the summary figures for the week, we must take the number of people absent on each day divided by the total number of people absent during the entire week. A bar chart showing this information might look as follows, with each asterisk representing 10 percent:

```
                    Monday Tuesday Wednesday Thursday Friday
        Percent

         100%
          90%
          80%
          70%
          60%
          50%
          40%       *
          30%       *
          20%       *         *                             *
          10%       *         *         *          *        *
```

This chart would be interpreted as follows: 40 percent of the total absences across the company were on Monday, 20 percent were on Tuesday, and so on.

We can represent this chart as a two-dimensional array with 10 rows and 5 columns. The rows will represent the percentages to the nearest tenth. For each day the percentage of employees absent will be calculated and then rounded to the nearest tenth. This percentage will determine how many asterisks are put in each column.

Input: Five lines of absentee data, each line containing the number of people out for each of six departments

PSIA

Figure 13-10
Absentee Data

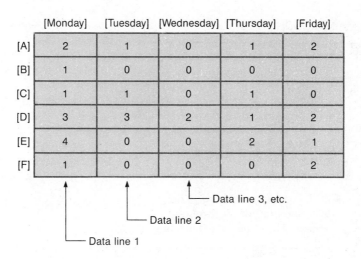

	[Monday]	[Tuesday]	[Wednesday]	[Thursday]	[Friday]
[A]	2	1	0	1	2
[B]	1	0	0	0	0
[C]	1	1	0	1	0
[D]	3	3	2	1	2
[E]	4	0	0	2	1
[F]	1	0	0	0	2

Data line 3, etc.

Data line 2

Data line 1

Output:

Table showing absentee figures and percentage differences from the average for each day of the week for each department

Bar chart showing the percentage of total absenteeism that occurs on each day of the week

Data Structures:

Two-dimensional array for holding the input (AbsenteeData)

One-dimensional array for holding the average daily absentee figures for each department (Averages) (Figure 13-11)

Two-dimensional array for holding the asterisks to be printed in the bar chart (Figure 13-12)

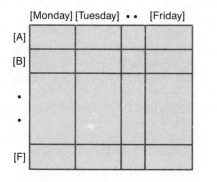

[Monday] [Tuesday] • • [Friday]

[A]
[B]
•
•
[F]

Figure 13-11

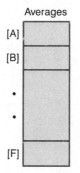

Averages

[A]
[B]
•
•
[F]

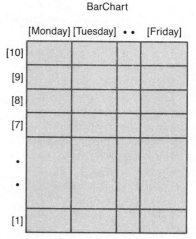

BarChart

[Monday] [Tuesday] • • [Friday]

[10]
[9]
[8]
[7]
•
•
[1]

Figure 13-12

PSIA

MAIN MODULE   Level 0

```
Get Data
Compute the departmental averages
Print Table
Calculate Summary
Print Bar Chart
```

GET DATA   Level 1

```
FOR days Monday through Friday
  FOR departments A through F
    Read AbsenteeData[Department, Day]
```

COMPUTE AVERAGES

We can use the general algorithm we developed to sum the rows of the table. The average is this sum divided by 5.

PRINT TABLE

We can use the algorithm developed in Program Election to print the table, adding an algorithm to calculate the percentage difference when needed.

CALCULATE PERCENTAGE DIFFERENCE   Level 2

```
Difference ⟵ AbsenteeData[Department, Day]
             − Averages[Department]
PercentDif ⟵ Round(Difference * 100.0
             / Averages[Department])
```

CALCULATE SUMMARY

We can first use either row processing or column processing to sum the entire table (Total Absences). We can then use column processing to sum each column, dividing the column sum by the total sum to get the percent of the total absences for each day.

Next we must put the appropriate number of asterisks into the bar chart. This will need expanding as module SetAsterisks.

SET ASTERISKS   Level 2

The number of asterisks needed in the bar chart can be used as an index to tell us how many blanks and how many asterisks to store in a column. For example, if Monday had 38 percent of the absences, we would fill the first column as shown in Figure 13-13.

PSIA _____

Figure 13-13

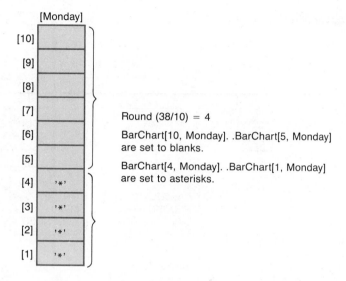

Round (38/10) = 4

BarChart[10, Monday]. .BarChart[5, Monday]
are set to blanks.

BarChart[4, Monday]. .BarChart[1, Monday]
are set to asterisks.

```
Index ⟵ Round(Percent / 10)
FOR Count going from 10 DOWNTO Index + 1
    BarChart[Count, Day] ⟵ ' '
FOR Count going from Index DOWNTO 1
    BarChart[Count, Day] ⟵ '*'
```

PRINT BARCHART   Level 1

We can use row processing to print the bar chart with appropriate headings. Note, however, that the array BarChart needs to be printed upside down. We have used the index to correspond to the nearest tenth of a percent. Therefore, we will have to print from row 10 down to row 1 to display the chart in the usual form.

```
FOR Count going from 10 DOWNTO 1
    Write Count '0%'
    FOR Days going from Monday TO Friday
        Write BarChart[Count, Days]
```

PSIA

Module Structure Chart:

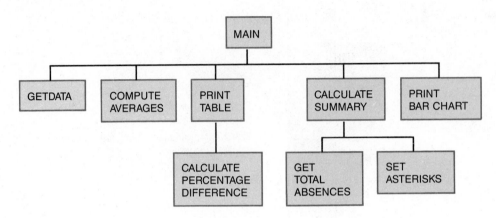

```
PROGRAM Absent (Output, Data, Report);

(* Absentee data are examined across departments for a week.  Percentage
   differences from the average per department are printed.  A summary
   bar chart showing percent of total absences on each day of the week
   is printed *)

CONST
  NumberOfDepartments = 6;

TYPE
  DayType = (Monday, Tuesday, Wednesday, Thursday, Friday);
  DepartmentType = (A, B, C, D, E, F);
  Tens = 1..10;
  TableType = ARRAY[DepartmentType, DayType] OF Integer;
  ChartType = ARRAY[Tens, DayType] OF Char;
  ColumnType = ARRAY[DepartmentType] OF Real;

VAR
  AbsenteeData:      (* Absences by department and day *)
    TableType;
  BarChart:          (* Summary charts of percentages  *)
    ChartType;
  Report,            (* Output file                    *)
  Data:              (* Input file                     *)
    Text;
  Averages:          (* Array of department averages   *)
    ColumnType;

(***********************************************************************)
```

PSIA

```
PROCEDURE GetData (VAR AbsenteeData:     (* Table of absences *)
                              TableType);

(* Data are read from the globally accessed file Data *)

VAR
  Department:             (* Loop counter *)
    DepartmentType;
  Day:                    (* Loop counter *)
    DayType;

BEGIN (* GetData *)
  FOR Day : = Monday TO Friday DO
    BEGIN
      FOR Department : = A TO F DO
        Read(Data, AbsenteeData[Department, Day]);
      Readln(Data)
    END
END;   (* GetData *)
```

(***)

```
PROCEDURE ComputeAverage (     AbsenteeData:     (* Table of absences *)
                              TableType;
                          VAR Averages:          (* Average per dept. *)
                              ColumnType);

(* Averages across the rows are calculated *)

VAR
  Department: .           (* Loop counter                        *)
    DepartmentType;
  Day:                    (* Loop counter                        *)
    DayType;
  Total:                  (* Total absences for each department *)
    Integer;

BEGIN (* ComputeAverage *)
  FOR Department : = A TO F DO
    BEGIN
      Total : = 0;
      FOR Day : = Monday TO Friday DO
        Total : = AbsenteeData[Department, Day] + Total;
      Averages[Department] : = Total / 5.0
    END
END;   (* ComputeAverage *)
```

(***)

PSIA ━━━

```
PROCEDURE PrintTable (AbsenteeData:      (* Table of absences        *)
                          TableType;
                      Averages:          (* Average per department *)
                          ColumnType);

(* Table showing percentage differences from the averages and
   original data is printed.  File Report is accessed globally *)

VAR
   Department:         (* Loop counter                      *)
      DepartmentType;
   Day:                (* Loop counter                      *)
      DayType;
   PerCentDif:         (* Percent different from average *)
      Integer;

BEGIN (* PrintTable *)
   Writeln(Report, 'ABSENTEE    DATA':40);
   Writeln(Report, 'Monday':13, 'Tuesday':13, 'Wednesday':13,
           'Thursday':13, 'Friday':13);
   FOR Day := Monday TO Friday DO
      Write(Report, '    Value    %');
   Writeln(Report);
   FOR Department := A TO F DO
      BEGIN
        FOR Day := Monday TO Friday DO
          BEGIN
            Write(Report, AbsenteeData[Department, Day]:6);
            PerCentDif := Round((AbsenteeData[Department, Day]
               - Averages[Department]) * 100.0 / Averages[Department]);
            Write(Report, PerCentDif:7)
          END;
        Writeln(Report)
      END
END;   (* PrintTable *)

(*****************************************************************************)

PROCEDURE Summary (    AbsenteeData:     (* Table of absences        *)
                          TableType;
                   VAR BarChart:         (* Charts of percentages *)
                          ChartType);

(* Total percentages by day are calculated and represented
   in a bar chart *)
```

PSIA

```
VAR
  Department:          (* Loop counter          *)
    DepartmentType;
  Day:                 (* Loop counter          *)
    DayType;
  PerCent:             (* Percent per day        *)
    Real;
  Total,               (* Total of entire table *)
  TotalColumn:         (* Total per day          *)
    Integer;

(*******************************************************************)

PROCEDURE SetAsterisks (VAR BarChart:      (* Charts of percentages *)
                          ChartType;
                        Day:                (* Chart index            *)
                          DayType;
                        Percent:            (* Percentage to chart    *)
                          Real);

(* Asterisks are stored to represent each 10 percent.
   Blanks are stored in balance of chart *)

VAR
  Index:               (* Percent in integer form *)
    0..10;
  Counter:             (* Loop counter            *)
    Tens;

BEGIN (* SetAsterisks *)
  Index := Round(Percent / 10.0);
  FOR Counter := 10 DOWNTO Index + 1 DO
    BarChart[Counter, Day] := ' ';
  FOR Counter := Index DOWNTO 1 DO
    BarChart[Counter, Day] := '*'
END;   (* SetAsterisks *)

(*******************************************************************)
```

PSIA ━━━━━

```
FUNCTION TotalAbsences (AbsenteeData:      (* Table of absences *)
                             TableType):
                                 Integer;


VAR
  Department:           (* Loop counter    *)
    DepartmentType;
  Day:                  (* Loop counter    *)
    DayType;
  Total:                (* Total absences *)
    Integer;

BEGIN (* TotalAbsences *)
  Total := 0;
  FOR Department := A TO F DO
    FOR Day := Monday TO Friday DO
      Total := Total + AbsenteeData[Department, Day];
  TotalAbsences := Total
END;   (* TotalAbsences *)


(********************************************************************)


BEGIN (* Summary *)
  Total := TotalAbsences(AbsenteeData);
  FOR Day := Monday TO Friday DO
    BEGIN
      TotalColumn := 0;
      FOR Department := A TO F DO
        TotalColumn := TotalColumn + AbsenteeData[Department, Day];
      Percent := (TotalColumn / Total) * 100.0;
      SetAsterisks(BarChart, Day, Percent)
    END
END;   (* Summary *)


(********************************************************************)


PROCEDURE PrintBarChart (BarChart:       (* Charts of percentages *)
                           ChartType);

(* Summary data are represented in a bar chart *)

VAR
  Counter:      (* Loop control *)
    Tens;
  Day:          (* Loop control *)
    DayType;
```

PSIA

```pascal
BEGIN (* PrintBarChart *)
  Writeln(Report);
  Writeln(Report, 'BAR CHART:   ABSENCES BY DAY':40);
  Writeln(Report, '        Monday     Tuesday     Wednesday Thursday',
          '   Friday');
  FOR Counter := 10 DOWNTO 1 DO
    BEGIN
      Write(Report, Counter:2, '0%');
      FOR Day := Monday TO Friday DO
        Write(Report, BarChart[Counter, Day]:5, '      ');
      Writeln(Report)
    END
END;   (* PrintBarChart *)


(**************************************************************************)

BEGIN (* Absent *)
  Rewrite(Report);
  Reset(Data);
  GetData(AbsenteeData);
  ComputeAverage(AbsenteeData, Averages);
  PrintTable(AbsenteeData, Averages);
  Summary(AbsenteeData, BarChart);
  PrintBarChart(BarChart);
END.   (* Absent *)
```

Testing: The program was run with the following test data, which included at least one zero in each row and column. Exam Preparation Exercise 2 asks you to outline a complete testing strategy for this program.

On file Data:

```
0 6 3 3 4 1
1 0 1 3 0 3
1 1 0 2 1 1
1 0 1 0 0 1
2 3 4 2 1 0
```

PSIA

Listed below are the results written on file Report.

ABSENTEE DATA

Monday		Tuesday		Wednesday		Thursday		Friday	
Value	%	Value	%	Value	%	Value	%	Value	%
0	−100	1	0	1	0	1	0	2	100
6	200	0	−100	1	−50	0	−100	3	50
3	67	1	−44	0	−100	1	−44	4	122
3	50	3	50	2	0	0	−100	2	0
4	233	0	−100	1	−17	0	−100	1	−17
1	−17	3	150	1	−17	1	−17	0	−100

BAR CHART: ABSENCES BY DAY

	Monday	Tuesday	Wednesday	Thursday	Friday
100%					
90%					
80%					
70%					
60%					
50%					
40%	*				
30%	*				*
20%	*	*			*
10%	*	*	*	*	*

Something looks a little strange: the percentages in the bar chart total to 110 percent. How can this be? In Chapter 8 we mentioned that strange things can happen with real numbers. In changing each percentage figure to an integer for use as an index, we rounded to the nearest 10 percent.

When we noticed that the percentages added up to 110, we went back and put an intermediate print statement in the program to monitor what was happening. The percentages (in decimal form) and the rounded values used as an index are shown below.

Percent	Index
0.369	4
0.173	2
0.130	1
0.065	1
0.260	3
0.997	11

This is a classic example of round-off error. Preprogramming Exercise 9 asks you to rewrite the procedures that create the bar chart using a smaller interval so that an asterisk represents 5 percentage points instead of 10.

ANOTHER WAY OF DEFINING TWO-DIMENSIONAL ARRAYS

One way of looking at a two-dimensional array is as a structure in which each component has two features. In the absentee problem, each component represents the number of people who have been absent. We know two things about each person represented in a particular place in the table: which department he or she works for and on which day of the week he or she was absent. Our data structure uses one dimension to represent the departments and the other dimension to represent days of the week.

In Pascal a two-dimensional array can also be defined as an array of arrays. That is, the component type of an array does not have to be a scalar type; it can be a structured type. For example, AbsenteeData could have been defined as follows:

```
TYPE
   DayType = (Monday, Tuesday, Wednesday, Thursday, Friday);
   DepartmentType = (A, B, C, D, E, F);
   DayArray = ARRAY[DayType] OF Integer;
   TableType = ARRAY[DepartmentType] OF DayArray;

VAR
   AbsenteeData:
      TableType;
```

With this definition, the components of the data type TableType are one-dimensional arrays of type DayArray. The components of the data type DayArray are integers representing absent employees. We can access each row as an entity: AbsenteeData[B] accesses the array containing the number of people absent from department B for five days, Monday through Friday. We can also access each individual component of AbsenteeData by giving its place on each dimension: AbsenteeData[B, Monday] accesses the number of people absent from department B on Monday.

Does it matter which way we define a two-dimensional array? No, in most cases it doesn't matter. However, the features of the data—the department and the day—are more clearly shown if the array is defined the way it was originally in the program (shown below).

```
   TableType = ARRAY[DepartmentType, DayType] OF Integer;
```

The program is more self-documenting when the features being represented by each dimension are clearly set out.

There is one situation in which it is advantageous to define an array as an array of arrays. If the rows have been defined first as a one-dimensional array, each can be passed to a procedure expecting a one-dimensional array of the same type as a parameter.

For example, the following procedure takes a list and returns the index to the largest value in the list.

```
PROCEDURE MaxValue (    List:
                          ListType;
                        Length:
                          Integer;
                    VAR Index:
                          IndexType);
```

```
(* The index of the maximum value in List is returned in Index *)
```

```
VAR
  Counter:
    IndexType;
```

```
BEGIN (* MaxValue *)
  Index := 1;
  FOR Counter := 2 TO Length DO
    IF List[Counter] > List[Index]
      THEN
        Index := Counter
END;    (* MaxValue *)
```

If we redefine the table used in Program Election to be an array of arrays, we can pass the rows of the table to MaxValue in order to determine which candidate got the most votes in each precinct.

```
CONST
    NumberOfPrecincts = 4;
    NumberOfCandidates = 4;

TYPE
    PrecinctRange = 1..NumberOfPrecincts;
    CandidateRange = 1..NumberOfCandidates;
    ListType = ARRAY[CandidateRange] OF Integer;
    VoteCount = ARRAY[PrecinctRange] OF ListType;

VAR
    Votes:
      VoteCount;
```

The following code segment will print the name of the candidate who got the most votes in each precinct.

```
FOR Precincts := 1 TO NumberOfPrecincts DO
  BEGIN
    MaxValue(Votes[Precincts], NumberOfCandidates, Index);
    Writeln(Names[Index], ' received the most votes in precinct ',
        Precincts)
  END;
```

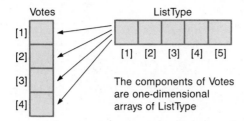

Figure 13-14
A One-Dimensional
Array

The components of Votes
are one-dimensional
arrays of ListType

The rows of Votes are passed to the procedure MaxValue, which treats them like any other one-dimensional array of ListType. (See Figure 13-14.) We are able to pass the rows as a parameter because the rows of VoteCount and the formal parameter of MaxValue are of the same named data type. The ability to use rows of a two-dimensional array as a parameter to a procedure expecting a one-dimensional array can be very helpful at times.

MULTIDIMENSIONAL ARRAYS

Pascal does not place a limit on the number of dimensions that an array can have. We can generalize our definition of an array to cover all cases.

Array A collection of components, all of the same type, ordered on N dimensions (N > =1). Each component is accessed by N indices, each of which represents the component's position within that dimension.

You should have guessed from the syntax diagrams that you can have as many dimensions as you want. How many should you have in a particular case? As many as there are features that describe the data being represented as components in the array.

Take, for example, a chain of department stores. Monthly sales figures must be kept for each item by store. There are three important pieces of information about each data item that has been sold: the month in which it was sold, the store from which it was purchased, and the item number. We can define an array to summarize this data as follows:

```
CONST
    NumberOfItems = 100;
    NumberOfStores = 10;

TYPE
    ItemNumbers = 1..NumberOfItems;
    Stores = 1..NumberOfStores;
    Months = 1..12;
    SalesType = ARRAY[Stores, Months, ItemNumbers] OF Integer;
```

```
VAR
   Sales:
      SalesType;
   Item:
      ItemNumbers;
   Store:
      Stores;
   Month:
      Months;
   NumberSold:
      Integer;
   CurrentMonth:
      Months;
```

A graphical representation of the array variable Sales is shown in Figure 13-15. The number of components in Sales is 12000 (10 × 12 × 100).

If it is currently only June (CurrentMonth = 6), then we won't have any sales information in part of the array. As with one-dimensional and two-dimensional arrays, we can keep track of the part of the array actually being used. The following program fragment will sum and print the total number of each item sold this year to date by the chain of stores.

```
FOR Item := 1 TO NumberOfItems DO
   BEGIN
      NumberSold := 0;
      FOR Store := 1 TO NumberOfStores DO
         FOR Month := 1 TO CurrentMonth DO
            NumberSold := NumberSold + Sales[Store, Month, Item];
      Writeln('Item #', Item:3, ' Sales to date = ', NumberSold:6)
   END;
```

Notice that for each item we hold Item constant in the outer FOR loop while we sum that item's sales by Month and Store. If we want to find the total sales for each store in the chain of stores, we hold Store constant in the outer FOR loop while we sum that store's sales by Month and Item.

Figure 13-15
Graphical
Representation of
Array Variable
Sales

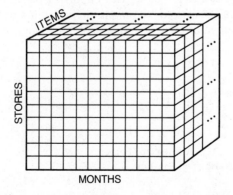

```
FOR Store := 1 TO NumberOfStores DO
  BEGIN
    NumberSold := 0;
    FOR Item := 1 TO NumberOfItems DO
      FOR Month := 1 TO CurrentMonth DO
        NumberSold := NumberSold + Sales[Store, Month, Item];
    Writeln('Store #', Store:3, ' Sales to date = ', NumberSold:6)
  END;
```

It takes two loops to access each component in a two-dimensional array; it takes three loops to access each component in a three-dimensional array. The task to be done determines which index controls the outer loop, the middle loop, and the inner loop. If we want to calculate monthly sales by store, Month controls the outer loop and Store controls the middle loop. If we want to calculate monthly sales by item, Month controls the outer loop and Item controls the middle loop.

If we want to keep track of the departments that sell each item, we can add a fourth dimension.

```
Departments = (A, B, C, D, E, F, G);
SalesType = ARRAY[Stores, Months, ItemNumbers, Departments] OF Integer;
```

How would we visualize this new structure? Not very easily! Fortunately, we do not have to be able to visualize a structure in order to write algorithms to process it. Preprogramming Exercise 6 asks you to initialize an array variable of type SalesType to 0. Preprogramming Exercise 7 asks you to write a procedure to calculate the total number of items sold during a year by each department in each store.

A multidimensional array is a structure that allows us to access a particular item directly by describing where the item is located within the various dimensions. For example, if we want the number of sales for item number 4, in department C, in store 1, for the month of May, we can access this value directly: Sales[1, 5, 4, C]. All of the components in the array represent the same thing: number of items sold.

CHOOSING A DATA STRUCTURE

During our analysis of a problem, we specify the input and the required output. The task of the program is to take the input and perform operations on it until it is in the form of the required output.

In our top-down design, at the top levels the operations on the data are only specified in general terms. When we reach the modules that actually perform the operations on the data, we must know exactly how the data will be represented. That is, the data structures must be specified.

We start at the top levels with a vague idea of what the data structure should be and clarify our ideas as our modules get more specific. That is, the specification of our data structures is done in parallel with our top-down design. As we introduce more data structures, we will try to give you guidelines on how to choose among them.

In both Program Election and Program Absent we could have used parallel arrays instead of a two-dimensional array to hold the data. How did we choose between these two data structures? Let's examine this question in the context of our two problems.

Even if an array is defined as an array of arrays, it is ultimately composed of components of some scalar type. For this reason, an array is called a *homogeneous* structure. All the components of an array are of the same type; they represent the same thing.

In determining whether to use parallel arrays or a multi-dimensional array, we must keep in mind two points:

1. All scalar components in an array must be of the same data type.
2. Each dimension in an array represents a different feature or facet of the item that the component represents. That is, the indices describe the component.

In Program Election we could have defined four one-dimensional arrays, one for each candidate in the election. The first component in each of the arrays would have referred to the first precinct; the second, to the second precinct; and so on.

In Program Absent we could have defined five one-dimensional arrays, one for each day of the week. The first component in each of the arrays would have referred to department A; the second component, to department B; and so on.

Two-dimensional arrays, however, were more appropriate than parallel arrays in both cases. In Program Election the components were votes, described by which precinct they were cast in and which candidate they were cast for. In Program Absent the components were employees who were absent, described by which department they worked for and which day of the week they were absent. In each program the components all represented the same thing.

In contrast, look at an example where we want to process information on the number of items sold, the cost of each item, and the percent tax to be charged for each item. We could define a table with the following table headings to hold this information:

Item Number   Number Sold   Cost per Item   Tax Rate

If we kept the item number and the number sold as real numbers, we could define a two-dimensional array of type Real with four columns, where the first column held the item number, the second column held the number of items sold, and so on. In this case, however, four parallel arrays would be more appropriate.

The components are all of the same data type, but they represent different things. The components in the Item Number column represent an identifying number. The components in the Number Sold column represent the quantity of items sold. The components in the Cost per Item column are prices representing the value of an item. The components in the Tax Rate column are the percent tax to be charged for an item.

In the next chapter we will look at a data structure called a record which would be even more appropriate than parallel arrays in this case. A record is a structure that allows us to group nonhomogeneous items.

TESTING AND DEBUGGING

Errors with multidimensional arrays fall into two major categories: index range errors and type conflict errors. In addition, an undefined-value error may result from trying to access undefined (uninitialized) components.

As the number of dimensions increases, so does the likelihood of a subtle logic error. The syntax of your nested loop structure may be valid, but what you intended to have happen may not be what you coded. Using meaningful identifiers for your loop control variables will help. If you were to use I, J, and K as the loop control variables in the department store chain example, it would be easy to interchange them by mistake. If you use Item, Store, and Month, you are less likely to confuse the indices. Use enumerated or other distinct types for indices; then the compiler will find any interchanged index variables.

Remember that any variables with the same type identifier can be assigned to each other. The key words here are "same type identifier." For example, for the declarations

```
TYPE
    Months = 1..12;
    Years = 1950..1990;
    Item = ARRAY[Months] OF Integer;
    Table1 = ARRAY[Years] OF Item;
    Table2 = ARRAY[Years, Months] OF Integer;

VAR
    TableA:
        Table1;
    TableB:
        Table2;
    TableC:
        ARRAY[Years] OF Item;
    NewItem,
    OldItem:
        Item;
```

the following are examples of valid and invalid assignments:

Statement	Status	Reason
NewItem := OldItem	Valid	One-dimensional array assignment
TableA[1976] := NewItem	Valid	First dimension (row) of two-dimensional array assigned value of a one-dimensional array
OldItem := Table[1984]	Valid	One-dimensional array assigned value of a row of a two-dimensional array
TableA := TableB	Invalid	Different named types
TableC := TableA	Invalid	Different types—one is named, the other is not
TableB[1976] := NewItem	Invalid	Different named types

Be careful when comparing arrays. Strings can be compared as units, but all other arrays must be compared component by component. For example, the following code would find whether TableA[1975] is equal to OldItem.

```
Equal  : = True;
Month  : = 1;
WHILE Equal AND  (Month <= 12)  DO
   IF TableA[1975, Month]  = OldItem[Month]
      THEN
         Month  : = Month + 1
      ELSE
         Equal  : = False;
```

A WHILE loop had to be used in the preceding fragment because there are two ending conditions on the loop. A FOR loop can be used only for a loop that is a simple count-controlled loop.

Testing and Debugging Hints

1. Initialize all components of an array if there is any chance that you will attempt to access the entire array.
2. Use subrange types for index variables and be careful when passing parameters to avoid array index range errors.
3. Use meaningful identifiers for index variables.
4. Define all data types globally to prevent type mismatches when using array references in assignment statements or when passing arrays as parameters.
5. Use the proper number of indices with array names when referencing a cell in an array.

SUMMARY

Two-dimensional arrays are very useful for processing information that is naturally represented in table form. Processing data in two-dimensional arrays usually takes one of two forms: processing by row or processing by column.

Two-dimensional arrays are useful for representing games like chess, tic-tac-toe, or Scrabble. Several of the programming exercises involve writing procedures to simulate moves in a game. They are also useful in graphics, where the screen is thought of as a two-dimensional array.

A multidimensional array is a collection of like components, ordered on more than one dimension. Each component is accessed by a set of indices, one for each dimension, which represents the component's position on the various dimensions.

Program design and selection of data structure occur in parallel. The data structure should accurately reflect the relationships inherent in the data itself. Two-dimensional arrays and parallel arrays can be used to hold the same data. An analysis of what the data means can help you to make the appropriate choice.

QUICK CHECK _____

1. Define a two-dimensional array data type, called Chart, with 30 rows and 10 columns. The component type of the array is Real. (pp. 496–500)

2. Assign the value 27.3 to the component in row 13, column 7 of an array variable, called Plan, of type Chart. (pp. 496–500)

3. Write a program fragment that will initialize array Plan from question 2 to all zeroes. (pp. 508–511)

4. Nested FOR loops can be used to sum the values in each row of array Plan. What range of values would the outer FOR loop count through in order to do this? (p. 511)

5. Nested FOR loops can be used to sum the values in each column of array Plan. What range of values would the outer FOR loop count through in order to do this? (p. 512)

6. Write a program fragment that will print the contents of array Plan. (p. 513)

7. Given the type definitions

```
TYPE
   OneDimIndex = 'A'..'Z';
   TwoDimIndex = 1..100;
   OneDim = ARRAY[OneDimIndex] OF Integer;
   TwoDim = ARRAY[TwoDimIndex] OF OneDim;
```

rewrite the definition of type TwoDim without referring to type OneDim. (pp. 525–527)

8. How many components does the following data type contain? (pp. 527–529)

```
CONST
   MaxIndex = 10;

TYPE
   Range = 1..MaxIndex
   FourDim = ARRAY[Range, Range, Range, Range] OF Char;
```

9. Write a program fragment that will fill a variable of type FourDim, called Quick, with blanks. (pp. 527–529)

10. Suppose you are writing a program to process a table of employee numbers, names, and pay rates. Is a two-dimensional array an appropriate data structure for this problem? Explain. (pp. 529–530)

Answers:
1. ```
   CONST
      MaxRow = 30;
      MaxColumn = 10;

   TYPE
      Rows = 1..MaxRow;
      Columns = 1..MaxColumn;
      Chart = ARRAY[Rows, Columns] OF Real
   ```
2. `Plan[13, 7] := 27.3;`
3. ```
   FOR Row := 1 TO 30 DO
      FOR Column := 1 TO 10 DO
        Plan[Row, Column] := 0.0;
   ```

```
4. FOR Row := 1 TO 30 DO
5. FOR Column := 1 TO 10 DO
6. FOR Row := 1 TO 30 DO
      BEGIN
        FOR Column := 1 TO 10 DO
          Write(Plan[Row, Column]:8:1);
        Writeln
      END
7. TYPE
      TwoDim = ARRAY[TwoDimIndex, OneDimIndex] OF Integer
8. Ten thousand (10 * 10 * 10 * 10)
9. FOR Dim1 := 1 TO MaxIndex DO
      FOR Dim2 := 1 TO MaxIndex DO
        FOR Dim3 := 1 TO MaxIndex DO
          FOR Dim4 := 1 TO MaxIndex DO
            Quick[Dim1, Dim2, Dim3, Dim4] := ' ';
```

10. A two-dimensional array is inappropriate because the data types of the columns are not the same. Parallel arrays are more appropriate in this case.

EXAM PREPARATION EXERCISES _____

1. Outline a testing strategy that will fully test Program Election.

2. Outline a testing strategy that will fully test Program Absent.

3. Given the declarations

```
CONST
   NumberOfWeeks = 5;
   NumberOfTeams = 6;

TYPE
   WeekRange = 1..NumberOfWeeks;
   TeamRange = 1..NumberOfTeams;
   SoldType = ARRAY[TeamRange, WeekRange] OF Integer;

VAR
   Weeks:
      WeekRange;
   Teams:
      TeamRange;
   Tickets:
      SoldType;
```

answer the following questions:

(a) What is the number of rows in Tickets?

(b) What is the number of columns in Tickets?

(c) How many Integer variables have been declared?

(d) What kind of processing (row or column) would be needed to total the ticket sales by weeks?

(e) What kind of processing (row or column) would be needed to total the ticket sales by teams?

4. Given the declarations

```
CONST
  NumberOfSchools = 10;

TYPE
  SchoolIndex = 1..NumberOfSchools;
  SportType = (FootBall, BasketBall, VolleyBall);
  ParticipantType = ARRAY[SchoolIndex, SportType] OF Integer;
  MoneyType = ARRAY[SportType, SchoolIndex] OF Real;

VAR
  KidsInSports:
    ParticipantType;
  CostOfSports:
    MoneyType;
  Schools:
    SchoolIndex;
  Sports:
    SportType;
```

answer the following questions:
   (a) What is the number of rows in KidsInSports?
   (b) What is the number of columns in KidsInSports?
   (c) What is the number of rows in CostOfSports?
   (d) What is the number of columns in CostOfSports?
   (e) How many Integer variables have been declared?
   (f) How many Real variables have been declared?
   (g) What kind of processing (row or column) would be needed to total the amount of money spent on each sport?
   (h) What kind of processing (row or column) would be needed to total the number of children participating in sports at a particular school?

5. (a) Define an enumerated type Teams made up of the clubs on your campus.
   (b) Define an Integer array type RecordType indexed by Teams.
   (c) Declare an array variable WinLoss to be of type RecordType.

6. Declare the array variables described below. Use good style.
   (a) A table with five rows and six columns that will contain Boolean values.
   (b) A table indexed from −5 to 0 and 'A' to 'F' that will contain Real values.
   (c) A Char table with rows indexed by uppercase letters and columns indexed by lower-case letters.

7. A logging operation keeps records of 37 loggers' monthly production for purposes of analysis, using the following array structure:

```
CONST
  NumberLoggers = 37;

TYPE
  LoggerIndex = 1..NumberLoggers;
  MonthType = 1..12;
  CutType = ARRAY[LoggerIndex, MonthType] OF Integer;
```

```
VAR
  LogsCut:
    CutType;
  MonthlyHigh,
  MonthlyTotal,
  YearlyTotal,
  High:
    Integer;
  Month,
  BestMonth:
    MonthType;
  Logger,
  BestLogger:
    LoggerIndex;
```

(a) The following statement would assign the January log total for logger number 7 to Monthly Total. (True or False?)

```
MonthlyTotal := LogsCut[7, 1]
```

(b) The following statements would compute the yearly total for logger number 11. (True or False?)

```
YearlyTotal := 0;
FOR Month := 1 TO 12 DO
  YearlyTotal := YearlyTotal + LogsCut[Month, 11]
```

(c) The following statements would find the BestLogger (most logs cut) in March. (True or False?)

```
MonthlyHigh := 0;
FOR Logger := 1 TO NumberLoggers DO
  IF LogsCut[Logger, 3] > MonthlyHigh
    THEN
      BEGIN
        BestLogger := Logger;
        MonthlyHigh := LogsCut[Logger, 3]
      END;
```

(d) The following statements would find the logger with the highest monthly production and the logger's best month. (True or False?)

```
High := 0;
FOR Month := 1 TO 12 DO
  FOR Logger := 1 TO NumberLoggers DO
    IF LogsCut[Logger, Month] > High
      THEN
        BEGIN
          High := LogsCut[Logger, Month];
          BestLogger := Logger;
          BestMonth := Month
        END;
```

8. Declare the Real array variables described below. Use good style.
   (a) A three-dimensional array where the first dimension is indexed from −1 to +3, the second dimension is indexed from 'A' to 'Z', and the third dimension is indexed from 1 to 20.
   (b) A four-dimensional array where the first two dimensions are indexed from 1 to 10 and the third and fourth dimensions are indexed from 'a' to 'f'.

PREPROGRAMMING EXERCISES _____

1. Write a Pascal function that returns True if all the values in a two-dimensional array are positive and False otherwise. The array, the number of columns, and the number of rows should be passed as parameters.

2. Write a Pascal procedure to initialize the diagonals of a two-dimensional Char array to a specified character. The array (Data of type DataType), the dimensions of the array (Length), and the specified character (Character) should be passed as parameters.

3. Write a Pascal procedure Copy that takes an Integer array Data, defined to be MaxRows by MaxColumns, and copies the values into a second array Data2, defined the same way. Data and Data2 are of type DataType. The constants MaxRows and MaxColumns may be accessed globally.

4. Using the declarations in Exam Preparation Exercise 3, write procedures to do the following tasks. Use good style. Only constants may be accessed globally.
   (a) Determine the team that sold the most tickets during the first week of ticket sales.
   (b) Determine the week in which the second team sold the most tickets.
   (c) Determine the week in which the most tickets were sold.
   (d) Determine the team that sold the most tickets.

5. Using the declarations in Exam Preparation Exercise 4, write procedures to do the following tasks. Use good style. Only constants may be accessed globally.
   (a) Determine which school spent the most money on football.
   (b) Determine which sport the last school spent the most money on.
   (c) Determine which school had the most students playing basketball.
   (d) Determine which sport the third school had the most students participating in.
   (e) Determine the total amount spent by all the schools on volleyball.
   (f) Determine the total number of students playing all sports. (Assume that each student plays only one sport.)
   (g) Determine which school had the most students participating in sports.
   (h) Determine which was the most popular sport in terms of money spent.
   (i) Determine which was the most popular sport in terms of student participation.

6. Write a Pascal procedure to initialize an array of type SalesType, described on page 529, to 0. The constants NumberOfStores and NumberOfItems may be accessed globally. The array should be passed as a parameter.

7. Sales figures are kept on items sold by store, by department, by month. Write a Pascal procedure to calculate the total number of items sold during the year by each department in each store. The data is stored in an array of type SalesType, described on page 529. The array containing the data should be passed as a parameter. The constants Number-OfStores and NumberOfItems may be accessed globally.

8. Write a Pascal function that will return the sum of the elements in a specified row of an array. The array, the number of columns, and which row is to be summed are to be passed as parameters.

9. Rewrite procedure SetAsterisks on page 521 so that an asterisk represents five percentage points instead of 10.

PROGRAMMING PROBLEMS _____

1. A deck of playing cards can be represented as a two-dimensional array where the first dimension is rank and the second dimension is suit. Read in a bridge hand (13 cards) and determine whether the player should pass or bid. Each card should be input on a line by itself, with the suit given first and rank next.

   The decision to pass or bid is based on the number of points the hand is worth. Points are counted as follows:

   An ace is worth 4 points.

   A king is worth 3 points.

   A queen is worth 2 points.

   A jack is worth 1 point.

   Add up the points in the hand and print one of the following messages.

Below 13 points,	'Pass'
Between 13 and 16 points,	'Bid one of a suit'
Between 17 and 19 points,	'Bid one no trump'
Between 20 and 22 points,	'Bid one of a suit'
Over 22 points,	'Bid two of a suit'

2. Write an interactive program that plays tic-tac-toe. Represent the board as a three-by-three character array. Initialize the array to blanks and ask each player in turn to input a position. The first player's position will be marked on the board with an "O" and the second player's position will be marked with an "X."

   Continue the process until a player wins or the game is a draw. To win a player must have three marks in a row, in a column, or on a diagonal. A draw occurs when the board is full and no one has won.

   Each player's position should be input in the form of an index into the tic-tac-toe board. That is, a row number, space, and column number. Make the program user friendly.

   After each game print out a diagram of the board showing the ending positions. Keep a count of the number of games each player has won and the number of draws. Before the beginning of each game, ask each player if he or she wishes to continue. If either player wishes to quit, print out the statistics and stop.

3. Photos taken in space by the Voyager spacecraft are sent back to earth as a stream of numbers. Your job is to take a matrix (two-dimensional array) of numbers and print it as a negative picture.

   If the numbers received represent levels of brightness, then one approach to generating a picture is to print a dark character (like a $) when the brightness level is low and print a light character (like a blank or a period) when the level is high.

   Unfortunately, errors in transmission sometimes occur. Thus your program should first attempt to find and correct these errors. Assume a value is in error if it differs by more than 1 from each of its four neighboring values. Correct the bad value by giving it the average of its neighboring values, rounding it to the nearest integer.

Example:

    5   The 2 would be regarded as an error and would

4 2 5   be given a corrected value of 5.

    5

NOTE: Values on the corners or boundaries of the matrix will have to be processed differently from values on the interior.

Finally, your program should print a negative image of the corrected picture on a new page.

4. The following diagram represents an island surrounded by water (shaded area). Two bridges lead out of the island. A mouse is placed on the black square. Write a program to make the mouse take a walk across the island. The mouse is allowed to travel one square at a time either horizontally or vertically. A random number between 1 and 4 should be used to decide which direction the mouse is to take. The mouse drowns when he hits the water or escapes when he crosses a bridge. What are the mouse's chances? You may generate a random number up to 100 times. If the mouse does not find his way by the 100th try, he will die of starvation. Restart the mouse in a new array and go back and repeat the whole process. Count the number of times he escapes, drowns, and starves.

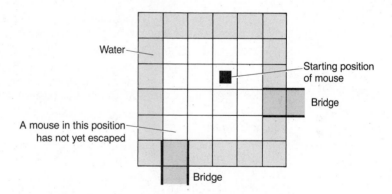

Input:

First record—the size of the array, including border of water and bridges (will not be larger than 20 × 20)

Next N records—the rows of the two-dimensional array, where the positions containing negative numbers represent the water, the positions in the edge containing a 0 represent the bridges, the position containing a 1 represents the starting position of the mouse, and all other positions contain zeroes

Output: For each trip by the mouse you should print the following (double space between trips):

A line stating whether the mouse escaped, drowned, or starved

A line showing the mouse's starting position and the position of the two bridges

A map showing the frequency of the visits of the mouse to each position

5. In competitive diving, each diver makes three dives of varying degrees of difficulty. Nine judges score the dive from 0 to 10 in steps of 0.5. The total score is obtained by discarding the lowest and highest of the judges' scores, adding the remaining scores, and then multiplying the scores by the degree of difficulty. The divers take turns, and when the competition is finished, they are ranked according to score. Write a program to do the above, using the following input and output specifications.

Input:

Number of divers

Diver's name (10 characters), difficulty (Real), and judges' ratings (Real)

There will be a record like the above for each diver. All of the records for Dive 1 will be grouped together, then all for Dive 2, then all for Dive 3.

Output:

Input data echo printed in tabular form with appropriate headings, e.g., Name, Difficulty, judges' number (1–9)

A table that contains the following information sorted by final total, in descending order (highest diver first):

Name   Dive 1   Dive 2   Dive 3   Total

where name is the diver's name; Dive 1, Dive 2, and Dive 3 are the total points received for a single dive as described above, and Total is the overall total

6. You work for the Jet Propulsion Laboratory. They want you to write a program that will take an array containing the digitized representation of a picture of the night sky and locate the stars on it. Each element of the array represents the amount of light hitting that portion of the image when the picture was taken. Intensities range from 0 to 20.

Sample Input:

```
0   3  4   0  0  0   6  8
5  13  6   0  0  0   2  3
2   6  2   7  3  0  10  0
0   0  4  15  4  1   6  0
0   0  7  12  6  9  10  4
5   0  6  10  6  4   8  0
```

A star is probably located in the area covered by the array element i,j if the following is the case:

$$(A(i, j) + \text{sum of the 4 surrounding intensities}) / 5 > 6.0$$

Ignore possible stars along the edges of the array.

The desired output is a star map containing asterisks where you have found a star and blanks elsewhere, such as

```
- - - - - - - - - - - - - - - - - - - - - - - -
:
:    *
:
:        *
:        *   *  *
:
:
```

Input:

A title

An array of intensities

Output: A star map. Print two blanks for the "no star" case. The presence of a star should be indicated by a blank followed by an asterisk. The chart should have a border and be labeled with the title.

■ *To be able to define a record data type.*

■ *To be able to access a field in a record variable.*

■ *To be able to use arrays of records to solve a given problem.*

■ *To be able to define a hierarchical record structure.*

■ *To be able to access values stored in a hierarchical record variable.*

■ *To be able to use the WITH statement to simplify accessing fields in records.*

■ *To be able to choose and design an appropriate array and/or record data structure for a given problem.*

14

Records and Data Abstraction

In the last three chapters, we have looked in depth at a homogeneous structured data type called an array. We have discussed common algorithms that are applied to arrays: sorting, linear searching, and binary searching. We have added a data structures section to our top-down design. Clearly, how we choose to represent our data is an important aspect of the programming process.

Although the array is an extremely useful data structure, it can only be used when the components are all of the same data type. In this chapter we will examine a nonhomogeneous structured data type called a *record*. The components of a record do not have to be of the same data type. The record differs from the array in another aspect: the components are accessed by name rather than by relative position.

The last chapter closed with a discussion of how to choose a data structure. We will continue this discussion at the end of this chapter, including the record among the possible choices.

RECORDS

Up until now, the data structures we've examined could only contain components of a single data type. Now we will examine a built-in Pascal data structure that allows us to group related components together regardless of the types of the components—the record. Each component in a record is given a name called a *field identifier*, which is used to access the component.

Record A structured data type with a fixed number of components that are accessed by name, not by an index. The components may be of different types.

Field Identifier The name of a component in a record.

The syntax diagram for the record data type is given below.

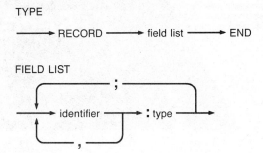

As an example, let's use a record to describe a student in a class. We want to keep the first and last name, the overall grade point average prior to this class, the grade on programming assignments, the grade on quizzes, the final exam grade, and the final course grade.

```
CONST
   NameLength = 15;

TYPE
   NameIndex = 1..NameLength;
   GradeType = (A, B, C, D, F);
   NameString = PACKED ARRAY[NameIndex] OF Char;
   StudentRecord = RECORD
                      FirstName,
                      LastName : NameString;
                      GPA : Real;
                      ProgramGrade : 0..400;
                      QuizGrade,
                      FinalExam : 0..300;
                      CourseGrade : GradeType
                   END;   (* Record *)

VAR
   Student:
      StudentRecord;
   Grade:
      Integer;
```

FirstName, LastName, GPA, ProgramGrade, QuizGrade, FinalExam, and CourseGrade are field identifiers within the record type StudentRecord. These field identifiers make up the field list. Note that each field identifier is given a type.

FirstName and LastName are of type NameString, which is a packed array of Char. GPA is a Real field. ProgramGrade is an Integer field in the subrange 0 to 400. QuizGrade and FinalExam are Integer fields in the subrange 0 to 300. CourseGrade is an enumerated data type made up of the grades A through F.

Figure 14-1
Pattern for a
Record

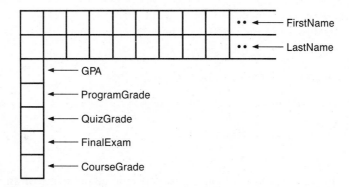

StudentRecord is a pattern for a record. This pattern is shown in Figure 14-1.
Student is a variable of type StudentRecord. The fields of the record variable
Student are accessed by giving the name of the record variable, a period, and the
field identifier. This expression is called a *field selector*. The syntax diagram is

Field selectors are used to access the fields of a record.

Field Selector The expression used to access components of a record variable, formed using
the record variable name and the field identifier, separated by a period.

The component of a record accessed by the field selector can be treated just like
any other variable of the same type. Figure 14-2 shows the record variable Student
with the field selectors for each field. In this example, some processing has already
taken place so values are stored in some of the components.

Let's demonstrate the use of these field selectors in a code segment that reads in
a final exam grade, adds up the program grade, the quiz grade, and the final exam
grade, and then assigns a letter grade to the result.

Figure 14-2
Record Variable
Student with Field
Selectors

| 'A' | 'l' | 'i' | 'c' | 'e' | | •• ← ———— Student.FirstName |

| 'B' | 'r' | 'o' | 'w' | 'n' | | •• ← ———— Student.LastName |

| 3.4 | ← ———— Student.GPA |

| 325 | ← ———— Student.ProgramGrade |

| 275 | ← ———— Student.QuizGrade |

| | ← ———— Student.FinalExam |

| | ← ———— Student.CourseGrade |

```
Read(Student.FinalExam);
Grade := Student.FinalExam + Student.ProgramGrade + Student.QuizGrade;
IF  Grade  <=  900
   THEN
      Student.CourseGrade := A
   ELSE
      IF  Grade  <=  800
         THEN
             Student.CourseGrade := B
   ELSE  ...
```

Just as we can read values into specific components of an array, we can read values into fields of a record. Read(Student.FinalExam) reads a value from Input and stores the value into the FinalExam field of the record variable Student. When using text files, we *cannot* read in whole records; we must read values into a record one field at a time. In the next chapter we will look at a different kind of file from which whole records can be read at once.

The component Student.LastName is an array. How do we access the individual elements in the component? Just as we would for any other array: we give the name of the array followed by the index, which is enclosed in brackets.

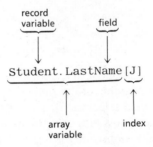

For the record structure defined earlier, Student.LastName[1] would access the first letter in the last name. Student.FirstName[NameLength] would access the last position in the first name, and so on.

In addition to being able to access individual components of a record variable, we can manipulate records as a whole. Records can be formal parameters for procedures or functions. Let's define a function that takes our example record as a parameter.

The task of the function is to determine if a student's grade in a course is consistent with his or her overall GPA. Consistent is defined to mean that the course grade is the same as the rounded GPA. The GPA is calculated on a 4-point scale where A is 4, B is 3, C is 2, D is 1, and F is 0. If the rounded GPA is 4 and the course grade is A, then the function returns True. If the rounded GPA is 4 and the course grade is not A, then the function returns False. Each of the other grades is tested the same way.

Function Consistent is coded below. The formal parameter AStudent is a record of type StudentRecord.

```
FUNCTION Consistent (AStudent:
                         StudentRecord):
                         Boolean;

(* This function returns True if the course
   grade is consistent with the overall GPA *)

TYPE
  GPA = 0..4;

VAR
  IntGPA:
    GPA;

BEGIN (* Consistent *)
  IntGPA := Round(AStudent.GPA);
  CASE IntGPA OF
    0 : Consistent := (AStudent.CourseGrade = F);
    1 : Consistent := (AStudent.CourseGrade = D);
    2 : Consistent := (AStudent.CourseGrade = C);
    3 : Consistent := (AStudent.CourseGrade = B);
    4 : Consistent := (AStudent.CourseGrade = A)
  END (* Case *)
END;    (* Consistent *)
```

One record variable can be assigned to another record variable of the same type. For example, if AnotherStudent is declared to be of StudentType, the statement

```
AnotherStudent := Student
```

assigns the entire contents of the record variable Student to the record variable AnotherStudent.

Let's review the syntax and semantics of the record data type in the context of another example. A parts wholesaler wants to computerize her operation. Until now she has kept the inventory on handwritten 8 × 10 cards. A typical inventory card contains the following data:

Part number: 1A3321

Description: cotter pin

Cost: 0.012

Quantity on hand: 2100

A record would be a natural choice for describing a part. Each item on the inventory card could be a field of the record. The record definition would look like this:

```
TYPE
   PartType = RECORD
                 PartNumber : PACKED ARRAY[1..6] OF Char;
                 Description : PACKED ARRAY[1..20] OF Char;
                 Cost : Real;
                 Quantity : Integer
              END;    (* Record *)

VAR
   Part:
      PartType;
```

The reserved words RECORD and END bracket the field declarations. Each field identifier is followed by a colon and a type, *just like the declaration of any variable.* Field identifiers must be unique within a record type just as variable identifiers must be unique within a VAR section.

Once a record variable has been declared, the field selectors of the record variable are treated and used in the same way as any other declared variable. Field selectors can be used in expressions such as

```
Part.Quantity := Part.Quantity + 24;
IF Part.Cost <= 5.00
   THEN
      Writeln('Cost is ', Part.Cost:4:2);
```

If the parts wholesaler supplied inventory data that looked like

```
2B3310Ring, piston         2.95  15
```

then the following program segment would read and store the data in the appropriate fields.

```
FOR Count := 1 TO 6 DO
   Read(Part.PartNumber[Count]);
FOR Count := 1 TO 20 DO
   Read(Part.Description[Count]);
Readln(Part.Cost, Part.Quantity);
```

Part.PartNumber, Part.Description, Part.Cost, and Part.Quantity are the field selectors for the fields of the record variable Part.

The PACKED option may be applied to records. This means that the compiler is instructed to pack as many fields as possible into one computer word. On machines with a small word size, very little memory space is saved using this option; on machines with a large word size, the use of the packed option will save considerable memory space.

A packed record variable is accessed and manipulated exactly like a nonpacked record variable. There are no special features associated with a packed record.

There is always a tradeoff when using the packed option. Memory space will be saved at the expense of execution time. It takes longer to access a field or a character that is packed in a word with another field or character.

Our examples have shown record types being defined within the TYPE section— that is, as named types. You can also define record types in the VAR section; however, we do not recommend that you do so. Defining any data type in the VAR section is anonymous typing. All the arguments given previously against anonymous typing apply to record types as well.

ARRAYS OF RECORDS

Although single records can be useful, many applications require a collection of records. For example, a business will need a list of parts records and a teacher will need a list of students in a class. Arrays are ideal for these applications. We simply define an array whose components are records.

Let's define a grade book to be a list of students as follows:

```
CONST
    NameLength = 15;
    MaxStudents = 150;
    TestPoints = 300;
    ProgPoints = 400;

TYPE
    TestIndex = 0..TestPoints;
    ProgramIndex = 0..ProgPoints;
    NameIndex = 1..NameLength;
    StudentIndex = 1..MaxStudents;
    GradeType = (A, B, C, D, F);
    NameString = PACKED ARRAY[NameIndex] OF Char;
    StudentRecord = RECORD
                        FirstName,
                        LastName : NameString;
                        GPA : Real;
                        ProgramGrade : ProgramIndex;
                        QuizGrade,
                        FinalExam : TestIndex;
                        CourseGrade : GradeType
                    END;   (* Record *)
    Students = ARRAY[StudentIndex] OF StudentRecord;
```

```
VAR
    Grade:
        Integer;
    Count:
        StudentIndex;
    GradeBook:
        Students;
    Length:
        Integer;
```

This structure can be visualized as shown in Figure 14-3.

An element of GradeBook is selected by an index. GradeBook[3] is the third component in the array variable GradeBook. Each component of GradeBook is a record of type StudentRecord. In order to access the course grade of the third student, we use the following expression:

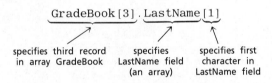

GradeBook[3] . CourseGrade

specifies third record   specifies CourseGrade
in array GradeBook   field in record
                            GradeBook[3]

If we want to access the first character in the last name of the third student, we use the following expression:

GradeBook[3] . LastName[1]

specifies third record   specifies   specifies first
in array GradeBook   LastName field character in
                          (an array)   LastName field

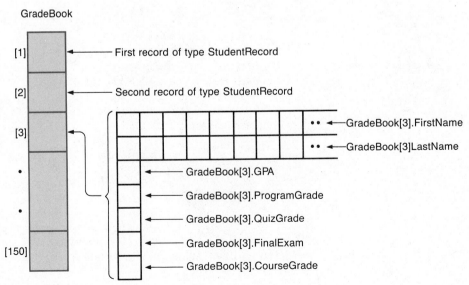

Figure 14-3
Array Gradebook
with Records as
Elements

The following code fragment will print the first and last name of each student in the class:

```
FOR Count := 1 TO Length DO
Writeln(GradeBook[Count].FirstName,' ', GradeBook[Count].LastName)
```

Problem Solving in Action

Problem: You have a pocket address book that you have used for years. It is now falling apart. Instead of copying all the items into a new book, you decide to automate your address book, including the following information for each entry:

Name: _____

Address: _____
        (street)

        _____
        (city)   (state)   (zip)

Telephone: (_____) _____-_____

Birthdate: _____/_____/_____

Discussion: There are all kinds of interesting things we could do with the address book information if we had it on a computer file: print a listing, input a name and have the phone number printed, print a list of the people with birthdays each month, print names and addresses in zip code order to facilitate sending cards, and so on.

However, let's not be too ambitious. We had better do the program in stages. In the first stage we'll create the address book and save the information on a file. Since we will want to enhance the program at a later time, we need to make the data structure as flexible as possible. As we do the top-down design, we will pay particular attention to the development of the data structure.

Just as there is no algorithm for writing algorithms, there is no algorithm for choosing a data structure. There are, however, heuristics. In fact, the applicable heuristics are some of the same ones we apply to algorithm design: (1) look at the structure you would use if you were to do the problem by hand, and (2) defer details as long as possible.

Remember that refinement of the data structure should be done in parallel with the top-down design. At the top level we think of our data structures in very general terms. As our modules get more specific, so do our ideas about our data structures. Only when our modules deal with specific algorithms on the data structures do we have to finalize our structured data type.

As we start our design phase for this problem, we will call all the information about one person an entry. We know that we want to keep our entries in order by last name so that we can use a binary search to locate specific people. We can either enter the entries in alphabetical order or enter them in any order and then sort them. Since some last names have changed over the years and we have not bothered to copy them on the appropriate page, it will be easier to let the program sort them than to enter them in alphabetical order.

PSIA ▬▬▬▬▬▬

Input: A series of entries containing a first and last name, a phone number, and a birthdate. Exact form of an entry to be determined.

Output: The entries in alphabetical order on file FriendList

Data structure: To be determined

MAIN MODULE   Level 0

```
WHILE more entries DO
   Get Entry
   Insert Entry in alphabetical order
Write Entries on file
```

Before we can write the module for procedure GetEntry, we have to decide what information we will keep on each person. Since we mainly use this address book to look up telephone numbers, we need each person's name and phone number. We will skip addresses for now, but include birthdates.

GET ENTRY   Level 1

```
Get Name
Get Number
Get Birthdate
```

GET NAME   Level 2

```
Get first name
Get last name
```

GET PHONE NUMBER

```
Get area code
Get phone number
```

GET BIRTHDATE

```
Get Month, Day, Year
```

PSIA ▰▰▰▰▰

WRITE ENTRIES   Level 1

Writeln FirstName, ' ', LastName
Writeln AreaCode, PhoneNumber
Writeln Month, '/', Day, '/', Year

Now we must decide what data types to use. We began with the general concept of an entry. We refined it to include the items needed in the entry. To go any further, we must decide how we will represent these items in Pascal. Up to this point, our design has been independent of any programming language, but now we must design specific algorithms for our data structures: reading in items, sorting items, and printing items.

What are the items? Two of the items are names, that is, strings of alphabetic characters. These can be represented as strings—packed one-dimensional arrays of type Char. The area code and number could be integer numbers. However, the phone number might be larger than MaxInt on some machines. Therefore, the area code will be an integer number but the phone number will be a string. We can represent birthdates as three integer numbers: Month, Day, and Year. Thus an entry will be represented by the seven components shown in Figure 14-4.

How do we create a structure that can hold more than one of these? We could use a set of parallel arrays. FirstName, LastName, and PhoneNumber would be arrays of strings; AreaCode, Month, Day, and Year would be one-dimensional arrays of integers. Each parallel row would represent the information for one entry. This set of structures is shown in Figure 14-5.

This seems a very clumsy way of representing this logical structure: a parallel structure made up of seven different arrays. Yet this is the structure that you will have to use for this type of problem if your programming language does not have the record data type—and some do not. However, it makes more sense to define an entry using the record data type if it is available.

Figure 14-4
Entry for
Addressbook

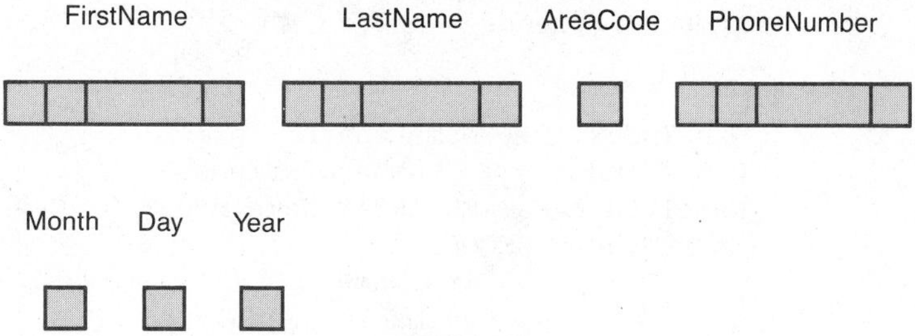

FirstName   LastName   AreaCode   PhoneNumber

Month   Day   Year

PSIA

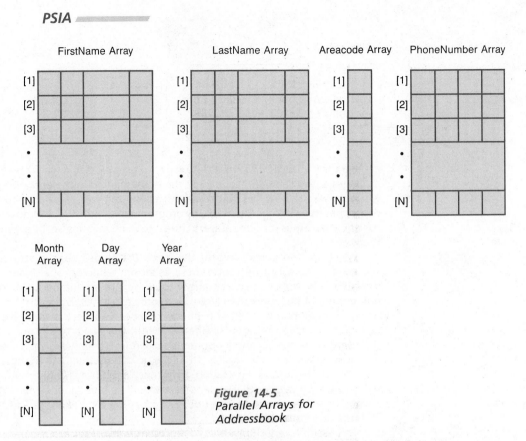

Figure 14-5
Parallel Arrays for
Addressbook

Let's now look at an alternative data structure in which a record is used to represent an entry and an array of records to represent the address book. The following declarations describe this structure:

```
CONST
    NameLength = 15;
    NumberOfFriends = 150;

TYPE
    NameIndex = 1..NameLength;
    FriendIndex = 1..NumberOfFriends;
    NameType = PACKED ARRAY[NameIndex] OF Char;
    EntryType = RECORD
                FirstName,
                LastName : NameType;
                AreaCode : 0..999;
                PhoneNumber : PACKED ARRAY[1..8] OF Char;
                Month : 1..12;
                Day : 1..31;
                Year : 1900..2020
            END;  (* Record *)
    BookType = ARRAY[FriendIndex] OF EntryType;
```

PSIA ▰▰▰▰▰

```
VAR
   AddressBook:
   BookType;
```

FirstName, LastName, AreaCode, PhoneNumber, Month, Day, and Year are field identifiers within the record type EntryType. These field identifiers will be used to access the different components of the record variables of type EntryType stored in the array variable AddressBook.

FirstName and LastName are strings of type NameType. AreaCode is an integer in the subrange 0 to 999. It could have been represented in a three-element character array, but a simple integer will suffice. PhoneNumber is defined as an eight-element character array. Phone numbers have only seven digits, but we decided to include the hyphen between the first three digits and the last four digits since this is how phone numbers are usually printed.

Month is an integer in the subrange 1 to 12. Day is an integer in the subrange 1 to 31. Year is an integer in the subrange 1900 to 2020. A complete entry with values stored in the record variable AddressBook[1] is shown in Figure 14-6.

We have now defined the data structure to hold the information in our address book. Before we can finish the algorithms to read the data, we will have to decide how we want to enter the data. We can create a file ahead of time or enter the data interactively. Let's enter the data interactively. The user can be prompted to enter each component. End of line can be used to end the first and last name.

Since the first name and the last name are both character strings of length 15, we can use the same procedure to input both the first name and the last name. The only thing that will differ is the user prompt. The correct prompt can be issued before the

Figure 14-6
Entry for Record
Variable
Addressbook[1]

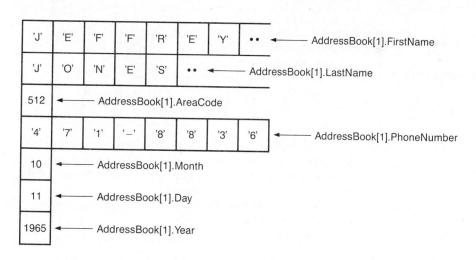

PSIA ▰▰▰▰▰▰

routine is called. Procedure GetName will therefore have to be changed. Our design
for this portion of the algorithm now looks like this:

GET NAME   Level 2

```
Writeln 'Enter first name and press return.'
Get Name String (first name)
Writeln 'Enter last name and press return.'
Get Name String (last name)
```

GET NAME STRING   Level 3

```
Name ⟵ Blanks
Index ⟵ 1
REPEAT
  Read(Character)
  Name[Index] ⟵ Character
  Index ⟵ Index + 1
UNTIL  EOLN OR Index > NameLength
```

We can also redo the module for getting the phone number.

GET PHONE NUMBER   Level 2

```
Read(Areacode)
Index ⟵ 1
REPEAT
  Read(Character)
  PhoneNumber[Index] ⟵ Character
  Index ⟵ Index + 1
UNTIL  Index > 8
```

In Chapter 12 we wrote procedures Insert and SearchOrd to insert an item into its
proper place in a list. These procedures were used in Program Exam to insert last names
as they were read into an array of last names. We can use the same procedures here
with the following minor modification.

The statement that compared the item being inserted with the components already in the list was

$$\text{IF Item} > \text{List[Index]}$$
$$\text{THEN}$$

Since our data structure is an array of records, Item and List[Index] are records—
not simple variables. Therefore the name of the field that is being compared must be
added as follows:

$$\text{IF Item.LastName} > \text{List[Index].LastName}$$
$$\text{THEN}$$

PSIA

When coding the design, we will need to remember to write the prompts for the phone number and the birthdate. Also, we haven't made any provision for keying errors. This is not very realistic. After an entry has been read and before it is entered into the address book, let's ask the user whether the entry is correct. If the user says it is, the entry can be stored. If the user says it is not, the entry will not be saved.

We also have not determined how to end the reading process. Let's ask the user after each entry whether another entry is to be read. The main module now needs rewriting.

MAIN MODULE   Level 0

```
REPEAT
  Get Entry
  Writeln 'Is this entry correct? (Y or N)'
  Readln(Character)
  IF Character IN ['y', 'Y']
    THEN
      Insert Entry
  Writeln 'Do you wish to continue? (Y or N)'
  Readln(Character)
UNTIL Character IN ['n', 'N']

WHILE more entries
  Write Entries
```

Module Structure Chart:

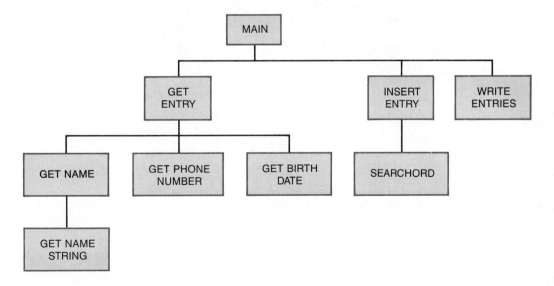

PSIA ▬▬▬▬

```
PROGRAM Friends (Input, Output, FriendList);

(* First names, last names, phone numbers and birthdates are read
   from the terminal.  An alphabetical listing is written on file
   Friendlist *)

CONST
  NameLength = 15;
  NumberOfFriends = 150;
  Blanks = '               ';

TYPE
  NameIndex = 1..NameLength;
  FriendIndex = 1..NumberOfFriends;
  FriendCount = 0..NumberOfFriends;
  NameType = PACKED ARRAY[NameIndex] OF Char;
  EntryType = RECORD
                FirstName,
                LastName : NameType;
                AreaCode : 0..999;
                PhoneNumber : PACKED ARRAY[1..8] OF Char;
                Month : 1..12;
                Day : 1..31;
                Year : 1900..2020
              END;   (* Record *)
  BookType = ARRAY[FriendIndex] OF EntryType;
  ItemType = EntryType;
  ListType = BookType;

VAR
  AddressBook:      (* Array of friend records          *)
    BookType;
  Character:        (* For response from terminal        *)
    Char;
  Entry:            (* Current record being entered      *)
    EntryType;
  Length:           (* Number of entries in AddressBook *)
    FriendCount;
  FriendList:       (* Entries saved to use later        *)
    Text;

(***************************************************************************)


PROCEDURE Insert (VAR List:        (* List being inserted into    *)
                        ListType;
                  VAR Length:       (* Number of entries in List *)
                        Integer;
                      Item:         (* Item being inserted         *)
                        ItemType);
```

PSIA ▰▰▰▰▰▰

```
(*  Item is inserted into its proper place in the sorted list List.
    Assumption:  Length is less than MaxLength.  If a match occurs,
    Item will be inserted before the one that is there. *)

VAR
  PlaceFound:        (* Flag set if match occurs *)
    Boolean;
  Index,             (* Current position in List *)
  Count:             (* Loop control variables   *)
    Integer;


(******************************************************************)

PROCEDURE SearchOrd (    List:         (* List being searched      *)
                           ListType;
                         Item:         (* Item being searched for *)
                           ItemType;
                         Length:       (* Number of items in List *)
                           Integer;
                     VAR Found:        (* Match flag               *)
                           Boolean;
                     VAR Index:        (* Position to insert item *)
                           Integer);

(* List is searched for an occurrence of Item.  If Item is found,
   Found is True and Index is the place in the List where Item
   occurs.  Otherwise, Found is False and Index is Length + 1.
   Assumption:  List is sorted in ascending order. *)

VAR
  Stop:          (* Loop control flag *)
    Boolean;


BEGIN (* SearchOrd *)
  Index := 1;
  Stop := False;
  List[Length+1] := Item;
  (* Exit loop when value is found or not there *)
  WHILE NOT Stop DO
     (* Item is not in List[1]..List[Index-1] *)
     IF Item.LastName > List[Index].LastName
       THEN
           (* Item is not in List[1]..List[Index] *)
           Index := Index + 1
       ELSE
           (* Item is either found or not there *)
           Stop := True;
  (* Determine whether Item was found or not there *)
```

PSIA ⬛━━━━━

```
      Found := (Index <> Length + 1)
   END;   (* SearchOrd *)


   (**********************************************************************)


BEGIN (* Insert *)
   SearchOrd(List, Item, Length, PlaceFound, Index);
   (* Shift List[Index]..List[Length] down one *)
   FOR Count := Length DOWNTO Index DO
     List[Count+1] := List[Count];
   List[Index] := Item;                          (* Insert Item *)
   Length := Length + 1                    (* Increment Length *)
END;   (* Insert *)


   (**********************************************************************)


PROCEDURE GetName (VAR Entry:          (* Record receiving names *)
                        EntryType);

(* GetNameString is called twice: Once to get the first name and once
   to get the last name *)

VAR
   Name:
     NameType;


   (**********************************************************************)


   PROCEDURE GetNameString (VAR Name:          (* Name typed in *)
                                  NameType);

   (* Characters are read and stored in Name until end of line or
      NameLength characters have been read.  The balance of the line
      is skipped. *)

   VAR
     Index:              (* Loop control variable *)
       0..NameLength;
     Character:          (* Character typed in    *)
       Char;

   BEGIN (* GetNameString *)
     Name := Blanks;
     Index := 0;
     WHILE NOT EOLN AND (Index < NameLength) DO
       BEGIN
         Index := Index + 1;
```

PSIA ◢▬▬▬▬▬▬▬▬

```
        Read(Character);
        Name[Index] := Character;
      END;
    Readln
  END;   (* GetNameString *)


  (****************************************************************)


BEGIN (* GetName *)
  Writeln('Enter first name and press return.');
  GetNameString(Name);
  Entry.FirstName := Name;
  Writeln('Enter last name and press return.');
  GetNameString(Name);
  Entry.LastName := Name
END;   (* GetName *)


(****************************************************************)


PROCEDURE GetPhoneNumber (VAR Entry:          (* Record receiving number *)
                                EntryType);

(* Area code and phone number are read and returned *)

VAR
  Index:
    1..9;
  Character:
    Char;


BEGIN (* GetPhoneNumber *)
  Writeln('Enter area code, blank, and the number. Include '-'.');
  Read(Entry.AreaCode);
  Read(Character);                                 (* Skip over blank *)
  Index := 1;
REPEAT
    Read(Character);
    Entry.PhoneNumber[Index] := Character;
    Index := Index + 1;
  UNTIL Index > 8;
  Readln
END;   (* GetPhoneNumber *)


(****************************************************************)


PROCEDURE GetEntry (VAR Entry:           (* Record being built *)
                          EntryType);

(* A complete entry is built and returned. GetName and GetPhoneNumber
   are called. *)
```

PSIA ▰▰▰▰

```
BEGIN  (* GetEntry *)
  GetName(Entry);
  GetPhoneNumber(Entry);
  Writeln('Enter birthdate as three integers: Month, Day, Year');
  Readln(Entry.Month, Entry.Day, Entry.Year)
END;   (* GetEntry *)


(***********************************************************************)


PROCEDURE WriteEntries (     AddressBook:     (* Array of friends   *)
                               BookType;
                             Length:          (* Number of entries  *)
                               FriendCount;
                         VAR FriendList:      (* File receiving list *)
                               Text);


(* All the entries are written on file FriendList *)


VAR
  Counter:
    FriendIndex;

BEGIN (* WriteEntries *)
  FOR Counter := 1 TO Length DO
    BEGIN
      Writeln(FriendList, AddressBook[Counter].FirstName, ' ',
              AddressBook[Counter].LastName);
      Writeln(FriendList, '(', AddressBook[Counter].AreaCode:3, ') ',
              AddressBook[Counter].PhoneNumber);
      Writeln(FriendList, AddressBook[Counter].Month:2, '/',
              AddressBook[Counter].Day:2, '/',
              AddressBook[Counter].Year:4);
      Writeln(FriendList)
    END
END;   (* WriteEntries *)


(***********************************************************************)
```

PSIA ▰▰▰▰▰▰

```
BEGIN  (* Friends *)
   Length : = 0;
   Rewrite(FriendList);
   REPEAT
     GetEntry(Entry);
     Writeln('Is this entry correct?  (Y or N)');
     Readln(Character);
     IF Character IN ['y', 'Y']
        THEN
           Insert(AddressBook, Length, Entry);
     Writeln('Do you wish to continue?  (Y or N)');
     Readln(Character);
   UNTIL Character IN ['n', 'N'];
   WriteEntries(AddressBook, Length, FriendList)
END.  (* Friends *)
```

Testing: This is an interactive program in which the user has a great deal of control. The user is prompted to enter data, then is asked if the data has been entered correctly. If the user indicates that there has been an error, the data is not saved. After the information about a person is entered, the user is asked whether he or she wishes to continue.

In testing of this program, each of the options must be selected by the user at least once. When testing an interactive program you may be tempted to sit down and just enter data randomly. However, if you don't keep a record of the data entered, the saved file will only show the correct entries. You won't know whether the sections of code that allow the program to ignore an incorrect entry were tested.

It is important to plan how you are going to test a program in advance. First, make a list of all the cases that must be tested. Then design data sets to test all the cases. Only when you have written out all of the data sets and are convinced that they will thoroughly test the program should you sit down at the console and begin entering data.

As you enter the data in an interactive program, note the results on the written copy of the data set. If there is output that is saved and printed later, check these results carefully against the output. Don't assume the program ran correctly because it had no run-time errors.

HIERARCHICAL RECORDS

Just as the components of an array can be of any type, so can the components of a record. We have seen cases where the type of a field identifier is an array. A component of a record can also be another record. Records whose components are themselves records are called *hierarchical records*.

Hierarchical Records Records in which at least one of the fields is itself a record.

Another structure for the entries in our automated address book would be one where AreaCode and PhoneNumber were grouped together into a record and Month, Day, and Year were grouped together into another record.

```
TYPE
   NameIndex = 1..NameLength;
   FriendIndex = 1..NumberOfFriends;
   NameType = PACKED ARRAY[NameIndex] OF Char;
   DateType = RECORD
                 Month : 1..12;
                 Day : 1..31;
                 Year : 1900..2020
              END;   (* Record *)
   PhoneType = RECORD
                 AreaCode : 0..999;
                 Number : PACKED ARRAY[1..8] OF Char
              END;   (* Record *)
   EntryType2 = RECORD
                 FirstName
                 LastName : NameType;
                 Phone : PhoneType;
                 BirthDate : DateType
              END;   (* Record *)

VAR
   Entry:
      EntryType2;
```

We build the accessing expressions (field selectors) for the fields of the embedded records from left to right, beginning with the record variable name. Following are some expressions and the components they access.

Expression	Component accessed
Entry.Phone	PhoneType record variable
Entry.Phone.AreaCode	AreaCode field of a PhoneType record variable
Entry.Phone.Number	Number field of a PhoneType record variable
Entry.Phone.Number[1]	First digit in the Number field

Figure 14-7
Hierarchical
Records in Entry

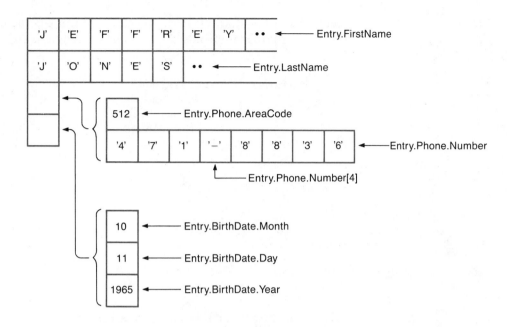

Figure 14-7 is a pictorial representation of Entry with values. Look carefully at how each component is accessed.

We can, of course, have an array of hierarchical records. If AddressBook were defined to be an array of EntryType2 records,

```
AddressBook[1].BirthDate.Year
```

would access the year in which the first person in the address book was born.

WITH STATEMENT

In working with record variables, we often need to access one or more fields of a record variable repeatedly in a small section of code. As we have seen, field selectors can get rather long and cumbersome. The WITH statement allows us to abbreviate the notation of field selectors by specifying the record name once and then using just the field identifiers to select the record components.

The form of the WITH statement is

```
WITH record variable DO
   statement
```

Let's look at how the WITH statement would simplify the code of procedure WriteEntries in Program Friends. The original procedure is shown below.

```
PROCEDURE WriteEntries (     AddressBook:
                               BookType;
                             Length:
                               FriendIndex;
                        VAR FriendList:
                               Text);

(* All the entries are written on file FriendList *)

VAR
  Counter:              (* Loop control variable *)
    FriendIndex;

BEGIN (* WriteEntries *)
  FOR Counter := 1 TO Length DO
    BEGIN
      Writeln(FriendList, AddressBook[Counter].FirstName, ' ',
              AddressBook[Counter].LastName);
      Writeln(FriendList, '(',AddressBook[Counter].AreaCode, ') ',
              AddressBook[Counter].PhoneNumber);
      Writeln(FriendList, AddressBook[Counter].Month, '/',
              AddressBook[Counter].Day, '/',
              AddressBook[Counter].Year);
      Writeln(FriendList)
    END
END;   (*WriteEntries *)
```

The body of this procedure is rewritten below using the WITH statement.

```
    FOR Counter := 1 TO Length DO
      WITH AddressBook[Counter] DO
        BEGIN
          Writeln(FriendList, FirstName, ' ', LastName);
          Writeln(FriendList, '(', AreaCode, ') ', PhoneNumber);
          Writeln(FriendList, Month, '/', Day, '/', Year);
          Writeln(FriendList)
        END
```

Within the scope of the WITH statement, each field name refers to the record variable named in the WITH statement. In this case, each field name refers to the record variable AddressBook[Counter]. Thus within the scope of the WITH statement, each record component can be selected by the field identifier alone; the full field selector is not necessary.

WITH statements can be nested to reference hierarchical records. For example, the statement

```
WITH AddressBook[1] DO
  WITH BirthDate DO
    BEGIN
      Day := 10;
      Month := 2;
      Year := 1984
    END;
```

would store 10, 2, and 1984 into the respective fields of the record of type BirthDate nested within the first record variable in AddressBook. This nested form can be abbreviated as

```
WITH AddresssBook[1], BirthDate DO
  BEGIN
        .
        .
  END;
```

Let's look at another example where a hierarchical structure is appropriate and see how the components are accessed using the WITH statement.

Information is to be kept about machines in a small machine shop. There is descriptive information such as the identification number, a verbal description of the machine, the purchase date, and the cost. Statistical information must also be kept such as the number of downdays, the failure rate, and the date of last service.

What is a reasonable way to represent all this information? This information can be divided into two groups: information that changes and information that does not. There are also two dates to be kept: date of purchase and date of last service. These observations suggest use of a record describing a date, a record describing the statistical data, and an overall record containing the other two as components. The following type definition reflects this structure.

```
CONST
  NumberOfMachines = 25;
  LengthOfDescription = 50;

TYPE
  MachineIndex = 1..NumberOfMachines;
  DescriptionIndex = 1..LengthOfDescription;
  DescriptionType = PACKED ARRAY[DescriptionIndex] OF Char;
  DateType = RECORD
               Month : 1..12;
               Day : 1..31;
               Year : 1900..2020
             END;  (* Record *)
```

```
StatisticsType = RECORD
                    FailRate : Real;
                    LastServiced : DateType;
                    DownDays : Integer
                 END;   (* Record *)
MachineRecord = RECORD
                   IdNumber : Integer;
                   Description : DescriptionType;
                   History : StatisticsType;
                   PurchaseDate : DateType;
                   Cost : Real
                END;   (* Record *)
InventoryType = PACKED ARRAY[MachineIndex] OF MachineRecord;

VAR
  Inventory:
    InventoryType;
  Machine:
    MachineRecord;
  Counter:
    MachineIndex;
  CurrentDate:
    DateType;
  Sum:
    Integer;
```

Two of the components of the record type MachineRecord are themselves records. PurchaseDate is of record type DateType, and History is of record type StatisticsType. One of the components of record type StatisticsType is a record of type DateType.

The following code segment would print out the IdNumber and year of purchase of each machine with a failure rate of more than 8 percent:

```
FOR Counter := 1 TO NumberOfMachines DO
   WITH Inventory[Counter] DO
      WITH History DO
         IF FailureRate > 0.08
            THEN
               Writeln(IdNumber, PurchaseDate.Year);
```

The following code segment would count the number of machines that have not been serviced within the current year:

```
Sum := 0;
FOR Counter := 1 TO NumberOfMachines DO
   WITH Inventory[Counter], History DO
      IF CurrentDate.Year <> LastServiced.Year
         THEN
            Sum := Sum + 1;
```

MORE ON CHOOSING DATA STRUCTURES

Representing Logical Entities with Hierarchical Records

We have demonstrated how we design our algorithms and data structures in parallel. We progress from the logical or abstract data structure envisioned at the top level through the refinement process until we reach the concrete coding in Pascal.

We have shown two different ways to represent the logical structure of the entry in our automated address book. The first way used a record where all the components in an entry were defined (made concrete) at the same time. The second way used a hierarchical record where the date and phone number were defined in a lower-level record.

Let's look again at the two different structures we declared to represent our logical data structure the entry.

```
CONST
   NameLength = 15;

TYPE
   NameIndex = 1..NameLength;
   NameType = PACKED ARRAY[NameIndex] OF Char:

   (*1*)
   EntryType = RECORD
                   FirstName,
                   LastName : NameType;
                   AreaCode : 0..999;
                   PhoneNumber : PACKED ARRAY[1..8] OF Char;
                   Month : 1..12;
                   Day : 1..31;
                   Year : 1900..2020
               END;   (* Record *)


   (*2*)
   DateType = RECORD
                   Month : 1..12;
                   Day : 1..31;
                   Year : 1900..2020
               END;   (* Record *)
   PhoneType = RECORD
                   AreaCode : 0..999;
                   Number : PACKED ARRAY[1..8] OF Char
               END;   (* Record *)
   EntryType2 = RECORD
                   FirstName,
                   LastName : NameType;
                   Phone : PhoneType;
                   BirthDate : DateType
               END;   (* Record *)
```

Which of these two representations is better? The second one is better for two reasons.

First, it groups elements together logically. The telephone number and the date are entities within themselves. We may want to have a date or a phone number in another record structure. If we define date and phone number only within EntryType (as in the first structure), we have to define them again for every other data structure that needs them, which gives us multiple definitions of the same logical entity.

Second, the details of the entities (telephone number and date) are pushed down to a lower level in the second structure. How a telephone number or a date will be represented is not relevant to our concept of an entry. The details of what a date or a phone number should look like do not need to be specified until it is time to write the algorithms to manipulate a date or a phone number.

In Chapter 10 we discussed control abstraction, in which the control structures are separated from their implementation. The principle of deferring details to as low a level as possible should be applied to designing data structures as well as to designing algorithms. By pushing the implementation details to a lower level, we are separating the logical description from the implementation. The separation of the logical properties of a data structure from its implementation details is called *data abstraction* and is a goal of good programming.

Data Abstraction The separation of the logical properties of a data structure from its implementation.

Eventually all the logical entities will have to be specified and routines written to manipulate them. If, however, each logical entity is a structure by itself, the same routines can be used to manipulate the entity, no matter what structure it is embedded in. For example, if we have a routine to compare dates, that routine can be used to compare dates representing birthdays of people or dates representing days on which equipment was bought or maintained.

The concept of designing a low-level structure and writing routines to manipulate it is the basis for the next Problem Solving in Action.

Problem Solving in Action

Dates are very often necessary pieces of information. Both the address book example and the machine shop example had a date as a part of the data. In fact, the machine shop example had two dates: the date of purchase and the date of last service. Each time we needed a date, we defined it again.

Often our processing of dates calls for us to compare two dates, print out a date, or determine the date a certain number of days away. So we write the code to do these operations again and again. Let's stop this duplication of effort and do the job once and for all.

Problem: Create a structure to represent a date and write a set of routines to operate on the structure. Make the structure and the routines general enough that they can be

PSIA

used in any program that needs to have these operations performed on dates. The operations are defined below.

Compare two dates: Take as input two dates and determine whether the first comes before the second, is the same as the second, or comes after the second.

Print out a date: Take as input a date and write it in the following form:

Month day ',' year (example: January 1, 1990)

Determine the date a certain number of days away: Take as input a date and an integer value DaysAway. Return a date that is the input date plus DaysAway. For example, given the date January 1, 1987, and the value 20 for DaysAway, the routine should return the date January 21, 1987.

Discussion: We will discuss each of the routines separately after we have determined a common data structure for representing a date. Note that we are using the terms routines and modules rather than procedures and functions at this stage. One of the decisions to be made in each case is whether the routine should be coded as a procedure or a function.

To make this structure as useful as possible, we must make our representation as general as possible. Month and day can remain as subranges as we have defined them in the previous examples. However, the year should not be limited; we will make it a positive integer.

```
TYPE
  DateType = RECORD
               Month : 1..12;
               Day : 1..31;
               Year : 0..MaxInt
             END;   (* Record *)
```

The format for this Problem Solving in Action will have to be a little different. There will be no Input and Output sections, since these routines will not read from or write to external files. Instead we will give the formal parameter lists that define the input and output for the routines.

Data Structures: All of the routines will operate on one or more record variables of type DateType.

Compare two dates: This operation will take two dates (Date1 and Date2) and determine whether the first one comes before the second one, they are the same, or the first one comes after the second one. We will define an enumerated type with three values: Before, Same, After. The operation can then be coded as a function of the enumerated type. The interface between the operation and any module that uses it is the function heading

```
FUNCTION Compare (Date1,
                  Date2:
                   DateType):
                   Relation;
```

PSIA ▬▬▬▬

where Relation is the enumerated type (Before, Same, After).

If we were to compare dates in our head, we would first look at the years. If the years were different, we could immediately determine which date came first. If the years were the same, we would look at the months. If the months were different, we could determine which came first. If the months were the same, we would have to look at the days. As so often happens, this algorithm can be used directly in our function.

COMPARE

```
IF Date1.Year < Date2.Year
   Compare ⟵ Before
ELSE
   IF Date1.Year > Date2.Year
      Compare ⟵ After
   ELSE
      IF Date1.Month < Date2.Month
         Compare ⟵ Before
      ELSE
         IF Date1.Month > Date2.Month
            Compare ⟵ After
         ELSE
            IF Date1.Day < Date2.Day
               Compare ⟵ Before
            ELSE
               IF Date1.Day > Date2.Day
                  Compare ⟵ After
               ELSE
                  Compare ⟵ Same
```

Function Compare is coded below. Note that the enumerated type Relation

```
TYPE
   Relation = (Before, Same, After);
```

must be defined in the main program.

```
FUNCTION Compare (Date1,          (* Date record to be compared *)
                  Date2:          (* Date record to be compared *)
                     DateType):
                     Relation;

(* If Date1 is before Date2, Before is returned.  If Date1 is equal
   to Date2, Same is returned.  If Date1 is after Date2, After is
   returned *)
```

PSIA

```
BEGIN (* Compare *)
  IF Date1.Year < Date2.Year                    (* Compare year *)
    THEN
      Compare : = Before
    ELSE
      IF Date1.Year > Date2.Year
        THEN
          Compare : = After
        ELSE
          IF Date1.Month < Date2.Month          (* Compare month *)
            THEN
              Compare : = Before
            ELSE
              IF Date1.Month > Date2.Month
                THEN
                  Compare : = After
                ELSE
                  IF Date1.Day < Date2.Day       (* Compare day *)
                    THEN
                      Compare : = Before
                    ELSE
                      IF Date1.Day > Date2.Day
                        THEN
                          Compare : = After
                        ELSE
                          Compare : = Same
END;   (* Compare *)
```

Testing: In testing this function, each path must be taken at least once. Preprogramming exercise 11 asks you to design test data for this function and to write a driver that does the testing.

Print out a date: To make this routine more general, we should make the file on which the date is to be written a formal parameter. If the date is to be written on the screen, Output can be used as the actual parameter.

The date is to be printed in the form month, day, comma, and year. Since the month is represented as an integer in the subrange 1..12, we can use a CASE statement to print out the month in word form. We will need a blank to separate the month and the day and a comma followed by a blank to separate the day and the year. This is so straightforward that no further discussion is necessary. The procedure heading forms the interface between the operation and the modules that will use it.

```
PROCEDURE PrintDate (VAR OutFile:        (* File to write date on      *)
                          Text;
                          Date:          (* Date record to be written *)
                          DateType);
```

PSIA

```
(* The date is printed out in standard form, with the month followed by
   the day followed by the year.  The month is not abbreviated *)

BEGIN (* PrintDate *)
  CASE   Date.Month  OF
     1 : Write(OutFile, 'January ');
     2 : Write(OutFile, 'February ');
     3 : Write(OutFile, 'March ');
     4 : Write(OutFile, 'April ');
     5 : Write(OutFile, 'May ');
     6 : Write(OutFile, 'June ');
     7 : Write(OutFile, 'July ');
     8 : Write(OutFile, 'August ');
     9 : Write(OutFile, 'September ');
    10 : Write(OutFile, 'October ');
    11 : Write(OutFile, 'November ');
    12 : Write(OutFile, 'December ')
  END;   (* Case *)
  Write(OutFile, Date.Day:1, ',', Date.Year:5)
END;   (* PrintDate *)
```

Testing: In testing of this procedure, each month should be printed at least once. The year and the day should each be tested at their end points and several points in between.

Determine the date a certain number of days away: The algorithm to calculate a date in the future is more complex than the previous two algorithms dealing with dates. If the current date plus DaysAway is still within the same month, there is no problem. If the current date plus DaysAway is within the next month, then the day must be calculated and the month must be changed. DaysAway could, in fact, be several months away or even in the next year (or the next, or the next . . .).

We can determine whether the given date (call it Date) plus DaysAway is within the current month by adding DaysAway to the day field of the date (call it NewDay) and comparing this value with the maximum number of days in the current month. If NewDay is greater than the number of days in the month, the month must be incremented and NewDay adjusted.

This process can be repeated until NewDay is within the current month. We must not forget to increment the year when the month changes from December to January and check for leap year when the month is February. The procedure heading can be defined as follows:

```
                    PROCEDURE AdjustDate(     Date:
                                                DateType;
                                              DaysAway:
                                                Integer;
                                          VAR NewDate:
                                                DateType);
```

PSIA ▬▬▬

ADJUST DATE

```
NewDay ⟵ Current.Day + DaysAway
NewDate ⟵ Date
REPEAT
  DaysInMonth ⟵ number of days in Date.Month
  IF NewDay <= DaysInMonth
    NewDate.Day ⟵ NewDay
    Finished ⟵ True
  ELSE
    NewDay ⟵ NewDay − DaysInMonth
    NewDate.Month ⟵ (NewDate.Month MOD 12) + 1
    IF NewDate.Month = 1
      NewDate.Year ⟵ NewDate.Year + 1
      Finished ⟵ False
UNTIL  Finished
```

We can use the old rhyme "Thirty days hath September, April, June, and November . . ." to determine how many days are in each month.

NUMBER OF DAYS

```
CASE Month
  9,4,6,11 : DaysInMonth ⟵ 30
  1,3,5,7,8,10,12 : DaysInMonth ⟵ 31
  2 : IF (Date.Year MOD 4 = 0) AND NOT (Date.Year MOD 100 = 0)
    THEN DaysInMonth = 29
    ELSE DaysInMonth = 28
```

The algorithm for finding the number of days in a month can be coded as an integer function which takes NewDate as a parameter. This function can be embedded within procedure AdjustDate.

```
PROCEDURE AdjustDate (     Date:          (* Initial date record   *)
                           DateType;
                           DaysAway:      (* Number of days to add *)
                           Integer;
                      VAR NewDate:        (* Resulting date record *)
                           DateType);

(* NewDate is the date DaysAway from Date. DaysAway must be nonnegative. *)
```

PSIA ▰▰▰▰▰▰

```
VAR
  NewDay,          (* DaysAway + Date.Day                            *)
  NumberOfDays:    (* Number of days in month                        *)
    Integer;
  Finished:        (* NewDate has been calculated when Finished is True *)
    Boolean;


(***************************************************************************)

FUNCTION DaysInMonth (Date:
                          DateType):
                          Integer;

(* DaysInMonth returns the number of days in Date.Day.
   Leap year is considered *)

BEGIN (* DaysInMonth *)
  WITH Date DO
    CASE Month OF
      9,4,6,11 : DaysInMonth := 30;
      1,3,5,7,8,10,12 : DaysInMonth := 31;
      2 : IF (Year MOD 4 = 0) AND NOT (Year MOD 100 = 0)
            THEN                                          (* Leap year *)
              DaysInMonth := 29
            ELSE
              DaysInMonth := 28
    END (* Case *)
END;   (* DaysInMonth *)


(***************************************************************************)

BEGIN (* AdjustDate *)
  NewDay := Date.Day + DaysAway;
  (* Initialize NewDate to Date *)
  NewDate := Date;
  REPEAT
    NumberOfDays := DaysInMonth(NewDate);
    IF NewDay <= NumberOfDays
      (* This is the correct month *)
      THEN
        BEGIN
          NewDate.Day := NewDay;
          Finished := True
        END;
```

PSIA _____

```
ELSE
(* Increment month and continue *)
   BEGIN
      NewDay := NewDay - NumberOfDays;
      NewDate.Month := (NewDate.Month MOD 12) + 1
      IF NewDate.Month = 1
         THEN
            NewDate.Year := NewDate.Year + 1;
      Finished := False
   END;
UNTIL Finished
END;   (* AdjustDate *)
```

Testing: To test this procedure, we will need to construct a driver that will call procedure AdjustDate with different values for both Date and DaysAway. The values for DaysAway must include 28, 29, 30, and 31, as well as multiples of these values and numbers less than 28. Leap year must be tested; a year with the last two digits 00 must be tested. Values that cause the year to change must be tested, as must values that cause the year to change more than once.

Preprogramming exercise 12 asks you to carry out this testing.

We have said that data abstraction is an important principle of good style. What we have done here is a good example of data abstraction. From now on when a problem needs a date, we can stop our decomposition at the logical level. We do not need to worry about the implementation details each time.

A date is a logical entity for which we have now developed an implementation. It is made up of the day, the month, and the year. The operations that we have defined on a date have been implemented and tested. We have created a date data type that we can use whenever we have the date as a part of our data. If a particular problem requires an additional operation on a date, it can be implemented, tested, and added to our set of date operations.

Style Considerations in Choice of Data Structure

Just as there are style considerations in writing programs, there are also style considerations in choosing a data structure. A program can produce a correct answer, yet be a poor program. It can be difficult to debug, read, or modify. A data structure can be used to solve a problem, yet not accurately reflect the relationships within the problem. If the data structure does not reflect these relationships, it is not a good structure for that program.

A data structure is a framework for holding data. This framework should be tailored to each particular problem. The relationships among data values should be

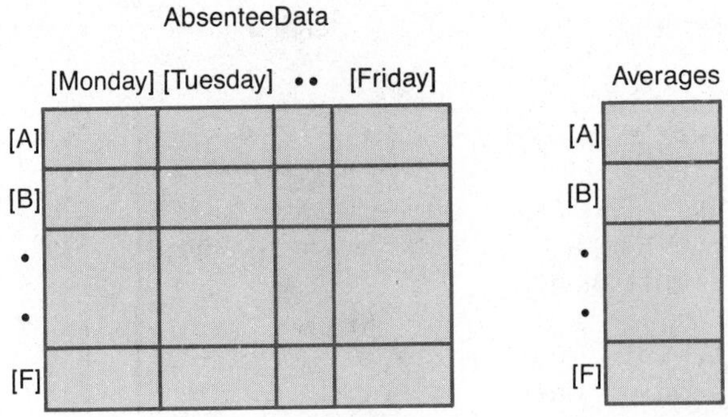

Figure 14-8
Arrays
AbsenteeData and
Averages

Figure 14-8 Arrays AbsenteeData and Averages

reflected in the framework, making it easy for users to see how the data items are related and how they should be processed to produce the required output.

Since each problem is different and the data structure should be tailored to the problem, it is impossible to give a set of rules by which to judge a good data structure. What we will do is examine the choices within a specific context, discuss the issues involved, and make some generalizations.

In Program Absent in Chapter 13, absentee data was analyzed. The data was made up of the number of people who were absent from each of six departments of a company during a particular week. The data was broken down further by day of the week.

The main data structure that was used was a two-dimensional array AbsenteeData, where the first dimension represented the departments and the second dimension represented the days of the week. Each component was an integer value that represented the number of people who were absent. A one-dimensional array Averages was used to hold the average daily absentee figures for each department. (See Figure 14-8.)

Would a record structure be a better choice to represent this information? Let's look at two possible representations of this same information as an array of records and discuss the implications of each representation.

```
TYPE
    DayType = (Monday, Tuesday, Wednesday, Thursday, Friday);
    DepartmentType = (A, B, C, D, E, F);
    AbsencesByWeek = RECORD
                        ByDepartment : ARRAY[A..F] OF Integer
                     END;   (* Record *)
    AbsencesByDept = RECORD
                        ByWeek : ARRAY[Monday..Friday] OF Integer
                     END;   (* Record *)
    Table1Type = ARRAY[Monday..Friday] OF AbsencesByWeek;
    Table2Type = ARRAY[A..F] OF AbsencesByDept;

VAR
    Table1:
      Table1Type;
    Table2:
      Table2Type;
```

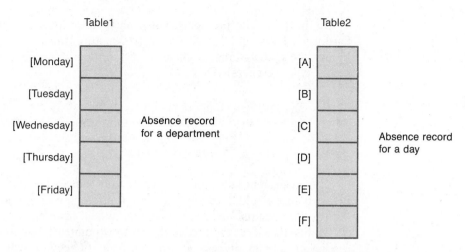

Figure 14-9
Absence Records
by Day

Table1

[Monday]

[Tuesday]

[Wednesday]

[Thursday]

[Friday]

Absence record
for a department

Table2

[A]

[B]

[C]

[D]

[E]

[F]

Absence record
for a day

Figure 14-10
Absence Records by Department

Table1 represents the data by day of the week. Table2 represents the data by department. These two representations are pictured in Figures 14-9 and 14-10.

Table1 and Table2 provide another example of abstraction. In the first representation, the fact that the absences are recorded by day of the week is the important feature. The detail that the absences are further broken down by department is pushed to a lower level. Conversely, in the second representation, the fact that the absences are recorded by department is the important feature, and the fact that the absences are further broken down by day of the week is pushed to a lower level. In the two-dimensional array representation, both features—recording by department and by day of the week—are equally important. (See Figure 14-11.)

The best representation for a particular problem is the one that reflects the emphasis of the processing within the problem. This emphasis can be determined by looking at the questions that are being asked—that is, the results to be computed.

If the primary processing involves absences by day of the week, the first structure is best. If the primary processing involves absences by department, the second representation is best. If both aspects of the processing are equally important, the two-dimensional array representation is best.

Figure 14-11
Two-Dimensional
Array of Absentee
Data

AbsenteeData

[Monday] [Tuesday] •• [Friday]

[A]

[B]

•

•

[F]

In this particular problem, management asked for absentee patterns across departments. Therefore, the second record structure, Table2, would be a better choice. In fact, the array Averages, which is used in the processing, can be incorporated in record type AbsencesByDept.

```
AbsencesByDept = RECORD
                   ByWeek: ARRAY[Monday..Friday] OF Integer;
                   Average: Real
                 END; (* Record *)
```

If management had wanted to know the averages for each day of the week, the first structure would have been more appropriate. If both averages had been needed, the two-dimensional array representation would have been more appropriate.

Notice that if all the processing on a two-dimensional array is either row processing *or* column processing, then an array of records will probably reflect the problem and the processing better than a two-dimensional array.

Data structures that accurately reflect the relationships among the data values in a problem lead to good programs. The logic of the program will be easier to understand because the data structures mirror the problem. The code of the program will be easier to maintain because the logic of the program is clearer. The program will be easier to modify because the data structure accurately represents the problem.

We should make one additional point here. The best structure is the *simplest* one that accurately reflects the problem and the processing. For example, don't use either an array or a record if simple variables will suffice.

When you are deciding whether to use a structured data type, ask yourself, "Can I process as I read, or must all the data be read in before I can begin processing?" For example, if you are finding the average of a set of test grades, each test grade can be added into the sum as it is read. All you need are simple variables—no structured data types are necessary.

What happens, however, if you want to compare each grade to the average? Since the average cannot be calculated until all the grades have been read, each individual grade must be kept in memory. Therefore the test grades should be stored in an array. Of course, if the grades are on a file, the file could be reset and the grades reread. However, rereading the grades takes much more time than storing them in an array and retrieving them.

This discussion presupposes that you know where to begin. What if you look at a problem and don't even know what the choices are? Go back and carefully examine the problem statement. Do you understand what is being asked? Could you do what is being asked by hand? If so, what sorts of forms would you use? Would you set up a table with rows and columns on a sheet of paper? Would you set up a column and make hash marks? More than likely an appropriate data structure will resemble the forms you would create to do the job by hand.

If you could not do the job by hand, your problem is more fundamental than the choice of a data structure. You need to clarify the problem. Try writing down everything you know about the problem. Then write down what your output must be. Next try writing down what you must have as input to produce that output. Refer, if necessary, to the problem-solving heuristics in Chapter 2.

Problem Solving in Action

Problem: In Chapter 10 we commented that everyone has at least one friend who never forgets important dates in the lives of his or her friends. Let's write a program to go through our address book and print the names and phone numbers of all the people who have birthdays within the next two weeks, so that we can give them a call.

Input:

A date (from the keyboard)

A list of names, phone numbers, and birthdates (file FriendList)

Output: The names, phone numbers, and birthdays of anyone whose birthday is within the next two weeks

Discussion: When looking for birthdays, we are interested in month and day only—the year is not important. If we were going through a conventional address book checking for birthdays by hand, we would write down the month and day of the date two weeks away and compare it to the month and day of each friend's birthdate.

We can use the same algorithm in our program. Procedure Adjust can be used to calculate the date two weeks (14 days) from the current date. Procedure Compare can be used to determine whether a friend's birthday comes before or on the date two weeks away. How do we ignore the year? We set the year of each friend's birthdate to the current year for the comparison.

Data Structure: Date data types

MAIN MODULE   Level 0

```
Get Current Date
Adjust Date (CurrentDate, 14, TargetDate)
WHILE NOT EOF (FriendList)
   Get Entry
TempDate ⟵ Entry.BirthDate
TempDate.Year ⟵ TargetDate.Year
IF Compare(TempDate,TargetDate) <= Same
   Print Entry
```

GET CURRENT DATE   Level 1

```
Write 'Please input current date as month, day, and year.'
Writeln 'Use digits for month.  Separate with blanks.'
Readln(CurrentDate.Month, CurrentDate.Day, CurrentDate.Year)
```

PRINT ENTRY

```
Write FirstName, LastName
Write Phone Number
Print Birthday
```

PSIA ▱▱▱▱▱▱

Since AdjustDate, Compare, and PrintDate already exist, no more decomposition is necessary.

```
PROGRAM BirthdayCalls (Input, Output, FriendList);

(* A date is read from the console, and a date two weeks away is
   calculated.  Names, phone numbers, and birthdays of all those on
   file FriendList whose birthdays come on or before the date two
   weeks away are printed. *)

CONST
  NameLength = 15;
  DaysHence = 14

TYPE
  NameIndex = 1..NameLength;
  NameType = PACKED ARRAY[NameIndex] OF Char;
  DateType = RECORD
                 Month : 1..12;
                 Day : 1..31;
                 Year : 0..MaxInt
             END;  (* Record *)
  PhoneType = RECORD
                  AreaCode : 0..999;
                  Number : PACKED ARRAY[1..8] OF Char
              END;   (* Record *)
  EntryType2 = RECORD
                   FirstName,
                   LastName : NameType;
                   Phone : PhoneType;
                   BirthDate : DateType
               END;   (* Record *)
  Relation = (Before, Same, After);

VAR
  Entry:            (* Current record from FriendList being checked *)
    EntryType2;
  CurrentDate,      (* Month, Day and Year of current day          *)
  TempDate,         (* Month and Day of BirthDate, current year    *)
  TargetDate:       (* Two weeks from current date                 *)
    DateType;
  FriendList:       (* Input file of friend records                *)
    Text;


(***********************************************************************)


PROCEDURE GetCurrentDate (VAR CurrentDate:   (* Today's date *)
                                  DateType);
```

PSIA ▬▬▬

```
(* Current date is entered from the console *)

BEGIN (* GetCurrentDate *)
  Writeln('Please input current date as month, day, and year.');
  Writeln('Use digits for month.  Separate with blanks.');
  Readln(CurrentDate.Month, CurrentDate.Day, CurrentDate.Year)
END;   (* GetCurrentDate *)

(*******************************************************************)

FUNCTION Compare (Date1,              (* Date record to compare *)
                  Date2:              (* Date record to compare *)
                     DateType):
                     Relation;

(* If Date1 is before Date2, Before is returned.  If Date1 is equal
   to Date2, Same is returned. If Date1 is after Date2, After is
   returned. *)

BEGIN (* Compare *)
  IF Date1.Year < Date2.Year                    (* Compare year *)
    THEN
      Compare : = Before
    ELSE
      IF Date1.Year > Date2.Year
        THEN
          Compare : = After
        ELSE
          IF Date1.Month < Date2.Month          (* Compare month *)
            THEN
              Compare : = Before
            ELSE
              IF Date1.Month > Date2.Month
                THEN
                  Compare : = After
                ELSE
                  IF Date1.Day < Date2.Day       (* Compare day *)
                    THEN
                      Compare : = Before
                    ELSE
                      IF Date1.Day > Date2.Day
                        THEN
                          Compare : = After
                        ELSE
                          Compare : = Same
END;   (* Compare *)

(*******************************************************************)
```

PSIA ▬▬▬

```
PROCEDURE PrintDate (VAR OutFile:        (* File receiving date *)
                             Text;
                         Date:           (* Date being written  *)
                             DateType);
```

(* The date is printed out in standard form, with the month followed by
   the day followed by the year. The month is not abbreviated. *)

```
BEGIN (* PrintDate *)
  CASE Date.Month OF
     1 : Write(OutFile,  'January ');
     2 : Write(OutFile,  'February ');
     3 : Write(OutFile,  'March ');
     4 : Write(OutFile,  'April ');
     5 : Write(OutFile,  'May ');
     6 : Write(OutFile,  'June ');
     7 : Write(OutFile,  'July ');
     8 : Write(OutFile,  'August ');
     9 : Write(OutFile,  'September ');
    10 : Write(OutFile,  'October ');
    11 : Write(OutFile,  'November ');
    12 : Write(OutFile,  'December ')
  END;   (* Case *)
  Write(OutFile, Date.Day:1, ',', Date.Year:5)
END;   (* PrintDate *)
```

(**)

```
PROCEDURE AdjustDate (    Date:         (* Starting date          *)
                              DateType;
                          DaysAway:      (* Number of days to add *)
                              Integer;
                      VAR NewDate:       (* Calculated new date    *)
                              DateType);
```

(* NewDate is the date DaysAway from Date. DaysAway must be nonnegative. *)

```
VAR
  NewDay,            (* DaysAway + Date.Day                         *)
  NumberOfDays:      (* Number of days in month                     *)
     Integer;
  Finished:          (* NewDate has been calculated when Finished is True *)
     Boolean;
```

(**)

PSIA

```
FUNCTION DaysInMonth (Date:              (* Date being checked *)
                         DateType):
                         Integer;

(* DaysInMonth returns the number of days in Date.Day.
   Leap year is considered. *)

BEGIN (* DaysInMonth *)
  WITH Date DO
    CASE Month OF
       9,4,6,11 : DaysInMonth := 30;
       1,3,5,7,8,10,12 : DaysInMonth := 31;
       2 : IF (Year MOD 4 = 0) AND NOT (Year MOD 100 = 0)
            THEN                                              (* Leap year *)
               DaysInMonth := 29
            ELSE
               DaysInMonth := 28
    END (* Case *)
END;   (* DaysInMonth *)


(*****************************************************************************)

BEGIN (* AdjustDate *)
  NewDay := Date.Day + DaysAway;
  (* Initialize NewDate to Date *)
  NewDate := Date;
  REPEAT
    NumberOfDays := DaysInMonth(NewDate);
    IF NewDay <= NumberOfDays
       (* This is the correct month *)
      THEN
        BEGIN
          NewDate.Day := NewDay;
          Finished := True
        END;
      ELSE
        (* Increment month and continue *)
        BEGIN
          NewDay := NewDay - NumberOfDays;
          NewDate.Month := (NewDate.Month MOD 12) + 1
          IF NewDate.Month = 1
            THEN
               NewDate.Year := NewDate.Year + 1;
          Finished := False
        END;
```

PSIA ▰▰▰▰

```
    UNTIL Finished
END;   (* AdjustDate *)


(******************************************************************)

PROCEDURE PrintEntry (Entry:              (* Valid friend record       *)
                         EntryType2;
                      TempDate:            (* Birthday of friend this year *)
                         DateType);

(* The name, phone number, and birthdate are printed *)

BEGIN (* PrintEntry *)
  WITH Entry DO
    BEGIN
      Writeln(FirstName, ' ', LastName);
      Writeln(Phone.AreaCode:3, ' ', Phone.Number);
      PrintDate(Output, TempDate);
      Writeln;
      Writeln
    END
END;   (* PrintEntry *)


(******************************************************************)

PROCEDURE GetEntry (VAR FriendList:       (* Input file of friends *)
                      Text;
                    VAR Entry:            (* Next friend from file *)
                      EntryType2);

(* An Entry is read from file FriendList *)

VAR
  Character:          (* Input character      *)
    Char;
  Counter:            (* Loop control variable *)
    1..NameLength;

BEGIN (* GetEntry *)
  WITH Entry DO
    BEGIN
      FOR Counter := 1 TO NameLength DO
        BEGIN
          Read(FriendList, Character);
          FirstName[Counter] := Character
        END;
```

PSIA ▬▬▬▬▬

```
         (* Skip over blank *)
         Read(FriendList, Character);
         FOR Counter := 1 TO NameLength DO
           BEGIN
              Read(FriendList, Character);
              LastName[Counter] := Character
           END;
         Readln(FriendList);
         (* Skip over ( *)
         Read(FriendList, Character);
         Read(FriendList, Phone.AreaCode);
         (* Skip over ) and blank *)
         Read(FriendList, Character, Character);
         FOR Counter := 1 TO 8 DO
           BEGIN
              Read(FriendList, Character);
              Phone.Number[Counter] := Character
           END;
         Readln(FriendList);
         WITH BirthDate DO
           Readln(FriendList, Month, Character, Day, Character, Year);
         (* Skip over blank line *)
         Readln(FriendList)
      END
END;   (* GetEntry *)


(**********************************************************************)


BEGIN (* BirthdayCalls *)
  Reset(FriendList);
  GetCurrentDate(CurrentDate);
  AdjustDate(CurrentDate, DaysHence, TargetDate);
  WHILE NOT EOF(FriendList) DO
    BEGIN
      GetEntry(FriendList, Entry);
      TempDate := Entry.BirthDate;
      TempDate.Year := TargetDate.Year;
      IF (Compare(TempDate, TargetDate) <= Same) AND
         (Compare(TempDate, CurrentDate) >= Same)
        THEN
          PrintEntry(Entry, TempDate)
    END
END.   (* BirthdayCalls *)
```

Testing: The only portions of this program that need to be checked are the main program and the input and output routines. The operations on dates have already been thoroughly tested.

The input routine is the mirror image of the output routine from the program that created the address lists. The output routine simply prints out exactly what was read in for the name and telephone number. The date is written out in a different format, but the routine that writes the date has already been tested. Therefore, only the logic of the main program needs extensive testing.

The logic in the main program is very straightforward. The test data should include birthdays less than two weeks away, exactly two weeks away, and more than two weeks away. The current date should include the cases where two weeks away is within the same month, within the next month, and within the next year.

Note that 14 was defined in the program as a named constant DaysHence. The program can be run to print birthdays within any time period by changing this named constant.

TESTING AND DEBUGGING

As we have demonstrated in several examples, hierarchical records simplify the logical design of a program but make the coding more complicated. The deeper the nesting of a structure, the longer the field selector becomes. We showed that using the WITH statement is a way to simplify the field selector. The fields of the record variable listed on the WITH statement can be accessed by field name only within the scope of the WITH statement.

The good news is that the WITH statement is very useful. The bad news is that if you don't use the WITH statement carefully, you may wind up with unexpected errors. For example, look what happens if you accidentally put the WITH statement in the wrong place.

```
WITH Inventory[Counter] DO
   FOR Counter := 1 TO NumberOfMachines DO
      Writeln(IdNumber);
```

You would assume that this code would write out the IdNumbers of all the machines in the machine shop. However, one of two things will happen, neither one of which is correct.

The record in the WITH statement is Inventory[Counter]. If Counter was last used in a FOR statement, it will be undefined and a run-time error will occur. If Counter is defined and within the bounds of the array Inventory, Inventory[Counter] will refer to one of the records in the array. The FOR loop will then print out its IdNumber NumberOfMachines times. To make this code do what you expect, you must put the WITH statement within the scope of the FOR statement. The correct version is

```
FOR Counter := 1 TO NumberOfMachines DO
   WITH Inventory[Counter] DO
      Writeln(IdNumber);
```

Figure 14-12
Scope of Two WITH
Statements

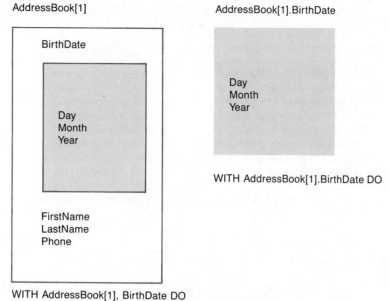

AddressBook[1]

BirthDate

Day
Month
Year

FirstName
LastName
Phone

WITH AddressBook[1], BirthDate DO

AddressBook[1].BirthDate

Day
Month
Year

WITH AddressBook[1].BirthDate DO

The use of the abbreviated form of the WITH for nested hierarchical records can also lead to problems if you are not careful. For example,

```
WITH AddressBook[1], BirthDate DO
   BEGIN
      .
      .
      .
   END;
```

allows you to access all of the fields of AddressBook[1] by field identifier. In addition, the fields of AddressBook[1].BirthDate can be accessed by field identifier.

Look what happens if the comma is replaced by a period:

```
WITH AddressBook[1].BirthDate DO
   BEGIN
      .
      .
      .
   END;
```

This form allows you to access only the fields of AddressBook[1].BirthDate by field identifier.

These two WITH statements look very similar, but are quite different. This subtle difference becomes clearer if we visualize the scope of the two statements. Those fields that can be accessed by field identifier only are shown in the boxes in Figure 14-12. The FirstName, LastName, and Phone fields of AddressBook[1] can still be accessed in the second case, but only by their full field selector, such as AddressBook[1].FirstName.

We said earlier that field names must be unique within a record. However, the temptation still exists to use the same field identifier in more than one record. For example, Name is such a meaningful identifier that it might logically be used in more than one record. Look at the following declarations:

```
CONST
  NameLength = 20;
  ClassSize = 150;
  NumberOfCities = 1000;

TYPE
  NameIndex = 1..NameLength;
  NameString = ARRAY[NameIndex] OF Char;
  Person = RECORD
             Name : NameString;
             Classification : (Freshman, Sophomore, Junior, Senior);
             Age : 0..100
           END;   (* Record *)
  City = RECORD
           Name,
           State : NameString;
           Elevation : Integer
         END;   (* Record *)
  Roster = ARRAY[1..ClassSize] OF Person;
  ListOfCities = ARRAY[1..NumberOfCities] OF City;

VAR
  Name:
    NameString;
  Student:
    Person;
  Students:
    Roster;
  Cities:
    ListOfCities;
```

The declarations are valid even though the identifier Name is used in three places: as a variable, as a field identifier in record Person, and as a field identifier in record City. No ambiguities arise because Name, Student.Name, Students[Counter].Name, and Cities[Counter].Name are all unique. No ambiguities arise for the compiler, that is. They could arise for someone reading the program, particularly if a WITH statement is being used. For example, which Name is being referred to in the following code segment?

```
WITH Students[Counter], Student DO
  BEGIN
    .
    .
    FOR K := 1 TO NameLength DO
      Read(Name[K]);
    .
    .
  END;
```

The Name in the above code refers to the Name field of the record variable Student. Is that what you thought? The reference is difficult to determine from the code, but the scope rules clarify it for the compiler. The Students[Counter] record overrides the variable Name. However, Student record overrides the Name field in the Students[Counter] record. Therefore, Name refers to the Name field in the Student record.

If a WITH statement refers to two record variables of the same type, a compiler error message will occur because the field names within the WITH statement are ambiguous.

Using the WITH statement can help the compiler generate better code. It can also save some writing and possibly make the program more readable. However, the WITH statement should be used with care, since it can sometimes lead to confusing results or hard to detect errors.

Testing and Debugging Hints

1. Be sure to specify the full field selector when referencing a component of a record variable. The only exception is when using a WITH statement where the record variable is already specified.
2. When using arrays in records or arrays of records, be sure to include the index with the array name when accessing individual components.
3. Process each field of a record separately, except when assigning one record variable to another (of the same type) or passing the record as a parameter.
4. Watch out for possible confusion or ambiguity when using the WITH statement.
5. Avoid using the same field identifiers in different record types, even though this is allowed.
6. If the record variable in a WITH statement is a record from an array of records, do not change the index of the specified record variable within the WITH statement.
7. Be careful when using the abbreviated form of the WITH for hierarchical records.

SUMMARY

The record is a useful data structure for grouping data relating to a single object. We can use a record variable to refer to the record as a whole, or we can use a field selector to access any individual field (component) of the record. Records of the same type may be assigned directly to each other. Comparison of records, however, must be done field by field. Reading and writing of records must also be done field by field. (There is an exception to this which is discussed in the next chapter.)

Since the components of arrays and records can be of any type, we can build quite complex structures made up of arrays of records where the components of the records are themselves arrays and records.

The design of our algorithms and our data structures must be done in parallel. At the top level of our design, we visualize our data structures as abstract objects such as tables, lists, and entries. As we refine our algorithms, we get more specific about data structure. Our tables take on shape; our entries become more concrete. When we reach the point in our design where a module must apply a specific algorithm to a data structure, then—and only then—do we determine the exact form our data structure will take.

Applying the top-down, defer-details principle to data structures is an example of data abstraction. The logical description of the data structure is at a higher level. The details of how the data structure will be implemented are pushed down to a lower level.

QUICK CHECK

1. Write the type definition for a record data type called Time, with three fields called Hour, Minute, and Second. The data type for the Hour field is a subrange from 0 through 23. The other two fields contain subranges from 0 through 59. (pp. 543–549)

2. Assume a variable called Now, of type Time, has been defined. Write the assignment statements necessary to store the time 8:37:28 into Now. (pp. 543–549)

3. Define a hierarchical record data type called Interval that consists of two fields of type Time. The fields are called Past and Present. (pp. 564–565)

4. Assume a variable called ChannelCrossing, of type Interval, has been defined. Write the assignment statements necessary to store the time 7:12:44 into the Past field of ChannelCrossing. Write the assignment statement that will store the value of variable Now into the Present field of ChannelCrossing. (pp. 564–565)

5. Define a data type called BoatTimes that is an array of Interval values indexed by an enumerated data type called BoatNames (assume BoatNames is already defined). (pp. 549–563)

6. Decide what form of data structure is appropriate for the following problem: A card in a library catalog system must contain the call number, author, title, and description of a single book. (pp. 569–570, 577–580)

7. What happens when a WITH statement refers to two record variables of the same type? (pp. 565–568, 588–591)

Answers:
```
1. TYPE Time = RECORD
                 Hour   :  0..23;
                 Minute :  0..59;
                 Second :  0..59
               END;   (* Record *)
2. Now.Hour   := 8;
   Now.Minute := 37;
   Now.Second := 28;
3. TYPE Interval = RECORD
                     Past,
                     Present : Time
                   END;  (* Record *)
4. ChannelCrossing.Past.Hour   := 7;
   ChannelCrossing.Past.Minute := 12;
   ChannelCrossing.Past.Second := 44;
   ChannelCrossing.Present := Now;
5. TYPE BoatTimes = ARRAY[BoatNames] OF Interval;
```

6. A simple record with four fields is sufficient.
7. A compiler error message is printed because references to the field names within the WITH statement are ambiguous.

EXAM PREPARATION EXERCISES _____

1. Define the following terms:

    record

    field identifier

    field selector

    hierarchical record

    data abstraction

2. Given the declarations

```
TYPE
    CodeRange = 1..25;
    TokenRange = 1..2000;
    SymbolRange = 1..20;
    GuideRange = 1..200;
    Code = ARRAY[CodeRange] OF Char;
    Ref = RECORD
            Token : ARRAY[TokenRange] OF Code;
            Symbol : ARRAY[SymbolRange] OF Code;
        END; (* Record *)
    Map = RECORD
            Mapcode : Code;
            Style : (Formal, Brief);
            Chart : Ref
        END; (* Record *)
    GuideType = ARRAY[GuideRange] OF Map

VAR
    Guide:
        GuideType;
    AMap:
        Map;
    ARef:
        Ref;
    I,
    Count:
        Integer;
    ACode:
        Code;
```

mark each of the following statements as valid or invalid. (Assume that all of the valid variables have defined values.)

Statement	Valid	Invalid

(a) IF Map.Style = Brief
     THEN
         Count := Count + 1
	____	____

(b) Guide[1].Chart.Token[2] := AMap	____	____
(c) Guide[6].Chart := ARef	____	____
(d) AMap.MapCode[1] := ARef.Token[1]	____	____
(e) Guide[100].Chart.Token[1,2] := ACode[2]	____	____
(f) Guide[20].Token[1] := ACode	____	____

(g) IF Guide[20].Style = Formal
     THEN
         Guide[20].Chart.Token[1,1] := 'A'
	____	____

(h) AMap := Guide[5]	____	____
(i) AMap.Chart := ARef	____	____

3. Using the declarations in exercise 2, write assignment statements to do the following:
   (a) Assign the value of the Chart field of the 71st element of Guide to the variable ARef.
   (b) Assign the 1st element of the Token field of the Chart field of the 88th element of Guide to the variable ACode.
   (c) Assign the value 'X' to the 1st element of the 23rd element of the Token field of the Chart field of the 94th element of Guide.
   (d) Assign the 4th element of the MapCode field of AMap to the 20th element of the Symbol field of ARef.

4. What are the two basic differences between a record and an array?

5. A hierarchical record structure may not contain another hierarchical record structure as a field. (True or False?)

6. If the fields of a record are all of the same data type, an array data structure could be used instead. (True or False?)

7. For each of the following descriptions of data, determine which general type of data structure is appropriate (array, record, array of records, or hierarchical record).
   (a) A payroll entry with a name, address, and pay rate
   (b) A person's address
   (c) An inventory entry for a part
   (d) A list of addresses
   (e) A list of hourly temperatures
   (f) A list of passengers on an airliner, including names, addresses, fare class, and seat assignment
   (g) A departmental telephone directory with last name and extension number
   (h) A street name.

8. Given the declarations

```
          TYPE
          Date = RECORD
                     Month : 1..12
                     Day : 1..31
                     Year : 0..MaxInt
                 END;  (* Record *)
```

```
                    Name = PACKED ARRAY[1..15] OF Char;
                    Person = RECORD
                                FirstName,
                                LastName : Name;
                                BirthDate : Date
                             END;  (* Record *)

            VAR
              Today:
                Date;
              AName:
                Name;
              Friend,
              Self:
                Person;
```

Show the value of each variable after the following program segment is executed.

```
              AName := '               ';
              Friend.FirstName := AName;
              Friend.LastName := AName;
              Today.Month := 1;
              Today.Day := 1;
              Today.Year := 1987;
              Friend.BirthDate := Today;
              Self := Friend;
```

9. Given the declarations in exercise 8, explain why the following program segment is invalid.

```
              WITH Friend, Self DO
                BirthDate := Today;
```

10. WITH statements cannot be nested. (True or False?)

PREPROGRAMMING EXERCISES _____

1. (a) Write a record declaration to contain the following information about a student:

   Name (string of characters)

   Social security number (string of characters)

   Class (freshman, sophomore, junior, senior)

   Grade point average

   Sex (M, F)

   (b) Declare a record variable of the type in part (a), and write a program segment that prints the information in each field of the variable.

   (c) Declare Roll to be an array variable of 3,000 records of the type in part (a).

2. Write a program segment to read in a set of part numbers and associated unit costs. Keep the data sorted by part number as you read it in. Use an array of records with two fields, Number and Price, to represent each pair of input values. Assume one pair of input values per line of data.

3. Write a hierarchical Pascal record definition to contain the following information about a student:

> Name (up to 30 characters)
>
> Student ID number
>
> Credit hours to date
>
> Number of courses taken
>
> Course grades (a list of up to 50 elements containing the course ID and the letter grade)
>
> Date first enrolled (month and year)
>
> Class (freshman, sophomore, junior, senior)
>
> Grade point average

Each record and user-defined enumerated type should have a separate type definition.

4. (a) Declare a record type called Apt for an apartment locator service. The following information should be included:

> Landlord (a string of up to 20 characters)
>
> Address (a string of up to 20 characters)
>
> Bedrooms (Integer)
>
> Price (Real)

   (b) Declare Available to be an array type of up to 200 records of type Apt.
   (c) Write a procedure to read values into the fields of a variable of type Apt. (The record variable should be passed as a parameter.) The order in which the data is read is the same as that of the items in the record.

5. Using the declarations given in Exam Preparation exercise 2, write statements to do the following:
   (a) Assign the value in the Chart field of AMap to ARef.
   (b) Assign AMap to the fourth element of Guide.
   (c) Assign ACode to the MapCode field of the 10th element of Guide.
   (d) Compare the first characters in ACode and in the MapCode field of the second element of Guide. If they are equal, then output the MapCode field and the Style field of the second element of Guide.
   (e) Compare AMap.Chart and ARef for equality. Show which elements (if any) are not equal by outputting the subscripts indicating the appropriate Token fields and/or Symbol fields. For example, if the second Token fields of both records were not equal, you would output "2," and so on for the remaining nonequal elements.

6. You are designing an automated library catalog system. The library contains 50,000 books. For each book, there is a catalog entry consisting of the call number (up to 10 characters), the number of copies in the library (an integer), the author (up to 30 characters), the title (up to 100 characters), and a description of the contents (up to 300 characters).

   (a) Write the type definitions necessary to contain this information.

   (b) Estimate how many characters of memory space will be required to hold all of the catalog information for the library (assume that an integer value occupies the equivalent of four characters in memory).

   (c) How many book records could a computer with 650,000 characters of memory hold?

7. Write a procedure that will read the information for a book into a record of the type defined in exercise 6. Write another procedure that will print the information contained in a record of the type defined in exercise 6. The record should be passed as a parameter to each of these procedures.

8. You are writing the subscription renewal system for a magazine. For each subscriber the system is to keep the following information:

   Name (first, last)

   Address (street, city, state, zip code)

   Expiration date (month, year)

   Date renewal notice was sent (month, day, year)

   Number of renewal notices sent so far

   Number of years for which subscription is being renewed (0 for renewal not yet received; otherwise 1, 2, or 3 years)

   Whether or not the subscriber's name may be included in a mailing list for sale to other companies.

   Write a hierarchical record type definition to contain this information. Each subrecord should be declared separately as a named data type.

9. You are writing a program that will keep track of the terminals that are connected to a company computer. The computer may have up to 30 terminals connected to it. For each terminal the following information must be kept:

   Brand and model (a string of up to 15 characters)

   Data rate (a subrange of 10 through 1920 characters per second)

   Parity (an enumerated type of Even, Odd, One, Zero, or None)

   Echoplex (an enumerated type of Half or Full)

   Data bits (a subrange of 7 through 8)

   Stop bits (a subrange of 1 through 2)

   Design a data structure for this problem and write the type definitions for all of the data types that will be needed to implement your design.

10. Rewrite the following program segment using a WITH statement.

```
FOR Term := 1 TO 30 DO
  BEGIN
    Write(TermList[Term].Model:16);
    Write(TermList[Term].Rate:7);
    CASE TermList[Term].Parity OF
      Odd  : Writeln(' Odd');
      Even : Writeln(' Even');
      One  : Writeln(' One');
      Zero : Writeln(' Zero');
      None : Writeln(' None')
    END (* Case *)
  END
```

11. Test function Compare (pages 572–573).
    (a) Design the data sets necessary to adequately test function Compare.
    (b) Write a driver and test function Compare using your test data.

12. Test procedure AdjustDate (pages 575–577).
    (a) Design the data sets necessary to adequately test procedure AdjustDate.
    (b) Write a driver and test procedure AdjustDate using your test data.

PROGRAMMING PROBLEMS

1. The Emerging Manufacturing Company has just installed its first computer and hired you as a junior programmer. Your first program is to read employee pay data and produce two reports: (1) an error and control report and (2) a report on pay amounts. The second report must contain a line for each employee and a line of totals at the end of the report.

Input

Transaction File

Set of five job site number/name pairs

One card or line for each employee containing ID number, job site number, and number of hours worked

These data items have been presorted by ID number.

Master File

ID number

Name

Pay rate per hour

Number of dependents

Type of employee (1 is management, 0 is union)

Job site

Sex (M, F)

This file is ordered by ID number.

NOTE: (1) Union members get time and a half for hours over 40; professionals (management) get nothing for hours over 40. (2) The tax formula for tax computation is as follows: If number of dependents is 1, tax rate is 15%; otherwise tax rate is

$$\left[1 - \left\{\frac{\text{No. of dep.}}{\text{No. of dep.} + 6}\right\}\right] \times 15\%$$

Output

Error and Control Report

Lists the input lines or cards for which there is no corresponding master record, or where the job site numbers do not agree. Continues processing with the next line or card of data.

Gives the total number of employee records that were processed correctly during the run.

Payroll Report (labeled for management)

Contains a line for each employee showing the name, ID number, job site name, gross pay, and net pay

Contains a total line showing the total amount of gross pay and total amount of net pay

2. The Emerging Manufacturing Company has decided to use its new computer for parts inventory control as well as payroll. You are writing a program that is to be run each night. It takes the stock tickets from the day's transactions, makes a list of the parts that need ordering, and prints an updated report that must be given to the five job site managers each morning. Note that you are not being asked to update the file.

Input

Transaction File

Set of five job site number/name pairs

One card or line for each stock transaction containing part ID number, job site number, and number of parts bought or sold (a negative number indicates that it has been sold)

This data has been presorted by site number within part number.

Master File

Part ID number

Part name (no embedded blanks)

Quantity on hand

Order point

Job site

This file is also ordered by job site number within part ID number. If a part is not in the master file and the transaction is a sale, an error message should be printed. If the transaction is a purchase, the part should be listed in the proper place in the parts report.

NOTE: There is a separate entry in the master file for parts at each job site.

Output

Error and Control Report

Contains error messages

Lists the parts that need to be ordered (those for which quantity on hand is less than order point)

A Report for *All* the Parts in the Master File

Contains the part number

Contains the part name

Contains the job site name

Contains the number on hand

Remember, this report is for management. Be sure it is written so managers can read it.

3. You have taken a job with the IRS, hoping to learn how to save on your income tax. They want you to write a toy tax computing program so that they can get an idea of your programming abilities. The program will read in the names of members of families and each person's income and compute the tax that the family owes. You may assume that people with the same last name who appear consecutively in input are in the same family. The number of deductions that a family can count is equal to the number of people listed in that family in the input data. Tax is computed as follows:

$$\text{adjusted-income} = \text{income} - (5000 * \text{number-of-deductions})$$

$$\text{tax-rate} = \text{adjusted-income}/100{,}000, \text{ if income} < 60{,}000$$
$$.50, \text{ otherwise}$$

$$\text{tax} = \text{tax-rate} * \text{adjusted-income}$$

There will be no refunds, so you must check for people whose tax would be negative and set it to zero.

Input entries will look as follows:

last name, first name. total income

Example

Jones,	Ralph.	19765.43
Jones,	Mary.	8532.00
Jones,	Francis.	
Atwell,	Humphry.	35678.12
Murphy,	Robert.	13432.20
Murphy,	Ellen.	
Murphy,	Paddy.	
Murphy,	Eileen.	
Murphy,	Conan.	

Murphy,   Nora.

Input The data as described above, with an end-of-file indicating the end of the run

Output A table containing all of the families, one family per line, with each line containing the last name of the family, their total income, and their computed tax

4. Your assignment is to write a program for a computer dating service. Clients will give you their names, phone numbers, and a list of interests. It will be your job to maintain lists of men and women using the service and to match up the compatible couples.

Data Structures The problem requires you to maintain two lists, one for men and one for women. The lists must include the following information: name (20 characters), phone number (8 characters), number of interests (maximum number is 10), interests (10 characters each; must be in alphabetical order), and a variable that gives the position of the client's current match (will be 0 if not matched). When a new client is added to the list, his or her name is added to the bottom of the appropriate list. (You do not keep the names of the clients in alphabetical order.)

Input

Number of current clients

Sex (7 characters), name (20 characters), phone number (8 characters), number of interests, list of interests (10 characters for each one; interests are separated by commas, with a period after the final interest.) There will be a record like this for each of the current clients.

The rest of the file will include data lines that look like one of the following (all of the lines will start with a 10-character word as outlined below; □ indicates a blank):

NewClient □ sex (7 characters), name (20 characters), number of interests, interests (10 characters for each one; see above for description)

If the keyword NewClient occurs, you should add the client to the appropriate list by storing the appropriate information. Match him or her with a member of the opposite sex. (A match occurs when three of the interests are the same. Use the fact that interests are sorted to make the matching process easier.) Make sure you then designate both persons as matched as described above. Print the name of the new client, his or her match, and both phone numbers. If no match is found, print an appropriate message.

OldClient□ name (20 characters)

Unmatch this name from its current match by setting the match variables for this name and its match to 0.

PrintMatch

Print a list of all matched pairs.

PrintNot□□

Print the names and phone numbers of clients who are not currently matched.

StopProg□□

This will be the last line in the file.

Output Information as described above, printed with appropriate titles

NOTE: Use an insertion sort to sort interests.

- To be able to define a nontext (binary) file data type.
- To be able to create and access a nontext (binary) file.
- To be able to merge the data in two or more files.
- To be able to access a file via its file buffer variable using the procedures Get and Put.
- To be able to define a pointer data type.
- To be able to create and access pointer variables.
- To be able to dynamically create and access pointer-referenced variables.
- To be able to destroy dynamic pointer-referenced variables.
- To be able to use pointers to improve program efficiency.

15

Files and Pointers

This chapter may seem somewhat redundant since you have been using files since Chapter 1. Files are so important that we had to describe how to use them at the very beginning. You couldn't have run your first program if you hadn't learned to create a file. Your programs would have been trivial if you hadn't known how to read in data values from a file.

In this chapter we will look at a file as a data structure. We will review Text files and define another type of file called a *binary file*. A binary file is a file that is created within one program to be read by another program or the same program at a later time. It takes less machine time to write or read a binary file than it does to write or read a Text file, so binary files should be used when possible.

Pointers are the last of the built-in data types in Pascal. A *pointer* is a simple data type that contains the address of a variable or structure rather than a data value. Pointers have two main purposes: they can make a program more efficient and they can be used to build very complex structures. We will demonstrate how they make a program more efficient in this chapter. Chapter 16 is devoted to how to build complex structures using pointers.

FILES

Files are exceedingly important data structures. Programs use files to communicate with the outside world and with each other. Data values are read from files. Results are written to a file that can be displayed.

A program can communicate with itself through the use of files. Data values that must be saved from one execution of the program to the next are written to a file. The output file from one run then becomes the input file for the next run. A program can communicate with another program in just the same way as it can communicate with itself. Output from one program can become the input for another program.

A file that is used to communicate with people or programs is called an *external file*. The external files used by a program are listed in the parameter list of the program statement.

External File A file that is used to communicate with people or programs. It is stored externally to the program.

A file can also be used strictly as an internal data structure. For example, a procedure or program may need more memory space for temporary data storage than is available. Data can be written to a file and then read back in when needed. A file that is used but not saved is called an *internal* or *scratch file.* It is used just like scratch paper.

Internal File A file that is created but not saved.

In Pascal the *file data type* is defined to be a collection of like components accessed sequentially.

File Data Type A collection of components, all of the same data type, accessed sequentially, one component at a time.

What makes the file data structure different from any other data structure we have studied is that only one component is available to the program at a time. You can think of a file as being like an array of components in secondary storage. You can access each component one at a time, beginning with the first component. Each time you access a component, you get the next one. The only way to access a component that you have accessed previously is to Reset the file and start from the beginning again.

We will now review Text files and see how the definition of the file data type relates to them.

Text Files Reviewed

The files we have used so far have all been of type Text. A file of type Text can be thought of as a file of characters broken up into lines. The components of Text files are characters. The built-in operations defined on Text files are reviewed below, where InFile and OutFile are files of type Text.

Reset(InFile) Opens file InFile and prepares to read file InFile from the beginning. If the file is empty or doesn't exist, the function EOF(InFile) is True. Otherwise, the function EOF(InFile) is False.

`Rewrite(OutFile)`	Opens file OutFile and prepares to write at the beginning. The old contents of the file (if any) are lost.
`EOF(InFile)`	Returns True if the next character to be read is the ⟨eof⟩ character (that is, no more characters remain in the file). Returns False otherwise.
`EOLN(InFile)`	Returns True if the next character to be read is the ⟨eoln⟩ character. Returns False otherwise.
`Read(InFile, ...)`	Reads values from InFile into the variables named on the parameter list.
`Readln(InFile, ...)`	Same as Read except that it skips to beginning of the next line before returning.
`Write(OutFile, ...)`	Writes values of expressions and variables named on the parameter list on OutFile.
`Writeln(OutFile, ...)`	Same as Write except that it writes the ⟨eoln⟩ character on OutFile before returning.

If we restrict our operations to character data only, these operations are consistent with our definition of a file data type. When character data are being input, the Read operation always accesses one character at a time sequentially along a line of input. When character data are being output, the Write operation always outputs one character at a time sequentially along a line of output.

The function EOLN is always consistent with the definition of the file data type because it asks if the next component (the next character) to be read is the ⟨eoln⟩ character. The function EOF is always consistent because it asks if the next component (the next character) to be read is the ⟨eof⟩ character.

When numeric data are being input or output, the Read or Write operation is not consistent with the definition of the file data type. The component of a Text file is a character, and a Read or Write with numeric parameters may access more than one character. This seeming inconsistency can be explained by the fact that the Read and Write procedures themselves actually access the file components sequentially, one character at a time.

If a parameter for a Read or Readln procedure is of type Char, the next component is accessed and stored in the parameter. If a parameter for a Read or Readln is of type Integer or Real, characters are accessed sequentially and converted from character form into numeric form.

If a parameter for a Write or Writeln procedure is of type Char, the next component (character) is written. If a parameter for a Write or Writeln is of type Integer or Real, the number is converted from its numeric form to its character representation and then written out, character by character.

In Chapter 5 we indicated that using the Read procedure in combination with EOF to input numeric data can cause a problem. The ⟨eoln⟩ character always follows the last number on a Text file. Therefore, EOF will not be True after the last value has been read and the loop will attempt to execute one more time. We said then that the only way to solve this problem is to read the numbers in as characters and convert them.

Let's review Text files by writing a procedure to read an unsigned integer number from a Text file and convert it to its numeric form. Some compilers allow any nondigit to separate numeric data; others require that blanks separate numeric data. We will write this procedure to recognize any nondigit as a separator.

This procedure, which is similar to the built-in Read procedure in Pascal, will have the following specifications:

```
PROCEDURE ReadInt (VAR DataFile:        (* Input file of characters    *)
                        Text;
                   VAR Number:          (* Resulting converted integer *)
                        Integer;
                   VAR Error:           (* Bad input indicator flag    *)
                        Boolean);
```

```
(* Reads and converts the next unsigned integer value encountered on
   Text file DataFile. There may be leading blanks. Any nondigit
   will mark the end of the number. If either EOF or a nondigit
   character is encountered before the first digit, Error is True and
   Number is undefined. Otherwise Error is False and Number contains
   the value *)
```

We will read in a digit in character form, convert it to its numeric value, multiply the previous value by 10 (to shift the number a digit position to the left), and add in the new digit. This process will continue until we find a character that is not a number.

READ INT

```
Number ←—— 0
Error ←—— False
Skip Blanks
IF Character is not a digit
   THEN
      Error ←—— True
   ELSE
      WHILE more digits
         Number ←—— Number * 10 + (Ord(Digit) − Ord('0'))
         Get another digit
```

SKIP BLANKS

```
Character ←—— ' '
WHILE NOT EOF AND Character is a blank
   Get another character
```

The code for procedure ReadInt is as follows:

```
PROCEDURE ReadInt (VAR DataFile:        (* Input file of characters    *)
                        Text;
                   VAR Number:          (* Resulting converted integer *)
                        Integer;
                   VAR Error:           (* Bad input indicator flag     *)
                        Boolean);

(* Reads and converts the next unsigned integer value encountered on
   Text file DataFile. There may be leading blanks. Any nondigit
   will mark the end of the number. If either EOF or a nondigit
   character is encountered before the first digit, Error is True and
   Number is undefined. Otherwise Error is False and Number contains
   the value *)

VAR
  Character:       (* Current input character being converted *)
    Char;

(**************************************************************************)

PROCEDURE SkipBlanks (VAR Character:        (* Returns first nonblank *)
                          Char);

(* Blanks are skipped.  First nonblank is returned. If EOF is
   encountered before a nonblank is found, character will be a blank *)

BEGIN (* SkipBlanks *)
  Character := ' ';
  WHILE NOT EOF(DataFile) AND (Character = ' ') DO
    Read(DataFile, Character)
END;   (* SkipBlanks *)

(**************************************************************************)

BEGIN (* ReadInt *)
  Error := False;
  SkipBlanks(Character);
  IF NOT (Character IN ['0'..'9'])
    THEN
      Error := True
    ELSE
      BEGIN
        Number := 0;
        WHILE Character IN ['0'..'9'] DO
          BEGIN
            Number := Number * 10 + (Ord(Digit) - Ord('0'));
            Read(DataFile, Character)
          END
      END
END;   (* ReadInt *)
```

*Figure 15-1
Code Walk-
Through of
Procedure ReadInt*

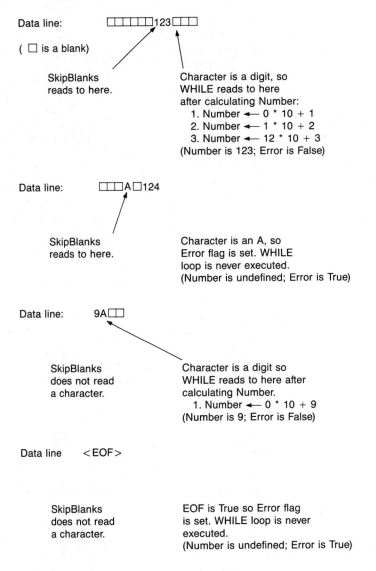

Data line: □□□□□□□123□□□

(□ is a blank)

SkipBlanks
reads to here.

Character is a digit, so
WHILE reads to here
after calculating Number:
   1. Number ◄— 0 * 10 + 1
   2. Number ◄— 1 * 10 + 2
   3. Number ◄— 12 * 10 + 3
(Number is 123; Error is False)

Data line: □□□A□124

SkipBlanks
reads to here.

Character is an A, so
Error flag is set. WHILE
loop is never executed.
(Number is undefined; Error is True)

Data line: 9A□□

SkipBlanks
does not read
a character.

Character is a digit so
WHILE reads to here after
calculating Number.
   1. Number ◄— 0 * 10 + 9
(Number is 9; Error is False)

Data line <EOF>

SkipBlanks
does not read
a character.

EOF is True so Error flag
is set. WHILE loop is never
executed.
(Number is undefined; Error is True)

Figure 15-1 contains diagrams describing the execution of Procedure ReadInt with four different lines of data. (Each example is independent of the others.)

Other Files

The components of a file can be of any type, simple or structured, except another file. The syntax diagram for defining a file in the TYPE section is

———► identifier ———► = ———► FILE ———► OF ———► type

The following declarations are all valid:

```
CONST
    StringLength = 15;
    ArrayLength = 20;

TYPE
    ArrayIndex = 1..ArrayLength;
    StringIndex = 1..StringLength;
    String = PACKED ARRAY[StringIndex] OF Char;
    Words = FILE OF String;
    Part = RECORD
                Description : String;
                IdNum : Integer;
                Cost : Real
            END;  (* Record *)
    Parts = FILE OF Part;
    Name = ARRAY[ArrayIndex] OF Char;
    Names = FILE OF Name;
    Integers = FILE OF Integer;

VAR
    InFile,
    OutFile:
        Text;
    Dictionary:     (* File of Strings          *)
        Words;
    AWord:          (* Component of Dictionary *)
        String;
    Inventory:      (* File of Parts            *)
        Parts;
    APart:          (* Component of Inventory  *)
        Part;
    Mail:           (* File of Names            *)
        Names;
    AName:          (* Component of Mail        *)
        Name;
    Data:           (* File of Integers         *)
        Integers;
    ANumber:        (* Component of Data        *)
        Integer;
```

InFile and OutFile are files of type Text. Dictionary is a file of strings. Inventory is a file of records. Mail is a file of arrays. Data is a file of integer numbers.

The built-in operations defined on nontext files are Reset, Rewrite, Read, Write, and EOF. Nontext files are not broken into lines, so EOLN, Readln, and Writeln *T,M,V* ↩ have no meaning with them.

Reset, Rewrite, and EOF have the same meaning for nontext files as they do for text files. Read and Write are simplified for nontext files because they operate in a manner consistent with the definition of a file: exactly one component of the file is read or written.

Read(Mail, AName)   The next component in file Mail is returned in AName.

Write(Mail, AName)   Aname is written on Mail.

The file marker operates with nontext files in exactly the same manner as it does with text files. After a call to the Read procedure for a text file, the file marker is at the next character to be read. After a call to the Read procedure for a nontext file, the file marker is at the next component to be read.

Using nontext files can simplify the coding of a program considerably. An entire data structure can be read or written at once, as shown in the following examples.

Read(Dictionary, AWord)   Inputs a string.

Read(Inventory, APart)   Inputs a record.

Read(Mail, AName)   Inputs an array.

Read(Data, ANumber)   Inputs an integer number.

Write(Inventory, APart)   Writes a record.

Write(Mail, AName)   Writes an array.

The good news is that nontext files are easy to read and write. The bad news is that we cannot create nontext files using an editor.

In nontext files data is stored in internal machine representation. There is no translation into a character format. All data entered from a console is in character format, as is output from an editor.

How then can nontext files be created? Nontext files are created when a program writes to a file that is not of type Text. That is, only a program can create a nontext file. A file in text format can be converted into nontext format by a simple translating program that reads the data from the text file and writes it out to a nontext file.

For example, the short program that follows will read data in from a text file and write it out on a nontext file.

```
PROGRAM Convert (Input, Output, PartsFile);

(* Data about parts are read from Input in character
   format and written out to file PartsFile *)

CONST
  StringLength = 10;
```

```
TYPE
   Range = 1..StringLength;
   NameType = PACKED ARRAY[Range] OF Char;
   Part = RECORD
             Name : NameType;
             IdNumber : Integer;
             Cost : Real
          END;  (* Record *)
   Parts = FILE OF Part;

VAR
   APart:        (* Part being entered from input *)
      Part;
   PartsFile:    (* File being constructed        *)
      Parts;
   Character:    (* Character read from input     *)
      Char;
   Counter:      (* Loop control variable         *)
      Range;

BEGIN (* Convert *)
   Rewrite(PartsFile);
   WHILE NOT EOF DO
      BEGIN
         (* Read a record from Input, a Text file *)
         FOR Counter := 1 TO StringLength DO
            BEGIN
               Read(Character);
               APart.Name[Counter] := Character
            END;
         Read(APart.IdNumber);
         Read(APart.Cost);
         Readln;
         (* Write a record to a binary file PartsFile *)
         Write(PartsFile, APart)
      END
END.  (* Convert *)
```

Nontext files are read and written faster than text files, since no time is lost in translating data from or into character form. Because nontext files are written in the internal representation of the machine, they are called *binary files*.

Binary File A file in which the data is written in the internal representation of a machine.

All internal files and those external files that are used as input from one program to another should be written as binary files.

Problem Solving in Action

Problem: A friend is running for City Council. It is getting down to the wire, and we want to call all those people who showed an interest in our friend and remind them to vote on election day.

The problem is that we have three different lists of people we should call. We don't want to annoy people by calling them twice or—worse still—three times, so we decide to merge the three lists and remove any duplicates. The three lists are each sorted in order by last name, and there are no duplicates within any of the lists. A dummy record with a last action of all Zs is appended at the end of each file.

Discussion: One of our problem-solving heuristics is to solve a simpler problem first. Let's solve the problem for two lists and then expand the solution to three lists.

How would we do this process by hand if we had two stacks of index cards? We would probably take the top card from each stack and compare the names. If they were the same, we would put one in a new stack and throw the other one away. If they weren't the same, we would put the card with the name that came first alphabetically in the new stack and take a replacement card from that stack.

We would repeat this process until one of the stacks of index cards became empty. Then we would move the rest of the other stack to the new one. Of course the lists might both end at the same time with a duplicate name.

This same process can be employed to solve this problem using two computer lists. Rather than having two stacks of index cards, we have two computer files. Reading in a name will be the equivalent of "take a replacement card from that stack."

Now that we have solved the problem for two files, we can expand the solution to three files. We can merge the first two files and store the result on a file. Then we can merge the third file with the file that contains the result of merging the first two files.

Input: The computer files were all generated from the same Pascal program. The components of each file are records that contain a person's last name, first name, and telephone number. The declarations used in the program that created the files are as follows:

```
CONST
  NameLength = 15;

TYPE
  NameIndex = 1..NameLength;
  NameString = PACKED ARRAY[NameIndex] OF Char;
  PhoneType = RECORD
                AreaCode : 0..999;
                Number : PACKED ARRAY[1..8] OF Char
              END; (* Record *)
  Data = RECORD
           LastName : NameString;
           FirstName : NameString;
           Phone : PhoneType
         END; (* Record *)
  DataList = FILE OF Data;
```

A dummy record signals the end of each file. This record contains all Zs for the last name and blanks in the other two fields.

PSIA

Output:

> Files One and Two merged on file TempFile (intermediate)
>
> Files Three and TempFile merged on file MasterList. File MasterList should have the same form as the three input files.
>
> Printed copy of file MasterList

Data Structures:

> Four external files of type DataList
>
> One scratch file of type DataList

MAIN MODULE   Level 0

```
Reset input files
Rewrite output files
Merge files One and Two onto TempFile
Reset TempFile
Merge files TempFile and Three onto MasterList
Print MasterList
```

MERGE   Level 1

```
Read a component from One (ComponentFromOne)
Read a component from Two (ComponentFromTwo)
WHILE neither component is the dummy record
   Process Components
Append Any Left
```

PROCESS COMPONENTS   Level 2

```
IF ComponentFromOne.LastName < ComponentFromTwo.LastName
   THEN
      Write ComponentFromOne
      Read ComponentFromOne
   ELSE IF ComponentFromOne > ComponentFromTwo
      THEN
         Write ComponentFromTwo
         Read ComponentFromTwo
   ELSE
      Write ComponentFromTwo
      Read ComponentFromOne
      Read ComponentFromTwo
```

PSIA ▰▰▰▰▰▰

Since Process Components is fairly simple, we have chosen to include it as part of procedure Merge in the program.

APPEND ANY LEFT

```
WHILE component on One not dummy
    Write ComponentFromOne
    Read ComponentFromOne
WHILE component on Two not dummy
    Write ComponentFromTwo
    Read ComponentFromTwo
Write dummy record
```

PRINT MASTER LIST   Level 1

```
Reset MasterList
Read component
WHILE component on MasterList not dummy
    Write component
    Read component
Write dummy record
```

Module Structure Chart:

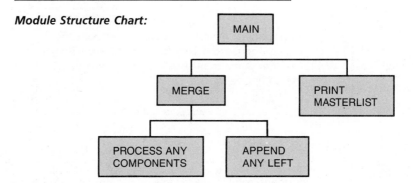

```
PROGRAM MergeLists (One, Two, Three, MasterList, Output);

(* Files One, Two, and Three are merged and
   written on File MasterList.  MasterList is printed. *)

CONST
   Dummy = 'ZZZZZZZZZZZZZZZ';
   NameLength = 15;

TYPE
   NameIndex = 1..NameLength;
   NameString = PACKED ARRAY[NameIndex] OF Char;
```

PSIA

```
PhoneType  = RECORD
                   AreaCode : 0..999;
                   Number : PACKED ARRAY[1..8] OF Char
               END; (* Record *)
Data = RECORD
          LastName : NameString;
          FirstName : NameString;
            Phone : PhoneType
          END; (* Record *)
  DataList = FILE OF Data;


VAR
  One,              (* Input file              *)
  Two,              (* Input file              *)
  Three,            (* Input file              *)
  MasterList,       (* Output file             *)
  TempFile:         (* Temporary file (internal) *)
    DataList;


(*************************************************************************)


PROCEDURE Append (VAR One,                 (* Input file, possibly empty *)
                      Two,                 (* Input file, possibly empty *)
                      Temp:                (* Output file             *)
                        DataList;
                      ComponentFromOne,    (* Active record from One    *)
                      ComponentFromTwo:    (* Active record from Two    *)
                        Data);


(* Remainder of either One or Two is appended to Temp *)


BEGIN (* Append *)
  (* Append rest of One, if there *)
  WHILE ComponentFromOne.LastName <> Dummy DO
    BEGIN
      Write(Temp, ComponentFromOne);
      Read(One, ComponentFromOne)
    END;
  (* Append rest of Two, if there *)
  WHILE ComponentFromTwo.LastName <> Dummy DO
    BEGIN
      Write(Temp, ComponentFromTwo);
      Read(Two, ComponentFromTwo)
    END;
  (* Write dummy record *)
  Write(Temp, ComponentFromTwo)
END;  (* Append *)


(*************************************************************************)
```

PSIA ━━━━━

```
PROCEDURE Merge (VAR One,              (* Input file to merge *)
                     Two,              (* Input file to merge *)
                     Temp:             (* Merged output file  *)
                       DataList);
```

(* Files One and Two are merged onto Temp. Constant Dummy is accessed
   globally. Assumption: Files have been reset *)

```
VAR
  ComponentFromOne,
  ComponentFromTwo:
    Data;

BEGIN (* Merge *)
  Read(One, ComponentFromOne);
  Read(Two, ComponentFromTwo);
  WHILE (ComponentFromOne.LastName <> Dummy) AND
        (ComponentFromTwo.LastName <> Dummy) DO
    IF ComponentFromOne.LastName < ComponentFromTwo.LastName
      THEN
        BEGIN
          Write(Temp, ComponentFromOne);
          Read(One, ComponentFromOne)
        END
    ELSE IF ComponentFromOne.LastName > ComponentFromTwo.LastName
      THEN
        BEGIN
          Write(Temp, ComponentFromTwo);
          Read(Two, ComponentFromTwo)
        END
    ELSE
      BEGIN
        Write(Temp, ComponentFromOne);
        Read(One, ComponentFromOne);
        Read(Two, ComponentFromTwo)
      END;
  Append(One, Two, Temp, ComponentFromOne, ComponentFromTwo)
END;  (* Merge *)
```

(***)

```
PROCEDURE Print (VAR MasterList:       (* File to print on output *)
                       DataList);
```

(* File MasterList is printed. Constant Dummy is accessed globally *)

```
VAR
  Component:
    Data;
```

PSIA ▰▰▰▰▰

```
BEGIN (* Print *)
  Reset(MasterList);
  Read(MasterList, Component);
  WHILE Component.LastName <> Dummy DO
    BEGIN
      Writeln(Component.LastName, ' ', Component.FirstName, ' ',
              Component.Phone.AreaCode:3, ' ', Component.Phone.Number);
      Read(MasterList, Component)
    END
END;   (* Print *)


(************************************************************************)


BEGIN (* MergeLists *)
  Reset(One);
  Reset(Two);
  Reset(Three);
  Rewrite(TempFile);
  Rewrite(MasterList);
  Merge(One, Two, TempFile);
  Reset(TempFile);
  Merge(Three, TempFile, MasterList);
  Print(MasterList)
END.   (* MergeLists *)
```

Testing: Since we have three input files, there are several cases to test:

1. File One is empty.
2. File Two is empty.
3. File Three is empty.
4. Files Two and Three are empty.
5. Files One and Three are empty.
6. Files One and Two are empty.
7. All three files are empty.
8. All three files have values.

There are data-dependent conditions that should be tested as well:

1. The files should be tested with each one containing the name that comes first in the alphabet.
2. The files should be tested with each pair containing duplicate names in the first position, an intermediate position, and the last position.
3. The files should be tested with each one containing the name that comes last in the alphabet.

Since files One, Two, and Three are binary files, a program will have to be written to create test data files. Test data files cannot be created with an editor because text editors create text files. It may be more trouble than it is worth to thoroughly test this program using the procedure outlined above. If it truly is a one-shot deal, three short files with values might suffice. If, however, this program is to be used more than once, it should be rigorously tested.

Before leaving this problem, we should say just a word about efficiency. We could have written two procedures that merge two files: the one we used here and one in which the components are printed as they are written to the file. That is, we could have had a different merge procedure to merge the third file and temporary file onto the MasterList. If we had done that, we would not have had to read Master-List back in to print it.

Input/output operations take longer to execute than any other operations performed on data. Operations on binary files take less time than operations on text files, but they are still time consuming. If this program were to be run several times, it would be worthwhile to recode this program so that the MasterList would not have to be reread. Preprogramming Exercise 9 asks you to recode Program Merge-Lists so that MasterList is printed as it is written. Programming Problem 1 asks you to rewrite this program using EOF instead of a dummy record to end each list.

FILE BUFFER VARIABLE

When we declare a file variable, another variable known as the *file buffer variable* is automatically created by the system. The file buffer variable is denoted by the file variable name followed by an up-caret (^). (You will sometimes see this written as an up-arrow ↑.) For example, the buffer variable for the file InFile is written

```
InFile^
```

This buffer variable allows us to access the data at the position of the file marker.

File Buffer Variable A variable of the same type as the components of the file with which it is associated.

We have said that Reset(InFile) opens or prepares the file for reading. What Reset(InFile) actually does is position the file marker at the first component in the file and assign the value of that component to InFile^, the file buffer variable.

The Read and Readln procedures also manipulate the file buffer variable. The file buffer variable always contains the next component of the file. The following table shows what happens to the file buffer variable as a series of statements is executed in sequence. InFile is a text file; A and B are Char variables.

Statements	Value read	File marker after statement	InFile^	EOLN
Reset(InFile)	None	FG⟨eoln⟩L⟨eoln⟩⟨eof⟩	'F'	False
Read(Infile, A)	A = 'F'	FG⟨eoln⟩L⟨eoln⟩⟨eof⟩	'G'	False
Read(Infile, B)	B = 'G'	FG⟨eoln⟩L⟨eoln⟩⟨eof⟩	' '	True
Readln(Infile)	None	FG⟨eoln⟩L⟨eoln⟩⟨eof⟩	'L'	False
Read(Infile, A)	A = 'L'	FG⟨eoln⟩L⟨eoln⟩⟨eof⟩	' '	True

The Rewrite, Write, and Writeln procedures also manipulate the file buffer variable. Rewrite prepares the file for writing by creating an empty file. The file buffer variable is undefined. When a variable is written, its contents are first copied into the file buffer variable. The file buffer variable is then appended to the end of the file. If a Writeln is used, ⟨eoln⟩ is appended immediately following the file buffer variable. After the file buffer variable has been appended to the file, it becomes undefined. EOF is always True for an output file at the completion of a Write, Writeln, or Rewrite.

We have demonstrated what happens to the file buffer variable when a Read or a Write is issued using a file of type Text. This is exactly what happens to the file buffer variable when any other file is used. Read and Write for text files can be more complicated, since a call to either can mask a series of file buffer variable manipulations.

Pascal provides two standard built-in procedures, Get and Put, that allow the programmer to manipulate the file buffer variable directly.

`Get(InFile)` Advances the file marker for file InFile to the next component and assigns the value of that component to the file buffer variable. Previous contents of InFile^ are lost.

`Put(OutFile)` Appends the value of the file buffer variable OutFile^ to the file OutFile.

These two procedures are the primitive operations out of which the procedures Read and Write are built. The statement

```
Read(InFile, Character)
```

is equivalent to

```
Character := InFile^;
Get(InFile)
```

The statement

```
Write(OutFile, Character)
```

is equivalent to

```
OutFile^ := Character;
Put(OutFile)
```

The following code fragment will copy binary file InFile to binary file TempFile using Get and Put.

```
                    Reset(InFile);
                    Rewrite(TempFile);
                    WHILE NOT EOF(InFile) DO
                      BEGIN
                        TempFile^ := InFile^;
                        Put(TempFile);
                        Get(InFile)
                      END;
```

Programming Problem 2 asks you to rewrite Program MergeLists using the file buffer variables directly.

Problem Solving in Action

Problem: Information on student athletes is available on a file. The names of all the students involved in both soccer and track must be printed so that they can be invited to a special sports banquet.

The data file is composed of records that contain the name of each student along with a set containing the names of the sports in which the student participates. The following declarations were used to create the structure for each student record:

```
CONST
   NameLength = 20;

TYPE
   SportType = (Tennis, Soccer, Football, Baseball,
                Basketball, Volleyball, Track);
   SportSetType = SET OF SportType;
   NameIndex = 1..NameLength;
   NameString = PACKED ARRAY[NameIndex] OF Char;
   StudentType = RECORD
                    Name : NameString;
                    Sport : SportSetType
                 END;  (* Record *)
```

Discussion: If the information were on paper, we would scan the list, checking to see if a student was in both soccer and track. If so, we would add the student's name to our list of students to invite.

That is exactly what the program will do. A constant set made up of soccer and track (FootSports) will be compared with the set that describes each student. If the intersection of the two sets is equal to FootSports, then that student is in both soccer and track.

Input: File of student records (StudentFile)

Output: The names of the students who participate in both soccer and track

Data Structure: A record containing a field with a packed array of 20 characters and a set with the component type SportType

PSIA ▰▰▰▰▰▰▰

MAIN MODULE   Level 0

```
FootSports ←── [Soccer, Track]
WHILE more students DO
   IF Sport field of student * FootSports = FootSports
   THEN
        Print Name field
```

The program is so simple that it can be coded directly.

```
PROGRAM SPORT (Input, Output, StudentFile);

CONST
   NameLength = 20;

TYPE
   SportType = (Tennis, Soccer, Football, Baseball,
                Basketball, Volleyball, Track);
   SportSetType = SET OF SportType;
   NameIndex = 1..NameLength;
   NameString = PACKED ARRAY[NameIndex] OF Char;
   StudentType = RECORD
                   Name  : NameString;
                   Sport : SportSetType
                 END; (* Record *)

VAR
   StudentFile:
      FileType;
   FootSports:
      SportSetType;
   AStudent:
      StudentType;

BEGIN (* Sport *)
   Reset(StudentFile);
   FootSports := [Soccer, Track];
   (* Get a student record and examine the sports *)
   WHILE NOT EOF(StudentFile) DO
      BEGIN
         Read(StudentFile, AStudent);
         IF AStudent.Sport * FootSports = FootSports
           THEN
              Writeln(AStudent.Name)
      END
END. (* Sport *)
```

PSIA

Testing: This is a very simple program involving only one input file. There are two cases to test. The data must include students who play both track and soccer and students who play only one of the two or neither. The following segment of code was used to generate a test file in which Athletes is an array of StudentType records.

```
BEGIN
  Rewrite(StudentFile);
  Athletes[1].Name := 'Susy          ';          (* Both *)
  Athletes[1].Sport := [Tennis, Soccer, Baseball, Track];
  Athletes[2].Name := 'Sarah         ';          (* Neither *)
  Athletes[2].Sport := [Volleyball, Baseball];
  Athletes[3].Name := 'June          ';          (* Neither *)
  Athletes[3].Sport := [];
  Athletes[4].Name := 'Bobby         ';          (* Both *)
  Athletes[4].Sport := [Tennis..Track];
  Athletes[5].Name := 'Judy          ';          (* One *)
  Athletes[5].Sport := [Track];
  Athletes[6].Name := 'Phil          ';          (* One *)
  Athletes[6].Sport := [Soccer, Tennis];
  FOR Counter := 1 TO 6 DO
    Write(StudentFile, Athletes[Counter]);
END.
```

Following is the output from running Program Sport with the StudentFile:

```
Susy
Bobby
```

POINTERS

We have only one data type left to cover: the *pointer*. Variables of this type are called pointers. Surprisingly, the word pointer isn't used in the type definition; the symbol ^ is used instead.

In many ways we've saved the best till last. Pointers are the most interesting data type of all. They are what their name implies: a variable that says where to go to get something else. That is, they contain the address or location of another variable. The variables that pointers point to are called *dynamic variables*. Dynamic variables are not declared in the declaration section of the program like other variables; they are created at execution time.

The advantage of being able to create variables at execution time is that we don't need to create any more of them than we actually need.

Let's begin this discussion by looking at pointers themselves. Then we will show how to use them to create dynamic variables.

Pointer A simple data type consisting of an unbounded set of values, each of which addresses or otherwise indicates the location of a variable of a given type. The operations defined on pointer variables are assignment and test for equality.

The syntax diagram for defining pointer types is

$$\longrightarrow \text{type identifier} \longrightarrow = \longrightarrow \wedge \longrightarrow \text{type identifier}$$

The following declaration section illustrates how pointers are defined:

```
TYPE
    Range = 1..25;
    RangePointer = ^Range;
    Color = (Red, Green, Blue);
    ColorPointer = ^Color;
    Date = RECORD
                Day : 1..31;
                Month : 1..12;
                Year : 1900..2020
            END; (* Record *)
    DatePointer = ^Date;

VAR
    RangePtr:
        RangePointer;
    ColorPtr:
        ColorPointer;
    DatePtr:
        DatePointer;
```

RangePtr, ColorPtr, and DataPtr are pointer variables. RangePtr is a pointer to a variable of type Range; ColorPtr is a pointer to a variable of type Color; and DatePtr is a pointer to a variable of type Date. These declarations cause the compiler to create three cells, RangePtr, ColorPtr, and DatePtr, the contents of which will be memory addresses. As in the case of all variables, their values are not yet defined.

RangePtr	ColorPtr	DatePtr
?	?	?

This declaration looks strange. We have declared three pointer variables but we haven't declared anything for them to point to—we haven't declared any variables of types Range, Color, or Date. The variables that RangePtr, ColorPtr, and DatePtr will point to will be created dynamically; that is, we will create variables of type Range, Color, and Date whenever they are needed during the execution of the program. To get a variable of the appropriate type for the pointer variable to point to, we use a built-in procedure called New.

New(RangePtr)	Creates a variable of type Range for RangePtr to point to and leaves its address in RangePtr.
New(ColorPtr)	Creates a variable of type Color for ColorPtr to point to and leaves its address in ColorPtr.
New(DatePtr)	Creates a variable of type Date for DatePtr to point to and leaves its address in DatePtr.

The call to procedure New always does two things: it creates a variable of the type to which its parameter points and returns the address of this variable in the parameter. The variable created by procedure New is a *dynamic variable.*

Dynamic Variable A variable created during execution of a program.

How do we access these newly created variables if we don't know their names? The pointer variable followed by ^ accesses the variable pointed to. Variables created this way are called *referenced variables* because they are not given a name but rather are referenced through a pointer variable.

Referenced Variable A variable created and accessed not by a name but by a pointer variable; a dynamic variable.

RangePtr^ is a referenced variable of type Range. It can contain any integer value in the range 1..25. ColorPtr^ is a referenced variable of type Color. It can contain Red, Green, or Blue. DatePtr^ is a referenced record variable of type Date. DatePtr^.Day is the Day field of DatePtr^. DatePtr^.Month is the Month field of DatePtr^. DatePtr^.Year is the Year field of DatePtr^. Notice how the accessing expression is built.

DatePtr	A pointer variable of type DatePointer
DatePtr^	A referenced record variable of type Date
DatePtr^.Year	The year field of a referenced record variable of type Date

If we defined Dates to be an array of pointers, we would access the Day field of the third date as follows:

Dates[3]^.Day

Referenced variables can be used in the same way as any other variable. The following statements are all valid:

```
RangePtr^ := 18;
ColorPtr^ := Red;
DatePtr^.Day := 3;
DatePtr^.Month := 12;
DatePtr^.Year := 1999;
Dates[3]^.Day := 4;
Dates[3]^.Month := 1
Dates[3]^.Year := 2020
```

Figure 15-2 shows the results of these assignments.

On most machines the value of a pointer is an integer, because memory locations have addresses ranging from zero to the size of memory minus one. However, a pointer type is *not* an integer type. We cannot assign an integer value to a pointer. We can't even assign RangePtr, ColorPtr, and DatePtr to each other, because they do not point to variables of the same type. Figure 15-3 pictures a pointer and the variable that it is referencing.

Figure 15-2
Results of
Assignment
Statements

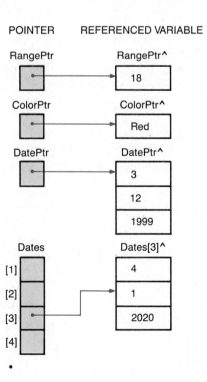

Figure 15-3
A Pointer and Its
Referenced
Variable

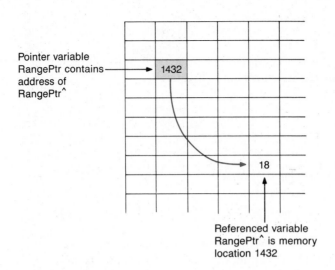

Pointer variable
RangePtr contains—
address of
RangePtr^

1432

18

Referenced variable
RangePtr^ is memory
location 1432

There are two operations that may be applied to pointer variables of the same type:

1. Pointer variables of the same type may be tested for equality. (See Figure 15-4a.)
2. Pointer variables of the same type may be assigned to one another. (See Figure 15-4b.)

Referenced variables, on the other hand, may be used in any way that is legal for named variables of the same type.

Referenced variables can be destroyed at any time during the execution of a program when they are no longer needed. The procedure Dispose is used to destroy a referenced variable.

`Dispose(RangePtr)`   Returns the locations used for the variable of type Range to the Pascal run-time support system to be used again. RangePtr is then undefined.

Figure 15-4
Operations on
Pointer Variables

(a) Pointer variables of the same type may be tested for equality.

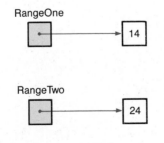

RangeOne

14

RangeTwo

24

RangeOne < > RangeTwo is True
RangeOne = RangeTwo is False

(b) Pointer variables of the same type may be assigned to one another.

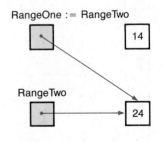

RangeOne := RangeTwo

14

RangeTwo

24

RangeOne < > RangeTwo is False
RangeOne = RangeTwo is True

Dispose (ColorPtr) Returns the locations used for the variable of type Color to the Pascal run-time support system to be used again. ColorPtr is then undefined.

Dispose (DatePtr) Returns the locations used for the variable of type Date to the Pascal run-time support system to be used again. DatePtr is then undefined.

Remember, any operation that is legal on a named variable of a certain type is legal on a referenced variable of that type. However, only assignment and test for equality are legal operations on pointer variables. For example, given the declarations

```
TYPE
    NumberRange = 1..50;
    NumberPointers = ^NumberRange;


VAR
    NumberOne,
    NumberTwo:
        NumberPointers;
```

we can do the following:

```
New(NumberOne);                          (* Creates a dynamic variable *)
New(NumberTwo);                          (* Creates a dynamic variable *)
(* Read value into dynamic variables *)
Read(NumberOne^, NumberTwo^);
(* Print out the sum of these dynamic variables *)
Writeln('The sum of ', NumberOne^:1, ' and ', NumberTwo^:1,
        ' is ', NumberOne^ + NumberTwo^:1);
NumberOne^ := NumberTwo^;                (* Assignment of dynamic variables *)
NumberOne := NumberTwo;                  (* Assignment of pointers          *)
Dispose(NumberTwo);                      (* Destroys a dynamic variable     *)
```

Notice that NumberOne^ + NumberTwo^ is legal, because we are adding the contents of two variables of type NumberRange pointed to by NumberOne and NumberTwo. We could not, however, add NumberOne and NumberTwo, because they are pointer variables.

NumberOne^ := NumberTwo^ Assigns the contents of the referenced variable NumberTwo^ to the referenced variable NumberOne^. (See Figure 15-5a.)

NumberOne := NumberTwo Assigns the contents of the pointer variable NumberTwo to the pointer variable NumberOne. (See Figure 15-5b.)

Dispose (NumberTwo) Returns the referenced variable NumberTwo^ back to the run-time support system to be used again. NumberTwo is undefined. (See Figure 15-5c.)

Figure 15-5
Results from
Sample Code
Segment

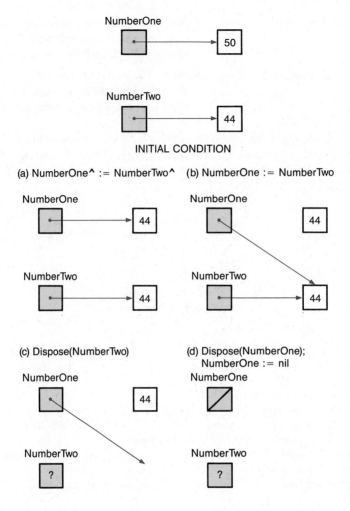

Notice that the variable that was referenced by NumberOne before the assignment statement shown in Figure 15-5b is still there. It cannot be accessed, however, unless there is another pointer variable referencing it. It is a bad practice not to dispose of dynamic variables when they are no longer needed. If this is done too often you may run out of memory.

Notice also that NumberOne is now referencing a variable that no longer exists. Both of these situations can be avoided by disposing of NumberOne before the assignment statement and setting NumberOne to NIL as follows:

```
Dispose(NumberOne);
NumberOne := NumberTwo;
Dispose(NumberTwo);
NumberOne := NIL
```

NIL is a special constant which is used to indicate that a pointer points to nothing. Now NumberOne is not referencing a variable that doesn't exist—it is defined to be pointing to nothing. (See Figure 15-5d.)

Although the concept of dealing with a pointer to a variable and not the variable itself may seem strange, this is not the first time we have seen it. The file name is a pointer to the next component in a file. The file buffer variable is the component to which it points. That's why we access the file buffer variable by the file name followed by an up-caret.

Let's review the syntax and semantics of pointers and dynamic variables in another short example. In the TYPE section we define a structure and a pointer to the structure. In the VAR section we declare a variable of the pointer type.

```
CONST
    StringLength = 20;

TYPE
    NameIndex = 1..StringLength;
    NameString = PACKED ARRAY[NameIndex] OF Char;
    DataType = RECORD
                   LastName,
                   FirstName : NameString
               END;  (* Record *)
    PointerType = ^DataType;

VAR
    Pointer:
        PointerType;
```

To get a record variable of DataType, we invoke the procedure New with Pointer as a parameter. Thus,

```
New(Pointer)
```

creates a record variable of type DataType. To access the record variable we give the pointer name followed by an up-caret.

`Pointer^`	Accesses the record pointed to by the pointer variable Pointer.
`Pointer^.LastName`	Accesses the LastName field.
`Pointer^.FirstName`	Accesses the FirstName field.

At the beginning of this chapter we said that pointers are used for two reasons: to make a program more efficient and to create complex data structures called linked structures. We will give an example of the use of pointers to make a program more efficient in the next Problem Solving in Action. Linked structures will be covered in a chapter by themselves (Chapter 16).

We have looked at two different sorting algorithms, the straight selection sort and the insertion sort. In both cases the contents of two variables are swapped during each iteration. Swapping the contents of two variables is a simple operation. If, however, very large records are being sorted, swapping the contents of two of them can be very time consuming.

The Pascal code to swap two records is the same, regardless of the size of the records. However, the length of time it takes to actually make the swap will vary greatly depending on the size of the records. For example, it may take 10 times as long to swap two records with 20 fields as it does to swap two records with 2 fields.

If we are dealing with very large records, we can make the sorting operation more efficient by sorting pointers to the records rather than the records themselves. In this way only simple pointer variables are swapped on each iteration, rather than the records themselves.

Problem Solving in Action

Problem: We have a file of personnel records. There is a great deal of data associated with each person. The task is to read in these records, sort them, and write them out again on the same file.

Discussion: In Chapter 12 we developed two general-purpose sort procedures: ExSort, which sorted an array of values already in memory, and Insert, which inserted new data items in order. Although either one would work here, let's use ExSort since we used Insert in the Problem Solving in Action in Chapter 12.

Procedure ExSort will have to be modified somewhat since we want to sort large records rather than single values. The size of the records indicates that it will be more efficient to swap pointers rather than whole records. Therefore, the records themselves will be dynamic variables. The pointers to each will be stored in an array. It is these pointers that will be shifted, not entire records, when the algorithm calls for the exchanging of two values.

Input: A file of personnel records in binary format written using the following declarations:

```
TYPE
    String20 = PACKED ARRAY[1..20] OF Char;
    String200 = PACKED ARRAY[1..200] OF Char;
    String100 = PACKED ARRAY[1..100] OF Char;
    PersonnelData = RECORD
                    FirstName : String20;
                    LastName  : String20;
                    Address   : RECORD
                                Street,
                                City,
                                State : String20;
                            END;  (* Record *)
                    WorkHistory : String200;
                    Education   : String100;
                    PayRollData : String200
                END;  (* Record *)
```

The number of records in the file MasterList is unknown. The maximum number of employees that the company has ever had is 1000.

PSIA ▬▬▬▬▬▬

Output: File MasterList with the records in order by LastName

Data Structures: An array (Person) of pointers to PersonnelData

There will be room for 1000 pointers set aside in memory for the Person array, but there will only be as many PersonnelData records in memory as there are records on the file. (See Figure 15-6.) Using dynamic variables saves memory. We have to define the array Person, which will hold pointers to the personnel records, to be the maximum we might need. However, we only have to create a PersonnelData record when we need one.

The Person array before and after sorting is shown in Figure 15-7. Note that when the algorithm says to swap the contents of two records, we will swap the pointers instead.

MAIN MODULE   Level 0

```
WHILE more records
   Get a dynamic variable
   Read record into dynamic variable
Sort pointers (use ExSort)
Write Records back on MasterFile
```

Figure 15-6
Array of Pointers
to Personnel Data
Records

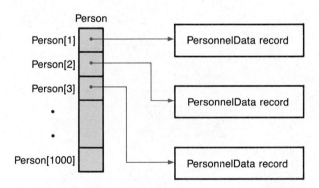

Figure 15-7
Person Array
Before and After
Sorting

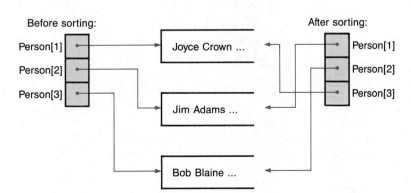

PSIA

Remember that the ExSort procedure we will use for sorting pointers finds the minimum value in the list of values and swaps it with the value in the first place in the array. Then the next smallest value in the list is swapped with the value in the second place. This process continues until all the values are in order.

The place in this algorithm that will have to be changed is where the minimum value is determined. Instead of comparing two components in the list, we will compare the last name fields in the records to which these components point. The statement that did the comparison in Procedure ExSort must be changed from

```
        IF List[PlaceCount] < List[MinIndex]
```

to

```
        IF List[PlaceCount]^.LastName< List[MinIndex]^.LastName
```

WRITE RECORDS   Level 1

```
    ┌────────────────────────────────────────────────────────┐
    │  FOR Index going from 1 to Length                      │
    │     Write PersonnelData record on MasterList           │
    │                                                        │
    └────────────────────────────────────────────────────────┘
```

Module Structure Chart:

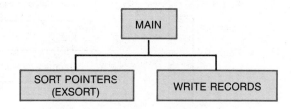

```
PROGRAM SortPointers (MasterList, Output);

(* Personnel records on file MasterList are sorted by last name and
   rewritten on MasterList. *)

CONST
  MaxLength = 1000;

TYPE
  String20 = PACKED ARRAY[1..20] OF Char;
  String200 = PACKED ARRAY[1..200] OF Char;
  String100 = PACKED ARRAY[1..100] OF Char;
```

PSIA ▬▬▬▬▬▬

```
            PersonnelData = RECORD
                              FirstName : String20;
                              LastName : String20;
                              Address : RECORD
                                          Street,
                                          City,
                                          State : String20
                                        END; (* Record *)
                              WorkHistory : String200;
                              Education : String100;
                              PayRollData : String200
                            END; (* Record *)
            IndexRange = 1..MaxLength;
            PersonPointer = ^PersonnelData;
            ListType = ARRAY[IndexRange] OF PersonPointer;
            PersonFile = FILE OF PersonnelData;


        VAR
          Person:              (* Array of pointers to personnel records  *)
            ListType;
          Length:              (* Number of valid pointers in Person       *)
            Integer;
          APerson:             (* Pointer to temporary record being built  *)
            PersonPointer;
          Index:               (* Loop control variable                    *)
            IndexRange;
          MasterList:          (* Input file of personnel records          *)
            PersonFile


    (**********************************************************************)

    PROCEDURE PointerExSort (VAR List:          (* Array of pointers        *)
                                  ListType;
                                  Length:        (* Total pointers in List  *)
                                  Integer);

    (* An unordered list with Length pointers is taken as input.  The same
        list is returned with the pointers ordered so that the records to
        which the pointers point are in ascending order by last name. *)

    VAR
      TempPointer:           (* Used for swapping        *)
        PersonPointer;
      PassCount,             (* Loop control variable    *)
      PlaceCount,            (* Loop control variable    *)
      MinIndex:              (* Index of minimum so far  *)
        IndexRange;
```

PSIA ▰▰▰▰▰▰▰▰▰

```
BEGIN (* PointerExSort *)
  FOR PassCount := 1 TO (Length - 1) DO
    (* The records pointed to by List[1]..List[PassCount - 1] are
       already sorted and contain the first PassCount - 1
       alphabetically last names *)
    BEGIN
      MinIndex := PassCount;
      (* Find the index of the pointer to the alphabetically first
         last name left in List[PassCount]..List[Length] *)
      FOR PlaceCount := PassCount + 1 TO Length DO
        IF List[PlaceCount]^.LastName < List[MinIndex]^.LastName
          THEN
            MinIndex := PlaceCount;
      (* Swap List[MinIndex] and List[PassCount] *)
      TempPointer := List[MinIndex];
      List[MinIndex] := List[PassCount];
      List[PassCount] := TempPointer
    END
END;   (* PointerExSort *)


(*****************************************************************************)


BEGIN (* SortPointers *)
  Reset(MasterList);
  Length := 0;
  (* Read and store personnel records *)
  WHILE NOT EOF(MasterList) DO
    BEGIN
      Length := Length + 1;
      New(APerson);
      Read(MasterList, APerson^);
      Person[Length] := APerson
    END;
  PointerExSort(Person, Length);
  Rewrite(MasterList);
  FOR Index := 1 TO Length DO
    Write(MasterList, Person[Index]^)
END.    (* SortPointers *)
```

Testing: There is only one file involved here, so testing the program completely requires only that we create a MasterFile with some records. Passive error detection has been used for the case where the file has more than 1000 records; the program will crash with a range error if this case arises.

Remember that a program must be written to generate the test data. Output from a text editor cannot be used directly. Binary files must be created by another Pascal program. The file can be created on a text editor, but it must be read as a text file and written out as a binary file.

PSIA ▬▬▬▬

In this particular case testing is difficult because of the large size of each record. It is time consuming to input such large records. To make this task somewhat easier, you can generate test records that contain only one field, the last name field. For the test runs, put comment indicators around the additional fields in Program SortPointers. This technique is shown in the revised declarations for Program SortPointers.

An editor is used to create a test file of names. Then Program Create reads this file and writes it out in binary (string20) format. The output from this program, MasterList, is then the input test file for Program SortPointers with the declaration of Personnel-Data modified as shown.

```
PROGRAM CreateData (Data, MasterList, Output);

(* Text file Data is read in Character format and written out on
   MasterList in binary format.  Data contains names, one per line. *)

CONST
  Blanks = '                    ';

TYPE
  String20 = PACKED ARRAY[1..20] OF Char;
  DataFile = FILE OF String20;

VAR
  Name:          (* Current name being read in  *)
    String20;
  Letter:        (* Used for reading characters *)
    Char;
  Data:          (* Input file of names         *)
    Text;
  MasterList:    (* Output file of names        *)
    DataFile;
  Index:         (* Loop counter                *)
    Integer;

BEGIN (* CreateData *)
  Reset(Data);
  Rewrite(MasterList);
  WHILE NOT EOF(Data) DO
    BEGIN
      Index := 0;
      (* Set name to all blanks *)
      Name := Blanks;
      WHILE NOT EOLN(Data) AND (Index < 20) DO
        BEGIN
          Index := Index + 1;
          Read(Data, Letter);
          Name[Index] := Letter
        END;
```

PSIA

```
(* Go to next line *)
Readln(Data);
Write(MasterList, Name)
    END
END.   (* CreateData *)
```

File Data:

```
Dale
MacDonald
Lilly
Weems
Jones
Brown
Vitek
Ripley
Kirshen
Gleason
Thompson
```

Program Create reads file Data and writes it out on file MasterList. File MasterList can then be used as test input for Program SortPointers. For this test, Program SortPointers should be modified in the following way:

```
PersonnelData = RECORD
         (*        FirstName : String20;              *)
                   LastName : String20;
         (*        Address : RECORD                   *)
         (*                  Street,                  *)
         (*                  City,                    *)
         (*                  State : String20;        *)
         (*             END; *) (* Record *)
         (*        WorkHistory : String200;           *)
         (*        Education : String100;             *)
         (*        PayRollData : String200;           *)
             END;  (* Record *)
```

The following is a listing of file MasterList after it was processed by Program SortPointers. The names are indeed in alphabetical order. (Note that what we have actually tested is that the program correctly sorts pointers to referenced variables of type String20.)

Brown	Dale	Gleason	Jones
Kirshen	Lilly	MacDonald	Ripley
Thompson	Vitek	Weems	

TESTING AND DEBUGGING

The error programmers most commonly make when working with files is to forget to put the file name as a parameter to the input statement. If the file name is not there, the default file Input is assumed. If Input is the keyboard, the program waits for data to be entered. If Input is a file, an end-of-file error will occur.

Other common errors are to run out of data prematurely and to lose the first or last component in the file. The only advice that we can give you here is to be very careful when designing the input section of your program. Always hand simulate the input before you code it. When checking your output, be sure to check whether the first and last components have been processed.

The most common error associated with the use of pointer variables is to confuse the pointer variable with the variable that it references. Again, the only general advice that we can give you is to be very careful when working with pointers.

Testing and Debugging Hints

1. Declare all Text file variables, other than Input and Output, and use Reset and Rewrite on these files. Specify the file variable when using Read, Readln, Write, Writeln, EOF, and EOLN for all Text files other than Input and Output.

2. Declare all nontext file variables. Specify the file variable when using Read, Write, Reset, Rewrite, and EOF.

3. Files passed as parameters must be VAR parameters.

4. Remember that a character read when EOLN is True returns a blank.

5. Readln, Writeln, and EOLN have no meaning with nontext files.

6. Don't use the value in an input file buffer variable when EOF is True for that file; the file buffer variable is undefined when EOF is True.

7. Nontext files must be created by programs. The output from a word processor or the keyboard is in text format.

8. Internal (scratch) files can be declared in procedures, but external files must be declared in the main program.

9. Pointers cannot be printed. Pointer variables contain memory addresses so the values they contain can not be printed. Even if they could, they might not tell us what we need to know to debug a program. Programs using pointers are therefore more difficult to debug than programs without them.

10. Pointers must point to variables of the same type in order to be compared or assigned one to another.

11. Do not confuse a pointer with the variable it points to (references).

`P := Q`	Copies the contents of Q into P.
`P^ := Q^`	Copies the contents of the variable to which Q points into the variable to which P points.

      P^ := Q   Is illegal because one is a pointer and one is the variable being pointed to.

      P := Q^   Is illegal because one is a pointer and one is the variable being pointed to.

12. Do not write pointer variables onto a file. Because memory is allocated differently from each program, the address stored in a pointer variable is only valid for a particular execution of a single program.

SUMMARY

Programs communicate with the outside world and with each other through files. Files, which are composed of a number of like components, reside in external storage. One component of a file is presented to the user at a time, in sequential order.

Input is the standard Pascal input file; Output is the standard Pascal output file. If no file name is listed on Read and Write statements, these standard files are assumed. Input and Output are Text files. Text files are files of characters broken up into lines. EOLN is a function that is used to determine if a Text file is at the end of the line.

The components of a file can be of any type other than another file. EOF is a function that is used to determine if the last component in the file has been accessed. The file name followed by an up-caret accesses the file buffer variable. The file buffer variable is the component at the file marker.

Pointers are a simple data type that can contain the address of another variable. They are used to create dynamic variables. The pointer is created at compile time, but the variable to which the pointer points is created at run time. The built-in procedure New creates a variable of the type the pointer references and returns the variable's address in the pointer. Dynamic variables are called referenced variables because they are not given a name but rather are referenced through a pointer variable.

The use of dynamic variables saves memory space because a variable is created only when it is needed. When a dynamic variable is no longer needed, it can be disposed of and those memory locations can be used again. The use of dynamic variables can also save machine time when large records are being sorted. The pointers to the large records can be sorted rather than the large records themselves.

QUICK CHECK

1. Given a user-defined data type called MapElement, how would you define a binary file data type called Map in which each component is a value of type MapElement? (pp. 608–611)

2. Given a binary file called Measures whose components are of type Integer, and an Integer variable called Length, how would you input a value from Measures into Length? (pp. 608–611)

3. When data in two files is being merged, what must be done if you run out of data on one file before running out of data on the other file? (pp. 612–618)

4. When data is being read from a file, what value is stored in the file buffer variable? When data is being written to a file, what value is stored in the file buffer variable? (pp. 618–620)

5. How would you define a pointer type called ToSomeNumber that will point to a variable of type Integer? (pp. 622–630)

6. (a) How would you dynamically create a referenced variable that is pointed to by a pointer variable called Number, of type ToSomeNumber? (b) How would you store the value 0 in the variable referenced by Number? (pp. 622–630)

7. How would you destroy the dynamic variable referenced by Number? (pp. 622–630)

8. What are two ways in which pointers may be used to improve program efficiency? (pp. 622–630)

Answers:
1. TYPE
     Map = FILE OF MapElement;
2. Read(Measures, Length);
3. The remainder of the nonempty file must be copied to the output file.
4. When reading, the file buffer variable contains the value at the marker position (one component ahead of the most recently read value). When writing, the file buffer variable contains the next value to be written. The file buffer variable is undefined after the file is written.
5. TYPE
     ToSomeNumber = ^Integer;
6. (a) New(Number) (b) Number^ := 0;
7. Dispose(Number);
8. Pointers improve memory space efficiency because we only create as many dynamic variables as are needed. It is more efficient in terms of time to move pointers than to move large data structures, as in the case of sorting large records.

EXAM PREPARATION EXERCISES _____

1. Given the data line

$$\square\square\square213\square$$

show the file operations at the component level that must occur to execute the statement Readln(Number), where Number is an integer variable.

2. What are the differences between accessing array elements and accessing file components?

3. Which of the following can be used with any file type?
   (a) Read
   (b) EOLN
   (c) EOF
   (d) Put
   (e) Writeln

4. When is it appropriate to use an internal file instead of an external file?

5. How many component types may be collected in one file?

6. Show a Read operation on a text file that is inconsistent with the definition of the file data type.

7. What Pascal procedure initializes the file buffer with the first component of the file?

8. What is wrong with the following type definition?

```
TYPE
    X = ARRAY[1..10] OF Char;
    Y = FILE OF X;
    Z = FILE OF Y;
```

9. What is the relationship between pointer variables and dynamic variables?

10. What Pascal procedure releases the space reserved for a dynamic variable back to the system?

11. How can the use of pointers make a program run faster?

12. What part of a Pascal program determines how much space is allocated when New(P) is executed?

13. What changes must be made in Program Sport so that the records are read into a referenced variable rather than into a named variable?

14. What changes must be made in Program Convert so that the records are read into a referenced variable rather than a named variable?

PREPROGRAMMING EXERCISES

1. Declare a file type Text2 that has component type Char.

2. Write the Pascal code needed to print the last character on every line of file Input.

3. Recode procedure ReadInt in this chapter to accept integers that are immediately preceded by a '+' or a '−' symbol. The output parameter Number should be negative if the integer started with the '−' symbol.

4. Write a declaration for a binary file type containing real numbers.

5. Write the Pascal code to advance the file marker for file Skipped without reading in a value.

6. Write a Boolean function that takes two binary files of type Datatype as input and returns True if the next records on the files are identical and False otherwise.

7. Write an integer function that returns the number of records on file Data.

8. Declare a pointer type that points to a record type named RefRec.

9. Recode Program MergeLists of this chapter so that the master list is printed (to the file Output) as it is written to the file MasterList.

10. Write an IF statement that compares the two dynamic integer variables pointed to by variables P and Q, puts the larger into the integer variable named Biggest, and gets rid of the original two dynamic variables.

11. Declare the variables used in exercise 10.

12. Write a Boolean function that takes as parameters two pointer variables Pointer1 and Pointer2. The function should return True if the two pointers reference the same variable and False otherwise.

13. Write a Boolean function that takes as parameters two pointer variables Pointer1 and Pointer2. The function should return True if their referenced variables are identical and False otherwise.

PROGRAMMING PROBLEMS _____

1. Program MergeLists merges three files into one, assuming that each file ends with a dummy record. Rewrite Program MergeLists using EOF. Assume that there are no dummy records on any of the files.

2. Rewrite Program MergeLists using Get and Put instead of Read and Write.

3. Program MergeLists merges three files by merging two files and then merging the third file with the result of merging the first two. Another way to solve the same problem is to merge three files at the same time, putting the result on a fourth file.

   Write a top-down design to solve the problem using this second strategy. Code your design in Pascal. Thoroughly test your program.

4. In Chapter 10 we introduced the problem of creating an automated address book with names, phone numbers, and birthdates. In Chapter 14 we printed the entry for each friend whose birthday was within two weeks of a given date. The data was on Text file FriendList.

   Complete the creation of an automated address book by writing a program to add each person's address to the file. Your program should read an entry from file FriendList, display the name on the screen, and prompt the user to enter the street address, city, state, and zipcode. The complete entry should be written on binary file AddressBook.

   Add a field to EntryType2 (Program BirthDayCalls) of type AddressType. AddressType should be a record which contains the street address, the city, the state, and the zipcode. The file AddressBook should be a file of EntryType2.

   Make the module that prompts the user for the address as user-friendly as possible. Give the user a chance to read and approve the address before the entry is written to AddressBook.

5. In Chapter 12, Program Exam printed the names of those students taking an exam and the names of those students missing an exam. Parallel arrays were used because the record data type had not yet been introduced. Rewrite Program Exam combining Students and Attendance into a record (type StudentType) with two fields: Name and Attendance. Make these records referenced variables rather than named variables. That is, Students should be an array of pointers to records of type StudentType.

- To be able to define a linked list data structure for a given problem.
- To be able to print the contents of a linked list.
- To be able to insert new items into a linked list.
- To be able to delete items from a linked list.
- To be able to define and use a stack data structure.
- To be able to define and use a queue data structure.
- To be able to define and use a binary tree data structure.

16

In the last chapter we saw that Pascal has a mechanism for creating dynamic variables. This means that we can define a type at compile time, but not actually create any variables of that type until run time. The built-in procedure New is used to create dynamic variables during run time.

These dynamic variables, which can be of any simple or structured type, can be created or destroyed at any time during execution of the program. A dynamic variable is referenced not by a name but through a pointer that contains the address (location) in memory of the dynamic variable referenced. Every dynamic variable created has an associated pointer by which it can be accessed.

In the last chapter we used dynamic variables to save space and machine time. In this chapter we will see how to use dynamic variables to build data structures that can grow and shrink as the program executes.

STATIC VERSUS DYNAMIC STRUCTURES

As we have already pointed out, many problems in computing involve lists of items. The structure we have used for implementing a list is the array, which is a static structure. A static structure is one whose size is fixed at compile time. A static structure exists as long as the part of the program (block) in which it is declared is executing.

Yet when we are working with lists, many times we have no idea of the number of components we will have. The usual approach in this situation is to declare an array large enough to hold the maximum amount of data we could logically expect.

Since we usually have less data than the maximum, the length of the subarray in which we have placed values is recorded and only that part of the array from the first

Figure 16-1
Array

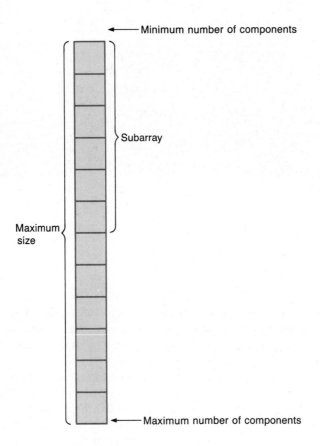

position to the recorded length is accessed. This subarray can vary in length during execution from zero to the maximum number of components in the array. The array itself, however, cannot vary; it is static. (See Figure 16-1.)

There is another technique for representing a list. In this technique the list components are dynamic variables, which are created only as they are needed. Rather than being *physically* next to each other as in an array, the components are *logically* next to each other. (See Figure 16-2.) Each component contains information about the location of the next component—a pointer to the next component in the list is stored with each component.

We don't have to know in advance how long the list will be. Such a list can expand or contract as the program executes. (See Figure 16-3.) The only limitation is the amount of available memory space. Data structures built using this technique are called *dynamic data structures.*

Dynamic Data Structure A data structure that can expand and contract during execution.

Figure 16-2
Physical vs. Logical
Ordering

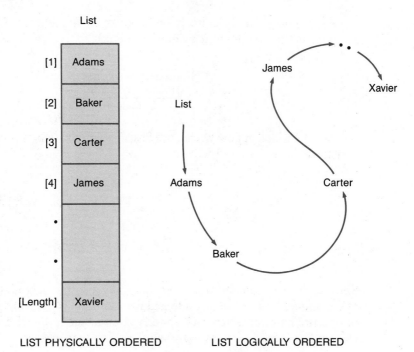

LIST PHYSICALLY ORDERED   LIST LOGICALLY ORDERED

Figure 16-3
Dynamic Data
Structure

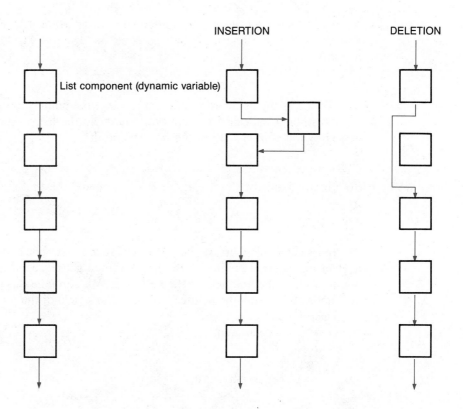

A dynamic data structure is built out of *nodes*. Each node is made up of a component (the data) and a pointer (the link).

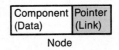

Node

Now let's look at how we can use Pascal pointer variables to create dynamic data structures.

LINKED LISTS

Since each node contains a pointer that links it to the next node, a dynamic list is called a *linked list*. Accessing a linked list is a little like playing the children's game of treasure hunt, in which each child is given a clue to the hiding place of the next clue and the chain of clues eventually leads to the treasure.

Linked List A list in which the order of the components is determined by an explicit link field in each node rather than by the sequential order of the components in memory.

We access the list by remembering (saving) the pointer to the first node in the list. This pointer is called the *external pointer* to the list. Every other node is accessed by the pointer field in the node before it.

External Pointer (to a list) A named pointer variable that references the first node in a linked list.

To create a linked list, we begin by getting the first node and saving the pointer to it in the external pointer to the list. We then get a second node and store the pointer to it in the link field of the first node. We continue this process—getting a new node and storing the pointer to it in the link field of the previous node—until we reach the end of the list.

Given the declarations

```
CONST
   NameLength = 10;
```

```
TYPE
   NameIndex = 1..NameLength;
   ComponentType = PACKED ARRAY[NameIndex] OF Char;
   NodePointer = ^NodeType;
   NodeType = RECORD
                 Component : ComponentType;
                 Link : NodePointer
              END;  (* Record *)

VAR
   List,                  (* External pointer to list *)
   Current,               (* Moving pointer           *)
   NewNode:
      NodePointer;
```

the following code fragment creates a linked list with the names Adams, Baker, and Carter as the components in the list.

```
New(List);
List^.Component := 'Adams    ';
New(NewNode);
NewNode^.Component := 'Baker    ';
List^.Link := NewNode;
Current := NewNode;
New(NewNode);
NewNode^.Component := 'Carter   ';
Current^.Link := NewNode;
NewNode^.Link := NIL;
Current := NewNode
```

Let's go through each of these statements, describing in words what is happening and showing the linked list as it appears after the execution of the statement.

`New(List)` A dynamic variable of NodeType is created. The pointer to this node is left in List. List will be the external pointer to the list we are building.

`List^.Component := 'Adams    '` The character string 'Adams   ' is stored in the Component field of the first node.

New (NewNode)

A dynamic variable of NodeType is created. The pointer to this node is left in NewNode.

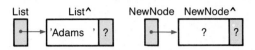

NewNode^. Component : = 'Baker   '

The character string 'Baker   ' is stored in the Component field of the new node.

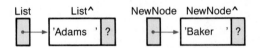

List^. Link : = NewNode

The pointer to the node containing 'Baker   ' in its Component field is stored in the Link field of List. NewNode still points to this node. The node can be accessed by both NewNode^ and List^.Link^.

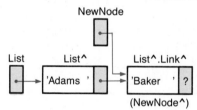

Current : = NewNode

The pointer to the new node is copied into Current. Current, NewNode, and List^.Link all point to this new node, which contains 'Baker   ' as its component.

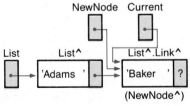

New (NewNode)

A dynamic variable of NodeType is created. The pointer to this node is in NewNode.

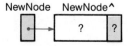

```
NewNode^.Component := 'Carter        '
```
The character string 'Carter   ' is stored in the Component field of the new node.

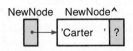

```
Current^.Link := NewNode
```
The pointer to the new node containing 'Carter   ' in the Component field is stored in the Link field of the node that contains 'Baker   ' in its Component field.

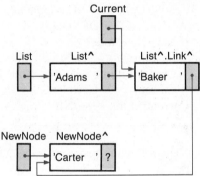

```
NewNode^.Link := NIL
```
The special pointer constant NIL is stored in the Link field of the last node in the list. When used in the Link field of a node, NIL means the end of the list. NIL is shown in the diagram as a / in the link field.

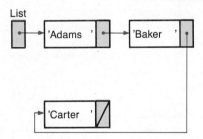

```
Current := NewNode
```
Current is updated.

Before we go on to generalize this algorithm for creating a linked list, a word should be said about the declarations. The pointer type NodePointer is defined to be a pointer to a record of type NodeType which has not yet been defined. This definition is an exception to the rule that identifiers must be defined before they are used. A pointer type may be defined to point to a type that has not yet been defined.

In the previous example, we used three pointers:

1. List, which was used to create the first node in the list and became the external pointer to the list,
2. NewNode, which was used to create a new node when it was needed, and
3. Current, which was updated to always point to the last node in the linked list.

When building any linked list, we will need three pointers to perform these same functions. The algorithm that we used is generalized below to apply to building a linked list of integer numbers from file Data. It is assumed that the file is not empty.

```
New(List)
Current ⟵ List
Readln(Data, List^.Component)
WHILE NOT EOF (Data)
  New(NewNode)
  Readln(Data, NewNode^.Component)
  Current^.Link ⟵ NewNode
  Current ⟵ NewNode
Current^.Link ⟵ NIL
```

The following program implements this algorithm:

```
PROGRAM CreateList (Output, Data);

(* Integers are read from file Data and stored in a linked list.
   List is the external pointer to the list.  Assumption: File
   is not empty *)

TYPE
   NodePointer = ^NodeType;
   NodeType = RECORD
                 Component : Integer;
                 Link : NodePointer
              END; (* Record *)

VAR
   List,              (* External pointer to the list        *)
   NewNode,           (* Pointer to the newest node          *)
   Current:           (* Pointer to the last node            *)
      NodePointer;
   Data:              (* A file of integer numbers, one per line *)
      Text;

BEGIN (*CreateList *)
   New(List);
   Current := List;
   Readln(Data, List^.Component);
```

```
WHILE NOT EOF (Data) DO
  BEGIN
    New (NewNode) ;
    (* Get a node *)
    Readln (Data, NewNode^. Component);
    (* Link it into list *)
    Current^. Link : = NewNode;
    (* Set Current to last node *)
    Current : = NewNode
  END;
  (* Set Link to end-of-list marker *)
  Current^. Link : = NIL
END.  (* CreateList *)
```

Let's do a code walkthrough and see just how this algorithm works.

`New (List) ;`	A variable of NodeType is created. The pointer is left in List. List will remain unchanged as the pointer to the first node. List is the external pointer to the list.
`Current : = List;`	Current now points to the last node in the list (the only node).
`Readln (Data, List^. Component)`	The first number is read into the Component field of the first node in the list.
`WHILE NOT EOF (Data) DO`	An event-controlled loop is used to read integer numbers from file Data until EOF.
`New (NewNode) ;`	Another variable of type NodeType is created, with NewNode referencing it.
`Readln (Data, NewNode^. Component)`	The next number on file Data is read into the Component field of the newly created node NewNode.
`Current^. Link : = NewNode;`	The pointer to the newly created node is stored in the Link field of the last node in the list.
`Current : = NewNode`	Current is again pointing to the last node in the list.
`Current^. Link : = NIL`	The Link field of the last node in the list is assigned the special end-of-list symbol NIL.

Following is the linked list that resulted when the program was run with the numbers 32, 78, 99, and 21 as data. The final values are shown for the auxiliary variables.

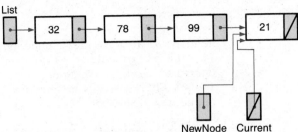

Problem Solving in Action

Problem: As an avid card player, you plan to write a program to play solitaire once you have become thoroughly comfortable with dynamic data structures. As a prelude to that program, you decide to write a procedure that will create a deck of playing cards. The playing cards will be structured as a linked list.

Discussion: The suits of the cards can be represented using an enumerated type. Rank can be represented using the numbers 1 through 13, with the ace as a 1 and the king as a 13. The first card can be generated and its pointer stored in the external pointer to the list. The balance of the 52 cards can be generated in a loop. After every thirteenth card, the suit will be incremented.

Input: None

Output: Deck, the external pointer to the linked list of playing cards

Data Structures: A linked list in which the components are cards represented as follows:

```
Cardtype = RECORD
             Suit : Suits;
             Rank : 1..13
           END;   (* Record *)
```

MAIN MODULE   Level 0

```
New(Deck)
Suit of Deck ⟵ Club
Rank of Deck ⟵ 1
Current ⟵ Deck
FOR Count going from 2 to 52
  New(NewNode)
  IF Rank of Current = 13
    THEN
       Suit of NewNode ⟵ Succ(Suit)
       Rank of NewNode ⟵ 1
    ELSE
       Suit of NewNode ⟵ Suit of Current
       Rank of NewNode ⟵ Rank of Current + 1
  Link of Current ⟵ NewNode
  Current ⟵ NewNode
```

PSIA ▬▬▬

The code for the global declarations and procedure follows:

```
TYPE
  NodePointer = ^NodeType;
  Suits = (Club, Diamond, Heart, Spade);
  CardType = RECORD
               Suit : Suits;
               Rank : 1..13                    (* 1 is ace.  13 is king *)
             END;  (* Record *)
  NodeType = RECORD
               Card : CardType;
               Link : NodePointer
             END;  (* Record *)

VAR
  Deck:                          (* External pointer to deck of cards *)
    NodePointer;


(**************************************************************************)

PROCEDURE CreateDeck (VAR Deck:          (* Pointer to list of cards *)
                          NodePointer);

(* Creates a list of 52 nodes.  Each node represents a playing
   card.  Deck is the external pointer to the list.  The cards are in
   order by suit and by rank *)

VAR
  NewNode,             (* Pointer to newest card   *)
  Current:             (* Pointer to previous card *)
    NodePointer;
  Count:               (* Loop control variable    *)
    Integer;

BEGIN (* CreateDeck *)
  New(Deck);
  Deck^.Card.Suit := Club;
  Deck^.Card.Rank := 1;
  Current := Deck;
  (* Loop to create balance of deck *)
  FOR Count := 2 to 52 DO
    BEGIN
      New(NewNode);
      (* Test for change of suit *)
      IF Current^.Card.Rank = 13
        THEN
          (* Change suit *)
          BEGIN
            NewNode^.Card.Suit := Succ(Current^.Card.Suit);
            NewNode^.Card.Rank := 1
          END
```

PSIA

```
  ELSE
    (* Increment rank *)
    BEGIN
      NewNode^. Card. Suit  : = Current^. Card. Suit;
      NewNode^. Card. Rank  : = Current^. Card. Rank + 1
    END;
  Current^. Link  : = NewNode;
  Current  : = NewNode
END;
(* Set end-of-list marker *)
Current^. Link  : = NIL
END;   (* CreateDeck *)
```

Algorithms on Linked Lists

Now that we have looked at three examples of creating a linked list, let's look at algorithms that process components in a linked list. For example, we will need to insert a component into a list, delete a component from a list, and print the components in lists. For each of these operations we will make use of the fact that NIL is in the Link field of the last node in a list.

The value NIL which was assigned to the last pointer field in the list is a reserved word. NIL can be assigned to any pointer variable. It means that the pointer points to nothing. Its importance lies in the fact that we can compare the Link field of each node to NIL to see when we have reached the end of the list.

As we develop these algorithms, we will use the following declarations:

```
TYPE
  NodePointer = ^NodeType;
  NodeType = RECORD
               Component : Integer;
               Link : NodePointer
             END; (* Record *)

VAR
  List:                    (* External pointer to list *)
    NodePointer;
```

Printing the components of a linked list is the easiest of the algorithms, so we will begin with it.

Printing a Linked List   To print the components of a linked list, we will need to access the nodes one at a time. This requirement implies an event-controlled loop where the event that stops the loop is reaching the end of the list.

We will use a pointer as a loop control variable. It will be initialized to the external pointer to the list. We will advance (increment) it by setting it equal to the Link field of the current node. When the loop control pointer becomes equal to NIL, the last node has been accessed.

PRINT

```
Current ⟵── List
WHILE Current <> end of the list
   Write Component of Current node
   Current ⟵── Link field of Current
```

This algorithm can be coded directly as the general procedure Print. Note that the algorithm will work even if List is empty (has no nodes).

```
PROCEDURE Print (List:                    (* Pointer to head of linked list *)
                 NodePointer);

(* The Component of the nodes in List are printed *)

VAR
   Current:             (* Loop control pointer *)
     NodePointer;

BEGIN (* Print *)
   Current := List;
   WHILE Current <> NIL DO
     BEGIN
       Write (Current^.Component);
       Current := Current^.Link
     END
END;  (* Print *)
```

Let's do a code walkthrough using the following list:

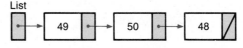

Current := List

Current and List both reference the first node in the list.

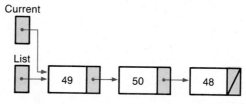

WHILE Current <> NIL

The loop is entered because Current is not NIL.

`Write(Current^.Component)`	The number 49 is printed.
`Current := Current^.Link`	Current now points to the second node in the list.

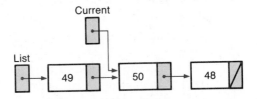

`WHILE Current <> NIL`	The loop repeats since Current is not NIL.
`Write(Current^.Component)`	The number 50 is printed.
`Current := Current^.Link`	Current now points to the third node in the list.

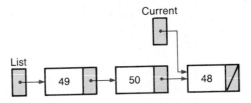

`WHILE Current <> NIL`	The loop repeats since Current is not NIL.
`Write(Current^.Component)`	The number 48 is printed.
`Current := Current^.Link`	Current is now NIL.

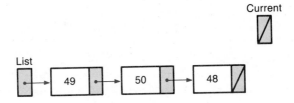

`WHILE Current <> NIL`	The loop is not repeated because Current is NIL.

Inserting into a Linked List A procedure for inserting a component into a linked list must have two parameters: the external pointer to the linked list and the item to be inserted. The phrase "inserting into" a linked list is ambiguous. It could mean either inserting the component at the top of the list (as the first node) or inserting the component into its proper place according to some ordering (alphabetic or numeric). Let's examine these two situations separately.

Inserting a component at the top of a list is easier because we don't have to search the list to find where the element belongs.

INSERT TOP

```
Get a new node (NewNode)
Component field of NewNode ⟵ Item
Link field of NewNode ⟵ External pointer
External pointer ⟵ NewNode
```

This algorithm is coded in procedure InsertTop.

```
PROCEDURE InsertTop (VAR List:        (* Pointer to head of linked list *)
                           NodePointer;
                         Item:        (* Number being placed on list    *)
                           Integer);

(* A node with Item in its component field is inserted as the top
   element in List.  Assumption: List has been initialized *)

VAR
  NewNode:            (* Temporary pointer *)
    NodePointer;

BEGIN (* InsertTop *)
  New(NewNode);
  NewNode^.Component := Item;
  NewNode^.Link := List;
  List := NewNode
END;   (* InsertTop *)
```

Before InsertTop is called the first time, the list must be initialized by setting List to NIL. The following code walkthrough shows the steps in inserting a component with the value of 20 as the first node in the linked list that was printed in the last section.

New(NewNode)   A new node is created.

NewNode^.Component := Item   The number 20 is stored in the Component field of the new node.

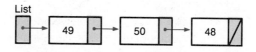

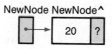

`NewNode^.Link := List`   The Link field of NewNode now points to the first node in the list.

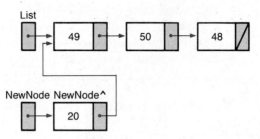

`List := NewNode`   The external pointer to the list now points to the node containing the new component.

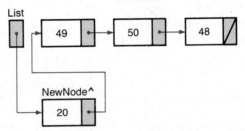

Inserting a component into its proper place in a list involves the additional step of finding its proper place. We will have to loop through all of the nodes until we find the place where the component belongs.

If the list is kept in increasing numeric order, we can recognize where a component belongs by finding the node in the list that contains a value *greater* than the one being inserted. Our new node should be inserted directly before the node with that value. Therefore we must keep track of the node *before* the current one in order to be able to insert our new node. We will call this node Previous. This method leads to the following algorithm:

INSERT IN PLACE

IF Item < List^.Component
  THEN
    InsertTop
  ELSE
    Get a new node (NewNode)
    Component field of NewNode ⟵ Item
    Previous ⟵ List
    Current ⟵ Link field of List
    WHILE Item > Component field of Current
        Previous ⟵ Current
        Current ⟵ Link field of Current
    Insert NewNode between Previous and Current

This algorithm is correct, but there is a problem associated with coding it. If the new component is larger than all of the other components in the list, the event that stops the loop (finding a node whose component is larger than the one being inserted) will not occur.

An infinite loop will not occur, however, because the process will be stopped by an error. Trying to access the referenced variable of a pointer that contains NIL will cause the program to crash. We can take care of this case by making sure that Current <> NIL. We would like to use the following expression to control the WHILE loop!

Current <> NIL AND Item > Component field of Current

However, this expression cannot be coded directly. Most Pascal compilers will evaluate both sides of an expression even if the first evaluates to False. That is, even if Current is equal to NIL, the other side of the expression will still be evaluated, giving us the error we are trying to avoid.

We will have to use our old friend the Boolean variable Found. We will have to move the comparison of component to the body of the loop and record the result in Found. Found is used in the loop control expression.

Procedure Insert implements our algorithm with these changes incorporated.

```
PROCEDURE Insert (VAR List:          (* Pointer to head of linked list *)
                      NodePointer;
                  Item:              (* Number being placed into list   *)
                      Integer);

(* A node with Item in its component field is inserted into its proper
   place in List.  Assumption: The Component fields are in increasing
   order *)

VAR
   Found:              (* True when insertion place found *)
      Boolean;
   Current,            (* Moving pointer                  *)
   Previous,           (* Node before Current             *)
   NewNode:            (* New node                        *)
      NodePointer;

BEGIN (* Insert *)
   IF Item < List^.Component
      THEN
         InsertTop(List, Item)
      ELSE
         BEGIN
            (* Set up node to be inserted *)
            New(NewNode);
            NewNode^.Component := Item;
            (* Find insertion point *)
            Previous := List;
            Current := List^.Link;
            Found := False;
```

```
            WHILE (Current <> NIL) AND NOT Found DO
              IF Item > Current^.Component
                THEN
                  BEGIN
                    Previous := Current;
                    Current := Current^.Link
                  END
                ELSE
                  Found := True;
              (* Insert NewNode *)
              NewNode^.Next := Current;
              Previous^.Link := NewNode
            END
      END;   (* Insert *)
```

There are two things to notice about this procedure. First, the parameter List has to be a VAR parameter in case the new node has to be inserted at the top. Second, this procedure can be made to work for any scalar component field by changing the type of Item in the procedure heading.

Let's go through this code for each of the three cases: inserting at the top (Item is 20), inserting in the middle (Item is 60), and inserting at the end (Item is 100). Each insertion will be into the list shown below.

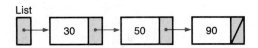

Insert(List, 20)

```
        IF Item < List^.Component
```

Since 20 is less than 30, Insert-Top is called to insert Item as the first component in the list. We will not repeat the walkthrough for that algorithm.

Insert(List, 60)

```
        IF Item < List^.Component
```

Since 60 is greater than 30, the ELSE branch is taken.

```
    New (NewNode)
    NewNode^.Component := Item
    Previous := List
    Current := List^.Link
    Found := False
```

These five statements initialize the variables used in the searching process. The variables and their contents are shown below.

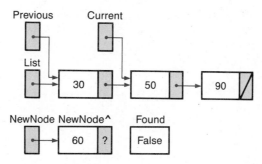

WHILE (Current <> NIL) AND NOT Found   This expression is True, so the loop is entered.

IF Item > Current^.Component   Since 60 is greater than 50, the THEN branch is taken.

Previous := Current
Current := Current^.Link   Pointer variables are advanced.

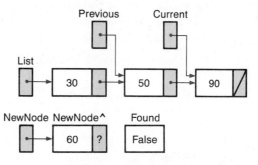

IF Item > Current^.Component   Since 60 is not greater than 90, the ELSE branch is taken.

Found := True

WHILE Current <> NIL AND NOT Found   This expression is False, so the loop is not repeated.

NewNode^.Next := Current   Set link field if NewNode

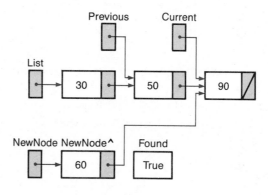

```
Previous^.Link := NewNode
```
The completed list is shown with the auxiliary variables removed.

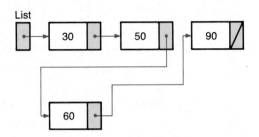

Insert(List, 100)

We will not repeat the first part of the search, but pick up the walkthrough where Previous is pointing to the node whose component is 50 and Current is pointing to the node whose component is 90.

```
IF Item > Current^.Component
```
Since 100 is greater than 90, the THEN branch is taken.

```
Previous := Current
Current := Current^.Link
```
The pointer variables are advanced.

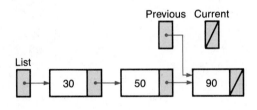

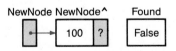

```
WHILE (Current <> NIL) AND NOT Found
```
Condition is False because Current is NIL.

```
NewNode^.Next := Current
Previous^.Link:= NewNode
```
NewNode is inserted between Previous and Current. List is shown with auxiliary variables removed.

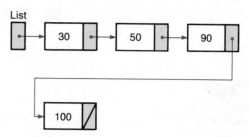

Deleting from a Linked List To delete a node from a linked list, we must know which node is to be deleted. We will look at the mirror image of our insertions: deleting the top node and deleting a node whose component is equal to an input parameter.

To delete the first node, we just change the external pointer to point to the second node. However, it seems reasonable that we should return the value in the node being deleted as an output parameter. The coding is so straightforward that it needs no further explanation.

```
PROCEDURE RemoveTop (VAR List:          (* Pointer to head of linked list *)
                          NodePointer;
                     VAR Item:          (* Number removed from the list   *)
                          Integer);

(* The top node is removed from List.  Its Component field is returned
   in Item.  Assumption: There is at least one node in List *)

VAR
   TempPointer:              (* Temporary pointer *)
      NodePointer;

BEGIN (* RemoveTop *)
   TempPointer := List;
   Item := List^.Component;
   List := List^.Link;
   Dispose(TempPointer)
END;   (* RemoveTop *)
```

Rather than show a complete code walkthrough, we will show the state of the data structure in two stages: after the first two statements and at the end. We will use one of our previous lists. Following is the data structure after the execution of the first two statements in the procedure.

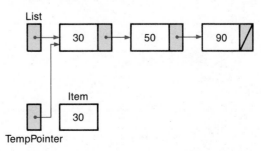

After the execution of the procedure, the structure looks as follows:

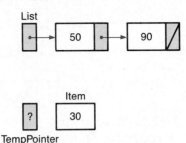

The procedure for deleting a node whose component contains a certain value is very similar to the Insert procedure. The difference is that we are looking for a match, not a Component field greater than our Item. If we make the assumption that the component we are looking for is in the list, our loop control is very simple. We don't have to worry about accessing a NIL pointer.

As in the Insert procedure, we will need the node before the one that is to be deleted in order to change its Link field. In the following procedure, we will demonstrate another technique for keeping track of the previous node. Instead of comparing Item with the Component field of Current, we will compare it with the Component field of the node that Current's Link field points to. That is, we will compare Item with Current^.Link^.Component. When Current^.Link^.Component is equal to Item, Current will be the previous node.

```
PROCEDURE Delete (VAR List:          (* Pointer to head of linked list *)
                     NodePointer;
                  Item:              (* Number within list to delete   *)
                     Integer);

(* The node whose Component field contains Item is deleted from List.
   The node is Disposed.  Assumptions: There is a Component field that
   equals Item.  The Components are in ascending order *)

VAR
   TempPointer,       (* Temporary pointer    *)
   Current:           (* Loop control pointer *)
      NodePointer;

BEGIN (* Delete *)
   (* Check if first node *)
   IF Item = List^.Component
      THEN
         (* Delete first node *)
         BEGIN
            TempPointer := List;
            List := List^.Link
         END
```

```
      ELSE
        BEGIN
          Current := List;
          (* Search for node in rest of list *)
          WHILE Current^.Link^.Component <> Item DO
            Current := Current^.Link;
          (* Delete Current^.Link *)
          TempPointer := Current^.Link;
          Current^.Link := Current^.Link^.Link
        END;
    Dispose(TempPointer)
  END;  (* Delete *)
```

Let's delete the node whose component is 90. The structure is shown below, with the nodes labeled as they would be when the WHILE loop is entered.

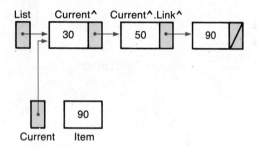

WHILE Current^.Link^.Component <> Item   Since 50 is not equal to 90, the loop is executed another time.

Current := Current^.Link   Pointer is advanced.

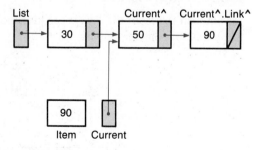

WHILE Current^.Link^.Component <> Item   Since 90 is equal to 90, the loop is exited.

```
TempPointer := Current^.Link
Current^.Link := Current^.Link^.Link
```

The Link field of the node whose component is 90 is stored in the Link field of the node whose component is 50. The Link field is NIL in this case.

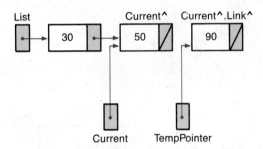

```
Dispose(TempPointer)
```

Locations used for TempPointer^ (the node that was deleted) are available to be used again. TempPointer is undefined.

Note that if the node whose component was 90 was not the last one in the list, a pointer to the next node, rather than NIL, would have been stored in Current^.Link.

Pointer Expressions

As you can see from the last procedure, pointer expressions can be quite complex. Let's look at some examples.

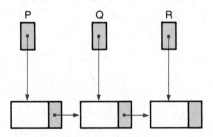

P, Q, and R point to nodes in a list. To access the fields of the nodes, we use P^, Q^, and R^. Use the preceding diagram to convince yourself that the following equivalences are true.

$$P\text{\textasciicircum}.\,Link\ =\ Q$$
$$P\text{\textasciicircum}.\,Link\text{\textasciicircum}\ =\ Q\text{\textasciicircum}$$
$$P\text{\textasciicircum}.\,Link\text{\textasciicircum}.\,Link\ =\ R$$
$$P\text{\textasciicircum}.\,Link\text{\textasciicircum}.\,Link\text{\textasciicircum}\ =\ R\text{\textasciicircum}$$
$$Q\text{\textasciicircum}.\,Link\ =\ R$$
$$Q\text{\textasciicircum}.\,Link\text{\textasciicircum}\ =\ R\text{\textasciicircum}$$

Remember the semantics of assignment statements.

P := Q — Assigns the value of pointer Q to pointer P.

P\^ := Q\^ — Assigns the value of the variable referenced by Q to the variable referenced by P.

Problem Solving in Action

Problem: There is a solitaire game that is fun to play on rainy days. It is quite simple, but seems very difficult to win. Let's write a program to play this solitaire and then run it a number of times to see if it really is that difficult to win or if we have just been unlucky.

Although this card game is played with a regular poker or bridge deck, the rules deal with suits only; the face values (ranks) are ignored. The rules are listed below. Rules 1 and 2 are initialization.

1. Take a deck of playing cards and shuffle it.
2. Place four cards side by side, left to right, face up on the table.
3. If the four cards (or right-most four if there are more than four on the table) are of the same suit, move them to a discard pile.

   Otherwise, if the first one and the fourth one (of the right-most four cards) are of the same suit, move the cards in between (second and third) to a discard pile.

   Repeat until no cards can be removed.
4. Take the next card from the shuffled deck and place it face up to the right of those already there.

   Repeat this step if there are less than four cards face up (assuming there are more cards in the deck).
5. Repeat steps 3 and 4 until there are no more cards in the deck. You win if all the cards are on the discard pile.

Figure 16-4 walks through the beginning of a typical game to demonstrate how the rules operate. Remember the game deals with suits only. There must be at least four cards face up on the table before the rules can be applied.

Discussion: A program that plays a game is an example of a *simulation program*. The program simulates what a human does when playing the game. Programs that simulate games or processes are very common in computing.

In developing a simulation, the first step is to decide how to represent in the program the physical items being simulated. In a card game, the basic item is, of course, a card. A deck of cards becomes a list of 52 cards in the program. Cards face up on the table, and the discard pile must also be simulated in this program.

Figure 16-4
Solitaire Game

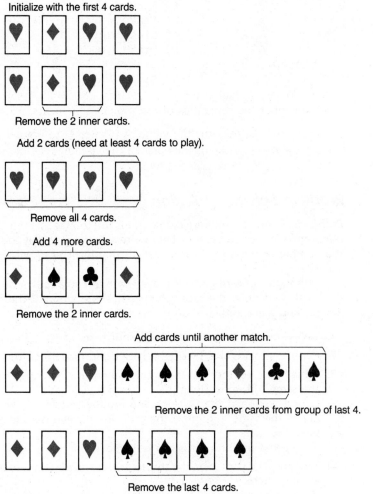

Initialize with the first 4 cards.

Remove the 2 inner cards.

Add 2 cards (need at least 4 cards to play).

Remove all 4 cards.

Add 4 more cards.

Remove the 2 inner cards.

Add cards until another match.

Remove the 2 inner cards from group of last 4.

Remove the last 4 cards.

Add cards until another match.

Remove the 2 inner cards from group of last 4.

Add cards until another match.

Remove all 4 cards.

PSIA ▬▬▬▬▬▬▬

Putting a card face up on the table means that a card is being taken from the deck and put on the table where the player can see it. The cards on the table can be represented by another list. The rules that determine whether cards can be moved to the discard pile are applied to the top four cards in this list—that is, the last four cards put in the list.

The discard pile is also a list of cards. At the end of the game, if no cards remain on the table (they are all on the discard pile), then the player has won. If any cards remain on the table face up, the player has lost.

A linked list seems a logical choice for representing these three lists (the deck, the cards face up on the table, and the discard pile). The simulation will require a lot of deleting from one list and inserting into another list. These operations are quite simple with a linked list. In fact, the procedures InsertTop and RemoveTop that we coded in a previous section can be used.

Using dynamic variables to represent our lists instead of arrays will save memory space. If an array representation were used, three arrays of 52 components each would have to be used. In a linked representation, we will use only 52 components in all, since a card can be in only one list at a time.

Now we are ready to complete the top-down design.

Input:

The number of times the simulation is to be run (NumberOfGames)

The number of times the deck is to be shuffled between games (NumberOfShuffles)

Output:

Number of games played

Number of games won

Data Structures:

A linked list representing a deck of cards (Deck)

A linked list representing the cards on the table (OnTable)

A linked list representing the discard pile (DiscardPile)

MAIN MODULE   · Level 0

```
Initialize
Create Deck of cards
WHILE more games to play
  Shuffle
  Play Game
  IF Won, increment won count
  Re-create Deck
Print number of games won
```

PSIA ━━━━━━

INITIALIZE   Level 1

```
Prompt for number of games to be played
Read number of games
Prompt for number of shuffles
Read number of shuffles
Initialize OnTable to NIL
Initialize DiscardPile to NIL
```

CREATE DECK

We can use the routine developed in an earlier section to create the deck. Although we won't use the rank field, it might as well be there. During debugging, we may want to print out the contents of the various lists. Some of the routines such as the one to shuffle the cards may be used elsewhere. They should be tested with a complete representation of a deck of cards.

SHUFFLE DECK

The shuffle module is a difficult one. Let's leave it to our "smart friend."

PLAY GAME

```
WHILE more cards in Deck
    Turn up card
    Try to Remove
```

WON

```
OnTable contains no cards at end of game
```

RE-CREATE DECK

```
WHILE more cards in OnTable
    Remove card from OnTable (RemoveTop)
    Insert into Deck (InsertTop)
WHILE more cards in DiscardPile
    Remove card from DiscardPile (RemoveTop)
    Insert into Deck (InsertTop)
```

TURN UP CARD   Level 2

```
Remove card from Deck (RemoveTop)
Insert into OnTable (InsertTop)
```

PSIA

TRY REMOVE

To play the game, check the first card and the fourth card first. If these do not match, we can't move any cards. If they do match, we check to see how many can be moved. This process continues until there are fewer than four cards face up on the table or until no move can be made.

```
Initialize flag Moved to True
WHILE Four on Table AND Moved
  IF First = Fourth
    THEN
      IF First, Second, and Third match
        THEN
          Move Four cards to DiscardPile
        ELSE
          Move Two (Second and Third) to DiscardPile
    ELSE
      Moved ⟵ False
```

MOVE FOUR   Level 3

```
FOR counter going from 1 to 4
  Remove top card from OnTable
  Insert in DiscardPile
```

MOVE TWO

```
Save top card from OnTable
Move top card from OnTable to DiscardPile
Move top card from OnTable to DiscardPile
Replace original top card
```

REMOVE CARD AND INSERT INTO DECK

We have already coded the procedures necessary to remove the top element from a list (Procedure RemoveTop) and to insert an element as the first in a list (Procedure InsertTop). We will modify variable names to reflect the nature of this program. We will also add a line of code to test whether or not there is an element to be moved.

FOUR ON TABLE

We need to know whether there are four cards on the table—that is, whether the list OnTable contains at least four cards. There are two ways to handle this problem: define a function that counts the number of cards in OnTable or keep a record of each insertion and deletion applied to OnTable. If all of OnTable had to be counted each

PSIA ▰▰▰▰▰▰

time, it would be better to keep track of how many insertions and deletions were made. However, the entire count is not needed. We only need to know whether there are at least four cards (nodes) in the list.

```
Count ⟵ 0
Pointer ⟵ OnTable
WHILE Count < > 4 AND Pointer < > NIL
    Count ⟵ Count + 1
    Pointer ⟵ Link field of Pointer
FourOnTable ⟵ Count = 4
```

In this discussion we have used First to stand for the suit of the first card on the table, Second to stand for the suit of the second card on the table, and so on. The values of these suits will have to be determined. We shall define four one-line functions of type Suits to determine these variables, as shown below.

FIRST   Level 3

```
First ⟵ Suit field of OnTable^.Card
```

SECOND

```
Second ⟵ Suit field of OnTable^.Link^.Card
```

THIRD

```
Third ⟵ Suit field of OnTable^.Link^.Link^.Card
```

FOURTH

```
Fourth ⟵ Suit field of OnTable^.Link^.Link^.Link^.Card
```

SHUFFLE   Level 1

When a human shuffles a deck of cards, he or she divides the deck into two nearly equal parts and then merges the two parts back together. This process can be simulated directly. (Yes, a simulation within a simulation!) The list Deck can be divided into two lists, HalfA and HalfB. Then these two lists can be merged back into Deck. We will use a random number generator to determine how many cards go into HalfA. The rest will go into HalfB.

PSIA

Although many computer systems have a random number generator built into the system software, we will include the code for one here. The procedure takes a seed value, which is set as a constant at the beginning of the program and returns a random number between 0.00 and 1.00 (RanNumber) each time it is executed. Since we want our random number to be between 1 and 52, we will use the following conversion formula:

$$\text{SizeOfCut} \longleftarrow (\text{Trunc}(\text{RanNumber} * 100) \text{ MOD } 52) + 1$$

The merge algorithm will be much simpler than the one developed in the last chapter, because a component is taken alternately from each list without regard to the contents of the component. Also, we know the exact length of each list. We will call the Merge procedure with four parameters: the shorter list, the longer list, the length of the shorter list, and the external pointer to the deck.

```
FOR counter going from 1 to SizeOfCut
    RemoveTop a card from Deck (TempCard)
    InsertTop TempCard into HalfA
HalfB ⟵ Deck
Deck ⟵ NIL
IF SizeOfCut <= 26
    THEN
        Merge(HalfA, HalfB, SizeOfCut, Deck)
    ELSE
        Merge(HalfB, HalfA, 52 − SizeOfCut, Deck)
```

MERGE(SHORTERLIST, LONGERLIST, LENGTH, DECK)   Level 2

```
FOR counter going from 1 to Length
    Remove a card from ShorterList (TempCard)
    Insert TempCard onto Deck
    Remove a card from LongerList (TempCard)
    Insert TempCard onto Deck
FOR counter going from 1 to (52 − Length * 2)
    Remove a card from LongerList (TempCard)
    Insert TempCard onto Deck
```

PSIA

Module Structure Chart:

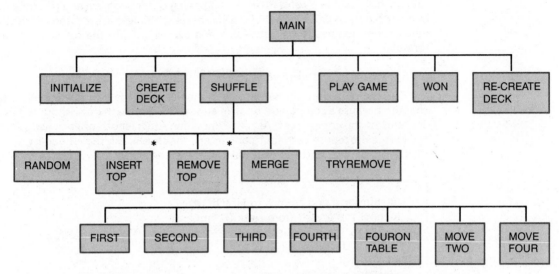

*REMOVETOP and INSERTTOP are also used by RE-CREATE DECK and MERGE

```
PROGRAM Solitaire (Input, Output);

(* This program is a simulation of a card game.
   See text for rules of the game. *)

CONST
  DeckSize = 52;
  HalfDeck = 26;

TYPE
  NodePointer = ^NodeType;
  Suits = (Club, Diamond, Heart, Spade);
  CardType = RECORD
               Suit : Suits;
               Rank : 1..13        (* 1 is Ace. 13 is King    *)
             END; (* Record *)
  NodeType = RECORD
               Card : CardType;
               Link : NodePointer
             END; (* Record *)
```

PSIA

```pascal
VAR
  Deck,                   (* External pointer to deck of cards *)
  OnTable,                (* NodeTypes face up on the table    *)
  DiscardPile:            (* NodeTypes on discard pile          *)
    NodePointer;
  NumberOfShuffles,       (* Number of shuffles per game        *)
  NumberOfGames,          (* Number of games to play            *)
  GamesPlayed,            (* Number of games played             *)
  GamesWon:               (* Number of games won                *)
    Integer;
  Seed:                   (* Used with random number generator *)
    Real;


(*********************************************************************)


PROCEDURE CreateDeck (VAR Deck:          (* Pointer to list of cards *)
                      NodePointer);

(* Creates a list of DeckSize nodes.  Each node represents a playing
   card.  Deck is the external pointer to the list.  The cards are in
   order by suit and by rank. *)

VAR
  NewNode,          (* Pointer to newest card   *)
  Current:          (* Pointer to previous card *)
    NodePointer;
  Count:            (* Loop control variable    *)
    Integer;

BEGIN (* CreateDeck *)
  New(Deck);
  Deck^.Card.Suit := Club;
  Deck^.Card.Rank := 1;
  Current := Deck;
  (* Loop to create balance of deck *)
  FOR Count := 2 to DeckSize DO
    BEGIN
      New(NewNode);
      (* Test for change of suit *)
      IF Current^.Card.Rank = 13
        THEN
          (* Change suit *)
          BEGIN
            NewNode^.Card.Suit := Succ(Current^.Card.Suit);
            NewNode^.Card.Rank := 1
          END
```

PSIA

```
        ELSE
          (* Increment rank *)
          BEGIN
            NewNode^.Card.Suit := Current^.Card.Suit;
            NewNode^.Card.Rank := Current^.Card.Rank + 1
          END;
      Current^.Link := NewNode;
      Current := NewNode;
    END;
  (* Set end-of-list marker *)
  Current^.Link := NIL;
END;   (* CreateDeck *)


(****************************************************************************)


PROCEDURE RemoveTop (VAR List:          (* Pointer to list of cards *)
                         NodePointer;
                     VAR Element:        (* Top card returned        *)
                         CardType);

(* The first card (node) is removed from List. The entire node is
   returned in Element. *)

VAR
  Pointer:            (* Temporary pointer *)
    NodePointer;

BEGIN (* RemoveTop *)
  IF List <> NIL
    THEN
      BEGIN
        Pointer := List;
        Element := List^.Card;
        List := List^.Link;
        Dispose(Pointer)
      END
END;   (* RemoveTop *)


(****************************************************************************)


PROCEDURE InsertTop (VAR List:          (* Pointer to list of cards *)
                         NodePointer;
                     Element:            (* Type of card to insert   *)
                         CardType);

(* Element is inserted as the first card (node) in List.  Assumption:
   List has been initialized to NIL. *)
```

PSIA

```
VAR
  Pointer:              (* Temporary pointer *)
    NodePointer;

BEGIN (* InsertTop *)
  New(Pointer);
  Pointer^.Card := Element;
  Pointer^.Link := List;
  List := Pointer
END;  (* InsertTop *)
```

(***)

```
PROCEDURE Shuffle (VAR Deck:           (* Pointer to list of cards *)
                       NodePointer;
                   NumberOfShuffles:  (* Times to perform shuffle *)
                       Integer);
```

(* Shuffle takes an input list of DeckSize nodes and returns the list
   with the nodes in a different order. The input list is divided into
   two parts which are then merged. The process is repeated
   NumberOfShuffles times. *)

```
VAR
  HalfA,               (* Half of the list      *)
  HalfB:               (* Half of the list      *)
    NodePointer;
  TempCard:            (* Temporary card        *)
    CardType;
  Count1,              (* Loop control variable *)
  Count2:              (* Loop control variable *)
    Integer;
  RanNumber:           (* Random real number    *)
    Real;
  SizeOfCut:           (* Size of HalfA         *)
    0..DeckSize;
```

(***)

```
PROCEDURE Random (VAR RanNumber:    (* Random generated value *)
                      Real);
```

(* Seed is accessed globally. *)

```
CONST
  Pi = 3.14159;
```

PSIA ▰▰▰▰▰▰

```
VAR
  Temp:            (* Temporary variable for computing random number *)
    Real;

BEGIN (* Random *)
  Temp := Seed + Pi;
  Temp := Exp(5.0 * Ln(Temp));
  Seed := Temp - Trunc(Temp);
  RanNumber := Seed
END;   (* Random *)


(***********************************************************************)


PROCEDURE Merge (     ShorterList,      (* Pointer to list of cards *)
                      LongerList:       (* Pointer to list of cards *)
                        NodePointer;
                      Length:           (* Length of shorter list   *)
                        Integer;
                  VAR Deck:             (* Resulting list of cards   *)
                        NodePointer);

(* ShorterList and LongerList are merged into Deck.  Length is number
   of nodes in ShorterList. *)

VAR
  Count:           (* Loop control variable *)
    Integer;
  TempCard:        (* Temporary card           *)
    CardType;

BEGIN (* Merge *)
  (* Merge two halves back into Deck *)
  FOR Count := 1 TO Length DO
    BEGIN
      RemoveTop(ShorterList, TempCard);
      InsertTop(Deck, TempCard);
      RemoveTop(LongerList, TempCard);
      InsertTop(Deck, TempCard)
    END;
  FOR Count := 1 TO (DeckSize - 2 * Length) DO
    BEGIN
      RemoveTop(LongerList, TempCard);
      InsertTop(Deck, TempCard)
    END;
END;   (* Merge *)


(***********************************************************************)
```

PSIA ▰▰▰▰▰

```
BEGIN (* Shuffle *)
  FOR Count1 := 1 TO NumberOfShuffles DO
    BEGIN
      Random(RanNumber);
      SizeOfCut := (Trunc(RanNumber * 100.0) MOD DeckSize) + 1;
      HalfA := NIL;
      HalfB := NIL;
      (* Divide Deck into two parts *)
      FOR Count2 := 1 TO SizeOfCut DO
        BEGIN
          RemoveTop(Deck, TempCard);
          InsertTop(HalfA, TempCard)
        END;
      FOR Count2 := SizeOfCut + 1 TO DeckSize DO
        BEGIN
          RemoveTop(Deck, TempCard);
          InsertTop(HalfB, TempCard)
        END;
      IF SizeOfCut <= HalfDeck
        THEN
          Merge(HalfA, HalfB, SizeOfCut, Deck)
        ELSE
          Merge(HalfB, HalfA, DeckSize - SizeOfCut, Deck)
    END
END;  (* Shuffle *)

(*********************************************************************)

FUNCTION First (OnTable:              (* Pointer to list of cards *)
                  NodePointer):
                    Suits;

(* First returns the suit of the first card (node) in OnTable *)

BEGIN (* First *)
  First := OnTable^.Card.Suit
END;  (* First *)

(*********************************************************************)

FUNCTION Second (OnTable:             (* Pointer to list of cards *)
                  NodePointer):
                    Suits;

(* Second returns the suit of the second card in OnTable *)

BEGIN (* Second *)
  Second := OnTable^.Link^.Card.Suit
END;  (* Second *)

(*********************************************************************)
```

PSIA ◢▬▬▬▬▬▬

```
FUNCTION Third (OnTable:                 (* Pointer to list of cards *)
                    NodePointer):
                      Suits;

(* Third returns the suit of the third card in OnTable *)

BEGIN (* Third *)
   Third := OnTable^.Link^.Link^.Card.Suit
END;   (* Third *)

(*****************************************************************)

FUNCTION Fourth (OnTable:                (* Pointer to list of cards *)
                    NodePointer):
                      Suits;

(* Fourth returns the suit of the fourth card in OnTable *)

BEGIN (* Fourth *)
   Fourth := OnTable^.Link^.Link^.Link^.Card.Suit
END;   (* Fourth *)

(*****************************************************************)

PROCEDURE MoveFour (VAR OnTable,          (* Pointer to list of cards *)
                        DiscardPile:      (* Pointer to list of cards *)
                        NodePointer);

(* The first four cards are moved from OnTable to DiscardPile *)

VAR
   TempCard:          (* Temporary card        *)
     CardType;
   Count:             (* Loop control variable *)
     Integer;

BEGIN (* MoveFour *)
   FOR Count := 1 TO 4 DO
      BEGIN
         RemoveTop(OnTable, TempCard);
         InsertTop(DiscardPile, TempCard)
      END
END;   (* MoveFour *)

(*****************************************************************)
```

PSIA ▰▰▰▰▰

```
PROCEDURE MoveTwo (VAR OnTable,            (* Pointer to list of cards *)
                       DiscardPile:        (* Pointer to list of cards *)
                       NodePointer);

(* The second and third cards are moved from OnTable to DiscardPile *)

VAR
  TempCard,          (* Temporary card *)
  First:             (* Temporary card *)
    CardType;

BEGIN (* MoveTwo *)
  RemoveTop(OnTable, First);
  (* Remove second card *)
  RemoveTop(OnTable, TempCard);
  InsertTop(DiscardPile, TempCard);
  (* Remove third card *)
  RemoveTop(OnTable, Tempcard);
  InsertTop(DiscardPile, Tempcard);
  (* Replace first card *)
  InsertTop(OnTable, First)
END;   (* MoveTwo *)

(************************************************************************)


FUNCTION FourOnTable (OnTable:             (* Pointer to list of cards *)
                       NodePointer):
                       Boolean;

(* FourOnTable is True if OnTable contains at least four cards *)

VAR
  Count:             (* Loop control variable *)
    Integer;

BEGIN (* FourOnTable *)
  Count := 0;
  WHILE (Count <> 4) AND (OnTable <> NIL) DO
    BEGIN
      Count := Count + 1;
      OnTable := OnTable^.Link
    END;
  FourOnTable := (Count = 4)
END;   (* FourOnTable *)

(************************************************************************)
```

PSIA

```
PROCEDURE TryRemove (VAR OnTable,          (* Pointer to list of cards *)
                         DiscardPile:       (* Pointer to list of cards *)
                         NodePointer);

(* If first (top) four cards are the same suit, they are moved from
   OnTable to DiscardPile.  If the first card and the fourth card are
   the same suit, the second and third card are moved from OnTable to
   DiscardPile.  Process continues until no further move can be made. *)

VAR
  Moved:           (* Flag to record whether a move has been made *)
    Boolean;

BEGIN (* TryRemove *)
  Moved := True;
  WHILE FourOnTable(OnTable) AND Moved DO
    IF First(OnTable) = Fourth(OnTable)
      THEN                                  (* A move will be made *)
        BEGIN
          IF (First(OnTable) = Second(OnTable)) AND
             (First(OnTable) = Third(OnTable))
            THEN
              (* Four alike *)
              MoveFour(OnTable, DiscardPile)
            ELSE
              (* First and fourth alike *)
              MoveTwo(OnTable, DiscardPile)
        END
      ELSE
        Moved := False
END;  (* TryRemove *)

(***********************************************************************)

PROCEDURE PlayGame (VAR Deck,              (* Deck of playing cards  *)
                        OnTable,           (* Cards face up on table *)
                        DiscardPile:       (* Cards on discard pile  *)
                        NodePointer);

(* Places the next card in the deck face up on the table
   and calls TryRemove to apply rules for moving *)

VAR
  Count:           (* Loop control variable *)
    Integer;
  TempCard:        (* Temporary card        *)
    CardType;
```

PSIA ▰▰▰▰▰▰

```
BEGIN (* PlayGame *)
  FOR Count := 1 to DeckSize DO
    BEGIN
      (* Turn up card *)
      RemoveTop(Deck, TempCard);
      InsertTop(OnTable, TempCard);
      TryRemove(OnTable, DiscardPile)
    END
END;  (* PlayGame *)
```

(***)

```
PROCEDURE ReCreate (VAR Deck,              (* Deck of playing cards  *)
                        OnTable,           (* Cards face up on table *)
                        DiscardPile:       (* Cards on discard pile  *)
                          NodePointer);

(* Gathers cards and puts them back into Deck *)

VAR
  TempCard:          (* Temporary card *)
    CardType;

BEGIN (* ReCreate *)
  (* Move cards from OnTable to Deck *)
  WHILE OnTable <> NIL DO
    BEGIN
      RemoveTop(OnTable, TempCard);
      InsertTop(Deck, Tempcard)
    END;
  (* Move cards from DiscardPile to Deck *)
  WHILE DiscardPile <> NIL DO
    BEGIN
      RemoveTop(DiscardPile, TempCard);
      InsertTop(Deck, TempCard)
    END
END;  (* ReCreate *)
```

(***)

PSIA

```
BEGIN (* Solitaire *)
  (* Initialize *)
  Seed := 4.0;
  GamesWon := 0;
  OnTable := NIL;
  DiscardPile := NIL;
  Writeln('Enter number of games to play.');
  Readln(NumberOfGames);
  Writeln('Enter number of shuffles per game.');
  Readln(NumberOfShuffles);
  CreateDeck(Deck);

  FOR GamesPlayed := 1 TO NumberOfGames DO
    BEGIN
      Shuffle(Deck, NumberOfShuffles);
      PlayGame(Deck, OnTable, DiscardPile);
      (* Determine if game was won *)
      IF OnTable = NIL
        THEN
          (* Game won *)
          GamesWon := GamesWon + 1;
      ReCreate(Deck, OnTable, DiscardPile)
    END;
  Writeln('Number of games played: ', NumberOfGames);
  Writeln('Number of games won:    ', GamesWon)
END.   (* Solitaire *)
```

Testing: In order to exhaustively test the portion of the program that plays the solitaire game, all possible configurations of a deck of 52 cards would have to be generated. Although this is theoretically possible, it is impractical. There are 52! (called 52 factorial) possible arrangements of a deck of cards. That is,

$$52 * 51 * 50 * \cdots 2 * 1$$

possible arrangements. (This is a *big* number. Try multiplying it out.)

Therefore another method of testing is required. At a minimum, the questions to be examined are

1. Does the program recognize a winning hand?

2. Does the program recognize a losing hand?

To answer these questions, we must examine at least one hand declared to be a winner and several declared to be losers. Rather than input specific hands, we let the program run on 100 cases to see if there were any winning hands in that number of cases. There were none.

From past experience we knew the solitaire was difficult. We let the simulation run 500 times and there was one winning hand. Intermediate prints were put in to examine the winning hand. It was correct.

PSIA ━━━━━━

Several losing hands were also printed; they were indeed losing hands. Satisfied that the program was working correctly, we set up runs that varied in length, number of shuffles, and seed for the random number generator. The results are listed below. There was no strategy behind the particular choices of parameters; they were random.

Number of games	Number of shuffles	Games won	Seed
100	1	0	3.00
100	2	0	4.00
500	3	1	4.00
1000	6	4	3.00
1000	1	6	4.00
10,000	4	41	4.00
10,000	4	48	3.00
10,000	4	44	1.37

CHOICE OF DATA STRUCTURE

We have now looked in detail at two ways of representing lists of components: one where the components are physically next to each other (an array) and one where the components are logically next to each other (a linked list). Let's look at common operations on lists and examine the advantages and disadvantages of each representation.

Common Operations

1. Read components sequentially into a list.
2. Access all the components in the list in sequence.
3. Insert or delete the first component in a list.
4. Insert or delete the last component in a list.
5. Insert or delete the Nth component in a list.
6. Access the Nth component in a list.
7. Sort the components in a list.
8. Search the list for a specific component.

Reading sequentially into a list is a little faster with an array representation because procedure New doesn't have to be called for each component. Accessing the components in sequence takes approximately the same amount of time with both structures.

Inserting or deleting the first component in a list is much faster using a linked representation. Conversely, the last component in a list can be inserted or deleted much more efficiently in an array representation, because there is direct access to the last component and no shifting is required. In a linked representation, the entire list must be searched to find the last component.

On the average, the time spent inserting or deleting the Nth component is about equal for the two types of lists. A linked representation would be better for small values of N, and an array representation would be better for values of N near the end of the list.

Accessing the Nth element is *much* faster in an array representation. We can access it directly by using N as the index into the array. In a linked representation, we have to access the first N − 1 components to reach the Nth one.

In sorting an existing linked list, we remove the elements one by one and insert them in their proper places in a second linked list. When the sorting is finished, we can set the external pointer of the original list to point to the first component of the new list. If we dispose of each node as we remove a component, no additional memory space is used for the sorted list. A linked list is limited to this type of sorting algorithm. With an array representation much faster sorting algorithms can be used.

In general, searching a list for a specific component is much faster in an array representation because a binary search can be used. If the components in the list to be searched are not ordered, the two representations are about the same.

When you are trying to decide whether to use an array representation or a linked representation, determine which operations will be applied most frequently. Use your analysis to determine which structure would be better in the context of your particular problem.

There is one additional point to consider. How accurately can you predict the maximum number of components in the list? Does the number of components in the list fluctuate widely? If you know the maximum and it remains fairly constant, an array representation is probably called for. Otherwise, it would be better to choose a linked representation in order to use memory more efficiently.

OTHER DATA STRUCTURES

Linked lists can be used to implement many more complicated data structures. The study of data structures forms a major topic in computer science education. Entire books and courses are developed to cover the subject. Our purpose in this section is not to make you an expert in data structures, but to pique your interest for the future.

In this section we will mention briefly three of the most useful structures: stacks, queues, and binary trees. A thorough treatment of these data structures is left to a data structures text.

Stacks

A stack is a data structure that can be accessed from only one end. We can insert an element at the top (as the first) and we can remove the top (first) element.

This data structure models a property commonly encountered in real life. Accountants call it LIFO, which stands for "last in, first out." The plate holder in a cafeteria has this property. You can take only the top plate. When you do, the one below it rises to the top so that the next person can take one. Cars in a noncircular driveway exhibit this property. The last car in has to be the first car out.

> **Stack** A data structure in which insertions and deletions can be made from only one end.

The term *push* is used for the insertion operation, and the term *pop* is used for the deletion operation. Figure 16-5 shows what happens when you push an element on a given stack and then pop the stack.

Stacks are used frequently in systems software. The Pascal run-time support system uses a stack to keep track of procedure and function parameters, local variables, and dynamic variables. The Pascal compiler uses a stack to translate arithmetic expressions. Expressions can be evaluated using a stack.

Program Solitaire made extensive use of a stack. The procedures InsertTop and RemoveTop operated on the stack principle. That is, the last component inserted was the first one removed. The MoveTwo and MoveFour procedures also made use of this principle.

Figure 16-5
Stack

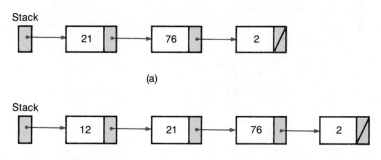

(a)

(b) Push(Stack, 12) pushes a new element on the stack with a value of 12

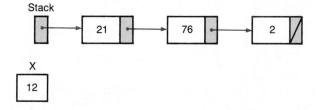

(c) Pop(Stack, X) pops an element from the stack and returns its value in X

Stacks are used whenever we wish to remember a sequence of objects or actions in the reverse order from that in which they occurred. The algorithm and code segment to read in a line of characters and print it out in reverse order using a stack is shown here.

REVERSE LINE

> Initialize Stack
> WHILE NOT EOLN
>   Read a character
>   Push character onto a stack
> WHILE More Characters on Stack
>   Pop character
>   Write character

INITIALIZE STACK

We are looking at implementing a stack as a linked list. Therefore, all we have to do is set Stack to NIL to initialize the stack. However, there are many ways in which a stack can be implemented. It is better style to create a procedure Initialize even if it is only one line of code. This way the algorithm that uses that stack will not have to be changed if the implementation is changed.

MORE CHARACTERS ON STACK

We will need to be able to determine when the stack is empty. This operation can also be done with one line: If Stack is NIL, the stack is empty. However, it is better style to make a one-line function Empty.

The program to implement this algorithm follows. InsertTop and RemoveTop have been renamed Push and Pop; their variable names have been changed to reflect the nature of the stack.

```
PROGRAM ReverseLine (Input, Output);

(* A line of characters is read in and printed in reverse order *)

TYPE
   StackPointer = ^StackType;
   ComponentType = Char;
   StackType = RECORD
                  Component : ComponentType;
                  Link : StackPointer
               END; (* Record *)

VAR
   Character:      (* Temporary character read in or written out *)
      Char;
   Stack:          (* Pointer to list of characters            *)
      StackPointer;


(*****************************************************************************)
```

```
PROCEDURE Pop (VAR Stack:              (* Pointer to top of stack   *)
                     StackPointer;
               VAR Component:          (* Object removed from stack *)
                     ComponentType);

(* The first component is removed from stack.
   Assumption:  Stack is not NIL. *)

VAR
  Pointer:            (* Temporary pointer *)
    StackPointer;

BEGIN (* Pop *)
  Pointer := Stack;
  Component := Stack^.Component;
  Stack := Stack^.Link;
  Dispose(Pointer)
END;   (* Pop *)


(********************************************************************)

PROCEDURE Push (VAR Stack:              (* Pointer to top of stack    *)
                      StackPointer;
                Component:              (* Object being put onto stack *)
                      ComponentType);

(* Component is inserted as the first component in Stack.
   Assumption:  Stack has been initialized to NIL. *)

VAR
  Pointer:            (* Temporary pointer *)
    StackPointer;

BEGIN (* Push *)
  New(Pointer);
  Pointer^.Component := Component;
  Pointer^.Link := Stack;
  Stack := Pointer
END;   (* Push *)


(********************************************************************)

PROCEDURE Initialize (VAR Stack:              (* Stack being initialized *)
                            StackPointer);

BEGIN (* Initialize *)
  Stack := NIL
END;   (* Initialize *)


(********************************************************************)
```

```
FUNCTION Empty (Stack:                (* Pointer to top of stack *)
                    StackPointer):
                    Boolean;

BEGIN (* Empty *)
  Empty := (Stack = NIL)
END;  (* Empty *)


(*******************************************************************)

BEGIN (* ReverseLine *)
  Initialize(Stack);
  (* Read and save characters *)
  WHILE NOT EOLN DO
    BEGIN
      Read(Character);
      Push(Stack, Character)
    END;
  (* Print characters in reverse order *)
  WHILE NOT Empty(Stack) DO
    BEGIN
      Pop(Stack, Character);
      Write(Character)
    END;
END.  (* ReverseLine *)
```

In Chapter 14 we wrote a set of procedures to operate on a date data type that we had defined. We have just done the same thing for the stack data structure. We have defined and coded the operations Push, Pop, Empty, and Initialize. The components on the stack can be of any data type. ComponentType can be an integer, a real, an array, a record—whatever needs to be accessed in the reverse order of their entry into a list. We will use these operations later without further comment.

We have adhered to the principle of abstraction by writing procedure Initialize and function Empty instead of inserting the code for these operations in the program that used the stack. The method of implementing a stack can then be changed without changing the main program.

Queues

A queue (pronounced like the letter "Q") is a data structure in which elements are entered at one end and are removed from the other end. Accountants call the property FIFO for "first in, first out." A waiting line in a bank or supermarket and a line of cars on a one-way street are types of queues. Indeed, queues are used to simulate situations like these in programs.

Queue A data structure in which insertions are made at one end and deletions are made at the other.

Whereas the terminology used to refer to the insert and remove operations on stacks is standard (Push, Pop), no such standardization exists with queues. The operation of inserting at the rear of the queue is called by many names in the literature: Insert, Enter, and Enqueue are three common ones. Correspondingly, the operation for removing from the front of the queue is variously called Delete, Remove, and Dequeue.

We have chosen to call our procedures Enqueue and Dequeue. Since we are accessing both ends, we will need two external pointers: Front and Rear. Figure 16-6 shows an empty queue (a), insertion into a queue (b), and deletion from a queue (c).

Figure 16-6
Queue Operations

(a) An empty queue

(b) Insertion into a queue

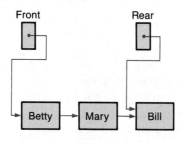

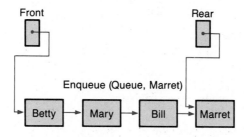

(c) Deletion from a queue

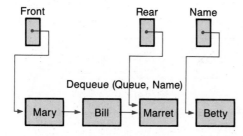

Since these operations are not ones we have coded before, we will develop them here using the following declarations:

```
CONST
   NameLength = 15;

TYPE
   NameIndex = 1..NameLength;
   NodePointer = ^NodeType;
   ComponentType = PACKED ARRAY [NameIndex] of Char;
   NodeType = RECORD
                   Component : ComponentType;
                   Link : NodePointer
               END; (* Record *)
   QueueType = RECORD
                   Front : NodePointer;
                   Rear : NodePointer
               END; (* Record *)

VAR
   Queue:
      QueueType;
```

To insert an Item at the Rear, we must take care of two cases: the one in which the queue is empty and the one in which it has at least one component. If the queue is empty, we must set both Rear and Front to point to the element that is entering the queue. If there is at least one component in the queue already, we have to insert the new component after Rear^ and redefine Rear to point to the new component.

ENQUEUE

```
Get a new node (NewNode)
Component field of NewNode ⟵ Component
IF Empty Queue
   THEN
      Front field of queue ⟵ NewNode
   ELSE
      Link field of last component ⟵ NewNode
Rear field of queue ⟵ NewNode
```

EMPTY QUEUE

```
Empty ⟵ Rear field of queue = NIL
```

Procedure Enqueue and function Empty are coded as follows:

```
            FUNCTION EmptyQ (Queue:              (* Head of queue to examine *)
                            QueueType):
                            Boolean;

            BEGIN (* EmptyQ *)
              EmptyQ := (Queue.Rear = NIL)
            END;   (* EmptyQ *)


            (*************************************************************************)


            PROCEDURE Enqueue (VAR Queue:              (* Head of queue          *)
                                   QueueType;
                               Component:       (* Item to insert into queue *)
                                   ComponentType);

            (* Component is inserted into the rear of Queue *)

            VAR
              NewNode:              (* New node *)
                QueuePointer;

            BEGIN (* Enqueue *)
              (* Initialize a new node *)
              New(NewNode);
              NewNode^.Component := Component;
              NewNode^.Link := NIL;
              WITH Queue DO
                BEGIN
                  IF EmptyQ(Queue)
                    THEN
                      Front := NewNode
                    ELSE
                      Rear^.Link := NewNode;
                  Rear := NewNode
                END
            END;   (* Enqueue *)
```

Removing an element from the front of the queue is actually just like popping a stack or removing the first node from any linked list. The name of the list is Front. The only additional thing that must be done is to check to see if the queue is empty after the node is removed. If it is, the rear pointer must be set to NIL.

```
            PROCEDURE Dequeue (VAR Queue:              (* Head of queue          *)
                                   QueueType;
                               VAR Component:       (* Item removed from queue *)
                                   ComponentType);

            (* The first node in the queue is removed. The Component field of the
               node is returned in Component. Assumption: There is at least one
               node *)
```

```
VAR
  Pointer:
    QueuePointer;

BEGIN (* Dequeue *)
  Pointer := Queue.Front;
  Component := Queue.Front^.Component;
  Queue.Front := Queue.Front^.Link;
  Dispose(Pointer);
  IF EmptyQ(Queue)
    THEN
      Queue.Rear := NIL
END;   (* Dequeue *)
```

To complete our set of queue operations we need an operation to initialize a queue. If an empty queue is one where Rear is NIL, then all we have to do is set Rear to NIL to initialize the queue.

```
PROCEDURE InitializeQ (VAR Queue:          (* Head of queue *)
                                  QueueType);

BEGIN (* InitializeQ *)
  Queue.Rear := NIL
END;   (* InitializeQ *)
```

Binary Trees

The concept of a linked list can be extended to structures containing nodes with more than one pointer field. One of these structures is known as a binary tree. The diagram in Figure 16-7 shows a binary tree.

The tree is referenced by an external pointer to the node called the *root* of the tree. The root has two pointers: one to its *left child* and one to its *right child.* Each child again has two pointers: one to its left child and one to its right child. The left child and the right child of a node are called *siblings.*

Figure 16-7
Binary Tree

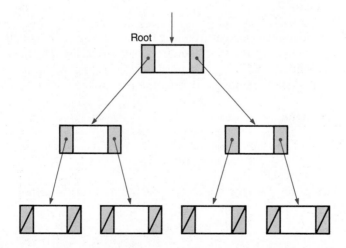

Root

For any node in a tree, the left child of the node is the root of the left subtree of the node. Likewise, the right child is the root of the right subtree. Nodes whose left and right children are both NIL are called *leaf nodes*.

Although Figure 16-7 shows a binary tree with only seven nodes, there is no theoretical limit on the number of nodes in a tree. It is easy to see why it is called binary—each node can have two branches. If you turn the figure upside down, you can see why it is called a tree.

There is a special kind of binary tree called a *binary search tree*. In binary search trees, the component in any node is greater than the component in its left child and any of its children (left subtree), and less than the component in its right child and any of its children (right subtree). This definition assumes no duplicates. The tree shown below is an example of a binary search tree.

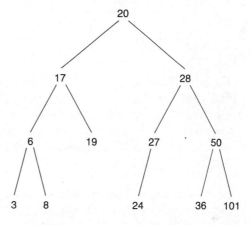

The reason a binary search tree is so useful is that if we are looking for a certain component, we can tell which half of the tree it is in by using just one comparison. We can then tell which half of that half the component is in with one more comparison. This process continues until either we find the component (number in this case) or we determine that it is not there. The process is analogous to a binary search of an array.

Let's search the tree for the number 50.

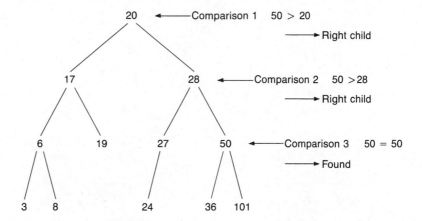

Now let's look for 18, a number that is not there.

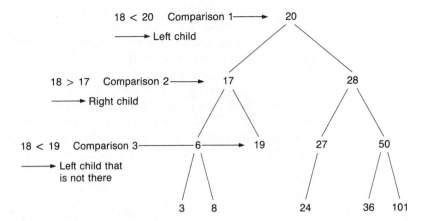

The left child of 19 is NIL, so we know that 18 isn't in the tree. Not only do we know that 18 is not there, but we are at the right place to insert 18 if we want to do so.

To summarize: We compared the item we were looking for with the component in a node in the tree and took the appropriate branch if the component and the item were not the same. When we started to take a branch that was NIL, we knew that the item was not there.

Let's develop and code the algorithm to search for an item in a binary search tree. If the item is there, we will increment an associated frequency; if the item is not there, we will insert a node containing the item and set the associated frequency to 1.

The components in the binary search tree will have two fields: Value and Count. The nodes in the binary search tree will have three fields: the component, Left (pointer to the left child), and Right (pointer to the right child). TreePtr is a pointer that we will use to keep our place in the tree. We will be finished either when we find the item or when we have inserted a node containing the item. The basic algorithm is as follows:

MAIN MODULE   Level 0

```
TreePtr ←—— Tree
Finished ←—— False
REPEAT
  IF TreePtr^.Component.Value = Item
    THEN
      Increment Count field
      Finished ←—— True
    ELSE IF TreePtr^.Component.Value > Item
    THEN
    (* Check left subtree *)
      IF TreePtr^.Left = NIL
        THEN
          Insert Item as LeftLeaf
        ELSE
          TreePtr ←—— TreePtr^.Left
    ELSE
    (* Check right subtree *)
    IF TreePtr^.Right = NIL
      THEN
        Insert Item as RightLeaf
      ELSE
        TreePtr ←—— TreePtr^.Right
UNTIL Finished
```

INSERT ITEM AS LEAF

RightLeaf and LeftLeaf are an enumerated type that tells which branch of TreePtr the new node is to be inserted into.

                                               Level 1

```
Initialize NewNode
CASE Leaf OF
  LeftLeaf : TreePtr^.Left ←—— NewNode
  RightLeaf : TreePtr^.Right ←—— NewNode
Finished ←—— True
```

INITIALIZE NEWNODE   Level 2

```
New(NewNode)
NewNode^.Right ←—— NIL
NewNode^.Left ←—— NIL
NewNode^.Component.Value ←—— Item
NewNode^.Component.Count ←—— 1
```

This algorithm is coded in three procedures, with the insertion procedure embedded within the main procedure SearchAndCount. The declarations are as follows:

```
TYPE
  TreePointer = ^TreeNode;
  ValueType = Integer;
  ComponentType = RECORD
                    Value : ValueType;
                    Count : Integer
                  END;  (* Record *)
  TreeNode = RECORD
               Component : ComponentType;
               Left,
               Right : TreePointer
             END;  (* Record *)

(********************************************************************)


PROCEDURE Initialize (VAR NewNode:         (* Node being initialized *)
                          TreePointer
                          Item:             (* Value for new node    *)
                          ValueType);

(* A Node is initialized with Item in the Value field and 1 in the Count
   field. Left and Right are set to NIL *)

BEGIN (* Initialize *)
  New(NewNode);
  NewNode^.Right := NIL;
  NewNode^.Left := NIL;
  NewNode^.Component.Value := Item;
  NewNode^.Component.Count := 1
END;  (* Initialize *)

(********************************************************************)


PROCEDURE SearchAndCount (VAR Tree:        (* Tree of scores      *)
                              TreePointer;
                              Item:         (* Input search value *)
                              ValueType);

(* SearchAndCount searches the binary search tree pointed to by Tree
   looking for the component Item.  IF Item is equal to a
   Component.Value in the tree, Component.Count is incremented.  ELSE
   Item is inserted into the tree with a Count field of 1.  Assumption:
   Tree contains at least one component. *)
```

```
TYPE
  LeafType = (RightLeaf, LeftLeaf);

VAR
  TreePtr:            (* Advancing pointer variable *)
    TreePointer;
  Finished:           (* Loop control flag          *)
    Boolean;


(************************************************************)


PROCEDURE Insert (VAR TreePtr:      (* Node new item is attached to *)
                      TreePointer;
                      Leaf:          (* Which pointer to attach to   *)
                      LeafType;
                      Item:          (* Value to put into new node   *)
                      ValueType;
                  VAR Finished:      (* Flag to stop insertion task  *)
                      Boolean);

(* Item is inserted into TreePtr as the Leaf child *)

VAR
  NewNode:            (* Pointer to node being linked to TreePtr's node *)
    TreePointer;

BEGIN (* Insert *)
  (* Initialize node *)
  Initialize(NewNode, Item);
  (* Insert node *)
  CASE Leaf OF
    LeftLeaf  : TreePtr^.Left  := NewNode;
    RightLeaf : TreePtr^.Right := NewNode
  END; (* Case *)
  Finished := True
END;   (* Insert *)


(************************************************************)
```

```
BEGIN (* SearchAndCount *)
  (* Initialize looping variables *)
  TreePtr := Tree;
  Finished := False;
  (* Search for Item in Tree *)
  REPEAT
    WITH TreePtr^ DO
      BEGIN
        IF Component.Value = Item
          THEN
            BEGIN                                      (* Match found *)
              Component.Count := Component.Count + 1;
              Finished := True
            END
          ELSE
            IF Component.Value > Item
              THEN                                     (* Search left subtree *)
                IF Left = NIL
                  THEN                                 (* Insertion place found *)
                    Insert(TreePtr, LeftLeaf, Item, Finished)
                  ELSE
                    TreePtr := Left
              ELSE                                     (* Search right subtree *)
                IF Right = NIL
                  THEN                                 (* Insertion place found *)
                    Insert(TreePtr, RightLeaf, Item, Finished)
                  ELSE
                    TreePtr := Right
      END
  UNTIL Finished;
END;    (* SearchAndCount *)
```

Problem Solving in Action

Problem: The admissions department has created a file containing the SAT scores of all the entering freshmen. They have asked us to print these scores in ascending numeric order along with a frequency count of the number of students making each score.

Discussion: In Chapter 12 we described a sorting algorithm based on inserting an element into an already sorted list (procedure Insert). We can use the same principle here. We can initialize a binary search tree with the first SAT score and then insert each new score into this binary search tree using the procedure we wrote in the last section.

The only problem is going to be how to print the values in the search tree in ascending order. We can look at the following binary search tree and read off the values in order: 2, 3, 4, 5, 7, 10, 13, 15, and 17. The question is, How did we do it?

PSIA

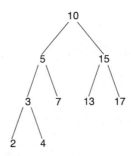

Let's make some observations about the values in this tree and see if we can generalize them into an algorithm. The smallest value is in the left-most node in the tree. The next smallest value is in the parent node of the smallest value. The third smallest value is in the sibling of the node containing the smallest value. These three nodes constitute the left subtree of the node containing 5. And 5 is the next node in order!

The algorithm so far then is to print the values in the left subtree of the node that contains 5 and then print the 5. What comes next? It's 7, the value in the right child of 5. (If the value 6 were in the tree, it would be the left child of 7 and would have to be printed first.) After 7 is printed, the next value is 10, the parent of 5, whose right child was just printed.

The process is to print the left subtree of a node, print the node, print the right subtree of a node, and then move back up to print the parent of the node. This process requires that we move back up the tree. Thus the nodes passed on the way down must be saved. When the values in a subtree have been printed, we back up and print the value in the parent node. This implies that the nodes must be retrieved in the reverse order from that in which they were saved. The stack data structure does exactly this.

The top-down design for this problem can now be completed.

Input: An unknown number of (unordered) SAT scores on file Freshmen (Freshmen is a file of integers)

Output: A numeric listing of all the SAT scores with associated frequencies

Data Structure: A binary search tree where each node contains an SAT score and its associated frequency of occurrence

MAIN MODULE   Level 0

```
Read first score
Initialize Tree
WHILE more scores
  Read a score
  Process score
Print scores and frequencies
```

"More scores" is an end-of-file loop.

PSIA

INITIALIZE TREE   Level 1

We can use procedure Initialize developed for procedure SearchAndCount.

PROCESS SCORE

To process the score we can use the procedure SearchAndCount that was developed previously with no modification.

PRINT

We also have already developed the broad outline for the print operation. We move down the tree as far to the left as possible, remembering the nodes we pass on the way by pushing them on a stack. We recognize that we have gone as far left as possible when the pointer we are advancing is NIL. We then back up and process the previous node. We back up by popping the stack on which we have been putting the nodes as we passed them. We have printed the last value when we have printed the right subchild of a node and can't back up any more—that is, when the stack is empty. We will use a function similar to EmptyQ to check whether the stack is empty.

```
Current ←—— Tree
REPEAT
  (* Move as far left as possible *)
  WHILE Current <> NIL
    Push Current on a stack
    Current ←—— Left child of Current
  (* Move back up the tree one node *)
  IF NOT Empty(Stack)
    Pop Current off stack
    Print SAT and Count fields of Component field of Current
    (* Move to right subtree *)
    Current ←—— Right child of Current
UNTIL Current = NIL AND stack is empty
```

Because this is a very complicated algorithm, an algorithm walkthrough is in order. We will use a portion of the tree we used before. We will refer to a node by its contents.

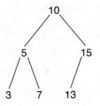

PSIA

Current ← Tree	Current now points to the node containing 10.
WHILE Current <> NIL	Current is not NIL. Loop is executed.
Push Current on a stack	Stack now contains 10.
Current ← Left child of Current	Current now points to node containing 5.
WHILE Current <> NIL	Current is not NIL. Loop is executed.
Push Current on a stack	Stack now contains 5 and 10.
Current ← Left child of Current	Current now points to node containing 3.
WHILE Current <> NIL	Current is not NIL. Loop is executed.
Push Current on a stack	Stack now contains 3, 5, and 10.
Current ← Left child of Current	Current now contains NIL.

The situation at this point is pictured below.

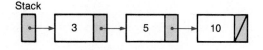

Stack

Current   What has been printed:

(nothing has been printed yet)

WHILE Current <> NIL	Current is NIL. Loop is skipped.
IF NOT Empty(Stack)	Stack is not empty.
Pop Current off stack	Current now contains pointer to 3.
Print . .	The number 3 is printed.
Current ← Right child of Current	Current is NIL.
UNTIL Current is NIL AND stack is empty	Current is NIL but stack is not empty.
WHILE Current <> NIL	Current is NIL. Loop is skipped.
IF NOT Empty(Stack)	Stack is not empty.
Pop Current off stack	Current contains pointer to 5.
Print . .	The number 5 is printed.
Current ← Right child of Current	Current is pointing to node containing 7.
UNTIL Current is NIL AND stack is empty	Current is not NIL and stack is not empty.

PSIA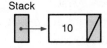

The situation at this point is pictured below.

Stack

```
10
```

Current   What has been printed:

3   5

```
7
```

WHILE Current <> NIL	Current is not NIL. Loop is executed.
Push Current on a stack	Stack now contains 7 and 10.
Current ← Left child of Current	Current is NIL.
WHILE Current <> NIL	Current is NIL. Loop is skipped.
IF NOT Empty(Stack)	Stack is not empty.
Pop Current off Stack	Current points to node containing 7.
Print . .	The number 7 is printed.
Current ← Right child of Current	Current is NIL.
UNTIL Current is NIL AND stack is empty	Current is NIL but stack is not empty.
WHILE Current <> NIL	Current is NIL. Loop is skipped.
IF NOT Empty(Stack)	Stack is not empty.
Pop Current off Stack	Current points to node containing 10.
Print . .	The number 10 is printed.
Current ← Right child of Current	Current now points to node containing 15.
UNTIL Current is NIL AND stack is empty	Current is not NIL but stack is empty.

PSIA

The situation at this point is pictured below.

Stack

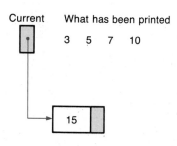

Current   What has been printed

3   5   7   10

15

WHILE Current <> NIL	Current is not NIL. Loop is executed.
Push Current on a stack	Stack contains 15.
Current ← Left child of Current	Current points to node containing 13.
WHILE Current <> NIL	Current is not NIL. Loop is executed.
Push Current on a stack	Stack contains 13 and 15.
Current ← Left child of Current	Current is NIL.
WHILE Current <> NIL	Current is NIL. Loop is skipped.
IF NOT Empty(Stack)	Stack is not empty.
Pop Current off stack	Current points to node containing 13.
Print . .	The number 13 is printed.
Current ← Right child of Current	Current is NIL.
UNTIL Current is NIL AND stack is empty	Current is NIL but stack is not empty.
WHILE Current <> NIL	Current is NIL. Loop is skipped.
IF NOT Empty(Stack)	Stack is not empty.
Pop Current off stack	Current points to node containing 15.
Print . .	The number 15 is printed.
Current ← Right child of Current	Current is NIL.
UNTIL Current is NIL AND stack is empty	Current is NIL and stack is empty. Loop exits.

PSIA

The situation at the end of the print module is shown below.

Stack

Current   What has been printed:

3   5   7   10   13   15

Module Structure Chart:

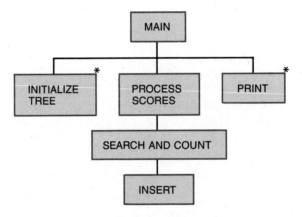

*PRINT uses stack operations.
INITIALIZE is also used by INSERT

```
PROGRAM SortSatScores (Freshmen, Output);

(* SAT scores are read from file Freshmen and sorted using a binary
   search tree.  Frequencies of each value are kept, and the sorted
   SAT scores with frequencies are printed. *)

TYPE
   TreePointer = ^TreeNode;
   ValueType = 0..1600;
   ComponentType = RECORD
                      Value : ValueType;
                      Count : Integer
                   END; (* Record *)
```

PSIA ▬▬▬▬

```
TreeNode = RECORD
              Component : ComponentType;
              Left,
              Right : TreePointer
           END;  (* Record *)
StackPointer = ^StackElement;
StackElement = RECORD
                  Element : TreePointer;
                  Link : StackPointer
               END;  (* Record *)
DataFile = FILE OF ValueType;

VAR
  Tree:            (* Pointer to tree of SAT scores *)
     TreePointer;
  SAT:             (* Temporary input SAT score    *)
     ValueType;
  Freshmen:        (* Input file of SAT scores      *)
     DataFile;

(****************************************************************)

PROCEDURE Initialize (VAR NewNode:            (* Node being initialized *)
                          TreePointer;
                      SAT:                     (* Score for new node    *)
                          ValueType);

(* Tree node is initialized to first SAT score *)

BEGIN  (* Initialize *)
  New(NewNode);
  NewNode^.Component.Value := SAT;
  NewNode^.Component.Count := 1;
  NewNode^.Right := NIL;
  NewNode^.Left := NIL;
END;   (* Initialize *)

(****************************************************************)

PROCEDURE SearchAndCount (VAR Tree:            (* Tree of scores     *)
                              TreePointer;
                          Item:                (* Input search value *)
                              ValueType);
```

PSIA ▬▬▬

```
(* SearchAndCount searches the binary search tree pointed to by Tree
   looking for the component Item.  IF Item is equal to a
   Component.Value in the tree, Component.Count is incremented.  ELSE
   Item is inserted into the tree with a Count field of 1.  Assumption:
   Tree contains at least one component. *)


TYPE
  LeafType = (RightLeaf, LeftLeaf);


VAR
  TreePtr:            (* Advancing pointer variable *)
    TreePointer;
  Finished:           (* Loop control flag          *)
    Boolean;


(********************************************************************)


PROCEDURE Insert (VAR TreePtr:        (* Node new item is attached to *)
                      TreePointer;
                      Leaf:           (* Which pointer to attach to    *)
                      LeafType;
                      Item:           (* Value to put into new node    *)
                      ValueType;
                  VAR Finished:       (* Flag to stop insertion task   *)
                      Boolean);

(* Item is inserted into TreePtr as the Leaf child *)

VAR
  NewNode:            (* Pointer to node being linked to TreePtr's node *)
    TreePointer;

BEGIN (* Insert *)
  (* Initialize node *)
  Initialize(NewNode, Item);
  (* Insert node *)
  CASE Leaf OF
    LeftLeaf  : TreePtr^.Left  := NewNode;
    RightLeaf : TreePtr^.Right := NewNode
  END; (* Case *)
  Finished := True
END;  (* Insert *)


(********************************************************************)
```

PSIA ▰▰▰▰▰▰▰

```
BEGIN (* SearchAndCount *)
  (* Initialize looping variables *)
  TreePtr : = Tree;
  Finished : = False;
  (* Search for Item in Tree *)
  REPEAT
    WITH TreePtr^ DO
      BEGIN
        IF Component.Value = Item
          THEN
            BEGIN                                            (* Match found *)
              Component.Count : = Component.Count + 1;
              Finished : = True
            END
          ELSE
            IF Component.Value > Item
              THEN                              (* Search left subtree *)
                IF Left = NIL
                  THEN                          (* Insertion place found *)
                    Insert(TreePtr, LeftLeaf, Item, Finished)
                  ELSE
                    TreePtr : = Left
              ELSE                              (* Search right subtree *)
                IF Right = NIL
                  THEN                          (* Insertion place found *)
                    Insert(TreePtr, RightLeaf, Item, Finished)
                  ELSE
                    TreePtr : = Right
      END;
    UNTIL Finished;
END;   (* SearchAndCount *)
```

(**)

```
FUNCTION Empty (Stack:               (* Pointer to top of stack *)
                StackPointer):
                Boolean;

(* Empty is True if there are no nodes on the stack *)

BEGIN (* Empty *)
  Empty : = (Stack = NIL)
END;   (* Empty *)
```

(**)

PSIA

```
PROCEDURE Push (VAR Stack:              (* Pointer to top of stack        *)
                     StackPointer;
                Component:              (* Tree node pointer being pushed *)
                     TreePointer);

(* Node containing Component is put on stack *)

VAR
  NewNode:              (* New node to put on top of stack *)
    StackPointer;

BEGIN (* Push *)
  New(NewNode);
  NewNode^.Element : = Component;
  NewNode^.Link : = Stack;
  Stack : = NewNode
END;   (* Push *)


(*********************************************************************)

PROCEDURE Pop (VAR Stack:              (* Pointer to top of stack        *)
                    StackPointer;
               VAR Component:          (* Tree node pointer being popped *)
                    TreePointer);

(* First node is removed from stack *)

VAR
  TempPointer:          (* Pointer to node being removed from stack *)
    StackPointer;

BEGIN (* Pop *)
  TempPointer : = Stack;
  Component : = Stack^.Element;
  Stack : = Stack^.Link;
  Dispose(TempPointer)
END;   (* Pop *)


(*********************************************************************)
```

PSIA

```
PROCEDURES Initializes (VAR Stack:    (* Stack being initialized *)

                               StackPointer);
BEGIN (* Initialize *)
  Stack := NIL
END;  (* Initialize *)

(*******************************************************************
PROCEDURE Print (Tree:           (* Pointer to tree of SAT scores *)
                 TreePointer);

(* SAT and frequency fields of nodes in Tree
   are printed in numeric order by SAT field *)

VAR
  Stack:             (* Pointer to stack being built from the tree *)
    StackPointer;
  Current:           (* Temporary pointer for traversing the tree  *)
    TreePointer;

BEGIN (* Print *)
  (* Initialize Stack *)
  Initializes(Stack)
  (* Initialize moving pointer *)
  Current := Tree;
  Writeln(' SAT ', '  Frequency');
  REPEAT
    (* Move as far left as possible *)
    WHILE Current <> NIL DO
      BEGIN
        Push(Stack, Current);
        Current := Current^.Left
      END;
    (* If there are any more nodes on the stack, pop the stack and pri
       the contents of the node and move to right subtree *)
    IF NOT Empty(Stack)
      THEN
        BEGIN
          Pop(Stack, Current);
          Writeln(Current^.Component.Value:5,
                  Current^.Component.Count:7);
          Current := Current^.Right
        END
  UNTIL (Current = NIL) AND (Empty(Stack))
END;  (* Print *)


(*******************************************************************
```

PSIA ▰▰▰▰▰

```
BEGIN (* SortSatScores *)
  Reset(Freshmen);
  Read(Freshmen, SAT);
  Initialize(Tree, SAT);
  (* Create binary search tree *)
  WHILE NOT EOF(Freshmen) DO
    BEGIN
      Read(Freshmen, SAT);
      SearchAndCount(Tree, SAT)
    END;
  (* Print the SAT scores and frequencies *)
  Print(Tree)
END.  (* SortSatScores *)
```

Testing: A test data file for this program must include some values once and some other values more than once. A rigorous testing would require multiple files, one to satisfy each of the following conditions:

1. The smallest SAT score is first (single value).
2. The smallest SAT score is first, with copies in other positions including last.
3. The largest SAT score is first (single value).
4. The largest SAT score is first, with copies in other positions including last.
5. The smallest SAT score is last (single value).
6. The largest SAT score is last (single value).

Sample input data including single values and multiple values is shown below. The output from Program SortSatScores follows the sample data.

Sample Input		Sample Output	
1200		SAT	Frequency
1300		300	1
600		400	1
400		600	3
1300		900	1
600		1200	2
600		1201	1
1200		1202	1
300		1300	2
900		1304	1
1201			
1202			
1304			

Comparison of Sorting Algorithms The sorting algorithm used in Program SortSatScores is a binary tree sort. Items are stored in a binary search tree and then written out in order. This algorithm is certainly more complex than both the exchange sort and the insertion sort which were discussed in Chapter 12. Is it a better sorting algorithm? This question can't be answered without first defining what is meant by "better."

If we define "better" to mean "takes less time to program," the answer is certainly no. Program SortSatScores is considerably longer than the others and has a much more complex data structure that is more difficult to debug. If we define "better" to mean "takes less time to run," the answer would depend on how many SAT scores there were to sort.

If the number of SAT scores is quite small, a simple sort like those in Chapter 12 is better. However, as the number of items to sort gets larger, the binary search tree sort gets relatively more and more efficient. Although the insertion sort is somewhat faster than the exchange sort, they are both classified as N-squared sorts. This means that the number of comparisons between two values in the center of the algorithm will be approximately $N \times N$.

The sort that uses a binary search tree is classified as an N log N sort. This means that the number of comparisons between two values in the center of the algorithm will be approximately N log N. The following table compares N-squared and N log N for increasing values of N. The values in the table are the number of comparisons in the center of the algorithm for various sizes of N, the number of elements to be sorted.

N	N-squared	N log N
4	16	8
8	64	24
32	1024	160
64	4096	384
128	16384	896
256	65536	2048
512	262144	4608

This table would seem to indicate that an N log N sort should be used for any value of N. This is not true, however, because N log N sorts are more complex; the parts of the algorithm that surround the comparison take longer to execute. A good rule of thumb is to use a simple, N-squared sort for sorting less than 40 components and an N log N sort for sorting more than 40 components.

Space also may be a consideration in determining what sort to use. The binary search tree sort uses more memory because there are two pointer variables in each node. If you are sorting a very large file on a small machine, you may have to use a slower sort that uses less space.

TESTING AND DEBUGGING

The assumptions listed for a procedure or function are like a contract between the procedure or function and the routine that calls it. These assumptions are often called *preconditions* because the calling routine guarantees that these assumptions will be met.

All the procedures that inserted a value into a linked list assumed that the list had been initialized. The routines that call these procedures must make sure that the lists have been initialized. There is no practical way to check that the list has been initialized from within a procedure. There is no test to see if a pointer is undefined. It is therefore reasonable for the procedure to make this assumption.

All the procedures that deleted a value from a linked list assumed that an item was there to be deleted (RemoveTop, Pop, and Dequeue) or that the specific item to be deleted was in the list (Delete). The calling routines were responsible for guaranteeing this assumption or precondition.

When deleting from a linked list, the procedure or function can easily detect that the component is not there or that there is not a component to remove. Should these procedures have been written to guard against trying to delete a component that is not there? It depends on the interface between the calling routine and the procedure. Either the calling routine takes responsibility for ensuring that the value is there to be deleted (guarantees the assumption) or the procedure should test for the case in which there is no value to delete or the specific value is not there. If the procedure does the testing, a flag should be returned to the calling routine showing whether or not the value was deleted.

It does not matter at which level the checking is done for this error condition. However, the higher-level module should determine which way the situation will be handled. Thus, when doing a top-down design, either don't call the delete module if the list is empty or have the delete module check for the error condition and return a flag indicating whether or not the delete was executed properly.

Following is a version of the Pop procedure in which error checking is included within the procedure itself. Notice that there is an additional parameter, UnderFlow.

```
PROCEDURE Pop (VAR Stack:              (* Pointer to top of stack    *)
                   StackPointer;
               VAR Component:           (* Object removed from stack  *)
                   ComponentType;
               VAR UnderFlow:           (* Error flag                 *)
                   Boolean);

(* If the stack is empty, UnderFlow will be True and Item will be
   undefined.  Otherwise, UnderFlow will be False, the first node will
   be deleted, and Item will contain the component field of the deleted
   first node.  Deleted node is disposed *)

VAR
   TempPointer:       (* Temporary pointer *)
     StackPointer;
```

```
BEGIN (* Pop *)
  IF Empty(Stack)
    THEN
      UnderFlow := True
    ELSE
      BEGIN
        TempPointer := Stack;
        Item := Stack^.Component;
        Stack := Stack^.Link;
        Dispose(TempPointer);
        UnderFlow := False
      END
END;  (* Pop *)
```

Whenever it is possible for an error condition to occur in a procedure, you must decide where to check for the condition. If your calling module is responsible for seeing that the situation does not occur, the assumption that the condition will not occur should be stated in the documentation of the procedure.

If the procedure is to do the checking for the error condition, your documentation of the procedure must state how the error will be handled if it occurs. Many times the procedure will test for the error condition and simply set a flag and return if the error occurs, leaving the determination of what to do about the error to the upper-level routine.

The key point about error detection is that the interface between a calling routine and a procedure must make it absolutely clear which level is responsible for the error checking.

Testing and Debugging Hints

1. Be sure that the pointer field in the last node in a linked list has been set to NIL.
2. When visiting the components in a linked list, be sure that you test for the end of the list in such a way that you don't try to access the component of a NIL pointer. Trying to access the variable a pointer references when the pointer is NIL will cause a run-time error.
3. Be sure to initialize the external pointer to each dynamic data structure.
4. Dispose(Pointer) leaves Pointer undefined; trying to access Pointer^ will cause a run-time error.
5. Dispose of all dynamic variables when they are no longer needed. If you don't do so in a large program, you may run out of memory space.
6. Pass as a parameter the pointer, not the object being pointed to.
7. Keep track of pointers carefully. Changing pointer values prematurely may cause problems when you try to get back to the referenced variable.
8. Be sure to test for possible error conditions when working with linked lists. There are two ways to handle error checking. The calling routine can check for the error condition and not call the procedure if the error occurs, or the procedure can test for the error condition. The documentation of both the calling routine and the procedure should state clearly which way error checking is being done.

SUMMARY

Dynamic data structures grow and contract during run time. They are made up of nodes that contain two kinds of fields: the component and one or more pointers to records of the same type. The pointer to the first record is saved in a named variable called the external pointer to the structure.

A linked list is a dynamic data structure in which the components are logically ordered by their pointer fields rather than physically ordered as they are in an array. The end of the list is indicated by the special pointer constant NIL.

A stack is a data structure in which insertions and deletions are made at the same end. Components are both inserted and removed from the beginning of the list. A stack is a "last in, first out" (LIFO) structure.

A queue is a data structure in which insertions and deletions are made at different ends. Components are inserted at the rear of the list and removed from the front of the list. A queue is a "first in, first out" (FIFO) structure.

A binary tree is a dynamic data structure in which each node has two pointers, one to the left child (left subtree) and one to the right child (right subtree). In a binary search tree all the values in the left subtree of a node are less than the value in the node and all the values in the right subtree of a node are greater than the value in the node.

Developing data structures and the algorithms to manipulate them is great fun. We hope that this introduction to the subject of data structures will stand you in good stead.

QUICK CHECK

1. What distinguishes a linked list from an array? (pp. 646–652)
2. When printing the contents of a linked list, what operation advances the current node pointer to the next node? (pp. 654–656)
3. What is the difference between the operations of inserting a new item at the top of a linked list, and inserting the new item in place? (pp. 656–662)
4. In deleting an item from a linked list, why do we need to keep track of the previous node (the node before the one to be deleted)? (pp. 663–666)
5. What is the difference between a stack and a linked list? (pp. 687–690)
6. What is the difference between a queue and a stack? (pp. 690–694)
7. What distinguishes a binary tree from the other linked data structures (linked list, stack, queue) covered in this chapter? (pp. 694–700)

Answers

1. Arrays are static data structures whose components are ordered by their relative locations in memory. Linked lists are dynamic data structures in which the ordering of the components is defined by an explicit link field in each node. 2. The current node pointer is set equal to the link field of the current node. 3. When inserting an item in place, the list must first be searched to find the proper place. We don't have to search the list when inserting at the top. 4. Because we must set the link field of the previous node equal to the link field of the current node as part of the deletion operation. 5. Items may be inserted or deleted anywhere in a linked list, but with a stack we may only insert or delete at the top of the structure. 6. Items are inserted and deleted at only one end of a stack, but with a queue we add items to one end and delete them from the other end. 7. A binary tree has multiple link fields in each node, while the other linked structures have only one link field per node.

EXAM PREPARATION EXERCISES _____

1. In a linked list elements are only logically next to each other, whereas in an array they are also physically next to each other. (True or False?)

2. Which of the following are always dynamic data structures?
   (a) linked list   (c) stack
   (b) binary tree   (d) array

3. The expression below can appear before the type name NodeType is defined. (True or False?)

```
          TYPE
             PtrType  =  ^NodeType;
```

4. Use the Pascal code below to identify the values of the variable references and Boolean comparisons that follow. The value may be undefined or the reference may be invalid.

```
     TYPE
        PtrNode = ^NodeType;
        NodeType = RECORD
                      Number : Integer;
                      Character : Char;
                      Link : PtrNode
                   END;    (* Record *)
     VAR
        Current,
        First,
        Last:
          PtrType;

     BEGIN
        First : = NIL;
        Last : = NIL;
        Current : = NIL;
        New(Current) ;
        Current^.Number : = 13;
        Current^.Character : = 'z';
        New(Current^.Link) ;
        Last : = Current^.Link;
        Last^.Number : = 9;
        New(First) ;
        Last^.Link : = First;
        First^.Number : = 9;
        First^.Character : = 'h';
        First^.Link : = Current;
        .

        .

        .
```

	Expression	*Value*

(a) `First^.Link^.Num` _____

(b) `First^.Link^.Link^.Character` _____

(c) `First^.Link^ = Last^` _____

(d) `Current.Link^.Num` _____

(e) `Current^.Link = Last^` _____

(f) `First^ = Last^.Link^` _____

(g) `Current < Last` _____

5. A stack is one of the abstract data structures that are often implemented with linked lists. (True or False?)

6. (a) Which element of a stack is the first to be removed? (b) Which element of a queue is the first to be removed?

7. Choose a data structure (array, linked list, or binary search tree) for each of the following situations. Assume unlimited memory but limited time.
   (a) A fixed list of 1000 elements to keep counts for particular values.
   (b) A fixed list of 1000 to 4000 (usually 1500) elements that will have elements printed according to position requests input to the program.
   (c) A list of an unknown number of elements that will be read, then printed in reverse order.

8. Choose a data structure (array, linked list, or binary search tree) for each of the following situations. Assume very limited memory but unlimited time.
   (a) A fixed list of 1000 elements to keep counts for particular values.
   (b) A fixed list of 1000 to 4000 (usually 1500) elements that will have elements printed according to position requests input to the program.
   (c) A list of an unknown number of elements that will be read, then printed in reverse order.

9. What is the difference between inserting an item into an empty queue and into one that has elements (assume a linked-list implementation)?

10. Which of the following are binary search trees?

    (a)

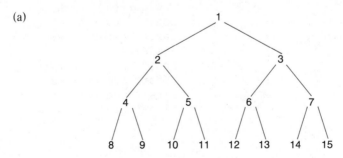

(b)

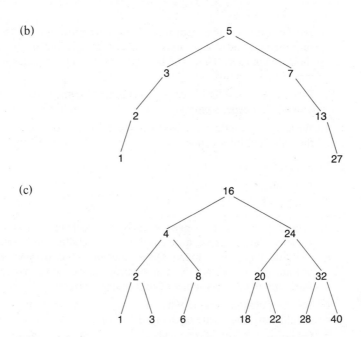

(c)

11. Referring to the binary tree in 10(c), write the values of the given items.

Item	Value
(a) the root	_____
(b) the largest value in the left subtree of 24	_____
(c) the parent of 4	_____
(d) the sibling of 8	_____
(e) the leaf nodes of the right subtree of 4	_____
(f) the right child of 20	_____

12. Will an N log N sort most likely become more time-consuming than an N-squared sort as the number of elements gets larger or smaller?

PREPROGRAMMING EXERCISES _____

1. To avoid special handling of empty linked lists for insertion and deletion routines, some programmers prefer to have a dummy node permanently in the list (the list is considered empty if it contains only the dummy node). Rewrite the queue subprograms Empty, Enqueue, Dequeue, and Initialize to use a dummy node whose component value is equal to a constant named Dummy. Do not keep any unnecessary code. *Hint:* The first element of the queue will follow the dummy node.

2. Use an array to implement a stack data structure limited to 100 elements. Write the subprograms and declarations necessary for this implementation (the component type should be Integer). *Hint:* The last item entered into the stack will be known by saving an array index position.

3. Rewrite procedure Dequeue in this chapter to immediately return a Boolean value that is True if the queue is empty.

4. Write the declarations needed to create a dynamic tree data structure whose nodes have the following information:

   Name (20 characters)

   Age (integer)

   Aptitude (real)

5. Write a procedure to receive a value N, pop N elements from a stack, and place them on a queue. Have the procedure check for any possible error conditions and return a Boolean True if an error is found. Determine what other parameters will need to be received or returned and declare them in the procedure heading. You may assume that the basic stack and queue operations of this chapter have already been coded.

6. Write a function CountQ which returns the number of nodes in a queue. The function should leave the queue unchanged.

7. Write a function CountList which returns the number of nodes in a linked list pointed to by its parameter List.

8. Write a procedure Copy which makes a copy of a linked list. The list to be copied is List and the copy is Copy.

PROGRAMMING PROBLEMS _____

1. In Program Solitaire in this chapter all insertions into a linked list were made using procedure InsertTop and all the deletions from a linked list were made using procedure RemoveTop. In some cases this was very inefficient. For example, procedure ReCreate takes the cards from OnTable and moves them one by one to Deck. Then the cards on the DiscardPile are moved one by one to Deck.

   Rewrite Program Solitaire to make it more efficient. Instead of using RemoveTop and InsertTop to re-create the deck, use the following algorithm.

   ```
   Deck ← OnTable
   Pointer ← Deck
   WHILE Pointer^.Link <> NIL
       Pointer ← Pointer^.Link
   Pointer^.Link ← DiscardPile
   ```

   Also use the same strategy to make procedure Merge more efficient.

2. Write a program to process file AddressBook as created in Programming Problem 4 in Chapter 15. Your program should read in the entries and store them in a linked list ordered by birthdate.

   The output should consist of a listing by month of the names and telephone numbers of the people who have birthdays each month.

3. Rewrite the program described in problem 2 using a binary search tree rather than a linked list.

4. A palindrome is a string of characters that reads the same forward and backward. Write a program that reads in a string of characters and determines if the string is a palindrome. Use EOLN to end the string. Echo print the string, followed by 'Is a palindrome' if the string is a palindrome and 'Is not a palindrome' if the string is not a palindrome.

   For example, given the following input string,

   Able was I ere I saw Elba

   the program would print 'Is a palindrome.' Consider upper- and lowercase letters to be the same. (*Hint:* Use a stack and a queue.)

- To be able to identify the base case(s) and the general case in a recursive definition.
- To be able to write a recursive algorithm for a problem involving only simple variables.
- To be able to write a recursive algorithm for a problem involving structured variables.
- To be able to write a recursive algorithm for a problem involving linked lists.
- To be able to write a recursive algorithm for a problem involving binary trees.

17

Recursion

In Chapter 8 we said that putting the name of a function in an expression within the function itself would cause the function to be called recursively. We cautioned that inadvertent recursive calls cause errors. In this chapter we will show you how to use recursion correctly. Recursion is a very powerful technique which can be used in place of iteration.

Recursion provides a different way of looking at repetition. Recursive solutions are generally less efficient than iterative solutions to the same problem. However, some problems that lend themselves to simple, elegant recursive solutions are exceedingly cumbersome to solve iteratively.

Many of the older programming languages do not allow recursion. FORTRAN, BASIC, and COBOL do not. Some languages are especially oriented to recursive algorithms—LISP is one of these. Pascal lets us take our choice: we can implement both iterative and recursive algorithms in Pascal.

Our examples will be broken into two groups: problems that use only simple variables and problems that use structured variables. If you are studying recursion before reading Chapter 11 on structured data types, then cover only the first set of examples and leave the rest until you have completed the chapters on structured data types.

WHAT IS RECURSION?

Have you ever seen a set of gaily painted Russian dolls which fit inside one another? Inside the first doll is a smaller doll, inside of which is an even smaller doll, inside of which is yet a smaller doll . . . . A recursive algorithm is like such a set of Russian dolls. It keeps reproducing itself with smaller and smaller examples of itself until a solution is found (there are no more dolls).

In our example in Chapter 8 we said that the ability of a function or a procedure to invoke itself was known as recursion. A better way of saying this is to state that procedures and functions that invoke themselves are recursive procedures or functions.

Let's review the one recursion problem that was included in Chapter 8. The problem was to calculate the result of taking a positive integer to a positive power. We noted that the formula for exponentiation could be successively rewritten as follows.

$$X^n = \underbrace{X * X * X * X * \cdots * X}_{n \text{ times}}$$

$$X^n = X * \underbrace{(X * X * \cdots * X)}_{(n-1) \text{ times}}$$

$$X^n = X * X * \underbrace{(X * X * \cdots * X)}_{(n-2) \text{ times}}$$

Another way of writing this formula would be

$$X^n = X * X^{n-1}$$

This definition is a classic *recursive definition:* the definition is given in terms of a smaller version of itself.

Recursive Definition A definition in which something is defined in terms of smaller versions of itself.

X^N is defined in terms of multiplying X times X^{N-1}. How is X^{N-1} defined? Why as $X * X^{N-2}$, of course! And X^{N-2} is $X * X^{N-3}$, X^{N-3} is $X * X^{N-4}$, and so on. In this example, "in terms of smaller versions of itself" means that the exponent is decremented each time.

When does the process stop? When we have reached a case where we know the answer without resorting to a recursive definition. In this example, it is the case where N equals 1: X^1 is X. The case (or cases) for which an answer is explicitly known is called the *base case;* the case for which the solution is expressed in terms of a smaller version of itself is called the recursive or general case.

Base Case The case for which the solution can be stated nonrecursively.

General Case (Recursive Case) The case for which the solution is expressed in terms of a smaller version of itself.

A *recursive algorithm* is an algorithm that expresses the solution in terms of a call to itself. The call to itself is known as a recursive call. A recursive algorithm must terminate; that is, it must have a base case.

Recursive Algorithm A solution that is expressed in terms of (a) smaller instances of itself and (b) a base case.

Figure 17-1 shows function Power with the base case and the recursive call marked. The function is embedded in a program that reads in a number and an exponent and prints the results.

Let's trace the execution of this recursive function, with Number equal to 2 and Exponent equal to 3. We will use a new format to trace recursive routines. We will number the calls and then discuss what is happening in paragraph form. For illustrative purposes, we will assume that each call creates a new version of the function Power.

Figure 17-1
Function Power

```
PROGRAM Exponentiation (Input, Output);

VAR
  Number,          (* Number that is being raised to power    *)
  Exponent,        (* Power the number is being raised to      *)
  Answer:          (* Result of raising the number to the power *)
    Integer;

(************************************************************************)

FUNCTION Power (X,            (* Number that is being raised to power *)
                N:            (* Power the number is being raised to   *)
                   Integer);
                   Integer;

(* This function computes X to the N power by multiplying X times the
   result of computing X to the N - 1 power *)

BEGIN (* Power *)
  IF N = 1
    THEN ◄──────────────────────────────────────── (* Base case *)
      Power := X
    ELSE
      Power := X * Power(X, N - 1)◄──────────── (* Recursive call *)
END;  (* Power *)

(************************************************************************)

BEGIN (* Exponentiation *)
  Readln(Number, Exponent);
  Answer := Power(Number, Exponent);◄──────────── (* Nonrecursive call *)
  Writeln(Answer)
END.  (* Exponentiation *)
```

Call 1: Power is called with Number equal to 2 and Exponent equal to 3. These are the formal parameters X and N, respectively. Therefore X is equal to 2 and N is equal to 3. N is not equal to 1, so Power is called with X and N − 1 as parameters. Execution of the call to the function halts until an answer is sent back from this recursive call.

Call 2: X is equal to 2 and N is equal to 2. Since N is not equal to 1, the function Power is called again, this time with X and N − 1 as parameters. Execution of this call to the function halts until an answer is sent back from this recursive call.

Call 3: X is equal to 2 and N is equal to 1. Since N is equal to 1, the value of X is stored in Power. This call to the function has finished executing, and Power is passed back to the place in the statement from which the call was made.

Call 2: This call to the function can now complete the statement that contained the recursive call because Power now has a value. This value (which is 2) is multiplied by X, and the result is stored in Power. This call to the function has finished executing, and Power is passed back to the place in the statement from which the call was made.

Call 1: This call to the function can now complete the statement that contained the recursive call because Power now has a value. This value (which is 4) is multiplied by X, and the result is stored in Power. This call to the function has finished executing, and Power is passed back to the place in the statement from which the call was made. Since the first call (the nonrecursive call) has now been completed, this is the final value of the function Power.

This trace is summarized in Figure 17-2. Each box represents a call to the function Power. The values for the parameters for that call are shown in each box.

What happens if there is no base case? We have infinite recursion, the equivalent of an infinite loop. For example, if the statement

$$IF \ N \ = \ 1$$

Figure 17-2
Execution of
Power(2, 3)

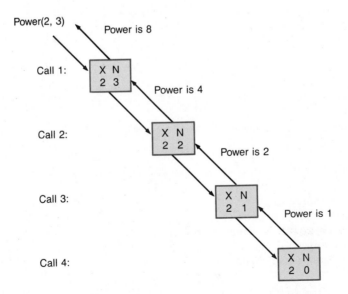

were omitted, Power would be called over and over again. Eventually, the program would halt with an error message such as "RUN-TIME STACK OVERFLOW."

RECURSIVE ALGORITHMS WITH SIMPLE VARIABLES

Let's look at another example: calculating a factorial. The factorial of a number N (written N!) is N multiplied by $N - 1, N - 2, N - 3, \ldots$. Another way of expressing factorial is

$$N! = N * (N - 1)!$$

Now this expression looks like a recursive definition. $(N - 1)!$ is a smaller instance of N!. It takes one less multiplication to calculate $(N - 1)!$ than it does to calculate N!. If we can find a base case, we can write a recursive algorithm. Fortunately, we don't have to look too far: 0! is defined to be 1. We can use that as our base case. When N is equal to 0, we can set the result to 1.

FACTORIAL

```
IF N is 0
   THEN
      Factorial ⟵ 1
   ELSE
      Factorial ⟵ N * Factorial (N − 1)
```

This algorithm can be coded directly.

```
FUNCTION Factorial  (N:                    (* Factorial number being computed *)
                        Integer):
                        Integer;

BEGIN (* Factorial *)
   IF N = 0
      THEN                                               (* Base case *)
         Factorial := 1
      ELSE
         Factorial := N * Factorial(N − 1)            (* General case *)
   END;  (* Factorial *)
```

Let's trace this function with an original N of 4.

Call 1: N is 4. Since N is not 0, the ELSE branch is taken. The assignment statement cannot be completed until the recursive call to function Factorial with $N - 1$ as the actual parameter has been completed.

Call 2: N is 3. Since N is not 0, the ELSE branch is taken. The assignment statement cannot be completed until the recursive call to function Factorial with $N - 1$ as the actual parameter has been completed.

Call 3: N is 2. Since N is not 0, the ELSE branch is taken. The assignment statement cannot be completed until the recursive call to function Factorial with N − 1 as the actual parameter has been completed.

Call 4: N is 1. Since N is not 0, the ELSE branch is taken. The assignment statement cannot be completed until the recursive call to function Factorial with N − 1 as the actual parameter has been completed.

Call 5: N is 0. Since N is equal to 0, Factorial is set to 1. This call to the function has finished executing. Factorial (which is 0) is sent back as the result.

Call 4: The assignment statement in this copy can now be completed. Factorial is Factorial times N. This call to the function has now finished executing. Factorial (which is 1) is returned as the result.

Call 3: The assignment statement in this copy can now be completed. Factorial is Factorial times N. This call to the function has now finished executing. Factorial (which is 2) is returned as the result.

Call 2: The assignment statement in this copy can now be completed. Factorial is Factorial times N. This call to the function has now finished executing. Factorial (which is 6) is returned as the result.

Call 1: The assignment statement in this copy can now be completed. Factorial is Factorial times N. This call to the function has now finished executing. Factorial (which is 24) is returned as the result. Since this is the last of the calls to Factorial, the recursive process is over. The value 24 is returned as the final value of the call to function Factorial with an actual parameter of 4.

Figure 17-3 summarizes the execution of function Factorial with an actual parameter of 4.

Figure 17-3
Execution of
Factorial(4)

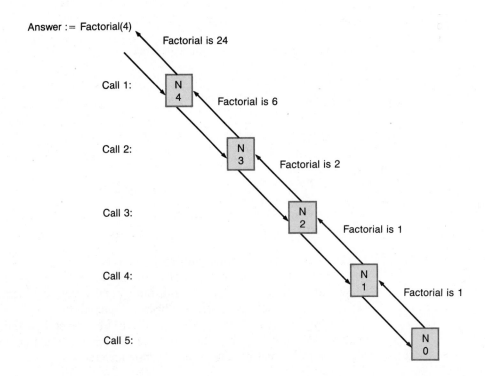

Let's organize what we have done in these two solutions into an outline for writing recursive algorithms.

1. Understand the problem. (We threw this in for good measure. It is always the first step.)
2. Determine the base case(s).
3. Determine the recursive case(s).

We have used the factorial and the power algorithms to demonstrate recursion because they are easy to visualize. In practice one would never want to calculate either of these functions using the recursive solution. In both cases the iterative solutions are simpler and much more efficient. Let's compare the code for the iterative and recursive versions of the factorial problem.

```
FUNCTION Factorial (N:
                        Integer):
                        Integer;
```

```
(* Iterative solution *)                    (* Recursive solution *)

VAR
  Factor,
  Counter:
    Integer;

BEGIN (* Factorial *)                       BEGIN (* Factorial *)
  Factor := 1;                                IF N = 0
  FOR Counter := 2 TO N DO                      THEN
    Factor := Factor * Counter;                   Factorial := 1
  Factorial := Factor                         ELSE
END;  (* Factorial *)                             Factorial := N * Factorial(N - 1)
                                            END;   (* Factorial *)
```

The iterative version has two local variables; the recursive version has none. A recursive procedure or function may have local variables, but there are fewer local variables in a recursive routine than in an iterative routine. The iterative version always has a loop; the recursive version always has a branch. A branching structure is the main control structure in a recursive routine. A looping structure is the main control structure in an iterative routine.

In the next section we will examine a more complicated problem—one in which the recursive solution is not immediately apparent.

Problem Solving in Action

Problem: Convert a decimal integer (base ten) into a binary integer (base two).

Discussion: The algorithm for this conversion is as follows:

1. Take the decimal number and divide it by two.
2. Make the remainder the right-most digit in the answer.

PSIA ▬▬▬▬▬

3. Replace the original dividend with the quotient.
4. Repeat, placing each new remainder to the left of the previous one.
5. Stop when the quotient is zero.

This is clearly a by-hand algorithm for a calculator and paper and pencil. Expressions such as "to the left of" are certainly not implementable in Pascal as yet. Let's do an example and get a feel for the algorithm before we try to write a computer solution. Remember, the quotient from one step becomes the dividend in the next.

Let's convert 42 from base ten to base two.

Step 1	*Step 2*
$\underline{21}$ ⟵ quotient	$\underline{10}$ ⟵ quotient
2⟌42	2⟌21
$\underline{4}$	$\underline{2}$
2	1
$\underline{2}$	$\underline{0}$
0 ⟵ remainder	1 ⟵ remainder

Step 3	*Step 4*
$\underline{5}$ ⟵ quotient	$\underline{2}$ ⟵ quotient
2⟌10	2⟌5
$\underline{10}$	$\underline{4}$
0 ⟵ remainder	1 ⟵ remainder

Step 5	*Step 6*
$\underline{1}$ ⟵ quotient	$\underline{0}$ ⟵ quotient
2⟌2	2⟌1
$\underline{2}$	$\underline{0}$
0 ⟵ remainder	1 ⟵ remainder

Answer: 1   0   1   0   1   0

(remainder from step   6   5   4   3   2   1)

It looks as though the problem could be implemented with a straightforward iterative algorithm. The remainder is, of course, the MOD operation, and the quotient is the DIV operation.

```
WHILE Number > 0
    Remainder ⟵ Number MOD 2
    Write Remainder
    Number ⟵ Number DIV 2
```

PSIA

Let's do an algorithm walkthrough to test this algorithm.

Number	Remainder
42	0
21	1
10	0
5	1
2	0
1	1

Answer: 0 1 0 1 0 1

(remainder from step 1 2 3 4 5 6)

The answer is backwards! An iterative solution (using only simple variables) doesn't work. We need to print the last remainder first. The first remainder should be printed only after the rest of the remainders have been calculated and printed.

In the case of our example this means that we should print 42 MOD 2 after (42 DIV 2) MOD 2 has been printed. But this in turn means that we should print (42 DIV 2) MOD 2 after ((42 DIV 2) DIV 2) MOD 2 has been printed.

Now this begins to look like a recursive definition. We can summarize by saying that for any given number, we should print Number MOD 2 after (Number DIV 2) MOD 2 has been printed.

This becomes the following algorithm:

CONVERT NUMBER

```
    :
IF Number < > 0
  Convert Number DIV 2
  Write Number MOD 2
```

If Number is 0, we have called Convert as many times as we need to and can begin printing the answer. The base case is simply when we stop making recursive calls. The recursive solution to this problem is encoded in procedure Convert.

```
PROCEDURE Convert (Number:              (* Number being converted to binary *)
                  Integer);

BEGIN (* Convert *)
   IF Number <> 0
     THEN                                          (* Recursive call *)
       BEGIN
         Convert(Number DIV 2);
         Write(Number MOD 2)
       END
   (* Empty ELSE branch is the base case *)
END;   (* Convert *)
```

PSIA ━━━

Let's do a code walkthrough of Convert(10). We will pick up our example at step 3, where the dividend is 10.

Call 1: Convert is called with an actual parameter of 10. Number is not equal to 0; execution of the THEN branch of this call halts until the recursive call to Convert with an actual parameter of (Number DIV 2) has been completed.

Call 2: Number is 5. Since Number is not equal to 0, execution of this call halts until the recursive call to Convert with an actual parameter of (Number DIV 2) has been completed.

Call 3: Number is 2. Since Number is not equal to 0, execution of this call halts until the recursive call to Convert with an actual parameter of (Number DIV 2) has been completed.

Call 4: Number is 1. Since Number is not equal to 0, execution of this call halts until the recursive call to Convert with an actual parameter of (Number DIV 2) has been completed.

Call 5: Number is 0. Execution of this call to Convert is completed. Control is passed back to the preceding call.

Call 4: Execution of this call resumes with the statement following the recursive call to Convert. Number MOD 2 (which is 1) is printed. Execution of this call to Convert is completed.

Call 3: Execution of this call resumes with the statement following the recursive call to Convert. Number MOD 2 (which is 0) is printed. Execution of this call to Convert is completed.

Figure 17-4
Execution of
Convert(10)

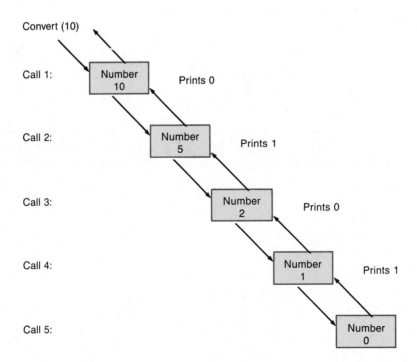

PSIA

Call 2: Execution of this call resumes with the statement following the recursive call to Convert. Number MOD 2 (which is 1) is printed. Execution of this call to Convert is completed.

Call 1: Execution of this call resumes with the statement following the recursive call to Convert. Number MOD 2 (which is 0) is printed. Execution of this call to Convert is completed. Since this is the nonrecursive call, execution resumes with the statement immediately following the original call.

Figure 17-4 shows the execution of procedure Convert with the values of the actual parameters.

TOWERS OF HANOI

One of your first toys may have been three pegs with colored circles of different diameters. If so, you probably spent countless hours moving the circles from one peg to another.

If we put some constraints on how the circles or disks can be moved, we have an adult game called the Towers of Hanoi. When the game begins, the circles are all on the first peg in order by size with the smallest on the top.

The object of the game is to move the circles, one at a time, to the third peg.

The catch is that a circle cannot be placed on top of one that is smaller in diameter. The middle peg can be used as an auxiliary peg, but it must be empty at the beginning and at the end of the game.

To get a feel for how this might be done, let's look at some sketches of what the configuration must be at certain points if a solution is possible. We will use four circles or disks. The beginning configuration is

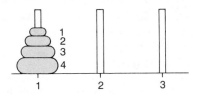

To move the largest circle (circle 4) to peg three, we must move the three smaller circles to peg two. Then circle 4 can be moved into its final place.

Let's assume we can do this. Now, to move the next largest circle (circle 3) into place, we must move the two circles on top of it onto an auxiliary peg (peg one in this case).

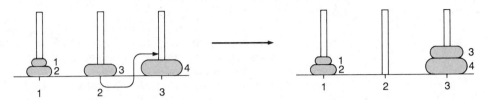

To get circle 2 into place, we must move circle 1 to another peg, freeing circle 2 to be moved to its place on peg three.

The last circle (circle 1) can now be moved into its final place. We are finished.

Notice that to free circle 4, we had to move three circles to another peg. To free circle 3, we had to move two circles to another peg. To free circle 2, we had to move one circle to another peg. This sounds like a recursive algorithm: to free the Nth circle, we have to move $N - 1$ circles.

Each stage can be thought of as beginning again with three pegs, but with one fewer circle each time. Let's see if we can summarize this process, using N instead of an actual number.

TO GET N CIRCLES MOVED FROM PEG 1 TO PEG 3

> Get $N - 1$ circles moved from peg 1 to peg 2
> Move Nth circle from peg 1 to peg 3
> Get $N - 1$ circles moved from peg 2 to peg 3

This algorithm certainly sounds simple; surely there must be more to it. Actually this really is all there is.

Let's write a recursive procedure that will implement this algorithm. We can't actually move disks, of course, but we can print out a message to do so.

Notice that the beginning peg, the ending peg, and the auxiliary peg keep changing during the algorithm. To make the algorithm easier to follow, we will call the pegs BeginPeg, EndPeg, and AuxPeg. These three pegs along with the number of circles on the beginning peg will be the parameters of the procedure.

We have the recursive or general case; what about a base case? How do we know when to stop the recursive process? The clue is in the expression "To get N circles moved." If we don't have any circles to move, we don't have anything to do. We are finished with that stage. Therefore, when the number of circles equals 0, we do nothing (that is, return).

```
PROCEDURE Towers  (Circles,          (* Number of circles to move          *)
                   BeginPeg,          (* Peg containing circles to move      *)
                   AuxPeg,            (* Peg holding circles temporarily     *)
                   EndPeg:            (* Peg receiving circles being moved   *)
                       Integer);

BEGIN (* Towers *)
   IF Circles > 0
     THEN
       BEGIN
         (* Move N - 1 circles from beginning peg to auxiliary peg *)
         Towers(Circles - 1, BeginPeg, EndPeg, AuxPeg);
         Writeln('move circle from peg', BeginPeg:2, 'to peg', EndPeg:2);
         (* Move N - 1 circles from auxiliary peg to ending peg *)
         Towers(Circles - 1, AuxPeg, BeginPeg, EndPeg)
       END
END;   (* Towers *)
```

It's hard to believe that such a simple algorithm will actually work. In fact, you probably don't really believe it will. We'll prove it to you.

Following is a driver program that calls procedure Towers. Remember that a driver program is a program whose sole purpose is to test a procedure or function. Write statements have been added so that you can see the values of the actual parameters with each recursive call. Since there are two recursive calls within the procedure, we have indicated which recursive statement issued the call.

```
PROGRAM TestTowers (Input, Output);

(* This program reads in a value from the console and calls procedure
   Towers with this value as the parameter *)

VAR
   Circles:        (* Number of circles on starting peg *)
     Integer;


(***********************************************************************)
```

```
PROCEDURE Towers (Circles,          (* Number of circles to move          *)
                  BeginPeg,         (* Peg containing circles to move      *)
                  AuxPeg,           (* Peg holding circles temporarily     *)
                  EndPeg:           (* Peg receiving circles being moved   *)
                     Integer);
```

(* This recursive procedure moves the number of circles in Circles from
    BeginPeg to EndPeg. All but one of the circles are moved from
    BeginPeg to AuxPeg, the last circle is moved from BeginPeg to EndPeg,
    then the circles are moved from AuxPeg to EndPeg. The subgoals of
    moving circles to and from AuxPeg are what involve recursion *)

```
BEGIN  (* Towers *)
  Writeln(Circles: 7, BeginPeg: 9, AuxPeg: 7, EndPeg: 7);
  IF Circles > 0
    THEN
      BEGIN
        Write('From  first: ');
        Towers(Circles - 1, BeginPeg, EndPeg, AuxPeg);
        Writeln(' ':48, ' move circle ', Circles: 2, ' from ',
                BeginPeg: 2, ' to ', EndPeg: 2);
        Write('From second: ');
        Towers(Circles - 1, AuxPeg, BeginPeg, EndPeg)
      END
END;   (* Towers *)


(************************************************************************)


BEGIN  (* TestTowers *)
  Writeln('Input number of Circles. ');
  Readln(Circles);
  Writeln('OUTPUT WITH ', Circles: 3, ' CIRCLES');
  Writeln;
  Write('CALLED FROM    #CIRCLES', 'BEGIN': 8, 'AUXIL. ': 8, 'END': 5);
  Writeln(' ':4, 'INSTRUCTIONS');
  Write('Original    : ');
  Towers(Circles, 1, 2, 3)
END.   (* TestTowers *)
```

The output from a run with three circles follows. "Original" means that the actual parameters listed beside it are from the nonrecursive call, which is the first call to procedure Hanoi. "From first:" means that the actual parameters listed are for a call issued from the first recursive statement. "From second:" means that the actual parameters listed are for a call issued from the second recursive statement. Notice that a call cannot be issued from the second recursive statement until the preceding call from the first recursive statement has completed execution.

```
OUTPUT WITH    3 CIRCLES

CALLED FROM      #CIRCLES    BEGIN    AUXIL.    END     INSTRUCTIONS

Original   :        3          1        2        3
From   first:       2          1        3        2
From   first:       1          1        2        3
From   first:       0          1        3        2
                                                        move circle 1 from 1 to 3
From second:        0          2        1        3
                                                        move circle 2 from 1 to 2
From second:        1          3        1        2
From   first:       0          3        2        1
                                                        move circle 1 from 3 to 2
From second:        0          1        3        2
                                                        move circle 3 from 1 to 3
From second:        2          2        1        3
From   first:       1          2        3        1
From   first:       0          2        1        3
                                                        move circle 1 from 2 to 1
From second:        0          3        2        1
                                                        move circle 2 from 2 to 3
From second:        1          1        2        3
From   first:       0          1        3        2
                                                        move circle 1 from 1 to 3
From second:        0          2        1        3
```

Since this procedure has two recursive calls, the diagrams that we have been using to show the execution would be too complicated. Therefore, the output from the driver program will have to suffice.

RECURSIVE ALGORITHMS WITH STRUCTURED VARIABLES

In our definition of a recursive algorithm, we said there were two cases: the recursive or general case and the base case for which an answer can be expressed nonrecursively.

In several of our algorithms nothing was done in the base case. That is, the base case was simply the return to the previous call.

In the general case in all our algorithms so far, a parameter was expressed in terms of a smaller value each time. When structured variables are used, the recursive case is often in terms of a smaller structure, rather than a smaller value.

We will examine the recursive definition for printing the components in a one-dimensional array of N components to show what we mean.

PRINT ARRAY

> IF more components
>   Write the value in the first component
>   Print array of N − 1 components

The recursive case is to print the values in an array that is one component smaller. That is, the size of the array gets smaller with each recursive call. The base case is where the size of the array becomes 0; there are no more components to print.

Our parameters must include the index of the first component (the one to be printed). How do we know when there are no more components to print (when the size of the array to be printed is 0)? We know we have printed the last component in the array when the index of the next component to be printed is beyond the length of the array. Therefore, the index of the last component in the array must be passed as a parameter. We will call the indexes First and Last. When First is greater than Last, we are finished. The name of the array will be List of type AryType.

```
PROCEDURE Print (List:          (* Array containing numbers to print    *)
                     AryType;
                 First,         (* Index first component in the array    *)
                 Last:          (* Index last  component in the array    *)
                     Integer);

BEGIN (* Print *)
   IF First <= Last
      THEN
         BEGIN
            Writeln(List[First]);
            Print(List, First + 1, Last)
         END
END;   (* Print *)
```

We will do a code walkthrough with the array shown at the left.

Call 1: First is 1 and Last is 5. First is less than Last, so the value in List[First] (which is 23) is printed. Execution of this call halts while the array from First + 1 to Last is printed.

Call 2: First is 2 and Last is 5. First is less than Last, so the value in List[First] (which is 44) is printed. Execution of this call halts while the array from First + 1 to Last is printed.

Call 3: First is 3 and Last is 5. First is less than Last, so the value in List[First] (which is 52) is printed. Execution of this call halts while the array from First + 1 to Last is printed.

Call 4: First is 4 and Last is 5. First is less than Last, so the value in List[First] (which is 61) is printed. Execution of this call halts while the array from First + 1 to Last is printed.

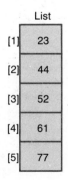

List

[1]	23
[2]	44
[3]	52
[4]	61
[5]	77

Print(List, 1, 5)

Call 5: First is 5 and Last is 5. First is equal to Last, so the value in List[First] (which is 77) is printed. Execution of this call halts while the array from First + 1 to Last is printed.

Call 6: First is 6 and Last is 5. First is greater than Last, so the execution of this call is completed. Control is passed back to the preceding call.

Call 5: Execution of this call is completed. Control is passed back to the preceding call.

Calls 4, 3, 2, and 1: Execution is completed in turn, and control is passed back to the preceding call.

Notice that once the deepest call (the call with the highest number) was reached, each of the calls before it returned without doing anything. When the only recursive call is the last statement in the procedure or function to be executed, the recursion is known as tail recursion. Tail recursion often indicates that the problem could be solved more easily using iteration. We used the array example because it made the recursive process easy to visualize; in practice, an array should be printed iteratively.

Figure 17-5 shows the execution of procedure Print with the values of the actual

Figure 17-5
Execution of
Print(List, 1, 5)

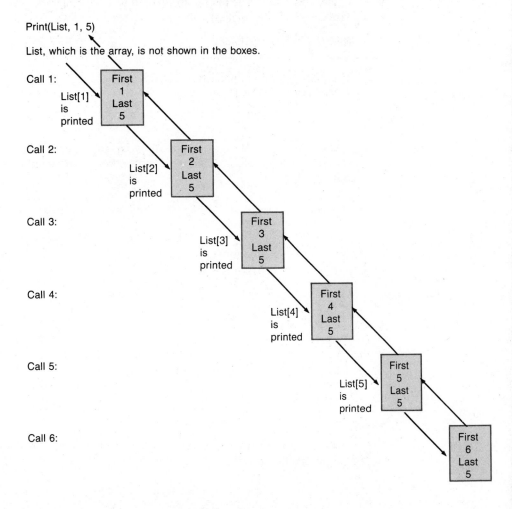

parameters for each call. Notice that the array gets smaller with each recursive call (List[First]..List[Last]).

If we wanted to print the components in the array in reverse order recursively, all we would have to do is interchange the two statements within the IF statement.

In the previous array example we stated the recursive definition and discussed why it works. Now let's take a problem and develop the recursive definition and algorithm.

Problem Solving in Action

Problem: Find the minimum value in an integer array indexed from 1 to Size.

Discussion: This problem is easy to solve iteratively, but the object here is to think recursively. This means that the problem has to be stated in terms of a smaller case of itself. Since this is a problem using an array, a smaller case will probably involve a smaller array.

How about this? The minimum value in an array of length Size will be the smaller of List[Size] and the smallest value in an array from List[1]..List[Size − 1].

MINIMUM(LIST[1]..LIST[SIZE])

```
IF List[Size] < Minimum(List[1]..List[Size − 1])
    Minimum ⟵—— List[Size]
```

This algorithm looks reasonable. All we need is a base case. When do we always know the minimum value? When there is only one value! So our base case will be when Size is 1.

```
FUNCTION Minimum (List:              (* Array containing numbers to print *)
                   AryType;
                  Size:              (* Index of last element in array     *)
                   Integer):
                    Integer;

BEGIN (* Minimum *)
  IF Size = 1
    THEN
      Minimum : = List[Size]
    ELSE
      IF List[Size]  < Minimum(List,  Size − 1)
        THEN
          Minimum : = List[Size]
  END;   (* Minimum *)
```

We will not do a code walkthrough for this function. A diagram showing the actual parameters for each call appears in Figure 17-6.

PSIA

*Figure 17-6
Execution of
Minimum(List, 5)*

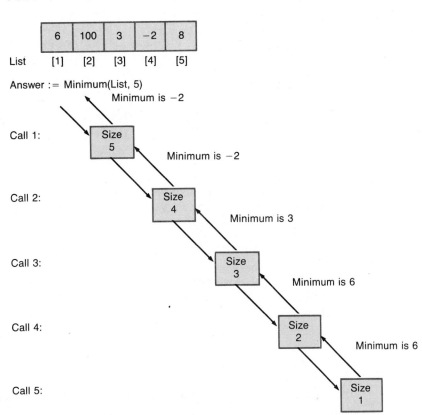

Testing: To test this function, we need a driver program that reads values into an array, calls the function, and prints the results. The cases to be tested are the end cases (Size equal to 1 and Size equal to MaxLength) and several cases in between.

RECURSION USING POINTER VARIABLES

The two previous recursive algorithms using one-dimensional arrays could have been done much more easily using iteration. Now we will look at two algorithms that cannot be done more easily with iteration: printing a linked list in reverse order and traversing a tree.

Printing a Linked List in Reverse Order

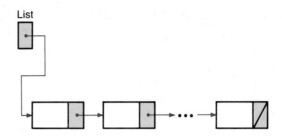

Printing a linked list in order from first to last is easy. We set a running pointer Pointer to List and cycle through the list until Pointer is NIL.

PRINT LIST

```
Pointer ⟵ List
WHILE Pointer < > NIL
   Write Pointer^.Component
   Pointer ⟵ Pointer^.Link
```

To print the list in reverse order, we must print the value in the last node first, then the value in the next-to-last node, etc. Another way of expressing this is to say that we can't print a value until all the values in all the nodes following it have been printed.

We might visualize the process as the first node's turning to its neighbor and saying, "Tell me when you have printed your value. Then I'll print my value." The second node says to its neighbor, "Tell me when you have printed your value. Then I'll print mine." That node, in turn, says the same to its neighbor. . . .

Since the number of neighbors gets smaller and smaller, we seem to have the makings of a recursive solution. We know when we have reached the end of the list: the running pointer is NIL. When that happens, the last node can print its value and send the message back to the one before it. That node can then print its value and send the message back to the one before it, and so on.

REVPRINT LIST

```
IF List is not NIL
   RevPrint rest of nodes in List
   Write current node in List
```

This algorithm can be coded directly into the following procedure:

```
PROCEDURE RevPrint (List:               (* Pointer to head of linked list *)
                     NodePointer) ;

(* The components of List are printed in reverse order *)

BEGIN  (* RevPrint *)
   IF List <> NIL
      THEN
         BEGIN                                        (* Recursive call *)
            RevPrint (List^.Link) ;
            Write (List^.Component)
         END
END;    (* RevPrint *)
```

This algorithm seems complex enough to warrant a code walkthrough. We will use the following list:

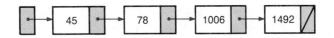

Call 1: List is a pointer pointing to the node containing 45. List is not NIL. Execution of this call halts until the recursive call with the actual parameter List^.Link has been completed.

Call 2: List is a pointer pointing to the node containing 78. List is not NIL. Execution of this call halts until the recursive call with the actual parameter List^.Link has been completed.

Call 3: List is a pointer pointing to the node containing 1066. List is not NIL. Execution of this call halts until the recursive call with the actual parameter List^.Link has been completed.

Call 4: List is a pointer pointing to the node containing 1492. List is not NIL. Execution of this call halts until the recursive call with the actual parameter List^.Link has been completed.

Call 5: List is NIL. Execution of this call is complete. Control is passed back to the preceding call.

Call 4: List^.Component (which is 1492) is printed. Execution of this call is complete. Control is passed back to the preceding call.

Call 3: List^.Component (which is 1066) is printed. Execution of this call is complete. Control is passed back to the preceding call.

Call 2: List^.Component (which is 78) is printed. Execution of this call is complete. Control is passed back to the preceding call.

Call 1: List^.Component (which is 45) is printed. Execution of this call is complete. Since this is the nonrecursive call, execution continues with the statement immediately following RevPrint(List).

Figure 17-7 shows the execution of procedure RevPrint. The actual parameters are pointers that cannot be printed, so ⟶ 45 means the pointer to the node whose component is 45.

Figure 17-7
Execution of
RevPrint(List)

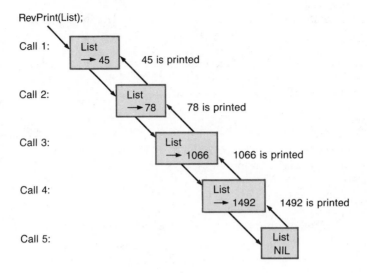

RevPrint(List);

Call 1:   List
          → 45   45 is printed

Call 2:   List
          → 78   78 is printed

Call 3:   List
          → 1066   1066 is printed

Call 4:   List
          → 1492   1492 is printed

Call 5:   List
          NIL

Recursion with Trees

In the last chapter we described a structure called a binary tree. Each node in a binary tree either is a leaf (that is, has no offspring) or has a left child and/or a right child. The left child of a node is the root of the left subtree of the node. The right child of a node is the root of the right subtree of the node.

A binary tree can be defined recursively as a finite set of nodes that either is empty or consists of a root and two disjoint binary trees called the left subtree and the right subtree.

We can make use of this recursive definition to traverse the tree. Traversing a tree means visiting each of the nodes in the tree in an organized fashion. "Visiting" implies any sort of action we wish—for example, printing, counting, or summing.

The following binary tree is a binary search tree because of the relationship among the values in the nodes of the tree. The value in a node is greater than any value in the nodes of its left subtree and less than any value in the nodes of its right subtree. (We are assuming no duplicates in this definition.)

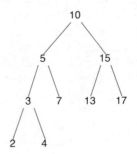

In the last chapter we developed an algorithm to print the values in a binary search tree in numeric order. Such a traversal is called an in-order traversal. In an in-order traversal, a node is visited in between visits to the nodes in its left subtree and the nodes in its right subtree. We will reexamine this algorithm and develop a recursive solution.

To print the values in the tree, we move as far down the tree to the left as possible. We print that value, print the value in the parent of that node, and then print the values in the right child of that node. We can generalize this process as follows:

> Print (in order) the values in the left subtree.
> Print the value in the node.
> Print (in order) the values in the right subtree

Like the solution to the Towers of Hanoi problem, this looks too simple. Yet it is the algorithm.

As in the Towers of Hanoi problem, the base case is a "do nothing" case. The end of the recursive calls is recognized when the root of the subtree is NIL—that is, the subtree is empty.

```
PROCEDURE InOrder (Tree:                (* Pointer to root of binary tree *)
                        Pointer);

(* Print the components of a binary search tree in order *)

BEGIN (* InOrder *)
   IF Tree <> NIL
     THEN
       BEGIN
         InOrder(Tree^.Left);
         Write(Tree^.Component);
         InOrder(Tree^.Right)
       END
END;    (* InOrder *)
```

In Chapter 16 we wrote a procedure to print a binary search tree using a stack. In fact, the Pascal compiler and the run-time support system implement recursion using a stack. Each time a procedure or function is called, its actual parameters are put on a stack. Let's do a code walkthrough indicating what is happening to the stack at each recursive call. Figure 17-8 shows the contents of the stack at the beginning of each call. The components (which are pointers) are shown one on top of the other. The most recently pushed element is on the top. The notation $\longrightarrow$ 10 refers to the pointer that points to the node containing 10.

Figure 17-8
Execution of
InOrder(Tree)

InOrder(Tree)

(a) Call   1: ⟶10

(b) Call 1L: ⟶ 5
          ⟶10

(c) Call 2L: ⟶ 3
         ⟶ 5
         ⟶10

(d) Call 3L: NIL
        ⟶ 3
        ⟶ 5
        ⟶10

(e) Call 2L: ⟶ 3
         ⟶ 5
         ⟶10

(f) Call 1R: NIL
        ⟶ 3
        ⟶ 5
        ⟶10

(g) Call 2L: ⟶ 3
         ⟶ 5
         ⟶10

(h) Call 1L: ⟶ 5
          ⟶10

(i) Call 1R: ⟶ 7
         ⟶ 5
         ⟶10

(j) Call 2L: NIL
        ⟶ 7
        ⟶ 5
        ⟶10

(k) Call 1R: ⟶ 7
         ⟶ 5
         ⟶10

(l) Call 2R: NIL
        ⟶ 7
        ⟶ 5
        ⟶10

(m) Call 1R: ⟶ 7
         ⟶ 5
         ⟶10

(n) Call 1L: ⟶ 5
          ⟶10

(o) Call   1: ⟶10

(p) Call 1R: ⟶15
         ⟶10

(q) Call 2L: ⟶13
         ⟶15
         ⟶10

(r) Call 3L: NIL
        ⟶13
        ⟶15
        ⟶10

(s) Call 2L: ⟶13
         ⟶15
         ⟶10

(t) Call 2R: NIL
        ⟶13
        ⟶15
        ⟶10

(u) Call 2L: ⟶13
         ⟶15
         ⟶10

(v) Call 1R: ⟶15
         ⟶10

(w) Call 2R: NIL
        ⟶15
        ⟶10

(x) Call 1R: ⟶15
         ⟶10

(y) Call   1: ⟶10

(z) Stack is empty

We will use the same subtree that we used in Chapter 16. Since there are two recursive calls, we will distinguish them by using L for the call with Tree^.Left and R for the call with Tree^.Right.

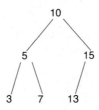

Call 1 (nonrecursive, Figure 17-8a):   Tree (which is pointing to the node that contains 10) is on the stack. Tree is not NIL, so InOrder is called with Tree^.Left as the actual parameter. This pointer (Tree^.Left) is put on the stack.

Call 1L (Figure 17-8b): Tree is pointing to the node that contains 5. Tree is not NIL, so InOrder is called with Tree^.Left as the actual parameter. Tree^.Left is put on the stack.

Call 2L (Figure 17-8c): Tree is pointing to the node that contains 3. Tree is not NIL, so InOrder is called with Tree^.Left as the actual parameter. Tree^.Left is put on the stack.

Call 3L (Figure 17-8d): Tree is NIL. Execution of this call is complete. The stack is popped.

Call 2L (Figure 17-8e): Tree^.Component (which is 3) is printed. InOrder is called with Tree^.Right as the actual parameter. Tree^.Right is put on the stack.

Call 1R (Figure 17-8f): Tree is NIL. Execution of this call is complete. The stack is popped.

Call 2L (Figure 17-8g): Execution of this call is now complete. Control is now passed back to the preceding call. The stack is popped.

Call 1L (Figure 17-8h): Tree^.Component (which is 5) is printed. InOrder is called with Tree^.Right as the actual parameter. Tree^.Right is put on the stack.

Call 1R (Figure 17-8i): Tree is not NIL. InOrder is called with Tree^.Left as the actual parameter. Tree^.Left is put on the stack.

Call 2L (Figure 17-8j): Tree is NIL. Execution of this call is complete. The stack is popped.

Call 1R (Figure 17-8k): Tree^.Component (which is 7) is printed. InOrder is called with Tree^.Right as the actual parameter. Tree^.Right is put on the stack.

Call 2R (Figure 17-8l): Tree is NIL. Execution of this call is complete. The stack is popped.

Call 1R (Figure 17-8m): Execution of this call is complete. The stack is popped.

Call 1L (Figure 17-8n): Execution of this call is complete. The stack is popped.

Call 1 (nonrecursive, Figure 17-8o): Tree^.Component (which is 10) is printed. InOrder is called with Tree^.Right as the actual parameter. Tree^.Right is put on the stack.

Call 1R (Figure 17-8p): Tree is not NIL. InOrder is called with Tree^.Left as the actual parameter. Tree^.Left is put on the stack.

Call 2L (Figure 17-8q): Tree is not NIL. InOrder is called with Tree^.Left as the actual parameter. Tree^.Left is put on the stack.

Call 3L (Figure 17-8r): Tree is NIL. Execution of this call is complete. The stack is popped.

Call 2L (Figure 17-8s): Tree^.Component (which is 13) is printed. InOrder is called with Tree^.Right as the actual parameter. Tree^.Right is put on the stack.

Call 2R (Figure 17-8t): Tree is NIL. Execution of this call is complete. The stack is popped.

Call 2L (Figure 17-8u): Execution of this call is now complete. The stack is popped.

Call 1R (Figure 17-8v): Tree^.Component (which is 15) is printed. InOrder is called with Tree^.Right as the actual parameter. Tree^.Right is put on the stack.

Call 2R (Figure 17-8w): Tree is NIL. Execution of this call is complete. The stack is popped.

Call 1R (Figure 17-8x):   Execution of this call is now complete. The stack is popped.

Call 1 (nonrecursive, Figure 17-8y):   Execution of this call is now complete. The stack is popped (Figure 17-8z). Execution continues with the first statement following the original call to procedure InOrder.

Another way of looking at recursion is as an automatic stack data structure mechanism. Often we can use recursion as a substitute for writing complicated stack handling declarations and procedures. For example, the string reversal problem in the last chapter could more easily be written as a recursive procedure.

The iterative algorithm was as follows.

Initialize stack
WHILE NOT EOLN
    Read a character
    Push character onto a stack
WHILE More Characters on Stack
    Pop character
    Write character

The recursive algorithm for the same task is as follows.

REVERSE

IF NOT EOLN
    THEN
        Read a character
        Reverse
        Write character

It is the number of characters left on a line of input that gets smaller with each call. The base case is when there are no more characters to be read. The code for the recursive procedure is shown embedded within Program ReverseLine.

```
PROGRAM ReverseLine (Input, Output);

(* A line is read from the keyboard and printed in reverse order *)

(*****************************************************************************)
```

```
        PROCEDURE Reverse;

     (* A character is read from the keyboard, but before it is printed
        Reverse calls itself recursively.  When EOLN is ultimately
        encountered, the routine returns to the previous call, writes out
        the character that was read in then, and returns again.  The process
        continues until all characters have been printed, with the first
        character read in being the last printed. *)

     VAR
        Character:          (* The character read in during current call *)
           Char;

     BEGIN (* Reverse *)
        IF NOT EOLN
           THEN                                          (* Recursive case *)
              BEGIN
                 Read(Character);
                 Reverse;
                 Write(Character)
              END
        (* Empty ELSE is the base case *)
     END;    (* Reverse *)


     (*********************************************************************)

     BEGIN (* ReverseLine *)
        Reverse
     END.    (* ReverseLine *)
```

RECURSION OR ITERATION?

Recursion is an alternative form of program control. When iterative control structures are used, processes are made to repeat by embedding code in a looping structure such as a WHILE, FOR, or REPEAT-UNTIL. In recursion, a process is made to repeat by having a procedure or function call itself. A selection statement is used to control the repeated calls.

Each time a recursive call is made, space must be assigned for all local variables. The overhead involved in any procedure or function call is time consuming. If an iterative solution is obvious, use it; it will be more efficient. There are, however, problems for which the recursive solution is the more obvious, such as the Towers of Hanoi problem and tree traversals.

Computer science students should be aware of the power of recursion. If the definition of a problem is inherently recursive, then a recursive solution should certainly be considered.

TESTING AND DEBUGGING

Recursion is a powerful technique when used correctly. Improperly used, recursion can cause bugs that are very hard to diagnose. The best way to debug a recursive algorithm is to construct it correctly in the first place. Being realistic, however, we will give a few hints about where to look if an error occurs.

Testing and Debugging Hints

1. Be sure that there is a base case. If there is no base case, the algorithm will continue to issue recursive calls until all the memory has been used. Each time the procedure or function is called, either recursively or nonrecursively, space is assigned for the parameters. If there is no base case to end the recursive calls, eventually all the memory will have been assigned. An error message such as "STACK OVERFLOW" indicates that the base case is missing.

2. Be sure you have not used a WHILE structure. The basic structure in a recursive algorithm is the IF-THEN-ELSE. There must be at least two cases: the recursive case and the base case. The base case may be to do nothing, in which case the ELSE branch is not present. The branching structure, however, must be there. If a WHILE statement is used in a recursive algorithm, the WHILE statement usually should not contain a recursive call.

3. Do not reference global variables directly within a recursive procedure or function.

4. Formal parameters that relate to the size of the problem must be value parameters. Actual parameters that relate to the size of the problem are usually expressions. Only value parameters can be expressions.

SUMMARY

A recursive algorithm is an algorithm that is expressed in terms of a smaller instance of itself. It must include a recursive case for which the algorithm is expressed in terms of itself and a base case for which the algorithm is expressed in nonrecursive terms.

In many recursive problems the "smaller instance" refers to a numeric parameter that is being reduced with each call. In other problems, the "smaller instance" refers to the size of the data structure being manipulated. The base case will be the one in which the size of the problem (value or structure) reaches a point where an explicit answer is known.

In the case of finding the minimum using recursion, the size of the problem was the size of the array being searched. When the array size became 1, the solution was known. If there is only one component, it must be the minimum (as well as the maximum).

In the case of the Towers of Hanoi, the size of the problem was the number of disks to be moved. When there was only one left on the beginning peg, it could be moved to its final destination.

QUICK CHECK _____

1. What distinguishes the base case in a recursive algorithm? (pp. 723–727)

2. What is the base case in the Towers of Hanoi algorithm? (pp. 733–737)

3. In work with simple variables, the recursive case is often in terms of a smaller value. What is typical of the recursive case in work with structured variables? (pp. 737–740)

4. In recursively printing a linked list in reverse order, what is the base case? (pp. 741–744)

5. What is the base case for the in-order binary tree traversal? (pp. 744–749)

ANSWERS
1. The base case is the simplest case: the case where the solution can be stated nonrecursively. 2. When there are no more circles left to move. 3. It is often stated in terms of a smaller structure. 4. When the current node pointer is NIL. 5. When the subtree is empty: when an offspring pointer is NIL.

EXAM PREPARATION EXERCISES _____

1. Recursion is an example of
   (a) selection
   (b) a data structure
   (c) repetition
   (d) data-flow programming

2. A procedure can be recursive and a function cannot be recursive. (True or False?)

3. When a procedure is called recursively, the actual parameters and local variables of the calling version are saved until its execution is resumed. (True or False?)

4. Given the recursive formula $F(N) = -F(N - 2)$ with base case $F(0) = 1$, what are the values of $F(4)$ and $F(6)$? What is the value of $F(5)$?

5. When can one have infinite recursion?

6. What control structure most commonly appears in a recursive procedure?

7. If you develop a recursive algorithm that employs tail recursion, what should you consider?

8. A recursive algorithm depends on making something smaller. When the algorithm works on a data structure, what may become smaller?
   (a) distance from a position in the structure
   (b) the data structure
   (c) the number of variables in the recursive procedure

9. What is a base case of a recursive procedure that traverses a binary tree?

10. What abstract data structure does Pascal use to save information for pending recursive calls of a procedure or function?

PREPROGRAMMING EXERCISES _____

1. Write a Pascal function that implements the recursive formula: $F(N) = F(N - 1) + F(N - 2)$ with base cases $F(0) = 1$ and $F(1) = 1$.

2. Add whatever is necessary to fix the function below so that F(3) = 10.

```
FUNCTION Funct (N:
                      Integer):
                      Integer

BEGIN
  F := F(N - 1) + 3
END;
```

3. Rewrite procedure LinePrint without using recursion.

```
PROCEDURE LinePrint (Infile:
                            Text;

VAR
  Charact:
  Char;

BEGIN (* LinePrint *)
  IF NOT EOF(Infile)
    THEN
      BEGIN
        IF NOT EOLN(Infile)
          THEN
            BEGIN
              Read(Infile, Charact);
              Write(Charact)
            END
          ELSE
            Writeln;
            LinePrint(X)
      END
END
```

4. Rewrite procedure SquarePrint using recursion.

```
PROCEDURE SquarePrint;

VAR
  Count:
  Integer;

BEGIN
  FOR Count := 1 TO 10 DO
    Writeln(Count, Count * Count)
END;
```

5. Modify function Factorial of this chapter to print its parameter and returned value in-

dented two spaces for each level of call to the function. The call Factorial(3) should produce the output:

```
3
  2
    1
      0
    1
  1
2
6
```

7. Write a recursive procedure to print the nodes of a binary tree so that the components are printed after their children are printed.

8. Using the stack procedures of Chapter 16, write a recursive procedure that prints the contents of a stack bottom first and reconstructs it before returning control to the calling routine.

PROGRAMMING PROBLEMS _____

1. Write a recursive palindrome checker. (See Programming Problem 4, Chapter 16.)

2. Write a program to place eight queens on a chess board in such a way that no queen is attacking any other queen. This is a classic problem that lends itself to a recursive solution.

   The chess board should be represented by an 8 × 8 Boolean array. If a square is occupied by a queen, the value is True. Otherwise, the square is False. The status of the chess board when all eight queens have been placed is the solution.

3. A maze is to be represented by a 10 × 10 array of an enumerated data type made up of the three values Path, Hedge, and Exit. There is one exit from the maze. Write a program to determine if it is possible to exit the maze from a given starting point.

   You may move vertically or horizontally in any direction that contains Path; you may not move to a square that contains Hedge. If you move into a square that contains Exit, you have exited.

   The input data consists of two parts: the maze and a series of starting points. The maze is entered as 10 lines of 10 characters (P, H, and E). Each succeeding line contains a pair of integers that represents a starting point (that is, row and column numbers). Continue processing entry points until EOF.

4. Rewrite Program SortSatScores (see Chapter 16) so that the scores are printed in reverse order. That is, the largest score is printed first. (Do not change the elements in the binary search tree.)

Appendixes

Appendix A   Reserved Words

AND	END	MOD	REPEAT
ARRAY	FILE	NIL	SET
BEGIN	FOR	NOT	THEN
CASE	FORWARD	OF	TO
CONST	FUNCTION	OR	TYPE
DIV	GOTO	PACKED	UNTIL
DO	IF	PROCEDURE	VAR
DOWNTO	IN	PROGRAM	WHILE
ELSE	LABEL	RECORD	WITH

(EXTERN, FORTRAN, GLOBAL, LOCAL, OTHERWISE, VALUE and others may be reserved words in some implementations. FORWARD is technically not a reserved word—it is a special word called a required directive. However, in the context of this text it may be considered to behave exactly like a reserved word.)

Appendix B   Standard Identifiers

Standard Constants

False   True   MaxInt

Standard Types

Integer   Boolean   Real   Char   Text

Standard Files

Input   Output

Standard Functions

	Parameter type	Result type	Returns
Abs(X)	Integer or Real	Same as parameter	Absolute value of X
ArcTan(X)	Integer or Real	Real	Arctangent of X in radians
Chr(X)	Integer	Char	Character whose ordinal number is X
Cos(X)	Integer or Real	Real	Cosine of X (X is in radians)
EOF(F)	File	Boolean	End-of-file test of F
EOLN(F)	File	Boolean	End-of-line test of F
Exp(X)	Real or Integer	Real	e to the X power
Ln(X)	Real or Integer	Real	Natural logarithm of X
Odd(X)	Integer	Boolean	Odd test of X
Ord(X)	Ordinal (scalar except Real)	Integer	Ordinal number of X
Pred(X)	Ordinal (scalar except Real)	Same as parameter	Unique predecessor of X (except when X is the first value)
Round(X)	Real	Integer	X rounded
Sin(X)	Real or Integer	Real	Sine of X (X is in radians)
Sqr(X)	Real or Integer	Same as parameter	Square of X
Sqrt(X)	Real or Integer	Real	Square root of X
Succ(X)	Ordinal (scalar except Real)	Same as parameter	Unique successor of X (except when X is the last value)
Trunc(X)	Real	Integer	X truncated

Standard Procedures

	Description
Dispose(P)	Destroys the dynamic variable referenced by pointer P by returning it to the available space list.
Get(F)	Advances the current position of file F to the next component and assigns the value of the component to F^.
New(P)	Creates a variable of the type referenced by pointer P, and stores a pointer to the new variable in P.
Pack(U, I, P)	Copies the elements beginning at subscript position I of array U into packed array P beginning at the first subscript position of P.
Page(F)	Advances the printer to the top of a new page before printing the next line of text file F.
Put(F)	Appends the value of the buffer variable F^ to the file F.
Read(F, variable list)	Reads data values from text file F (if F is not specified, default is Input) and assigns these values to the variable(s) in the variable list in order until the list is satisfied.
Readln(F, variable list)	Same as Read except advances the file pointer past the end-of-line after satisfying its variable list.

Reset(F)	Resets file F to its beginning for reading.
Rewrite(F)	Resets file F to its beginning for writing; old contents of F are lost.
Unpack(P, U, I)	Copies the elements beginning at the first subscript position of packed array P into array U beginning at subscript position I.
Write(F, parameter list)	Writes the data in the order specified in the parameter list to text file F (if F is not specified, default is Output).
Writeln(F, parameter list)	Same as Write except generates an end-of-file after satisfying its parameter list.

(Some compilers provide additional types, files, functions and/or procedures. Check the manual for your specific implementation to see what is available.)

Appendix C   Pascal Operators and Symbols

Standard symbol	Alternate symbol	
+		plus or set union
−		minus or set difference
*		times or set intersection
/		real divide
DIV		integer divide
MOD		remainder from integer divide (modulus)
<		is less than
<=		is less than or equal to
=		is equal to
<>		is not equal to
>=		is greater than or equal to
>		is greater than
AND		Boolean conjunction
OR		Boolean inclusive disjunction
NOT		Boolean negation
IN		test set membership
:=		is assigned the value of
,		separates items in a list
;		separates statements
:		separates variable name and type; separates case label and statement; separates statement label and statement
'		delimits character and string literals
.		decimal point, record selector and program terminator
..		subrange specifier
∧	@	file and pointer variable indicator
(		starts parameter list or nested expression
)		ends parameter list or nested expression
[	(.	starts index list or set expression
(*	{	starts a comment
*)	}	ends a comment
]	.)	ends index list or set expression

Appendix D Precedence of Operators

NOTE

1. Parentheses can be used to change the order of precedence.
2. When operators of equal precedence are used, they are executed in left to right order.

NOT	Highest precedence
* / DIV MOD AND	
+ - OR	
< <= = >= > <> IN	Lowest precedence

Appendix E Syntax Diagrams

PROGRAM

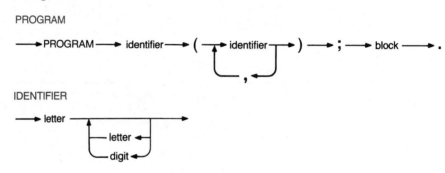

IDENTIFIER

BLOCK

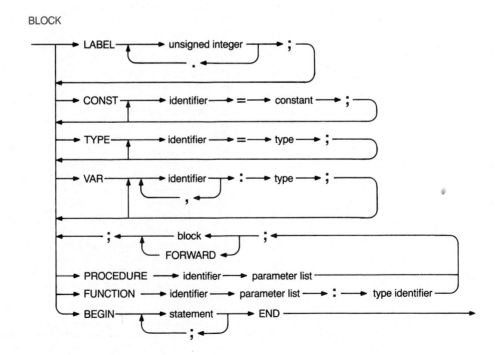

CONSTANT

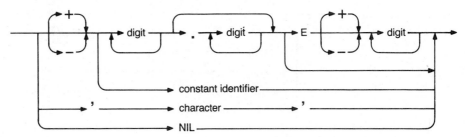

TYPE

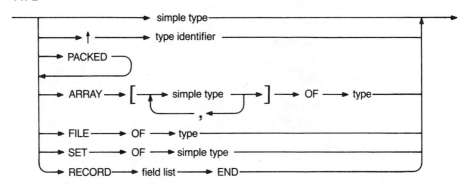

SIMPLE TYPE

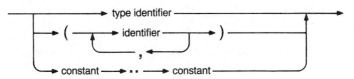

FIELD LIST

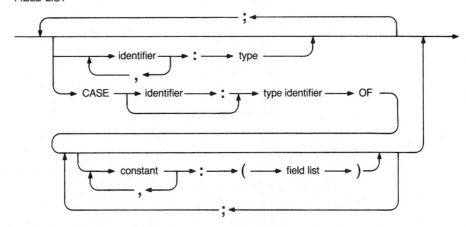

PARAMETER LIST

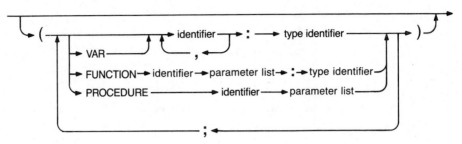

STATEMENT

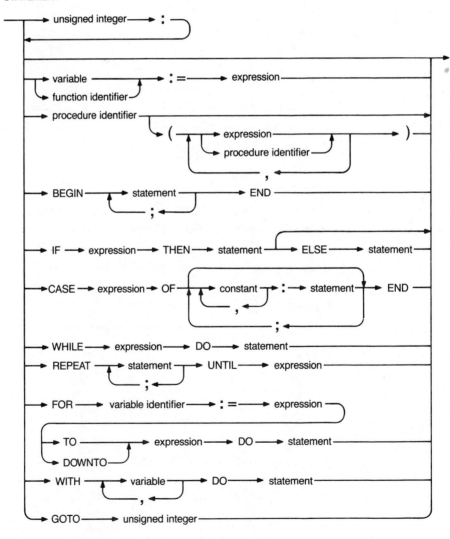

VARIABLE

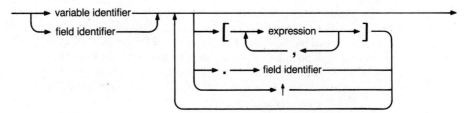

EXPRESSION

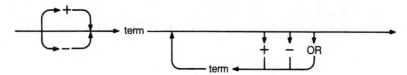

SIMPLE EXPRESSION

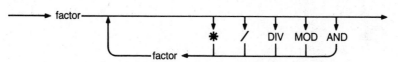

TERM

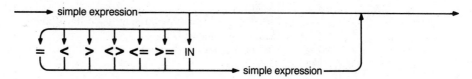

FACTOR

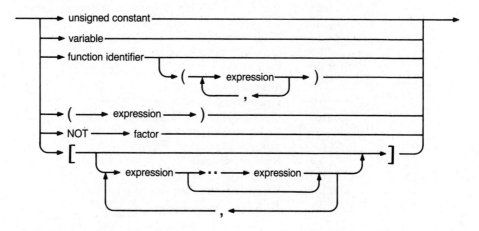

Appendix F   Compiler Error Messages

The following error codes are produced by the compiler to inform the user of a compiler error. The list defines the error code number and a description of the meaning of the error. This list is based on the Pascal User Manual and Report by Jensen and Wirth. Many compilers do not use this notation for errors. You should consult the manual for your compiler to determine the exact meaning of any error message. This list is simply intended to give you an idea of the types of error messages you may encounter when compiling a Pascal Program.

1:	Error in simple type
2:	Identifier expected
3:	'PROGRAM' expected
4:	')' expected
5:	':' expected
6:	Illegal symbol (possibly missing ';' on line above)
7:	Error in parameter list
8:	'OF' expected
9:	'(' expected
10:	Error in type
11:	'[' expected
12:	']' expected
13:	'END' expected
14:	';' expected (possibly on line above)
15:	Integer expected
16:	'=' expected
17:	'BEGIN' expected
18:	Error in declaration part
19:	Error in <field-list>
20:	',' expected
21:	'*' expected
50:	Error in constant
51:	':=' expected
52:	'THEN' expected
53:	'UNTIL' expected
54:	'DO' expected
55:	'TO' or 'DOWNTO' expected in FOR statement
56:	'IF' expected
57:	'FILE' expected
58:	Error in <factor> (bad expression)
59:	Error in variable
101:	Identifier declared twice
102:	Lower bound exceeds upper bound
103:	Identifier is not of the appropriate class
104:	Undeclared identifier
105:	Sign not allowed
106:	Number expected
107:	Incompatible subrange types
108:	File not allowed here
109:	Type must not be Real

110: <tagfield> type must be scalar or subrange
111: Incompatible with <tagfield> type
112: Index type must not be Real
113: Index type must be scalar or subrange
114: Base type must not be Real
115: Base type must be scalar or a subrange
116: Error in type of standard procedure parameter
117: Unsatisfied forward reference
118: Forward referenced type identifier in variable declaration
119: Must not repeat parameter list for a FORWARD declared procedure

120: Function result type must be scalar, subrange or pointer
121: File value parameter not allowed
122: Must not repeat result type for a FORWARD declared function
123: Missing result type in function declaration
124: E-format for reals only
125: Error in type of standard function parameter
126: Number of parameters does not agree with declaration
127: Illegal parameter substitution
128: Result type does not agree with declaration
129: Type conflict of operands

130: Expression is not of set type
131: Tests on equality allowed only
132: Strict inclusion not allowed
133: File comparison not allowed
134: Illegal type of operand(s)
135: Type of operand must be Boolean
136: Set element type must be scalar or subrange
137: Set element types must be compatible
138: Type of variable is not array
139: Index type is not compatible with declaration

140: Type of variable is not record
141: Type of variable must be file or pointer
142: Illegal parameter substitution
143: Illegal type of loop control variable
144: Illegal type of expression
145: Type conflict
146: Assignment of files not allowed
147: Label type incompatible with selecting expression
148: Subrange bounds must be scalar
149: Index type must not be Integer

150: Assignment to standard function is not allowed
151: Assignment to formal function is not allowed
152: No such field in this record
153: Type error in Read
154: Actual parameter must be a variable
155: Control variable must be local and not a parameter
156: Multidefined case label
157: Too many cases in CASE statement

158: No such variant in this record
159: REAL or string tagfields not allowed
160: Previous declaration was not FORWARD
161: Previously declared as FORWARD
162: Parameter size must be constant
163: Missing variant in declaration
164: Substitution of standard procedure/function not allowed
165: Multidefined label
166: Multideclared label
167: Undeclared label
168: Undefined label
169: Base type of set exceeds implementation limit

170: Value parameter expected
171: Standard file was re-declared
172: Undeclared external file
173: FORTRAN procedure or function expected
174: Pascal procedure or function expected
175: Missing file Input in program heading
176: Missing file Output in program heading

Appendix G   Program Style, Formatting, and Documentation

Throughout this text we encourage the use of good programming style and documentation. Although the programs you write for class assignments may not be looked at by anyone except the person grading your work, outside of class you will write programs that will be used by others.

Useful programs have very long lifetimes, during which they must be modified and updated. When maintenance work must be done, either you or another programmer will have to do it. Good style and documentation are essential if another programmer is to understand and work with your program. You will also discover that, after not working with your own program for a few months, you'll be amazed at how many of the details you've forgotten.

General Guidelines

The style used in the programs and fragments throughout this text provides a good starting point for developing your own style. Our goals in creating this style were to make it simple, consistent, and easy to read.

Style is of benefit only for a human reader of your program—differences in style make no difference to the computer. Good style includes the use of meaningful variable names, comments, and indentation of control structures, all of which help others to understand and work with your program. Perhaps the most important aspect of program style is consistency. If the style within a program is not consistent, then it becomes misleading and confusing.

Sometimes, a particular style will be specified for you by your instructor or by the company you work for. When you are modifying someone else's code, you will use his or her style in order to maintain consistency within the program. However, you will also develop your own, personal programming style based on what you've been taught, your own experience, and your personal taste.

Comments

Comments are extra information included to make a program easier to understand. You should include a comment anywhere the code is difficult to understand. However, don't overcomment. Too many comments in a program will obscure the code and be a source of distraction.

In our style, there are four basic types of comments: headers, definitions, in-line, and sidebar.

1. *Header comments* appear at the top of the program immediately following the program heading, and should include your name, the date that the program was written, and its purpose. It is also useful to include the input, output, and assumptions sections from your top-down design. Think of the header comments as the reader's introduction to your program. Here is an example:

```
(* This program computes the sidereal time for a given date and
    solar time.

    Written By: Your Name

    Date Completed: 4/8/86

    Input: A date and time in the form of MM DD YY HH MM SS

    Output: Sidereal time in the form of HH MM SS

    Assumptions: Solar time is specified for a longitude of 0
          degrees (GMT, UT, or Z time zone)                    *)
```

Header comments should also be included for all user-defined procedures. (See Chapters 6, 7, and 8.)

2. *Definition comments* accompany all declarations and definitions in the program. Anywhere that an identifier is declared, a comment should appear that explains its purpose. In programs in the text, definition comments appear to the right of the identifier being declared. For example:

```
CONST
    E = 2.718281828459     (* The base of the natural logarithms *)

VAR
    DeltaX,                (* The difference in the X direction *)
    DeltaY:                (* The difference in the Y direction *)
       Real;
```

Notice that aligning the comments gives the code a neater appearance and is less distracting.

3. *In-line comments* are used to break long sections of code into shorter, more comprehensible fragments. These are usually the names of modules in your top-down design, although you may occasionally choose to include other information. In-line comments should be surrounded by blank lines to make them stand out. (This was not done in this text to save space. We used color printing instead.) For example:

```
BEGIN   (* Main *)

  (* Initialize *)

  Reset(Infile);
  MinTemp := MaxInt;

  (* Get Data *)

  Readln(InFile, NumTemps);
```

Blank lines may be inserted wherever there is a logical break in the code that you would like to emphasize.

4. _Sidebar_ comments appear to the right of statements in the body of the program and are used to shed light on the function of the statement. Sidebar comments are often just pseudocode statements from the lowest levels of your top-down design. If a complicated Pascal statement requires some explanation, the pseudocode statement should be written to the right of the Pascal statement. For example:

```
IF EOF(File1) <> EOF(File2)   (* If one of the files is empty *)
  THEN
      .

      .
```

In addition to the four main types of comments that we have discussed, there are some miscellaneous comments that we should mention: (1) comments should be included at the main BEGIN and END of each procedure, function, and the main program; (2) a row of asterisks in a comment should appear before and after each procedure or function to help it to stand out. For example:

```
(*********************************************************)

PROCEDURE Balance (VAR Param1:      (* Definition of Param1 *)
                        Real);

BEGIN (* Balance *)
  .

  .
END;   (* Balance *)

(*********************************************************)
```

(3) We also recommend that you comment the END associated with every RECORD declaration and CASE statement to make them easier to debug. For example,

```
CASE Command OF
      .

      .
END; (* Case *)
```

Identifiers and Keywords

The most important consideration in choosing a name for an object or process in a program is that the name convey as much information as possible about what the object is or what the process does. The name should also be readable in the context in which it is used. For example, the following names convey the same information but one is more readable than the other:

> DateOfInvc   InvoiceDate

Identifiers for types, constants, or variables should be nouns, while names of procedures should be verbs. Because of the way that functions are called, function names should be nouns or occasionally adjectives. Here are some examples:

Variables	Address, Price, Radius, MonthNumber
Constants	Pi, TaxRate, StringLength, ArraySize
Data Types	Names, CarMakes, RoomLists, Hours
Procedures	GetData, ClearTable, PrintBarChart
Functions	CubeRoot, Greatest, Color, AreaOf

Although an identifier may be a series of words, very long identifiers can become quite tedious, and can make the program difficult to read.

The best approach to designing an identifier is to try writing out different names until you reach an acceptable compromise—and then write an especially informative definition comment next to the declaration.

Capitalization is another consideration when choosing an identifier. Some systems require the use of all capital letters, but most permit you to mix upper- and lowercase. In programs in the text, the first letter of every word in an identifier is capitalized.

We have written Pascal keywords in all capital letters to distinguish them from identifiers. Making the keywords stand out also helps you to quickly locate a particular statement in a long program.

Formatting Lines and Expressions

In general, it is best never to include more than one statement on a line. One exception would be when you must initialize a large array with specific values, where it is acceptable to neatly align the assignment statements in multiple columns. For example:

```
(* Initialize state abbreviations table *)

State[1]    := 'AL';          State[25]  := 'MT';
State[2]    := 'AK';          State[26]  := 'NE';
State[3]    := 'AZ';          State[27]  := 'NV';
State[4]    := 'AR';          State[28]  := 'NH';
    .  .

    .

State[24]  := 'MO';          State[50]  := 'WY';
```

When a long statement must be broken in the middle and continued onto the next line, it's important to choose a breaking point that is logical and readable. Compare the readability of the following code fragments.

```
Writeln('For a radius of ', Radius:1, 'the diameter of the cir',
        'cle is ', Diameter:1);

Writeln('For a radius of ', Radius:1,
        ' the diameter of the circle is ', Diameter:1);
```

When you must split an expression across multiple lines, try to end each line with an operator. Also, try to take advantage of any repeating patterns in the expression. For example,

```
MeanOfMaxima := Maximum(Set1Value1, Set1Value2, Set1Value3) +
                Maximum(Set2Value1, Set2Value2, Set2Value3) +
                Maximum(Set3Value1, Set3Value2, Set3Value3) / 3.0;
```

When writing expressions, also keep in mind that spaces improve readability. Usually you should include one space on either side of the := and most operators. Occasionally spaces are left out to emphasize the order in which operations are performed. Here are some examples:

```
IF X+Y > Y+Z
  THEN
    Maximum := X + Y
  ELSE
    Maximum := Y + Z;
Mileage := (FillUp1+FillUp2+FillUp3) / (EndMiles-StartMiles);
```

Indentation

The purpose of indenting statements in a program is to provide visual cues to the reader and to make the program easier to debug. When a program is properly indented, the way the statements are grouped is immediately obvious. Compare the following two program fragments:

```
WHILE Count <= 10 DO          WHILE Count <= 10 DO
BEGIN                         BEGIN
Readln(Num);                    Readln(Num);
IF Num = 0                      IF Num = 0
THEN                              THEN
BEGIN                               BEGIN
Count := Count + 1;                   Count := Count + 1;
Num := 1                              Num := 1
END;                                END;
Writeln(Num:1);                   Writeln(Num:1);
Writeln(Count:1)                  Writeln(Count:1)
END;                          END;
```

As a basic rule in this text, each nested or lower-level item is indented by two spaces.

Exceptions to this rule are formal parameters and statements that are split across two or more lines. Indenting by two spaces is really just a minimum. Many people prefer to indent by three, four, or even five spaces.

The remainder of this section is devoted to presenting examples of indentation for each Pascal statement, according to the style used in this book.

DECLARATIONS

In the text, constant and variable declarations are indented in the same way. The keyword (CONST or VAR) appears on a line by itself, indented to the same level as the program, procedure, or function heading that immediately precedes it. On succeeding lines, each constant or variable is listed, one per line, indented by two spaces, with a defining comment to the right. For variable declarations, all of the variables of a given type are grouped together, with the data type following on a separate line, indented by two additional spaces. Here is an example:

```
CONST
  Pi = 3.141592654;       (* Ratio of circumference to diameter *)
  E = 2.718281828;        (* Base of the natural logarithms      *)

VAR
  Radius,                 (* Radius of a circle       *)
  Diameter,               (* Diameter of a circle     *)
  Area:                   (* Area of a circle         *)
    Real;
  Count,                  (* Example number           *)
  MaxCircle,              (* Number of greatest circle *)
  MinCircle:              (* Number of smallest circle *)
    Integer;
```

Data type declarations are generally indented like constant declarations.

In the text, two different indentation styles are used in procedure and function declarations. When space permits, the parameter list begins on the same line as the procedure or function name. Each formal parameter is listed on a separate line, in a style similar to that used for the VAR declaration. In the following example, notice that blanks are used to highlight the formal value parameter:

```
PROCEDURE GetSum (    Number:    (* Number of values to be read *)
                        Integer;
                  VAR Sum:        (* Sum of values read          *)
                        Real);
```

Occasionally, we need more room for the comments. In such a case, we use a second style in which the parameter list appears on lines following the procedure or function name. In the following example, note that the parameter list is indented by two spaces.

```
PROCEDURE GetDataAverage
  (VAR Infile:        (* File of test scores                      *)
```

```
       Text;
   NumScores:    (* The number of scores to be read from Infile *)
       Integer;
VAR Average:     (* The average of the test scores              *)
       Real);
```

The local declarations and body of a procedure or function follow the same guidelines as the declarations and body of the main program. The only difference is that nested procedures or functions should be indented by two spaces for each level of nesting.

STATEMENTS

In general, any statement that is part of another statement is indented by two spaces in programs in the text; including compound statements, assignment statements, procedure calls, and nested statements.

Because the IF-THEN-ELSE contains two statements, separated by the keyword ELSE, the ELSE and THEN are written on separate lines, indented two spaces to the right of the IF. The statements within the branches of the IF-THEN-ELSE are then indented by two additional spaces. The IF-THEN statement is indented like the IF-THEN-ELSE, but without the ELSE branch. Here are examples of the IF-THEN-ELSE and IF-THEN.

```
IF Sex = Male
  THEN
    BEGIN
      MaleSalary := MaleSalary + Salary;
      MaleCount := MaleCount + 1
    END
  ELSE
    FemaleSalary := FemaleSalary + Salary;


IF Count > 0
  THEN
    Average := Total / Count;
```

For nested IF-THEN-ELSE statements that form a generalized CASE Statement (see Chapter 9), a special style of indentation is used in the text. Here is an example:

```
IF Month = January
  THEN
    MonthNumber := 1
  ELSE IF Month = February
  THEN
    MonthNumber := 2
  ELSE IF Month = March
  THEN
    MonthNumber := 3
  ELSE IF Month = April
      .
      .
```

```
                    ELSE
                       MonthNumber : = 12
```

The remaining Pascal statements all follow the basic indentation guideline mentioned previously. For reference purposes, here are examples of each.

```
WHILE Count <= 10 DO
   BEGIN
      Readln(Value);
      Sum : = Sum + Value;
      Count : = Count + 1
   END;

REPEAT
   GetAnswer(Letter);
   PutAnswer(Letter)
UNTIL Letter = 'N';

FOR Count : = 1 TO NumSales DO
   Write('*');

FOR Count : = 10 DOWNTO 1 DO
   BEGIN
      Readln(Infile, Data);
      Writeln(Outfile, Data, Count)
   END;

CASE Color OF
   Red     : Writeln('Red');
   Orange  : Writeln('Orange');
   Yellow  : Writeln('Yellow');
   Green,
   Blue,
   Indigo,
   Violet  : Writeln('Short visible wavelengths');
   White,
   Black   : BEGIN
                Writeln('Not valid colors');
                Color : = None
             END
END;  (* Case *)

WITH EmployeeRec DO
   BEGIN
      Writeln(Name);
      Writeln(Street);
      Writeln(City, State, Zip)
   END
```

Appendix H Additional Features of Pascal

Standard Pascal has some additional features not usually covered in a first course. The syntax diagrams in Appendix E describe the complete Pascal language and show some of these additional features.

For the sake of completeness, the additional features that are available in Pascal are described in this appendix. They include another structuring option for records (variant records), the use of functions and procedures as parameters, and a mechanism for forward referencing procedures and functions.

GOTO Statement

A GOTO statement, or unconditional branch, is provided in most common programming languages. Pascal is no exception, but, because all the control structures already exist, the GOTO should be rarely needed. In other languages an IF and a GOTO statement must be used to construct control structures. In Pascal the IF, CASE, WHILE, FOR, and REPEAT control structures are more convenient and make programs more readable; they make the flow of control clearer.

The GOTO statement passes control directly from one point in a program to another. The GOTO must specify the label of a statement to which control is transferred. The label must be declared in the declaration section of the block. These are the rules concerning the GOTO statement:

1. All labels must be declared.
2. Label declarations precede all others in the block.
3. Labels are unsigned integers in the range 0 to 9999.
4. Each label may be declared only once, and it may be used to label only one statement.
5. A GOTO branch into a control structure or block (procedure or function) is not permitted. A GOTO branch out of a control structure or a block is permitted.

In the following example, the commented statements are the equivalent control structures for the code using the GOTO.

```
PROGRAM Jump (Input, Output);

LABEL
   10, 20, 30, 40;

CONST
  N = 2000;

VAR
   Value, Sum:
     Integer;

BEGIN (* Jump *)
  Sum := 0;
  10: IF EOF                (* WHILE NOT EOF DO            *)
        THEN GOTO 20;       (*    BEGIN                    *)
      Readln(Value);        (*      Readln(Value);         *)
      Sum := Sum + Value;   (*      Sum := Sum + Value     *)
```

```
      GOTO 10;                 (*    END;                      *)
 20: IF Sum <= N               (* IF  Sum > N                  *)
       THEN GOTO 30;           (*                              *)
     Writeln('Minority');      (*     THEN Writeln('Minority') *)
     GOTO 40;                  (*                              *)
 30: Writeln('Majority');      (*     ELSE Writeln('Majority') *)
 40:
 END.     (* Jump *)
```

Structured programming is characterized by the use of control structures with only one entry and one exit. Use of the GOTO leads to unstructured programming: multiple entry and exits from control structures. This makes programs harder to read, understand, modify and debug. Because of this the GOTO should be avoided. Use it only for exceptional circumstances and forward (not backward) jumps, such as exiting a procedure or program due to certain error conditions.

Overuse of the GOTO statement in Pascal is poor programming practice. Pascal contains all the control structures necessary to write a program without the GOTO.

Variant Records

Within a record type, there may be some fields that are mutually exclusive. That is, fields A and B may never be in use at the same time. Instead of declaring a record variable large enough to contain all the possible fields, you can use the variant record provided in Pascal.

The variant record has two parts: the fixed part where the fields are always the same and the variant part where the fields will vary. Since only a portion of the variant fields are in use at any one time, they may share space in memory. The compiler need allocate only enough space for the record variable to include the largest variant.

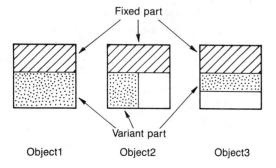

Fixed part

Variant part

Object1   Object2   Object3

If a record has both a fixed part and a variant part, the fixed part must be defined first. The following is an example of a record definition that contains a variant part.

```
TYPE
    Item = (Assembly, Nut, Bolt, Washer, Lock);
    PartType = RECORD
                   Id  : PACKED ARRAY[1..10] OF Char;
                   Qty : Integer;
                   Tag : Item;
                   CASE Item OF
```

```
              Assembly : (DrawingId : PACKED ARRAY
                                      [1..5] OF CHAR;
                     Code : 1..12;
                     Class : (A, B, C, D) );
          Nut, Bolt, Washer : ();
          Lock : (KeyNo : Integer)
       END;   (* Record *)
```

```
VAR
   Part:
      PartType;
```

When using a variant record variable, the user is responsible for accessing fields that are consistent with the Tag field. For example, if the Tag field is Nut, Bolt, or Washer, only the fixed fields can be accessed. If the Tag field is Lock, Part.KeyNo is a legal field reference. If the Tag field is Assembly, Part.DrawingId, Part.Code, and Part.Class are all legal references.

Several points should be made about defining and using variant records. We will use the above definition to illustrate.

1. A record definition may contain only one variant part, although field lists in the variant part may contain a variant part (nested variant).
2. All field identifiers within a record definition must be unique.
3. The tag field (Tag) is a separate field of a record (if present).
4. The tag field is used to indicate the variant used in a record variable.
5. The case clause in the variant part is not the same as a CASE statement.
   (a) There is no matching END for the CASE; the END of the record definition is used.
   (b) The case selector is a type (Item).
   (c) Each variant is a field list labeled by a case label list. Each label is a constant of the tag type (Item).
   (d) The field lists are in parentheses.
   (e) The field lists define the fields and field types of that variant.
6. The tag type can be any ordinal type, but it must be a type identifier.
7. Several labels can be used for the same variant (Nut, Bolt, Washer).
8. A field list can be empty, which is denoted by "( )".
9. The variant to be used is assigned at run-time. The variant can be changed by assignments to other variant fields and the tag field. When a variant is used, data (if any) in a previous variant is lost.
10. The tag field does not appear in the field selectors for the variant fields.
11. It is an error to access a field that is not part of the current variant.

The case clause in the variant part of the record definition is often matched by a CASE statement in the body of the program. For example, the following program fragment could be used to print data about a record.

```
Writeln('Part Id - ', APart.ID);
Writeln('Qty - ', APart.Qty:1);
CASE Tag OF
   Assembly : Writeln('Assembly : ', APart.DrawingID);
   Nut      : Writeln('Nut');
   Bolt     : Writeln('Bolt');
   Washer   : Writeln('Washer')
```

```
                           Lock :  Writeln('Lock, Key Attached')
                       END;    (* Case *)
```

Functions and Procedures as Parameters

In addition to variable and value parameters, Pascal allows procedures and functions to be passed as parameters. That is, the actual parameter is a procedure or function identifier. The only restriction is that only user defined procedures and functions may be passed as actual parameters.

This is a syntax diagram for a formal parameter list:

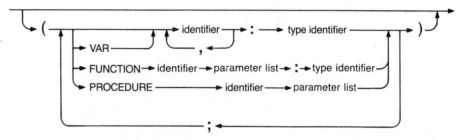

As an example, suppose we need a procedure that will find the minimum and maximum values of various functions within a specified range. The functions can be passed as a parameter to the procedure which can check the function's value at specified intervals.

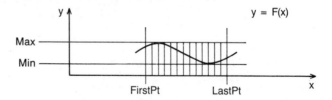

The following procedure will evaluate the function F at intervals between FirstPt and LastPt and return the minimum and maximum values in Min and Max.

```
PROCEDURE MinMax (Function F (Pt: Real: Real;  (* Function name        *)
                   FirstPt,                     (* First point to evaluate *)
                   LastPt,                      (* Last point to evaluate  *)
                   Interval:                    (* Interval between points *)
                     Real;                      (* to be evaluated         *)
              VAR
                   Min, (* Minimum value returned by F*)
                   Max: (* Maximum value returned by F*)
                     REAL;
VAR
  Result,              (* Value returned from function F*)
  EvalPt:              (* Point to be evaluated  '       *)
     REAL;
BEGIN (* MinMax *)
  (*Initialize Min and Max to first function value *)
  Min := F(FirstPt);
```

```
   Max := Min;
   EvalPt := FirstPt + Interval;
   WHILE EvalPt <= LastPt DO
      BEGIN
         Result := F(EvalPt);              (* Evaluate function F at EvalPt *)
         IF Result < Min
            THEN
               Min := Result;
         IF Result > Max
            THEN
               Max := Result;
         EvalPt := EvalPt + Interval
      END
END;      (* MinMax *)
```

The procedure calls the function specified for F in the call to MinMax. For example, the calls

```
MinMax (UserSIN, 0.5, 0.9, 0.01, Min, Max);
MinMax (Response, A, B, T, Min, Max);
MinMax (Poly, D1, D2, S, Min, Max)
```

are all valid calls to the procedure if UserSIN, Response, and Poly are declared real functions, with one real formal parameter each. The other actual parameters must be real—all parameters must match in type.

The call to function F within MinMax would substitute the function specified in the call to MinMax. For example,

```
Result := F(EvalPt)
```

within MinMax would be evaluated as

```
Result := Response(EvalPt)
```

if Response was specified in the call to MinMax.

Forward Statement

Identifiers in Pascal must be defined before being used (the type identifier in the pointer type definition is an exception). Recursion was defined as a procedure or function calling itself. There are recursive situations where one procedure or function calls another which in turn calls the first. This is called mutual recursion.

.

.

```
(*************************************************************)

PROCEDURE One (VAR A : AType);
BEGIN

   .

   .

   Two (X);

   .

   .
```

```
END;

(*******************************************************************)

PROCEDURE Two  (VAR B : BType);
BEGIN
    .
    .
  One (Y) ;
    .
    .
END;

(*******************************************************************)
    .
    .
```

In the above example, the call to procedure Two in the body of procedure One is not allowed because procedure Two has not yet been defined. The solution to this problem is to make a forward reference to procedure Two by using the FORWARD directive.

```
    .
    .

(*******************************************************************)

PROCEDURE Two  (VAR B : BType);
FORWARD;

(*******************************************************************)

PROCEDURE One  (VAR A : AType);
BEGIN
    .
    .
  Two (X) ;
    .
    .
END;

(*******************************************************************)

PROCEDURE Two;
BEGIN
    .
    .
  One (Y) ;
    .
    .
END;

(*******************************************************************)
```

Notice that the parameter list (and the result type for a function) is written in the forward reference; it is *not* repeated in the actual declaration of the procedure (or function). The compiler "remembers" the parameter declarations when it encounters the actual procedure.

Appendix I   Implementations

(This appendix is not written for the beginning student; an understanding of Pascal is assumed.)

This book has presented standard Pascal as described in international and American standards (ISO/DIS 7185 and ANSI/IEEE 770 × 3.97-1983). Although Pascal was originally designed as a teaching tool, its popularity as a commercial language has grown. Today, almost every major brand of computer, from microcomputers to mainframes, has at least one Pascal compiler written for it. Pascal implementations for use in commercial environments generally have extensions to the original language such as interactive I/O, random access to file components and additional character string processing and manipulation features.

Brief descriptions of two popular implementations of Pascal, including some of their extensions to standard Pascal, are given in this appendix. CDC Pascal 6000 is a mainframe implementation that is fairly close to standard Pascal. UCSD Pascal (developed at the University of California at San Diego) is representative of a number of microcomputer implementations.

CDC Pascal 6000

Pascal was originally implemented on a CDC 6600. This implementation is in widespread use, especially at universities. This implementation conforms closely to standard Pascal but includes some additional features which we will describe here.

There are now two principal implementations of Pascal for CDC machines. These are CDC Pascal and University of Minnesota Pascal 6000. The two implementations are very similar.

CDC Pascal is an ISO standard implementation of Pascal with some extensions and limitations that are specific to CDC machines. For example, CDC Pascal requires programs to be written in the CDC scientific character set, which does not include lowercase letters.

Minnesota Pascal 6000 is very similar to CDC Pascal. It is essentially ISO standard with only a few minor differences. In Minnesota, Pascal includes the CDC extensions and even more. In particular, with release 4 of Pascal 6000, the user is allowed to choose between the CDC scientific character set and the ASCII character set. The latter permits programs to be written in upper- and lowercase. Pascal 6000 also provides a facility for separately compiling collections of subprograms that can then be used in other programs.

This section describes the features that are common to both of these implementations. Keep in mind, however, that each implementation of Pascal will have restrictions imposed by the particular machine. CDC machines can have one of several character sets. You will need to check your implementation for this and other features such as the value of MaxInt or the precision of real numbers.

If no fieldwidth is specified in the Write statement, the following default values will be used.

integer	10 columns
real	22 columns
Boolean	10 columns
char	1 column

Sets are limited to 59 components. Trailing blanks in lines of text files may be truncated (do not assume lines to be 80 characters), so use the EOLN function to check for line boundaries. The file list in the program heading must contain the file Output.

CDC Pascal and Minnesota Pascal 6000 contain some extensions to the language including segmented files, the provision to call external library routines (procedures and functions) and a string type called Alfa. Additional built-in procedures and functions are also provided.

Segmented files allow faster access to any part of a file. A segmented file is composed of segments. A file Data can be declared as a segmented file

```
VAR Data : Segmented File of component type;
```

and additional built-in procedures and functions used to manipulate it. Reset(Data), Rewrite(Data), EOLN(Data) and Put(Data) work as usual. Get(Data) must not be used if either EOS(Data) or EOF(Data) is True. Read and Write can be used with segmented textfiles.

EOS(Data) returns True if file Data is positioned at the end of a segment, otherwise False. Returns True whenever EOF(Data) is True.

PutSeg(Data) terminates a segment of file Data. Used after data has been written to the file with a Write or Put.

GetSeg(Data) positions the file Data at the beginning of the next segment. Get or Read may then be used to read the next component.

GetSeg(Data, N) positions the file Data at the beginning of the Nth segment from the current file position. N > 0 causes a forward count; N < 0 causes a backward count; N = 0 positions the file at the beginning of the current segment.

Rewrite(Data, N) prepares the file Data for writing at the beginning of the Nth segment from the current file position.

Precompiled library routines external to the program can be called from the program. The declaration to these external procedures (or functions) is in the form

```
PROCEDURE Example (VAR Par1 : Integer; Par2 : Real);
Extern;
```

or

```
PROCEDURE Example2 (VAR Par1 : Integer; Par2 : Real);
FORTRAN;
```

depending on whether a Pascal or FORTRAN library is being accessed.

Alfa is an additional predefined type

```
TYPE Alfa = PACKED ARRAY[1..10] OF Char;
```

that is, a string variable of exactly 10 characters. It can be used like any packed array as described in this book.

The following are some of the additional built-in procedures:

Date(string)	assigns the current date in the format "yy/mm/dd" to the string variable (of type Alpha) specified.
Time(string)	assigns the current time in the format "hh.mm.ss" to the string variable (of type Alpha) specified.
Message(string)	writes the string specified into the dayfile. (Maximum string length of 40.)
Halt	aborts the program and prints a post-mortem dump.

and functions:

Clock	returns the number of milliseconds of elapsed processor time since job initiation.
Card(set)	returns the cardinality (number of members) of the set specified.
Expo(number)	returns the contents of the exponent part of the real number specified.
Undefined(number)	returns True if the value of the number specified is indefinite or out-of-range.

This description of CDC Pascal and Minnesota Pascal 6000 is based upon the discussion of the implementation in the _Pascal User Manual and Report,_ by Jensen and Wirth. Newer versions will vary, and you should refer to the manual for your local implementation. For example, some versions provide for interactive I/O. One approach lets Input be declared as the keyboard if a slash is placed in the program heading.

```
PROGRAM Inter (Input/, Output);
```

This approach also requires that a Readln with no parameters appear between the first input prompt and the corresponding Read or Readln that gets the data. For example,

```
Writeln('Enter a number: ');
Readln;
Read(Number);
```

UCSD Pascal

UCSD Pascal includes its own operating system and utilities such as a filter, editor, linker, and assembler. We only discuss its variations from, and extensions to, standard Pascal here. You should refer to the manual for information on using its operating system and system utilities.

There are several versions of UCSD Pascal in existence, and some limits and capabilities will vary among versions.

This implementation has some differences from standard Pascal. Boolean variables cannot be printed by a Write statement. Procedures and functions cannot be used as parameters to procedures or functions. The Dispose procedure is not implemented, but memory can be recovered by using the additional procedures Mark and Release. The procedures Pack and Unpack are not provided since their operation is automatic when manipulating a packed variable in UCSD Pascal. Sets are limited to 4080 components (may be different in your version). Arrays or records of the same type can be compared for equality or inequality ('=' or '<>'). If none of the case labels in a CASE statement matches the value of the case selector, then no action is taken and execution continues with the next statement. The file list in the program heading is ignored (and is therefore unnecessary); filenames are specified in the procedures Reset and Rewrite.

Interactive I/O is provided by the additional file type Interactive. Input, Output and Keyboard are defined as being of type Interactive. Input is composed of characters typed at the terminal keyboard which are echoed on the terminal screen. Keyboard is the same as Input except there is no echo on the screen. Output is the screen. Input from interactive files is different from normal files. A

```
Read (F,  CH)
```

from an Interactive file F is equivalent to

```
Get (F) ;
Ch  : = F^
```

which is the reverse of a normal file. When the Interactive file is opened, the file buffer is empty since a character has not been typed yet. EOLN and EOF for interactive files remain False until the explicit end-of-line character (carriage-return) for EOLN or the end-of-file character for EOF is typed. Your code will probably need to be modified when reading from interactive files as opposed to normal text files.

Files internal to the program use Reset and Rewrite as usual. Reset is automatically performed on Input and Keyboard, as is Rewrite on Output. Other external files require a special form of Reset and Rewrite to associate the file variable with a specific file or device.

Reset(F, 'filename')   performs a reset of the file specified by 'file-name' (can be a string variable or constant) and associates the file variable F with this file.

Rewrite(F, 'filename')   as above in Reset but opens the file for writing.

Random access to any record in a file of records is provided by the Seek procedure. The syntax to this extension is in the form

```
Seek (file variable,  record number) ;
```

where the records are numbered sequentially from zero to the last record in the file. Performing a Seek for a record number that is too large causes EOF(file variable) to be True. After performing a Seek for a particular record, it can be read using the Get procedure or overwritten using the Put procedure. Two Seeks in succession to the same file without an intervening Get or Put should not be attempted.

A predefined type String is provided for easier string manipulation. Variables of type String are actually packed arrays of type Char but with a length attribute that can vary dynamically from zero to a maximum of 255. The default length of this type is 80,

```
TYPE
    String = PACKED ARRAY[1..80] OF Char;
```

but this limit can be set to any length up to 255.

```
VAR
    Line : String;          (* Default maximum length of 80 *)
    Word : String[10];      (* Maximum length of 10         *)
    Para : String[255];     (* Maximum length of 255        *)
```

The actual length of the string variable is determined by the data stored in it (blank fill is not required). Unequal length strings may be compared (the ordering is based upon the lexicographic ordering of the character set). Any size string value may be assigned to a string variable as long as it does not exceed the maximum length of the variable. String variables may be indexed (a particular character accessed) as in any array as long as the current dynamic length of the string is not exceeded (otherwise an index-out-of-range error is generated).

Direct string Reads are allowed. However, only one string should be read at a time since the termination of an input string is indicated by <eoln>. If S1 and S2 are variables of type String and the statement

```
Readln(S1, S2)
```

is executed, the string S2 will be empty.

If a string variable is a parameter of a Write statement, only the actual string is printed (in a field width equal to the current dynamic length).

To manipulate strings more easily and increase their usefulness, UCSD Pascal provides several additional string functions:

Length(string)	returns the integer value of the length of the string specified.
Copy(source string, index, size)	returns a string of the size specified taken from the source string beginning at the index position of the source string.
Concat(string list)	returns a string which is the concatenation of the strings specified. The string list is composed of any number of source strings separated by commas.
Pos(pattern string, source string)	returns the beginning index position of the first occurrence in the source string of the pattern string. If no match is found, Pos returns 0.

and procedures:

Delete(destination string, index, size)	removes a substring of the size specified from the destination string beginning at the index specified.

Insert(source string, desti-   inserts the source string into the destination string begin-
nation string, index)   ning at the index specified of the destination string.

An individual character value may be assigned to a specific cell in a string by specifying the index. However, such an assignment does not affect the Length of a string, so the length can become incorrect. To maintain the integrity of the Length of a string, use a full string (nonindexed) assignment or a string procedure or function to change the value of a string.

Since a memory word length in microcomputers severely limits the value of MaxInt, another scalar type, Long Integer, is provided. Long integers may be up to 36 digits. They are declared by using a length attribute in the type definition. For example, a long integer variable that could have a value of up to 15 digits in length could be declared by

```
VAR
  Big : Integer[15];
```

Long integers are used just like integers; however, long integer results cannot be assigned to integer variables. A long integer value can be converted to an integer value by using the Trunc procedure as long as the value is less than MaxInt.

UCSD supports the separate compilation of program modules. This is convenient for several reasons. Commonly used procedures can be kept in an external library of routines and called when needed. Also, program modifications can be made without requiring the entire program to be compiled again. This is particularly time-saving during program development when bugs can crop up frequently. These separate program modules are called units.

There are three kinds of units: intrinsic, regular, and separate. Intrinsic units are stored in the system library. Regular units actually become part of the calling program's codefile. Separate units are like regular units, but only those portions actually used by the calling program are placed in the calling program's codefile.

All units are composed of a heading, an Interface part, an Implementation part, and initialization code. The heading specifies the type of unit (intrinsic, regular, or separate). The Interface includes all of the declarations and definitions available to the calling program. The Implementation part contains the code for procedures and functions declared in the Interface part and any other declarations and definitions needed (these are not accessible to the calling program). The initialization code is used to initialize the unit and is not accessible to the calling program. The following is an example of a regular unit.

```
UNIT JustAnExample;                              (* Unit heading *)

(*******************************************************************)

INTERFACE                 (* Global declarations and definitions *)
  CONST
    Pi= 3.14;
  TYPE
    Blob = (Soft, Hard, Squishy);
  VAR
    Framus : String[15];
  PROCEDURE DoWhatcha(Num : Integer);
  FUNCTION Devious(LowDown : Real) : Boolean;

(*******************************************************************)
```

```
IMPLEMENTATION           (* Local declarations and definitions *)
  CONST
    OnlyHere = 22;
  TYPE
    Light = 1..6;
  VAR
    Ctr:
      Integer;
    Name:
      String[20];
    Flag:
      Boolean;


(***********************************************************)


  PROCEDURE DoWhatcha;
  BEGIN
    (* Procedure body *)
  END;


(***********************************************************)


  FUNCTION Devious;
  BEGIN
    (* Function body *)
  END;


(***********************************************************)


BEGIN                              (* Unit initialization code *)
  (* Initialization code *)
END.
```

Units used in a calling program must be declared immediately after the program heading. For example, the calling program indicates that it uses the above Unit JustAnExample as follows.

```
PROGRAM Caller;
Uses JustAnExample;
CONST ...
      .

      .
```

Large programs may easily fill available memory, especially on a microcomputer. To allow programs to be larger than available memory, UCSD Pascal provides for a memory overlay technique through SEGMENT procedures and functions. This means that not all of the program has to be in memory at the same time, only the part being executed.

To declare a procedure or function as a program segment requires only that the additional reserved word SEGMENT precede the procedure or function declaration.

```
PROGRAM Segmented;

(* Declarations *)

(************************************************************)

Segment Procedure One;
BEGIN (* One *)

  (* Procedure body *)

END; (* One *)

(************************************************************)

SEGMENT Function Two;
BEGIN (* Two *)

  (* Function body *)

END; (* Two *)

(************************************************************)

PROCEDURE Three;
BEGIN (* Three *)

  (* Procedure body *)

END; (* Three *)

(************************************************************)

BEGIN (* Segmented *)

  (* Main program *)

END. (* Segmented *)
```

Segment procedures and functions must precede any other executable blocks of code (procedures, functions or main program) in the program. The number of segments allowed depends on the version of UCSD Pascal you are using (anywhere from seven to 255). Each unit as well as the main program counts as a segment.

The GOTO statement is more restricted in UCSD Pascal than in standard Pascal: only a branch to a label that is local to the same block containing the GOTO is allowed. The Exit statement is provided to permit a clean exit from a procedure, function or program. It is useful for exiting a block (particularly a complicated or deeply nested block) when an error is encountered. Exit requires a parameter to indicate the procedure, function or program to be exited.

Exit (identifier)

The Exit statement must be within the scope of its parameter. As with the GOTO, the Exit should be used sparingly and with care to avoid poor program structure.

The following are some of the additional built-in procedures:

Mark(heappointer)	assigns to the heappointer the current top-of-heap. The heappointer is a user-defined pointer of type ^Integer used to keep the location of the heap in memory.
Release(heappointer)	assigns to the top-of-heap pointer the value of the heap-pointer.
MoveLeft(source, destination, length)	moves from the source string to the destination string, starting from the left, the number of characters specified by length.
MoveRight(source, destination, length)	moves from the source string to the destination string, starting from the right, the number of characters specified by length.
FillChar(destination, length, character)	fills the destination string with the character specified to the length specified.
GoToXY(x-coordinate, y-coordinate)	positions the cursor on the terminal screen at the coordinates specified. The top-left corner of the screen is position (0, 0).

and functions:

SizeOf(type or variable identifier)	returns the size in bytes of the entity specified by the identifier.
MemAvail	returns the number of words of memory available (the memory words between the top-of-stack and top-of-heap).
Scan(length, partial expression, array)	returns the number of characters scanned of the array. Termination of the scan is caused by matching the specified length or satisfying the expression. The partial expression may be either '<>' or '=' followed by a character value.
Log(number)	returns the log base 10 of the number.
PwrOften(exponent)	returns the value of 10 to the exponent power.

Appendix J   Character Sets

The following charts show the ordering of the most common character sets: ASCII (American Standard Code for Information Interchange), EBCDIC (Extended Binary Coded Decimal Interchange Code) and CDC Scientific. Only printable characters are shown. The ordinal number for each character is shown in decimal. The blank character is denoted by a "□".

Left Digit(s)	Right Digit → ASCII 0	1	2	3	4	5	6	7	8	9
3			□	!	"	#	$	%	&	'
4	(	)	*	+	,	−	.	/	0	1
5	2	3	4	5	6	7	8	9	:	;
6	<	=	>	?	@	A	B	C	D	E
7	F	G	H	I	J	K	L	M	N	O
8	P	Q	R	S	T	U	V	W	X	Y
9	Z	[	\	]	^	_	`	a	b	c
10	d	e	f	g	h	i	j	k	l	m
11	n	o	p	q	r	s	t	u	v	w
12	x	y	z	{	|	}	~			

Codes 00–31 and 127 are nonprintable control characters.

Left Digit(s)	Right Digit → EBCDIC 0	1	2	3	4	5	6	7	8	9
6					□					
7					¢	.	<	(	+	|
8	&									
9	!	$	*	)	;	¬				
10							^	,	%	—
11	>	?								
12			:	#	@	'	=	"		a
13	b	c	d	e	f	g	h	i		
14						j	k	l	m	n
15	o	p	q	r						
16			s	t	u	v	w	x	y	z
17								\	{	}
18	[	]								
19				A	B	C	D	E	F	G
20	H	I								J
21	K	L	M	N	O	P	Q	R		
22							S	T	U	V
23	W	X	Y	Z						
24	0	1	2	3	4	5	6	7	8	9

Codes 00–63 and 250–255 are nonprintable control characters.

Left Digit(s)	Right Digit → CDC 0	1	2	3	4	5	6	7	8	9
0	:	A	B	C	D	E	F	G	H	I
1	J	K	L	M	N	O	P	Q	R	S
2	T	U	V	W	X	Y	Z	0	1	2
3	3	4	5	6	7	8	9	+	−	*
4	/	(	)	$	=	□	,	.	≡	[
5	]	%	≠	↱	∨	∧	↑	↓	<	>
6	≤	≥	¬	;						

Glossary

actual parameter   a variable constant or expression listed in the call to a procedure (Ch. 6)

algorithm   a step-by-step procedure for solving a problem in a finite amount of time; a verbal or written description of a logical sequence of actions (Ch. 1)

ALU   see *arithmetic/logic unit*

anonymous type   a type defined in the VAR section of a program, so called because it does not have an identifier (a name) associated with it (Ch. 10)

arithmetic/logic unit (ALU)   the computer component that performs arithmetic operations (addition, subtraction, multiplication, division) and logical operations (comparison of two values) (Ch. 1)

array   a collection of components, all of the same type, ordered on N dimensions (N >= 1); each component is accessed by N indices, each of which represents the component's position within that dimension (Ch. 13)

assembler   a program that translates an assembly language program into machine code (Ch. 1)

assembly language   a low-level programming language in which a mnemonic is used to represent each of the machine language instructions for a particular computer (Ch. 1)

assignment   the action that gives the value of an expression to a variable (Ch. 2)

assignment compatible   implies that the types are compatible and the value being stored in a variable is within the range allowed for that variable (Ch. 10)

atomic data type   a data type that allows only a single value to be associated with an identifier of that type (Ch. 9)

automatic range-checking   the automatic detection of the assignment of an out-of-range value to a variable (Ch. 10)

auxiliary storage device   a device that stores data in coded form, external to the computer's memory (Ch. 1)

base case   the case for which the solution can be stated nonrecursively (Ch. 17)

batch processing   a technique for entering data and executing programs without intermediate user interaction with the computer (Ch. 1)

binary   expressed in terms of combinations of the numbers 1 and 0 only (Ch. 1)

binary file   a file that is created within one program to be read by another program or by the same program at a later date; such a file is written in the internal representation of a machine (Ch. 15)

binary search   a search algorithm for sorted lists that involves dividing the list in half and determining, by value comparison, whether the item would be in the upper or lower half; the process is performed repeatedly until either the item is found or it is determined that the item is not on the list (Ch. 12)

binary search tree   a binary tree in which the information in any node is greater than the information in its left child and any of its children (left subtree) and less than the information in its right child and any of its children (right subtree) (Ch. 16)

bit   short for binary digit; a single 1 or 0 (Ch. 1)

block   the declaration and statement sections of a program, procedure, or function (Ch. 2)

Boolean   data type consisting of only two values: True and False (Ch. 2)

Boolean operators   operations applied to values of the type Boolean; in Pascal these are the special symbols AND, OR, and NOT (Ch. 4)

Boolean expression an assertion that can be evaluated as being either True or False, the only values of the Boolean data type (Ch. 4)

booting the system the process of starting up a computer by loading the operating system into its main memory (Ch. 1)

branch see *selection*

branching control structure see *selection control structure*

case label list a list of values of the same type as the case selector, appearing in the body of the CASE statement (Ch. 9)

case selector the ordinal expression or variable whose value determines which case label list is selected (cannot be Real) (Ch. 9)

central processing unit (CPU) the part of the computer that executes the instructions of a program stored in memory; computer component composed of the arithmetic/logic unit (ALU), memory unit and control unit (Ch. 1)

char data type consisting of one alphanumeric character (letter, digit, or special symbol) (Ch. 2)

Chr an operation that takes an ordinal position and returns the character in that position (Ch. 10)

coding translating an algorithm into a programming language; also, the process of assigning bit patterns to pieces of information (Ch. 1)

collating sequence the ordering of the elements of a set or series, such as the characters (values) in a character set (Ch. 10)

compatibility a property of data types if they have the same type definition or type identifier, if they are subranges of the same host type, or if one is a subrange of the other (Ch. 10)

compiler a program that translates a high-level language (such as Pascal, COBOL, or FORTRAN) into machine code (Ch. 1)

compiler listing a copy of a program into which have been inserted messages from the compiler (indicating errors in the program that prevent its translation into machine language if appropriate) (Ch. 1)

composite data type a data type that allows a collection of values to be associated with an identifier of that type (Ch. 9)

compound statement any group of statements enclosed by the keywords BEGIN and END (Ch. 2)

computer a programmable electronic device that can store, retrieve, and process data (Ch. 1)

computer program a sequence of instructions outlining steps to be performed by a computer (Ch. 1)

computer programming the process of planning a sequence of instructions for a computer to follow (Ch. 1)

constant an item in a program whose value is fixed at compile time and cannot be changed during execution (Ch. 2)

control abstraction the separation of the logical properties of a control structure from its implementation (Ch. 10)

control unit the computer component that controls the actions of the other components in order to execute instructions (the program) in sequence (Ch. 1)

count-controlled loop a loop that executes a known number of times (Ch. 5)

counter a variable whose value is incremented to keep track of the number of times a process or event occurs (Ch. 5)

CPU see *central processing unit*

crash the cessation of a computer's operations as a result of the failure of one of its components (Ch. 1)

cursor control keys a special set of keys on a computer keyboard, which allow the user to move the cursor up, down, right, and left to any point on the screen (Ch. 1)

data information that has been put into a form usable by a computer—that is, a form suitable for analysis or decision making (Ch. 1)

data abstraction the separation of the logical properties of a data structure from its implementation (Ch. 14)

data type the general form of a class of data items; a formal description of the set of values (called the domain) that a variable or constant of that type can have and of the basic set of operations that can be applied to values of that type (Ch. 2, Ch. 10)

data validation a test added to a program or a procedure that checks for errors in the data (Ch. 7)

debugging the process by which errors are removed from a program so that it does exactly what it is supposed to do (Ch. 1)

decision see *selection*

declaration a statement that associates an identifier with a process or object so that the user can refer to that process or object by name (Ch. 2)

documentation written text and comments that make a program easier for others to understand, use, and modify (Ch. 1)

down a descriptive term applied to a computer when it is not in a usable condition (Ch. 1)

driver a simple dummy main program that is used to call a procedure or function being tested (Ch. 7)

dynamic data structure a data structure that can expand and contract during program execution (Ch. 16)

dynamic variable   a variable created during execution of a program and hence not declared in the declaration section of a program (Ch. 15)

echo printing   printing the data values input to a program so that it can be verified that they are correct (Ch. 3)

editor   an interactive program that is used to create and modify source programs or data (Ch. 1)

empty set   the set with no members at all (Ch. 9)

enumerated data type   an ordered set of literal values (identifiers) defined as a data type in a program (Ch. 10)

event-controlled loop   a loop that terminates when something happens inside of the loop body to signal that the loop should be exited (Ch. 5)

event counter   a counter variable that is incremented each time a particular event occurs (Ch. 5)

executing   the action of a computer performing as instructed by a given program (Ch. 1)

execution summary   a computer-generated list of all commands processed and any system messages generated during batch processing (Ch. 1)

external file   a file that is used to communicate with people or programs and is stored externally to the program (Ch. 15)

external pointer (to a list)   a named pointer variable that references the first node in a linked list (Ch. 16)

field identifier   the name of a component in a record (Ch. 14)

field selector   the expression used to access components of a record variable, formed using the record variable name and the field identifier, separated by a period (Ch. 14)

fieldwidth   the total number of columns (character positions) allotted to an output value in a Write or Writeln statement (Ch. 2)

file   an area in the computer's memory that has a name and is used to hold a collection of data; the collection of data itself (Ch. 1)

file buffer variable   a variable of the same type as the components of the file with which it is associated; it is automatically created by the system when a file variable is declared and is denoted by the file variable name followed by an up arrow ($\uparrow$) or up caret (^) (Ch. 15)

file data type   a collection of components, all of the same data type, accessed sequentially, one component at a time (Ch. 15)

flag   a Boolean variable that is set in one part of the program and tested in another to control the logical flow of a program (Ch. 5)

floating point number   the value stored in a type Real variable, so called because part of the memory

location is assumed to hold the exponent and the balance of the location the number itself, with the decimal point floating as necessary among the significant digits (Ch. 8)

flow of control   the order of execution of the statements in a program (Ch. 4)

formal parameter   a variable declared in a procedure heading (Ch. 6)

formal parameter declaration   the code that associates a formal parameter identifier with a data type and a passing mechanism (Ch. 6)

formatting   the planned positioning of statements or declarations and blanks on a line of a program; the arranging of program output so that it is neatly spaced and aligned (Ch. 2)

function   a subprogram that is called from within an expression, and in which a single value (for example, the square root of a number) is computed and returned to the main program through the subprogram name (Ch. 2, 8)

functional modules   in top-down design, the structured tasks and subtasks that are solved individually to create an effective program (Ch. 3)

functional problem description   a description that clearly states what a program is to do (Ch. 3)

function call   an expression in the main program requiring the computer to execute a function subprogram (Ch. 3)

function definition   that portion of a function subprogram appearing in a declaration section (Ch. 8)

function result   the value computed by the function subprogram and then returned to the main program; often called just the result (Ch. 2)

function result type   the data type of the result value returned by a function; often referred to simply as function type (Ch. 8)

function type   see *function result type*

general case   in a recursive definition, the case for which the solution is expressed in terms of a smaller version of itself; recursive case (Ch. 17)

global   a descriptive term applied to any identifier declared in the main program, because it is accessible to everything that follows it (Ch. 7)

hardware   the physical components of a computer (Ch. 1)

heuristics   assorted problem-solving strategies used to solve problems (Ch. 2)

hierarchical records   records in which at least one of the fields is itself a record (Ch. 14)

homogeneous   a descriptive term applied to structures in which all components are of the same data type (such as an array) (Ch. 13)

identifiers   names associated with processes and objects and used to refer to those processes and objects within a program; in Pascal they are made up of letters and numbers, but must begin with a letter (Ch. 2)

implementation phase the second set of steps in programming a computer: translating (code) the algorithm into a programming language; testing the resulting program by running it on a computer, checking for accuracy, and making any necessary corrections; using the program (Ch. 1)

implementing coding and testing an algorithm (Ch. 1)

infinite loop a loop whose termination condition is never reached and which therefore is never exited without intervention from outside of the program (Ch. 5)

infinite recursion the situation in which a subprogram calls itself over and over without end (Ch. 8)

information any knowledge that can be communicated (Ch. 1)

in place describes a kind of sorting algorithm in which the components in an array are sorted without the use of a second array (Ch. 12)

input the process of placing values from an outside data set into variables in a program; the data may come from either an input device (terminal keyboard or card reader) or an auxiliary storage device (such as a disk or tape) (Ch. 3)

input/output (I/O) devices the parts of a computer that accept data to be processed (input) and/or present the results of the processing (output) (Ch. 1)

input prompts messages printed by an interactive program, explaining what data is to be entered (Ch. 3)

insertion sort a sorting algorithm in which values are placed one at a time into their proper position within a list that was originally empty (Ch. 12)

integer number a positive or negative whole number made up of a sign and digits (when the sign is omitted, a positive sign is assumed) (Ch. 2)

interactive system a system for direct communication between the user and the computer; a terminal/computer connection allowing direct entry of programs and data and providing immediate feedback to the user (Ch. 1)

interface a connecting link (such as a computer terminal) at a shared boundary, permitting independent systems (such as the user and the computer) to meet and act on or communicate with each other; the combination of formal and actual parameters that allows communication between a main program and a procedure (Ch. 1, Ch. 6)

internal file a file that is created but not saved; also called a scratch file (Ch. 15)

invoke to call on a subprogram, causing the subprogram to execute before control is returned to the statement following the call (Ch. 6)

iteration an individual pass through, or repetition of, the body of a loop (Ch. 5)

iteration counter a counter variable that is incremented for each iteration of a loop (Ch. 5)

leaf nodes nodes in a binary tree structure whose left child and right child are both NIL (Ch. 16)

left child (of a node) root of left subtree of the node (Ch. 16)

length in reference to an array, the number of actual data values contained therein (Ch. 11)

linked list a list in which the order of the components is determined by an explicit link field in each node rather than by the physical order of the components in memory (Ch. 16)

literal constant any constant value written in a program (Ch. 2)

local variable variable declared within a procedure subprogram and accessible only within the block in which it was declared; the value of this variable is destroyed when the procedure returns control to the calling program (Ch. 6)

logging off informing a computer—usually through a simple command—that no further commands will follow (Ch. 1)

logging on taking the preliminary steps necessary to identify one's self to a computer so that it will accept one's commands (Ch. 1)

logical order the order in which the user wants the statements in a program to be executed, which may differ from the physical order in which they appear (Ch. 4)

loop a method of structuring statements so that they are repeated while certain conditions are met (Ch. 1)

loop control variable (LCV) a variable whose value is used to determine whether the loop will execute another iteration or exit (Ch. 5)

loop exit the point in the execution of a loop when repetition of the body ends and control passes to the first statement following the loop (Ch. 5)

loop invariant those conditions that must exist at the start of each iteration of a particular loop in order for the loop to execute properly (Ch. 5)

machine language the language used directly by the computer and composed of binary-coded instructions (Ch. 1)

mainframe a large computing system designed for high-volume processing or for use by many people at once (Ch. 1)

maintenance the modification of a program, after it has been completed, in order to meet changing requirements or to take care of any errors that show up (Ch. 1)

mantissa with respect to floating point representation of Real numbers, the digits representing a number itself and not its exponent (Ch. 8)

MaxInt the predefined identifier in Pascal whose value is set to the largest integer number that can be represented in a given computer (Ch. 2)

memory unit the internal data storage of a computer (Ch. 1)

minicomputer a computer system larger than a personal computer but smaller than a mainframe; sometimes called an entry-level mainframe (Ch. 1)

modular programming see *top-down design*

module nesting chart a chart that depicts the nesting structure of modules and shows calls among them (Ch. 7)

named constant a location in memory, referenced by a constant name (identifier), where a data value is stored (this value cannot be changed) (Ch. 2)

name precedence the priority treatment (precedence) accorded to a local identifier over a global identifier with the same spelling in any references that the procedure or function makes to that identifier (Ch. 7)

named type a type defined in the TYPE section of a program, procedure, or function (Ch. 10)

nested control structure a program structure consisting of one control statement (selection, iteration, or procedure) embedded within another control statement (Ch. 4)

nested IF an IF that is within another IF (Ch. 4)

nested loop a loop that is within another loop (Ch. 5)

nested procedure a procedure that is defined within another procedure (Ch. 7)

nodes the building blocks of dynamic structures, each made up of a component (the data) and a pointer (the link) to the next node (Ch. 16)

nonlocal a descriptive term applied to any identifier declared outside of a given block (Ch. 7)

nonlocal access access by a procedure of any identifier declared outside of its own block (Ch. 7)

null statement an empty statement (Ch. 2)

object program the machine language version of a program that results when a compiler translates a source program into the binary codes for a particular computer (Ch. 1)

Odd a predefined Boolean function that takes an Integer operand and gives a value of True if the operand is odd (not divisible by 2) or False otherwise (Ch. 4)

one-dimensional array a structured collection of components of the same type, given a single name; each component is accessed by an index that indicates its position within the collection (Ch. 11)

operating system a set of programs that manages all computer resources; it can input a program, call the compiler, execute the resulting object program, and carry out any other system commands (Ch. 1)

Ord an operation that returns the position of a value in the ordering of an ordinal data type (Ch. 10)

ordinal data types data types in which each value (except the first) has a unique predecessor and each value (except the last) has a unique successor (Ch. 10)

packed array a special type of one-dimensional array in which data is stored in as little memory space as possible. A packed array whose elements are of type Char is called a string and has special properties in Pascal (Ch. 12)

parameter list a mechanism for communicating with a subprogram, via which data may be given to the subprogram and/or results received from it (Ch. 2)

password a unique series of letters assigned to a user (and known only by that user) by which that user identifies himself or herself to a computer during the logging on procedure; a password system protects information stored in a computer from being tampered with or destroyed (Ch. 1)

PC see *personal computer*

peripheral device an input, output, or auxiliary storage device of a computer (Ch. 1)

personal computer (PC) a small computer system (usually intended to fit on a desk top) that is designed to be used primarily by a single person (Ch. 1)

pointer a simple data type consisting of an unbounded set of values, each of which addresses or otherwise indicates the location of a variable of a given data type; operations defined on pointer variables are assignment and test for equality (Ch. 15)

precision the maximum number of significant digits that can be represented (Ch. 8)

precondition an assumption written into a procedure that a specific condition will (or will not) occur; this assumption places on the calling module the responsibility for making sure the procedure is not called when that condition is present (or absent) (Ch. 12, Ch. 16)

Pred an operation that returns the unique predecessor of a value of an ordinal data type (Ch. 10)

priming Read an initial reading of a set of data values before entry into an event-controlled loop in order to establish values for the variables (Ch. 5)

problem-solving phase the first set of steps in programming a computer: analyze the problem; develop an algorithm; test the algorithm for accuracy (Ch. 1)

procedure a structure that allows replacement of a group of statements with a single statement; often called a subprogram or subroutine; it is used by writing a statement consisting of the subprogram name, often followed by a parameter list (Ch. 1, Ch. 2)

procedure call a statement that transfers control to a procedure; the name of the procedure followed by a list of actual parameters (Ch. 3, Ch. 6)

procedure declaration the procedure code, from the heading to the end of the associated block (Ch. 6)

programming the planning, scheduling, or performing of a task or an event; see also *computer programming* (Ch. 1)

programming language a set of rules, symbols, and special words used to construct a program (Ch. 1

proper subset a subset contained within another set that holds all the elements in the subset and at least one element not in the subset (Ch. 9)

queue a data structure in which insertions are made at one end and deletions are made at the other (Ch. 17)

range the interval within which values must fall, specified in terms of the largest and smallest allowable values (Ch. 8)

Read a statement that causes the computer to get values from a data set and place them into variables (Ch. 3)

Readln a statement that causes the computer to get values from a data set and place them into variables; the computer then skips over any extra values on the line and goes to the start of the next line (or card) (Ch. 3)

read mode the status of a file that is to be used to input data; a file is put into read mode through use of the Reset statement (Ch. 3)

real number a number that has a whole and a fractional part and an optional exponent (Ch. 2, Ch. 8)

record a structured data type with a fixed number of components that are accessed by name, not by an index; the components may be of different types (Ch. 14)

recursion the situation in which a subprogram calls itself (Ch. 7, Ch. 8, Ch. 17)

recursive algorithm a solution that is expressed in terms of (a) smaller instances of itself and (b) a base case (Ch. 17)

recursive call a subprogram call in which the subprogram being called is the same as the one making the call (Ch. 8)

recursive case see *general case*

recursive definition a definition in which something

is defined in terms of smaller versions of itself (Ch. 17)

referenced variable a variable created during the execution of a program and accessed not by a name but by a pointer variable; a dynamic variable (Ch. 15)

refinement in top-down design, the expansion of a module specification to form a new module that solves a major step in the computer solution of a problem (Ch. 3)

relational operators operators that state that a relationship exists between two values; in Pascal, symbols that cause the computer to perform operations to verify whether or not the indicated relationship exists (Ch. 4)

representational error arithmetic error caused by the fact that the precision of the true result of arithmetic operations is greater than the precision of the machine (Ch. 8)

reserved word a word that has special meaning in the Pascal language and cannot be used as an identifier (Ch. 2)

Reset the statement that prepares a file for reading by putting the file into read mode and setting the file marker to the first piece of data in the file (Ch. 3)

result see *function result*

return the point at which execution of a subprogram is completed and execution resumes with the statement immediately following the call (Ch. 6)

Rewrite the statement that prepares a file for writing by putting the file into write mode and placing the file marker at the start of the file, erasing whatever information the file previously contained (Ch. 3)

right child (of a node) root of the right subtree of the node (Ch. 16)

right-justified placed as far to the right as possible within a fixed number of character positions (Ch. 2)

robust a descriptive term for a program that can recover from erroneous inputs and keep running (Ch. 5)

root in reference to a binary tree structure, a node with two pointers (left child and right child) and which is not itself the child of any other node; the tree is referenced by an external pointer to the root (Ch. 16)

scalar data types data types in which the set of values is ordered and each value is atomic (indivisible) (Ch. 10)

scope see *scope of access*

scope of access all of the places from which an identifier can be accessed; often referred to just as its scope (Ch. 7)

scope rules   the rules that determine where in a program a given identifier may be accessed (Ch. 7)

scratch file   see *internal file*

selection control structure   a form of program structure allowing the computer to select one among possible actions to perform based on given circumstances; also called a branching control structure (Ch. 4, 9)

self-documenting code   a program containing meaningful identifiers as well as judiciously used clarifying comments (Ch. 3)

semantics   the set of rules that gives the meaning of instructions written in a programming language (Ch. 2)

sentinel   a special data value used in certain event-controlled loops as a signal that the loop should be exited (Ch. 5)

sequence   a structure in which statements are executed one after another (Ch. 1)

set   an unordered collection of distinct values (components) chosen from the possible values of a single atomic data type (other than Real) called the component or base type (Ch. 9)

siblings   the left child and right child of a node in a binary tree structure (Ch. 16)

side effect   any effect of one module (a procedure, a function, or the main program) on another module that is not part of the explicitly defined interface between them (Ch. 7)

significant digits   within a number, those digits from the first nonzero digit on the left to the last nonzero digit on the right (plus any zero digits that are exact) (Ch. 8)

simulation   a problem solution that has been arrived at through the application of an algorithm designed to model the behavior of physical systems, materials, or processes (Ch. 5)

software   the computer programs; the set of all programs available to a computer (Ch. 1)

sorting   arranging the components of a list in order (for instance, words in alphabetical order, numbers in ascending or descending order) (Ch. 12)

source program   a program written in a high-level programming language (Ch. 1)

stack   a data structure in which insertions and deletions can be made from only one end (Ch. 17)

standard identifier   a predefined identifier in Pascal (like MaxInt); may be redefined by user.

standardized   made uniform; most high-level languages are standardized, as official descriptions of them exist (Ch. 1)

stepwise design   see *top-down design*

string   a collection of characters that is interpreted

as a single data item; a packed character array (Ch. 12)

structured data type   a collection of components whose organization is characterized by the method used to access individual components (Ch. 11)

stub   a simple dummy procedure or function that assists in testing part of a program; it has the same name and interface as the procedure or function that would actually be called by the part of the program being tested, but is usually much simpler (Ch. 7, Ch. 10)

styles   the individual manners in which computer programmers translate algorithms into a programming language (Ch. 1)

subprogram   see *procedure*

subrange type   a data type composed of a specified range of any ordinal type (Ch. 10)

subroutine   see *procedure*

subset   a set including only elements that are common to the containing set (Ch. 9)

Succ   an operation that returns the unique successor of a value of an ordinal data type (Ch. 10)

syntax   the formal rules governing how one writes valid instructions in a programming language (Ch. 2)

system software   a set of programs—including the compiler, the operating system, and the editor—that improves the efficiency and convenience of the computer's processing (Ch. 1)

team programming   the use of two or more programmers to design a program that would take one programmer too long to complete (Ch. 7)

termination condition   the condition that causes a loop to be exited (Ch. 5)

testing   checking a program's output by comparing it to hand-calculated results; running a program with data sets designed to discover any errors (Ch. 2)

Text   a predefined file data type whose components are characters organized as lines that are separated by ⟨eoln⟩ marks. Input and output are of type Text. The subprograms Readln, Writeln, and EOLN may only be applied to files of type Text (Ch. 3)

top-down design   a technique for developing a program in which the problem is divided into more easily handled subproblems, the solutions of which create a solution to the overall problem; also called stepwise refinement and modular programming (Ch. 3)

two-dimensional array   a collection of components, all of the same type, structured in two dimensions; each component is accessed by a pair of indices which represent the component's position within each dimension (Ch. 13)

type compatible   implies that types have the same

type definition or type identifier, that they are subranges of the same host type, or that one is a subrange of the other (Ch. 10)

type definition a definition of a data type in the TYPE declaration of a block, with the type identifier to the left of the equal sign and the description of the data type to the right (Ch. 10)

universal set the set containing all of the values of the component type (Ch. 9)

user name the name by which a computer knows you, the entry of which is necessary to log onto a mainframe (Ch. 1)

value parameter a type of formal parameter through which only a copy of the value—not the location of the actual parameter—is given to the procedure, preventing the procedure from changing the value of the actual parameter (Ch. 6, Ch. 7)

variable a location in memory, referenced by a variable name (identifier), where a data value can be stored (this value can be changed) (Ch. 2)

variable (VAR) parameter a type of formal parameter through which the actual parameter's location in memory, not its value, is passed to the procedure, so called variable because the procedure in which it is used may change the value of the actual parameter (Ch. 6)

visible accessible; a term used in describing a scope of access (Ch. 7)

Write a subprogram that causes a computer to write out the value of variables, constants, or expressions (Ch. 2)

Writeln a subprogram that causes a computer not only to write out the value of variables, constants, or expressions but also to print the following output on the next line (Ch. 2)

write mode the status of a file that is to be used to output data; a file is put into write mode through use of the Rewrite statement (Ch. 3)

Chapter 1 Exam Preparation Exercises

2. The compiler takes as input the *source* file that contains the program created (by the programmer) with the editor. The compiler produces one file that contains the *listing* of the program (along with any errors found in the source and other information relevant to the programmer) and another file that contains the *object* code (the translation of the source program).

3. The following are peripheral devices: disk drive, tape drive, printer, card reader, auxiliary storage, terminal. The arithmetic/logic unit, the memory, and the control unit are not peripherals.

Chapter 2 Exam Preparation Exercises

1. (a) invalid   (b) valid   (c) valid   (d) invalid   (e) valid   (f) invalid
   (g) valid   (h) invalid

3. False

5. program—15; algorithm—14; compiler—13; identifier—11; translation phase—12; execution phase—10; variable—1; constant—2; memory—3; syntax—6; semantics—8

6. (a) Real: 13.333333   (b) Integer: 2   (c) Integer: 5   (d) Real: 13.75
   (e) Integer: −4   (f) Real: 1.0   (g) Illegal: 10/3 is Real but MOD expects an integer.

8. (a) reserved   (b) user-defined   (c) user-defined   (d) reserved
   (e) user-defined

14.
```
Cost is
    300
Price is      30Cost is     300
Grade A Costs     300
```

Chapter 2   Preprogramming Exercises

1.
```
PROGRAM Exercise (Output);

CONST
  Lbs = 15;

VAR
  Price, Cost:
    Integer;
  Ch:
    Char;

BEGIN
  Price := 30;
  Cost := Price * Lbs;
  Ch := 'A';
  Writeln('Cost is ');
  Writeln(Cost);
  Writeln('Price is ', Price, 'Cost is ', Cost);
  Write('Grade ', Ch, 'Costs ');
  Writeln(Cost)
END.
```

2. Quadratic formula. All variables are assumed to be of type Real.

```
Determinant := Sqrt(Sqr(B) - 4.0 * A * C);
Denominator := 2.0 * A;
Solution1   := (-B + Determinant) / Denominator;
Solution2   := (-B - Determinant) / Denominator;
```

Chapter 3   Exam Preparation Exercises

2. Variable E will contain 17, variable F will contain 13, and leftover values 7 and 3 will be skipped over and lost.

5. True.

6. Code segments (b) and (d) will skip one entire line of data.

8. Errors with the program are as follows: file InData is missing from the program header, file OutData is missing from the declarations section, file InData should be reset (not rewritten), and file InData is missing as the first parameter of the Read statement.

9. Assuming that the program run is the corrected version of the program in exercise 8, file InData will still contain the 144 after the program is executed. File OutData will also contain 144.

Chapter 3   Preprogramming Exercises

1.
```
Read(Length, Height, Width);
```

3.
```
Readln(Length1, Height1);
Readln(Length2, Height2);
```

4. ```
   Readln(Chr1);
   Readln(Chr2);
   Readln(Chr3);
   ```

7. ```
   PROGRAM CopyFour (DataIn, ResultsOut, Output);

   VAR
     Value1,
     Value2,
     Value3,
     Value4:
       Integer;
     DataIn,
     ResultsOut:
       Text;

   BEGIN (* CopyFour *)
     Reset(DataIn);
     Rewrite(ResultsOut);
     Read(DataIn, Value1, Value2, Value3, Value4);
     Writeln(ResultsOut, Value1, Value2, Value3, Value4);
   END.   (* CopyFour *)
   ```

9. Starting an automobile with a manual transmission and an automatic choke. Note that the problem statement said nothing about getting into the car, adjusting seatbelts, checking the mirror, or driving away. Presumably those tasks, along with starting the car, are subtasks of a larger design such as "Go to the store." Here we are concerned only with starting the car itself.

   Main Module
     Ensure car won't roll.
     Disengage gears.
     Attempt ignition.

   Ensure car won't roll.
     Engage parking brake.
     Turn wheels into curb.

   Disengage gears.
     Push in clutch with left foot.
     Move gearshift to neutral.
     Release clutch.

   Attempt ignition.
     Insert key into ignition slot.
     Turn key to ON position.
     Pump accelerator once.
     Turn key to START position.
     Release after engine catches or 5 seconds, whichever comes first.

Chapter 4   Exam Preparation Exercises

2. (a) (I = J) OR K   (b) ((I >= J) OR (I <= J)) AND K *or*
   (I >= J) OR ((I <= J) AND K)   (c) (NOT K) OR K
   (d) NOT (L AND L)

4. (a) 4   (b) 2   (c) 5   (d) 3   (e) 1

6. (a) IF-THEN-ELSE   (b) IF-THEN   (c) IF-THEN   (d) IF-THEN-ELSE

7. The error message is printed because there is a semicolon before the ELSE.

10. Yes; the expression X $<>$ Y tests the same condition as (X OR Y) AND NOT (X AND Y).

Chapter 4   Preprogramming Exercises

1.
```
Available := NumberOrdered <= (NumberOnHand - NumberReserved);
```

4. `LeftPage := NOT ODD(PageNumber);`

6.
```
IF Year MOD 4 = 0
   THEN
      Writeln(Year, ' is a leap year. ');
IF Year MOD 4 <> 0
   THEN
      BEGIN
         Year := Year + 4 - Year MOD 4;
         Writeln(Year, ' is the next leap year. ')
      END;
```

8.
```
IF Age > 64
   THEN
      Write('Social Security')
   ELSE IF Age < 18
      THEN
         Write('Exempt')
   ELSE
      Write('Taxable');
```

10.
```
BEGIN
   (* This is a nonsense program *)
   A := 10;
   IF A > 0
      THEN
         IF A < 20
            THEN
               Writeln('A is in range')
            ELSE
               BEGIN
                  Writeln('A is too high');
                  A := 10
               END
```

```
            ELSE
              IF  A  =  0
                THEN
                   Writeln('A is null')
                ELSE
                  BEGIN
                     Writeln('A is too low');
                     A  := 10
                  END
        END.
```

Chapter 5 Exam Preparation Exercises

2.
```
Number  := 1;
WHILE Number < 11 DO
  BEGIN
    Writeln(Number: 7);
    Number  := Number + 1
  END;
```

3. The number of iterations executed by the loop is 6.

5. Invariant. Count is in range from 0 to 21; Sum contains sum of integers from zero up to current value of Count.

6. Telephone numbers read in with integer form have many different values that could be used as sentinels. In the United States, a standard telephone number is a positive seven-digit integer (ignoring things like area codes), and may not start with 0, 1, 411, or 911. Therefore, a "good" sentinel may be negative, greater than 9999999, or less than 2000000.

9. (1) Change < to <=; (2) Change 1 to 0; (3) Change 20 to 21. Changes (1) and (3) have Count range from 1 to 20; change (2) has Count range from 0 to 19.

Chapter 5 Preprogramming Exercises

1.
```
Danger  := False;
WHILE NOT Danger DO
  BEGIN
    Read(Pressure);
    IF Pressure > 510.0
      THEN
         Danger  := True
  END;
```

or

```
Danger  := False;
WHILE NOT Danger DO
  BEGIN
    Read(Pressure);
    Danger  := (Pressure > 510.0)
  END;
```

```
2. Count := 0;
   Count28 := 0;
   WHILE Count < 100 DO
     BEGIN
       Count := Count + 1;
       Read(Number);
       IF Number = 28
         THEN
           Count28 := Count28 + 1
     END;

5. Positives := 0;
   Negatives := 0;
   WHILE NOT EOF DO
     BEGIN
       Read(Number);
       IF Number > 0
         THEN
           Positives := Positives + 1;
       IF Number < 0
         THEN
           Negatives := Negatives + 1
     END;
   Writeln('Number of positive numbers ', Positives);
   Writeln('Number of negative numbers ', Negatives);

6. Sum := 0;
   Count := 16;
   WHILE Count <= 26 DO
     BEGIN
       Sum := Sum + Count;
       Count := Count + 2
     END;

8. Hour := 1;
   TenMinute := 0;
   Minute := 0;
   AM := True;
   Done := False;
   WHILE NOT Done DO
     BEGIN
       Write(Hour:2, ':', TenMinute:1, Minute:1);
       IF AM
         THEN
           Writeln(' A.M.')
         ELSE
           Writeln(' P.M.');
       Minute := Minute + 1;
       IF Minute > 9
         THEN
           BEGIN
             Minute := 0;
```

```
                        TenMinute := TenMinute + 1;
                        IF TenMinute > 5
                          THEN
                            BEGIN
                              TenMinute := 0;
                              Hour := Hour + 1;
                              IF Hour = 13
                                THEN
                                    Hour := 1;
                              IF Hour = 12
                                THEN
                                    AM := NOT AM;
                            END
                  END;
            IF (Hour = 1) AND (TenMinute = 0) AND (Minute = 0) AND AM
               THEN
                    Done := True
        END;
```

Chapter 6   Exam Preparation Exercises

2. 13571 (the address of the cell that belongs to variable Widgets).

3. Widgets and Clunkers are synonyms for the same memory location, so after the assignment statement both Widgets and Clunkers have the value 77.

6. The answers are   12   10   3   10

7. (3) Readln(Value3, Value1);
   (4) Value2 := Value1 + 10
   (1) Writeln('Exercise');
   (2) Logical(Number1, Number2);
   (5) Writeln(Number1:6, Number2:6)

8. Only one of the marked statements is not a procedure call: the assignment to Value2.

Chapter 6   Preprogramming Exercises

3. PROCEDURE Increment (VAR Number:
                                    Integer);

```
BEGIN (* Increment *)
   Number := Number + 15
END;   (* Increment *)
```

4. (a) Procedure definition

```
PROCEDURE ScanHeart (VAR Normal:
                          Boolean);

VAR
   HeartRate:
     Integer;
```

```
BEGIN (* ScanHeart *)
  (* Initialize to impossible value *)
  HeartRate := -MaxInt;
  WHILE ((HeartRate > 80) OR (HeartRate < 60)) AND NOT EOF DO
    Readln(HeartRate);
  (* Only way to this point is if normal heartrate or EOF, *)
  (* but can't check for EOF here because after the last value in the *)
  (* file is read in EOF is set, and that last value could be normal *)
  Normal := ((HeartRate <= 80) AND (HeartRate >= 60))
END;   (* ScanHeart *)
```

(b) Procedure invocation

```
ScanHeart(Normal);
```

5. (a) Procedure definition:

```
PROCEDURE Rotate (VAR FirstValue,      (* Input/Output *)
                      SecondValue,     (* Input/Output *)
                      ThirdValue,      (* Input/Output *)
                          Integer);
```

```
(* This procedure takes in three variables and returns their values
   in a shifted order *)
```

```
VAR
  Temp:     (* Intermediate holding variable *)
    Integer;
```

```
BEGIN (* Rotate *)
  (* Save value in local variable *)
  Temp := FirstValue;
  (* Shift next two variables *)
  FirstValue := SecondValue;
  SecondValue := ThirdValue;
  (* Replace final variable with saved value *)
  ThirdValue := Temp
END;   (* Rotate *)
```

(b) Driver program:

```
PROGRAM RotateTest (Input, Output);

VAR
  Value1,
  Value2,
  Value3:
    Integer;

(* PROCEDURE Rotate, as above, goes here *)

BEGIN  (* RotateTest *)
  Writeln('Enter three values');
  Readln(Value1, Value2, Value3);
```

```
        Writeln('Before: ', Value1, Value2, Value3);
        Rotate(Value1, Value2, Value3);
        Writeln('After: ', Value1, Value2, Value3)
   END.  (* RotateTest *)
```

Chapter 7 Exam Preparation Exercises

3. True

7. (a) False   (b) False   (c) False   (d) True   (e) False   (f) True
   (g) False   (h) True   (i) True   (j) True

9. Variables in Sample just before Change is called: A = 10; B = 7. Variables in Change when it is first called (before any statements are executed): X = 10; Y = 7; B = undefined. Variables in Sample after return from Change: A = 10 (X in Change is a value parameter, no result returned.); B = 17.

10. 4   7   6

Chapter 7 Preprogramming Exercises

1. (a) Procedure definition:

```
PROCEDURE SumSquare (     Number1,
                          Number2,
                          Number2:
                              Integer;
                  VAR Result:
                              Integer;
                  VAR AllPositive:
                              Boolean);

BEGIN (* SumSquare *)
   Result := Sqr(Number1) + Sqr(Number2) + Sqr(Number3);
   AllPositive := (Number1 > 0) AND (Number2 > 0) AND (Number3 > 0)
END; (* SumSquare *)
```

(b) Calling statement:

```
SumSquare(A, B, C, Result, AllPositive);
```

4. Procedure heading

```
PROCEDURE GetAverage (     DeptNum:
                              Integer;
                     VAR AvgSales:
                              Real);
```

5. Another procedure heading

```
PROCEDURE RocketSimulation (     Thrust:
                                    Real;
                             VAR Weight:
                                    Real;
                                 TimeStep,
                                 TotalTime:
                                    Integer;
                             VAR Velocity:
                                    Real;
                             VAR OutOfFuel:
                                    Boolean);
```

7. Except for Skipblanks, procedures in Transpose are not quite usable here.

```
PROGRAM Acronym (Input, Output);

CONST
  Blank = ' ';

VAR
  Ch:
    Char;

PROCEDURE SkipBlanks (VAR Ch:
                                Char);

BEGIN (* SkipBlanks *)
  Read(Ch);
  WHILE Ch = Blank DO
    Read(Ch)
END;

PROCEDURE SkipNonBlanks (VAR Ch:
                                    Char);

BEGIN (* SkipNonBlanks *)
  Read(Ch);
  WHILE Ch <> Blank DO
    Read(Ch)
END;    (* SkipNonBlanks *)

BEGIN (* Acronym *)
  WHILE NOT EOLN DO
    BEGIN
      SkipBlanks(Ch);
      Write(Ch);
      SkipNonBlanks(Ch)
    END;
  Readln;
  Writeln
END.   (* Acronym *)
```

Chapter 8   Exam Preparation Exercises

2. False

4. Yes

5. (a) 1.4E+12 (to 10 digits)   (b) 100.0 (to 10 digits)   (c) 3.2E+5 (to 10 digits)

7.
```
Sum := 0.0;                (* Sum is now of type Real *)
WHILE NOT EOF DO
  BEGIN
    Read(Amount);
    Sum := Sum + Amount
  END;
Writeln(Round(Sum):6);
```

10. It is poor programming practice to use formal VAR parameters in a function declaration because it provides a mechanism for side effects to escape from the function. A function returns one value as its result through its name, which is then used in the expression that called the function. If a VAR parameter in a function declaration is changed, that function would be returning more than one result, which is not obvious from the way the function is used. The only time a VAR formal parameter must be in a function declaration is when a file is passed as a parameter; even then the only operations that should be performed on the file are the EOLN and EOF tests that do not have side effects.

Chapter 8   Preprogramming Exercises

2.
```
FUNCTION Equal (Num1,
               Num2,
               Difference:
                 Real):
                   Boolean;
```

5.
```
FUNCTION Hypotenuse (Side1,
                     Side2:
                       Real):
                       Real;


BEGIN (* Hypotenuse *)
  Hypotenuse := Sqrt(Sqr(Side1) + Sqr(Side2))
END;   (* Hypotenuse *)
```

6.
```
FUNCTION SameStatus (VAR File1,
                         File2:
                           Text):
                             Boolean;
```

7.
```
FUNCTION CompassHeading (TrueCourse,
                        WindCorrAngle,
                        Variance,
                        Deviation:
                          Real):
                            Real;

BEGIN (* CompassHeading *)
  CompassHeading := TrueCourse + WindCorrAngle + Variance + Deviation
END;   (* CompassHeading *)
```

10. The type of CostPerOunce and the function return type are real so that cost can be expressed in terms of dollars and cents (i.e., $1.23 = 1.23$). These types could be integer if cost is expressed in terms of cents only (i.e., $1.23 = 123$).

```
FUNCTION Postage (Pounds,
                  Ounces:
                    Integer;
                  CostPerOunce:
                    Real):
                      Real;

BEGIN (* Postage *)
  Postage := (Pounds * 16 + Ounces) * CostPerOunce
END;    (* Postage *)
```

Chapter 9   Exam Preparation Exercises

2. No, this is not a valid declaration of a set variable:

```
VAR Digits : ['0'..'9'];
```

This is confusing because it looks almost correct. However, the notation ['0'..'9'] refers to a set constant (not a type) that could be assigned to variable Digits, as in the following statement:

```
Digits := ['0'..'9'];
```

The proper declaration should be

```
VAR Digits : SET OF '0'..'9';
```

4. (a) ['0'..'9'] (same as Digits)   (b) ['1']   (c) ['0', '2'..'9']   (d) True, expression reduces to: ['1'..'3'] $<=$ ['0'..'9']   (e) False, expression reduces to: ['1'..'9'] $>$ ['0'..'2', '8'..'9'] and '0' is not a member of ['1'..'9']   (f) False, expression reduces to: ['0', '2', '4', '6', '8'] = ['2', '4', '6', '8']   (g) True, expression reduces to: ['0'..'9'] $>$ ['1'..'9']   (h) ['1', '3', '5', '7', '9'] (same as Odds; odds has no elements that are also in Evens, so no elements are removed from Odds)   (i) ['1', '3', '5', '7', '9'] (same as Odds)   (j) False, expression reduces to: [] $>$ []; For this to be True there would have to be one element in the left-hand set which is not in the right-hand set. Note that [] $>=$ [] is True.

8. (a) False   (b) True   (c) True   (d) False

10. False

12. False

Chapter 9   _Preprogramming Exercises_

1. (a) I IN [1..24]   (b) Ch IN ['A', 'J', 'K']   (c) X IN [1, 51..100]

5. REPEAT
```
    Writeln('ENTER Y for Yes, N for No');
    GetYesOrNo(Response);
    Write('Valid Response')
  UNTIL Response = 'N';
```

8. This solution returns proper results for values of Exponent greater than or equal to zero only. It returns correct values for $(Base^0) = 1$, $(0^{Exponent}) = 0$, and the special case of $(\infty) = 1$.

```
  FUNCTION Power (Base,
                  Exponent:
                    Integer):
                      Integer;

  VAR
    Count,
    Temp:
      Integer;

  BEGIN (* Power *)
    Temp := 1;
    FOR Count := 1 to Exponent DO
      Temp := Temp * Base;
    Power := Temp
  END;   (* Power *)
```

9. CASE Grade OF
```
      'A' : Sum := Sum + 4;
      'B' : Sum := Sum + 3;
      'C' : Sum := Sum + 2;
      'D' : Sum := Sum + 1;
      'F' : Writeln('Student is on probation')
    END; (* Case *)
```

10. IF Grade IN ['A'..'D', 'F']
```
      THEN
        CASE Grade OF
          'A' : Sum := Sum + 4;
          'B' : Sum := Sum + 3;
          'C' : Sum := Sum + 2;
          'D' : Sum := Sum + 1;
          'F' : Writeln('Student is on probation')
        END (* Case *)
      ELSE
        Writeln('Invalid letter grade');
```

Chapter 10 Exam Preparation Exercises

3. Pred, Succ, and Ord

6. 0, error, DiorEssence

8. False

10. Two types are type compatible when they have the same type definition or type identifier, they are subranges of the same type, or one is a subrange of the other.

13. True

Chapter 10 Preprogramming Exercises

2.
```
TYPE
   NationalFootball = (Cowboys, Giants, Eagles, Cardinals, Redskins,
                       Bears, Lions, Packers, Vikings, Buccaneers,
                       Falcons, Rams, Saints, SF49ers);
```

4.
```
TYPE
   UpperCase = 'A'..'Z'
```

6.
```
TYPE
   CharDigits = '0'..'9'
```

8. Any set of procedures with meaningful information to be printed.

Chapter 11 Exam Preparation Exercises

1. False

4.
```
   TYPE
(a)    BirdType = (Cardinal, BlueJay, HummingBird, Robin);
(b)    SitingType = ARRAY[BirdType] OF Integer;

   VAR
(c)    Sitings:
          SitingType;
```

5. (a) 100   (b) 8   (c) Colors   (d) Range   (e) 8   (f) 100

Chapter 11 Preprogramming Exercises

1.
```
   PROCEDURE Initialize (VAR Failing:
                             FailType;
                         Length:
                             IndexType);

   VAR
     Counter:        (* Loop control variable *)
        IndexType;
```

```
      BEGIN   (* Initialize *)
        FOR Counter := 1 TO MaxLength DO
          Failing[Counter] := False
      END;   (* Initialize *)
```

3. PROCEDURE AlsoCheckScore (VAR Passing:
                                        PassType;
                                   Score:
                                        ScoreType;
                                   Length:
                                        IndexType);

```
      VAR
        Counter:             (* Loop control variable *)
          IndexType;

      BEGIN   (* AlsoCheckScore *)
        FOR Counter := 1 TO Length DO
          IF Score[Counter] >= 60
            THEN
              Passing[Counter] := True
      END;   (* AlsoCheckScore *)
```

6. PROCEDURE PassingGrade (VAR Passing:
                                        PassType;
                                   Score:
                                        ScoreType;
                                   Length:
                                        IndexType;
                                   Grade:
                                        Integer);

```
      VAR
        Counter:
          IndexType;

      BEGIN   (* PassingGrade *)
        FOR Counter := 1 TO Length DO
          IF Score[Counter] > Grade
            THEN
              Passing[Counter] := True
      END;   (* PassingGrade *)
```

Chapter 12 Exam Preparation Exercises

3. (a) valid   (b) valid   (c) valid   (d) valid   (e) invalid   (f) invalid
   (g) valid

5.   CONST
         MaxNumber = 1000;

```
              TYPE
(a)    CarType = (Ford, Honda, Jaguar, Puegot, Morris);
       InventoryRange = 1..MaxNumber;
(b)    Inventory = ARRAY[InventoryRange] OF CarType;

              VAR
(c)    Cars : Inventory;
```

6. (a) valid   (b) invalid   (c) valid   (d) valid   (e) valid   (f) invalid

Chapter 12   Preprogramming Exercises

```
3. FUNCTION Found (List:
                       RealAry;
                   Item:
                       Real;
                   Length:
                       IndexType):
                       Boolean;

   VAR
     Counter:
       Integer;

   BEGIN    (* Found *)
     Counter := 1;
     Found := False;
     WHILE (Counter <= Length) AND NOT Found DO
       IF List[Counter] > Item
         THEN
           Found := True
         ELSE
           Counter := Counter + 1
   END;     (* Found *)

7. PROCEDURE SetPresent (VAR Present:
                             BooleanAry);

   VAR
     Counter:
       Integer;

   BEGIN    (* SetPresent *)
     FOR Counter := 1 TO MaxLength DO
       Present[Counter] := False
   END;      (* SetPresent *)
```

10. Procedure BinSearch remains the same until the last assignment statement. This statement should be replaced with the following code segment:

```
IF Found
   THEN
      Index := Middle
   ELSE
      Index := First
```

The documentation should read "Otherwise, Found is False and Index is where Item should be inserted."

11. Replace the call to SearchOrd with a call to BinSearch.

Chapter 13   Exam Preparation Exercises

3. (a) 6   (b) 5   (c) 30   (d) column   (e) row

5.
```
      TYPE
(a)      Teams = (NOW, YoungDemocrats, YoungRepublicans);
(b)      RecordType = ARRAY[Terms] OF Integer;

      VAR
(c)      WinLoss : RecordType;
```

7. (a) True   (b) False   (c) True   (d) True

8.
```
(a)   TYPE
      FirstIndex = -1..3;
      SecondIndex = 'A'..'Z';
      ThirdIndex = 1..20;
      ThreeDArray = ARRAY[FirstIndex, SecondIndex, ThirdIndex] OF Real;
(b)   TYPE
      Index1and2 = 1..10;
      Index3and4 = 'a'..'f';
      FourDArray = ARRAY[Index1and2, Index1and2,
                         Index3and4, Index3and4] OF ItemType
```

Chapter 13   Preprogramming Exercises

```
2. PROCEDURE SetDiagonals (VAR Data
                                  DataType;
                           Length:
                                  IndexType;
                           Character:
                                  Char);

      VAR
        Counter:
            IndexType;
```

```
      BEGIN   (* SetDiagonals *)
        FOR Counter := 1 TO Length DO
          BEGIN
            Data[Counter, Counter] := Character;
            Data[Counter, Length - Counter + 1] := Character
          END
      END;    (* SetDiagonals *)
```

6. ```
   PROCEDURE Initialize (VAR Sales:
                                    SalesType);

       VAR
         Store:
           Stores;
         Item:
           ItemNumber;
         Month:
           Months;
         Department:
           Departments;

       BEGIN   (* Initialize *)
         FOR Store := 1 TO NumberOfStores DO
           FOR Item := 1 TO NumberOfItems DO
             FOR Months := 1 TO 12 DO
               FOR Department := A TO G DO
                 Sales[Store, Month, Item, Department] := 0
       END;    (* Initialize *)
   ```

8. ```
   FUNCTION SumRowI (Table:
                             TableType;
                       WhichRow:
                         Integer;
                       ColLimit:
                         Integer):
                             Integer;

       VAR
         Col,
         Sum:
           Integer;

       BEGIN   (* SumRowI *)
         Sum := 0;
         FOR Col := 1 TO ColLimit DO
           Sum := Sum + Table[WhichRow, Col];
         SumRow := Sum
       END;    (* SumRowI *)
   ```

Chapter 14 Exam Preparation Exercises

2. (a) invalid   (b) invalid   (c) valid   (d) invalid   (e) valid   (f) invalid
    (g) valid   (h) valid   (i) valid

3. (a) ARef := Guide[71].Chart   (b) ACode := Guide[88].Chart.Token[1]
    (c) Guide[94].Chart.Token[23,1] := 'X'
    (d) ARef.Symbol[20] := AMap.MapCode[4]

5. False

7. (a) hierarchical record   (b) record   (c) record   (d) array of records
    (e) array   (f) array of hierarchical records   (g) array of records   (h) packed
    array of Char

9. Reference to the field name in this statement is ambiguous. Friend and Self are both of
    type Person.

Chapter 14 Preprogramming Exercises

1.  ```
    CONST
        NameLength = 20;

    TYPE
        NameIndex = 1..NameLength;
        SSIndex = 1..11;
        Classification = (Freshman, Sophomore, Junior, Senior);
        SexType = (M, F);
        NameString = PACKED ARRAY[NameIndex] OF Char;
        SSString = PACKED ARRAY[SSIndex] OF Char;
        PersonType = RECORD
                        Name : NameString;
                        SSNumber : SSString;
                        Class : Classification;
                        GPA : Real;
                        Sex : SexType
                     END;   (* Record *)
    ```

3.  ```
    CONST
        NameLength = 20;
        MaxCourses = 50;

    TYPE
        NameIndex = 1..NameLength;
        CourseIndex = 1..MaxCourses;
        NameString = PACKED ARRAY[NameIndex] OF Char;
        DateType = RECORD
                      Month : 1..12;
                      Year  : 1950..2020
                   END;   (* Record *)
        ClassType = (Freshman, Sophomore, Junior, Senior);
        GradeType = (A, B, C, D, F, Q);
    ```

```
GradeRecord = RECORD
                  CourseId : Integer;
                  Grade : GradeType
              END;    (* Record *)
GradeArray = ARRAY[CourseIndex] OF GradeRecord;
StudentType = RECORD
                  Name : NameString;
                  StudentID : Integer;
                  HoursToDate : Integer;
                  CoursesToDate : 0..MaxCourses;
                  CourseGrades : GradeArray;
                  FirstEnrolled : DateType;
                  Class : ClassType;
                  GPA : Real
              END;    (* Record *)
```

10.
```
FOR Term := 1 TO 30 DO
   WITH TermList[Term] DO
      BEGIN
        Write(Model:16);
        Write(Rate:7);
        CASE Parity OF
          Odd : Writeln(' Odd');
          Even : Writeln(' Even');
          One : Writeln(' One');
          Zero : Writeln(' Zero');
          None : Writeln(' None')
   END;    (* Case *)
```

Chapter 15   Exam Preparation Exercises

3. (a) Read   (c) EOF   (d) Put

6. Read(Character) or Read(N), where N is a single digit.

8. One cannot use a file type as the component type of another file.

10. The Pascal procedure Dispose releases the space reserved for a dynamic variable back to the system.

12. TYPE section, where P is defined.

Chapter 15   Preprogramming Exercises

1. `Text2 = FILE OF Char;`

2.
```
WHILE NOT EOF DO
   BEGIN
     WHILE NOT EOLN DO
        Read(Ch);
     Writeln(Ch);
     Readln
   END
```

4. TYPE
   ```
   RealFile = FILE OF Real;
   ```

6. FUNCTION IdentBuffers (VAR File1, File2:
   ```
                                   Datatype):
                                       Boolean;
   ```

   ```
   BEGIN
     IdentBuffers := File1^ = File2^
   END;
   ```

8. TYPE
   ```
   PtrRefRec = ^RefRec;
   ```

Chapter 16   Exam Preparation Exercises

1. True. In a linked list, elements are only logically next to each other; in an array, they are also physically next to each other.

6. (a) The top or last-entered element of a stack is the first to be removed.   (b) The front or first-entered element of a stack is the first to be removed.

8. When an item is inserted into an empty queue, a front and rear pointer must be set to point to the component.

9. (b) and (c) Every element is smaller than the elements to its right and larger than those to its left.

11. An N log N sort would most likely be more time-consuming than an N-squared sort because the number of elements gets smaller.

Chapter 16   Preprogramming Exercises

3. PROCEDURE Dequeue (VAR Queue:
   ```
                                   QueueType;
                       VAR Component:
                                   ComponentType;
                       VAR Underflow:
                                   Boolean);
   ```

   ```
   VAR
     Pointer:
       NodePointer;
   ```

```
         BEGIN
           IF NOT EmptyQ(Queue) THEN
             BEGIN
               Pop(Queue.Front, Component);
               IF Empty(Queue.Front) THEN
                 Queue.Rear := NIL
             END
           ELSE
             Underflow := True
         END;
```

5.
```
   PROCEDURE QStack(    N:
                            Integer
                      VAR Error:
                            Boolean;
                      VAR Stack:
                            NodePointer;
                      VAR Queue:
                            QueueType;

     VAR
       Item:
         ComponentType;
       I:
         Integer;

     BEGIN
       I := 1;
       WHILE (I <= N) AND NOT Empty(Stack) DO
         BEGIN
           Pop(Stack, Item);
           Enqueue(Queue, Item);
           I := I + 1
         END;
       Error := I < N
     END;
```

7.
```
   FUNCTION CountList(List:
                         NodePointer):
                            Integer;

     VAR
       Count:
         Integer;

     BEGIN
       Count := 0;
       WHILE List <> NIL DO
         BEGIN
           List := List^.Link;
```

```
            Count := Count + 1
         END;
      CountList := Count
   END;
```

Chapter 17 Exam Preparation Exercises

2. False. Both procedures and functions can be recursive.

4. F(4) = 1; F(6) = −1; F(5) is undefined.

6. An IF statement is the control structure that most commonly appears in a recursive procedure.

9. The root pointer being NIL (or both descendent links being NIL) is a base case of a recursive procedure that traverses a binary tree.

Chapter 17 Preprogramming Exercises

1.
```
FUNCTION F (N:
                 Integer):
                 Integer;

BEGIN
  IF (N = 0) OR (N = 1) THEN
    F := 1
  ELSE
    F := F (N − 1) + F (N − 2)
END;
```

3.
```
PROCEDURE LinePrint (Infile:
                            Text);

VAR
  C:
    Char;

BEGIN
  WHILE NOT EOF (Infile) DO
    BEGIN
      WHILE NOT EOLN (Infile) DO
        BEGIN
          Read (X, C);
          Write (C)
        END
      Readln (Infile);
      Writeln
    END
END;
```

```
7.  PROCEDURE PrintStack(VAR Stack:
                                  NodePointer);

    VAR
      Component:
        ComponentType;

    BEGIN
      IF NOT Empty(Stack) THEN
        BEGIN
          Pop(Stack, Component);
          PrintStack(Stack);
          Writeln(Component);
          Push(Stack, Component)
        END
    END;
```

INDEX

Absent, Program, 518–525, 530, 578–580
Abstraction
  control, 397, 570
  data, 570, 577, 579
Active error detection, 398
Actual parameters, 236, 237, 239–242, 260
Ada, 117
Algorithm(s), 3, 4–6, 37
  comparison of sorting, 713
  on linked lists, 654–666
  on lists, 449–465
  recursive, 724–725
    with simple variables, 727–729
    with structured variables, 737–740
Analogy, problem-solving by, 39–40
Anonymous type, 385–386, 549
Arithmetic/logic unit (ALU), 9
Array(s)
  defined, 527
  of records, 549–551
  representation, 685–686
Array processing, 508–509
  initializing table, 510–511
  printing table, 513
  summing columns, 512
  summing rows, 511
Arrays, multidimensional, 495, 527–529
  errors with, 531
Arrays, one-dimensional, 407, 408, 449, 496
  accessing individual components, 416
  defined, 414–415
  examples of defining and accessing, 416–420
  passing, as parameters, 438
  problems requiring, 409–414, 424–437
  processing, 421–422
  testing and debugging, 439–440
  using, in programs, 423–424
Arrays, packed, 449
  and strings, 466–469
Arrays, parallel, 423, 530
Arrays, two-dimensional, 495–500
  another way of defining, 525–527
  and array processing, 503–513
ASCII, 366, 367, 368, 369, 370
Assembler, 17
Assembly language, 16–17
Assignment, 53–57
Assignment compatibility, 387
Atomic data type, 334
Automatic range-checking, 384
Auxiliary storage device, 12

Base case, 724
BASIC, 22, 117, 723
Batch input/output, 105
Batch processing, 13
Batch program entry, 31
Binary, 7
Binary digit, see Bit
Binary file, 603, 611, 618
Binary search, in ordered list, 461–465
Binary search tree, 695–696, 713, 744–745
Binary tree data structure, 694–700, 713, 744
Birthday, Program, 64–65, 78
BirthdayCalls, Program, 582–588
BirthdayReminder, Program, 392–397, 398–401, 449, 469–473
Bit, 7
Blocks, 61
  procedures and, 235–236
Boole, George, 49
Boolean data types, 47, 49, 333, 365–367
  relational operators with real and, 142
Boolean expressions, 136–140
  writing, 141–142
Boolean function Odd, 142
Boolean functions, 306–307
Boolean operators, 138–140
Boolean variables, 137
Booting the system, 25
Building-block approach, to problem-solving, 40

Cancellation error, 322
Case label list, 349–351
Case selector, 349–351
CASE statement, 333, 349–352, 356, 357
CategoryCount, Program, 340–343
CDC-Scientific, 366, 369
Central processing unit (CPU), 8–9
Character(s)
  data, reading, 100–103
  data type (Char), 47, 48–49, 333, 365–367
  output, formatting integer and, 74–76
CharCount, Program, 427–432, 436, 449, 450
CheckLists, Program, 412–414, 415
Chess, two-dimensional arrays for, 495
Chr operation, 369–370
COBOL, 17, 22, 117, 723
Code walkthrough, 209
Coding, 5, 7
Collating sequence, 366
Compiler, 17
Compiler listing, 30

Composite data type, 334, 407–408
Compound statements, 61, 145–146
Computer
  components of, 8–13
  defined, 1, 8
  program, 2–3
  programming, 2–3
  See also Mainframes; Minicomputers;
    Personal computers (PCs)
Constants, 52–53, 280
Control abstraction, 397, 570
Control unit, 9
CountAll Program, 434–437, 449
Count-controlled loops, 176–177
Counters, 176
Counting loops, 183–184
Crash, 25
CreateData, Program, 635–636
CreateList, Program, 650–652
Cursor control keys, 27–28

Data abstraction, 570, 577, 579
Data error checking, 282
Data formats, impact of, on program design,
  112
Data input, 95–105
Data representation, 7–8
Data storage, 49–53
Data structures
  binary tree, 694–700, 713
  choosing, 529–530, 569–580, 685–686
  queue, 690–694
  stack, 687–690
  static vs. dynamic, 643–646
Data type(s), 47–49, 333, 365–370, 401
  anonymous, 385–386, 549
  atomic, 334
  compatibility of, 386–389
  composite, 334
  definition of, 370–371
  enumerated, 371–375
  file, 604, 605
  named, 385, 386
  ordinal, 367
  scalar, 366
  structured, 407–408
  subrange, 383–385
  user-defined scalar, 370–386
Data validation, 282
Debugging, 6, 30
  See also Errors
Declaration, 50–51
Disk drives, 12
Documentation, 119
  program, 6–7

Down, 25
Drivers, 288–290
Dynamic data structures, static vs., 643–646
Dynamic variables, 622–624, 628, 629

EBCDIC, 366, 367, 369
Echo printing, 104
Editor, 18, 20
  entering program with line-oriented, 26–27
  entering program with screen, 27–29
Editor programs, 26
Election, Program, 503–509, 526–527, 530
Empty set, 334, 336
Enumerated data types, 371–375
EOF loops, 180–181, 189, 218
⟨eoln⟩, 99–100
EOLN loops, 181–182, 189
Error detection
  active, 398
  passive, 398
Error messages, 126–128
Errors
  cancellation, 322
  representational, 319, 320, 321, 322
  semantic, 162–163
  subscript range, 531
  syntactic, 162–163
  type conflict, 531
  undefined-value, 531
Event-controlled loops, 176, 177–183
Event counter, 185, 189–190
Exam, Program, 477–485, 556
Example, Program, 59–60, 271–272, 275–277
Exchange sorts, 454–455
Executing, 5
Execution summary, 31
Exercise, Program, 229–230, 233, 234–235,
  241–242
Exponentiation, Program, 725–727
Extended command mode, 29
External file, 604
External pointer, 646

Field identifier, 543–545, 548, 589–590
Field selector, 545–546, 548, 564, 565, 588,
  589
Fieldwidth, 58, 75
FIFO ("first in, first out") structure, 690
File(s), 27, 106–107, 603–604
  binary, 603, 611, 618
  buffer variable, 618–620, 629
  data type, 604, 605
  declaring, in VAR section, 108
  errors made with, 637
  external, 604

File(s) *(cont.)*
  internal or scratch, 604
  names in program heading, listing, 107–108
  other, 608–611
  preparing, with Reset or Rewrite, 108–110
  specifying, in read, readln, write, and writeln,
    110–111
  text, 603, 604–608, 618
  using, 107
Flag, 182
Flag-controlled loops, 182–183, 190
Floating point number, 320
Flow of control, 143
Formal parameter declaration, 232
Formal parameters, 236, 237, 239–242, 260
  See also Value parameters; Variable (or VAR)
    parameters
Formatting
  integer and character output, 74–76
  output, 73–74
  program, 62–63
ForMom, Program, 77–79
FOR statement, 333, 346–348, 352, 356, 357,
    588
  guidelines for using, 348
  problem illustrating use of, 352–355
FORTRAN, 17, 22, 117, 162, 723
Friends, Program, 557–563, 566–567
Function(s), 58, 81, 303–306
  Boolean, 306–307
  definition, 304
  interface design and side effects, 307
  problems making use of, 308–316
  result type, 305
  testing and debugging, 326–327
  when to use, 308
Functional modules, 113
Functional problem description, 113
Function call, 102
Function result, 81

Game, Program, 378–383
General case, 724
GetInitialDriver, Program, 289
Global constants, 271, 272, 280
Global declarations, *see* Local vs. global
    declarations
Global procedure, 271
Global variable, 271, 272
GradeList, Program, 354–355, 389
Graph, Program, 247–249, 280, 282–287

HalfLife, Program, 199–201, 218
Hardware, 12
Heuristics, 42

Hierarchical records, 564–565, 588, 589
  representing logical entities with, 569–570
Homogeneous structure, 530

Identifiers, 45–47
IF statement, 135–136, 143, 206, 333, 352
  IF-THEN-ELSE form of, 144–145, 146, 333,
    351–352, 357, 750
  IF-THEN form of, 147–148
  nested, 151–152, 156–157
Implementation phase, 3
Implementing, 5
In, 261
Incomes, Program, 195–196, 218
Index value, 423
Indices with semantic content, 424
Infinite loop, 177, 218
Infinite recursion, 326
Information, 7–8
  See also Data representation
In-order traversal, 745
In/out, 261
In place, 454
Input, 96
Input/output
  batch, 105
  interactive, 103–105
Input/output (I/O) devices, 9
Input prompts, 104
Inserting, into ordered list, 458–461
Integer and character output, formatting, 74–76
Integer numbers, 322
  data type, 47–48, 333, 365–367
Integrate, Program, 314–316
Interactive input/output, 103–105
Interactive program entry, 25–31
Interactive system, 13
Interface, 12, 249–250
  design, 260–262
  design and side effects, function, 307
Internal file, 604
International Standards Organization (ISO), 22,
    108, 350
Invocation, *see* Procedure call
Invoice, Program, 215–218
Iteration, 175, 723, 749
Iteration counter, 184, 189–190

Language, *see* Programming language
Leaf nodes, 695
Left child, 694
LIFO ("last in, first out") structure, 687
Linked lists, 629, 646–652, 685–686
  algorithms on, 654–666
  deleting from, 663–666

error checking with, 714–715
  inserting into, 656–662
  pointer expressions, 666–667
  printing, 654–656
  printing of, in reverse order, 742–744
Liquid crystal displays (LCDs), 9
LISP, 723
List
  binary search in ordered, 461–465
  inserting into ordered, 458–461
  sequential search in sorted, 456–458
  sequential search in unordered, 450–453
Literal, literal value, 52
Local constants, 271
Local vs. global declarations, 270–272
Local procedures, 271
Local variables, 242–243, 270–272
Logging off, 30–31
Logging on, 26
Logical entities, representing, with hierarchical
    records, 569–570
Logical order, 173
Loop control variable (LCV), 176, 347
Loop design, 186–191
  problems related to, 191–206
Loop exit, 175
Looping statement, guidelines for choosing, 348–
    349
Looping subtasks, 183–185
Loop invariant, 186–188, 218
  determining, 188
Loop structure, 20
Loops using WHILE statement, 175–185

Machine language, 16
Magnetic tape drives, 12
Mainframes, 13
  getting started on, 25–26
Maintenance, program, 6–7
Mantissa, 320
Means-ends analysis, for problem-solving, 40–42
Memory, 49–50
  programs in, 86
Memory unit, 8
Mental blocks, to problem-solving, 42–43
Mercury space program, 323
Mileage, Program, 82–85, 86, 107, 111
Minicomputers, 16
Mnemonic, 16
Modular programming, 113
  See also Top-down design
Modula-2, 22
Module nesting chart, 281
Modules, 78–79, 113–117

Multidimensional arrays, *see* Arrays, multidimen-
    sional

Named constant, 52–53
Named type, 385, 386
Name precedence, 271
Needs, 261, 307
Needs/returns, 261, 307
Nested IF statements (nested control structure),
    151–152, 156–157
Nested loops (nested logic), 173, 206–209
  designing, 209–210
  printing headings and columns for, 210–212
  problems illustrating, 212–217
Nesting, designing programs with, 280–281
Nodes, 646
  leaf, 695
NoGlobals, Program, 290
Nonlocal, 272–273
Nonlocal access, 273
Notices, Program, 158–161, 164
Null statement, 61
Numerical integration, 311, 322
"NUMERIC DATA EXPECTED" error message,
    126, 127

Object program, 18
One-dimensional arrays, *see* Arrays, one-dimen-
    sional
Operating system, 18, 20
Order, Program, 369
Ordinal data types, 367
Ord operation, 367–368, 369, 370
OTHERWISE clause, 350
Out, 261
"OUT OF DATA" error message, 126–127
Output, 57–59
  appearance of, 72–76
  formatting, 73–74
  formatting integer and character, 74–76
Overflow, 321–322

Packed arrays, *see* Arrays, packed
Packed option, applied to records, 548–549
Parallel arrays, *see* Arrays, parallel
Parameter list, 58–59
Parameters, 103, 236, 237, 239–242
  passing arrays as, 438
Parentheses, use of, 140–141
Pascal, Blaise, 21
Pascal, defined, 21–24
Passive error detection, 398
Password, 26
Payroll, Program, 23–24, 43, 46, 48, 49, 62–63
Peripheral devices, 10, 12

Personal computers (PCs), 13–16
  getting started on, 25
Pointer(s), 603, 622–630
  errors made with, 637
  expressions, 666–667
  external, 646
  and linked lists, 649–650
  variables, recursion using, 741–749
Pop, 687
PossibleWords, Program, 309–310, 324
Posttest loop, 345
Precedence of operators, 140–141
Precedence rules, 80–81, 140
Precision, 316–317, 318, 320
  practical implications of limited, 322–323
Precondition, of the procedure, 487, 714
Pred operation, 367, 368
Pretest loop, 345
Priming Read, with sentinel-controlled loops, 178–180
Problem-solving phase, 3
Problem-solving process, 37–38
  asking questions, 38
  breaking up problems into smaller units, 38–39
  building-block approach, 40
  looking for familiar things, 38
  means-ends analysis, 40–42
  mental blocks to, 42–43
  solving by analogy, 39–40
Procedure(s), 20, 58, 103
  and blocks, 235–236
  difference between functions and, 303
  multiple calls to same, 243–249
  overview of user-defined, 234–237
  top-down structured design with, 227–234
  when to use, 234–235
Procedure call (invocation), 103, 238–239
  flow of control in, 234
Procedure declaration, 232, 238
ProdSum, Program, 149–150, 161–162
Program, computer, 2–3
Program construction, 59–63
Program entry, *see* Batch program entry; Interactive program entry
Programming, 1–2
  computer, 2–3
  defined, 3–7
Programming language, 5
  defined, 16–20
Programs in memory, 86
Prompts, input, 104
Pseudocode, 116–117
Push, 687

Questions, asking, for problem-solving, 38
Queue data structure, 690–694

Range, 320
Reading marker, 99–100
Readln statement, 98–99, 103
  specifying files in, 110–111
Read mode, 109
Read statement, 96–98, 103
  specifying files in, 110–111
ReadWrite, Program, 468
Read/write head, 12
Real numbers, 47
  arithmetic with, 319
  data type, 48, 333, 365–367
  defined, 320
  how Pascal implements, 320–323
  representation of, 316–318
Records, 543–549
  arrays of, 549–551
  hierarchical, 564–565
  and WITH statement, 565–568
Recursion, 277, 323–326, 723, 749
  defined, 723–727
  infinite, 326
  tail, 739
  testing and debugging, 750
  with trees, 744–749
  using pointer variables, 741–749
Recursive algorithms, 724–725
  with simple variables, 727–729
  with structured variables, 737–740
Recursive call, 305, 323, 326, 723, 724, 739–740
Recursive case, 724
Recursive definition, 724
Referenced variables, 624–628
Refinement, 118
Relational operators, 137–138
  with real and Boolean data types, 142
REPEAT statement, 333, 343–346, 352, 356, 357
  guidelines for using, 348–349
  problem illustrating use of, 352–355
Representational error, 319, 320, 321, 322
Reserved words, 51
Reset statement, preparing files with, 108–110
Result, 81
Returns, 239, 261, 307
ReverseLine, Program, 688–690, 748–749
Rewrite statement, preparing files with, 108–110
Right child, 694
Right-justified numeric values, 58
Root, 694

Scalar data types, 366
  user-defined, 370–386
Scope rules, 272–277
Scrabble, two-dimensional arrays for, 495
Scratch file, 604
Secondary storage device, *see* Auxiliary storage
    device
Selection, 20
Selection control structures
  compound statements, 145–146
  flow of control, 143
  IF statement, 143
  IF-THEN-ELSE form of IF statement, 144–
    145
  IF-THEN form of IF statement, 147–148
  nested IF statements, 151–152, 156–157
  selection, 143
Self-documenting code, 119, 375
Semantic content, indices with, 424
Semantic errors, 162–163
Semantics, 44–57
  defined, 44
Sentinel-controlled loops, 177–178, 189
  priming Read with, 178–180
Sentinel value, 177–178, 179–180
Sequence, 20
Sequential search
  in sorted list, 456–458
  in unordered list, 450–453
Sets, 333–338, 389
  problem demonstrating use of, 338–343
Siblings, 694
Side effects, 261, 277–280
  function interface design and, 307
Significant digits, 317, 320
Software, 12
Solitaire, Program, 674–685, 687
Sorting, 453–456
  algorithms, comparison of, 713
SortPointers, Program, 632–635, 636
SortSatScores, Program, 706–713
Source program, 18
Sport, Program, 155, 163–164, 621–622
Stack data structure, 687–690
Standardized languages, 18
Static vs. dynamic data structures, 643–
    646
Stepwise refinement, 113
  See also Top-down design
Straight selection, 454
String or string variables, 466–469, 487
Structured data types, 407–408
Stubs, 287–290
Style, programming, 5

Style considerations, in choice of data structure,
    577–580
Subarray processing, 423
Subprogram, 57–58, 103
  See also Function(s); Procedure(s)
Subrange type, 383–385
Subscript range errors, 531
Subsets, 334
Subtasks, looping, 183–185
Succ operation, 367, 368
Summing loops, 184–185
Syntactic errors, 162–163
Syntax, 44–57
  defined, 44
  diagrams, 44–45
System software, 18

Tail recursion, 739
Team programming, 290
TempStat, Program, 204–206
Terminal, 12–13
Termination condition, 175
Termination control, 175
Terms, Program, 243
TestAve, Program, 122–123
TestTowers, Program, 735–736
Text data type, 333
Text files, 603, 604–608, 618
Tic-tac-toe, two-dimensional arrays for, 495
Top-down design, 112–113
  documentation of, 119
  methodology of, 117–118
  modules in, 113–117
Top-down structured design, with procedures,
    227–234
Tower of Hanoi, 733–737, 745
Transpose, Program, 266–270, 271, 273, 280,
    281, 288–289
Trees, recursion with, 744–749
Tree structure, 113
Triangle, Program, 125–126
Trouble, Program, 279
Turing Award, 21
Two-dimensional arrays, *see* Arrays, two-dimen-
    sional
Type compatibility, 386–389
Type conflict errors, 531
Type definition, 370
Type Test, 51, 108

Undefined-value error, 531
Underflow, 321
Universal set, 334, 336, 337
User name, 25

Value
  index, 423
  keeping track of previous, 185
  literal, 52
Value parameter, 240, 259–260, 291
  interface design, 260–262
  problem illustrating, 263–270
  semantics, 260
  syntax, 262
Variable(s), 50–51
  Boolean, 137
  dynamic, 622–624, 628, 629
  file buffer, 618–620, 629
  global, 271, 272
  local, 242–243, 270–272
  recursion using pointer, 741–749
  recursive algorithms with simple, 727–729
  recursive algorithms with structured, 737–740
  referenced, 624–628
Variable (or VAR) parameters, 240, 282, 283, 291

passing arrays as, 438
problem illustrating, 263–270
vs. value parameters, 259–262
VAR Section, declaring files in, 108
Visible scope of access, 273

WHILE statement, 173–175, 206, 356, 750
  guidelines for using, 348–349, 357
  loops using, 175–185
  and REPEAT statement, 344–346
Wirth, Niklaus, 21
WITH statement, 565–568, 588–591
Words, working with, 466–469
Writeln statement, 70–72, 103, 218–219
  specifying files in, 110–111
Write mode, 109
Write statement, 57–59, 70, 103
  specifying files in, 110–111